HUMAN COMMUNICATION

HUMAN COMMUNICATION

THE BASIC COURSE FOURTH EDITION

Joseph A. DeVito

HUNTER COLLEGE CITY UNIVERSITY OF NEW YORK

 HarperCollins*Publishers*

Sponsoring Editor: Barbara Cinquegrani
Project Editor: Thomas Farrell
Text Design: Tamara O'Bradovich, Woods End Studio
Cover Design: Edward A. Butler
Cover Art and Frontispiece: Edward A. Butler
Text Art: Vantage Art, Inc.
Photo Research: Mira Schachne
Production Manager: Jeanie Berke
Production Assistant: Paula Roppolo
Compositor: Ruttle, Shaw & Wetherill, Inc.
Printer and Binder: R. R. Donnelley & Sons Company
Cover Printer: The Lehigh Press, Inc.

Human Communication: The Basic Course, Fourth Edition
Copyright © 1988 by HarperCollins, Publishers, Inc.

Library of Congress Cataloging-in-Publication Data

DeVito, Joseph A., Date
    Human communication.

    Includes index.
    1. Communication.   I. Title.
P90.D485 1987   001.51   87-11982
ISBN 0-06-041608-4

    90 9 8 7 6

ABOUT THE AUTHOR

Joseph A. DeVito is Professor of Communication at Hunter College of the City University of New York. After earning his M.A. at Temple University and Ph.D. at the University of Illinois, he did postdoctoral studies at Illinois and at the University of Minnesota's Human Learning Institute. He has taught a variety of communication courses for over twenty years. Dr. DeVito has written widely for major scholarly journals such as the *Quarterly Journal of Speech, Communication Monographs,* the *Journal of Communication,* and *Communication Education.* He is the author of a number of textbooks, including *The Interpersonal Communication Book, The Elements of Public Speaking,* and *The Communication Handbook,* all published by Harper & Row.

Books by the Author

The Psychology of Speech and Language: An Introduction to Psycholinguistics
Communication: Concepts and Processes (Third Edition)
General Semantics: Nine Lectures
General Semantics: Guide and Workbook (Revised Edition)
Language: Concepts and Processes
Psycholinguistics
Articulation and Voice: Effective Communication
The Interpersonal Communication Book (Fourth Edition)
The Elements of Public Speaking (Third Edition)
The Communication Handbook: A Dictionary

To Maggie

CONTENTS IN BRIEF

Preface   xxv

PART ONE **PRELIMINARIES**   1

1 PRELIMINARIES TO HUMAN COMMUNICATION: NATURE, COMPONENTS, AND PURPOSES   2
2 EIGHT POSTULATES OF COMMUNICATION   17
3 THE SELF IN COMMUNICATION: AWARENESS AND DISCLOSURE   28
4 PERCEPTION   47
5 LISTENING   61

PART TWO **LANGUAGE AND VERBAL INTERACTION**   79

6 PRELIMINARIES TO LANGUAGE AND VERBAL INTERACTION: LANGUAGE, SYMBOLS, AND MEANING   80
7 BARRIERS IN LANGUAGE AND VERBAL INTERACTION   91
8 PRINCIPLES OF LANGUAGE AND VERBAL INTERACTION   103
9 SOCIAL ASPECTS OF LANGUAGE AND VERBAL INTERACTION   118

PART THREE **NONVERBAL COMMUNICATION**   133

10 PRELIMINARIES TO NONVERBAL COMMUNICATION: FUNCTIONS AND UNIVERSALS   134
11 BODY COMMUNICATION   145
12 SPACE, TERRITORIALITY, AND TOUCH COMMUNICATION   155
13 PARALANGUAGE AND TIME   170

PART FOUR **INTERPERSONAL COMMUNICATION AND RELATIONSHIPS**   185

14 PRELIMINARIES TO INTERPERSONAL COMMUNICATION AND RELATIONSHIPS: DEFINITIONS, CHARACTERISTICS, AND INTERPERSONAL ATTRACTION   186

15 RELATIONSHIP DEVELOPMENT AND DETERIORATION   201
16 IMPROVING INTERPERSONAL COMMUNICATION AND
   CONFLICT MANAGEMENT   219

PART FIVE GROUP AND ORGANIZATIONAL
COMMUNICATION   245

17 PRELIMINARIES TO GROUP COMMUNICATION: TYPES,
   PROCEDURES, AND FORMATS   246
18 MEMBERS AND LEADERS IN GROUP COMMUNICATION   258
19 ORGANIZATIONAL COMMUNICATION   273
20 INTERVIEWING   290

PART SIX PUBLIC COMMUNICATION   309

21 PRELIMINARIES TO PUBLIC COMMUNICATION: STEPS IN SPEECH
   PREPARATION (IN BRIEF) AND SPEAKER APPREHENSION   310
22 ORGANIZING THE PUBLIC SPEECH   326
23 STYLE AND LANGUAGE IN THE PUBLIC SPEECH   349
24 DELIVERY IN PUBLIC SPEAKING   362
25 THE INFOMATIVE SPEECH   378
26 THE PERSUASIVE SPEECH   394

PART SEVEN INTERCULTURAL COMMUNICATION   423

27 PRELIMINARIES TO INTERCULTURAL COMMUNICATION:
   IMPORTANCE, DIFFICULTIES, AND FORMS   424
28 INTERCULTURAL COMMUNICATION: BARRIERS AND
   GATEWAYS   435

PART EIGHT MASS COMMUNICATION   453

29 PRELIMINARIES TO MASS COMMUNICATION: COMPONENTS,
   FORMS, AND FUNCTIONS   454
30 THEORIES OF MASS COMMUNICATION   472

A HANDBOOK OF EXPERIENTIAL VEHICLES IN HUMAN
COMMUNICATION   H-1

   Glossary   G-1
   Index   I-1

CONTENTS IN DETAIL

Preface   xxv

PART ONE   PRELIMINARIES   1

1 PRELIMINARIES TO HUMAN COMMUNICATION: NATURE,
   COMPONENTS, AND PURPOSES   2
   Communication: A Definition   4
     Communication Context   4
     Sources-Receivers   5
     Encoding-Decoding   6
     Communicative Competence   6
     Messages and Channels   7
     Feedback   8
     Noise   9
     Field of Experience   10
     Communication Effects   10
     Ethics and the Notion of Choice   10

   The Purposes of Communication   12
     Personal Discovery   12
     Discovery of the External World   13
     Establishing Meaningful Relationships   13
     Changing Attitudes and Behaviors   14
     Play and Entertainment   14

   Summary   14
   Sources   16

2 EIGHT POSTULATES OF COMMUNICATION   17
   Communication Is a Transactional Process   18
     Communication Is a Process   18
     Components Are Interrelated   18
     Communicators Act as Wholes   18

   Communication Is Inevitable   19
   Communication Is Irreversible   19
   Communication Is a Package of Signals   20
     Contradictory Messages   20

   Communication Involves Content and Relationship Dimensions   21
     The Failure to Distinguish Content and Relationship   21

   Communication Is a Process of Adjustment   22
   Communication Sequences Are Punctuated for Processing   23

Communication Involves Symmetrical and Complementary Transactions   24
Rigid Complementarity   24
Progressive Differentiation   26

Summary   26
Sources   27

3   **THE SELF IN COMMUNICATION: AWARENESS AND DISCLOSURE   28**

Self-Awareness   29
The Open Self   29
The Blind Self   30
The Unknown Self   31
The Hidden Self   32

Growing in Self-Awareness   33
Dialogue with Yourself   33
Listen   34
Reduce Your Blind Self   34
See Your Different Selves   34
Increase Your Open Self   35

Self-Disclosure   35
The Nature of Self-Disclosure   35
Factors Influencing Self-Disclosure   36
Self-Disclosure Avoidance   37
The Rewards of Self-Disclosure   38
The Dangers of Self-Disclosure   40

Self-Disclosure Guidelines   41
Guidelines for Self-Disclosing   41
Guidelines for Responding to Self-Disclosures   43

Summary   44
Sources   45

4   **PERCEPTION   47**

The Perception Process   48
Sensory Stimulation Occurs   48
Sensory Stimulation Is Organized   48
Sensory Stimulation Is Interpreted-Evaluated   49

Processes Influencing Perception   50
Primacy-Recency   50
Self-Fulfilling Prophecy   51
Perceptual Accentuation   51
Implicit Personality Theory   52
Consistency   52
Stereotyping   53

Attribution   55
Consensus   56
Consistency   56
Distinctiveness   56
Behaviors Revealing of Internal Motivation   57
Self-Attribution   57

　　　　　Summary   58
　　　　　Sources   59

5　LISTENING   61
　　　　　The Significance of Listening   62
　　　　　The Nature of Listening   62
　　　　　　　Listening: A Definition   62
　　　　　　　Types of Listening   63

　　　　　Listening Effectively   64
　　　　　　　Active and Passive Listening   65
　　　　　　　Empathic and Objective Listening   65
　　　　　　　Nonjudgmental and Judgmental Listening   66
　　　　　　　Surface and Deep Listening   67

　　　　　Active Listening   69
　　　　　　　The Functions of Active Listening   70
　　　　　　　The Techniques of Active Listening   71

　　　　　Summary   72
　　　　　Sources   72

　　　SKILL DEVELOPMENT SUMMARY   74

　　PART TWO LANGUAGE AND VERBAL INTERACTION   79

6　PRELIMINARIES TO LANGUAGE AND VERBAL INTERACTION:
　　LANGUAGE, SYMBOLS, AND MEANINGS   80
　　　　　Language as a Symbol System   81
　　　　　　　Implications for Human Communication   82

　　　　　Language as a Meaning System   83
　　　　　　　A Process View of Meaning   83
　　　　　　　Implications for Human Communication   84
　　　　　　　Denotative and Connotative Meanings   86

　　　　　Phatic Communion   88
　　　　　Summary   89
　　　　　Sources   90

7　BARRIERS IN LANGUAGE AND VERBAL INTERACTION   91
　　　　　Polarization   92
　　　　　Intensional Orientation   93
　　　　　　　Prestige Suggestion   94

　　　　　Fact-Inference Confusion   94
　　　　　　　Pragmatic Implications   95
　　　　　　　Differentiating Facts from Inferences   96

　　　　　Bypassing   96
　　　　　　　Correctives   97

　　　　　Allness   97
　　　　　　　Allness and Conflict   99
　　　　　　　End Statements with Etc.   99

　　　　　Static Evaluation   99
　　　　　　　Date Statements   100

Indiscrimination   100
Index Terms   101

Summary   101
Sources   102

8   PRINCIPLES OF LANGUAGE AND VERBAL INTERACTION   103
In-Group Talk   104
Inclusion   104

Downward and Upward Talk   105
Downward Talk   105
Upward Talk   106
Equality   107

Criticism and Complimenting   107
Honest Appraisal   107

Lying   108
Reasons for Lying   108
Is Lying Effective?   109
Honesty   111

Self-Talk and Other-Talk   111
Balance   111

Offensive Language: Racism, Sexism, Etc.   112
Fairness   112

Gossip   112
Some Problems of Gossip   113
Ethical Implications   114
Confidentiality   114

Disconfirmation   114
Confirmation   115
Differences Between Disconfirmation and Confirmation   115

Summary   116
Sources   117

9   SOCIAL ASPECTS OF LANGUAGE AND VERBAL INTERACTION   118
Language as a Social Institution   119
Functions of Sublanguages   120
Subcultural Communication   120
Subcultural Identification   121
Communication Privacy   121
The Impressing and Confusing of Outsiders   122

Kinds of Sublanguages   123
Language Taboo and Euphemism   124
Taboo Origins   124
Taboo Variations   124
Taboo Effects   125
Taboo Alternatives: Euphemisms   126

Summary   126
Sources   127

SKILL DEVELOPMENT SUMMARY   128

PART THREE   NONVERBAL COMMUNICATION   133

10 **PRELIMINARIES TO NONVERBAL COMMUNICATION:**
    FUNCTIONS AND UNIVERSALS   134
    Functions of Nonverbal Communication   135
    Universals of Nonverbal Communication   136
        Communicative   136
        Determined   139
        Contextual   139
        Believable   140
        Rule-Governed   141
        Metacommunicational   142

    Summary   143
    Sources   143

11 **BODY COMMUNICATION   145**
    Body Movements   146
        Emblems   146
        Illustrators   147
        Affect Displays   147
        Regulators   147
        Adaptors   148

    Facial Movements   148
        Affect Displays   149
        Encoding-Decoding Accuracy   149
        Micromomentary Expressions   150

    Eye Movements   150
        Functions of Eye Communication   151
        Eye Avoidance Functions   152
        Pupil Dilation   152

    Summary   153
    Sources   153

12 **SPACE, TERRITORIALITY, AND TOUCH COMMUNICATION   155**
    Space Communication   156
        Spatial Distances   156
        Influences on Space Communication   158

    Territoriality   160
        Territorial Encroachment   161
        Reactions to Encroachment   161
        Markers   162

    Touch Communication   162
        The Meanings of Touch   162
        Touch Avoidance   164
        Who Touches Whom Where   164

    Summary   168
    Sources   168

13 **PARALANGUAGE AND TIME   170**
    Paralanguage   171
        Judgments About People   171
        Judgments About Conversational Turns   173
        Judgments About Communication Effectiveness   174

    Temporal Communication   175
        Biological Time   175
        Cultural Time   176
        Psychological Time   177
        Time and Status   178
        Time and Appropriateness   178

    Summary   179
    Sources   179

SKILL DEVELOPMENT SUMMARY   181

PART FOUR **INTERPERSONAL COMMUNICATION AND RELATIONSHIPS   185**

14 **PRELIMINARIES TO INTERPERSONAL COMMUNICATION AND RELATIONSHIPS: DEFINITIONS, CHARACTERISTICS, AND INTERPERSONAL ATTRACTION   186**
    Interpersonal Communication   187
        A Componential Definition   187
        A Relational (Dyadic) Definition   187
        A Developmental Definition   188

    Interpersonal Relationships   189
        Relationships Are Established in Stages   189
        Relationships Vary in Breadth and Depth   192

    Interpersonal Attraction   194
        Attractiveness (Physical and Personality)   195
        Proximity   195
        Reinforcement   196
        Similarity   198
        Complementarity   198

    Summary   199
    Sources   200

15 **RELATIONSHIP DEVELOPMENT AND DETERIORATION   201**
    Relationship Development   202
        Reasons for Relationship Development   202
        Initiating Relationships: The First Encounter   203

    Relationship Deterioration   206
        The Nature of Relationship Deterioration   206
        Some Causes of Relationship Deterioration   207
        Communication in Relationship Deterioration   214

    Summary   217
    Sources   217

16 IMPROVING INTERPERSONAL COMMUNICATION AND
    CONFLICT MANAGEMENT   219
    A Humanistic Approach to Interpersonal Effectiveness   221
        Openness   221
        Empathy   222
        Supportiveness   223
        Positiveness   224
        Equality   225

    A Pragmatic Approach to Interpersonal Effectiveness   226
        Confidence   226
        Immediacy   227
        Interaction Management   227
        Expressiveness   228
        Other-Orientation   230

    A Social Exchange Approach to Interpersonal Effectiveness   230
        Exchange Rewards   231
        Bear Your Share of the Costs   232
        Intensify the Exchange of Rewards in Times of Rising Costs   232
        Increase Rewards to Reduce the Attractiveness of Alternatives   232

    Conflict Management   233
        Unproductive Conflict Management   233
        Effective Conflict Management   236

    Summary   237
    Sources   238

    SKILL DEVELOPMENT SUMMARY   240

PART FIVE   GROUP AND ORGANIZATIONAL
COMMUNICATION   245

17 PRELIMINARIES TO GROUP COMMUNICATION:
    TYPES, PROCEDURES, AND FORMATS   246
    The Small Group   247
    The Problem-Solving Group   248
        Steps to Successful Group Problem Solving   248

    The Idea-Generation Group   251
    The Personal Growth Group   252
        Some Popular Personal Growth Groups   252
        How One Type of Group Works   253

    The Educational or Learning Group   254
    Small Group Formats   255
    Summary   256
    Sources   256

18 MEMBERS AND LEADERS IN GROUP COMMUNICATION   258
    Members in Small Group Communication   259
        Member Roles   259
        Member Participation   261
        Groupthink   263

A Group Membership Evaluation Form   264

Leaders in Small Group Communication   **264**
Leader's Functions   266
Leadership Styles   268
A Leadership Evaluation Form   269

Summary   **271**
Sources   **271**

19   ORGANIZATIONAL COMMUNICATION   **273**
Organization and Organizational Communication: Definitions   **274**
The Organization   274
The Communications   275

Approaches to Organizations   **276**
The Scientific Approach   276
The Human Relations Approach   277
The Systems Approach   277
The Cultural Approach   278

Communication Networks   **279**
The Network Structures   280
Network Productivity and Morale   281

Communication Flow in Organizations   **282**
Upward Communication   282
Downward Communication   283
Lateral Communication   284
Serial Communication   285
The Grapevine   286
Information Overload   287

Summary   **288**
Sources   **289**

20   INTERVIEWING   **290**
Interviewing Defined   **291**
Kinds of Interviews   **292**
The Information Interview   292
The Persuasive Interview   292
The Appraisal Interview   292
The Exit Interview   293
The Employment Interview   293
The Counseling Interview   293

The Interview Sequence   **294**
Before the Interview   295
During the Interview   297
After the Interview   302

Lawful and Unlawful Questions   **302**
Possible Strategies   303

Summary   **304**
Sources   **305**

SKILL DEVELOPMENT SUMMARY   **306**

PART SIX PUBLIC COMMUNICATION   **309**

21 PRELIMINARIES TO PUBLIC COMMUNICATION:
    STEPS IN SPEECH PREPARATION (IN BRIEF)
    AND SPEAKER APPREHENSION   **310**
    Preparing the Public Speech: A Capsule Summary   **311**
        Select the Subject and Purpose   *311*
        Analyze the Audience   *313*
        Research the Topic   *316*
        Formulate Your Thesis and Identify the Major Propositions   *316*
        Support the Major Propositions   *317*
        Organize the Speech Materials   *319*
        Wording the Speech   *321*
        Construct the Conclusion and the Introduction   *321*

    Speaker Apprehension   **322**
        Apprehension: Is It Normal? Is It Harmful?   *322*
        Dealing with Speaker Apprehension   *323*

    Summary   **324**
    Sources   **325**

22 ORGANIZING THE PUBLIC SPEECH   **326**
    The Thesis (Your Main Assertion)   **327**
        Using Thesis Statements to Generate Main Ideas   *327*

    The Proposition (Your Main Points)   **328**
    Transitions and Internal Summaries   **330**
        Transitions   *331*
        Internal Summaries   *331*

    Thought Patterns for Organizing Main Assertions   **332**
        Spatial Pattern   *332*
        Cause-Effect/Effect-Cause Pattern   *333*
        The Motivated Sequence   *333*

    Introductions   **335**
        Gain Attention   *335*
        Orient the Audience   *336*
        Some Common Faults with Introductions   *337*

    Conclusions   **337**
        Summarize   *338*
        Provide Closure   *338*
        Some Common Faults with Conclusions   *339*

    Before the Introduction and After the Conclusion   **339**
        Before the Introduction   *340*
        After the Conclusion   *340*

    Constructing the Outline   **340**
        Preface the Outline with Identifying Data   *340*
        Outline the Introduction, Body, and Conclusion as Separate Parts   *341*
        Insert Transitions and Internal Summaries   *341*
        Append a List of References   *341*

Some Mechanics of Outlining   342
Use a Consistent Set of Symbols   342
Use Visual Aspects to Reflect and Reinforce the Organizational Pattern   343
Use One Discrete Idea per Symbol   344
Use Complete Declarative Sentences   344

The Delivery Outline   345
Be Brief   345
Be Clear   345
Be Delivery-Minded   345
Rehearse Your Speech with This Outline   346

Summary   346
Sources   347

23 **STYLE AND LANGUAGE IN THE PUBLIC SPEECH   349**
Oral Style   350
Word Choice   351
Clarity   351
Vividness   353
Appropriateness   355
Personalness   356
Forcefulness   357

Sentence Construction   359
Summary   360
Sources   361

24 **DELIVERY IN PUBLIC SPEAKING   362**
Methods of Delivery   363
The Impromptu Method of Delivery   363
The Manuscript Method of Delivery   363
The Memorized Method of Delivery   364
The Extemporaneous Method of Delivery   364

Voice   365
Volume   365
Rate   366
Pitch   366
Quality   367
Articulation and Pronunciation   368
Pauses   370

Bodily Action   371
Eye Contact   371
Facial Expression   371
Gestures   371
Movement   372
Proxemics   372

Using Notes   373
Rehearsal: Practicing and Improving Delivery   373
Goals of Rehearsal   374
Rehearsal Procedures   374

Summary   376
Sources   377

25 **THE INFORMATIVE SPEECH**   378
    General Types and Purposes   379
        Speeches of Description   379
        Speeches of Definition   380
        Speeches of Demonstration   380

    Specific Purposes   381
        Speeches of Description   381
        Speeches of Definition   381
        Speeches of Demonstration   381

    Principles of Informative Speaking   382
        Limit the Amount of Information   382
        Stress Relevance and Usefulness   382
        Present Information at the Appropriate Level   382
        Relate New Information to Old   383

    Amplifying Materials in Informative Speeches   384
        Examples and Illustrations   384
        Testimony   385
        Definition   386
        Audiovisual Aids   388

    Summary   392
    Sources   393

26 **THE PERSUASIVE SPEECH**   394
    Attitudes, Beliefs, and Behaviors   395
    Types and Purposes of Persuasive Speaking   396
        Specific Purposes   397
    Principles of Persuasion   398
        The Attractiveness Principle   398
        The Selective Exposure Principle   398
        The Audience Participation Principle   399
        The Inoculation Principle   399
        The Magnitude of Change Principle   400

    Arguments in Persuasive Speeches   401
        Reasoning from Analogy   402
        Reasoning from Causes and Effects   403
        Reasoning from Sign   404
        Reasoning from Specific Instances and Generalizations   405

    Psychological Appeals in Persuasive Speeches   406
        Fear   406
        Power, Control, and Influence   407
        Self-Esteem and Approval   407
        Achievement   408
        Financial Gain   408
        Status   409

Credibility Appeals in Persuasive Speeches   409
Forming Credibility Impressions   410
Increasing Credibility   411

Summary   414
Sources   416

SKILL DEVELOPMENT SUMMARY   **417**

PART SEVEN   **INTERCULTURAL COMMUNICATION   423**

27   **PRELIMINARIES TO INTERCULTURAL COMMUNICATION:
     IMPORTANCE, DIFFICULTIES, AND FORMS   424**
     An Excursion into Intercultural Communication   425
     The Importance of Intercultural Communication   426
     Mobility   426
     Economic Interdependence   427
     Communication Technology   428
     Immigration Patterns   428
     Political Well-Being   428

     The Difficulty in Studying Intercultural Communication   428
     Ethnocentricism   429
     Mindlessness and Mindfulness   430

     The Nature of Intercultural Communication   430
     Subcultures   431
     The Forms of Intercultural Communication   432

     Summary   433
     Sources   434

28   **INTERCULTURAL COMMUNICATION: BARRIERS AND
     GATEWAYS   435**
     Language and Cultural Relativity   436
     Some Semantic Aspects of Language Relativity   437
     Some Structural Aspects of Language Relativity   439
     Implications for Human Communication   441

     Barriers to Intercultural Communication   442
     *Barrier One: Ignoring Differences Between Yourself and the Culturally
         Different   442*
     Barrier Two: Ignoring Differences Among the Culturally Different Group   442
     *Barrier Three: Ignoring Meaning Differences in Verbal and Nonverbal
         Messages   443*
     *Barrier Four: Violating the Cultural Rules and Customs That Regulate the Content
         and Flow of Communication   443*
     Barrier Five: Evaluating Differences Negatively   443
     Barrier Six: Culture Shock   444

     Gateways to Intercultural Communication   445
     Avoiding Barriers   446
     Employing the Principles of Effective Interpersonal Interaction   446

     Summary   448
     Sources   448

SKILL DEVELOPMENT SUMMARY   **450**

PART EIGHT   MASS COMMUNICATION   453

29 PRELIMINARIES TO MASS COMMUNICATION:
    COMPONENTS, FORMS, AND FUNCTIONS   454
    A Definition of Mass Communication   455
    Source   455
    Audience   455
    Messages   457
    Process   457
    Context   457

    Forms of Mass Communication   458
    Television   458
    Radio   460
    Newspapers   460
    Magazines   461
    Films   461
    Books   462
    Records-Tapes-Cassettes-Compact Discs   462

    The Functions of Mass Communication   463
    To Entertain   463
    To Reinforce   463
    To Change or Persuade   464
    To Educate   464
    To Confer Status   465
    To Activate   466
    To Narcotize   466
    To Create Ties of Union   467
    To Ethicize   467
    Evaluating Media Functions   468

    Summary   469
    Sources   470

30 THEORIES OF MASS COMMUNICATION   472
    Step Theories   473
    The One-Step Theory   473
    The Two-Step Theory   474
    The Multistep Theory   475

    Play Theory   475
    Diffusion of Innovations Theory   476
    Uses and Gratification Theory   478
    Opinion Leaders and Gatekeepers   478
    Opinion Leaders   478
    Gatekeepers   480

    Summary   482
    Sources   482

SKILL DEVELOPMENT SUMMARY   484

A HANDBOOK OF EXPERIENTIAL VEHICLES IN HUMAN COMMUNICATION   H-1

1. Models of Communication   H-2
2. Analyzing an Interaction   H-4
3. I'd Prefer to Be   H-8
4. Self-Disclosure Questionnaire   H-9
5. A Self-Disclosure Experience   H-10
6. Ethical Issues in Human Communication   H-12
7. Causal Attribution   H-13
8. Sequential Communication   H-14
9. Practicing Active Listening   H-16
10. Facts and Inferences   H-17
11. Haptics: Body Accessibility   H-18
12. Gender Differences in Nonverbal Communication   H-19
13. Who?   H-20
14. The Greeting Card   H-22
15. Male and Female   H-23
16. Up and Down with Jack and Jill   H-24
17. The Ideal Relational Couple   H-26
18. Win as Much as You Can   H-27
19. Group Communication Patterns   H-29
20. Interviews: Experiencing and Analyzing   H-31
21. Dealing with Unlawful Questions   H-32
22. Analyzing the Public Speech   H-33
23. The Teacher and the Student   H-35
24. Motivational Analysis and the Advertisement   H-37
25. Television and Values   H-37

Glossary   G-1
Index   I-1

PREFACE

Human Communication: The Basic Course is addressed to the introductory college course in communication that surveys the entire field of communication, and to students who have little or no prior background in communication. It is addressed to those students who will take this course as their only communication course, as well as to those who will take additional and advanced courses or who are beginning to major in communication.

The fourth edition of *Human Communication: The Basic Course* remains in the tradition of its earlier editions, while incorporating significant improvements.

POINT OF VIEW

In writing this book I tried to provide the student with the best—the most insightful, reliable, and recent—of what is known about communication. I have therefore drawn freely on all those who have contributed to the development of contemporary communication study—psychologists, sociologists, philosophers, linguists, and, of course, communication researchers and theorists themselves. After completing this text, the student should have a firm grasp of the theoretical and research foundations of communication and also should have developed significant new skills and improved old ones. I am concerned here with the student growing both in understanding communication and in mastering the arts of effective communication in a wide variety of contexts—interpersonal, small group, public, intercultural, and mass communication.

PLAN OF THE BOOK

Human Communication: The Basic Course is divided into eight parts and a handbook. The first three parts cover the fundamental concepts and principles applicable to all forms and contexts of communication.

1. "Preliminaries" covers the nature of human communication, the general principles of communication, the role of the self in communication, and the processes of receiving messages: perception and listening.
2. "Language and Verbal Interaction" covers the verbal message code and discusses the nature of language, some of the most important barriers to effective interaction, some useful principles to guide everyday communications, and the social aspects of language and verbal interaction and how these influence communication.
3. "Nonverbal Communication" focuses on the role of nonverbal messages in

human interaction and considers such aspects as body, facial, and eye communication, communication by space, touch, paralanguage, and time.

The next five parts focus on the major contexts or forms of human communication.

4. "Interpersonal Communication and Relationships" covers two-person communication and emphasizes communication encounters between intimates and how those encounters, including conflict encounters, may be made more effective. How and why interpersonal relationships develop and deteriorate and how we can achieve greater control over those relationships command considerable attention.

5. "Group and Organizational Communication" deals with small groups serving a wide variety of purposes, and focuses on our understanding of the nature and patterns of group interaction and how they may be made more effective. Problem-solving groups, personal growth groups, interviewing situations, and organizational networks are all approached with a view toward improving our own effectiveness.

6. "Public Communication" focuses on the art of public speaking and explains theoretical principles of organization, style, delivery, information processing, and persuasion, as well as practical guidelines for the preparation and presentation of a wide variety of public speeches. These units seek to increase our understanding of ourselves and our abilities as speakers, consumers, and critics of public discourse.

7. "Intercultural Communication" covers communication between members of different cultures and identifies some of the foundations and the major forms of intercultural communication. In these units, primary attention is given to explaining the major barriers to and guidelines for effective intercultural communication.

8. "Mass Communication" focuses on the structure and function of the various mass communication systems and especially how we as consumers of the media may interact more effectively and intelligently with the media systems. Here we explain some of the major theories of mass communication, especially as they apply to identifying the ways in which the media exert their influence on us and on society generally.

Each of these eight parts begins with a unit titled "Preliminaries," designed to provide an overview of the essential principles needed to understand the particular area to ensure that all readers begin the study of each topic with comparable backgrounds. The remaining units in each part cover the specific dimensions or aspects of these eight major topics.

THE UNIT APPROACH

There are 30 relatively brief units rather than the traditional longer chapters characteristic of most texts. This system of short units makes reading the text easier and more enjoyable and at the same time makes for more effective learning. One great advantage of this approach is that it enables the units to be read at almost any time. Since we learn most effectively when we learn in small doses, I recommend that no more than one unit be read at any given sitting. It will prove most valuable if one unit is read and then time is spent digesting it, thinking about its contents, and considering how it relates to your own communication behaviors.

LEARNING GOALS

Each unit begins with a set of learning goals. They will help you focus on the major concepts contained in the unit. Read those goals before beginning the unit to fix those essential concepts in your mind. After reading the unit, return to those goals to see if you are, in fact, able to achieve them. If you are not, reread the unit or those parts that caused difficulty, focusing on the goal or goals you were not able to achieve. In this way you will have an easy-to-follow guide to mastery of the material.

SUMMARY STATEMENTS AND
SKILL DEVELOPMENT SUMMARIES

Summary statements conclude each of the units. They are designed to highlight the essential concepts and processes discussed in the text.

Skill development summaries follow each of the eight parts of the text and spell out in brief the communication skills covered in the preceding units that the student should master (in varying degrees). Over 200 skills in human communication are highlighted.

SOURCE NOTES

At the end of each unit is a note on sources. Those notes include both the references I used in preparing the text and the references I suggest for further reading. That procedure serves the pleasant function of keeping the text free from burdensome notes that often interfere with reading and also provides me with the opportunity to comment on the recommended readings, to express my own indebtedness, and to characterize the readings in terms of their importance and appropriateness.

EXPERIENTIAL VEHICLES

The Handbook of Experiential Vehicles in Human Communication contains 25 exercises designed to enable you to work actively with the concepts discussed in the text. They are means for enabling you to internalize the concepts and principles. Some instructors will prefer to devote a considerable amount of class time to these experiential vehicles and have the readings done independently. Others will prefer to devote some time to the experiences and some to an explanation or elaboration of text material. Still others will prefer to devote all class time to theoretical and/or textual material. Regardless of what procedure is followed in your particular class, the experiences should prove a useful way for thinking about the concepts discussed in the text and for working actively with them.

GLOSSARY

At the end of the text is a glossary of significant terms used in the study of communication. These brief definitions should give you a clear understanding of the concepts and processes essential to an understanding of communication. As the course progresses, you will find it useful to add any new terms used in the course to this glossary so that you will have all the terms in one convenient place. A more complete guide to the terminology of communication may be found in my *Communication Handbook: A Dictionary.*

INSTRUCTOR'S MANUAL AND HARPER TEST

I have prepared an Instructor's Manual (available from the publisher) for use in connection with this text. The manual contains suggested syllabli, guidelines for using the experiential vehicles contained in the text, additional experiential vehicles, and a bibliography of useful teacher resources.

A test bank of short-answer questions is available in hard copy and on disk (Harper Test) and may be secured from the publisher.

THE MAJOR ADDITIONS AND REVISIONS

A few of the major improvements of this new edition are identified here:

1. Two new units of intercultural communication have been added (Units 27 and 28), covering the nature of intercultural communication, the common barriers, and principles for increasing intercultural communication effectiveness.
2. The section on public speaking has been expanded to give justice to such matters as organization, style, delivery, amplifying materials, and logical, psychological, and ethical appeals.
3. Coverage of nonverbal communication has been greatly revised and enlarged to reflect more accurately the expanding research literature and its general importance in the field of human communication.
4. The section on interpersonal effectiveness has been greatly expanded to include principles derived from a pragmatic model and from a social ex-

change and equity model, as well as from the humanistic model used in the previous editions. Again, this expansion more accurately reflects current thinking and research in the field.

5. Both theory and application have been highlighted in this edition—theory in the summary propositions following each of the units, and application in the skill development summaries following each of the major parts of the text.

6. Material on the processes involved in initiating relationships (including interpersonal attraction) and in relational deterioration has been expanded and updated.

7. Additional topics have been introduced throughout the text as appropriate. Some of the more important are types of noise, growing in self-awareness, guidelines in self-disclosure, bypassing, pragmatic implication, disconfirmation, and small group formats. Group membership and leadership evaluation forms have also been added.

8. Eleven experiential vehicles, including several dialogues for analysis, are new to this edition.

In addition, the glossary has been updated, new and helpful headings have been added, and the style has been improved to achieve greater clarity and economy.

THE PAYOFFS

For every course and for every textbook, a student has a right to ask: "What will I get out of this?" I would like to identify here some of the major payoffs that should be, and I think will be, derived from this text. These payoffs concern both the development of skills and the understanding of theory, neither of which can effectively be developed without the other. After reading this text you should be able to

1. understand a wide variety of communication forms and the principles governing them

2. apply these communication principles in a variety of situations as source, receiver, and critic

3. understand the role of self-concept and self-awareness in communication and how these may be heightened

4. understand and better control self-disclosure

5. understand the ways in which we perceive others, the ways they perceive us, how these processes influence communication and interaction generally, and how perception may be made more accurate

6. understand what listening is and how it can be made more effective

7. listen more effectively and efficiently in a wide variety of communication situations, and effectively employ the skills of active listening

8. understand what language is and what its role is in human communication generally

9. understand the language principles for effective interpersonal interaction and incorporate these principles into your verbal interactions

10. understand the common barriers to verbal interaction and communicate more effectively by avoiding these barriers

11. understand the social aspects of language and how these influence everyday verbal interactions

12. understand how nonverbal communication operates and how meanings are communicated through body movements, spatial relationships, touch, variations in voice, and treatment of time

13. communicate more effectively through these nonverbal codes as both sender and receiver

14. develop an increased appreciation for the wide variety of cultural differences in both verbal and nonverbal communication patterns, and better understand the hidden meanings these differences may communicate

15. understand the nature of interpersonal relationships and the role of communication in their development, maintenance, and deterioration

16. communicate more effectively to initiate relationships and to arrest relational deterioration

17. understand how conflict develops in relationships, some of the unproductive ways in which it is frequently dealt with, and some of the productive and effective ways for dealing with it

18. engage in interpersonal conflict in more productive and more constructive ways

19. understand the wide variety of group encounters and the roles of members and leaders

20. understand the nature of interviewing and the wide variety of interviewing situations

21. understand the role of communication within organizational settings and some of the ways in which organizational communications may be improved

22. communicate more effectively as a group member and as a group leader in a wide variety of situations—for example, in learning groups, problem-solving groups, therapeutic groups, and idea-generation groups

23. communicate more effectively in interview situations—from the initial preparation through the actual interview situation to the follow-up

24. understand the role of public speaking in a democratic society and the varied benefits to be derived from its mastery

25. understand the principles of organization, style, and delivery governing an effective public speech, and improve your abilities to apply these principles to your own speeches

26. understand the principles of information processing and persuasion

27. understand how to construct logical, psychological, and ethical appeals in all forms of communication

28. function more effectively as a public speaker in communicating information and in persuading others to alter their attitudes, values, and behaviors

29. understand the nature of intercultural communication and the difficulties involved in effective cross-cultural encounters

30. improve your abilities to communicate in intercultural situations by over-coming the common barriers and by employing the principles of effective-ness
31. understand the nature and functions of the mass media in our society, and how we are influenced by and in turn influence the media
32. master a vocabulary for thinking about and talking about communication in all its forms

The most general payoff is this: an increased understanding and control of human communication in interpersonal, group, public, intercultural, and mass communication situations. More specific payoffs in the form of learning goals preface each of the 30 units of the text.

ACKNOWLEDGMENTS

It is always a pleasure to thank the many people who have had an influence on the writing and production of a book. My major debt is to those colleagues who reviewed this and previous editions and who gave freely of their insights, suggestions, criticisms, time, and energy. Their input resulted in substantial improvements for which I am most grateful. Thank you, John Amsbary, North Dakota State University; Roy M. Berko, Lorain County Community College; Nancy Wood Bliese; David Brenders, Indiana University; Bernard J. Brommel, Northeastern Illinois University; Jerry Butler, University of Arkansas, Little Rock; Gil Clardy, Washburn University; Pamela Cooper, Northwestern University; Carley H. Dodd, Abilene Christian University; William A. Donahue, Michigan State University; Fran Franklin, University of Arkansas; Anne S. Garrard-Alley, James Madison University; Joseph Giordano, University of Massachusetts, Amherst; William Gourd, Saginaw Valley State College; Catherine Konsky, Illinois State University; Michael L. Lewis, Abilene Christian University; Jon F. Nussbaum, University of Oklahoma; Lynn A. Phelps, Ohio University; Sam Riccillo, University of Wyoming; Armeda C. Reitzel, Humboldt State University; Mary Lynn Sandoz, Mississippi State University; Jo Sprague, San Jose State University; and Sanford B. Weinberg, St. Joseph's University.

The staff at Harper & Row likewise contributed to the final product. Thank you, Barbara Cinquegrani, sponsoring editor; Thomas Farrell, project editor; Mira Schachne, photo researcher; and Karla Philip, director of art and design.

Joseph A. DeVito

HUMAN COMMUNICATION

PART ONE
PRELIMINARIES

1. PRELIMINARIES TO HUMAN COMMUNICATION: NATURE, COMPO-
NENTS, AND PURPOSES

2. EIGHT POSTULATES OF COMMUNICATION

3. THE SELF IN COMMUNICATION

4. PERCEPTION

5. LISTENING

In this first part of *Human Communication* we cover some of the fundamental principles and concepts relevant to communication in all its forms, whether interpersonal, group, public, intercultural, or mass communication. The nature of communication, its essential components, and its major purposes are considered in the first unit. Subsequent units focus on the elementary principles of human communication, self-awareness, and self-disclosure, and the processes involved in receiving messages—namely, perception and listening.

The major purpose of this first part is to answer the questions "What is human communication?" and "How does it work?"

UNIT 1 PRELIMINARIES TO HUMAN COMMUNICATION:
Nature, Components, and Purposes

LEARNING GOALS

After completing this unit, you should be able to

1. discuss the nature of the universals of communication
2. define the following terms: *communication context, sources-receivers, encoding-decoding, competence, messages, channel, feedback, noise, field of experience, communication effect,* and *ethics*
3. explain the transactional nature of communication
4. diagram the model of the universals of communication presented in this unit, labeling all its parts
5. explain the nature of communication competence
6. identify and explain the five purposes of communication

Of all the knowledge and skills we possess, those concerning communication are among the most significant and useful. Through **interpersonal communication** we interact with others, learn about them and ourselves, and reveal ourselves to one another. Whether with new acquaintances, old friends, lovers, or family, it is through interpersonal communication that our personal relationships are established, maintained, and sometimes destroyed (and sometimes repaired). Through **small group communication** we interact with others—solving problems, developing new ideas, and sharing knowledge and experiences. Our work and our social lives are lived largely in groups—from the employment interview to the executive board meeting, from the informal social group having coffee to the formal meeting discussing issues of national and international concern. Through **public communication** we are informed and persuaded, and we in turn inform and persuade others—to do, to buy, or to think in a particular way, or to change an attitude, opinion, or value. Through **intercultural communication** we learn about other cultures and about living with different customs, roles, and rules. Perhaps most important, we learn through intercultural communication to understand new ways of thinking and new ways of behaving. Intercultural cooperation begins with mutual understanding. Through **mass communication** we are entertained, informed, and persuaded by the media—movies, television, radio, newspapers, and books. Likewise, through our viewing habits and buying patterns, we in turn influence the media in form and content.

Not surprisingly, the importance of communication in all aspects of our lives is reflected by its increased popularity as a topic in colleges and universities throughout the country. We, as a society in general, seem to be more acutely aware of how communication influences the success of our day-to-day interactions.

This book, then, is about these communications and about your communications. It seeks both to explain the theories and concepts important to the many forms of communication and to enhance your own skills and abilities as senders, receivers, and critics of communication.

This book is relatively long, simply because communication is an enormous field and for many of you this is your first academic exposure to communication. In order to do justice to this expanding and rapidly developing area and to the students enrolled in an introductory communication course, it was necessary to write the rather heavy volume you now hold. No legitimate purpose would be served by eliminating significant areas, concepts, or theories of communication or by glossing over complexities. Fortunately, the time and effort that will be required by this book and this course will be more than repaid by the knowledge you will gain and by the essential skills you will acquire and improve.

We begin our study of communication by looking at the definition of communication and at its essential components and processes.

3

COMMUNICATION: A DEFINITION

Communication refers to the act, by one or more persons, of sending and receiving messages that are distorted by noise, occur within a context, have some effect, and provide some opportunity for feedback.

Figure 1.1 illustrates what we might call the universals of communication—the elements present in every communication act, regardless of whether it is intrapersonal (with oneself), interpersonal (with one or two others), small group, public speaking, or mass communication. Each of these components will be explained in depth.

Communication Context

Communication always takes place within a *context*. At times this context is subtle and unobtrusive; it seems to be so natural that it is ignored, like background music. At other times, the context stands out boldly, and the ways in which it restricts or stimulates our communications are obvious. Compare, for example, the differences in communicating in a funeral home, a football stadium, or a quiet restaurant.

The context of communication has at least three dimensions: physical, social-psychological, and temporal. The room or hallway or park—that is, the tangible or concrete environment—in which communication takes place is the *physical context*. This physical context, whatever it is, exerts some influence on the content as well as the form of our messages.

The *social-psychological dimension* of context includes, for example, the status relationships among the participants, the roles and the games that people play, the norms and cultural mores of the society in which they are communicating, and the friendliness or unfriendliness, formality or informality, and seriousness or humorousness of the situation. Communications are permitted at a graduation party that would not be permitted at a funeral or in a hospital.

The *temporal dimension* includes the time of day as well as the time in history in which the communication act takes place. For many people, the morning is not a time for communication; for others, the morning is ideal. Time in history is no less important, because the appropriateness, importance, impact, and effectiveness of messages depend in great part on the time in which they are uttered. Consider, for example, how messages on racial, sexual, or religious attitudes and values would be differently framed and responded to in different times in history. Henry Miller's *Tropic of Cancer*, D. H. Lawrence's *Lady Chatterley's Lover*, and Vladimir Nabokov's *Lolita* were all, at various times, banned from publication and distribution; now they are frequently found on required reading lists in colleges throughout the world. Another and perhaps more important dimension of time refers to how a particular message fits into the sequence of communication events. For example, consider the varied meanings a "simple" compliment paid to a friend would have depending on whether it occurred immediately after your friend paid you a compliment, immediately prior to your asking your friend for a favor, or during an argument.

These three dimensions of context interact with one another; each influ-

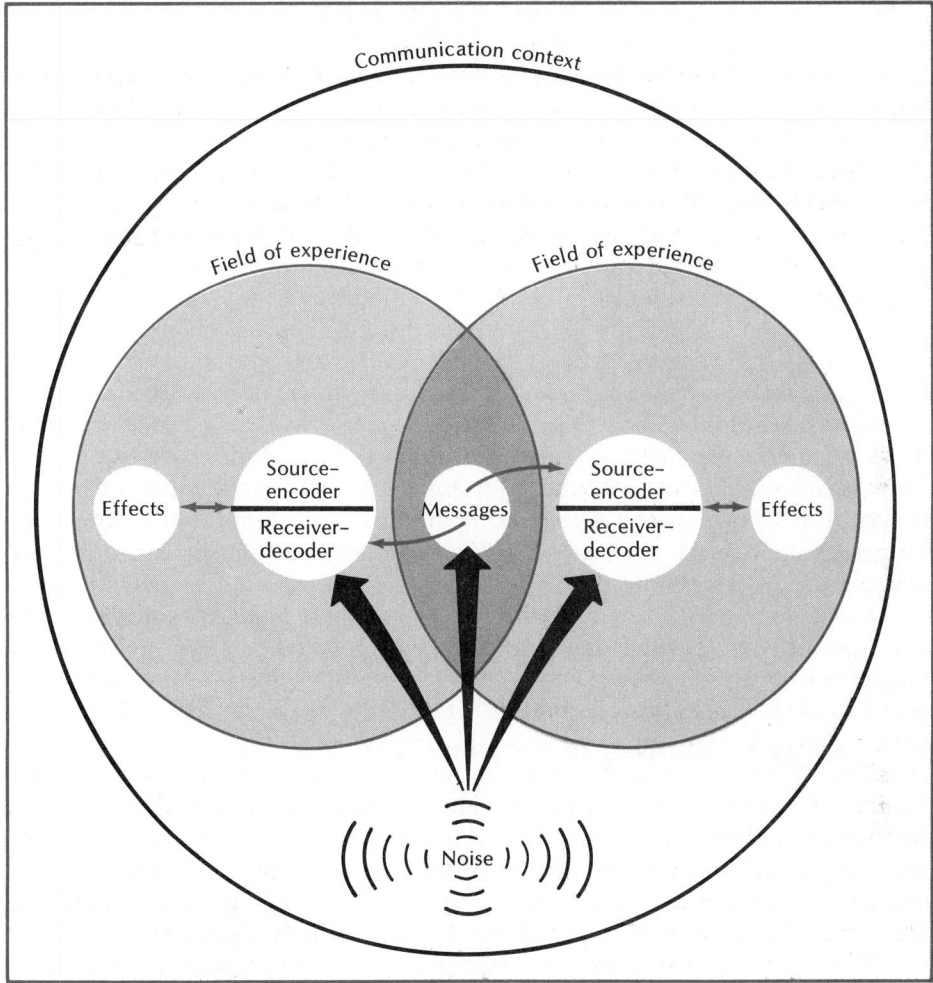

FIGURE 1.1 The universals of communication.

ences and is influenced by the others. For example, arriving late for a date (temporal context) may lead to changes in friendliness-unfriendliness (social-psychological context), which may lead, for example, to changes in physical closeness and in the selection of the restaurant for dinner (physical context). And these changes may lead to a host of other changes; the process is ongoing and never static.

Sources-Receivers

In the model of communication presented in Figure 1.1, communication is illustrated as taking place between two persons. If we wanted the diagram to illustrate *intra*personal communication, we would view the two "participants" as two roles or functions of the same person. Communication demands that someone send signals and someone receive them.

We use the hyphenated *sources-receivers* to emphasize this dual function. We send messages in speaking, writing, gesturing, or smiling; we receive messages in listening, reading, smelling, and so on. As you are speaking, you are also receiving messages. You are receiving your own messages (you hear yourself, you feel your own movements, you see many of your own gestures) and you are receiving the messages of the other person—visually, auditorily, or even through touch or smell. Notice that as you speak to anyone, you are looking at that person for responses—for approval, understanding, sympathy, agreement, and so on. As you decipher these nonverbal signals, you are performing receiving functions.

What people say and how they say it are functions of who they are, what they know, what they believe in, what they value, what they want, and what they are told, how intelligent they are, what their attitudes are, and so on. Likewise, the particular messages they receive and how they receive them are functions of who they are. A rich, pampered, well-educated child and a poor, neglected, uneducated child do not talk about the same things in the same way, nor will they receive messages identically. Even if they were to view the same television program, each would derive a unique and different meaning. Who you are can never be divorced from the messages you send or the messages you perceive.

Encoding-Decoding

In communicology (the study of communication) the processes of speaking and understanding, or writing and comprehending, are referred to as *encoding* and *decoding*. The act of producing messages—for example, speaking or writing—is termed *encoding*. By putting our ideas into sound waves we are putting these ideas into a code, hence *en*coding. By translating sound waves into ideas we are taking them out of the code they are in, hence *de*coding. Thus we may refer to speakers or writers as encoders, and listeners or readers as decoders. As with *source-receiver*, we hyphenate *encoding-decoding* to emphasize that the functions are performed *simultaneously;* as we are speaking (encoding) we are also deciphering the responsive messages of the other individual (decoding).

Communicative Competence

Communicative competence refers to our knowledge of the more social aspects of communication. It includes such "knowledges" as the role the context plays in determining the substance and form of communication messages—for example, the knowledge that in certain contexts and with certain auditors one topic is appropriate and another is not.

Knowledge of the role of silence in communication would represent another aspect of communication competence—specifically, a knowledge concerning when to speak and when to remain silent, when silence is uncomfortable and when it is welcomed. Knowledge concerning the rules of nonverbal behavior—

for example, the appropriateness of touching, vocal volume, and physical close-ness—would also be part of communication competence.

We learn communication competence much as we learn how to eat with a knife and fork—by observing others, by explicit instruction, by trial and error, and so on. Some have learned better than others, though, and such people are generally the ones we find both interesting and comfortable to talk with; they are the ones who seem to know what to do and how and when to do it. One of the major goals of this text and this course is to spell out the nature of communication competence and to increase your own communication compe-tence. By increasing your competence, you will have available a greater number of performance options.

Put differently, the more you know about communication (that is, the greater your competence), the more choices you will have available for your day-to-day communications. The process is comparable to learning vocabulary: The more vocabulary you know (that is, the greater your vocabulary compe-tence), the more ways you will have available for expressing yourself. Thus, the aim of this book is to increase your communicative competencies so that you will have available a broader range of options in performing your various communication activities.

Messages and Channels

The *messages* that are sent and received in communication may take any form; they may be sent and received through any one or any combination of sensory organs. Although we customarily think of communication messages as being verbal (oral or written), these are not the only kinds of messages that communicate. We also communicate nonverbally (without words). For example, the clothes we wear communicate something to other people and probably also communicate to ourselves as well. The way we walk communicates, as does the way we shake hands, cock our heads, comb our hair, sit, or smile or frown. In fact, everything about us communicates. And this is true whether it is our intention or not to communicate. Thus, a slip of the tongue or an overheard whisper communicates just as does a carefully prepared speech. All this infor-mation (verbal and nonverbal, intentional and unintentional) constitutes com-munication messages.

We may think of the communication *channel* as the medium through which the messages pass. Communication rarely takes place over only one channel; rather, two, three, or four different channels are used simultaneously. Thus, for example, in face-to-face interactions we speak and listen (vocal-auditory channel), but we also gesture and receive these signals visually (gestural-visual channel) and we also emit odors and smell them (chemical-olfactory channel). Often we touch one another, and this too communicates (cutaneous-tactile channel).

The amount of time that information stays in the communication channel has changed drastically over the last several decades. John Naisbitt, in his *Megatrends: Ten New Directions Transforming Our Lives,* notes this as one of the major changes taking place in our move from an industrial to an informational society. The faster the information moves through the communication channel, the closer together are sender and receiver brought. With electronic communication (for example, electronic mail), a process that formerly took two to four days now takes just seconds. This process Naisbitt refers to as "collapsing the information float." He notes further that this acceleration of communication will function to accelerate all aspects of life and commerce.

Feedback

Feedback is information that is sent back to the source. Feedback may come from oneself (the source) or from others (the receivers), may be positive or negative, and may be immediate or delayed. Each of these dimensions should be considered briefly.

Sources of Feedback

When we send a message—say, in speaking to another person—we also hear ourselves. We get feedback from our own messages—we hear what we say, we feel the way we move, we see what we write, and so on. On the basis of this information we may correct ourselves, rephrase something, or perhaps smile at a clever turn of phrase. In addition to this self-feedback, there is the feedback we get from others. In speaking with another individual, not only are we constantly sending messages, we are also constantly receiving messages. The receiver's messages (sent in response to the source's messages) are also termed *feedback*. This feedback, like other messages, can take many forms—a frown or a smile, a yea or a nay, a pat on the back or a punch in the mouth are all types of feedback. In the diagram of the universals of communication (Figure 1.1), the arrows from source-receiver to effect and from one source-receiver to the other source-receiver are drawn going in both directions to illustrate the notion of feedback. We perceive our own messages and we perceive the responses and reactions of the other communicator to our own messages.

Positive and Negative Feedback

Feedback may be positive or negative. Positive feedback tells the source that everything is fine and that one should continue as one has been going. Negative feedback tells the source that all is not well and that a reassessment of one's communication behavior is necessary. Negative feedback serves a corrective function by informing the communicator that something needs changing and adjustment. Effectiveness in communication seems largely due to the ability of the communicator to respond appropriately to feedback. Teaching effectiveness may also be seen in the same way.

Immediate and Delayed Feedback

The immediacy of feedback has often been used to distinguish interpersonal from mass communication. With interpersonal communication the feedback we get is usually immediate: We see the frown or smile, we hear the agreeing or disagreeing responses immediately. With mass communication, the feedback is usually delayed; for example, a "letter to the editor" arrives a week after the article appears. Now, however, this is changing; much of the feedback to the media is now relatively immediate. For example, viewers can now register their political opinions and even their preferences for videos or films by dialing special 900 numbers. Audience responses can be channeled to the source almost immediately, given the proper computer hookups. In the next several years, these mechanisms for immediate commentary and response will increase tremendously. In the not-too-distant future, when we turn on the television our choice will be automatically recorded in some central data bank and we will be able to communicate our responses—not merely "yea" or "nay," but detailed and intricate reactions—with immediacy and ease not only to this central data bank, but to all others who have the requisite equipment.

Noise

In the early development of communication theory, noise was viewed as a disturbance in the channel—as in the telephone cables connecting speaker and hearer. But there are many other kinds of disturbances that need to be identified and analyzed, and it has become convenient to refer to any such interference as *noise*. Noise, in this extended sense, can enter any communication system and constitutes anything that distorts or interferes with the message. Noise is present in a communication system to the extent that the message sent differs from the message received. Three major types of noise may be identified.

Physical Noise

Physical noise interferes with the physical transmission of the signal or message. Examples of this include the hum of a computer, a speaker's lisp, and sunglasses, because each interferes with the transmission of signals from one person to another. Physical noise is also present in written communication and includes blurred type, smudges on the paper, illegible writing, and, in fact, anything that prevents a reader from getting the message sent by the writer.

Psychological Noise

Biases, prejudices, preconceptions, erroneous assumptions, closed-mindedness, and similar mental sets that lead to distortions in receiving and processing information would be considered *psychological noise*.

Semantic Noise

Semantic noise leads to the receiver's failing to grasp the meaning intended by the source. In its extreme form, semantic noise occurs between people speaking widely differing languages. In more common form, semantic noise is evident when speakers use technical or complex terms that are not fully understood by the listener. Such noise also occurs, and perhaps more frequently, when a term is used to which speaker and listener assign different meanings. Consider, for example, such terms as *communism, religion, lesbian, education, freedom,* and *death.* These terms will almost invariably be given different meanings by different communicators. When these differences in meaning are ignored, we have semantic noise interfering with the accurate transmission of a message from one person to another.

Noise is inevitable. All communications contain noise of some kind, and although we cannot eliminate noise completely, we can reduce noise and its effects. Making our language more precise; acquiring the skills for sending and receiving nonverbal messages; and improving our perceptual, listening, and feedback skills—covered throughout this text—are some of the ways in which we can effectively combat the interference of noise in our messages.

Field of Experience

The circles in Figure 1.1 refer to what is called a *field of experience*. The assumption here is that communication can take place only to the extent that the participants have had the same experiences (illustrated by the overlapping portions of the circles). Communication is ineffective to the extent that the participants have not had the same experiences. Parents have difficulty communicating with their children, in this view, because the children cannot share the parental experience and because the parents have forgotten what it is like to be a child or do not know what it is like to be a child today. When management forgets what it is like to be labor and when labor does not share any of management's experiences, communication becomes extremely difficult. Differences among people serve to make communication more and more difficult, and the larger the differences, the more difficult communication becomes. Although many differences cannot be eliminated, communication is not hopeless. While we cannot, for example, share the actual experiences of our parents, we can perhaps attempt to role-play what it is like being a parent and perhaps in that way extend the field of experience.

Communication Effects

Communication *always* has some effects on one or more persons involved in the communication. For every communication act, there is some consequence. The effect may be either on one participant or on both. Further, the effect may involve such diverse consequences as (1) the acquisition of knowledge or learning how to analyze, synthesize, or evaluate something (that is, intellectual or cognitive effects); (2) the acquisition of or changes in one's attitudes, beliefs, emotions, and feelings (that is, affective effects); and (3) the learning of gross and finely coordinated bodily movements such as throwing a ball or painting a picture, as well as the learning of appropriate verbal and nonverbal behaviors (that is, psychomotor effects).

Ethics and the Notion of Choice

To the degree that communication has an effect, it also has an *ethical dimension*. Because communication has consequences, there is a right-versus-

All forms of communication (interpersonal, small group, public, intercultural, and mass) have numerous elements in common. How many of the elements discussed in this unit can you identify in this photo?

wrong aspect to any communication act. Unlike principles of effective communication, principles of ethical communication are difficult to formulate. Often we can observe the effect of communication and, on the basis of the observations, formulate principles of effective communication. We cannot, however, observe the rightness or wrongness of a communication act. The ethical dimension of communication is further complicated by the fact that it is so interwoven with one's personal philosophy of life that it is difficult to propose universal guidelines. Given these difficulties, we nevertheless include ethical considerations as being integral to any communication act. The decisions we make concerning communication must be guided by considerations of ethics as well as effectiveness.

The major determinant of whether communications are ethical or unethical is to be found in the notion of choice and the assumption that people have a right to make their own choices. Communications are ethical to the extent that they facilitate an individual's freedom of choice by presenting that person with accurate bases for choice. Communications are unethical to the extent that they interfere with an individual's freedom of choice by preventing that person from securing information relevant to the choice. Unethical communications, there-fore, would be those that force people (1) to make choices they would not normally make, and/or (2) to decline to make choices they would normally make.

The ethical communicator, then, provides others with the kind of infor-mation that is helpful in making their own choices. In this ethic based on choice, however, there are a few qualifications that may restrict one's freedom. It is assumed that these individuals are of an age and mental condition to allow the reasonable execution of free choice, and that a free choice in their situation will not prevent the free choice of others. A child of 5 or 6 is not ready to make certain choices, so someone else must make them instead. Similarly, some mentally disadvantaged individuals need others to make certain decisions for them. In addition, the circumstances under which one is living can restrict free choice; for example, persons in the military will at times have to give up free choice and eat hamburger rather than steak, wear uniforms rather than jeans, and march rather than stay in bed. By entering the armed forces, one at least partially relinquishes the right to make one's own choices. Finally, the free choices we make must not prevent others from making their free choices. We cannot permit a thief to have freedom of choice to steal, because in granting that freedom we effectively prevent the victims from exercising their free choice.

These, then, are some of the qualifications that must be considered in any theory of choice as an ethical guide. Admittedly, it is not always easy to determine when people possess the mental ability to make their own decisions or when the choice of one person actually precludes the choices of another. Yet these are decisions we must face in any theory concerned with the morality of human behavior.

THE PURPOSES OF COMMUNICATION

Five significant purposes of communication should be noted here. These pur-poses may also be viewed as the motives or reasons for communicating.

Purposes need not be conscious, nor is it essential that individuals agree about their purposes for communicating. Purpose may be subconscious as well as conscious, and unrecognizable as well as recognizable. Further, although communication technologies are changing rapidly and drastically—we send and receive electronic mail, work at computer terminals, and telecommute, for example—the purposes of communication are likely to remain essentially the same throughout the electronic revolution and whatever revolutions follow.

Personal Discovery

One of the major purposes of communication concerns personal discovery. When we communicate with another person, we learn a great deal about ourselves as well as about the other person. In fact, our self-perceptions result largely from what we have learned about ourselves from others during com-munications, especially our interpersonal encounters.

By talking about ourselves with another individual we are provided with an excellent source of feedback on our feelings, thoughts, and behaviors. From this type of encounter we learn, for example, that our feelings about ourselves, others, and the world are not so different from someone else's feelings. And the same is true about our behaviors, fears, hopes, and desires. This positive reinforcement helps us to feel "normal."

Social Comparison Processes

Another way in which we increase personal discovery is through comparing our abilities, accomplishments, attitudes, opinions, values, and failings with those of others. That is, we evaluate ourselves largely by comparing ourselves with the people we know and with whom we interact. Different people will deal with these evaluations in different ways. On the basis of social comparison, one may see oneself as worthless and develop feelings of depression, while another may appear as a "super" individual and yet another as mediocre and "just one of the crowd." Some people may use these social comparisons as motivation to acquire new knowledge and skills. Regardless of how we evaluate ourselves and what we do with the information, it is clear that social comparisons are essential in the development of our self-concept and that we make these social comparisons largely through our communication interactions and experiences.

Discovery of the External World

Much as communication gives us a better understanding of ourselves and the person with whom we are communicating, it also gives us a better understanding of the external world—the world of objects, events, and other people. Today, we rely on the various communications media to inform us about entertainment, sports, war, economic developments, health and dietary concerns, new products to buy, and so on. Much of what we acquire from the media interacts with what we learn from our interpersonal interactions; we seem to acquire a great deal of information from the media, discuss it with other people, and ultimately learn or internalize the material as a result of the interaction of these two sources.

Establishing Meaningful Relationships

One of our strongest motivations is to establish and maintain close relationships with others. We want to feel loved and liked, and in turn we want to love and like others. Much of our communication time and energy is devoted to establishing and maintaining social relationships. You communicate with your close friends in school, at work, and probably on the phone; you talk with your parents, children, and brothers and sisters; you interact with your relational partner. All told, this takes a great deal of your time and attests to the importance of this purpose of communication.

Changing Attitudes and Behaviors

The mass media exist largely to change our attitudes and behaviors; the media survive on advertisers' money, which is directed at getting us to buy a variety of items we can easily do without. Right now you probably spend a great deal of time as consumers rather than originators of these mass media messages. But in the not-too-distant future you will no doubt be originating messages—working on newspapers, editing magazines, and working in ad agencies, television stations, and a variety of other communication-related fields.

But we also spend a great deal of our time engaged in interpersonal persuasion, as both sources and receivers. In our everyday interpersonal encounters we attempt to change the attitudes and behaviors of others—to get them to vote a particular way, to try a new diet, to buy a particular item, to see a movie, to read a book, to take a specific course, to believe that something is true or false, to value or devalue some idea, and so on. The list is endless. Few of our interpersonal communications, in fact, do *not* seek to change attitudes or behaviors.

Play and Entertainment

Much of our communication behavior is devoted to play and entertainment. We listen to comedians, speeches, the jokes of friends, songs, and movies largely for entertainment. Similarly, much of our own communication behavior is devoted to the entertainment of others—we tell jokes, we say clever things, and we try, in short, to entertain others, sometimes as an end in itself and sometimes merely as a way of holding their attention.

In thinking about these purposes of communication, keep a few facts clearly in mind. First, no list of communication purposes can be exhaustive; obviously there are others. The five considered here seem the major ones and were therefore singled out for discussion. Second, no communication act is motivated by just one factor. Single causes do not seem to exist in the real world, and so any communication is probably motivated by a combination of purposes rather than only one. Third, since communication involves at least one other person, all five of these purposes affect both the self and other(s). These purposes also motivate each individual in different ways and to different degrees depending on the nature of the individuals involved—their needs, wants, and histories; the context in which the communication takes place; and the numerous other factors we have already noted as being essential to any communication act.

SUMMARY

1. *Communication* refers to the act, by one or more persons, of sending and receiving messages that are distorted by noise, occur within a context, have some effect, and provide some opportunity for feedback.

2. The universals of communication—the elements present in every communication act—are these: context, source-receiver, message, channel, noise, sending or encoding processes, receiving or decoding processes, feedback, and effect.

3. The communication context has at least three dimensions: physical (the tangible or concrete environment), social-psychological (the roles, norms, and mores of the society), and temporal (the time in history as well as the position of the communication in the sequence of events).

4. The hyphenated term *source-receiver* is used to emphasize that each individual engaged in communication is both a source (or sender) and a receiver. Similarly, the hyphenated term *encoding-decoding* is used to emphasize that each person involved in communication both sends and receives messages.

5. *Communication competence* refers to knowledge of the elements and rules of communication.

6. Communication *messages* may be of varied forms and may be sent and received through any one or any combination of sensory organs: vocal-auditory, gestural-visual, chemical-olfactory, or cutaneous-tactile. The communication *channel* is the medium through which the messages are sent in their passage from sender to receiver.

7. *Feedback* refers to messages or information that is sent back to the source and may come from the source itself (as when listening to oneself) or from the receiver (in the form of applause, looks of puzzlement, or nods of agreement, for example). Feedback may be positive or negative, and immediate or delayed.

8. *Noise* refers to anything that distorts the message; it is present to some degree in every communication transaction. Noise is present to the degree that the message received differs from the message sent.

9. The *field of experience* refers to the total experiences of an individual that influence the individual's meanings. In some views, meaningful communication can take place only to the extent that the fields of experience of the sender and receiver overlap.

10. Communication always has an *effect*. Effects may be cognitive (intellectual or cerebral), affective (emotional or attitudinal), and/or psychomotor (referring to motor or perceptual motor skills).

11. *Communication ethics* refers to the rightness or wrongness—the morality—of a communication transaction and is an integral part of each and every communication transaction.

12. Communication may serve at least five general purposes: personal discovery, discovery of the external world, establishing meaningful relationships, changing attitudes and behaviors, and play and entertainment.

13. Through social comparison processes we compare ourselves with others to assess and evaluate ourselves. We may assess, for example, our abilities, attitudes, beliefs, and shortcomings in this way.

SOURCES

For communication concepts, see Joseph A. DeVito, *The Communication Handbook: A Dictionary* (New York: Harper & Row, 1986), and Tracy Daniel Connors, *Longman Dictionary of Mass Media and Communication* (New York: Longman, 1982). An excellent overview of the entire field of communication, though one that may prove somewhat advanced in parts, is Stephen W. Littlejohn, *Theories of Human Communication*, 2d ed. (Belmont, Calif.: Wadsworth, 1983). John Naisbitt's *Megatrends: Ten New Directions Transforming Our Lives* (New York: Warner, 1984) provides a wealth of insights into the changes taking place in communication and how these changes will influence our lives.

UNIT 2
EIGHT POSTULATES OF COMMUNICATION

LEARNING GOALS

After completing this unit, you should be able to

1. explain the transactional nature of communication
2. explain the inevitability of communication
3. explain what is meant by communication being an irreversible process and identify the implications of this irreversibility
4. explain why communication is viewed as a package of signals
5. define and distinguish between the content and the relationship dimensions of communication
6. explain the principle of adjustment in communication
7. explain the concept of punctuation
8. define and distinguish between symmetrical and complementary transactions

In the previous unit, we defined communication and explained some of its components and characteristics. In this unit, we continue to elaborate on the nature of communication by presenting eight postulates or principles of communication—propositions that are essential to an understanding of communication in all its forms and functions.

COMMUNICATION IS A TRANSACTIONAL PROCESS

Communication is a transaction. By *transaction* I mean to specify that communication is a process, that its components are interrelated, and that communicators act and react as wholes.

Communication Is a Process

Communication is a process; communication is an ongoing activity. Although we may talk about communication as if it were static and at rest, it is never so. Consequently, everything in communication is in a state of constant change. We are constantly changing, the people with whom we are communicating are changing, and our environment is changing. Sometimes these changes go unnoticed; sometimes they intrude in obvious ways. But they are always occurring. Nothing in communication ever remains static.

Components Are Interrelated

In any transactional process, each element is integrally related to every other element; the elements of communication are interdependent (never independent); each exists in relation to the others. For example, there can be no source without a receiver; there can be no message without a source; there can be no feedback without a receiver. Because of this interdependence, a change in any one element of the process produces changes in the other elements. For example, you are talking with a group of your friends and your mother enters the group. This change in "audience" will lead to a number of other changes—perhaps in the style of the communications, the content of what is said, the frequency with which certain people talk, and so on. Regardless of what change is introduced, other changes will be produced as a result.

Communicators Act as Wholes

Each person involved in communication acts and reacts as a whole. We are biologically designed to act as whole beings. One cannot react, for example, solely on an intellectual or an emotional level; we are not so compartmentalized. Rather, we respond emotionally and intellectually, physically and cognitively; we respond with body-and-mind. Perhaps the most important corollary of this characteristic is that our actions and reactions in communication are determined not only by what is said, but also by our interpretation of what is said. Our responses to a movie, for example, do not depend solely on the words and pictures in the movies but on our entire being—on our previous experiences, present emotions, knowledge, physical well-being, and a host of other factors. Thus, two people listening to the same message will often derive two very different meanings. Although the words and symbols are the same, they will be interpreted very differently by different people. Each individual's interpretation of any communication will be unique; each interpretation will be different from every other interpretation.

COMMUNICATION IS INEVITABLE

Often we think of communication as being intentional, purposeful, and consciously motivated, and in many instances it is. But in other instances we are communicating even though we might not think we are or might not even want to communicate. Take, for example, the student sitting in the back of the room with an expressionless face, perhaps staring at the front of the room or out the window. Although the student might claim not to be communicating with the teacher or with the other students, that student is obviously communicating a great deal—perhaps lack of interest, boredom, a concern for something else, or a desire for the class to be over with as soon as possible. In any event, the student is communicating with or without wanting to. We cannot *not* communicate.

Further, when we are in an interactional situation with this seemingly uncommunicative person, we must respond in some way. Even if we do not actively or overtly respond, that lack of response is itself a response and communicates. Like the student's silence, our silence in response also communicates. We cannot *not* respond.

COMMUNICATION IS IRREVERSIBLE

The processes of some systems can be reversed. For example, we can turn water into ice and then reverse the process by turning the ice back into water. And we can repeat this reversal process for as long as we wish. Other systems, however, are irreversible: The process can go in only one direction. Communication is such an irreversible process. What has been communicated remains communicated; we cannot uncommunicate. Although we may try to qualify, negate, or somehow reduce the effects of our message, the message itself, once it has been sent and received, cannot be reversed.

This principle has a number of important implications for communication in all its forms. For example, in interpersonal interactions we need to be careful that we do not say things we may be sorry for later. Especially in conflict situations, when tempers run high, we must avoid saying things we may wish to withdraw later. Commitment messages—the "I love you" messages and their variants—need to be similarly monitored lest we commit ourselves to a position we may not be happy with at some later time. In public and in mass communication situations, when the messages are heard by hundreds, thousands, and even millions of people, it is especially crucial that we recognize the irreversibility of our communications.

COMMUNICATION IS A PACKAGE OF SIGNALS

Communication behaviors, whether they involve verbal messages, the movements of the hands or eyes, or some combination, normally occur in "packages" in which the various verbal and nonverbal behaviors reinforce or support each other. All parts of our message system normally work together to communicate a particular meaning. We do not express fear with our verbalizations while the rest of our body relaxes as if sleeping. We do not express anger through our posture while our face smiles. Rather, the entire body—verbally and nonverbally—works together to express our thoughts and feelings.

In any form of communication, whether interpersonal, small group, public speaking, or mass media, we generally pay little attention to the packaged nature of communication; it is so expected that it goes unnoticed. But when there is an incongruity—when the weak handshake belies the verbal greeting, when the nervous posture belies the focused stare, when the constant preening belies the expressions of being comfortable and at ease—we take notice. Invariably we are led to question the credibility, the sincerity, and the honesty of the individual.

Contradictory Messages

A person who says "I'm so glad to see you," but who avoids direct eye contact and looks around as if to see who else is present is sending contradictory messages. Contradictory messages (also called "mixed messages" by some writers) are seen frequently in couples (whether newly dating or long married) who say they love each other but seem to go out of their way to hurt each other nonverbally—for example, by being late for important dates, by dressing in ways the other person dislikes, by flirting with others, by avoiding direct eye contact, or by not touching each other.

Ernst Beier has argued that these messages—which he refers to as "discordance"—are the result of the desire of the individual to communicate two different emotions or feelings. For example, we may like someone and want to communicate this positive feeling, but we may also dislike this person and want to communicate this negative feeling as well. The result is that we communicate both feelings, one verbally and one nonverbally.

COMMUNICATION INVOLVES CONTENT AND RELATIONSHIP DIMENSIONS

Communications, to a certain extent at least, refer to the real world or to something external to both speaker and hearer. At the same time, however, communications also refer to the relationships between the parties. For example, a teacher may say to a student, "See me after class." This simple message has a *content aspect,* which refers to the behavioral responses expected—namely, that the student see the teacher after class—and a *relationship aspect*, which tells us how the communication is to be dealt with. Even the use of the simple command states that there is a status difference between the two parties such that the teacher can command the student. This is perhaps seen most clearly when we visualize this command being made by the student to the teacher. It appears awkward and out of place simply because it violates the normal relationship between teacher and student.

In any communication situation the content dimension may stay the same but the relationship aspect may vary, or the relationship aspect may be the same with the content being different. For example, the teacher could say to the student either "You had better see me after class," or "May I please see you after class?" In each case the content is essentially the same; that is, the message being communicated about the behavioral responses expected is about the same in both cases. But the relationship dimension is very different. In the first it signifies a very definite superior-inferior relationship and even a put-down of the student. In the second a more equal relationship is signaled and a respect for the student is shown. Similarly, at times the content may be different but the relationship essentially the same. For example, a teenager might say to his or her parents, "May I go away this weekend?" and "May I use the car tonight?" The content of the two messages is clearly very different, yet the relationship dimension is essentially the same. It is clearly a superior-inferior relationship in which permission to do certain things must be secured.

The Failure to Distinguish Content and Relationship

Many problems between people are caused by the failure to recognize the distinction between the content and the relationship levels of communication. Consider the engaged couple arguing over the fact that Pat made plans to study during the weekend with friends without first asking Chris if that would be all right. Probably both would have agreed that to study over the weekend was the right choice to make; thus the argument is not at all related to the content level. The argument centers on the relationship level: Chris expected to be consulted about plans for the weekend; Pat, in not doing this, rejected this definition of relationship.

Let me give you a personal example. My mother came up to stay for a week at a summer place I had. On the first day she swept the kitchen floor six times, though I had repeatedly told her that it did not need sweeping and that I would be tracking in dirt and mud from outside, so all this effort was just

How does the postulate that communication is a process of adjustment relate to the communications that take place in your typical college class? How might an understanding of this postulate help to improve classroom communication?

wasted. But she persisted in sweeping, saying that the floor was dirty and should be swept. On the content level, we were talking about the value of sweeping the kitchen floor. But on the relationship level we were talking about something quite different: We were each saying, "This is my house." When I realized this (though only after considerable argument), I stopped complaining about the relative usefulness of sweeping a floor that did not need sweeping and she stopped sweeping.

Arguments over the content dimension are relatively easy to resolve. Generally, we may look something up in a book or ask someone what actually took place. It is relatively easy to verify facts that are disputed. Arguments on the relationship level, however, are much more difficult to resolve, in part because we seldom recognize that the argument is in fact a relationship one.

COMMUNICATION IS A PROCESS OF ADJUSTMENT

Communication may take place only to the extent that the communicating parties use the same system of signals. This is obvious when dealing with speakers of different languages; one will not be able to communicate with the other to the extent that their language systems differ. This principle takes on particular relevance, however, when we realize that no two persons use identical signal systems. Parents and children, for example, not only have largely different vocabularies but, even more importantly, have different meanings for the terms they share. Different cultures and subcultures, even when they use a common language, often have greatly different nonverbal communication systems. To the extent that these systems differ, meaningful and effective communication will not take place.

Part of the art of communication is identifying the other person's signals, learning how they are used, and understanding what they mean. Someone who is in a close relationship with another—either as intimate friends or as romantic partners—realizes that learning the other person's signals takes a great deal of time and often a great deal of patience. If we want to understand what another person means (by a smile, by saying "I love you," by arguing about trivia, by self-deprecating comments), rather than simply acknowledging what the other person says or does, we have to learn that person's system of signals.

COMMUNICATION SEQUENCES ARE PUNCTUATED FOR PROCESSING

Communicating events are continuous transactions. There is no clear-cut beginning and no clear-cut ending. As participants in or observers of the communication act, we divide up this continuous, circular process into causes and effects, or stimuli and responses. That is, we segment this continuous stream of communication into a number of smaller pieces and label some of these causes or stimuli and others effects or responses.

Consider an example: The students are apathetic; the teacher does not prepare for classes. Figure 2.1(a) illustrates the sequence of events in which there is no absolute beginning and no absolute end. Each action (the student apathy and the teacher's lack of preparation) stimulates the other; each serves as the stimulus for the other, but there is no initial stimulus. Each of the events may be regarded as a stimulus and each of the events may be regarded as a response, but there is no way to determine which is which. Now, consider how the teacher might divide up this continuous transaction. Figure 2.1(b) illustrates the teacher's perception of this situation. From this point of view, the teacher sees the student apathy as the stimulus for a lack of preparation, and the lack of teacher preparation is seen as the response to the student apathy. In Figure 2.1(c) we see how the students might divide up the transaction. The students might see this "same" sequence of events as beginning with the teacher's lack of preparation as the stimulus (or cause) and their own apathy as the response (or effect).

This tendency to divide up the various communication transactions into sequences of stimuli and responses is referred to by Paul Watzlawick, Janet Beavin, and Don Jackson, in their influential *Pragmatics of Human Communication*, as *punctuation*. We each punctuate the continuous sequences of events into stimuli and responses for convenience of processing. And, as the example of the students and teacher illustrates, we most often punctuate communication in ways that allow us to look good and that are consistent with our own self-image.

If communication is to be effective, if we are to understand what the other person means from his or her point of view, then we have to imagine the sequence of events as punctuated by the other person. Further, we have to recognize that our punctuation does not reflect what exists in reality; rather, it reflects our own unique but fallible perception.

COMMUNICATION INVOLVES SYMMETRICAL AND COMPLEMENTARY TRANSACTIONS

In a *symmetrical relationship* the two individuals mirror each other's behavior. The behavior of one person is reflected in the behavior of the other. If one member nags, the other member responds in kind. If one member expresses jealousy, the other member expresses jealousy. If one member is passive, the other member is passive. The relationship is one of equality, with the emphasis on minimizing the differences between the two individuals.

In a *complementary relationship* the two individuals engage in different behaviors, with the behavior of one serving as the stimulus for the complementary behavior in the other. In complementary relationships the differences between the parties are maximized. In a complementary relationship, the parties occupy different positions, one superior and the other inferior, one passive and the other active, one strong and the other weak. At times such relationships are established by the culture—as, for example, the complementary relationship existing between teacher and student, or between employer and employee.

Problems may arise in both symmetrical and complementary relationships; two of the most significant are referred to as rigid complementarity and progressive differentiation.

Rigid Complementarity

Occurring in complementary relationships, *rigid complementarity* refers to an inability to change the type of relationship between oneself and another even though the individuals, the context, and a host of other variables have changed. Whereas the complementary relationship between mother and child was at one time vital and essential to the life of the child, the same relationship when the child is older, as Watzlawick, Beavin, and Jackson put it, "becomes a severe handicap for his further development, if adequate change is not allowed to take place in the relationship." Rigid complementarity is also seen frequently when, in the early stages of a heterosexual relationship, the man is more educated and makes more money than the woman. Initially his role is to guide and finance the relationship. But if the woman becomes the better educated of the two and/or begins to earn more money than the man, he is frequently unable to adjust to this change. He remains rigid, unable to alter his relationship to this "new" woman. This type of rigid complementarity seems to be one of the main reasons why couples in which the woman earns more money than the man are relatively unhappy ones—a finding well documented in the recent and extensive *American Couples*.

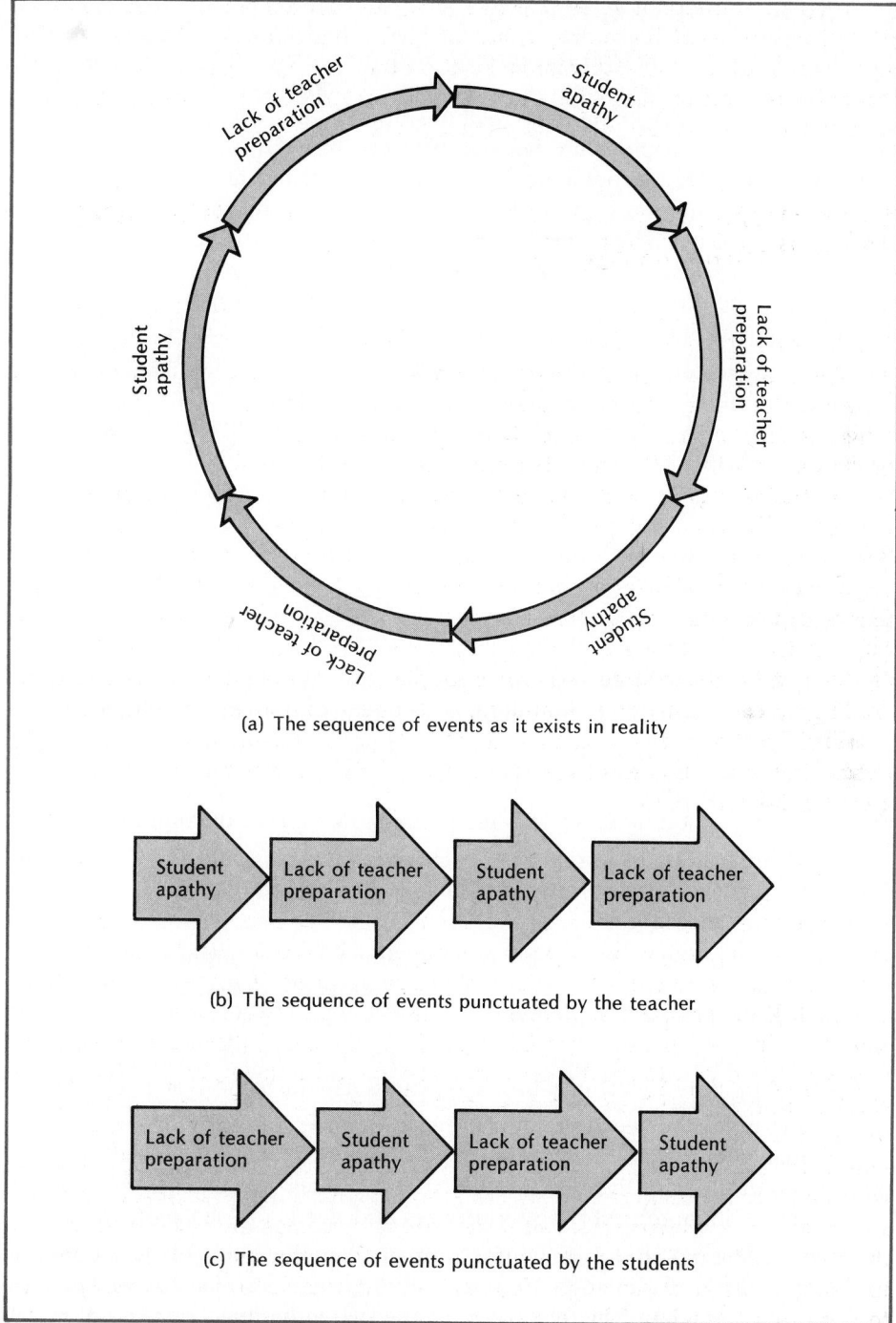

(a) The sequence of events as it exists in reality

(b) The sequence of events punctuated by the teacher

(c) The sequence of events punctuated by the students

FIGURE 2.1 The sequence of events.

Progressive Differentiation

The problem of *progressive differentiation* may result from either type of relationship—a condition Bateson called *schismogenesis*. Consider this development first in the complementary relationship. Let us say that we have two brothers and that the older brother overprotects the younger. This overprotection fosters increased dependency from the younger brother. As the younger brother becomes more and more dependent, the older brother becomes more and more protective. The result is often a breakdown in the relationship, with each coming to resent the behavior of the other and perhaps coming to dislike or even hate the other.

Progressive differentiation may also occur in a symmetrical relationship. Consider the situation of a husband and wife, both of whom are very aggressive. The aggressiveness of the husband fosters aggressiveness in the wife; the aggressiveness of the wife fosters aggressiveness in the husband. As this escalates, the aggressiveness can no longer be contained, and the relationship blows up.

SUMMARY

1. Communication is transactional: Communication is a process, its components are interrelated, and communicators act and react as wholes.

2. In any interactional situation, communication is inevitable; we cannot *not* communicate nor can we *not* respond to communication.

3. Communication is an irreversible process; we cannot uncommunicate.

4. Communication is normally a package of signals, each reinforcing the other. When communication signals contradict each other, we have contradictory messages.

5. Communication involves both content dimensions (references to the world outside the speaker and receiver) and relationship dimensions (references to the connections existing between speaker and receiver).

6. Communication is a process of adjustment and may take place only to the extent that the communicating individuals use the same system of signals.

7. Communication sequences are punctuated for processing. Different individuals divide up the communication sequence into stimuli and responses differently. This division (or punctuation) does not exist in reality but depends in large part on the purposes and needs of each participant.

8. Communication involves symmetrical and complementary transactions. In symmetrical relationships, the two individuals mirror each other's behavior. In complementary relationships, the two individuals engage in different behaviors, with the behavior of one serving as the stimulus for the complementary behavior in the other.

9. *Rigid complementarity* refers to the inability to change the kind of relationship existing between oneself and another even though the individuals and numerous other variables have changed.

10. *Progressive differentiation* refers to the unproductive and extreme increase in a particular behavior pattern that may occur in either symmetrical or complementary relationships.

SOURCES

For this unit I relied most heavily on Paul Watzlawick, Janet Helmick Beavin, and Don D. Jackson, *Pragmatics of Human Communication: A Study of Interactional Patterns, Pathologies, and Paradoxes* (New York: Norton, 1967). Another useful work in this area is Jurgen Ruesch and Gregory Bateson, *Communication: The Social Matrix of Psychiatry* (New York: Norton, 1951). Many of the ideas set forth in *Pragmatics* may be found in the work of Bateson. For a useful collection of Bateson's writings, see *Steps to an Ecology of Mind* (New York: Ballantine, 1972). For an application of many of these principles to the therapeutic process, see Paul Watzlawick, *The Language of Change: Elements of Therapeutic Communication* (New York: Basic Books, 1978). A useful collection of articles dealing with these concepts is provided by Paul Watzlawick, *How Real is Real? Confusion, Disinformation, Communication: An Anecdotal Introduction to Communications Theory* (New York: Vintage Books, 1977). I also relied (especially for the concepts of adjustment and packaging) on Robert E. Pittenger, Charles F. Hockett, and John J. Danehy, *The First Five Minutes: A Sampling of Microscopic Interview Analysis* (Ithaca, N.Y.: Paul Martineau, 1960). See Philip Blumstein and Pepper Schwartz, *American Couples: Money, Work, Sex* (New York: Morrow, 1983) for extensive data on relationships.

UNIT 3
THE SELF IN COMMUNICATION:
Awareness and Disclosure

LEARNING GOALS

After completing this unit, you should be able to

1. explain the structure and general function of the Johari Window
2. define the *open, blind, unknown,* and *hidden selves*
3. provide examples of information that might be contained in each of the four selves
4. identify and explain the five suggestions for increasing self-awareness
5. define *self-disclosure*
6. explain at least three rewards of self-disclosure
7. explain at least three dangers of self-disclosure
8. explain the operation of at least six factors that influence self-disclosing behaviors
9. explain the concept of and the gender differences in self-disclosure avoidance
10. explain at least five guidelines for self-disclosing and at least four guidelines to observe in responding to the disclosures of others

Of all the components of the communication act, the most important is the self. Who you are and how you perceive yourself and others influence your communications and your responses to the communications of others more than any other elements. In this unit, we explore some dimensions of the self. First, we examine self-awareness and look at our several selves. Second, we consider self-disclosure, that form of communication in which we reveal something of who we are.

SELF-AWARENESS

If we had to list some of the qualities we wanted to possess, self-awareness would surely rank high. We all wish to know ourselves better, because we control our thoughts and behaviors largely to the extent that we understand ourselves, to the extent that we are aware of ourselves.

This concept of self-awareness is basic to all forms and functions of communication and is best explained by the Johari Window, presented in Figure 3.1. (The name *Johari* was derived from the first names of the two persons who developed the model: Joseph Luft and Harry Ingham.) The window is broken up into four basic areas or quadrants, each of which contains a somewhat different self.

The Open Self

The *open self* represents all the information, behaviors, attitudes, feelings, desires, motivations, ideas, and so on that are known to the self and also known to others. The type of information included here might vary from one's name, skin color, and sex to one's age, political and religious affiliation, and batting average. Each individual's open self will vary in size depending on the time and on the individuals he or she is dealing with. At some times we are more likely than at others to open ourselves up. If, for example, we opened ourselves and got hurt because of it, we might then close up a bit more than usual. Similarly, some people make us feel comfortable and support us; to them, we open ourselves wide, but to others we prefer to leave most of ourselves closed.

The size of the open self also varies greatly from one individual to another (Figure 3.2). Some people are prone to reveal their innermost desires and feelings, whereas others prefer to remain silent about both the significant and the insignificant things in their lives. Most of us, however, open ourselves to some people about some things at some times.

"The smaller the first quadrant," says Luft, "the poorer the communication." Communication depends on the degree to which we open ourselves to

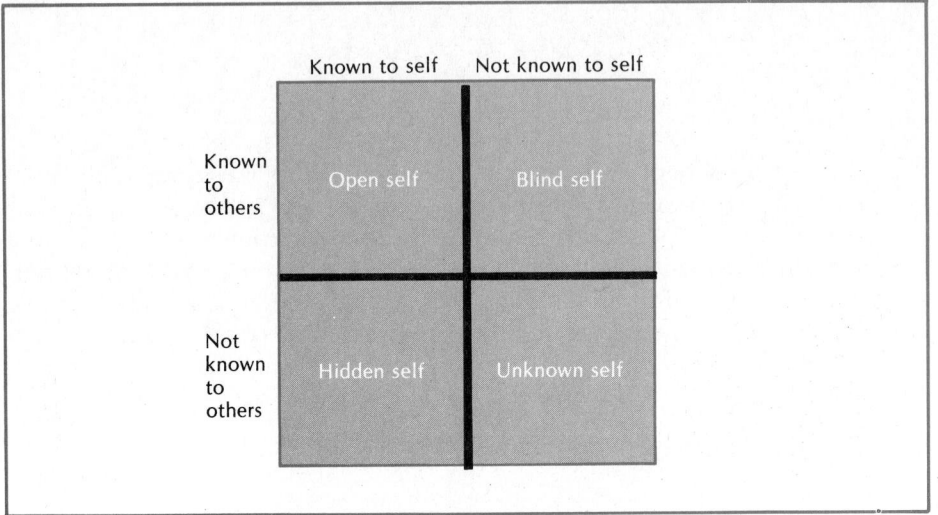

FIGURE 3.1 The Johari Window. *Source:* Joseph Luft, *Group Process: An Introduction to Group Dynamics* (Palo Alto, Calif.: Mayfield, 1970), p. 11.

others and to ourselves. If we do not allow others to know us (that is, if we keep the open self small), communication between them and us becomes extremely difficult, if not impossible. We can communicate meaningfully only to the extent that we know one another and to the extent that we know ourselves. To improve communication, we have to work first on enlarging the open self.

A change in the open area—or in any of the quadrants—will bring about a change in the other quadrants. Visualize the entire window as being of constant size, with the size of each pane variable—sometimes small, sometimes large. As one pane becomes smaller, one or more of the others must become larger. Similarly, as one pane becomes larger, one or more of the others must become smaller. Thus, these several selves are not separate and distinct but are interacting selves, each dependent on the others.

The Blind Self

The *blind self* represents all those things about ourselves that others know but of which we are ignorant. This may vary from the relatively insignificant habits of saying "you know," rubbing your nose when you get angry, or having a peculiar body odor, to something as significant as defense mechanisms, fight strategies, or repressed past experiences.

Some people have a very large blind self and seem to be totally oblivious to their own faults and sometimes (though not as often) their own virtues. Others seem overconcerned with having a small blind self. They seek therapy at every turn and join every consciousness-raising group. Some are even convinced that they know everything there is to know about themselves, that they have reduced the blind self to zero. Still others only pretend to want to reduce the size of the blind self; they profess a total willingness to hear all about

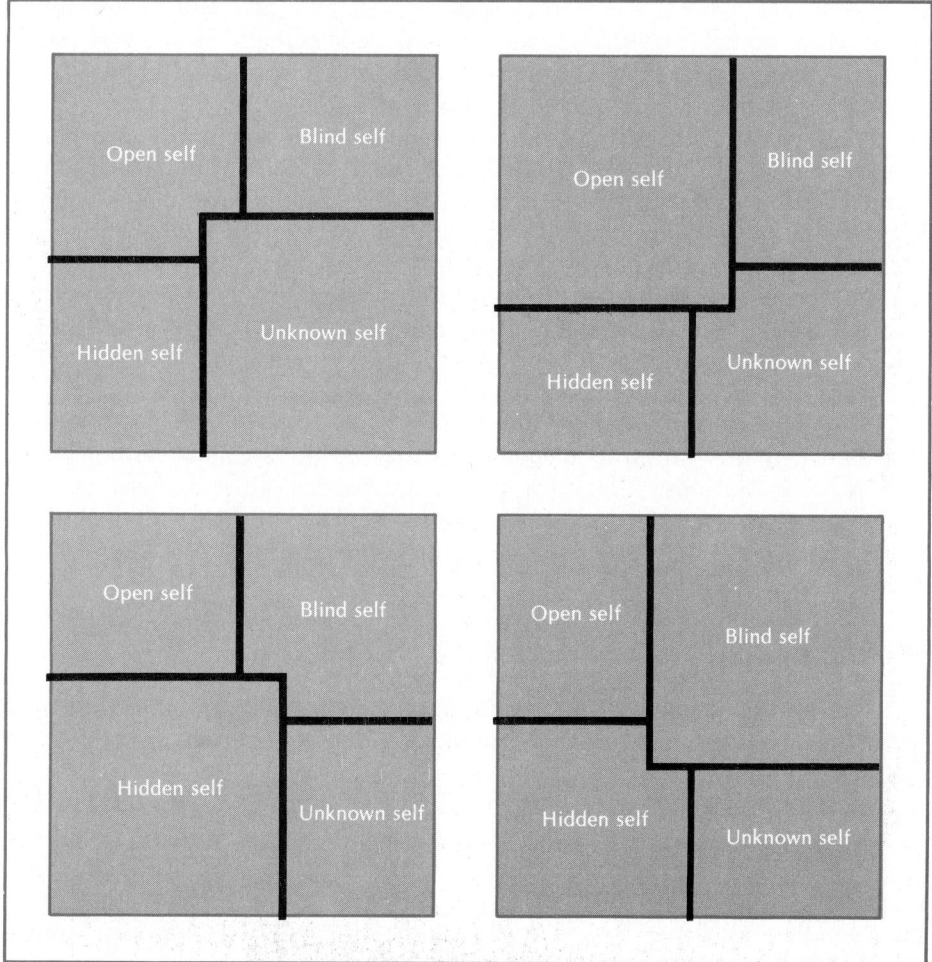

FIGURE 3.2 Johari Windows of varied structure.

themselves, but when they are confronted with the first negative comment, the defenses and denials go up with amazing speed. In between these extremes lie most of us.

Communication depends in great part on both parties possessing the same basic information about each other. To the extent that blind areas exist, communication will be made difficult. Yet blind areas will always exist for each of us. Although we may be able to shrink our blind areas, we can never totally eliminate them.

The Unknown Self

The *unknown self* represents those parts of ourselves that exist but about which neither we nor others know. One could argue that if neither we nor anyone else knows what is in this area, we cannot know that it exists at all. Actually, we do not *know* that it exists; rather, we *infer* that it exists. We assume that some aspects of ourselves are confined to our subconscious and are therefore currently unknown to ourselves as well as to others.

We may gain insight into the unknown self from a number of different sources. Sometimes this area is revealed through temporary changes brought about by drug experiences, through special experimental conditions such as hypnosis or sensory deprivation, or through various projective tests or dreams. There seem to be sufficient instances of such revelations to justify our including this unknown area as part of the self. The exploration of the unknown self through open, honest, and empathic interaction with trusted and trusting others—parents, friends, counselors, children, lovers—is one of the most effective ways of gaining insight into this unknown self.

Although we cannot easily manipulate this area, recognize that it does exist and that there are things about ourselves that we do not and will not know. This may be the most important step in increasing self-awareness. A clear recognition that our knowledge of self is incomplete coupled with a determination to increase that knowledge constitute prerequisites to increasing self-awareness.

The Hidden Self

The *hidden self* contains all that you know of yourself and others but keep to yourself. This area includes all your successfully kept secrets about yourself and others.

At the extremes we have the overdisclosers and the underdisclosers. The overdisclosers tell all. They keep nothing hidden about themselves or others. They will tell you their family history, sexual problems, marital difficulties, financial status, goals, failures and successes, and just about everything else. For them the hidden self is very small, and had they sufficient time and others sufficient patience it would be reduced to near zero. The problem with these overdisclosers is that they do not discriminate. They do not distinguish between those to whom such information should be disclosed and those to whom it should not be disclosed, nor do they distinguish among the various types of information that should and should not be disclosed.

The underdisclosers tell nothing. They will talk about you but not about themselves. Depending upon our relationship with these underdisclosers, we might feel that they are afraid to tell anyone anything for fear of being laughed at or rejected, or we may feel somewhat rejected for their refusal to trust us. Never to reveal anything about yourself comments on what you think of the people with whom you are interacting. On one level, at least, it communicates "I don't trust you enough to reveal myself to you."

The vast majority of us fall somewhere between these two extremes. We keep certain things hidden and we disclose other things; we disclose to some people and we do not disclose to others. We are, in effect, selective disclosers.

The way in which we view ourselves will greatly influence how we send and how we receive messages. How does your own self image influence your communication behavior as speaker and as listener? How does the self image of others (as you perceive it) influence the ways in which you communicate with these other people?

GROWING IN SELF-AWARENESS

Embedded in the foregoing discussion were suggestions on how to increase your own self-awareness. Some of these may now be made explicit.

Dialogue with Yourself

No one knows you better than you do; the problem is that we seldom if ever ask ourselves about ourselves. It can be interesting and revealing. There are a number of ways to do this. One way is to take a "Who Am I?" test informally. Take a piece of paper, head it "Who Am I?" and write 10, 15, or 20 times, "I am . . . ." Then complete the sentence each time. Try not to give only positive or socially acceptable responses; just respond with what comes to mind first. Second, take another piece of paper and divide it into two columns. Head one column "Strengths" or "Virtues" and the other column "Weaknesses" or "Vices." Fill in each column as quickly as possible. Third, using these first two "tests" as a base, take a third piece of paper, head it "Self-Improvement Goals," and complete the statement "I want to improve my . . . " as many times as you can in, say, five minutes. Whether or not these particular methods are used is not important; what is important is that you begin a dialogue with yourself about yourself.

Further, remember that you are constantly changing; consequently, these self-perceptions and goals also change, often in drastic ways; they therefore need to be updated at regular and frequent intervals.

Listen

We can learn a great deal about ourselves from seeing ourselves as others do. Conveniently, others are constantly giving us the very feedback we need to increase self-awareness. In every interpersonal interaction, people comment on us in some way—on what we do, what we say, how we look. Sometimes these comments are explicit; most often they are only implicit. Often they are "hidden" within the way in which others look at us, in what they talk about, in their interest in what we say. Pay close attention to this kind of information (both verbal and nonverbal) and use it to increase your self-awareness. In the discussions of verbal and nonverbal communication that follow, suggestions and insights for reading these hidden messages are offered.

Reduce Your Blind Self

Actively seek out information to reduce your blind self. Generally, people will reveal more when they are encouraged to do so. You need not be so blatant as to say, "Tell me about myself" or "What do you think of me?" But you can use some of the situations that arise every day to gain self-information: "Do you think I came down too hard on the instructor today?" or "Do you think I was assertive enough when asking for the raise?" Do not, of course, seek this information constantly; your friends would then surely and quickly find others with whom to interact. But you can make use of some situations—perhaps those in which you are particularly unsure of what to do or how you appear—to reduce your blind self and increase self-awareness.

See Your Different Selves

Each of us is viewed differently by each of our friends and relatives; to each we are a somewhat different person. Yet we are really *all* of these. Practice seeing yourself as do the people with whom you interact. For starters, visualize how you are seen by your mother, your father, your teachers, your best friend, the stranger you sat next to on the bus, your employer, your neighbor's child. Each of these people sees you differently. Because you are, in fact, a composite of all of these views, it is important that you for a moment see yourself through the eyes of these others. The experience will surely give you new and valuable perspectives on yourself.

Increase Your Open Self

The extent to which you reveal yourself to others—the degree to which you increase your open self—influences at least two dimensions of self-awareness. First, when you reveal yourself to others, you reveal yourself to yourself at the same time. At the very least, you bring into consciousness or into clearer focus what you may have buried within. As you discuss yourself, you may see connections that you had previously missed, and with the aid of feedback from others, you may gain still more insight. All this helps to increase your self-awareness. Second, by increasing the open self, you increase the likelihood that a meaningful and intimate dialogue will develop, and it is through such interactions that you best get to know yourself.

There are risks involved in revealing yourself, and these need to be taken into consideration. The risks (and advantages) of self-disclosure are considered in the next section.

SELF-DISCLOSURE

When we reveal information from our hidden self, we are engaging in what is called self-disclosure. In this section we look at self-disclosure from a number of vantage points: the nature of self-disclosure, the factors influencing self-disclosure, self-disclosure avoidance, the rewards or benefits to be derived from self-disclosure, and the potential dangers of self-disclosure.

The Nature of Self-Disclosure

Self-disclosure is a type of communication in which information about the self that is normally kept hidden is communicated to another person. Special note should be taken of several aspects of this elementary definition.

Self-disclosure is a type of communication. Thus, overt statements pertaining to the self as well as slips of the tongue, unconscious nonverbal movements, and public confessions would all be classified as self-disclosing communications. Usually, however, the term *self-disclosure* is used to refer to the conscious revealing of information.

Self-disclosure is information, in the information theory sense, meaning something previously unknown by the receiver. Information is new knowledge. In order to constitute self-disclosure, some new knowledge has to be communicated.

Self-disclosure is information about oneself; about one's own thoughts, feelings, and behaviors; or about one's intimates that has a significant bearing on oneself. Thus, self-disclosure could refer to your own actions or the actions of, say, your parents or children, since these have a direct relationship to who you are.

Self-disclosure involves information that is normally and actively kept hidden. It is not simply information that you have not previously revealed; it is information that you usually refuse to reveal and actively work at keeping secret.

Self-disclosure involves at least one other individual. To constitute self-disclosure, the communication act must involve at least two persons; it cannot be an intrapersonal act. Furthermore, we are not really disclosing when we make it impossible for the other person to understand us: This is not a disclosure at all. Also, we cannot write in diaries that no one reads and call this self-disclosure. To be self-disclosure, the information must be received and understood by another individual.

Factors Influencing Self-Disclosure

Self-disclosure occurs more readily under certain circumstances than others. Here, several of the factors influencing self-disclosure are identified.

Group Size   Perhaps because of the numerous fears we have about revealing ourselves, self-disclosure is more likely to occur in small groups than in large groups. Dyads are generally the most hospitable environment for self-disclosure. A dyad seems more suitable than a larger group because it is easier for the self-discloser to deal with the reactions and responses of one person than with those of three, four, or five. With one listener, the self-discloser can attend to the responses carefully, and on the basis of this support or lack of support can monitor the disclosures, continuing if the situation is supportive and stopping if it is not. With more than one listener such monitoring becomes difficult, since the responses are sure to vary among the listeners.

Closeness and Liking   Some research studies have found that we disclose more often to those who are close to us—for example, our spouses, family, or close friends. Husbands and wives self-disclose to each other more than they do to any other person or group of persons.

Other studies claim that we disclose to people we like or love and do not disclose to people we dislike, regardless of how close they are to us. Thus, someone may disclose to a well-liked teacher even though they are not particularly close and yet not disclose to a brother or sister who is close but is not liked very much. Recently, John Berg and Richard Archer reported that not only do we disclose to those we like, but we also seem to come to like those to whom we disclose.

Still other studies claim that self-disclosure is more likely to occur in temporary than permanent relationships—for example, between prostitute and client, or even between strangers on a train or plane. Michael McGill, in *The McGill Report on Male Intimacy,* refers to this type of relationship as "in-flight intimacy," wherein an intimate self-disclosing relationship is established during some brief travel period but is not pursued beyond that point.

Dyadic Effect   We tend to self-disclose when the person we are with also self-discloses. This dyadic effect probably leads us to feel more secure and, in fact, reinforces our own self-disclosing behavior. Berg and Archer also report that disclosures are generally more intimate when they are made in response to the disclosures of others.

Competence Competent people engage in self-disclosure more than less competent people. "It may very well be," note James McCroskey and Lawrence Wheeless, "that people who are more competent also perceive themselves to be more competent, and thus have the self-confidence necessary to take more chances with self-disclosure. Or, even more likely, competent people may simply have more positive things about themselves to disclose than less competent people."

Trust Mutual trust seems to be a prerequisite to self-disclosing behaviors. Generally, the more we trust someone the more likely it is that we will self-disclose to that person. Trust, however, is not a sufficient condition for self-disclosure; we do not self-disclose to everyone we trust.

Personality Generally, people who are highly sociable and extroverted self-disclose more than those who are less sociable and more introverted. Both general and specific anxiety affect our degree of self-disclosure, either increasing it significantly or reducing it to a minimum.

Topics We are more likely to disclose about some topics than others. For example, we are more likely to self-disclose information about our jobs or hobbies than about our sex lives or financial situations. We also disclose favorable information more readily than unfavorable information. Generally, the more personal and the more negative the topic, the less likely we are to self-disclose.

Gender The most important factor influencing self-disclosure is gender. Generally, men disclose less than do women. Judy Pearson, however, has argued that it is sex role rather than biological gender that accounts for the differences in self-disclosure. "Masculine women," for example, self-disclosed to a lesser extent than did women who scored low on masculinity scales. Further, "feminine men" self-disclosed to a greater extent than did men who scored low on femininity scales.

Self-Disclosure Avoidance

Men and women give different reasons for avoiding self-disclosure. The main reason for avoiding self-disclosure, however, is common to both men and women: "If I disclose, I might project an image I do not want to project." In a society where one's image is so important—where one's image is often the basis for success or failure—this reason for avoiding self-disclosure is expected. Other explanations, however, are unique to men and to women. Here are some reasons that men report: "If I self-disclose, I might give information that makes me appear inconsistent," "If I self-disclose, I might lose control over the other person," and "Self-disclosure might threaten relationships I have with people other than close acquaintances." Lawrence Rosenfeld sums up the male reasons for self-disclosure avoidance: "If I disclose to you, I might project an image I do not want to project, which could make me look bad and cause me to lose control over you. This might go so far as to affect relationships I have with people other than you." The principal objective of men in avoiding self-disclosure is to maintain control.

In addition to fearing the projection of an unfavorable image, women avoid self-disclosure for the following reasons: "Self-disclosure would give the other person information that he or she might use against me at some time," "Self-disclosure is a sign of some emotional disturbance," and "Self-disclosure might hurt our relationship." Rosenfeld gives the general reason for women to avoid self-disclosure: "If I disclose to you I might project an image I do not want to project, such as my being emotionally ill, which you might use against me and which might hurt our relationship." The principal objective for women's avoiding self-disclosure is "to avoid personal hurt and problems with the relationship."

Since self-disclosure depends so greatly on the role our culture dictates for both men and women and since these roles are changing so rapidly, we should be seeing significant changes in male and female self-disclosure patterns.

Rosenfeld summarizes the results of his investigation by observing: "The stereotyped male role—independent, competitive, and unsympathetic—and the stereotyped female role—dependent, nonaggressive, and interpersonally oriented—were evident in the reasons indicated for avoiding self-disclosure. Seeking different rewards from their interpersonal relationships, many males and females go about the business of self-disclosing, and *not* self-disclosing, differently." You might wish to test some of these findings yourself by talking with your peers about the reasons they avoid self-disclosure and about the reasons for their reasons. That is, why do men and women have different reasons for avoiding self-disclosure? What is there in the learning histories of the two sexes that might account for such differences?

The Rewards of Self-Disclosure

The obvious question when the topic of self-disclosure arises is "why?" Why should anyone self-disclose to anyone else? What is it about this type of communication that merits its being singled out and discussed at length? There is no clear-cut answer to these very legitimate questions, nor is there a great body of statistical research findings that attests to the usefulness or importance of self-disclosure. Yet there is evidence in the form of testimony, observational reports, and the like that has led a number of researchers and theorists to argue that self-disclosure is perhaps the most important form of communication in which we can engage. Here we identify some of the benefits ascribed to self-disclosure.

Self-Knowledge

One argument for self-disclosure is that we cannot know ourselves as fully as possible if we do not self-disclose to at least one other individual. It is assumed that by self-disclosing to another we gain a new perspective on ourselves and a deeper understanding of our own behavior. In therapy, for example, very often the insight does not come directly from the therapist; while the client is self-disclosing, he or she recognizes some previously unknown facet of behavior or relationship. Through self-disclosure, then, we may come to understand ourselves more thoroughly. Jourard, in *The Transparent Self*, notes that self-disclosure is an important factor in counseling and psychotherapy and argues that people may need such help because they have not previously disclosed significantly to other people.

Coping Abilities

Closely related is the argument that we will be better able to deal with our problems, especially our guilt, through self-disclosure. One of the great fears many people have is that they will not be accepted because of some deep dark secret, because of something they have done, or because of some feeling or attitude they might have. Because we feel these things are a basis for rejection, we develop guilt. If, for example, you do not love—or perhaps you hate—one of your parents, you might fear being rejected if you were to self-disclose such a feeling; thus a sense of guilt develops. By self-disclosing such a feeling, and by receiving support rather than rejection, we become better prepared to deal with the guilt and perhaps to reduce or even eliminate it. Even self-acceptance is difficult without self-disclosure. We accept ourselves largely through the eyes of others. If we feel that others would reject us, we are apt to reject ourselves as well. Through self-disclosure and subsequent support, we put ourselves in a better position to perceive the positive responses to us and will more likely respond by developing a positive self-concept.

Available Energies

Keeping our various secrets to ourselves and not revealing who we are to others takes a great deal of energy and leaves us with that much less energy for other things. We must be constantly on guard, for example, lest someone see in our behavior what we consider to be a deviant orientation, attitude, or behavior pattern. We might avoid talking to certain people for fear that they will be able to tell this awful thing about us, or we may avoid situations or places because if we are seen there others will know how terrible we really are. By self-disclosing we rid ourselves of the false masks that otherwise must be worn.

Communication Efficiency

Self-disclosure improves communication. We understand the messages of others largely to the extent that we understand the other individuals; we can understand what someone says better if we know that individual well. We can tell what certain nuances mean, when the person is serious and when joking, when the person is being sarcastic out of fear and when out of resentment, and so on. Self-disclosure is an essential condition for getting to know another individual. You might study a person's behavior or even live together for years, but if that person never self-discloses, you are far from understanding that individual as a complete person.

Relational Depth

Perhaps the main reason for the importance of self-disclosure is that it is necessary if a meaningful relationship is to be established between two people. Without self-disclosure, relationships of any meaningful depth seem impossible. There are, it is true, relationships that have lasted for many years without self-disclosure. Many married couples would fall into this category, as would many coworkers or neighbors. Without self-disclosure, however, these relationships are probably not terribly meaningful, or at least are not as meaningful as they might be. By self-disclosing we are in effect saying to other individuals that we trust them, respect them, and care enough about them and our relationship to reveal ourselves to them. This in turn leads the other individual to self-disclose, and forms at least the start of a meaningful relationship, one that is honest and open and goes beyond the surface trivialities.

The Dangers of Self-Disclosure

The numerous advantages to be gained from self-disclosure should not blind us to the fact that self-disclosure often involves very real risks. Here we discuss a few of the major dangers.

Personal and Social Rejection

When we self-disclose we usually do so to a person whose responses we can be fairly sure of; we don't self-disclose to just anyone, but rather to someone we feel will be supportive of our disclosures. Realize, of course, that we can only make guesses, and sometimes we guess wrong; the person we think will be supportive may turn out to reject us. Parents, normally seen as the most supportive of all our interpersonal relations, have frequently rejected children who self-disclosed their homosexuality, their plans to marry someone of a different religion, their decision to avoid the draft, or their belief in another faith. Our best friends, our closest intimates, may reject us for similar self-disclosures.

Material Loss

Not infrequently, self-disclosures result in severe material losses of various kinds. Politicians who disclose that they have been seeing a psychiatrist may later find that their own political party no longer supports their candidacy and that voters are unwilling to risk having someone who needed analysis in a position of political influence. Teachers who disclose former or present drug behavior or cohabitation with one of their students may find themselves denied tenure, teaching undesirable schedules, and eventually being victims of "budget cuts." In the corporate world, where alcoholism and drug addiction are persistent problems and where we might assume a supportive atmosphere would exist, self-disclosures relevant to such problems are often dealt with by dismissal, demotion, or transfer.

Intrapersonal Difficulties

When the reactions of others to our self-disclosures do not go as predicted, intrapersonal difficulties may result. When you are rejected instead of supported, when your parents say that you disgust them instead of hugging you, and when your friends ignore you at school rather than seeking you out as before, you are in line for some intrapersonal difficulties. No one likes to be rejected, and those with fragile egos might well consider what damage such rejection could bring.

Any significant self-disclosure imposes a burden on the other person. At the very least it imposes the burden of secrecy; some people, as you no doubt know, have great difficulty keeping secrets. In self-disclosing to them, we are creating this added difficulty for them. But some situations are much more complex. Consider, for example, the parent who swears the children to secrecy and then discloses an ongoing affair with a neighbor. This type of situation puts an unreasonable burden on the children, who are now in a bind to either break the promise of secrecy or allow the other parent to go on believing a lie.

In addition, remember that self-disclosure, like any communication, is irreversible. We cannot self-disclose to someone and then take it back; once we have disclosed, the disclosure is permanent, as if etched in stone. Regardless of how many times we may attempt to qualify something, "take it back," or deny it, once something is said it cannot be withdrawn. Nor can we erase the conclusions and inferences listeners have made on the basis of our disclosures.

SELF-DISCLOSURE GUIDELINES

Because self-disclosure involves both potential rewards and dangers, we need to examine carefully the likely consequences before deciding whether or not to self-disclose. Almost equally difficult is responding appropriately to the disclosures of others. Because self-disclosure is so important and so delicate a matter, guidelines are offered here for (1) deciding whether to self-disclose and how, and (2) responding to the disclosures of others.

Guidelines for Self-Disclosing

Each person has to make her or his own decisions concerning self-disclosure; there is no universal answer. Further, your decision will be based on numerous variables, many of which were considered in the foregoing discussion. The following guidelines will help you raise the right questions before making what must be *your* decision.

The Motivation for the Self-Disclosure

Self-disclosure should be motivated out of a concern for the relationship, for the others involved, and for oneself. Some people self-disclose out of a desire to hurt the listener. For example, a woman who tells her parents that they never did love her or that they hindered rather than helped her emotional development may be disclosing out of a desire to hurt and punish rather than to improve the relationship. Nor, of course, should self-disclosure be used to punish oneself (perhaps because of some guilt feeling or unresolved conflict). Self-disclosure should not represent an exercise in exhibitionism or an opportunity to parade one's sexual fantasies, past indiscretions, or psychological problems. Self-disclosure should serve a useful and productive function for all involved.

The Appropriateness of the Self-Disclosure

Self-disclosure should be appropriate to the context and to the relationship between speaker and listener. Before making any significant self-disclosure, ask if this is the right time and place. Could a better time and place be arranged? Ideally, self-disclosures should grow naturally out of the developing situation and relationship. Is this self-disclosure appropriate to the relationship? Generally, the more intimate the disclosures, the closer the relationship should be. It is probably best to resist intimate disclosures with nonintimates, with casual acquaintances, or in the early stages of a relationship. This suggestion applies especially to intimate negative disclosures.

The Opportunity Available for Open and Honest Responses

Self-disclosure should occur in an atmosphere that encourages open and honest responses. Don't hit and run. Avoid self-disclosure when the people involved are under time pressure or are in a situation that will not allow them to respond freely. Ask yourself, then, if there is sufficient time and if the atmosphere will allow the listener to respond at length to your self-disclosures if she or he wishes. If the answer is no, wait for another time and place.

The Clarity and Directness of the Self-Disclosure

The goal of self-disclosure is to inform, not to confuse, the other person. If you are going to self-disclose, consider the extent of the disclosure and be prepared to disclose enough to ensure the necessary understanding.

The most important suggestion in this regard is to disclose gradually. Disclose in small increments. When disclosures are made too rapidly and all at once, it is impossible to monitor your listener's responses and to retreat if the responses are not positive enough. Further, you prevent the listener from responding with his or her own disclosures, thereby upsetting the natural balance so helpful in this kind of communication exchange.

The Disclosures of the Other Person

During your disclosures, give the other person a chance to reciprocate with his or her own disclosures. If such reciprocal disclosures are not made, reassess your own self-disclosures. The lack of reciprocity may be a signal that for this person at this time and in this context, your disclosures are not welcomed or appropriate.

The Possible Burdens Self-Disclosure Might Entail

Any potential self-discloser should carefully weigh any problems that may be incurred as a result of a disclosure. Can you afford to lose your job if you disclose your previous prison record? Are you willing to risk failing the course if you confess to having plagiarized your term paper?

Ask yourself whether you are making unreasonable demands on the listener. Parents often place unreasonable burdens on their children by self-disclosing marital problems, infidelities, or self-doubts without realizing that the children may be too young or too emotionally involved to accept this information. Often such disclosures do not make the relationship a better one but instead add tension and friction, something we can all do without. Often such disclosures are made to ease one's own guilt without considering the burden this places on the other person.

Guidelines for Responding to Self-Disclosures

When someone discloses to you, it is usually a sign of trust and affection. In serving this most important receiver function, keep the following in mind.

Use Effective and Active Listening Skills

In Unit 5 we identify the skills of effective listening. These are especially important when listening to self-disclosures. Listen actively, listen for different levels of meaning, listen with empathy, and listen with an open mind. Paraphrase the speaker so that you can be sure you understand both the thoughts and the feelings communicated. Express understanding of the speaker's feelings to allow the speaker the opportunity to see these more objectively and through the eyes of another individual. Ask questions to ensure your own understanding and to signal your own interest and attention.

Support the Discloser

Express support for the person during and after the disclosures. Refrain from evaluation during the disclosures; concentrate on understanding and empathizing with the discloser. Allow the discloser to choose her or his own pace; don't rush the discloser with the too-frequent "So how did it all end?" type of response. Make your supportiveness clear to the discloser through your verbal and nonverbal responses—for example, maintaining eye contact, leaning toward the speaker, asking relevant questions, and echoing the speaker's thoughts and feelings.

Reinforce Disclosing Behaviors

The difficulty of self-disclosure makes it important that you reinforce the disclosing behavior throughout the experience. No reinforcement or too little reinforcement is likely to be interpreted as indifference or disapproval, with the result that the self-disclosing stops short. Both verbally and nonverbally, indicate your positive attitudes toward the discloser and the act of disclosing.

Maintain Confidentiality

When a person discloses to you, it is because she or he wants you to know these feelings and thoughts. If the discloser wishes others to share these, then it is up to her or him to disclose them. If you reveal these disclosures to others, all sorts of negative effects are bound to occur. Such indiscretion will likely inhibit future disclosures from this individual to anyone in general and to you in particular, and it is probable that your relationship will suffer considerably. Those to whom you reveal these disclosures will likely feel that since you have betrayed a confidence once, you will do so again, perhaps with their own self-disclosures. A general climate of distrust is easily established. But most important, betraying a confidence is unfair; it debases what could be and should be a significant and meaningful interpersonal experience.

Don't Use the Disclosures Against the Person

This is one of the most often abused rules concerning self-disclosures. Many self-disclosures expose some kind of vulnerability or weakness. If we later turn around and use these against the person, as we might in beltlining (hitting "below the belt"), we betray the confidence and trust invested in us. Regardless of how angry we might get, we should resist the temptation to use self-disclosures as weapons. If we do use disclosures against the person, the relationship is sure to suffer and may never fully recover.

SUMMARY

1. In the Johari Window model of the self, there are four major areas, each containing different information: the *open self* contains information that is known to both the self and others, the *blind self* contains information known to others and not to the self, the *hidden self* contains information known to the self but not to others, and the *unknown self* contains information unknown to both the self and others.

2. Suggestions for increasing self-awareness include asking yourself about yourself, listening to others to see yourself as others do, actively seeking information from others about yourself, seeing yourself from different perspectives, and increasing your open self.

3. *Self-disclosure* refers to a form of communication in which information about the self that is normally kept hidden is communicated to another person.

4. Self-disclosure is more likely to occur under the following conditions: when the potential discloser is with one rather than a group of people, when the discloser feels close to and likes or loves the listener, when the listener also discloses, when the discloser feels competent, when the discloser trusts the listener, when the discloser is highly sociable and extroverted, and when the topic of disclosure is fairly impersonal and is also positive.

5. Both men and women resist self-disclosure for fear of presenting a negative image of themselves. Other reasons for not disclosing are unique to each sex. Men resist disclosing for fear of appearing inconsistent, losing control, and damaging a relationship. Women resist disclosing for fear that the disclosed information will be used against them and will damage their relationships or lead to personal hurt.

6. A number of rewards have been identified for self-disclosure: increase in self-knowledge, increase in the ability to cope with difficult situations and guilt, increase in available energy, increase in communication efficiency, and increase in the chances for a meaningful relationship.

7. A number of dangers may also be identified for self-disclosure: personal and social rejection, material loss, and intrapersonal difficulties.

8. Before self-disclosing to another, consider the following issues: the motivation for the self-disclosure, the appropriateness of the self-disclosure, the opportunity available for open and honest responses, the clarity and directness of the self-disclosure, the disclosures of the other person, and the possible burdens that your self-disclosure might impose on you and on your listener.

9. In listening to the disclosures of others, keep the following in mind: practice the skills of effective and active listening, support the disclosure, reinforce the disclosing behaviors, keep the disclosures confidential, and do not use the disclosures as weapons against the person.

SOURCES

The Johari model is most thoroughly discussed in the works of Joseph Luft, particularly *Group Processes: An Introduction to Group Dynamics,* 2d ed. (Palo Alto, Calif.: Mayfield Publishing Company, 1970), and *Of Human Interaction* (Palo Alto, Calif.: Mayfield Publishing Company, 1969). Patricia Niles Middlebrook, in her *Social Psychology and Modern Life* (New York: Knopf, 1974), provides a thorough overview of the social-psychological dimensions of the self. A thorough overview of research and theory in self-awareness is provided by Chris L. Kleinke, *Self-Perception: The Psychology of Personal Awareness* (San Francisco, Calif.: Freeman, 1978).

On self-disclosure, see Sidney M. Jourard, *Disclosing Man to Himself* (New York: Van Nostrand Reinhold, 1968), and *The Transparent Self,* rev. ed. (New York: Van Nostrand Reinhold, 1971). In writing this unit I relied heavily on the insights of Gerard Egan; see especially his *Encounter: Group Processes for Interpersonal Growth* (Belmont, Calif.: Brooks/Cole, 1970). Overviews of self-disclosure in communication are provided by W. Barnett Pearce and Stewart M. Sharp, "Self-Disclosing Communication," *Journal of Communication* 23 (December 1973): 409–425, and James McCroskey and Lawrence Wheeless, *Introduction to Human Communication* (Boston: Allyn and Bacon, 1976). Another excellent review is by Paul Cozby, "Self-Disclosure: A Literature Review," *Psychological Bulletin* 79 (1973): 73–91.

A great deal of research is currently being conducted on self-disclosure. On the relationship between trust and self-disclosure, see Lawrence R. Wheeless and Janis Grotz, "The Measurement of Trust and Its Relationship to Self-Disclosure," *Human Communication Research* 3 (spring 1977): 250–257. For the study on self-disclosure avoidance, see Lawrence Rosenfeld, "Self-Disclosure Avoidance: Why I Am Afraid to Tell You Who I Am," *Communication Monographs* 46 (March 1979): 63–74. On sex roles and self-disclosure, see Judy C. Pearson, "Sex Roles and Self-Disclosure," *Psychological Reports* 47 (1980): 640. A thorough and readable analysis of self-disclosure (and the lack of it) in men is provided by Steven Naifeh and Gregory White Smith, *Why Can't Men Open Up? Overcom-*

ing Men's Fear of Intimacy (New York: Clarkson N. Potter, 1984). Also see Michael E. McGill, *The McGill Report on Male Intimacy* (New York: Harper & Row, 1985). The relationship between liking and disclosure is explored in John H. Berg and Richard L. Archer, "The Disclosure-Liking Relationship," *Human Communication Research* 10 (winter 1983): 269–281.

UNIT 4
PERCEPTION

LEARNING GOALS

After completing this unit, you should be able to

1. define *perception*
2. explain the three stages in the perception process
3. define *primacy* and *recency* and explain their influence on perception
4. define the *self-fulfilling prophecy* and explain how it influences perception
5. define *perceptual accentuation* and explain its influence on perception
6. define *implicit personality theory* and explain how it influences the perception process
7. define *consistency* and explain how it influences perception
8. define *stereotyping* and explain its influence on perception
9. define *attribution* and its principles of *consensus, consistency,* and *distinctiveness* and explain how this approach enables us to understand human behavior
10. explain the process of self-attribution and how the self-serving bias operates in this process

Perception is the process by which we become aware of the many stimuli impinging on our senses. It is a process that influences what stimuli or messages we take in and, perhaps more importantly, what meaning we give them once they reach awareness. Perception is therefore central to the study of communication in all its forms and functions. Here we look at (1) the perception process as a whole, identifying the three main stages in the process; (2) the psychological processes that influence perception; and (3) attribution, the process through which we make sense of the behaviors of ourselves and of others.

THE PERCEPTION PROCESS

Perception is complex. There is no one-to-one relationship between the messages that occur "out there" in the world—in the vibrations of the air and in the black marks on paper—and the messages that eventually get to our brain. What occurs "out there" may differ greatly from what reaches our brain. Examining how and why these messages differ is crucial to understanding communication. Perhaps the best way to illustrate how perception works is to explain the three steps involved in the process. These stages are not discrete and separate, as the following discussion might imply; in reality they are continuous and blend into and overlap one another (see Figure 4.1).

Sensory Stimulation Occurs

At this first stage the sense organs are stimulated—we hear a new recording, see someone we have not seen for years, smell perfume on the person next to us, taste a slice of pizza, feel a sweaty palm as we shake hands. But even when we have the sensory ability to perceive stimuli, we do not always do so. For example, when you are daydreaming in class, you do not hear what the teacher is saying until your own name is called. Then you wake up. You know your name was called, but you do not know why. This is a clear example of our perceiving what is meaningful to us and not perceiving what seems not to be meaningful.

Sensory Stimulation Is Organized

At the second stage, the sensory stimulations are organized according to various principles. One of the more frequently used "principles" is that of *proximity*: people or messages that are physically close to one another (people who are often seen together or live together, or messages uttered one immediately after the other) are perceived together, or as a unit. We infer that they

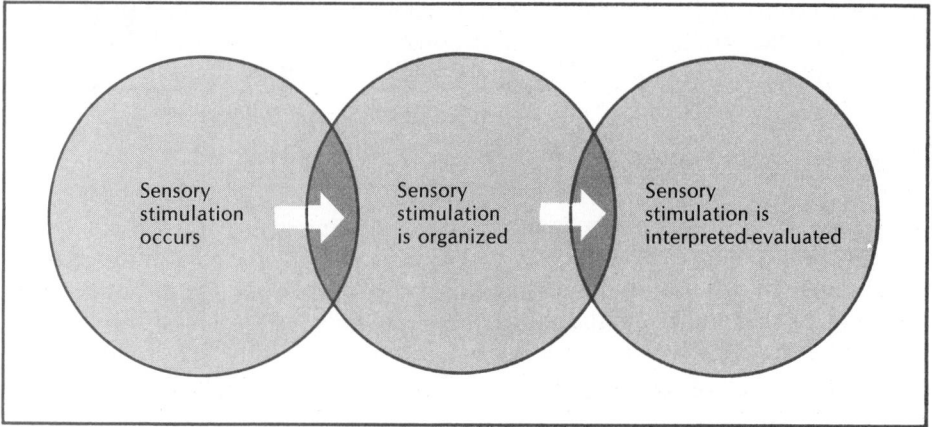

FIGURE 4.1 The perception process.

are related in some meaningful and nonarbitrary way. Another such principle is that of *closure:* We will perceive as closed or complete a figure or message that is in reality unclosed or incomplete. For example, a broken circle will be perceived as a circle even though part of it is missing. Even a series of dots or dashes arranged in a circular pattern will be perceived as a circle.

Proximity and closure are just two of the many organizing principles that may be cited. Exactly how any given stimulation will be organized and exactly what principles such organization will follow is not always clear or agreed upon by theorists. What we do know and what is especially important to remember is that what is perceived is organized into a pattern that is meaningful to the perceiver.

Sensory Stimulation Is Interpreted-Evaluated

The third step in the perceptual process is *interpretation-evaluation,* terms that we hyphenate and consider together to emphasize that in reality they cannot be separated. This third step is inevitably a subjective process involving evaluations on the part of the perceiver. Our interpretations-evaluations are not based solely on the external stimulus. They are greatly influenced by our past experiences, needs, wants, value systems, beliefs about the way things are or should be, physical or emotional states at the time, expectations, and so on.

It should be clear from even this very incomplete list of influences that there is much room for disagreement. Although we may all be exposed to a single external stimulus, the way it is interpreted-evaluated will differ for each person and from one time to another for the same person. The sound of a popular rock group may be heard by one person as terrible noise and by another as great music. The sight of someone we have not seen for years may bring joy to one person and anxiety to another. The smell of perfume may be pleasant to one person and repulsive to another. A sweaty palm may be perceived by one person to indicate nervousness and by another to indicate excitement.

These individual differences should not blind us to the validity of some generalizations. While these generalizations do not necessarily hold for any specific individual, they seem true enough for a significant majority.

PROCESSES INFLUENCING PERCEPTION

Between the occurrence of the stimulation (the uttering of the message, presence of the person, smile, or wink of the eye) and the evaluation or interpretation of that stimulation, perception is influenced by a number of significant psychological processes. Here we identify six major ones (see Figure 4.2).

Primacy-Recency

Assume for a moment that you have taken a course in which half the classes were extremely dull and half were extremely exciting. At the end of the semester you evaluate the course. Will the evaluation be more favorable if the dull classes constituted the first half of the semester and the exciting classes constituted the second half, or if the order were reversed? If what came first exerts the most influence, we have what is called a *primacy effect*. If what came last (or is the most recent) exerts the most influence, we have a *recency effect*.

In an early study on the effects of primacy-recency in people perception, Solomon Asch read a list of adjectives describing a person to a group of subjects and found that the effects of order were significant. A person described as "intelligent, industrious, impulsive, critical, stubborn, and envious" was evaluated as more positive than a person described as "envious, stubborn, critical,

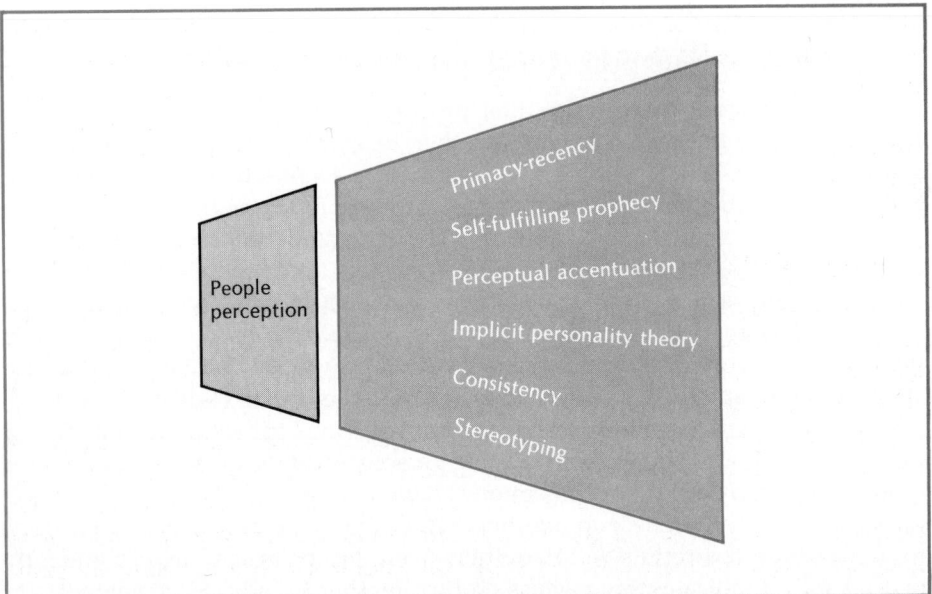

FIGURE 4.2 Some psychological processes influencing perception.

impulsive, industrious, and intelligent." The implication here is that we rely on the early information for a general idea of what a person is like, and the later information to make this general idea or impression more specific.

Self-Fulfilling Prophecy

A *self-fulfilling prophecy* occurs when we make a prediction or formulate a belief that proves true *because* we have made the prediction and have acted on it as if it were true. Identifying the four basic steps in the self-fulfilling prophecy should clarify this important concept and its implications for interpersonal perception.

1. We make a prediction or formulate a belief about a person or a situation. (For example, we predict that Pat is awkward in interpersonal encounters.)
2. We act toward that person or situation as if that prediction or belief is in fact true. (For example, we act toward Pat as if Pat were in fact awkward.)
3. Because we act as if the belief is true, it becomes true. (For example, because of the ways in which we act toward Pat, Pat becomes tense and manifests awkwardness.)
4. We observe *our* effect on the person or the resulting situation and what we see strengthens our beliefs. (For example, we observe Pat's awkwardness and this reinforces our belief that Pat is in fact awkward.)

If we expect people to act a certain way or if we make a prediction about the characteristics of a situation, our predictions will frequently come true because of the self-fulfilling prophecy phenomenon.

Consider, for example, people who enter a group situation convinced that the other members will dislike them. Almost invariably they are proved right; the other members do dislike them. What the newcomers may be doing is acting in such a way as to encourage other people to respond negatively. They made a prophecy and then fulfilled it. We must consciously monitor our perceptions and the manner in which we act on them to ensure that we are not creating for ourselves and others stumbling blocks to accurate and effective perception.

Perceptual Accentuation

"Any port in a storm" is a common enough phrase that, in its variants, appears throughout our communications. To many, even an ugly date is better than no date at all. Spinach may ordinarily taste horrible to you, but when you are starving, it can taste excellent. And so it goes.

In terms of people perception, *perceptual accentuation* leads us to see what we expect to see and what we want to see. We see people we like as better-looking than people we do not like; we see people we like as smarter than people we do not like. The obvious counterpart to this is that we actually prefer good-looking and smart people—not that people we like are seen as being handsome and smart. But perhaps that is not the entire story.

As social psychologist Zick Rubin describes it, male undergraduates participated in what they thought were two separate and unrelated studies; actually they were two parts of a single experiment. In the first part each subject read a passage; half the subjects were given a sexually arousing seduction scene to read, and half were given a passage about seagulls and herring gulls. In the second part of the experiment, subjects were asked to rate a female student on the basis of her photograph and a self-description. As might be expected, the subjects who read the arousing scene rated the woman as significantly more attractive than did the other group. Further, the subjects who expected to go on a blind date with this woman rated her as more sexually receptive than did the subjects who were told they had been assigned to date someone else. How can we account for such findings?

Although this experiment was a particularly dramatic demonstration of perceptual accentuation, the same process occurs every day. We magnify or accentuate what will satisfy our needs and wants. The thirsty person sees a mirage of water, the sexually deprived person sees a mirage of sexual satisfaction, and only very rarely do they get their mirages mixed up.

Implicit Personality Theory

We each have a theory of personality, complete with rules, although we may not be able to verbalize either. More specifically, we have a system of rules that tells us which characteristics of an individual go with which other characteristics. Consider, for example, the following brief statements. Note the characteristic in parentheses that best seems to complete the sentence:

- John is energetic, eager, and (intelligent, stupid).
- Joe is bright, lively, and (thin, fat).
- Jim is handsome, tall, and (flabby, muscular).
- Jane is attractive, intelligent, and (likable, unlikable).
- Mary is bold, defiant, and (extroverted, introverted).
- Susan is cheerful, positive, and (attractive, unattractive).

It is not important which words you selected; certainly there are no right or wrong answers. What should be observed, however, is that certain words "seemed right" and others "seemed wrong." What made some seem right was our implicit personality theory, the system of rules that tells us which characteristics go with which other characteristics. The theory may tell us, for instance, that a person who is energetic and eager is also intelligent rather than stupid, although there is no logical reason that a stupid person could not be energetic and eager.

Consistency

There is a rather strong tendency to maintain balance or consistency among our perceptions. We strive to maintain balance among our attitudes; we expect certain things to go together and others not to. On a purely intuitive basis, for example, respond to the following sentences by noting the expected response.

1. I expect a person I like to (like, dislike) me.
2. I expect a person I dislike to (like, dislike) me.
3. I expect my friend to (like, dislike) my friend.
4. I expect my friend to (like, dislike), my enemy.
5. I expect my enemy to (like, dislike) my friend.
6. I expect my enemy to (like, dislike) my enemy.

According to most consistency theories, our expectations would be as follows: We would expect a person we liked to like us (1) and a person we disliked to dislike us (2). We would expect a friend to like a friend (3) and to dislike our enemy (4). We would expect our enemy to dislike our friend (5) and to like our other enemy (6). All of these statements should be intuitively satisfying.

We expect someone we like to possess those characteristics we like or admire, and we expect our enemies not to possess those characteristics. Conversely, we expect people we like to lack unpleasant characteristics and people we dislike to possess unpleasant characteristics.

In terms of people perception, this tendency for balance and consistency may influence the way in which we see one another. It is easy to see our friends as possessing fine qualities and our enemies as possessing unpleasant qualities. Donating money to the poor, for example, can be perceived as an act of charity (if from a friend) or of pomposity (if from an enemy). We laugh harder at a joke told by a well-liked comedian than at that same joke told by an unpopular comedian.

Stereotyping

One of the most frequently used shortcuts in people perception is that of *stereotyping*. Originally, ''stereotype'' was a printing term that referred to the plate that printed the same image over and over again. A sociological or psychological stereotype, then, is a fixed impression of a group of people. We all have stereotypes, whether they be of national groups, religious groups, racial groups, or occupational groups, such as criminals, prostitutes, teachers, plumbers, or artists.

When we have these fixed impressions we will often, upon meeting someone of a particular group, see that person primarily as a member of that group. All the characteristics we attribute to members of that group are then applied to this individual. If we meet someone who is a prostitute, for example, we have a host of characteristics for prostitutes that we are ready to apply to this person. To further complicate matters, we will often see in this person various characteristics that we would not have seen if we had not known this person was a prostitute. Stereotypes distort our ability to perceive people accurately. They prevent us from seeing an individual as an individual; instead, the individual is seen only as a member of a group.

Forming impressions from stereotypes and forming them from implicit personality theories are somewhat similar processes. The main difference is that stereotypes are organized around national, religious, ethnic, and other group identifications; we reason that since an individual is a member of a

Regardless of where or with whom we interact, we form impressions of others and they form impressions of us based on a variety of factors. These impressions, in turn, will influence our subsequent communications. How would you go about discovering the impressions that others (say, your fellow classmates) form of you? What cues do others make use of in formulating these impressions of you? How accurate do you think these initial impressions are?

particular group, he or she must possess certain characteristics. Implicit personality theories are organized in clusters of characteristics; from two or three known characteristics, we reason that this other, unknown characteristic is also a part of this individual.

For example, with stereotypes we reason that since certain people are Venusians, they are also energetic and courageous. With an implicit personality theory we reason that since these people are energetic and courageous, they are also intelligent (since intelligence, in our hypothetical theory, goes with energy and courage). As can be appreciated, both stereotypes and implicit personality theory rely heavily on our need for consistency. It is psychologically comfortable for us to see an unknown Venusian as conforming to our stereotype of all Venusians. Similarly, it is psychologically comfortable for us to see an energetic and courageous person as intelligent, since this conforms to our expectations.

ATTRIBUTION

Perhaps the most interesting theoretical approach to perception is that of *attribution theory,* developed largely by E. E. Jones and K. E. Davis and expanded and clarified greatly by H. H. Kelly. Attribution is a process through which we attempt to understand the behaviors of others (as well as our own), particularly the reasons or motivations for these behaviors. Most of our inferences about a person's motivations—a person's reasons for behaving in various ways—come from our observations of the person's behaviors.

If our eventual aim is to discover the causes of another's behavior, then our first step is to determine whether the individual is responsible for the behavior or if some outside factor is responsible. That is, we first have to determine whether the cause of the behavior is *internal* (for example, when the behavior is due to the person's personality or to some such enduring trait), or *external* (for example, when the behavior is due to some situational factor). Internal and external causality are the two kinds with which attribution theory is concerned.

Consider an example. We look at a teacher's grade book and observe that 10 Fs were assigned on a cultural anthropology examination. In an attempt to discover what this behavior (assignment of the 10 Fs) reveals about the teacher, we first have to determine whether the teacher was in fact responsible for the behavior or whether it could be attributed to outside or external factors. If we discover that the examination was made up by a faculty committee and that the committee set the standards for passing or failing, we could not attribute any particular motives to this individual teacher. The behavior was externally caused (in this case by the department committee in conjunction with each student's performance on the examination).

On the other hand, let us assume that this teacher made up the examination without any assistance from other faculty and that no department or university standards were used—the teacher made up the standards for passing and failing. Now we would be more apt (though perhaps not fully ready) to attribute the 10 Fs to internal causes. We would be strengthened in our belief that there was something within this teacher, some personality characteristic, for example, that led to this behavior if we discovered that (1) no other teacher in anthropology gave out nearly as many failures, (2) this particular teacher frequently gives out Fs in cultural anthropology, and (3) this teacher frequently gives Fs in other courses as well. These three bits of added information would lead us to conclude there was something in this teacher that motivated the behavior. Each of these three new items of information represents one of the three principles we use in making causal judgments in interpersonal perception: consensus, consistency, and distinctiveness.

Consensus

When we focus on the principle of *consensus* we ask essentially, "Do other people react or behave in the same way as the person on whom we are focusing?" That is, are they acting in accordance with the general consensus? If the answer is "no," we are more likely to attribute the behavior to some internal cause. In the teacher example, we were strengthened in our belief that there was something internal causing the Fs when we learned that other teachers did not do this—there was low consensus. When one person acts contrary to the norm, we are likely to attribute that person's behavior to some internal motivation. If all teachers gave a great number of Fs (that is, if there was a high consensus), we would be more likely to look for causality outside the individual teacher and to conclude, for example, that the anthropology department uses a particular curve in determining grades or that the students were not very bright.

Consistency

When we focus on the principle of *consistency* we ask whether this person repeatedly behaves the same way in similar situations. If the answer is "yes," there is high consistency, and we are likely to attribute the behavior to some internal motivation. The fact that this teacher frequently gives lots of Fs in cultural anthropology leads us to attribute cause to the teacher rather than to outside sources. If, on the other hand, there was low consistency—that is, if this teacher rarely gives Fs—we would be more likely to look for reasons external to the teacher. We might consider, for example, the possibility that this specific class was not terribly bright or that the department required the teacher to start giving out failures, and so on.

Distinctiveness

When we focus on the principle of *distinctiveness,* we ask if this person acts in similar ways in different situations. If the answer is "yes," there is low distinctiveness and we are likely to conclude there is an internal cause. Low distinctiveness indicates that the situation is not distinctive and that this person acts in similar ways in different situations. The fact that the teacher acted the same way (gave lots of Fs) in similar situations led us to conclude that this particular class was not distinctive and that the reason or motivation for the behavior could not be found in this situation. We further concluded that the behavior must be due to the teacher's inner motivation. Consider the alternative: Assume that this teacher gave all high grades and no failures in all other courses (that is, that the cultural anthropology class situation was distinctive). Then we would conclude that the motivation for the failures was to be found in sources outside the teacher and for reasons unique to this class.

Low consensus, high consistency, and low distinctiveness lead us to attribute a person's behavior to internal causes. High consensus, low consistency, and high distinctiveness lead us to attribute a person's behavior to external causes.

Behaviors Revealing of Internal Motivation

Of course, not all behaviors are equally revealing of internal motivations. Some behaviors tell us a great deal about an individual; other behaviors fail to distinguish this person from thousands of others. First, behaviors that are produced by one motivation are more revealing than behaviors produced by various and numerous motivations. Second, behaviors that are uncommon or are drastically different from those of other people are more revealing than behaviors common to everyone.

Single Motivation   Consider attempting to account for a friend's taking a position with Hulk Industries. The job is a boring one and the work required is physically demanding and unpleasant, but it pays well. Further, our friend has turned down easier and more exciting jobs that do not pay well. From this we would conclude that this individual was motivated by money. The behavior of taking the position with Hulk Industries could be accounted for (assuming we had all the facts) only on the basis of the money factor. Accepting work at Hulk is therefore more revealing of motivation than taking a position with Wonder, Inc., where the job is interesting, the work easy and pleasant, and the money is good. Here we would not be able to make a strong inference concerning which motive operated to produce the given behavior.

Uncommon Behaviors   Likewise, uncommon behaviors are more revealing than common behaviors. Consider the mother who buys her children new clothes, sees that they go to bed on time, and supervises their homework. These are the functions of many mothers and hence would not be particularly revealing; they would not enable us to distinguish this mother from thousands of others. However, take the mother who beats her child for hanging her new dress on a wire hanger—as in the book and film *Mommie Dearest* (whether accurately or falsely I do not know). This bit of behavior is uncommon enough for us to find it revealing; it tells us something about this individual and enables us to distinguish her from thousands of other mothers.

Self-Attribution

When we use *self-attribution*—the attempt to account for our own behaviors—we follow the same general patterns with two main differences. First, there is a general tendency to see the behaviors of others as internally caused, but our own behaviors as externally caused. In part this may occur because, in accounting for our own behaviors, we have a great deal more information. For example, we know that we have acted differently in other situations and therefore can more easily attribute a particular behavior to a particular situation. Also, since we cannot focus directly on our own behaviors and see them as objectively as we see the behaviors of others, we focus most of our attention on the environment or situation. Both tendencies lead us to attribute the majority of our own behaviors to situational factors.

The second major difference in self-attribution involves the *self-serving bias*. Generally, this bias leads us to take credit for the positive and to deny responsibility for the negative. Thus, when attempting to account for our negative behaviors, we would be more apt to attribute them to situational or environmental factors, and when accounting for our positive behaviors, we are likely to attribute them to internal factors.

Generally, then, in self-attribution, we attribute our behaviors to situational factors—especially when they are negative. When our behaviors are positive, the self-serving bias tends to have greater force and leads us to attribute the behavior to some internal factor, to our positive personality characteristics.

SUMMARY

1. *Perception* refers to the process by which we become aware of the many stimuli impinging on our senses.

2. The process of perception may be visualized as occurring in three stages: sensory stimulation occurs, sensory stimulation is organized, and sensory stimulation is interpreted-evaluated.

3. The following processes have been found to influence perception: (1) primacy-recency, (2) self-fulfilling prophecy, (3) perceptual accentuation, (4) implicit personality theory, (5) consistency, and (6) stereotyping.

4. *Primacy-recency* refers to the relative influence of stimuli as a result of their order. If what occurs first exerts greatest influence, we have a primary effect; if what occurs last exerts greatest influence, we have a recency effect.

5. The self-fulfilling prophecy occurs when we make a prediction or formulate a belief that comes true *because* we have made the prediction and acted on it as if it were true.

6. Perceptual accentuation leads us to see what we expect and what we want to see.

7. *Implicit personality theory* refers to the private personality theory that individuals hold and that influence how they perceive other people.

8. *Consistency* refers to the tendency of people to perceive what will enable them to achieve psychological balance or comfort among various attitude objects and the connections between and among them.

9. *Stereotyping* refers to the tendency to develop and maintain fixed, unchanging perceptions of groups of people and to use these perceptions to evaluate individual members of these groups, ignoring their individual, unique characteristics.

10. *Attribution* refers to the process by which we attempt to understand our own and others' behaviors and the reasons or motivations for these behaviors. In this process we utilize three types of data: *consensus* (the degree to which the person whose behavior we are attempting to understand is similar to or different from others), *consistency* (the degree to which this person repeatedly behaves in the same way in similar situations), and

distinctiveness (the degree to which this person reacts in similar ways in different situations). Low consensus, high consistency, and low distinctiveness lead us to attribute an individual's behavior to internal causes (for example, to personality). High consensus, low consistency, and high distinctiveness lead us to attribute an individual's behavior to external causes (for example, to outside pressures).

11. Behaviors stimulated by one motivation (rather than several) and behaviors that are uncommon (rather than common or frequently observed) are more revealing of internal motivation.

12. Using self-attribution in our attempt to account for our own behaviors, we follow the same general principles as when accounting for the behaviors of others. There are two major exceptions: we have a general tendency to see our own behaviors as externally rather than internally caused, and we generally operate with a self-serving bias (the tendency to take credit for positive behaviors and to deny responsibility for negative behaviors).

SOURCES

A thorough summary of perception is contained in Mark Cook's *Interpersonal Perception* (Baltimore: Penguin, 1971), on which I relied heavily. A brief but insightful account of people perception is provided by Albert Hastorf, David Schneider, and Judith Polefka in *Person Perception* (Reading, Mass.: Addison-Wesley, 1970). I also found Zick Rubin's *Liking and Loving: An Invitation to Social Psychology* (New York: Holt, 1973) a useful source. Much of the discussion of the perceptual processes is based on the insights provided by Rubin. The cited study by Solomon Asch is "Forming Impressions of Personality," *Journal of Abnormal and Social Psychology* 41 (1946): 258–290. A brief overview is provided by Robert A. Baron and Donn Byrne, *Social Psychology: Understanding Human Interaction*, 4th ed. (Boston: Allyn and Bacon, 1984), and a more thorough review by Chris L. Kleinke, *Self-Perception: The Psychology of Personal Awareness* (San Francisco, Calif.: Freeman, 1978). An excellent review of perception in interpersonal communication is provided by Alan L. Sillars and Michael D. Scott, "Interpersonal Perception Between Intimates: An Integrative Review," *Human Communication Research* 10 (fall 1983): 153–176.

The self-fulfilling prophecy was originally formulated by Robert K. Merton in *Social Theory and Social Structure* (New York: Free Press, 1957). For the original Pygmalion studies, see R. Rosenthal and L. Jacobson, *Pygmalion in the Classroom* (New York: Holt, Rinehart and Winston, 1968). Although a number of studies failed to replicate these original findings, the most recent studies seem now to again support the Pygmalion effect. An excellent collection of articles on the self-fulfilling prophecy may be found in Paul M. Insel and Lenore F. Jacobson, eds., *What Do You Expect? An Inquiry into Self-Fulfilling Prophecies* (Menlo Park, Calif.: Cummings, 1975).

On attribution theory, see E. E. Jones and K. E. Davis, "From Acts to Dispositions: The Attribution Process in Person Perception," in L. Bukowitz,

Advances in Experimental Social Psychology, vol. 2, (New York: Academic Press, 1965), pp. 219–266. H. H. Kelley offers several works: "Attribution Theory in Social Psychology," in D. Levine, ed., *Nebraska Symposium on Motivation* (Lincoln: University of Nebraska Press, 1967), pp. 192–240; "The Process of Causal Attribution," *American Psychologist* 28 (1973): 107–128; and *Personal Relationships: Their Structures and Processes* (Hillsdale, N.J.: Erlbaum, 1979). For a recent review of attribution theory, see Susan T. Fiske and Shelley E. Taylor, *Social Cognition* (Reading, Mass.: Addison-Wesley, 1984).

UNIT 5
LISTENING

LEARNING GOALS

After completing this unit, you should be able to

1. explain the significance of listening
2. define *listening*
3. identify and define the three types of listening
4. define and distinguish between *active* and *passive* listening
5. define and distinguish between *empathic* and *objective* listening
6. define and distinguish between *nonjudgmental* and *judgmental* listening
7. define and distinguish between *surface* and *deep* listening
8. define *active listening*
9. identify at least three functions of active listening
10. describe three techniques for practicing active listening

There can be little doubt that we listen a great deal. Upon awakening we listen to the radio. On the way to school we listen to friends, people around us, screeching cars, singing birds, or falling rain. In school we listen to the teacher, to other students, and sometimes even to ourselves. We listen to friends at lunch and return to class to listen to more teachers. We arrive home and again listen to family and friends. Perhaps we listen to records, radio, or television. All in all, we listen for a good part of our waking day.

THE SIGNIFICANCE OF LISTENING

If we measured importance in terms of the time we spend on an activity, then listening would be our most important communication activity. We spend most of our communication time engaged in listening. A glance at Figure 5.1, which diagrams the results of two studies, should illustrate this point. Note that in both studies (one conducted in 1929 using adults as subjects and one in 1980 with college students), listening occupied more time than any other communication activity. The results of studies using, for example, people in business further support the importance of listening.

Most of us are relatively poor listeners, and our listening behavior could be made more effective. Given the amount of time we engage in listening, the improvement of that skill would seem well worth the effort. And it does take effort. Effective listening is not easy; it takes time and energy.

THE NATURE OF LISTENING

Because listening is often only vaguely and sometimes inaccurately understood, we need to examine the nature of listening—specifically, its definition and its major types.

Listening: A Definition

By *listening*, we mean an active process of receiving aural stimuli. Contrary to popular conception, listening is an *active* rather than a passive process. Listening does not just happen; we must make it happen. Listening takes energy and commitment.

Listening involves *receiving* stimuli and is thus distinguished from hearing as a physiological process. The word *receiving* is used here to emphasize that stimuli are taken in by the organism and are in some way processed or utilized. For at least some amount of time, the signals received are retained. Listening involves *aural* stimuli—that is, signals (sound waves) received by the ear. Lis-

62

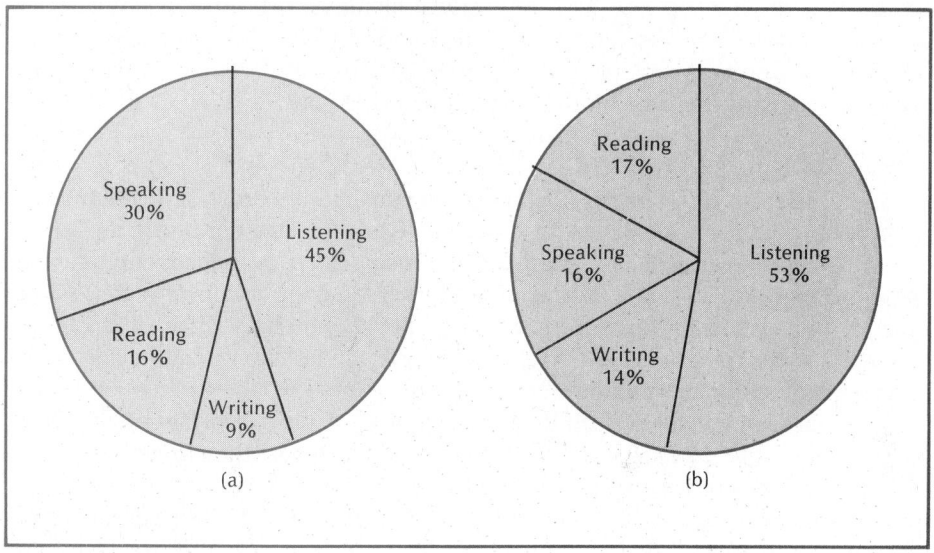

FIGURE 5.1 The time spent in listening.

tening therefore is not limited to verbal signals, but encompasses all signals sent by means of fluctuations in air—noises as well as words, music as well as prose. Make special note of the fact that nothing in this definition implies that listening as a skill is limited to formal speaking situations, such as when a public speaker addresses a large audience. Listening is a skill that is of crucial importance in interpersonal and in small group communication, as well as in public speaking, intercultural, and mass communication.

Jesse S. Nirenberg, in his *Getting Through to People*, distinguishes three levels of listening; these may further clarify what we mean by listening. First, there is the level of *nonhearing*. Here the individual does not listen at all; rather, he or she looks at the speaker and may even utter remarks that seem to imply attention, such as "OK," "yes," and "mm," but there is really no listening. Nothing is getting through. The second level is the level of *hearing*. Here the person hears what is being said and even remembers it, but does not allow any of the ideas to penetrate beyond the level of memory. Third is the level of *thinking*, wherein the listener not only hears what the speaker is saying, but also thinks about it. The listener here evaluates and analyzes what is being said. It is this third level, the level of *listening-thinking*, that we are defining.

Types of Listening

Just as we speak for a variety of purposes, we also listen for different purposes. Three general types of listening may be distinguished.

Listening for Enjoyment

Listening for enjoyment occupies a good deal of our listening time. We listen to music, a sports broadcast, or a television comedy or drama basically for enjoyment. Here we suspend our critical faculties, rid ourselves of competing stimuli, relax, and enjoy the stimulation. Our listening here is relatively passive. We don't attempt to evaluate or critically analyze these messages, nor do we probe for deep and hidden meanings.

Listening for Information

As students, your primary listening responsibilities center on listening for information; in class you listen to the instructor and to other students. When you turn on the car radio to listen for game scores, your objective again is to gain information. In small group and interpersonal situations, much of your time is spent listening for information—what happened to Chris and Pat last weekend, what friends are planning to do over the holiday, what happened in the sociology class you missed.

At times, our goal is simply the acquisition of new information, to learn some isolated bits of data we did not already know. At other times, we listen for information so we can acquire some new skill or engage in some behavior more effectively—operating a computer, throwing a curve, preparing a particular dinner. In still other cases, we listen for information so that we may later offer an evaluation, judgment, or criticism. In a public speaking class, we listen to the speeches of others to acquire information so that we may eventually evaluate the speech and render a critical judgment.

These two types of listening—listening for enjoyment and listening for information—are often intertwined: Often we learn something even from our entertainment, and often we are entertained by our informative listening. The mass media have been particularly sensitive to the importance of mixing entertainment with informative programs and have recently made great changes, for example, in news broadcasts. Programs such as "Sesame Street," "60 Minutes," and "20/20" may best illustrate this close connection between entertainment and information.

Listening to Help

The helping function of listening is a crucial one to which we turn repeatedly. When we listen to someone complain, or talk about their problems, or attempt to make a decision, we are often listening with a view to helping them. Perhaps the help will come simply from providing them with a receptive and supportive audience. Just being there, ready to listen and willing to help, is often a great comfort. At other times, the help we give may be more direct, as when we make suggestions and offer advice.

LISTENING EFFECTIVELY

Because we listen for different reasons and toward different ends, the principles we follow in listening effectively should vary from one situation to another. Here we identify four dimensions of listening and illustrate the appropriateness of different listening modes for different communication situations.

Active and Passive Listening

The art of effective listening in most interpersonal, small group, public, or mass communication situations lies in being an active participant. Perhaps the best preparation for active listening is to act like an active listener, physically and mentally. Recall, for example, how your body almost automatically reacts to important news: you quickly assume an upright posture, turn your head to the speaker, and remain relatively still and quiet. We do this almost reflexively because this is how we listen most effectively. This is not to say that we should be tense and uncomfortable, but only that our bodies should reflect our active minds. Even more important than this physical alertness is a mental alertness, an active listening attitude. As listeners we need to enter the communication interaction—whether interpersonal, small group, or public speaking—as equal partners with the speakers, as persons emotionally and intellectually ready to engage in the sharing of meaning.

Passive listening, however, is not without merit. Listening without talking and without nonverbally directing the speaker in any way constitutes one of the most powerful means for communicating acceptance. Passive listening allows the other person to develop his or her thoughts and ideas in the presence of another person who accepts but does not evaluate, who supports but does not intrude. Passive listening serves the often useful purpose of allowing the other person free reign and is especially helpful in the beginning of a person's attempt to unravel his or her thoughts. With passive listening we do not direct; rather, we simply provide a supporting and receptive environment. After that acceptance and support have been communicated, we may wish to contribute in a more active way both verbally and nonverbally.

Another form of passive listening is just to sit back, relax, and let the auditory stimulation work you over and massage you without your exerting any significant energy or effort, and especially without your directing the stimuli in any way. Listening to music for pure enjoyment (rather than critically) may be the best example. But listening to the wind howl, the birds sing, and a crowd of people chatter may be better accomplished with a passive attitude and psychological set.

Empathic and Objective Listening

If we are to understand what a person means and feels, we need to listen with empathy. To *empathize* with others is to see the world as they see it and to feel what they feel. Only when we achieve empathy will we be able to understand another's meaning fully.

There is no fast method for achieving empathy with another individual, but it is something we should work toward. It is important that we see the teacher's point of view, and equally it is important for the teacher to see the student's point of view. Popular college students might intellectually understand why an unpopular student is depressed, but that will not enable them to understand these feelings emotionally. What popular students need to do is to put themselves in the position of the unpopular student, to role-play a bit and begin to feel his or her feelings and think his or her thoughts. Then these students will be in a somewhat better position to "really understand," to empathize.

Although empathic listening is, for most communication situations, the preferred mode of responding, there are times when we need to go beyond standing in the other person's shoes and measure the meanings and the feelings against some objective reality. It is important to listen to a friend tell us how the entire world hates him or her and to understand how our friend feels and perhaps why he or she feels this way. But then we need to look a bit more objectively at our friend and at the world and perhaps see the paranoia or the self-hatred. Sometimes we have to put our empathic responses aside and listen with objectivity and detachment.

Nonjudgmental and Judgmental Listening

Effective listening seems characterized by both nonjudgmental and judgmental responses—listening openly with a view toward understanding, and listening critically with a view toward making some kind of evaluation or judgment. Clearly, we should first listen for understanding while suspending judgment; only after we have fully understood the relevant messages should we evaluate or judge. Listening with an open mind is extremely difficult. It is not easy for us, for example, to listen to arguments against some cherished belief. It is not easy to listen to statements condemning what we so fervently believe. It is not easy to listen to criticisms of what we think is just great.

We need to listen fairly, even though some signal has gone up in the form of an out-of-place expression or a hostile remark. Listening often stops when such a remark is made. Admittedly, to continue listening with an open mind is difficult, yet here it is particularly important.

If meaningful communication is to take place, we need to supplement our open-minded listening with critical listening. Listening with a critical mind will help us to analyze our understanding and to evaluate messages judiciously. As intelligent and educated citizens, it is our responsibility to evaluate critically what we hear. This is especially true in the college environment. While it is very easy simply to listen to a teacher and take down what is said, it is extremely important that what is said be evaluated and critically analyzed. Teachers have biases too; at times consciously and at times unconsciously, these biases creep into scholarly discussions. They need to be identified and brought to the surface by the critical listener. Contrary to what most students will argue, the vast majority of teachers will appreciate the responses of critical listeners: Such responses demonstrate that someone is listening.

Two particularly dangerous tendencies that interfere with the judicious application of nonjudgmental and judgmental listening are prejudging messages and filtering out certain messages.

Prejudging Messages

Be especially careful of *prejudgment*. There is often a strong tendency to prejudge the communications of others as uninteresting, irrelevant, or invalid before we even hear them. By prejudging a communication, we are in effect lifting the burden of listening from our shoulders. We just tune out the speaker and let our minds recapture last Saturday night. It is an easy trap to fall into. Most communications are at least potentially interesting and relevant. If we prejudge them and tune them out, we will never be proved wrong. At the same time, however, we close ourselves off from potentially useful information. Most important, perhaps, is that we are not giving the other person a fair hearing.

Filtering Out Messages

Avoid filtering out difficult messages. Depending on our own intellectual equipment, many of the messages we confront will need careful analysis and scrutiny. Listening will be difficult, but the alternative—to miss out on what is said—seems even less pleasant than stretching and straining our minds a bit.

Also avoid filtering out unpleasant messages. None of us wants to be told that something we believe in is untrue, that people we care for are unpleasant, or that ideals we hold are self-destructive. And yet these are the very messages we need to listen to with great care. These are the very messages that will lead us to examine and reexamine our unconscious assumptions. If we filter out this kind of information, we will be left with a host of unstated and unexamined assumptions that will influence us without our influencing them.

Surface and Deep Listening

In Shakespeare's *Julius Caesar,* Mark Antony, in giving the funeral oration for Caesar, says: "I come to bury Caesar, not to praise him./The evil that men do lives after them,/the good is oft interred with their bones." And later: "For Brutus is an honourable man;/So are they all, all honourable men." But Antony, as we know, did not come to bury Caesar and certainly not to convince the crowd that Brutus was, in fact, an honorable man. Instead he came to incite the crowd to avenge the death of Caesar, his friend.

In most messages there is an obvious meaning that a literal reading of the words and sentences enables us to derive. But there is often another level of meaning; sometimes, as in *Julius Caesar,* it is the opposite of the expressed literal meaning; sometimes it seems totally unrelated to the literal meaning of the verbalized messages. In reality, few messages have only one level of meaning. Most messages function on at least two or three levels at the same time. Consider some of the frequently heard messages: A friend asks you how you like his new haircut. Another friend asks you how you like her painting. On one level, the meaning is clear: Do you like the haircut? Do you like the painting? But it seems reasonable to assume that on another and perhaps a more impor- tant level, they are asking you to say something positive about them—about his appearance, about her artistic ability. The parent who verbalizes how hard he or she has worked at the office or in the home may well be asking for some expression of appreciation rather than merely complaining. The college student who expresses the desire to quit school and get a full-time job may be asking for encouragement or perhaps for some understanding of the soon-to-be-re- ceived, not-so-great grades.

Noise is always present in any communication system. Physical noise, as illustrated in this photo, is especially obvious and for the most part relatively easy to combat. Psychological and semantic noise, however, are more difficult to identify and to combat. What instances of psychological and semantic noise can you identify from your own recent communication interactions?

In interpersonal listening we have to be particularly sensitive to the different levels of meaning because if we respond only to the surface level communication (only to the literal meaning), we will miss the opportunity to make contact with the other person's feelings and real needs. If we say to the parent, "You're always complaining. I bet you really love working so hard," we are failing to meet the need of this call for understanding and appreciation.

Examining the Levels of Meaning

In attempting to decipher the different levels of meaning, a few principles prove useful. Meaning is communicated both verbally and nonverbally, by what is said as well as by what is done with the face, the eyes, the hands, and so forth. Sweating hands, shaking knees, a limp handshake, a wink of the eye, or the avoidance of direct eye contact, when used in conjunction with verbal messages, alter those messages in significant ways and tell us that there is more to them than their literal meaning. Further, recognize that the meaning of a communication lies also in what is omitted. The parents of teenagers who talk about the teenage drug problem of everyone else's teenagers but never once mention their own children (and may never even think of their own children in this connection) are communicating some important information.

Earlier we noted that all messages have a content and a relationship dimension. Listening for different levels of meaning will be enhanced if we focus on both relational and content aspects. The student who constantly criticizes or challenges the teacher is on one level communicating disagreement over content; the student is debating the issues. On another level, however—the relationship level—the student may well be voicing objections to the instructor's authority or perhaps to the instructor's authoritarianism. If the instructor is to deal effectively with the student, both types of messages must be listened to and both must receive a response.

In listening for the different levels of meaning, recognize that one inevitably talks about oneself, from one's own point of view, on the basis of one's own previous experiences, colored by one's needs, wants, and desires, and so on. Whatever a person says is, in part, a function of who that person is, and to listen for the different levels of meaning is to attend to those personal, self-referential messages.

All this is not to say that we should disregard the literal meaning of interpersonal messages or that we should constantly focus attention on what else the speaker might be attempting to communicate. If we do this, we will quickly find that our listening problems are over; no one will be talking with us anymore. We need to walk a reasonable line between the literal and the underlying meanings in the messages we receive. We need to become sensitive to the underlying meanings in many messages but not become preoccupied with them to the point that we see and hear nothing else. We need to be ready to respond to the underlying messages while not becoming obsessed with uncovering everyone's hidden meanings. Perhaps the best guideline to use is to respond to the various levels of meaning in the messages of others as you would like others to respond to yours—sensitively but not obsessively, readily but not overanxiously.

ACTIVE LISTENING

Earlier we noted the distinction between active and passive listening and observed that generally we should be active participants in the communication encounter. There is, however, another kind of active listening that should be considered. This type is one of the most important communication skills we can learn, and so we need to consider it in some depth. Consider the following brief exchange:

SPEAKER: That creep gave me a C on the paper. I really worked on that project and I get a lousy C.

LISTENER 1: That's not too bad; most people got around the same grade. I got a C too.

LISTENER 2: So what? This is your last semester. Who cares about grades anyway?

LISTENER 3: You should be pleased with a C. Peggy and Michael both failed and John and Judy got Ds.

LISTENER 4: You got a C on that paper you were working on for the last three weeks? You sound really angry and hurt.

All four listeners are probably anxious to make the speaker feel better. But they go about it in very different ways and, we can be sure, with very different outcomes. The first three listeners give fairly typical responses. Listeners 1 and 2 both try to minimize the significance of a C grade. This is an extremely common response to someone who expresses displeasure or disappointment. It is also a most inappropriate response, which may be well-intended but does little to foster meaningful communication and understanding. Listener 3 tries to make the C grade take on a more positive meaning. Note, however, that in the process these listeners are also saying a great deal more. All three listeners are also saying that the speaker should not be feeling as he or she does, and that the feelings are not legitimate ones and should be replaced with feelings that are more logical. These responses deny the validity of the speaker's feelings. They put the speaker into the position of having to defend his or her own feelings.

Listener 4, however, is different; listener 4 uses what is called *active listening*, a process of sending back to the speaker what you as a listener think the speaker meant—both in terms of content and in terms of feelings. Active listening is not a process of merely repeating back to the speaker the exact words, but rather one of putting together into some meaningful whole the listener's understanding of the speaker's total message—the verbal and the nonverbal, the content and the feelings.

The Functions of Active Listening

Active listening serves a number of important functions. First, it enables the listener to check on his or her understanding of what the speaker said and, more important, what the speaker meant. When the listener reflects back to the speaker what he or she perceived to be the speaker's meanings, the listener gives the speaker an opportunity to confirm or disconfirm the listener's perceptions and to clarify whatever may need clarification. In this way, future messages will have a better chance of being relevant and purposeful.

Second, through the process of active listening the listener expresses acceptance of the speaker's feelings. Note that in the sample responses given above, the first three listeners challenged the speaker's feelings; they refused to give these feelings legitimacy. The active listener who reflected back to the speaker what he or she thought was said gave the speaker acceptance. The speaker's feelings were not challenged; rather, they were echoed in a sympathetic and empathic manner. Note too that in the first three responses the feelings of the speaker are denied without ever actually being identified. Listener 4, however, not only accepts the speaker's feelings but identifies them explicitly ("You sound really angry and hurt"), again allowing an opportunity for correction.

Third, and perhaps most important, is that active listening stimulates the speaker to explore feelings and thoughts. With the response of listener 4, the speaker has an opportunity to elaborate on his or her feelings without having to defend any feelings that others may have unfairly minimized. Active listening helps create a climate that encourages the speaker further to explore and express thoughts and feelings. Active listening sets the stage for meaningful dialogue, a dialogue of mutual understanding rather than a dialogue in which one person must defend his or her feelings. In stimulating this further exploration, active listening also encourages the speaker to solve his or her own problems by providing the opportunity to talk through those problems.

The Techniques of Active Listening

Three simple techniques may prove useful in learning the process of active listening.

Paraphrase the Speaker's Thoughts

State in your own words what you think the speaker meant. This paraphrase will help to ensure understanding, since the speaker will be able to correct or modify your restatement. It will also serve to show the speaker that you are interested and are attending to what is being said. Everyone wants to feel attended to, especially when angry or depressed. The active listening response confirms this attention to the speaker. The paraphrase also provides the speaker with the opportunity to elaborate or extend what was originally said. Thus, when the listener echoes the C grade thought, this may provide the speaker with the opportunity to elaborate on why that C was an important one—perhaps a fear that the history paper will receive a similar grade, perhaps an increase in anxiety about the next paper, and so on. In your paraphrase, be especially careful that you do not lead the speaker in the direction you think he or she should go; paraphrases should be objective descriptions.

Express Understanding of the Speaker's Feelings

In addition to paraphrasing the content, echo the feelings you felt were expressed or implied. Just as the paraphrase enables you to check on your perception of the content, the expression of feelings will enable you to check on your perception of the speaker's feelings. This expression of feelings will also provide the speaker with the opportunity to see his or her feelings more objectively. It is helpful especially when an individual is feeling angry or hurt or depressed. We need that objectivity; we need to see our feelings from a somewhat less impassioned perspective if we are to deal with them effectively.

When we echo the speaker's feelings, we also provide a stimulus for elaboration and extension of these feelings. Most of us hold back on our feelings until we are certain they will be accepted; when we feel they are accepted, we then feel free to go into more detail. Active listening provides the speaker with this important opportunity. In echoing these feelings, be careful that you do not maximize or minimize the speaker's emotions and feelings. Just try to echo these feelings as accurately as you can.

Ask Questions

Ask questions to ensure your own understanding of the speaker's thoughts and feelings and to secure additional relevant information. The questions should be designed to provide just enough stimulation and support for the speaker to express the thoughts and feelings he or she wants to express, but not to pry into areas that are not germane to the issue or that challenge the speaker in any way. These questions will further confirm your interest and concern for the speaker.

SUMMARY

1. *Listening* may be defined as an active process of receiving aural stimuli.

2. We listen for a variety of reasons: for enjoyment, for information, and to help.

3. Effective listening involves adjusting our behaviors on the basis of at least four dimensions: active and passive listening, empathic and objective listening, nonjudgmental and judgmental listening, and surface and deep listening.

4. A particular type of listening has been termed *active listening;* this refers to listening in which we send back to the speaker what we think the speaker said and felt. Active listening thus enables us to check on our understanding, express acceptance of the speaker's feelings, and stimulate the speaker to explore further his or her feelings and thoughts.

5. Three major techniques are recommended for active listening: (1) paraphrasing the speaker's thoughts, (2) expressing understanding of the speaker's feelings, and (3) asking relevant questions.

SOURCES

Listening is currently experiencing renewed popularity in both the theoretical and the applied spheres. Perhaps the classic in listening is Ralph Nichols and Leonard Stevens, *Are You Listening?* (New York: McGraw-Hill, 1957). Nichols's "Do We Know How to Listen? Practical Helps in a Modern Age," *Communication Education* 10 (1961): 118–124, contains 10 suggestions for improving listening. Most of the suggestions for listening improvement, including some of those presented here, owe their formulation to the work of Nichols.

The two studies referred to in Figure 5.1 are Paul Rankin, "Listening Ability," *Proceedings of the Ohio State Educational Conference's Ninth Annual Session,* 1929; and Larry Barker, R. Edwards, C. Gaines, K. Gladney, and F. Holley, "An

Investigation of Proportional Time Spent in Various Communication Activities by College Students," *Journal of Applied Communication Research* 8 (1980): 101–109.

Other treatments include Lyman K. Steil, Larry L. Barker, and Kittie W. Watson, *Effective Listening: Key to Your Success* (Reading, Mass.: Addison-Wesley, 1983), and Florence I. Wolf, Nadine C. Marsnik, William S. Tacey, and Ralph G. Nichols, *Perceptive Listening* (New York: Holt, Rinehart and Winston, 1983). One of the most readable and penetrating discussions of listening, on which I drew for the discussion of active and passive listening, is Thomas Gordon, *P.E.T.: Parent Effectiveness Training* (New York: New American Library, 1975). The theories and experimental research bearing on the issues of attention, memory, and comprehension—all relevant to listening and listening effectiveness—are surveyed in David H. Dodd and Raymond M. White, Jr., *Cognition: Mental Structures and Processes* (Boston: Allyn and Bacon, 1980). Listening from the viewpoint of a philosopher (but with much practical advice) is covered in Mortimer J. Adler, *How to Speak, How to Listen* (New York: Macmillan, 1983). A useful guide to listening improvement, especially in business, is Warren H. Reed, *Positive Listening: Learning to Hear What People Are Really Saying* (New York: Franklin Watts, 1985).

SKILL DEVELOPMENT SUMMARY

1. Become sensitive to **contexts** of communication; recognize that changes in the physical, social-psychological, and/or temporal contexts will alter meaning.

2. Look for **meaning** not only in words but in nonverbal behaviors as well.

3. Become sensitive to the **feedback** that you give to others and that others give to you, and respond to that feedback by taking corrective actions or by continuing your performance so that communication may be made more effective and more satisfying.

4. Combat the effects of physical, psychological, and semantic **noise** that distort messages by eliminating or lessening the sources of physical noise, making language more precise, improving listening and feedback skills, securing agreement on meanings, and, in general, following the numerous suggestions for improving communication offered throughout the text.

5. Recognize that we can communicate effectively only to the degree that we share a common **field of experience.** Seek to expand this commonality by sharing experiences, listening actively, disclosing as appropriate, and encouraging the disclosures of the other.

6. Remember that **communication is inevitable,** that we cannot not communicate, and that all behavior in an interactional situation communicates. Look carefully for these real but often hidden meanings.

7. Recognize the **irreversibility of communication**—that we cannot uncommunicate. Therefore, be especially cautious in communicating messages that you may later wish to withdraw—for example, words spoken in anger and commitment messages.

8. Because communication is a **package of signals,** make your verbal and nonverbal messages reinforce rather than contradict each other.

9. Respond to **contradictory messages** by identifying the dual meanings communicated and by discussing these openly.

10. Become conscious of the **relational messages** you and others communicate and respond to the relational messages of others in order to increase meaningful interaction.

11. Recognize that each person punctuates the communication sequence differently. Look for the **punctuation** pattern that you and others use in order to understand the meanings communicated.

12. Be conscious of the potential problems caused by **progressive differentiation** and **rigid complementarity** so that these spiraling patterns and their problems may be arrested.

13. Increase **self-awareness** by talking with yourself, listening to others, reducing your blind self, seeing yourself from different perspectives, and increasing your open self.

14. **Self-disclose** (as appropriate) in order to gain self-knowledge, increase your coping abilities, increase your available energy, improve communication efficiency, and increase relational depth.

15. Be especially careful of **self-disclosing too early** in a relationship with disclosures that might be perceived as too intimate or too negative.

16. Be conscious of the potential **dangers of self-disclosure**—for example, personal and social rejection, material loss, and intrapersonal difficulties.

17. **Self-disclose** when the motivation for the disclosure is to improve the relationship, when the disclosure is appropriate to the context and to the relationship between you and the listener, when there is ample opportunity for open and honest responses, when the disclosures will be made with clarity and directness, when the other person discloses also, and only after analyzing the potential burdens self-disclosure might entail.

18. In **responding to the disclosures of others** use effective and active listening skills, support the discloser, reinforce the disclosing behaviors, maintain confidentiality, and do not use the disclosures against the person.

19. Recognize the operation of **primacy-recency,** which states that the temporal position of a stimulus within the sequence of events (for example, whether first or last) may influence your perception of the whole. Be careful that your first impressions do not prevent your accurate perceptions of subsequent events. Also, recognize that first impressions are extremely important; therefore, be at your very best during first encounters.

20. Do not allow the **self-fulfilling prophecy** to obscure or distort reality. Take a second look at your perceptions when they conform too closely to your expectations.

21. Be aware of the operation of **perceptual accentuation;** be careful that your perception of an event is not unduly influenced by what you expect or what you want to see. Both your expectations and the occurring events influence perception; discriminate between these.

22. Bring to consciousness your **implicit personality theories** so that they will not distort your perceptions of people and events; avoid drawing too-definite conclusions about others on the basis of these theories.

23. Be careful that your need for balance or **consistency** does not lead you to distort your perceptions of people by "perceiving" what you expect to see instead of what really is.

24. Avoid **stereotyping** and instead learn to see individuals as individuals, not merely as members of groups.

25. From **attribution theory,** remember, in attempting to account for behavior, that low consensus, high consistency, and low distinctiveness are good signs that the behavior is internally motivated, whereas high consensus, low consistency, and high distinctiveness are good signs that the behaviors are externally motivated.

26. In **analyzing the motivations for behavior,** remember that not all behaviors are equally revealing; behaviors that have a single motive or are uncommon generally reveal more about internal motivation than do behaviors that are governed by numerous motives or are relatively common.

27. In attempting to account for your own behavior, be especially sensitive to the possible operation of the **self-serving bias,** which may lead you to distort your analysis by leading you to take credit for the positive and to deny responsibility for the negative.

28. Improve your **listening** by adjusting your behavior between active and passive listening, empathic and objective listening, nonjudgmental and judgmental listening, and surface and deep listening.

29. Be especially careful that you do not **prejudge messages** or **filter out messages** that may appear too complex or too unpleasant.

30. Practice the skills of **active listening** by paraphrasing the speaker's thoughts, expressing understanding of the speaker's feelings, and asking questions to check on your understanding of the speaker, to express acceptance and support for the speaker's feelings, and to encourage the speaker to explore further her or his thoughts and feelings.

PART TWO
LANGUAGE AND VERBAL INTERACTION

6. PRELIMINARIES TO LANGUAGE AND VERBAL INTERACTION: LANGUAGE, SYMBOLS, AND MEANINGS

7. BARRIERS IN LANGUAGE AND VERBAL INTERACTION

8. PRINCIPLES OF LANGUAGE AND VERBAL INTERACTION

9. SOCIAL ASPECTS OF LANGUAGE AND VERBAL INTERACTION

In this part we focus on the verbal message system. First, we cover the nature of language and meaning. The next two units identify some of the major barriers to effective verbal interaction and offer a variety of useful antidotes or principles for making verbal interactions more meaningful and effective. In the last unit in this part, we look at language and verbal interaction in the broader context of social groups and explore the ways in which language and verbal interaction reflect and preserve the social order. A major concern of this unit is to identify the varieties and functions of sublanguages and the role of taboo and euphemisms in everyday speech.

UNIT 6
PRELIMINARIES TO LANGUAGE AND VERBAL INTERACTION:
Language, Symbols, and Meanings

LEARNING GOALS

After completing this unit, you should be able to

1. define the following terms: *productivity, displacement, rapid fading, arbitrariness,* and *cultural transmission*
2. explain at least four implications for human communication of the view of language presented here
3. explain the process view of meaning
4. identify at least four implications for human communication of this process view of meaning
5. define and distinguish between *denotation* and *connotation*
6. define *phatic communion*

In this unit we explore the concept of verbal messages by focusing on some essential preliminaries. First, the nature of the human language system (the system of words and grammatical rules that governs the creation of our verbal messages) is explained, and its essential characteristics are identified and defined. Once the nature of language in general is understood, we focus on meaning.

LANGUAGE AS A SYMBOL SYSTEM

Language may be thought of as the code, or system of symbols, utilized in the construction of verbal messages. Language may be defined as a productive system capable of displacement and composed of rapidly fading, arbitrary, culturally transmitted symbols. Each of these characteristics will be explained briefly.

Productivity

Human verbal messages evidence productivity—sometimes referred to as openness or creativity. That is, our verbal messages are novel utterances; each utterance is generated anew. There are exceptions to this general rule, but these seem few and trivial. For example, messages such as "How are you?," "What's new?," and "Good luck" do not evidence productivity; they are not newly created each time they are uttered. Such exceptions aside, all verbal messages are created at the time of utterance. When you speak, you are not repeating memorized sentences but are creating your own sentences. Similarly, your understanding of verbal messages evidences productivity in that you can understand new utterances as they are uttered. Your ability to comprehend verbal messages is not limited to previously heard and learned utterances.

Another dimension of productivity is that human message systems allow the introduction of new words. When something is discovered or invented, we can create new words to describe it. And it does not seem to matter whether we create the new word by joining together old words or parts of old words or by starting from scratch. What does matter is that the language system is open to expansion—a feature that seems absent from just about all known animal communication systems.

Displacement

Human language can be used to talk about things that are remote in both time and space; we can talk about the past and the future as easily as the present. And we can talk about things that we have never seen and will never see—about mermaids and unicorns and supernatural beings from other planets. We can talk about the unreal as well as the real, the imaginary as well as the actual. *Displacement* also refers to the fact that messages may have effects or consequences that are independent of their context. Thus, for example, statements uttered in one place today may have effects elsewhere tomorrow.

Rapid Fading

Speech sounds fade rapidly; they are evanescent. They must be received immediately after they are emitted or else they will not be received at all. Although mechanical devices now enable sound to be preserved much as writing is preserved, this is not a characteristic of human language. Rather, these are extralinguistic means of storing information and aiding memory. Of course, all signals fade; written symbols and even symbols carved in rock are not permanent. In relative terms, however, speech signals are probably the least permanent of all communicative media.

Arbitrariness

Language signals are arbitrary; they do not possess any of the physical properties or characteristics of the things for which they stand. The word *wine* is no more tasty than the word *sand*, nor is the latter any less wet. Names are arbitrary in large part; there is no real relationship between the name and the individual. And yet, names are not totally arbitrary; many names indicate the ethnic group to which an individual belongs and usually indicate sex.

Cultural Transmission

The form of any particular human language is culturally or traditionally transmitted. The child raised by English-speakers learns English as a native speaker, regardless of the language of his or her biological parents. The genetic endowment pertains to human language in general rather than to any specific human language.

Implications for Human Communication

Within the nature of language as defined there are a number of important implications for human communication. Here are a few.

Rules of Language and Productivity   Productivity enables us to create an infinite number of sentences that were never uttered before—yet these sentences must conform to the rules of the language if they are to be understood by others. That is, productivity operates within a clearly defined system of rules specifying what may and what may not be done. Effective communication begins with and within the rules of language.

The Ability to Lie   Displacement, together with productivity, makes lying possible. We are able to lie because we are able to form new utterances (productivity) and because our utterances are not limited to what is in our immediate environment (displacement). Thus, for example, we can say, "I found a sunken treasure off the coast of Manhattan" without this sentence's ever having been uttered before and without any concern for what is actually present in our environment. No linguistic limitations restrict our utterances to accurate descriptions of reality. Most important is the fact that truthful and untruthful sentences have identical forms. Truth or falsehood cannot be determined by any linguistic analysis.

Instant Intelligibility   Because of rapid fading, our oral messages must be instantly intelligible; if they are not, they are lost. Clarity is therefore the most important element in oral communication. Because written messages may be reread at leisure, they need not possess this quality of instant intelligibility.

Meanings and Arbitrariness   Because all linguistic symbols are arbitrary, we need to look for meaning not merely in the words and sentences but also in the person communicating. We need to know not so much what a person said as what the person meant. Someone who uses obscenity may mean merely to emphasize a point; the listener, however, may be offended. To the speaker, the obscenity meant emphasis; to the listener, it meant vulgarity and a lack of social grace. Such different perceptions are commonplace. We need, therefore, to check back with the speaker to see what meanings were intended instead of just substituting our meanings for the speaker's words.

Language Learning and Cultural Transmission   One consequence of cultural transmission is that any human language can be learned by any normal human being. All human languages—English, Mandarin Chinese, Italian, Russian, Bantu, or any other of the approximately 3,000 languages—are equally learnable; no single language should present any greater difficulty for a child to learn than any other. Note, however, that this ability to learn any language holds only at particular times in the life of an individual. One generally cannot learn to speak a language with native fluency after passing a certain age, usually around puberty.

LANGUAGE AS A MEANING SYSTEM

If it were not for the desire of one person to communicate meaning to another person, language would probably not exist. Of all the functions of language, the communication of meaning from one person to another is surely the most significant. Consequently, meaning must be placed at the center of any attempt to explain language.

A Process View of Meaning

Meaning is an active process created in cooperation between source and receiver, speaker and listener, writer and reader. This is illustrated in the model developed by Wendell Johnson, leading semanticist, and depicted in Figure 6.1. The surrounding rectangle indicates that communication takes place in a context that is external to both speaker and listener and to the communication process as well. The twisted loop indicates that the various stages of communication are actually interrelated and interdependent.

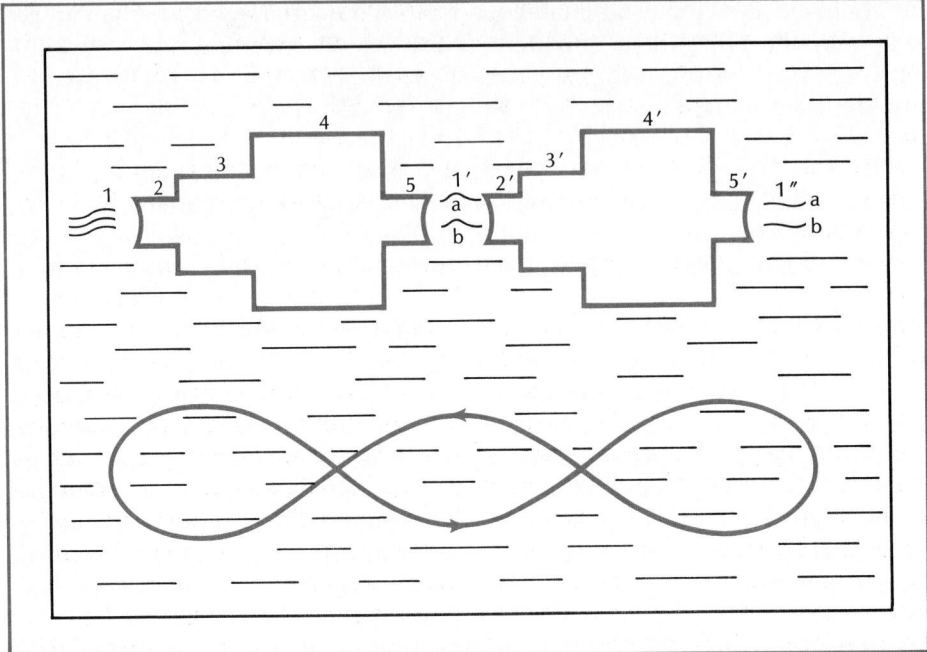

FIGURE 6.1 Johnson's model of communication. *Source:* Wendell Johnson, "The Spoken Word and the Great Unsaid," *Quarterly Journal of Speech* 37 (1951): 421.

The actual process begins at 1, which represents the occurrence of an event—anything that can be perceived. This event is the stimulus. At stage 2 the observer is stimulated through one or more sensory channels. The opening at 2 is purposely illustrated as being relatively small to emphasize that out of all the possible stimuli in the world, only a small part of these actually stimulate the observer. At stage 3 organismic evaluations occur; nerve impulses travel from the sense organs to the brain, causing certain bodily changes—for example, in muscular tension. At 4 the feelings aroused at 3 are beginning to be translated into words—a process that takes place in accordance with the individual's unique language habits. At stage 5, from all the possible linguistic symbols, certain ones are selected and arranged into some pattern.

At 1′ the words that the speaker utters or writes serve as stimulation for the hearer (by means of sound or light waves, respectively), much as the outside event at 1 served as stimulation for the speaker. At 2′ the hearer is stimulated, at 3′ there are organismic evaluations, at 4′ feelings are beginning to be translated into words, at 5′ certain of these symbols are selected and arranged, and at 1″ these symbols, in the form of sound and/or light waves, are emitted and serve as stimulation for another hearer. The process is a continuous one.

Implications for Human Communication

Johnson's process model of meaning offers a number of implications for human communication; here just a few are identified.

Meanings Are in People   Meanings are not in words but in people. We use words to approximate the meanings we wish to communicate, but these words are imperfect and incomplete representations of our meanings. Similarly, the meanings that a listener derives from our messages will be quite different from the meanings we may have intended to communicate. Communication is a process through which we attempt to reproduce what is in our minds, in the minds of our listeners. The reproduction is only a partial process and is always subject to error.

One of the best examples of the confusion that can result when the relatively simple fact of imperfect reproduction is not taken into consideration is provided by Laing, Phillipson, and Lee in *Interpersonal Perception* and analyzed with insight by Paul Watzlawick in *How Real Is Real?* A couple on the second night of their honeymoon was sitting at a hotel bar. The woman struck up a conversation with the couple next to her. The husband refused to communicate with the couple and became antagonistic to his wife as well as to the couple. The wife then became angry because he created such an awkward and unpleasant situation. Each became increasingly disturbed, and the evening ended with a bitter conflict in which each was convinced of the other's lack of consideration. Eight years later they analyzed this argument. Apparently "honeymoon" had meant very different things to them; to the husband it had meant a "golden opportunity to ignore the rest of the world and simply explore each other." His wife's interaction with the other couple implied to him that something lacking in him made her seek out additional people with whom to interact. To the wife "honeymoon" had meant an opportunity to try out her new role as a wife. "I had never had a conversation with another couple as a wife before," she said. "Previous to this I had always been a 'girlfriend' or 'fiancée' or 'daughter' or 'sister.'"

Meanings Change   Words are relatively static; many of the words we use today were also used 200 or 300 years ago. But the meanings of these words change constantly; and this is especially true of the emotional dimension of meaning. Compare, for example, the meanings given years ago and those of today for such terms as *premarital sex, drugs, religion, entertainment,* and *marriage.*

Meanings Need Referents   Although not all communication has reference to some external stimulus or to some referents in the real world, communication makes sense, Johnson argues, only when it relates in some way to the external world. This quality, it might be added, is often used to distinguish healthy from unhealthy communication and normal from abnormal persons (for example, those suffering from paranoia).

Beware of High-Order Abstractions   Closely related to the idea that meanings need referents is the communication problem that arises from using high-order abstractions without linking them to observable, concrete referents. For example, when we talk of *love, friendship, happiness, goodness, evil,* and similar abstract concepts without linking them to specifics, we will fail to achieve a sharing of meaning. Abstractions need to be connected to objects, events, and behaviors in the real world. When we have done this, we will be able to share what *we* mean by these terms and not leave the entire communication act to chance.

Meanings Are Shared Through Communication   All meanings are, in a sense, private. Each individual assigns different meanings to each term, event, and person. Communication may thus be viewed as a process of taking these private meanings and sharing them with another. Communication is not merely a process of exchanging words but of exchanging meanings and sharing your meanings with another person.

Meanings Are Infinite in Number   At any given time, the words of language are finite in number, but the meanings we have are infinite. Consequently, most words have multiple meanings and these may create communication problems when the same word is given different meanings by the two people communicating. When in doubt about meanings, inquire rather than assume; disagreements may well evaporate when each person's meaning is identified.

Meanings Are Communicated Only Partially   The meanings we derive from an event are multifaceted and extremely complex, but the words we use to describe these meanings represent only a small part of our experience. Much of our meaning remains in our heads. Our messages communicate only a small portion of these meanings. Consequently, true understanding—a complete sharing of meaning—is probably an unattainable ideal toward which we may strive but can never really achieve.

Denotative and Connotative Meanings

Although many types of meaning may be identified, two general types are essential to identify in communication: denotation and connotation. In order to explain these two types of meaning, let us take as an example the word *death*. To a doctor this word might simply mean, or denote, the time when the heart stops. It may be an objective description of a particular event. On the other hand, to the dead person's mother (upon being informed of her son's death), the word means much more than that. It recalls to her the son's youth, ambition, family, illness, and so on. To her it is a highly emotional, subjective, and personal word. These emotional, subjective, or personal reactions are the word's connotative meaning. The *denotation* of a word is its objective definition; the *connotation* of a word is its subjective or emotional meaning.

Snarl Words and Purr Words   Semanticist S. I. Hayakawa coined the terms *snarl words* and *purr words*, which may help in clarifying the distinction between denotation and connotation, especially as these concepts are used in human communication. Snarl words are highly negative ("He's a pig," "She's an idiot," "They're a bunch of losers"). Purr words are highly positive ("He's a dream," "She's a real sweetheart," "They're tops").

Snarl and purr words, although they may sometimes seem to have denotative meaning and to refer to the "real world," are actually connotative in

Understanding denotative meaning is relatively easy with the aid of good dictionaries and thesaurases, now even easier with the numerous computer software programs. Understanding connotative meaning, however, is quite different. What would a dictionary (in book or software form) of connotative meaning look like? What elements would you seek to include in a word's dictionary entry? What would be your major difficulty in constructing this dictionary?

meaning. These terms do not describe people, objects, or events in the real world, but rather describe the speaker's feelings about these people, objects, or events.

Variations in Denotative and Connotative Meanings   Some words are primarily and perhaps even completely denotative. Such words as *the, of,* and *a* may be purely denotative; no one seems to have emotional reactions to such words. Some other primarily denotative words are *perpendicular, parallel, cosine, adjacent,* and the like. Of course, even these words might have strong connotative meanings for some people. For example, the student who failed geometry might have a very strong emotional reaction to the word *geometry.* Other words, such as derogatory racial names and curse words, are primarily connotative and often have little denotative meaning. The point here is that words may vary from highly denotative to highly connotative. A good way to determine the word's connotative meaning is to ask where it would fall on a good-bad scale.

If "good" and "bad" do not seem to apply to the word, then it has little, if any, connotative meaning for you. If, however, the term can be placed on the good-bad scale with some degree of conviction, then it has connotative meaning for you.

General Agreement on Denotative and Connotative Meanings   Another distinction between the two types of meaning has already been implied. The denotative meaning of a word is fairly general or universal—that is, most people agree on the denotative meanings of words and have similar definitions. Connotative meanings, however, are extremely personal, and few people would agree on the precise connotative meaning of a word. If this does not seem correct, try to get a group of people to agree on the connotative meanings of words such as *religion, God, democracy, wealth,* and *freedom.* Chances are very good that it will be impossible to get agreement on such words.

Learning Denotative and Connotative Meanings   The denotative meaning of a term can be learned from a good dictionary. When we consult a dictionary, it is the denotative meaning we are seeking. The dictionary would tell us, for example, that *south* means "a cardinal point of the compass directly opposite to the north, the direction in which this point lies," and so on. Connotative meaning, on the other hand, cannot be found in a dictionary. Instead it must be found in the person's reactions or associations to the word. To some people, for example, *south* might mean poverty, to others it might mean wealth and good land investment, and to still others it might recall the Civil War, or perhaps warmth and friendliness. Obviously, no dictionary could be compiled for connotative meanings, simply because each person's meaning for a word is unique.

Changes in Denotative and Connotative Meanings   Denotative meaning differs from connotative meaning in yet another way. Denotative meanings are relatively unchanging and static. Although definitions of all words change through time, denotative meanings generally change very slowly. The word *south,* for example, meant (denotatively) the same thing a thousand years ago that it does now. But the connotative meaning changes rapidly. A single favorable experience in the south, for example, might completely change one's connotative meaning of the word.

PHATIC COMMUNION

No discussion of language and verbal interaction can omit *phatic* (pronounced *fáttik*) *communion*—the small talk that precedes the big talk, the talk that opens the channels of communication so that the important and significant issues may be discussed.

In content, phatic communion is trivial—"Hello," "How are you?" "Fine weather, isn't it?" "Have a nice day," and the like. But in establishing and maintaining relationships, phatic talk is extremely important. For one thing, phatic communication assures us that the social customs are in effect; the general rules of communication that we expect to operate will operate here also.

The teacher who says, "Turn to Chapter Three" before greeting us presents us with a situation in which the normal rules seem not to operate.

In first encounters, phatic communion enables us to reveal something of ourselves and at the same time to gain some preliminary information about the other person. Even if it is only to hear the tone or quality of voice, something is gained. Sometimes the important benefit is that phatic talk allows us time to look each other over and to decide on our next move. Phatic communion also shows us that the other person is willing to communicate, that in fact the channels of communication are open and there is some willingness to pursue the interaction.

Phatic communion, by its nature and because of the purposes it serves, is noncontroversial; with phatic talk there is little chance for conflict or fighting. Similarly, the topics considered are unemotional and hence not ego-involving. They are not intellectually demanding, nor are they too personal. In phatic talk the parties avoid extreme positions; rather, they seem to engage in what appears to be rather bland chatter. But we need to see that what on the surface is shallow is actually a foundation for later and more significant communication.

The person who says, "Haven't I seen you here before?" is probably asking not whether you have been here before, but "Would you like to talk with me?" To answer the literal question and fail to respond to the underlying and more significant question is a clear example of miscommunication on the listener's part.

SUMMARY

1. Language is productive; new elements may be added to the system and elements may be arranged in new ways to form new sentences.

2. Language is displaced; language can be used to talk about matters remote in both time and space—about the not-now and the not-here.

3. Spoken language consists of rapidly fading symbols.

4. Language symbols are arbitrary; there is no real or inherent connection between the word and the thing it symbolizes.

5. Language is culturally, not biologically, transmitted; language is learned from the culture in which the individual grows up. Human beings do have a biological predisposition to acquire language, but this predisposition refers to language in general and not to any specific language.

6. Among the implications of this view of language are (1) effective communication begins with and within language rules: (2) displacement and productivity make it possible to lie; false statements, however, cannot be distinguished from true statements on the basis of form or structure; (3) because of rapid fading, oral messages must be instantly intelligible; (4) meanings must be looked for in the person speaking and not merely in the words used; and (5) all human languages are equally learnable by any normal individual, but the period of this language readiness begins to fade after puberty.

7. Meaning is created by the persons communicating and is a function not only of messages but of the interaction of these messages and the individuals' thoughts, feelings, and attitudes.

8. Among the implications of this process view of meaning are (1) meanings are in people; (2) meanings (especially emotional meanings) change constantly though words remain static; (3) words make sense when they are anchored in some way to referents in the real world; (4) communication may be viewed as the process of sharing one's private meanings with others; (5) disagreements frequently arise when we forget that the same word may have multiple meanings; and (6) words communicate only a small part of any individual's total meaning.

9. Two major types of meaning are distinguished: *denotative meaning* refers to the objective, descriptive, or dictionary meaning; *connotative meaning* refers to the emotional or affective dimension of meaning.

10. *Snarl* and *purr* words are descriptions of the speaker's feelings, not descriptions of people, objects, or events; they are connotative rather than denotative in meaning.

11. *Phatic communion* refers to the small talk that precedes the big talk—the talk that opens the channels of communication so that other and more significant talk may take place.

SOURCES

For universal characteristics of language, I relied on the work of Charles F. Hockett, particularly "The Problem of Universals in Language," in J. H. Greenberg, ed., *Universals of Language* (Cambridge, Mass.: MIT Press, 1963). The concepts of language universals are thoroughly surveyed in Greenberg's *Universals of Language*. Most of the material, however, presumes a rather thorough knowledge of linguistics.

On language universals, see also Jean Aitchison, *The Articulate Mammal* (New York: McGraw-Hill, 1977), and Neil A. Stillings *et al.*, *Cognitive Science: An Introduction* (Cambridge, Mass.: MIT Press, 1987). On these universals and the ways in which human communication differs from animal communication, see A. Akmajian, R. A. Demers, and R. M. Harnish, *Linguistics: An Introduction to Language and Communication* (Cambridge, Mass.: MIT Press, 1979). A more popular introduction to language, describing studies on teaching language to apes, may be found in Herbert S. Terrace, *Nim: A Chimpanzee Who Learned Sign Language* (New York: Washington Square Press, 1981). On snarl and purr words and abstraction, see, for example, S. I. Hayakawa, *Language in Thought and Action*, 4th ed. (New York: Harcourt Brace Jovanovich, 1978). The role of language in the development and maintenance of interpersonal relationships is covered in Charles R. Berger and James J. Bradac, *Language and Social Knowledge: Uncertainty in Interpersonal Relations* (London: Edward Arnold, 1982).

UNIT 7
BARRIERS IN LANGUAGE AND VERBAL INTERACTION

LEARNING GOALS

After completing this unit, you should be able to

1. define *polarization, intensional orientation, fact-inference confusion, bypassing, all-ness, static evaluation,* and *indiscrimination*
2. identify examples of these seven misevaluations in the media
3. identify examples of these seven misevaluations from your interpersonal interactions
4. explain the relevance of intensional orientation to research in prestige suggestion
5. explain the nature of pragmatic implication and relate this concept to fact-inference confusion
6. explain the role of the *etc.*, the date, and the index in reducing the barriers in language and verbal interaction

Although communication may break down at any point in the process from sender to receiver, perhaps the most obvious site of breakdown is in the actual message. Breakdown, of course, may occur in any form of communication, and the breakdowns noted here are applicable to all forms of communication.

POLARIZATION

Polarization refers to the tendency to look at the world in terms of opposites and to describe it in terms of extremes—good or bad, positive or negative, healthy or sick, intelligent or stupid, rich or poor, and so on. It is often referred to as the "fallacy of either-or" or "black and white." Although it is true that magnetic poles may be described as positive or negative and that certain people are extremely rich and others are extremely poor, the vast majority of cases are clearly in the middle. Most people exist somewhere between the extremes of good and bad. health and sick, intelligent and stupid, rich and poor. Yet there seems to be a strong tendency to view only the extremes and to categorize people, objects, and events in terms of these polar opposites.

We can easily illustrate this tendency by attempting to fill in the polar opposites for such words as the following:

hot	————————⟶	———————
high	————————⟶	———————
good	————————⟶	———————
popular	————————⟶	———————
sad	————————⟶	———————

Filling in these opposites should have been relatively easy and quick. Also, the words should have been fairly short. Further, if a number of people supplied opposites, we should find a high degree of agreement among them.

Now attempt to fill in the middle positions with words meaning, for example, "midway between high and low," "midway between hot and cold," and so on. These midway responses, compared with the opposites, were probably more difficult to think of and took more time. The words should also have been fairly long or phrases of two, three, four, or more words. Further, we would probably find rather low agreement among different people completing this same task.

It might be helpful to visualize the familiar bell-shaped curve. Few items exist at either of the two extremes, but as we move closer to the center, more and more items are included. This is true of any random sample. If we selected a hundred people at random we would find that their intelligence, height, weight, income, age, health, and so on would, if plotted, fall into a bell-shaped or "normal" distribution. Yet our tendency seems to be to concentrate on the extremes at either end of this curve and ignore the middle, which contains the vast majority of cases.

In certain areas it is legitimate to phrase statements in terms of two absolutes. For example, this thing that you are holding is either a book or it is not. Clearly the classes of book and not-book include all possibilities, so there is no problem with this kind of statement. Similarly, we may say that the student will pass this exam or will not pass it, these two categories including all possibilities.

We create problems, however, when we use the absolute form in inappropriate situations—for example, "The politician is either for us or against us." Note that these options do not include all possibilities; the politician may be for us in some things and against us in other things, or may be neutral. During the Vietnam War there was a tendency to categorize people as either hawk or dove, but clearly there were many people who were neither and many who were probably hawks on certain issues and doves on others.

Beware of implying and believing that two extreme classes include all possible classes—that an individual must be a hawk or a dove, with no other alternatives. "Life is either a daring adventure or nothing," said Helen Keller. But for most people it is neither a daring adventure nor nothing, but something somewhere in between these two extremes.

INTENSIONAL ORIENTATION

Intensional orientation (the *s* in intensional is intentional) refers to the tendency to view people, objects, and events in terms of their labels rather than in terms of their reality. *Extensional orientation,* on the other hand, is the tendency to look first to the actual people, objects, and events and only afterwards to their labels; it is the tendency to be guided by what we see happening rather than by the label used for what is happening.

Intensional orientation is evident when we act as if the labels are more important than the things they represent—when we act as if the map is more important than the territory. An extreme form of intensional orientation is shown by the person who, afraid of dogs, begins to sweat when shown a picture of a dog or when hearing people talk about dogs. Here the person is responding to the label (a picture of a dog) as if it were the actual thing (a dog).

One of the most ingenious examples of intensional orientation requires that you role-play for a minute and picture yourself seated with a packet of photographs before you. Each photograph shows a person you have never seen. You are asked to scratch out the eyes in each photograph. You are further told that this is simply an experiment and that the individuals whose pictures you have will not be aware of anything that has happened here. As you progress through the pictures, scratching out the eyes, you come upon a photograph of your mother. What do you do? Are you able to scratch out the eyes as you have done with the pictures of the strangers, or have you somehow lost your ability to scratch out eyes? If, like many others, you are unable to scratch out the eyes, you are responding intensionally. You are, in effect, responding to the map (in this case the picture) as if it were the territory (your own mother).

An experiment conducted with stutterers should further illustrate this phenomenon. This experiment used two findings from earlier studies. First, stutterers stutter more when talking with people in authority than with subordinates. Stutterers will stutter very little when talking with children or addressing animals, for example, but when it comes to teachers or employers, they stutter a great deal. Second, as a stutterer reads a particular passage, he or she will stutter less on each successive reading; this is called *adaptation*. Using these findings, the researcher in this experiment obtained from the stutterers the names of those to whom they had most difficulty speaking. At a later date the researchers had each stutterer read a passage five times. As predicted, the stuttering decreased on each reading to the point of being almost entirely absent on the fifth reading. Before the sixth reading the experimenter placed in front of the stutterer a photograph of the person the stutterer had named as being most difficult to speak to, and on the sixth reading the stuttering increased approximately to the level of the first reading. Again, the individual was responding to the photograph as if it were the actual person.

Prestige Suggestion

Intensional orientation may be seen clearly in the results of the numerous studies on prestige suggestion. Basically, these studies demonstrate that we are influenced more by a message when it comes from a prestigious personality than we are when it comes from an average individual. Such studies have shown that if given a painting, we will evaluate it highly if we think it was painted by a famous artist, but we will give it a low evaluation if we think it was produced by a little-known artist. Other studies have focused on our agreement with dogmatic statements, our judgments of literary merit, our perception of musical ability, and so on. In all these studies the influencing factor is not the message itself—that is, the statement, the literature, the music—but the name attached to it. Advertisers, of course, have long known the value of this type of appeal and have capitalized on it quite profitably. Labels are certainly helpful guides, but they are not the things for which they are the symbols and should not be confused with them.

FACT-INFERENCE CONFUSION

We can make statements about the world we observe, and we can make statements about what we have not observed. In form or structure these statements are similar and cannot be distinguished by any grammatical analysis. For example, we can say, "She is wearing a blue jacket," as well as "He is harboring an illogical hatred." If we diagramed these sentences they would yield identical structures, and yet we know quite clearly that they are very different types of statement. We can observe the jacket and the blue color, but how do we observe "illogical hatred"? Obviously, this is not a descriptive but an inferential statement. It is a statement we make on the basis not only of what we observe, but on what we conclude.

There is nothing wrong with making inferential statements; we must make them to talk about much that is meaningful to us. The problem arises in acting as if those inferential statements are factual statements. Consider, for example, the following anecdote: A woman went for a walk one day and met a friend whom she had not seen, or heard from, or heard of in 10 years. After an exchange of greetings, the woman said: "Is this your little boy?" and her friend replied, "Yes, I got married about six years ago." The woman then asked the child, "What is your name?" and the little boy replied, "Same as my father's." "Oh," said the woman, "then it must be Peter."

How did the woman know the boy's father's name when she had not seen, heard from, or heard of her friend in the last 10 years? The answer, of course, is obvious, but it is obvious only after we recognize that in reading this short passage we have made an unconscious inference that is preventing us from answering a simple question. Specifically, we have inferred that the woman's friend is a woman. Actually, the friend is a man named Peter.

Perhaps the classic example of this type of fact-inference confusion concerns the case of the "empty" gun that unfortunately proves to be loaded. With amazing frequency we find in the newspapers examples of someone's being so sure that a gun is empty that the person points at another individual and fires. Many times, of course, the gun is empty. Unfortunately, many times it is not. Here one makes an inference (that the gun is empty), but acts on the inference as if it is a fact.

Pragmatic Implications

A related communication barrier is raised by what linguistic philosophers call *pragmatic implication*. Consider the following: We hear that our biology teacher has been replaced for next year. Further, we know that our biology class has not been very exciting and that many students complained about the poor instruction. On the basis of this knowledge, we draw a pragmatic implication. Unlike a logical implication which must be true, a pragmatic implication is an inference that is probably but not necessarily true. In this example we infer that the teacher was fired for ineffective teaching. Note that here we have two pragmatic implications: (1) The teacher was fired, and (2) the reason for the firing was ineffective teaching. Again, there is nothing wrong with drawing pragmatic implications; we all do it. The problem is created, in a way, by our memory systems. After making such pragmatic implications we forget that they are in fact inferences and not observed facts. We remember these inferences just as we remember the fact that the biology teacher has been replaced.

This type of situation happens every day. We see two friends in a quiet romantic restaurant. We draw the pragmatic implication that they are dating or that they are somehow romantically involved. We forget that this is only an inference and remember it as observed fact. When, on subsequent occasions, we see these same friends with different partners, the plot thickens and we begin to draw pragmatic implications on top of pragmatic implications, again failing to distinguish between what was observed fact and what was inference. In the process we move further and further away from facts and observations without ever realizing that we are doing so.

Differentiating Facts from Inferences

Some of the essential differences between factual and inferential statements are summarized in Table 7.1. Distinguishing between these two types of statement does not imply that one type is better than the other. We need both types of statements; both are useful, both are important. The problem arises when we treat an inferential statement as if it were a factual statement.

Inferential statements need to be accompanied by tentativeness. Recognize that such statements may prove to be wrong, and be aware of that possibility. Inferential statements should leave open the possibility of alternatives. If, for example, we treat the statement "The United States should enforce the blockade" as factual, we eliminate the possibility of any alternatives. When making inferential statements, we are psychologically prepared to be proved wrong. This requires a great deal of effort, but when we are psychologically prepared to be proved wrong, we will be less hurt if and when we are shown to be incorrect.

TABLE 7.1 DIFFERENCES BETWEEN FACTUAL AND INFERENTIAL STATEMENTS

Factual Statements	Inferential Statements
1. May be made only after observation	1. May be made at any time
2. Are limited to what has been observed	2. Go beyond what has been observed
3. May be made only by the observer	3. May be made by anyone
4. May only be about the past or the present	4. May be about any time—past, present, future
5. Approach certainty	5. Involve varying degrees of probability
6. Are subject to verifiable standards	6. Are not subject to verifiable standards

BYPASSING

Bypassing is a pattern of misevaluation in which people fail to communicate their intended meanings. William Haney defines it as "the miscommunication pattern which occurs when the *sender* (speaker, writer, and so on) and the *receiver* (listener, reader, and so forth) *miss each other with their meanings.*"

Bypassing can take either of two forms. In the first form, two people use different words but give them the same meaning. On the surface there is apparent disagreement but at the level of meaning there is agreement. Consider the following brief dialogue:

PAT: I want a permanent relationship. I'm not interested in one-night stands. [Meaning: I want to date you exclusively and I want you to date me exclusively.]

CHRIS: I'm not ready for that [thinking and meaning: marriage]. Let's keep things the way they are [meaning: let's continue dating only each other].

Here we have a not-uncommon situation in which two people agree but assume, because they use different words (some of which may actually never be verbalized), that they disagree.

The second type of bypassing and the more common type occurs when two people use the same words but give the words different meanings. Here there is apparent agreement but underlying disagreement. Consider this brief dialogue:

> PAT: I don't really believe in religion [meaning: I don't really believe in God].
>
> CHRIS: Neither do I [meaning: I don't really believe in organized religions].

Here Pat and Chris assume they agree but actually disagree. At some later date the implications of these differences may well become crucial.

Numerous other examples could be cited. Dating couples who say they are "in love" may mean very different things: One may mean "a permanent and exclusive commitment" while the other may mean "a sexual involvement." "Come home early" may mean one thing to the anxious parent and quite another to the teenager.

The underlying assumption in bypassing is that words have intrinsic meanings, so that when two people use the same word they mean the same thing, and when they use different words those words have different meanings. But words do not have meaning; meaning is in people.

Correctives

One obvious corrective for this misevaluation, as Haney points out, is to look for meaning in the person and not in the words. Remember, as was pointed out in the discussion of Johnson's model of meaning, that words may be assigned a wide variety of meanings by different people and, alternatively, people may assign different words the same meaning.

A second corrective is to use the active listening techniques discussed in Unit 5. By paraphrasing the speaker you will be able to check on whether there is agreement or disagreement, not in the words but in the communicators. By reflecting back the speaker's thoughts and feelings, you will be able to see whether you understand the speaker and you will also be providing the speaker with an opportunity to clarify any misunderstanding or ambiguity. By asking questions you will be able to check on your own perception of the speaker's meanings.

ALLNESS

Because the world is infinitely complex, we can never know all or say all about anything—at least we cannot logically say all about anything. This is particularly true in dealing with people. We may *think* we know all there is to know about individuals or about why they did what they did, yet clearly we do not know all. We can never know all the reasons we ourselves do something, and yet we often think that we know all the reasons why our parents, our friends, or our enemies did something. And because we are so convinced that we know all the reasons, we are quick to judge and evaluate the actions of others with great confidence that what we are doing is justified.

We may, for example, be assigned a textbook to read and, because previous texts have been dull or perhaps because the first chapter was dull, we infer that all the rest will be dull. Of course, it often turns out that the rest of the book is even worse than the beginning. Yet it could be that the rest of the book would have proved exciting had we read it with an open mind. The problem here is that we run the risk of defining the entire text (on the basis of previous texts and perhaps the first chapter) in such a way as to preclude any other possibilities. If we tell ourselves that the book is dull, it probably will appear dull. If we say a course will be useless ("all required courses are useless"), it will be extremely difficult for the instructor to make the course anything but what we have defined it to be. Only occasionally do we allow ourselves to be proved wrong; for the most part we resist rather fiercely.

The parable of the six blind men and the elephant is an excellent example of an "allness" orientation and its attendant problems. You may recall from elementary school the poem by John Saxe that concerns six blind men of Indostan who came to examine an elephant, an animal they had only heard about. The first blind man touched the elephant's side and concluded that the elephant was like a wall. The second felt the tusk and said the elephant must be like a spear. The third held the trunk and concluded the elephant was much like a snake. The fourth touched the knee and knew the elephant was like a tree. The fifth felt the ear and said the elephant was like a fan. And the sixth grabbed the tail and concluded that the elephant was like a rope. Each reached his own conclusion regarding what this marvelous beast, the elephant, was really like. Each argued that he was correct and that the others were wrong. Each, of course, was correct; but at the same time each was wrong.

The point this poem illustrates is that we are all in the position of the six blind men. We never see all of something; we never experience anything fully. We see part of an object, an event, a person—and on that limited basis conclude what the whole is like. This procedure is a relatively universal one; we have to do this since it is impossible to observe everything. And yet we must also recognize that when we make judgments of the whole based only on a part, we are actually making inferences that can later be proved wrong. If we assume that we know all of anything, we have stumbled into the pattern of misevaluation called *allness*.

Disraeli once said that "to be conscious that you are ignorant is a great step toward knowledge." That observation is an excellent example of a *nonallness* attitude. If we recognize that there is more to learn, more to see, and more to hear, we will leave ourselves open to additional information and will be better prepared to assimilate it into our existing structures.

Allness and Conflict

In conflict situations, negative allness statements—especially those containing *always* and *never*—are particularly troublesome. Allness statements ("You *always* criticize me in front of your friends," "You *never* do what I want," "You're *always* nagging," "You *never* want to visit my family") encourage defensiveness and are more in the nature of attacks than attempts to pinpoint and resolve problems.

It would be just as easy and much more constructive to say, for example, "At Pat's party, you talked about my being a terrible cook. That really embarrassed me. I don't know if you realized it, but I felt hurt. If you want to criticize something, I think it should be kept private and said when we're alone." Expressed in this way, there is no attack and no encouragement of defensiveness. Instead, there is a clear and descriptive statement of the problem and a proposed solution that can be discussed reasonably.

End Statements with *Etc.*

A useful device to help us remember our nonallness orientation is to end each statement, verbally or mentally, with an *etc.*—a reminder that there is more to learn, more to know, and more to say, and a reminder that every statement is inevitably incomplete.

STATIC EVALUATION

Often when we form an abstraction of something or someone—when we formulate a verbal statement about an event or person—that abstraction, that statement, has a tendency to remain static and unchanging while the object or person to whom it originally referred may have changed enormously. Alfred Korzybski, the founder of the study of language called General Semantics, used an interesting illustration in this connection: In a tank we have a large fish and many small fish, which are the natural food for the large fish. Given freedom in the tank, the large fish will eat the small fish. After some time we partition the tank with the large fish on one side and the small fish on the other, divided only by a clear piece of glass. For a considerable time the large fish will attempt to eat the small fish but will fail each time; each time it will knock into the glass partition. After some time it will "learn" that attempting to eat the small fish means difficulty and will no longer go after them. Now, however, we remove the partition and the little fish swim all around the big fish. But the big fish does not eat them and in fact will die of starvation. The large fish has learned a pattern of behavior, and even though the actual territory has changed, the map remains static.

While we would probably all agree that everything is in a constant state of flux, the relevant question is whether we act as if we know this. Put differently, do we act in accordance with the notion of change, instead of just accepting it intellectually? Do we realize, for example, that if someone does something to hurt us, they too are in a constant state of change? Our evaluations of ourselves and of others must keep pace with the rapidly changing real world; otherwise we will be left with attitudes about and beliefs in a world that no longer exists.

Date Statements

To guard against static evaluation, date your statements and especially your evaluations. Remember that Pat Smith$_{1984}$ is not Pat Smith$_{1988}$; academic abilities$_{1985}$ are not academic abilities$_{1989}$. T. S. Eliot, in *The Cocktail Party*, said that "what we know of other people is only our memory of the moments during which we knew them. And they have changed since then . . . at every meeting we are meeting a stranger."

INDISCRIMINATION

Nature seems to abhor sameness at least as much as vacuums, for nowhere in the universe can we find two things that are identical. Everything is unique—everything is unlike everything else.

The old one-room school house is now a relic of an almost forgotten past. Yet, even the average classroom contains students who differ from each other in numerous and significant ways. What are some of the major ways in which the students in your class differ from one another? What are the implications of these differences for effective teaching and effective communication?

Our language, however, provides us with common nouns, such as *teacher, student, friend, enemy, war, politician,* and *liberal,* which lead us to focus on similarities. Such nouns lead us to group all teachers together, all students together, and all friends together and perhaps serve to divert attention away from the uniqueness of each individual, each object, and each event. The misevaluation of *indiscrimination,* then, is one in which we focus on classes of individuals, objects, or events and fail to see that each is unique and needs to be looked at individually.

This misevaluation is at the heart of the common practice of stereotyping national, racial, and religious groups. A *stereotype* is a relatively fixed mental picture of some group that is applied to each individual of the group without regard to his or her unique qualities. It is important to note that although stereotypes are usually thought of as negative, they may also be positive. We can, for example, consider certain national groups as lazy, superstitious, mercenary, or criminal, but we can also consider them as intelligent, progressive, honest, hard-working, and so on. Regardless of whether such stereotypes are positive or negative, however, the problem they create is the same. They provide us with shortcuts that are often inappropriate. For example, when we meet a particular individual our first reaction may be to pigeonhole him or her into some category—perhaps religious, national, or academic. Regardless of the type of category we use, we invariably fail to devote sufficient attention to the unique characteristics of the individual before us.

There is nothing wrong with classifying. No one would argue that classifying is unhealthy or immoral. It is, on the contrary, an extremely useful method of dealing with any complex matter. Classifying helps us to deal with complexity; it puts order into our thinking. The problem arises not from classifying itself, but from classifying, applying some evaluative label to that class, and then utilizing that evaluative label as an "adequate" map for each individual in the group. Put differently, indiscrimination is a denial of another's uniqueness.

Index Terms

A useful antidote to indiscrimination is the *index,* a verbal or mental subscript that identifies each individual as an individual even though two individuals may be covered by the same label: $politician_1$ is not $politician_2$, $teacher_1$ is not $teacher_2$. The index helps us to discriminate *among* without discriminating *against.*

SUMMARY

1. *Polarization* refers to the tendency to divide reality into two unrealistic extremes—for example, black and white, or good and bad.

2. *Intensional orientation* refers to the tendency to respond to the way something is talked about or labeled rather than to the thing's reality; it is the tendency to respond to symbols as if they were things.

3. *Extensional orientation,* the opposite of *intensional orientation,* refers to the tendency to respond to things as they are rather than as they are labeled or talked about.

4. *Fact-inference confusion* refers to the tendency to respond to inferences as if they were facts.

5. *Bypassing* refers to the pattern of miscommunication that occurs when speaker and listener miss each other with their meanings—when different words are used but are given the same meaning; or when the same word is used but is given two different meanings.

6. *Allness* refers to the tendency to assume that one knows all there is to know, or that what has been said is all that there is to say.

7. *Static evaluation* refers to the tendency to ignore change and to assume that reality is static and unchanging.

8. *Indiscrimination* refers to the tendency to group unlike things together and to assume that because they have the same label, they are all alike. It is the tendency to ignore differences among items that are labeled in the same way.

SOURCES

The barriers to verbal interaction owe their formulation to the work of the General Semanticists. I would especially recommend J. Dan Rothwell's *Telling It Like It Isn't: Language Misuse & Malpractice/What We Can Do About It* (Englewood Cliffs, N.J.: Prentice-Hall, 1982), and Peggy Rosenthal, *Words and Values: Some Leading Words and Where They Lead Us* (New York: Oxford University Press, 1984). William Haney's *Communication and Organizational Behavior: Text and Cases,* 3d ed. (Homewood, Ill.: Irwin, 1973) covers bypassing as well as the other misevaluations and provides numerous cases for analysis. Much that appears in this unit appears in more detail in my *General Semantics: Guide and Workbook,* rev. ed. (DeLand, Fla.: Everett/Edwards, 1974), and on my cassette tape series *General Semantics: Nine Lectures* (DeLand, Fla.: Everett/Edwards, 1971).

UNIT 8
PRINCIPLES OF LANGUAGE AND VERBAL INTERACTION

LEARNING GOALS

After completing this unit, you should be able to

1. define *in-group talk* and the *principle of inclusion* and provide examples of each
2. define *downward* and *upward talk* and the *principle of equality* and provide examples of each
3. explain how criticism and complimenting can create interpersonal difficulties and how the principle of honesty can be used
4. explain some of the disadvantages of lying from a communication point of view
5. define *self-talk, other-talk,* and the *principle of balance* and provide examples of each
6. explain the principle of fairness in regard to offensive language
7. define *gossip* and explain how the principle of confidentiality should operate
8. define *disconfirmation* and *confirmation* and provide examples of each

The effects people have on us and we have on them result largely from the verbal messages sent and received—the way we talk, the way we express our ideas and our feelings, the way we verbalize our relationship to the other person. In this unit, we consider seven "turnoffs"—ways in which we may create negative effects—and their corresponding opposites—the principles that should be followed to avoid such negative reactions. At the same time, these principles should enable us to create a more positive environment for communication in all its forms.

IN-GROUP TALK

One of the most annoying and destructive verbal habits is the use of in-group talk in the presence of some out-group member—someone who is not a member of this "elite" in-group. When doctors get together and discuss medicine, there seems to be no problem. But when they get together with someone who is not a doctor, they often fail to adjust to this new person. Instead, they simply continue with discussions of prescriptions, symptoms, medication, and all the in-group talk that could interest only another doctor. Many professionals do the same thing; teachers talk teaching, lawyers talk lawyering, and so on. In-grouping makes for pretty boring conversation, even among in-group members. When nonmembers are involved, it makes for communication that is both ineffective and insulting.

A variant of this habit occurs when people of the same nationality get together within a larger, more heterogeneous group and use the language of their group, sometimes just isolated words, sometimes sentences, and sometimes even entire conversations. This is not merely a question of understandability: The use of these terms in the presence of a nonmember emphasizes that person's status as an outsider. In almost every instance, the foreign term could easily be translated. The use of the foreign expression does not aid communication; it serves no purpose other than to mark the in-group members as united and the out-group members as outsiders.

Inclusion

Instead of trying to emphasize the exclusion of one or more members, consider the *principle of inclusion*. Regardless of the type of communication situation, everyone needs to be included in an interaction. Even when we have to "talk shop" in the presence of a nonmember, that person can be included in a variety of ways. We might attempt to seek a nonmember's perspective on the issue, or perhaps draw an analogy with that person's field.

Practicing inclusion is so easy that I am amazed to see the principle violated so often. When inclusion is practiced, everyone seems to gain a great deal more satisfaction from the interaction.

DOWNWARD AND UPWARD TALK

In communication theory and particularly in the area of communication concerned with organizations (see Unit 19), downward and upward communication have very specific meanings. *Downward communication* refers to communication originating from a high-level source (for example, a manager or executive) and directed at a lower-level receiver (for example, a line worker). *Upward communication* is the reverse and refers to communication originating from an individual who is low on the organizational hierarchy and directed at someone higher up. As used here, however, the terms refer to that irksome habit of talking down or talking up to others.

Downward Talk

Here we feel that the speaker for some unknown reason has "the word" and is passing it on to the masses. We hear downward talk from the teacher who says, "This may be beyond your reach, but try to grasp it anyway" or the "friend" who puts himself or herself above others by using phrases such as "You probably didn't realize this but . . ." or "I know you don't keep up with the computer literature but . . . ." Regardless of who is doing the talking, we get the distinct feeling that somehow the speaker is above us for a multitude of reasons—intelligence, experience, knowledge, position, wealth, or whatever. We are put into the position of learner and subordinate.

Another way in which some people talk down is in telling others how to feel and how to act. Consider this scene: You are at a party with a group of people who are singing along with a record. One individual, perhaps because of shyness, perhaps because of some other reason, does not join in. The individual remains social but doesn't participate in the sing-along. Enter the problem communicator: "Come on, loosen up, sing with us." The person no doubt means well, but at the same time displays a total lack of respect for the other person's behaviors and feelings. If one member chooses not to sing along, that is her or his choice. As friends and associates, we need to respect that choice. To insist that the individual sing along (or smoke or drink) only creates further problems by throwing the spotlight on this individual, who may, by not singing, have wanted to escape attention.

There is usually little point in attempting to take on the responsibility for another person's feelings. It is far better to assume that each person can and prefers to make his or her own decisions. Few persons need us to tell them to loosen up, to have fun, or to do this or that.

Power Games

A variant of this downward-directed talk is seen in the individual who plays a power game with us. This power game takes many forms, but in all cases our communications are treated as second-rate, of only minor importance. The game is frequently played by men against women. When a man and a woman are engaged in a conversation or argument, the man will frequently interrupt the woman; rarely will the woman interrupt the man. Through years of cultural conditioning, women have been taught not to interrupt men and men have been taught that it is perfectly acceptable to interrupt women. Notice that people who interrupt are stating that their communications are more important than yours; consequently, they have a right to interrupt you, but you do not have a right to interrupt them. By allowing this to happen, we frequently give tacit agreement to this analysis, and the existing power structure is maintained.

Another power technique occurs when someone dismisses what you say with such phrases as "you can't be serious" or "you couldn't possibly mean that." Even the most secure among us begin to question ourselves when confronted by such powerful attacks. Such statements are like interruptions; they state that what you are saying is unimportant and unworthy of serious consideration.

Gobbledygook

A somewhat different form of talking down occurs when people use gobbledygook—double-talk, or language that is needlessly complex and confusing. Semanticist J. Dan Rothwell calls it "verbosity and circumlocution that buries a message in an avalanche of verbal rubble." Originally coined by Maury Maverick, a representative from Texas, the term *gobbledygook* refers to much around us, particularly in government documents, legal and medical contracts, and, unfortunately, much academic writing. We can gain perspective on this type of noncommunication by viewing it as a form of talking down.

Upward Talk

A type of communication equally difficult to deal with approaches you as if you have the answer and are the authority. Anyone who has been in this position knows that it is tiresome and difficult. You have to be at your very best at all times.

Sometimes the speaker talks upward in an attempt to manipulate or flatter you so that you will treat what is to be said kindly. In many instances, such speakers begin their communications with what are called disqualifiers: "I'm not sure of this, but . . . " or "I'm probably wrong, but I was wondering . . . " or "You know this better than I do, but would it be possible to . . . ." These disqualifiers appear to put the speaker one-down and the listener one-up. When these disqualifiers are genuine expressions of doubt and uncertainty, there is no problem. When they are just verbal manipulations to throw the other person off guard or to create an impression of the speaker as totally without power, problems do arise. At still other times, they can reflect an inferiority complex that manifests itself in constant attempts to put oneself down.

Equality

When used unfairly to intimidate or to manipulate, both downward and upward talk create problems for all involved. Although there are a number of ways to deal with these attempts, perhaps the most helpful is the *principle of equality*. As a receiver of messages that talk down to us or attempt to strip us of any power, we need to recognize that all parties in the communication act are equal in the sense that each person's communications are worthwhile and each person has something to contribute. Some of us may be using these power plays and manipulations without even being aware of them (only until now, I hope). Perhaps keeping the principle of equality in mind will lessen the likelihood of our doing this in the future. As a receiver, we need to recognize our own responsibility in these situations; when we allow people to interrupt us or somehow to treat our own communications as being of lesser importance, we are in effect encouraging and reinforcing this behavior. Demand communication equality. The simple statement "Excuse me but you're interrupting me; I'd like to finish my thought" is usually most effective. Also effective is: "Yes, I am serious and I would appreciate your dealing with my ideas and not with putting me down by saying 'you can't be serious.' I wouldn't say it if I wasn't serious."

CRITICISM AND COMPLIMENTING

Throughout our communication experiences we are expected to criticize, evaluate, and otherwise render some kind of judgment. Especially if we are in a helping profession like teaching, nursing, or counseling, criticism becomes an important and frequently used skill. In short, criticism is a most useful and important part of our interactions and communications generally. A communication problem develops when criticism is used outside its helping function, when it is used inappropriately, or when it is used to excess. We need to distinguish between a request for our criticism and a request for a compliment. Thus, when a friend asks how you like her new apartment, she may be searching for a compliment and not really be interested in itemizing all the things wrong with it. Often, too, we use such opportunities to hurt other people, sometimes even people we care for.

Sometimes the desire to be liked (or perhaps the need to be appreciated) is so strong that we go to the other extreme and paint everything with praise. I'm sure you know people who act this way. The most average jacket, the most ordinary thought, the most common meal are given extraordinary praise, far beyond their merits. The overly critical and the overly complimentary soon find that their comments are no longer responded to with concern or interest.

Honest Appraisal

As an alternative, consider the *principle of honest appraisal*. Tell the truth. But note that there is an art to truth-telling just as there is an art to all other forms of communication effectiveness. First, distinguish between instances when an honest appraisal or evaluation is asked for and times when the individual is in need of a compliment. Respond to the appropriate level of meaning. Second, if an honest appraisal is desired and if your honest appraisal is a negative one, give some consideration to how you phrase your criticism. Begin positively and proceed gently and always with a concern for the other person and for your relationship.

LYING

According to the *Random House Dictionary,* a *lie* is "a false statement made with deliberate intent to deceive; a falsehood; something intended or serving to convey a false impression." As this definition makes clear, lying may be both overt and covert. Although usually done by overt statements, lying may also be committed by omission. When we omit something relevant to the issue at hand, whose omission leads others to draw incorrect inferences, we have lied just as surely as if we had made a false statement on national television. Most of us can easily appreciate this by recalling when we were very young and our parents, suspicious for various reasons about what went on last night, asked us what happened. Many of us probably recited all the innocent things and conveniently omitted what our parents were really asking us about. It was a lie and we knew it.

Similarly, although most lies are verbal, some are nonverbal and most seem to involve at least some nonverbal elements. The innocent facial expression—despite the commission of some punishable act—and the knowing nod instead of the honest expression of ignorance are common enough examples of nonverbal lying. Lies may range from the "white" lie in which one "stretches the truth" to the big lie in which one formulates falsehoods so enormous that everyone comes to believe they are true.

Reasons for Lying

There are probably as many reasons for lying as there are lies; each situation is different and each situation seems to be governed by a different reason or set of reasons. But if we boiled it down, we would probably find that people lie for two main reasons: (1) to gain some reward or (2) to avoid some punishment. Carl Camden, Michael Motley, and Ann Wilson, in their study of white lies in interpersonal communication, have identified four major reward categories that seem to motivate lying behavior:

■ *Basic needs:* Lies told to gain or to retain objects that fulfill basic needs—for example, money or various material possessions.
■ *Affiliation:* Lies told to increase desired affiliations or to decrease undesired affiliations—for example, lies told to prolong desirable social interactions, avert interpersonal conflicts, avoid granting some request to halt undesirable interaction. Also included here are lies told to gain or maintain conversational control during interpersonal interaction—for example, lies told

to avoid certain self-disclosures or to manipulate the conversation in a desired direction.

- *Self-esteem:* Lies told to protect or increase the self-esteem of oneself, the person one is interacting with, or some third party—for example, lies told to increase one's perceived competence, taste, or social desirability.
- *Self-gratification:* Lies told to achieve some personal satisfaction—for example, lies told for the sake of humor or to exaggerate for some desired effect.

Very likely an in-depth analysis of the avoidance of punishment would yield categories similar to those identified for gaining rewards. That is, we probably lie *to avoid* such punishments as having our basic needs taken away (losing money, for example), decreasing desired affiliations, decreasing self-esteem, and losing or decreasing personal satisfaction.

Generally, people lie in order to achieve some reward or avoid some punishment for themselves, although some lies are motivated by a desire to benefit the person with whom one is interacting or some third party. From an analysis of 322 lies, Camden, Motley, and Wilson found that 75.8 percent benefited the liar, 21.7 percent benefited the other interactant, and 2.5 percent benefited some third party.

Generally, we know when we are lying and when we are not lying. No one has to tell us. And yet there are many gray areas where it is not clear when a statement is a lie and when it is not. Sometimes it is difficult to tell—for example, when someone is asking for an honest opinion or merely asking for a compliment. "What do you think of my new apartment?" may be designed to get a needed pat on the back and not an honest opinion of the decoration. Sometimes there is a tacit agreement between people to avoid telling the truth about certain issues. A couple, for example, may agree that extrarelational affairs are not to be disclosed and that the acceptable procedure is to make up some kind of innocent excuse—working late at the office and its variants—to cover up. In these instances, the context and the intent of the message would define whether something is or is not a lie. Thus, if in response to the question about the apartment, one said "It's really beautiful" because of the belief that the question was asking for a compliment, then I think there was no lie. Similarly, if the individuals have made it known that they do not want to deal with the truth about certain issues, then it seems it is not a lie to conform to this expectation or wish.

Is Lying Effective?

Lies have both ethical and effectiveness dimensions; both need to be considered. The ethical dimension concerns what is right and what is wrong. Lying is unethical simply because each person has a right to base his or her choices on the best information available. By lying we are withholding at least part of that information and contributing to decisions based on incorrect assumptions, falsehoods, and the like. The effectiveness dimension concerns whether the lie succeeds or fails in gaining the reward or avoiding the punishment. Many lies are effective; people have risen to the top of their professions and have amassed fortunes built on lies and deceit. There can be little doubt that in many instances lying works. And yet there are enough problems and enough disadvantages to lying that should make us pause and reconsider any decision to lie.

Lies and Inconsistent Packages

As already noted, communication messages are sent and received as packages. Lies are no exception. It is often difficult to lie nonverbally with any degree of conviction. Often our lies are betrayed nonverbally. It is far easier to lie with our mouths than with our faces and our bodies. And when the contradiction is observed, it is the nonverbal message that is generally believed. The result is that we have lied, but to no avail. Our reputation may suffer without our having achieved the reward or avoided the punishment. Perhaps the main disadvantage of lying is that it influences who we are and what we think of ourselves. When we believe that lying is wrong and yet lie ourselves, we are creating psychological imbalance and intrapersonal conflict, neither of which is particularly healthy. We seem to be designed to function as a consistent whole, with our thinking and our behavior echoing each other. When we believe one thing and do something else, we begin to develop various internal conflicts.

Lies and Energy to Conceal

As a result of lying, one has to expend a considerable amount of energy to maintain the lie. We realize, like F. M. Knowles in his *Cheerful Year Book*, "There is nothing so pathetic as a forgetful liar." The more people we lie to and the more complex the lie, the more energy we have to devote to keeping things straight in order to preserve that lie. This leaves us with that much less energy to use for other matters. This is similar to the burdensome aspects of self-disclosure; the more secrets we keep, the more energy has to be exerted to maintain those secrets.

Lies and Interpersonal Disapproval

Perhaps the most obvious disadvantage to lying is that there will be social disapproval when the lie is discovered. Although the vast majority of people lie—at some times and with some issues—the vast majority dislike lying and condemn it. Consequently, when our lie is discovered, we incur social disapproval. It may range from mild disapproval to total ostracism from a group or organization. It is interesting to note in this connection that Mark Comadena found that intimates are better lie detectors than are casual friends; further, women seem to be somewhat better at detecting lies than men.

The general upshot of all this is that the liar's communication effectiveness will be drastically impaired. When an individual is known to have lied or to be a liar, that person is seldom believed, even when telling the truth—because, after all, even liars tell the truth most of the time. We not only disbelieve the information this individual might wish to communicate, we also give no persuasive force to his or her arguments, frequently discounting them as lies. Even more important, it seems, is that one's relational messages and relational interactions generally become less meaningful. The most important messages an individual can communicate—the "I love you," "I enjoy being with you" messages—are discounted, since the listener can no longer ascertain whether or not they are true.

Honesty

Honesty, of course, never gives license to hurt another person, to destroy their illusions, or to make fun of their inadequacies and problems. Honesty can serve effectively only as a means for relating more closely, for exchanging feelings, for sharing, for responding to the deeper levels of communication. When viewed in this way, there is little chance that honesty will be confused with forcing others to see what they may not wish to see or what they may not be ready to see.

SELF-TALK AND OTHER-TALK

We are an egocentric society. Although we have long since learned that the sun does not revolve around the earth, we apparently have yet to learn that the world does not revolve around us. As children we believed it did, and for the most part, at least as far as our own world was concerned, it did revolve around us. Our every wish was responded to before we even learned to express it. Fortunately, most of us grew up. Yet there are many people who did not and who still act as if the world and its people exist only for their pleasure. They talk constantly about themselves—their jobs, accomplishments, families, love lives, problems, successes, and sometimes even failures. Rarely do they ask how we are, what we think (except perhaps about them), or what our plans are.

There are other people who go to the opposite extreme and never talk about themselves. These are the underdisclosers we discussed in Unit 3. These are the people who want to learn everything about you but are not willing to share themselves. They do not want to reveal anything about themselves that might make them vulnerable. As a result, we go away from the interaction with the feeling that they did not like us very much or did not trust us. Otherwise, we feel, they would have revealed something of themselves.

Balance

All our interactions need to be characterized by the *principle of balance*—some self-talk, some other-talk, and never all of one or the other. Communication is a two-way process; each person needs to function as source and as receiver; each person should have a chance to function as subject. Balanced communication interactions are more satisfying and result in a great deal more interesting interactions. We all get bored with too much about the other person—and, let's face it, others get bored with too much about us. The principle of balance seems a sorely needed guide.

OFFENSIVE LANGUAGE: RACISM, SEXISM, ETC.

No group is immune to being offended in language. Jokes and put-downs abound for just about every national, racial, and religious group. Each of the sexes and all of the sexual orientations are likewise treated to "humorous" offense. We are all victims in one way or another.

Perhaps the most obvious instances are verbal attacks on a person's race, with attacks on one's nationality a close second. We all know the disparaging terms for the various races, nationalities, and affectional orientations and there is no need to repeat them here. What we need to be reminded of is that they serve very little purpose other than offending certain people. Similarly, using the popular stereotypes for women and at the same time not according women equality in language does nothing but offend. To imply in our verbalizations that all doctors are men—with such statements as "woman doctor" or the use of the masculine pronoun before the sex of the doctor has even been identified— or that all secretaries are women merely perpetuates the stereotypes and makes it more and more difficult for both men and women to interact as equals.

Fairness

As an antidote, try the simple *principle of fairness*. Treat each person as you would want to be treated—an old rule but a badly neglected one. A good guide to follow might be to imagine that the person whose group you might disparage is in a position to offer you just the job you have been looking for at just the right salary. With that in mind, it might be a little more difficult to use language that others might find offensive or degrading.

GOSSIP

There can be no doubt that we spend a great deal of time in gossiping. According to the *Random House Dictionary, gossip* is defined as "idle talk or rumor, esp. about the personal or private affairs of others." A *gossiper*, then, is a person who engages in this idle talk; a *gossipmonger* is one who is addicted to this type of interpersonal interchange.

Gossip is an inevitable part of our daily interactions and to advise anyone to refrain from gossiping would be absurd. No one would listen and further, if people did listen, it would eliminate one of the most frequently employed and enjoyed forms of communication. Ogden Nash put it this way: "There are two kinds of people who blow through life like a breeze/And one kind is gossipers, and the other kind is gossipees." Clearly, we are not going to stop talking about the personal and private affairs of others. And, let us be equally clear, others are not going to stop talking about our personal and private affairs. I doubt that many of us would actually want them to; if they did, it would be testimony that our lives were too dull for gossip and that our friends and associates were indifferent to our feelings, thoughts, and behaviors.

Some Problems of Gossip

Nevertheless, gossip does create serious problems when not managed correctly or fairly, and it is to this point that our attention should be directed. When we tell someone our feelings about some third party, we normally expect that the conversation will be held in confidence; we do not expect this to be relayed to others and especially not to the individual talked about. If we wanted it relayed, we probably would have done that ourselves. When such a conversation is relayed without our knowledge or approval, we feel, and rightly so, that our confidence has been betrayed.

Consider the following fairly typical incident. You're talking with a friend and mention that a mutual friend, Pat, should really devote more attention to dressing properly. You might continue that you would like to invite Pat to your home to meet your parents, but Pat's constant use of vulgar language might embarrass your parents and make the evening difficult. Surely this is not a savage attack on Pat and may even have been said with a certain degree of kindness. But what happens when the "friend" relays to Pat that you said Pat doesn't know how to dress and that you are ashamed because Pat has such a filthy mouth. The effect of such an exchange is to create hostility toward all—

Although the women in the foreground might be communicating just about anything, what are some of the more probable assumptions people would make about what is being communicated here? What nonverbal cues are used in formulating these assumptions? What impressions of these women would you form? Why?

toward you for making the original observations and toward the person who repeated them. The person talked about is probably going to act in a less friendly manner and may respond in kind by repeating your personal conversations to others. The next result is that the entire situation snowballs, and what may well have been an innocent remark becomes the cause of a friendship breakdown.

Quite often the person who repeats such remarks is, perhaps subconsciously, seeking to create friction between the two individuals. And this motivation is usually recognized, sooner or later, by all parties involved. To claim— as some do—that they didn't realize you didn't want anything repeated is absurd. It is usually obvious from the context what should and what should not be held in confidence. We have little trouble in deciding when something is said in confidence, and it does not seem unreasonable to expect others to be equally discerning.

Ethical Implications

Gossip also has an ethical dimension. In some instances gossip is immoral. Sissela Bok, in *Secrets,* identifies three kinds of gossip that she considers unethical. First, it is unethical to reveal information that you have promised to keep secret. When we promise to keep something confidential, we should do so. When that is impossible (Bok offers the example of the teenager who confides a suicide plan), the information should be revealed only to those required to know it and not to the world at large.

Second, gossip is unethical when we know it to be false and nevertheless pass it on. When we attempt to deceive our listeners by spreading gossip we know to be false, our communications are unethical.

Third, gossip is unethical when it is invasive, when it invades the privacy that everyone has a right to. More specifically, invasive gossip is unethical when it concerns matters that are properly considered private and when the gossip can hurt the individual involved.

Bok does not argue that these conditions are easy to identify in any given instance of gossip. But they do provide us with excellent starting points for asking ourselves, "Is this talk about another person ethical?"

Confidentiality

I think the *principle of confidentiality* presents a good guideline for dealing with gossip: Keep confidential all private conversations about third parties. Messages that begin with "He said . . ." or "She thinks that you . . ." should be automatically suspect as potential violators of the principle of confidentiality. Remember too the *principle of irreversibility*—we cannot take messages back; once we say something, we cannot uncommunicate it.

DISCONFIRMATION

The psychologist William James once observed that "No more fiendish punishment could be devised, even were such a thing physically possible, than that one should be turned loose in society and remain absolutely unnoticed by all the members thereof." In this often-quoted observation James identifies the essence of disconfirmation.

Disconfirmation is a communication pattern in which we ignore someone's presence as well as that person's communications. We say, in effect, that this person and what this person has to say are not worth our attention or our effort—that this person and this person's contributions are so unimportant or insignificant that there is no reason to concern ourselves with them.

Note that disconfirmation is not the same as rejection. When we reject someone, we disagree with that person; we indicate our unwillingness to accept something the other person says or does. In disconfirming someone, however, we deny that person's significance; we claim that what this person says or does simply does not count.

Confirmation

Confirmation is the opposite communication pattern. In confirmation we not only acknowledge the presence of the other person but we also indicate our acceptance of this person, of this person's definition of self, and of our relationship as defined or viewed by this other person.

Differences Between Disconfirmation and Confirmation

Disconfirmation and confirmation may be communicated in a wide variety of ways. Here are just a few. As you review this list, try to imagine a specific illustration for each of the ways of communicating disconfirmation and confirmation.

Confirmation	Disconfirmation
1. Acknowledge the presence of the other verbally or nonverbally.	1. Ignore the presence of the other.
2. Acknowledge the contributions of the other by either supporting or taking issue with what the other says.	2. Ignore what the other says; express indifference.
3. Make nonverbal contact by maintaining direct eye contact, touching, hugging, kissing, and otherwise demonstrating acknowledgment of the other.	3. Make no nonverbal contact.
4. Engage in dialogue—communication in which both persons are speakers and listeners, both are involved, and both are concerned with and have respect for each other.	4. Engage in monologue—communication in which one person speaks and one person listens, there is no real interaction, and there is no real concern or respect for each other.

5. Demonstrate understanding.

5. Jump to interpretation or evaluation rather than working at understanding what the other means.

6. Reflect back the other's feelings.

6. Express one's own feelings, ignore feelings of the other, or give abstract intellectualized responses.

7. Ask questions of the other concerning both thoughts and feelings.

7. Make statements about oneself; ignore any lack of clarity in the other's remarks.

8. Positively stroke the other.

8. Praise oneself or third parties; appear indifferent to the other.

9. Acknowledge the other's requests; answer the other's questions, return phone calls, and answer letters.

9. Ignore the other's requests; fail to answer questions, return phone calls, and answer letters.

10. Encourage the other to express thoughts and feelings.

10. Interrupt or otherwise make it difficult for the other to express himself or herself.

11. Give responses that are relevant to what the other says.

11. Respond with irrelevant comments that indicate a failure to listen.

12. Respond directly and exclusively to what the other says.

12. Respond tangentially by acknowledging the other's comment but then shifting the focus of the message in another direction.

SUMMARY

1. *In-group talk* occurs when members belonging to a particular group talk about their group concerns and/or use their group's language in the presence of those who are not members of the group and who are therefore excluded from the interaction.

2. *Downward and upward talk* refers to the tendency to talk down and to talk up to others, rather than talking as equals.

3. *Criticism and complimenting* create communication barriers when they are excessive or when they are inappropriate to the person or the context.

4. *Lying*—communicating messages designed to mislead or deceive another person—creates communication problems by lessening the credibility of the individual (generally), by creating psychological imbalance for the liar, and by engendering social disapproval of the liar.

5. *Self-talk and other-talk,* when extreme, create communication problems by distorting the normal give-and-take (the reciprocal self-disclosing that nor-

mally occurs between two people) and substituting excessive talk of oneself, with nothing about the other, or excessive talk of the other, with nothing about oneself.

6. *Offensive language* refers to language that denigrates a particular group of people.

7. *Gossip,* although inevitable, creates problems when it betrays a confidence, when it is false and known to be false, or when it is used to hurt another person.

8. *Disconfirmation* refers to the process whereby we ignore the presence and the communications of other; *confirmation* refers to the process whereby we accept, support, and acknowledge the importance of the other person.

SOURCES

There are a number of excellent sources for eliminating problems in communication. Edmond G. Addeo and Robert E. Burger's *Egospeak: Why No One Listens to You* (New York: Bantam, 1973) covers a wide variety of verbal deterrents. J. Dan Rothwell's *Telling It Like It Isn't* (Englewood Cliffs, N.J.: Spectrum, 1982) likewise covers a variety of barriers and their corrections. Theodore Isaac Rubin's *One to One: Understanding Personal Relationships* (New York: Viking, 1983) discusses the relationship process and offers considerable insight into language and effective communication. On gobbledygook, see, for example, Rothwell's *Telling It Like It Isn't* and William Lambdin's *Doublespeak Dictionary* (Los Angeles, Calif.: Pinnacle Books, 1981). On lying, see Sissela Bok, *Lying: Moral Choice in Public and Private Life* (New York: Pantheon, 1978). The analysis of rewards for lying is taken from Carl Camden, Michael T. Motley, and Ann Wilson, "White Lies in Interpersonal Communication: A Taxonomy and (Preliminary) Investigation of Social Motivations," paper delivered at the International Communication Association convention (Dallas, Texas, 1983). On lie detection, see Mark Comadena, "Accuracy in Detecting Deception: Intimate and Friendship Relationships," in Michael Burgoon, ed., *Communication Yearbook 6* (Beverly Hills: Sage, 1982), pp. 446–472; and the summaries in Mark Knapp, *Nonverbal Communication in Human Interaction,* 2d ed. (New York: Holt, Rinehart and Winston, 1978) and Paul Ekman, *Telling Lies* (New York: W. W. Norton, 1985). The power games discussed here were taken from Claude Steiner, *The Other Side of Power* (New York: Grove, 1981). In *Secrets* (New York: Vintage Books, 1983), Sissela Bok continues her insightful analysis of ethics and focuses on such issues as gossip, whistleblowing, confidentiality, concealment, and revelation. On disconfirmation, see Paul Watzlawick, Janet Beavin, and Don D. Jackson, *Pragmatics of Human Communication* (New York: Norton, 1967), and Kathleen Galvin and Bernard J. Brommel, *Family Communication: Cohesion and Change,* 2d ed. (Glenview, Ill.: Scott, Foresman, 1986).

UNIT 9
SOCIAL ASPECTS OF LANGUAGE AND VERBAL INTERACTION

LEARNING GOALS

After completing this unit, you should be able to

1. define *sublanguage* and *subculture*
2. identify at least three functions served by sublanguages
3. define *argot, cant, jargon,* and *slang*
4. define *taboo* and *euphemism*
5. explain at least four variables that influence the use of taboo expressions

Language is a social institution; it exists because human beings interact in social groups, in societies. As a social institution, language both reflects and influences the society of which it is a part. In this unit, the social aspects of language and verbal interaction are considered. First, we examine language as a social institution and explain the notion of sublanguages, or languages used by smaller groups within the larger social or cultural group. Second, we examine some of the functions sublanguages serve. Third, we examine the variety of sublanguages—for example, argot, cant, jargon, and slang. Fourth, we look at language taboos and euphemisms, and how these reflect the society of which they are a part.

LANGUAGE AS A SOCIAL INSTITUTION

Language is a social institution designed, modified, and extended (some purists might even say distorted) to meet the ever-changing needs of the culture or subculture. As such, language differs greatly from one culture to another and, equally important though perhaps less obvious, from one subculture to another.

Subcultures are cultures within a larger culture and may be formed on the basis of religion, geographical area, occupation, affectional orientation, race, nationality, living conditions, interests, needs, and so on. Roman Catholics, Protestants, and Jews; New Yorkers, Californians, and mountain folk; teachers, plumbers, and musicians; gays and lesbians; blacks, Chinese, and American Indians; Germans, Italians, and Mexicans; prisoners, suburbanites, and ghetto dwellers; bibliophiles, drug addicts, and bird watchers; diabetics, the blind, and exconvicts may all be viewed as subcultures, depending, of course, on the context on which we focus. In New York, for example, New Yorkers would obviously not constitute a subculture, but throughout the rest of the world they would. In the United States as a whole, Protestants would not constitute a subculture (though Roman Catholics and Jews would). In New York City, on the other hand, Protestants would constitute a subculture. Blacks and Chinese would be subcultures only outside Africa and China.

As these examples illustrate, the majority generally constitutes the culture, and the various minorities generally constitute the subcultures. Yet this is not always the case. Women, although the majority in our culture, may be viewed as a subculture primarily because society as a whole is male-oriented. Whether a group should be regarded as a subculture or a culture, then, depends on the context being considered and the orientation of the society of which these groups are a part.

Each individual belongs to several subcultures. The importance of a given subcultural affiliation will vary greatly from one individual to another, from one context to another, from one time or circumstance to another. For example, to some people in some contexts an individual's religious affiliation may be inconsequential and his or her membership in this subculture hardly thought of. When, on the other hand, the individual wishes to marry into a particular family, this once inconsequential membership may take on great significance.

Because of the common interests, needs, or conditions of individuals constituting a subculture, sublanguages come into being. Like language in general, sublanguages exist to enable members of the group to communicate with one another. In addition, however, sublanguages serve a variety of other functions.

FUNCTIONS OF SUBLANGUAGES

Sublanguages exist and thrive because they serve useful functions. If they did not serve such functions, they would die of disuse.

Subcultural Communication

Sublanguages facilitate subcultural communication by providing a variety of terms and distinctions that are convenient to the subculture's members.

Variety of Terms

One of the most obvious facts about language and its relation to culture is that concepts important to a given culture are given a large number of terms. For example, in our culture money is extremely important; consequently, we have numerous terms for it: *finances, funds, capital, assets, pocket money, spending money, pin money, change, bread, loot, swag.* Transportation and communication are other concepts for which numerous terms exist in our language. Without knowing anything about a given culture, we could probably make some pretty good guesses as to the relative importance of concepts in that culture simply by examining one of its dictionaries or thesauruses. With sublanguages, the same principle holds.

Concepts that are of special importance to a particular subculture are given a large number of terms. Thus, one function of sublanguages is to provide the subculture with convenient synonyms for those concepts that are of great importance and hence are spoken about frequently. To prisoners, for example, a prison guard—clearly a significant concept and one spoken about a great deal—may be denoted by *screw, roach, hack, slave driver, shield,* and various other terms. Heroin, in the drug subculture, may be called *H, Harry, smack, Carga, joy powder, skag, stuff,* or just plain *shit.*

Convenient Distinctions

Sublanguages provide convenient distinctions that are important to the subculture but generally not to the culture at large—and thus distinctions that the general language does not make. For example, the general culture has no need for making distinctions among various drugs—all may be conveniently labeled *drugs.* But to members of the drug subculture it is essential to make distinctions. The general culture, for example, does not distinguish between "getting stoned" and "on a high." Yet to the members of the drug subculture, these are two different states that need to be distinguished.

This function is also clearly seen in the technical jargon of the academic world. Whereas to most people it is sufficient to distinguish between statements and questions, for example, the linguist and psycholinguist find these distinctions too gross. Consequently, they distinguish between active and passive questions, as well as tag and nontag, open and yes/no, and numerous other types. Whereas the term *learning* may be sufficient for the general population, the psychologist needs to distinguish between classical and instrumental learning, incidental and instructed learning, response and stimulus learning, and so on. In the field of communication, instead of using the general term *message,* we distinguish between digital and analogic messages, verbal and nonverbal messages, content and relational messages, content and metamessages, and so on. These distinctions are all helpful in conceptualizing and communicating the data and theories of a discipline.

Subcultural Identification

Sublanguages also serve as means of identification. By using a particular sublanguage, speakers identify themselves to hearers as members of that subculture—assuming, of course, that hearers know the language being used. Individuals belonging to various nationality-based subcultures will frequently drop a foreign word or phrase in the conversation to identify themselves to their hearers. Similarly, gays, lesbians, and exconvicts will at times identify themselves by using their sublanguage. When the subcultural membership is one that is normally hidden, as in the case of exconvicts, the clues to self-identification are subtle. Generally, they are given only after the individuals themselves receive some kind of positive feedback that leads them to suspect the hearer also belongs to the subculture in question or that the hearer is at least sympathetic. Similarly, sublanguages also function to express one's identification with that subculture. For example, blacks may address each other as *brother* and *sister* when meeting for the first time. The use of these terms by blacks, as well as the frequent use of foreign expressions by members of various national groups, communicates to others that the speaker feels a strong identification with the group.

Sublanguages serve to provide the group with a kind of identity and a sense of fraternity. Because exconvicts all over the country know the same sublanguage, they are, in a sense, bound together. Obviously, the greater the subculture's need to band together, the greater the importance of a specialized language.

Communication Privacy

Sublanguages also enable members of a subculture to communicate privately in the presence of nonmembers. A common example of this, which many of us may have heard but been unaware of, occurs in stores. Salespersons will describe arriving customers as "J.L." (just looking), "skank" (cheap individual),

"T.O" (turn over to an experienced salesperson), or "palooka" (one who is on a buying binge). In certain situations, of course, using a particular sublanguage would mark the speaker as a member of an undesirable subculture, and so he or she would refrain from using the sublanguage. This is often the case among criminals when in a noncriminal environment. At other times, however, the use of a sublanguage does not lead to an individual's identification as a subculture member, and the sublanguage serves the useful purpose of excluding nonmembers from the class of decoders.

The Impressing and Confusing of Outsiders

One of the less noble functions of sublanguages—capitalized on by numerous professionals—is to impress and at times confuse outsiders. The two functions, I think, often go hand in hand; many people are impressed in direct proportion to their confusion. Insurance policies and legal documents are perhaps the best examples. I suspect that in many instances this technical language is used to impress and confuse people. Then, when there is doubt about something, the claims adjuster and the lawyer begin with an advantage—they understand the language, whereas you and I do not. Similarly, in evaluating and eventually in signing such documents, we are unable even to ask the right

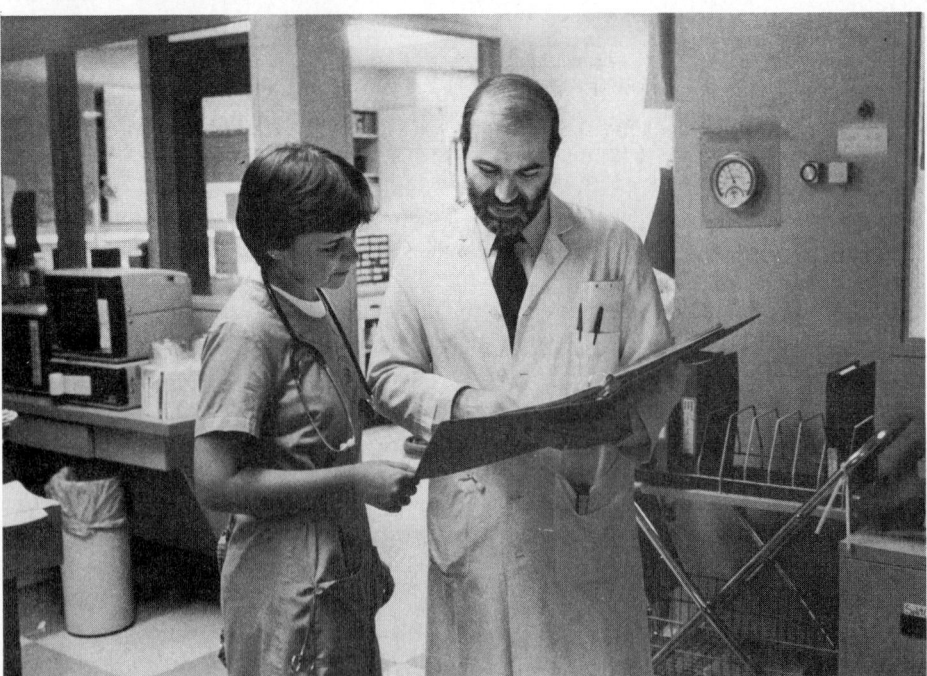

Most subcultures have developed their own sublanguage to serve a variety of functions. What subcultures do you belong to? Do these subcultures have sublanguages? How are they used in communication? Can you identify recent instances in which these sublanguages facilitated communication? Hindered communication?

questions, because there is so much we do not understand. Fortunately, as *Time* magazine has reported, "the forces of hereinafter, *res ipsa loquitur* and party of the first part are now clearly on the defensive." The Federal Trade Commission and the Department of Health, Education, and Welfare have enlisted the aid of communication experts to rewrite much of their incomprehensible prose.

KINDS OF SUBLANGUAGES

Sublanguage has been used here as a general term to denote a language that varies from the general language and that is used by a particular group of subculture existing within the broader, more general culture. More correctly, however, there are different kinds of sublanguages.

Argot *Argot* is the specialized vocabulary of some disreputable or underworld subculture. It is the sublanguage of pickpockets, murderers, dope peddlers, and prostitutes. Expressions such as *college* (meaning prison), *stretch* (jail sentence), *to mouse* (to escape from prison), and *lifeboat* (a pardon) are examples of argot. In its true form argot is not understood by outsiders. Today, with television and movies so much a part of our lives, it is difficult for any group, however specialized and "underground," to hide its specialized language. Consequently, many reputable people know some of these "disreputable" expressions.

Cant *Cant* designates the specialized vocabulary of any "nonprofessional" (usually noncriminal) group and includes, for example, the specialized sublanguage of the taxi driver, the truck driver, the CB operator, and the soldier. As is the case with argot, these vocabularies would ideally not be understood by nonmembers were it not for television and film. Expressions such as *dog* (meaning a motor vehicle inspector), *kidney buster* (hard-riding truck), and *sweatshop* (bulletproof cab with poor ventilation) are examples of cant.

Jargon *Jargon* is the technical language of a professional class—for example, college professors, writers, medical doctors, and lawyers. Terms such as *perceptual accentuation, inflationary spiral,* and *behavioral objectives* are examples of professional academic jargon, as are the writer's technical terms for proofreading and editing, the doctor's terms for diseases and medications, and the lawyer's terms for legal documents and criminal offenses.

Slang *Slang* is the most general of the terms and designates those words in our vocabulary that are derived from cant and argot particularly, and that are understood by most people but not often used in "polite society" or in formal written communications. "Slang," Carl Sandburg once observed, "is a language that rolls up its sleeves, spits on its hands and goes to work." Terms such as *skirt* (meaning woman), *skiddoo* (leave fast), *goo-goo eyes, hush money, booze, brass* (impudence), and *to knock off* (to quit working) are examples of slang. Usually slang is fairly short-lived; terms such as *skirt, skiddoo,* and *goo-goo eyes* are rarely used today and, when used, label the speaker as being out of touch with reality. There are, of course, exceptions to this short life span; some slang terms have been around for a long time and remain classified as slang. For example, according to the famous lexicographer H. L. Mencken, *booze* dates back to the fourth century, *brass* to 1594, and *knocking off* to 1662.

With the passage of time and increased usage, slang terms enter the general language as socially acceptable expressions. When this happens, new terms are needed and are coined by the subcultures. The old terms are then dropped from the sublanguage, since they now serve none of the functions for which they were originally developed. This type of transition is just one of the ways in which new words enter the language and in which sublanguages are kept distinct from the general language.

LANGUAGE TABOO AND EUPHEMISM

One of the best ways of examining language in general, and the social dimension of language in particular, is to focus on taboo and euphemism. *Language taboo* refers to verbal behavior forbidden by the society for reasons that are not always clear; generally, it is for some vague and seemingly irrational reason. When we think of taboo we often think of primitive societies with elaborate precautions against and punishments for uttering particular words and phrases. But language taboo is actually universal; all languages and all societies have language taboos built into their social structure.

Taboo Origins

Stephen Ullmann, in his *Semantics*, notes that there are three general origins of language taboo. The first are taboos rooted in fear. We may fear being punished by God, for example, and so we avoid naming the dead or avoid using the name of God or of the Devil. Similarly, fear may motivate our not taking the name of God in vain. The second is the taboo of delicacy. This taboo centers on an avoidance of unpleasant topics; it leads us to avoid talking of topics relating to death, illness, and disease. When we refer to someone who has a mental deficiency, for example, we avoid such expressions as *idiot* or *imbecile*, using instead *mentally retarded* or *intellectually impaired*. The third is the taboo of propriety. This leads us to avoid certain sexual references, swear words, and the names of various parts and functions of the body. And although it is true that we no longer say *limbs* or *benders* instead of *legs*, there are still many parts of the body for which we avoid speaking the terms we think, and instead employ some other term that is more socially acceptable.

Taboo Variations

Although taboo is a language universal, its form varies from one language to another and from one culture or subculture to another. Thus, the terms under taboo in our culture may not be under a taboo in other cultures. Even within any culture or subculture, what is and what is not taboo will vary on the basis of several factors. Taboo varies greatly with age, for example. Young people are more restricted in their language usage than are adults. Adults are allowed to talk about topics that are forbidden to children and in language that children would be punished for using. Taboo also varies on the basis of sex. Our society and, in fact, most societies allow men greater freedom. That these different taboos still operate is seen when the speech of men and women is analyzed; male speech contains a far greater number of taboo expressions than does female speech. Men also begin to use taboo expressions at an earlier age than women.

Taboo varies with the educational and intellectual level of the individual. Uneducated persons generally demonstrate greater freedom of expression—in part because they do not have alternative expressions. The educated do have these alternatives and, at least when in "polite society," will use these rather than the taboo expressions. The communication context also influences the frequency and strength of taboo expressions. Generally, as the formality of a situation increases, so does the linguistic restriction. There is, for example, greater restriction in a classroom than in the cafeteria.

Perhaps the most important variable influencing taboo is the speaker-listener relationship. If the speaker and listener are equals, there is usually less restriction on their speech than if they are of widely differing statuses. You know from your own experience that you will monitor your speech when you are talking to persons who are higher than you in status, as you also will with people you may be trying to impress. If you are talking with equals, you will be less likely to monitor and censor your expressions.

Taboo Effects

Some people use taboo expressions because this is their natural mode of communication and they do not monitor or censor any of it before speaking—"They calls it as they sees it." To such people, these expressions are natural rather than taboo. Others use taboo expressions because they are not aware of the inappropriateness of these expressions; they are not sensitive to the communication context or to the differences in speaker-listener status. Often, however, the listener is aware so that the focus shifts from the content of the communication to the taboo expression, and—for a while at least—real and meaningful communication breaks down. This is seen frequently when people talk during dinner about throwing up or about some particularly gory accident, or when two people who do not know each other well use expressions that prove offensive, crude, or gross to the other. Some people use taboo expressions for their shock value. They want to shock other people or to present particular images of themselves that taboo expressions help achieve.

When the language taboo is broken, various forms of punishment may be meted out. For the most part, we no longer have legal punishments, although taboo expressions uttered in court, for example, will often result in a fine, and the use of taboo expressions in print or on the air may in some cases bring similar penalties. But for the most part such penalties have been removed. Nevertheless, some severe punishments are still administered. Persons who make frequent use of taboo expressions will often find themselves laughed with over coffee but then not invited to more sophisticated functions; they may find themselves popular in the mail room, while corporate advancement eludes them.

Taboo Alternatives: Euphemisms

In all languages, alternative expressions are used instead of taboo expressions, and these are called *euphemisms*. Euphemisms are the nice words designed to replace taboo expressions and to sweeten topics that may be unpleasant or less than desirable—and so instead of *undertaker* we say *mortician*, and instead of *toilet* we say *rest room* (though few really rest there), *bathroom* (though we are not going to bathe), or *little boy's* or *little girl's room* (though we are grown men and women). H. L. Mencken, in his *American Language*, identifies hundreds of such euphemistic substitutions: *collection correspondent* for *bill collector*; *section manager* for *floor walker*; *superintendent* for *janitor*; and *sanitary officer* for *garbage man* (or *woman*). A friend of mine who works for the Department of Sanitation refers to himself as a "garbalogist."

William Safire, in his "On Language" column in *The New York Times*, identifies three main functions euphemisms serve. One function is to substitute a pretty word for an ugly thing; thus a financial loss is referred to as a *net profits revenue deficiency* or drug addiction is called a *chemical problem*. A second function is to rename a familiar activity with a pretentious name—for example, by calling a doorman an *access controller*. The third function is to use words as coverups for parts of the body we do not wish to talk about. Here we have, for example, the television commercial that refers to women with large breasts as *full-figured*.

SUMMARY

1. Language is a social institution designed, modified, and extended to meet the ever-changing needs of the culture or subculture.

2. Subcultures are cultures within a larger culture and may be formed on the basis of religion, occupation, affectional orientation, nationality, and so on. Each subculture develops its own sublanguage.

3. Sublanguages serve as a means for facilitating subcultural communication, identifying subcultural members, ensuring communication privacy, and impressing and confusing outsiders.

4. The most common forms of sublanguages are (1) *argot*, the specialized vocabulary of some disreptuable or underworld subculture; (2) *cant*, the specialized vocabulary of any nonprofessional, usually noncriminal, class; (3) *jargon*, the technical language of a professional class; and (4) *slang*, the language containing the terms derived from cant and argot that are understood by most people but are generally considered not proper in polite society.

5. *Language taboo* refers to verbal behavior forbidden by the society.

6. *Euphemism* refers to expressions used in place of taboo expressions; euphemisms are often overly polite.

SOURCES

On sublanguages, see H. L. Mencken, *The American Language* (New York: Knopf, 1971). Mencken's chapter entitled "American Slang" is a classic work and a very interesting one. I relied heavily on Mencken for the discussion of sublanguages. Much interesting research relevant to sublanguages is reported in the various works in sociolinguistics; for example, Joshua A. Fishman, *The Sociology of Language* (Rowley, Mass.: Newbury House, 1972), and Dell Hymes, *Foundations in Sociolinguistics: An Ethnographic Approach* (Philadelphia: University of Pennsylvania Press, 1974).

The broad area of sex differences in communication is surveyed in Barbara Eakins and R. Gene Eakins, *Sex Differences in Communication* (Boston: Houghton Mifflin, 1978), and in Judy Cornelia Pearson, *Gender and Communication* (Dubuque, Iowa: Wm. C. Brown, 1985). A sublanguage of a somewhat different type, the language of intimacy used by couples, is explored by Robert Hooper, Mark L. Knapp, and Lorel Scott, "Couples' Personal Idioms: Exploring Intimate Talk," *Journal of Communication* 31 (winter 1981): 23–33. J. Dan Rothwell, *Telling It Like It Isn't* (Englewood Cliffs, N.J.: Prentice-Hall, 1982), covers the social aspects of language and provides useful guidelines to its more effective use.

SKILL DEVELOPMENT SUMMARY

1. Because of **rapid fading,** spoken messages need to be instantly intelligible; take special care to make such messages clear and unambiguous.

2. **Meanings are in people;** look for meaning, therefore, not only in words but in people; ask questions whenever intended meaning is in doubt.

3. Words make sense only when they are in some way anchored to the real world. **Connect your words and meanings to the real world.**

4. Recognize that the same word may be given **different meanings** by different people; when in doubt, ask.

5. Recognize that **words communicate only part of the meaning** in a person's head. Words are never complete descriptions of thoughts or feelings.

6. Remember that words have both **denotations and connotations** and that it is the connotative meanings and differences among people that will often cause communication problems. Seek to understand not only the objective, denotative meanings but also the subjective, connotative meanings.

7. Recognize that **snarl and purr words** describe the speaker's feelings and not objective reality; they are connotative in meaning, not denotative.

8. Recognize that **phatic communion** serves the social purpose of opening the channels of communication; it indicates a desire or willingness to pursue an interpersonal interaction. Do not, therefore, look for objective meaning or deep significance in phatic messages.

9. Avoid **polarization**—the tendency to divide up the world into two extremes and to describe it with polar opposites such as *good* and *bad*, *rich* and *poor*. Most of the world and its people lie between these extremes. Use "middle" terms and qualifiers in describing the world and especially people.

10. Avoid allowing the labels or the way something is talked about to prevent you from clearly seeing people, objects, and events; avoid an **intensional orientation.** Instead, respond extensionally; look first at the reality and only then at the words.

11. Distinguish **facts from inferences;** respond to inferences with tentativeness.

12. Distinguish **logical from pragmatic implications.** Remember that these two types of inferences are often confused in our memories. Recognize that pragmatic inferences may be incorrect and treat these with tentativeness.

13. Recognize the forms of **bypassing:** (1) assuming that different words must have different meanings, and therefore assuming disagreement when

there is actually underlying agreement; and (2) assuming that the same word must have the same meaning when used by different people, and therefore assuming agreement when there is actually underlying disagreement. Look for meaning in people and practice the skills of active listening as correctives for bypassing.

14. Remember that we can **never say all** about anything; there is always more that could be said. End your statements with an explicit or an implicit *etc.*

15. Be especially careful in conflict situations to avoid **negative allness statements** (particularly those using *always* and *never*).

16. Avoid **static evaluation.** Recognize that the world is in a constant state of process, always changing. Language, however, is relatively static and often obscures or ignores changes. Therefore, date your statements.

17. Avoid **indiscrimination.** Recognize that the same word may be used to refer to different people, objects, and events. Index your terms and statements; remember, teacher$_{1986}$ is not teacher $_{1988}$, though both are referred to as *teacher.*

18. Avoid **in-group talk** in the presence of nonmembers and instead seek to include all persons in the interaction (both verbally and nonverbally).

19. Avoid **talking down** or **talking up** to others; instead, recognize that all parties in a transaction are potentially equal.

20. Avoid excessive or undeserved **criticism or complimenting;** instead, use the principle of honest appraisal: say what you feel without needless excess.

21. Recognize the problems involved with **lying** and avoid it. Also avoid using the truth to hurt others; say what you feel is the truth with gentleness.

22. Balance **self-talk** with **other-talk.** Too much or too little talk of self or other will lead to boring and meaningless interactions. Balance encourages equal sharing and interpersonal satisfaction.

23. Remember that **offensive language** (sexism, racism, and vulgarity, for example) serves no purpose other than offending; avoid it if you do not wish to offend others.

24. Avoid **gossip** when it betrays a confidence, when it is known to be false, or when it may be used to hurt another person.

25. Avoid **disconfirmation.** To foster meaningful communication, use responses that confirm the other person—for example, responses that acknowledge the presence, importance, and contributions of the other.

26. Use appropriate **sublanguages** as means of subcultural identification or to ensure communication privacy when this does not hurt or offend others.

27. Avoid allowing **sublanguages** (especially professional jargon) to impress or confuse; learn the relevant sublanguage vocabulary and ask questions when meanings are not clear.

28. Avoid **sublanguages** when inappropriate—for example, in the presence of nonmembers.

29. Learn appropriate **sublanguages** so that you will be better able to understand others and to share their experiences. Assist significant others to learn your sublanguages in order to foster more meaningful interpersonal interaction.

30. Avoid **taboo language** (generally), because it may lead others to see you in an unfavorable light; substitute euphemistic expressions when appropriate.

31. Do not allow the **taboo language** of others to unduly influence your perceptions of them or to interfere with comprehension. Remember: The meaning is not in the taboo expression but in the user.

PART THREE
NONVERBAL COMMUNICATION

10. PRELIMINARIES TO NONVERBAL COMMUNICATION: FUNCTIONS AND UNIVERSALS

11. BODY COMMUNICATION

12. SPACE, TERRITORIALITY, AND TOUCH COMMUNICATION

13. PARALANGUAGE AND TIME

In this part we focus on the nonverbal message system and identify the ways and means of communicating without words. In the first unit, the functions nonverbal communication serves and the characteristics common to all nonverbal messages are identified. With these preliminaries as a foundation, the next three units focus on the different types of nonverbal messages—body, facial, and eye movements in Unit 11; space, territoriality, and touch communication in Unit 12; and paralanguage (variations in, for example, rate, volume, and pausing) and time communication in Unit 13.

UNIT 10
PRELIMINARIES TO NONVERBAL COMMUNICATION:
Functions and Universals

LEARNING GOALS

After completing this unit, you should be able to

1. define and give examples of the six major functions of nonverbal communication
2. explain why nonverbal behaviors in an interactional situation always communicate
3. explain the determined nature of nonverbal communication
4. explain the principle holding that nonverbal communication occurs in a context
5. identify the reasons for assuming that nonverbal communication is highly believable
6. explain the *rule-governed* nature of nonverbal communication
7. define *metacommunication*
8. provide at least three examples of the ways in which nonverbal behavior is frequently metacommunicational

Nonverbal communication—what is popularly called "body language"—is surely among the buzzwords of the decade. Everyone seems interested in nonverbal communication—the messages that are communicated by body posture, eye movements, facial expressions, gestures, use of space, vocal volume and rate, and even silences. We want to learn to "read a person like a book," as one popular book put it. We want to be able to see what is behind the "obvious" verbal messages.

At the same time that we want to learn how to read other people, we want to be able to control our own nonverbal communications so that we can communicate more effectively. The young executive wants to learn how to communicate status, power, and control. The salesperson wants to communicate sincerity and belief in the merchandise. The interviewee wants to communicate competence, efficiency, and experience.

Clearly these are important goals, and we can easily identify with them. Unfortunately, nonverbal communication is too complex for us to achieve such goals easily. Further, we simply do not know enough to enable us to read a person's inner thoughts from the way he or she smiles, frowns, or winks, nor do we know enough to set down clear-cut rules for the nonverbal communication of status or power. Yet, we have recently learned much about nonverbal communication and its relationship to a host of significant characteristics, such as status, persuasion, credibility, control, friendship, and authority. Much of this insight is detailed in this unit and the three that follow.

In approaching this material, then, our goals should be realistic. The purpose of these units are (1) to increase our understanding of the nature and function of nonverbal communication, (2) to increase our understanding of ourselves and of others as nonverbal communicators, and (3) to increase our ability to communicate more effectively (as senders and receivers of nonverbal messages).

In the present unit we consider two topics: the major functions that nonverbal messages serve and those characteristics of nonverbal communication that are found in all forms of nonverbal communication.

FUNCTIONS OF NONVERBAL COMMUNICATION

Nonverbal communication can serve any number of significant functions. Six major functions are generally identified by nonverbal researchers.

To Accent   Nonverbal communication is often used to highlight or emphasize some part of the verbal message. We might, for example, smile to emphasize a particular word or phrase, bang our fist on the desk to emphasize our commitment to a statement, or look longingly into someone's eyes when saying "I love you."

To Complement   Nonverbal communication may also be used to reinforce the general tone or attitude communicated by the verbal message. Thus, we might smile when telling a humorous story, or frown and shake our heads when telling of someone's deceit.

To Contradict   We may also deliberately contradict our verbal messages with nonverbal movements, for example, by crossing our fingers or winking to indicate that what we are saying is a lie.

To Regulate   Nonverbal movements are frequently used to control or to indicate one's desire to control the flow of verbal messages, for example, as when we purse our lips, lean forward, or make hand movements to indicate that we want to say something. We might also put up our hand or vocalize our pauses (for example, "um") to indicate that we have not finished and are not ready to relinquish the floor to the next speaker.

To Repeat   We can also repeat or restate the meaning of the verbal message. We can, for example, follow our verbal "Is that alright?" with an "Okay?" sign made with our fingers, or motion with our head or hand to repeat our verbal "Let's go."

To Substitute   Nonverbal communication may also take the place of verbal messages. We can, for example, say "okay" with our hands without any verbalization. We can shake our heads to indicate "yes" or nod our heads to indicate "no."

UNIVERSALS OF NONVERBAL COMMUNICATION

Six general characteristics of nonverbal messages are identified here: nonverbal messages are communicative, determined, contextual, believable, rule-governed, and often metacommunicational. These characteristics may be found in all forms of nonverbal communication (hence the term *universals*) and should provide a framework through which the specifics of nonverbal communication may be viewed.

Communicative

Nonverbal behavior in an interactional situation always communicates. This observation is true of all forms of communication, but it seems particularly true of nonverbal communication. It is impossible not to behave, and consequently, it is impossible not to communicate. Regardless of what one does or does not do, regardless of whether it is intentional or unintentional, one's nonverbal behavior communicates. Further, these messages may be received consciously or subconsciously; we need not be consciously aware that we are receiving messages for them to communicate meaning to us.

Sitting silently in a corner and reading a book communicates to the other people in the room just as surely as verbalization. Staring out the window during class communicates something to the teacher just as surely as saying "I'm bored." Notice, however, an important difference between the nonverbal and the verbal statements. The student looking out the window, when confronted by the teacher's "Why are you bored?" can always claim to be momentarily distracted by something outside. Saying "I'm bored," however, prevents the student from backing off and giving a more socially acceptable meaning to the statement.

Even the less obvious and less easily observed behaviors communicate. The smaller movements of the eyes, hands, facial muscles, and so on also communicate, just as do the gross movements of gesturing, sitting in a corner, or staring out a window. These small movements are extremely important in interpersonal relationships. We can often tell, for example, when two people genuinely like each other and when they are merely being polite. If we had to state how we know this, we would probably have considerable difficulty. These inferences, many of which are correct, are based primarily on these small nonverbal behaviors of the participants—movement of the muscles around the eyes, the degree of eye contact, the way in which the individuals face each other, and so on. All nonverbal behaviors, however small-scale or transitory, are significant—each has a meaning, each communicates.

Behavioral Synchrony

One means often used to infer whether two individuals like each other is that of behavioral synchrony, which refers to the similarity in two people's nonverbal behavior. This synchrony may reflect one person's imitating the nonverbal behaviors of the other, or it may be simply that the two people behave "spontaneously" in the same way. Although we normally think of behavioral synchrony in connection with general bodily movements and hand gestures, nonverbal synchrony is also evidenced in posture (for example, one's way of standing, sitting, or crossing of legs) and in voice (for example, one's rate of speaking, loudness, or pausing patterns). Generally, behavioral synchrony is an index of mutual liking.

Gifts as Nonverbal Messages

A number of theorists have recently pointed out how we communicate even in our gift-giving. Aside from the obvious messages—remembering one's birthday or celebrating Christmas, for example—gifts often communicate less noble motives. For example, giving candy or chocolates to a diabetic or to someone who wants to lose weight, and giving a bottle of liquor to someone with a drinking problem are examples of giving destructive gifts. Their selection seems to communicate an underlying hostility. One type of gift has been referred to as the "Pygmalion gift," which is designed to change the recipient into what the donor wants the person to become. The husband who buys his wife sexy lingerie may be asking his wife to be sexy; the wife who buys her husband a weight-lifting machine or tight-fitting underwear may well be asking the same thing. The parent who repeatedly gives a child books or science equipment may be asking the child to be a scholar. The problem with some of these gifts is that the underlying motives—the underlying displeasures—may never be talked about and hence never resolved. When parents give a child a nonplay gift—for example, clothes or books—they may be responding to their own inability to play, to enjoy spontaneous and seemingly impractical pleasures.

This is not to say that all gifts with hidden messages are motivated by the more negative aspects of our personalities, but only to suggest that even in gift-giving there are messages communicated that are often overlooked and that often function below the level of conscious awareness. Such messages may have considerable impact on the recipient, the donor, and the relationship itself.

Artifactual Communication

Although we have concentrated here on behaviors, do not assume that all nonverbal communication takes place behaviorally. Numerous nonverbal mes-

All nonverbal behavior communicates in some way. Gift giving is a particularly interesting example that many people seldom think of as a form of communication. What meanings have recent gifts that you received communicated to you? What meanings did you communicate in the gifts that you gave to others? Were these the meanings you intended to communicate?

sages are communicated by clothing and other artifacts, such as jewelry, makeup, buttons, the car you drive, the home you live in, the furniture you have and its arrangement, and, in fact, just about every object with which you associate yourself. Your association with an Alfa Romeo, Fendi leather, and Missoni sweaters says something quite different from what your association with a Volkswagen, vinyl, and Acrilan would say. A Rolex and a Timex may both give you the correct time, but each communicates differently about you. Whatever you wear (or do not wear) and whatever you are associated with (or are not associated with) will communicate something about you.

Determined

Earlier it was pointed out that verbal messages evidence the quality of determinism—that is, all verbalizations are motivated in some way. This same quality holds for nonverbal messages as well. The smile or frown, the forward or backward glance, the strong or mild hug, the long or short kiss—all are motivated in different ways. Much as the smile and the frown, for example, will communicate different meanings to receivers, they will also reflect different meanings in the source. Smiling seems obviously motivated by a different set of factors from those for frowning. From this rather weak claim, many will make the further unsupported assumption that we can therefore learn a person's motives (or subconscious desires, repressed fears, or strengths and weaknesses) by analyzing her or his nonverbal behaviors.

Our analysis of nonverbal behaviors and our assumption of determinism may assist us in suggesting possible hypotheses about what is going on inside the person, but that is about as far as we can legitimately go with our present level of knowledge. People are different; one person's smile may mean "I'm happy," whereas another person's smile may cover up seething hostility. Social and cultural factors also influence what a person means by various nonverbal behaviors. One culture may encourage direct eye contact in interpersonal interaction; another culture may discourage it. These are just a few of the many influencing factors that should caution us against postulating specific meanings for specific nonverbal behaviors.

Contextual

Like verbal communication, nonverbal communication exists in a context, and that context helps to determine the meanings of any nonverbal behaviors. The same nonverbal behavior may have a totally different meaning when it occurs in another context. A wink of the eye to a beautiful person on a bus means something completely different from a wink of the eye over a poker table. Similarly, the meaning of a given bit of nonverbal behavior will differ depending on the verbal behavior it accompanies or is close to in time. Pounding the fist on the table during a speech in support of a particular politician means something quite different from that same fist pounding in response to news about someone's death.

It is the differing cultural contexts that seem to provide the most provocative examples of the ways in which nonverbal behaviors may differ in meaning. Weston La Barre, a cultural anthropologist, provides a number of fascinating examples. Spitting in most Western cultures is a sign of disgust and displeasure. However, for the Masai of Africa it is a sign of affection, and for the American Indian it may be an act of kindness. For example, the medicine man spits on the sick in order to cure them. Sticking out the tongue to Westerners is an insult; to the Chinese of the Sung dynasty, it served as a symbol to mock terror or to make fun of the anger of another individual; and to the modern South Chinese it serves to express embarrassment over some social mistake.

Mediterranean peoples have a number of hand gestures that communicate quite specific meanings. For example, kissing the fingers means approval, stroking the finger on the chin signifies ignorance of and concern over a particular event or statement, and forward movement of the hand with the palm downward means "don't worry," "take it slow." Since there is no real relationship between the gestures and the meanings they signify, the meanings cannot be deduced simply by observing the behaviors.

When any given bit of nonverbal behavior is divorced from the context, it is impossible to tell what that behavior may mean. Of course, even if we know the context in detail, we still might not be able to decipher the meaning of the nonverbal behavior.

Believable

For some reasons, not all of which are clear to researchers in nonverbal communication, we are quick to believe nonverbal behaviors even when they contradict the verbal behavior. The researcher Albert Mehrabian argues that the total impact of a message is a function of the following formula: *Total Impact = 0.07 verbal + 0.38 vocal + 0.55 facial.* This formula leaves very little influence for verbal messages. Over one-third of the impact is vocal (that is, paralanguage, rate, pitch, rhythm), and over half of the message is communicated by the face. Caution should be exercised in interpreting this formula. It was developed by Mehrabian and his colleagues from their studies on connotative meaning, or the emotional impact, of a message and is not applicable to all messages, as is sometimes implied by writers in nonverbal communication. According to researcher Judee Burgoon, Ray Birdwhistell's estimate that 60 to 65 percent of the meaning is communicated nonverbally is more reasonable. Although we cannot offer a specific percentage, researchers and theorists seem to agree that the meaning communicated nonverbally is significant and probably constitutes considerably more than 50 percent.

In any case, we do seem to believe the nonverbal over the verbal. It may be that we feel verbal messages are easier to fake, so when there is a conflict, we distrust the verbal and accept the nonverbal. Or it may be that the nonverbal messages are perceived without conscious awareness. We learned them without being aware of any such learning and we perceive them without conscious awareness. Thus when a conflict arises, we somehow get this "feeling" from the nonverbal. Since we cannot isolate its source, we assume that it is somehow correct.

Believability and Deception

Usually our verbal and nonverbal behavior is consistent. Thus when we lie verbally, we also try to lie nonverbally; we strive always for consistency. Yet both our verbal and our nonverbal behaviors often betray us. Researchers in nonverbal behavior have identified a number of behaviors that often accompany deception. Generally, a liar moves less than a person who is telling the truth, talks more slowly (perhaps to gain time to create the fabrication or mentally check on the consistency of the story), and makes more speech errors. The best indicator of lying, according to Albert Mehrabian, is that the liar uses fewer words, particularly in answering questions. The liar gives monosyllabic answers and generally does not elaborate on them.

In an investigation of paralinguistic and verbal leakage, Michael Cody, Peter Marston, and Myrna Foster discovered a number of other clues to deception. When compared with truth-tellers, liars paused longer before answering questions and used longer pauses throughout their communications; they also used fewer words, supporting the findings of Mehrabian noted above. Further, liars used more ''generalizing terms'' (for example, ''you know what I mean,'' ''stuff like that,'' and ''you know'' at the ends of sentences). Liars also used fewer concrete and specific terms. For example, they spoke of nonspecific activities (''hung out,'' ''had fun'') more often than truth-tellers. They also referred less frequently than did truth-tellers to specific persons and specific places.

Allan Pease, in *Signals,* and Desmond Morris, in *Manwatching,* note a number of gestures that seem to indicate lying. Most prominent among these are the mouth guard (hand over mouth and thumb on cheek), nose touching, and eye rubbing.

Do not forget that nonverbal (and verbal) behaviors must be interpreted as part of the context in which they occur; the behaviors just cited should be used to suggest hypotheses concerning deceit rather than firm conclusions. After reviewing the extensive literature on deception, Paul Ekman, in *Telling Lies,* cautions: ''Evaluating behavioral clues to deceit is hazardous. . . . The lie catcher must always estimate the *likelihood* that a gesture or expression indicates lying or truthfulness; rarely is it absolutely certain.''

Rule-Governed

Nonverbal communication, like verbal communication, is rule-governed. We learned both the ways to communicate nonverbally *and* the rules of appropriateness from observing the behaviors of the adult community. For example, we learned how to express sympathy along with the rules that our culture has established for why, where, and when to express sympathy. We learned that touch is permissible under certain circumstances but not under others, and we learned which type of touching is permissible and which is not.

Some of these rules, stated rather informally, would hold that lower-status persons may not initiate touching behavior with higher-status persons, but higher-status persons may initiate touching with lower-status persons. We learned that women may touch each other in public; for example, they may hold hands, walk arm in arm, engage in prolonged hugging, and even dance together. Men may not do this, at least not without social criticism.

Like the nonverbal behaviors themselves, these rules are learned outside conscious awareness. We learn them largely from observing others. The rules are brought to conscious awareness only in formal discussions of nonverbal communication, such as this one, and when the rules are violated and the violations are called to our attention—either directly by some tactless snob or indirectly through the examples of others. While linguists are attempting to formulate the rules for verbal messages, nonverbal researchers are attempting to formulate the rules for nonverbal messages—rules that native communicators know and use every day but cannot necessarily verbalize. A major function of the following units on nonverbal communication is to bring to consciousness some of these implicit rules and the meanings and implications behind their appropriate and inappropriate usage.

Metacommunicational

All behavior, verbal as well as nonverbal, can be metacommunicational. Any given bit of behavior can make reference to communication. We can say, "This statement is false," or "Do you understand what I am trying to communicate to you?" Both statements refer to communication and are therefore called *metacommunicational statements*.

Nonverbal behavior is often metacommunicational. Nonverbal behaviors frequently function to make a statement about some verbal statement. An obvious example is crossing one's fingers behind one's back when telling a lie. When someone makes a statement and winks, the wink functions as a comment on the statement. Consider more subtle metacommunication: On the first day of class, the teacher walks in and says something to the effect that he or she is the instructor for the course and might then say how the course will be conducted, what will be required, what the goals of the course will be, and so on. But notice that much metacommunication is also going on. Notice that the clothes the teacher wears and how he or she wears them, the length and style of hair, the general physical appearance, the way he or she walks, the tone of voice, and so on all communicate about the communication—as well as, of course, communicating in and of themselves. These nonverbal messages function to comment on the verbal messages the instructor is trying to communicate. On the basis of these cues, students will come to various conclusions. They might conclude that this teacher is going to be easy even though a long reading list was given or that the class is going to be enjoyable or boring or too advanced or irrelevant. Nonverbal communication may also comment on other nonverbal communication. For example, the individual who, when meeting a stranger, both smiles and presents a totally lifeless hand for shaking is a good example of how one nonverbal behavior may refer to another nonverbal behavior. Here the lifeless handshake may belie the enthusiastic smile.

Most often, when nonverbal behavior is metacommunicational it functions to reinforce (rather than contradict) other verbal or nonverbal behavior. You may literally roll up your sleeves when talking about cleaning up this room, smile when greeting someone, or arrive early for a party you verbally express pleasure in attending. On the negative, though still consistent side, you may arrive late for a dental appointment (presumably with a less than pleasant facial expression) or grind your teeth while telling off your boss.

This discussion should not be taken to imply that nonverbal communication may not refer to people, events, things, relationships, and so on (that is, be *object* communication) or that verbal communication may not be metacommunication. We merely stress here the role of nonverbal communication as metacommunication because of its frequent appearance in this role.

SUMMARY

1. Six major functions of nonverbal communication are identified: to accent, to complement, to contradict, to regulate, to repeat, and to substitute.

2. Nonverbal behavior is communicative; in an interactional situation, such behavior always communicates.

3. Nonverbal behavior is determined; all nonverbal messages are motivated in some way.

4. Nonverbal behavior is contextual; nonverbal communication exists in a context that helps to determine the meanings of any nonverbal behaviors.

5. Nonverbal communication is highly believable; generally, when verbal and nonverbal messages contradict each other, we believe the nonverbal message.

6. Nonverbal communication is rule-governed; like verbal communication, it follows a culturally learned set of rules stating when and where nonverbal behaviors are appropriate or inappropriate.

7. Nonverbal communication is frequently metacommunicational; nonverbal messages frequently serve to comment on other messages, both verbal and nonverbal.

SOURCES

Six excellent general introductions to nonverbal communication may be recommended: Mark Knapp, *Nonverbal Communication in Human Interaction*, 2d ed. (New York: Holt, Rinehart and Winston, 1978); Dale G. Leathers, *Successful Nonverbal Communication: Principles and Applications* (New York: Macmillan, 1986); Judee K. Burgoon and Thomas Saine, *The Unspoken Dialogue* (Boston: Houghton Mifflin, 1978); Loretta A. Malandro and Larry Barker, *Nonverbal Communication* (Reading, Mass.: Addison-Wesley, 1983); Mark L. Hickson and Don W. Stacks, *NVC: Nonverbal Communication: Studies and Applications* (Dubuque, Iowa: Brown, 1985); and Virginia Richmond, James McCroskey and Steven Payne, *Nonverbal Behavior in Interpersonal Relationships* (Englewood Cliffs, N.J.: Prentice-Hall, 1987). On behavioral synchrony, see M. LaFrance and C. Mayo, *Moving Bodies:*

Nonverbal Communication in Social Relationships (Monterey, Calif.: Brooks/Cole, 1978). The area of clothing is well surveyed by Alison Lurie, *The Language of Clothes* (New York: Vintage, 1983). For the functions of nonverbal communication, see Paul Ekman, "Communication through Nonverbal Behavior: A Source of Information about an Interpersonal Relationship," in S. S. Tomkins and C. E. Izard, eds., *Affect, Cognition and Personality* (New York: Springer, 1965). An excellent review of research and theory is provided by Judee Burgoon, "Nonverbal Signals," in Mark L. Knapp and Gerald R. Miller, eds., *Handbook of Interpersonal Communication* (Beverly Hills, Calif.: Sage, 1985), pp. 344–390.

UNIT 11
BODY
COMMUNICATION

LEARNING GOALS

After completing this unit, you should be able to

1. provide two or three examples of nonverbal behaviors meaning different things in different cultures
2. define and provide at least two examples each of *emblems, illustrators, affect displays, regulators,* and *adaptors*
3. identify instances of the five types of movement in the behaviors of others and in your own behaviors
4. identify the types of information communicated by the face
5. identify at least two problems in judging the meaning of facial expressions
6. explain how context and culture influence facial expressions and their decoding
7. explain micromomentary expressions
8. identify at least three functions of eye movements
9. explain the types of information communicated by pupil dilation and constriction

First among all the avenues of nonverbal communication is the body. Through body movements, facial movements, and eye movements we communicate our thoughts and our feelings vividly, accurately, and frequently. In this unit we look at body communication and examine the numerous ways in which body, face, and eyes communicate meaning.

BODY MOVEMENTS

For dealing with movements of the body, a classification offered by Paul Ekman and Wallace V. Friesen seems the most useful. These researchers distinguish five classes of nonverbal movement based on the origins, functions, and coding of the behavior (see Figure 11.1).

Emblems

Emblems are nonverbal behaviors that rather directly translate words or phrases. Emblems include, for example, the signs for "okay," "peace," "come here," "I'm hitchhiking and I need a lift," "up yours," and so on. Emblems are nonverbal substitutes for specific words or phrases and are probably learned in

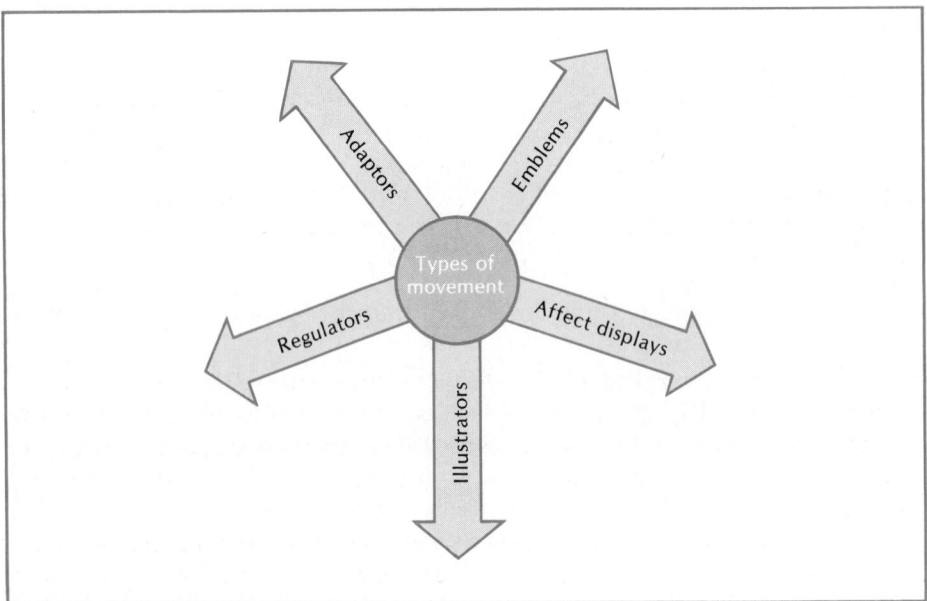

FIGURE 11.1 Types of movement.

essentially the same way as specific words and phrases—without conscious awareness or explicit teaching and largely through a process of imitation.

Although emblems seem rather natural to us and almost inherently meaningful, they are as arbitrary as any word in any language. Consequently, our present culture's emblems are not necessarily the same as the emblems of 300 years ago or the same as the emblems of other cultures.

Illustrators

Illustrators are nonverbal behaviors that accompany and literally "illustrate" verbal messages. In saying, "Let's go up," for example, you may move both your head and hands in an upward direction. In describing a circle or a square you are likely to make circular or square movements with your hands. So well learned are these movements that it is physically difficult to reverse them or to employ inappropriate ones.

We are only partially aware of the illustrators we use; at times they may have to be brought to our attention. Illustrators seem more natural, less arbitrary, and more universal than emblems. Because illustrators are more common throughout the world and throughout time, it is likely that they include some innate component as well as some learning.

Affect Displays

Affect displays are those facial movements that convey emotional meaning; they show anger and fear, happiness and surprise, eagerness and fatigue. Such facial expressions "give us away" when we attempt to present a false image and lead people to say, "You look angry today, what's wrong?" We can, however, consciously control affect displays, as actors do whenever they play a role. Affect displays are more independent of verbal messages than are illustrators and are less under conscious control than are emblems or illustrators.

Affect displays may be unintentional—as when they give us away—but they may also be intentional. We may want to show anger, love, hate, or surprise and, for the most part, we do a creditable job. Actors are often rated by the public for their ability to portray affect accurately by movements of their facial muscles.

Regulators

Regulators are nonverbal behaviors that "regulate," monitor, maintain, or control the speaking of another individual. When we are listening to another, we are not passive; rather, we nod our heads, purse our lips, adjust our eye focus, and make various paralinguistic sounds such as "mm-mm" or "tsk." Regulators are clearly culture-bound and are not universal.

Regulators in effect tell speakers what we expect or want them to do as they are talking—"Keep going," "What else happened?," "I don't believe that," "Speed up," "Slow down," and any number of other speech directions. Speakers in turn receive these nonverbal behaviors without being consciously aware

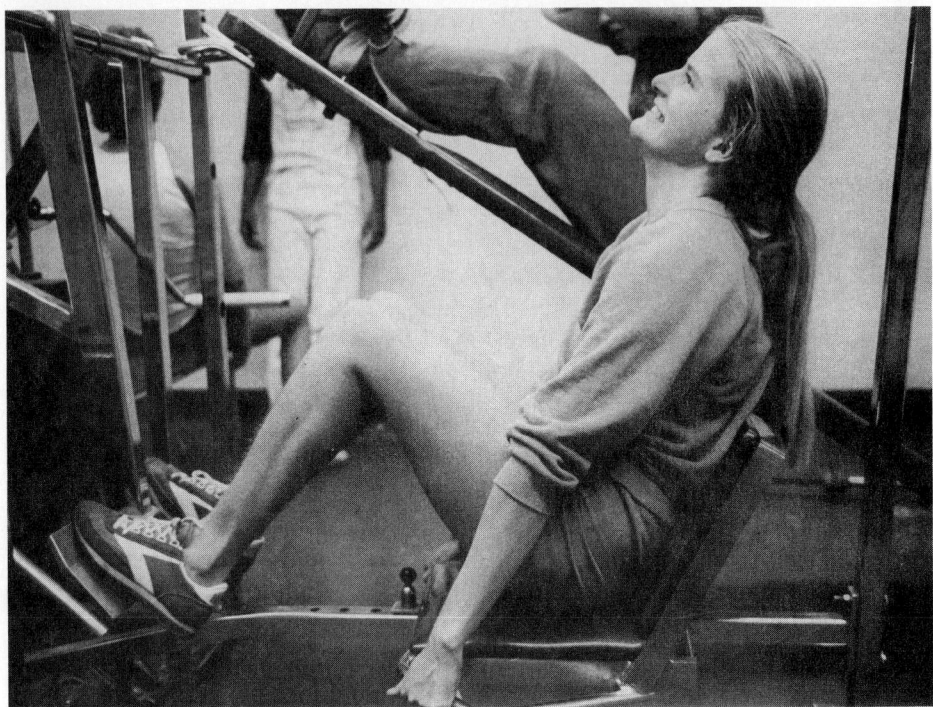

What messages do you derive from a person's body? What messages does your body communicate? How do you know this? How might you go about checking these initial assumptions?

of them. Depending on the speakers' degree of sensitivity, they modify their behavior in line with the directions supplied by the regulators.

Adaptors

Adaptors are nonverbal behaviors that when performed in private—or in public but without being seen—serve some kind of need and occur in their entirety. For example, when you are alone you might scratch your head until the itch is put to rest, or you might pick your nose until satisfied. In public, when people are watching us, we perform these adaptors only partially; you might put your fingers to your head and move them around a bit, but you probably would not scratch enough to eliminate the itch.

FACIAL MOVEMENTS

Facial messages communicate types of emotion as well as selected qualities or dimensions of emotion. Although opinion is divided, most researchers agree with Paul Ekman, Wallace V. Friesen, and Phoebe Ellsworth in claiming that facial messages may communicate at least the following "emotion categories":

happiness, surprise, fear, anger, sadness, and disgust/contempt. Nonverbal researcher Dale Leathers has proposed that facial movements may also communicate bewilderment and determination.

Affect Displays

The communication of the six emotions identified by Ekman and his colleagues are generally referred to as *primary affect displays*. These are relatively pure, single emotions. Other emotional states and other facial displays are combinations of these various primary emotions and are referred to as *affect blends*. Approximately 33 affect blends have been identified and are fairly consistently recognized by trained nonverbal analysts. These affect blends may be communicated by different parts of the face. Thus, for example, you may experience both fear and disgust at the same time. Your fear may be signaled by your eyes and eyelids, whereas your disgust may be signaled by movements of the nose, cheek, and mouth area. Sometimes different emotions are displayed within the same area; for example, one eyebrow may communicate one emotion, whereas the other eyebrow may communicate a different emotion.

Encoding-Decoding Accuracy

The accuracy with which people express emotions facially and the accuracy with which receivers decode these expressions have been the objects of considerable research. One problem is that it is difficult to separate the ability of the encoder from the ability of the decoder. Thus, an individual may be quite adept at communicating emotions, but the receiver may prove to be insensitive. On the other hand, the receiver may be quite good at deciphering emotions, but the sender may be inept. And, of course, there are tremendous differences between one person and another, as well as with the same person at different times.

Accuracy also varies with the emotions themselves. Some emotions are easier to communicate and to encode than others. Ekman, Friesen, and Carlsmith, for example, report that happiness is judged with an accuracy ranging from 55 to 100 percent, surprise from 38 to 86 percent, and sadness from 19 to 88 percent. All this is not to say that the results of these studies are of no value; rather, it is merely to inject a note of caution in dealing with "conclusions" from nonverbal research.

Try to communicate surprise using only facial movements. Do this in front of a mirror and attempt to describe in as much detail as possible the specific movements of the face that make up surprise. If you signal surprise like most people, you probably employ raised and curved eyebrows, long horizontal forehead wrinkles, wide-open eyes, a dropped-open mouth, and lips parted with no tension. Even if there were differences—and clearly there would be from one person to another—you could probably recognize the movements listed here as indicative of surprise. Paul Ekman has developed what he calls FAST—the Facial Affect Scoring Technique—in which the face is broken up into three main parts: eyebrows and forehead, eyes and eyelids, and the lower face from the bridge of the nose down. Judges then attempt to identify various emotions by observing the different parts of the face and writing descriptions along the lines of the one for surprise given above. As can easily be appreciated, certain areas of the face seem best suited to communicating certain emotions. For example, fear seems to be most clearly communicated by the eyes and eyelids, while disgust seems most clearly communicated by the nose, cheek, and mouth area.

Micromomentary Expressions

A frequently asked question in this regard concerns whether emotions can really be hidden or whether they somehow manifest themselves below the level of conscious awareness. Is our contempt encoded facially without our being aware of it or even without observers being aware of it? Although we do not have a complete answer to this question, some indication that we do communicate these emotions without awareness comes from research on micromomentary expressions. Haggard and Isaacs conducted studies in which they showed slow-motion films of therapy patients. They noted that often the patient's expression would change dramatically. For example, a frown would change to a smile and then quickly back to a frown. If the film was played at normal speed, the change to the smile would go unnoticed. Only when the film was played at slow speed was it apparent that the patient smiled in between frowning. Generally, if a facial expression lasts for less than two-fifths of a second, the expression goes unnoticed unless it is filmed and then played back at reduced speed. These extremely brief movements are called *micromomentary expressions*, and it has been proposed that they indicate an individual's real emotional state and that our conditioning leads us to repress such expressions.

EYE MOVEMENTS

From Ben Jonson's poetic observation "Drink to me only with thine eyes, and I will pledge with mine" to the scientific observations of contemporary researchers, the eyes are regarded as the most important nonverbal message system.

The messages communicated by the eyes vary depending on the duration, direction, and quality of the eye behavior. For example, in every culture there are rather strict, though unstated, rules for the appropriate duration for eye contact. In our culture the average length of gaze is 2.95 seconds and the average length of mutual gaze (two persons gazing at each other) is 1.18 seconds. When eye contact falls short of this amount, we may think the person is uninterested, shy, or preoccupied. When the appropriate amount of time is exceeded, we generally perceive this as indicating unusually high interest. The direction of our eye also communicates. Our cultural norm in communicating with another person states that we glance alternatively at the other person's face, then away, then again at the face, and so on. When these directional norms are broken, different meanings are communicated—abnormally high or low interest, self-consciousness, nervousness over the interaction, and so on. The quality—how

wide or how small our eyes get during interaction—also communicates meaning—especially, it seems, interest level and such emotions as surprise, fear, and
disgust.

Functions of Eye Communication

Among other researchers, Mark Knapp notes four major functions of eye
communication.

To Seek Feedback

The eyes are frequently used to seek feedback from others. In talking with
someone, we look at her or him intently, as if to say, "Well, what do you think?"
As you might predict, listeners gaze at speakers more than speakers gaze at
listeners. The percentage of interaction time spent gazing while listening, for
example, was observed in two studies to be 62 and 75 percent. The percentage
of time spent gazing while talking, however, was observed to be 38 and 41
percent.

Women make eye contact more and maintain it for longer periods of time
(both in speaking and in listening) than do men. This holds true whether the
woman is interacting with other women or with men. This difference in eye
behavior may be due to women's being more open in displaying their emotions
than men; eye contact is one of the most effective ways of communicating
emotions. Another possible explanation, as Evan Marshall observes, is that
women have been conditioned more than men to seek positive feedback from
others and may use eye contact in an attempt to seek this visual feedback.

To Inform Others to Speak

A second and related function of eye communication is to inform the other
person that the channel of communication is open and that he or she should
now speak. The clearest example of this is seen in the college classroom, when
the instructor asks a question and then locks eyes with a student. Without
saying anything, the instructor clearly expects that student to answer the question. Instructors who learn the names of their students do not have to use eye
contact to identify student-respondents. But whether names or eyes are used,
the function is essentially the same; it is a cue to speak.

To Signal the Nature of the Relationship

A third function of eye communication is to signal the nature of the relationship between two people—for example, one of positive or negative regard.
We may attempt to hide our feelings, and here we would avoid eye contact.
We may also signal status relationships with our eyes. This is particularly
interesting, because the same movements of the eyes may signal either subor-
dination or superiority. The superior individual, for example, may stare at the
subordinate or may glance away. Similarly, the subordinate may look directly
at the superior or perhaps to the floor.

Power is often signaled by what is called *visual dominance behavior*. The
average speaker maintains a high level of eye contact while listening and a

lower level while speaking. When powerful individuals want to signal dominance, they tend to reverse this "normal" pattern and maintain a high level of eye contact while talking but a much lower level while listening. Eye movements may also signal whether the relationship between two people is an amorous one, a hostile one, or one of indifference. Because some of the eye movements expressing these different relationships are so similar, we often utilize information from other areas, particularly the face, to decode the message before making any final judgments.

To Compensate for Increased Physical Distance

Last, eye movements are often used to compensate for increased physical distance. By making eye contact we overcome psychologically the physical distance between us. When we catch someone's eye at a party, for example, we become psychologically close even though we may be separated by a considerable physical distance. Eye contact and other expressions of psychological closeness, such as self-disclosure, have been found to vary in proportion to each other.

Eye Avoidance Functions

The eyes, sociologist Erving Goffman, in *Interaction Ritual*, observed, are "great intruders." When we avoid eye contact or avert our glance, we enable others to maintain their privacy. We frequently do this when a couple argues, say in the street or on a bus. We turn our eyes away (though our eyes may be wide open) as if to say, "We don't mean to intrude; we respect your privacy." Goffman refers to this behavior as *civil inattention*.

Eye avoidance can signal disinterest—in a person, a conversation, or some visual stimulus. At times, like the ostrich, we hide our eyes in an attempt to cut off unpleasant stimuli. Notice, for example, how quickly people close their eyes in the face of some extreme unpleasantness. Interestingly enough, even if the unpleasantness is auditory, we tend to shut it out by closing our eyes. Sometimes we close our eyes to block out visual stimuli and thus heighten our other senses; we often listen to music with our eyes closed. Lovers often close their eyes while kissing, and many prefer to make love in a dark or dimly lit room.

Pupil Dilation

In addition to eye movements, considerable research has been done on pupil dilation, or pupillometrics, largely as a result of the impetus of psychologist Ekhard Hess of the University of Chicago. In the fifteenth and sixteenth centuries in Italy, women used to put drops of belladonna (which literally means "beautiful woman") into their eyes to dilate the pupils so that they would look more attractive. Generally, contemporary research seems to support the logic of these women; dilated pupils are in fact judged to be more attractive.

Pupil size also indicates one's interest and level of emotional arousal. One's pupils enlarge when one is interested in something or when one is emotionally aroused. Perhaps we judge dilated pupils as more attractive because we judge an individual's dilated pupils to indicate interest in us. The dilation of the pupils also seems to vary depending on the degree of agreement one has with political figures. For example, it has been found that when black liberals were shown slides of Martin Luther King, their pupils dilated; the pupils constricted when shown slides of George Wallace. The pupils of white conservative students responded in the opposite way. More generally, Ekhard Hess has argued—with both experimental and intuitive support—that pupils dilate in response to positively evaluated attitudes and objects, and constrict in response to negatively evaluated attitudes and objects.

SUMMARY

1. Five classes or categories of nonverbal movements are distinguished: (1) *emblems* are nonverbal behaviors that rather directly translate words or phrases; (2) *illustrators* are nonverbal behaviors that accompany and literally "illustrate" the verbal messages; (3) *affect displays* are nonverbal movements that communicate emotional meaning; (4) *regulators* are nonverbal movements that coordinate, monitor, maintain, or control the speaking of another individual; and (5) *adaptors* are nonverbal behaviors that are emitted without conscious awareness and that usually serve some kind of need, as in scratching an itch.

2. Facial movements may communicate a wide variety of emotions; the most frequently studied are happiness, surprise, fear, anger, sadness, and disgust/contempt. Communications of these six emotions are generally referred to as *primary affect displays*.

3. *Micromomentary expressions* are extremely brief movements that are not consciously perceived and that are thought to reveal a person's real emotional state.

4. Eye movements may serve to seek feedback, to inform others to speak, to signal the nature of a relationship, and to compensate for increased physical distance.

5. Pupil size seems indicative of one's interest and one's level of emotional arousal. Pupils enlarge when one is interested in something or when one is emotionally aroused in a positive way.

SOURCES

Perhaps the most authoritative source for body communication is Ray L. Birdwhistell's *Kinesics and Context: Essays on Body Motion Communication* (New York: Ballantine Books, 1970). This paperback contains 28 articles by Birdwhistell on body communication plus a complete bibliography of research and theory in this area. The discussion and classification of types of body movements is from

P. Ekman and W. V. Friesen, "The Repertoire of Nonverbal Behavior: Categories, Origins, Usage, and Coding," *Semiotica* 1 (1969): 49–98. Good general introductions include Flora Davis, *Inside Institution* (New York: New American Library, 1973), and Gerald Nierenberg and Henry Calero, *How To Read a Person Like a Book* (New York: Pocket Books, 1971).

The studies referred to in the discussion of facial and eye communication are as follows: Paul Ekman, Wallace V. Friesen, and Phoebe Ellsworth, *Emotion in the Human Face: Guidelines for Research and an Integration of Findings* (New York: Pergamon Press, 1972); Paul Ekman, W. V. Friesen, and S. S. Tomkins, "Facial Affect Scoring Technique: A First Validity Study," *Semiotica* 3 (1971): 37–58; M. G. Cline, "The Influence of Social Context on the Perception of Faces," *Journal of Personality* 2 (1956): 142–185; E. A. Haggard and K. S. Isaacs, "Micromomentary Facial Expressions as Indicators of Ego Mechanisms in Psychotherapy," in L. A. Gottschalk and A. H. Auerbach, eds., *Methods of Research in Psychotherapy* (Englewood Cliffs, N.J.: Prentice-Hall, 1966). The Ekman, Friesen, and Carlsmith study may be found in *Emotion in the Human Face*.

On eye movements, see Ekhard H. Hess, *The Tell-Tale Eye* (New York: Van Nostrand Reinhold, 1975). For a discussion of visual dominance behavior, see R. V. Exline, S. L. Ellyson, and B. Long, "Visual Behavior as an Aspect of Power Role Relationships," in P. Pliner, L. Krames, and T. Alloway, eds., *Nonverbal Communication of Aggression* (New York: Plenum, 1975). Evan Marshall, in his *Eye Language: Understanding the Eloquent Eye* (New York: New Trend, 1983), covers both the folklore and the scientific research on eye communication. Allen Pease, in *Signals: How to Use Body Language for Power, Success and Love* (Bantam Books, 1984), provides a thorough popular account of the nature and meanings of body gestures.

In addition to these works, the works of Knapp, Leathers, Burgoon and Saine, Malandro and Barker, Hickson and Stacks, and Richmond, McCroskey, and Payne cited in the previous unit, were very helpful and should prove useful to anyone interested in the areas of body, facial, and eye movements.

UNIT 12
SPACE, TERRITORIALITY, AND TOUCH COMMUNICATION

LEARNING GOALS

After completing this unit, you should be able to

1. identify and explain the four spatial distances
2. give examples of the kinds of communication that would take place in each of the four spatial distances
3. identify and explain the operation of at least four influences on space communication
4. define *territoriality*
5. identify and explain territorial encroachment, distinguishing among violation, invasion, and contamination, and give examples of four possible reactions to encroachment
6. explain the concept of markers and distinguish among central, boundary, and ear markers
7. give examples of the operation of territoriality from your own experiences
8. explain the five major meanings communicated by touch
9. identify and explain the operation of some of the factors that influence whom one touches and where
10. explain the concept of touch avoidance and its relationship to apprehension, self-disclosure, age, and sex

In addition to communicating with words and with our hands, face, and eyes, we also communicate with space, territoriality, and touch. These forms of nonverbal communication figure in almost every communication transaction. In this unit, we focus on how these systems operate in human communication.

SPACE COMMUNICATION

Our use of space speaks just as surely and just as loudly as words and sentences. Speakers who stand close to their listener, with their hands on the listener's shoulders and their eyes focused directly on those of the listener, communicate something very different from the speaker who sits crouched in a corner with arms folded and eyes on the floor. Similarly, the executive office suite on the top floor with huge windows, private bar, and plush carpeting communicates something very different from the 6-by-6 cubicle occupied by the rest of the workers.

Space communication, often referred to as *proxemics,* a term coined by anthropologist Edward T. Hall, encompasses a number of interrelated behaviors. Some of the more frequently examined include the extent of visual contact people maintain as they communicate, the amount of body heat one person perceives from the other, the potential that exists for one person to touch another while communicating, the posture of the persons communicating, the physical directness of the communicators, and the extent to which one person can smell the other's body odor. In our discussion we will take a more macroscopic view of spatial communication and focus on some of the larger dimensions of proxemics. First, we identify the four major spatial distances that operate when people communicate. Second, we examine some of the influences on space.

Spatial Distances

In communication, space is especially important, although we seldom think about it or even consider the possibility that it might serve a function. Edward Hall distinguishes four distances that he claims define the type of relationship permitted. Each of these four has a close phase and a far phase, giving us a total of eight clearly identifiable distances (see Figure 12.1).

Intimate Distance
In *intimate distance,* ranging from the close phase of actual touching to the far phase of 6 to 18 inches, the presence of the other individual is unmistakable. Each person experiences the sound, smell, and feel of the other's breath. The *close phase* is used for lovemaking and wrestling, for comforting and protecting.

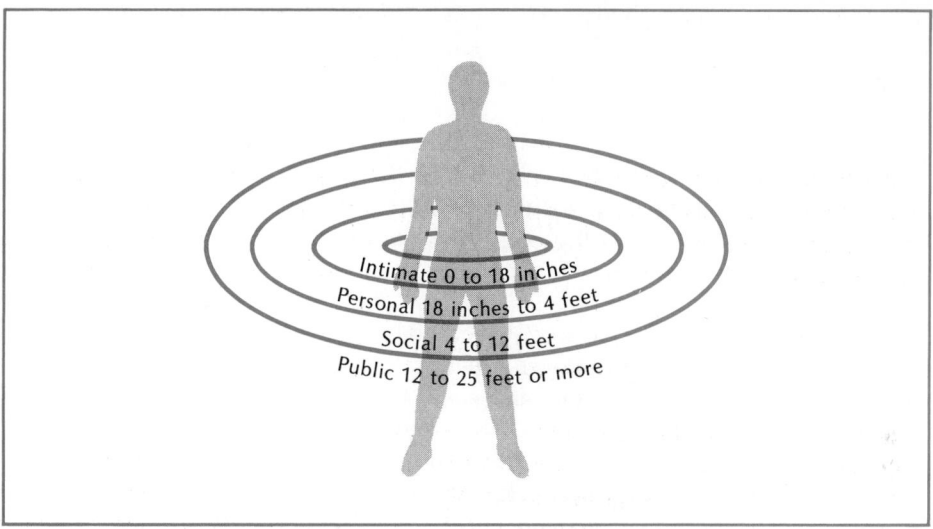

FIGURE 12.1 Proxemic distances.

In the close phase the muscles and the skin communicate, while actual verbalizations play a minor role. In this close phase even whispering, says Hall, has the effect of increasing the psychological distance between the two individuals. The *far phase* allows us to touch each other by extending our hands. This distance is still so short that it is not considered proper in public, and because of the feeling of inappropriateness and discomfort (at least for Americans), the eyes seldom meet; they remain fixed on some remote object.

Personal Distance

Each of us, says Hall, carries around with us a protective bubble defining our *personal distance,* which allows us to stay protected and untouched by others. In the *close phase* of personal distance (from 1½ to 2½ feet), we can still hold or grasp each other but only by extending our arms. We can then take into our protective bubble certain individuals—for example, loved ones. In the *far phase* (from 2½ to 4 feet), two people can touch each other only if they both extend their arms. This far phase represents the extent to which we can physically get our hands on things, and hence it defines, in one sense, the limits of our physical control over others.

Even at this distance we can see many details of an individual—the gray hairs, tooth stains, clothing lint, and so on. However, we can no longer detect body heat. At times we may detect breath odor, but generally at this distance etiquette demands that we direct our breath to some neutral corner so as not to offend (as the television commercials warn us we might do).

When personal space is invaded, we often become uncomfortable and tense. When people stand too close to us, our speech may become disrupted, unsteady, jerky, and staccato. We may have difficulty maintaining eye contact and may frequently look away from the person. This discomfort may also be manifested in excessive body movement. At other times we do not seem to mind the invasion of personal space and in fact would not even define it as invasion. For example, when others enter our personal space bubble at a crowded party, there is no tension or discomfort; in fact, we seem to enjoy this physical closeness. Similarly, when people we like enter our personal space we perceive the situation as being less crowded than when less-liked people enter the very same space. That is, people we like crowd us psychologically less than people we do not like, even though physically the situations are identical.

Social Distance

At the *social distance* we lose the visual detail we have in the personal distance. The *close phase* (from 4 to 7 feet) is the distance at which we conduct impersonal business and interact at a social gathering. The *far phase* (from 7 to 12 feet) is the distance we stand at when someone says, "Stand away so I can look at you." At this distance, business transactions have a more formal tone. In offices of high officials the desks are positioned so that the individual is assured of at least this distance when dealing with clients. Unlike intimate distance, where eye contact is awkward, the far phase of social distance makes eye contact essential—otherwise communication is lost. The voice is generally louder than normal at this distance, but shouting or raising the voice has the effect of reducing the social distance to a personal distance. It is at this distance that we can work with people but not constantly interact with them or appear rude.

Public Distance

In the *close phase* of *public distance* (from 12 to 15 feet), an individual seems protected by space. At this distance one is able to take defensive action when threatened. On a public bus or train, for example, we might keep at least this distance from a drunkard so that should anything come up (literally or figuratively), we could get away in time. Although at this distance we lose fine details of the face and eyes, we are still close enough to see what is happening.

At the *far phase* (more than 25 feet), we see people not as separate individuals, but as part of the whole setting. We automatically set approximately 30 feet around important public figures and we seem to do this whether or not there are guards preventing us from entering this space. This far phase is of course the distance from which actors perform on stage; consequently, their actions and voices have to be somewhat exaggerated to convey detail.

Influences on Space Communication

A number of variables have been found to have a significant effect on our treatment of space in communication situations. And although not all research findings are in agreement, a few generalizations seem warranted.

Status People of equal status generally maintain a shorter distance between themselves than do people of unequal status. When the status is unequal, the

The space that a person controls in an office is often indicative of that person's status within the organizational hierarchy. Can you identify the rank of your college instructors on the basis of their offices? What cues are most helpful in enabling you to draw these inferences?

higher-status person may approach the lower-status person more closely than the lower-status person may approach the higher-status person.

Culture Americans generally stand fairly far apart when conversing, at least compared with certain European and Middle Eastern cultures. Arabs, for example, stand much closer to each other than do Americans. Italians and Spaniards likewise maintain less distance in their interactions than many northern Europeans.

Context Generally, the larger the physical space we are in, the smaller the interpersonal space. Thus, for example, the space between two people conversing will be smaller in the street than in an apartment. The space will be smaller in a large room than in a small room. The larger the space, the more we seem to need to close it off and make the immediate communication context manageable.

Subject Matter If we talk about personal matters or share secrets, we maintain a short distance; when we talk about impersonal, general matters, the space is generally larger. Psychologically, it seems we are attempting to exclude others from hearing even though physically there may be no one within earshot. We maintain a shorter distance if we are being praised than if we are being blamed. It would seem that we want to move in closer to the praise lest it fall on someone else, and that we want to remove ourselves (physically) from the blame. Our body behavior seems to reflect this quite clearly.

Sex and Age   Generally, women stand closer to one another than do men; opposite sex pairs seem to stand the farthest apart. Similarly, women are allowed to touch each other more than men are and more than unacquainted opposite-sex pairs. Children generally stand closer to each other than do adults, indicating that the distances we maintain are learned rather than innately determined.

Positive and Negative Evaluation   We stand farther apart from enemies than from friends, from authority figures and higher-status persons than from peers, from the physically handicapped than from the nonhandicapped, and from those of a different racial group than from those of our group. We maintain more distance between ourselves and people we may subconsciously evaluate negatively.

TERRITORIALITY

One of the most interesting concepts in ethology (the study of animals in their natural surroundings) is *territoriality*. For example, male animals will stake out a particular territory and consider it their own. They will allow prospective mates to enter but will defend it against entrance by others, especially other males of the same species. Among deer, the size of the territory signifies the power of the buck, which in turn determines how many females he will mate with. Less powerful bucks will be able to control only small parcels of land and consequently will mate with only one or two females. This is a particularly adaptive measure, since it ensures that the stronger members of the society will produce most of the offspring. When the "landowner" takes possession of an area—either because it is vacant or because he gains it through battle, he marks it—for example, by urinating around the boundaries. The size of the animal's territory, then, indicates the status of the animal within the herd.

The size and location of human territory also indicate something about status. A townhouse on Manhattan's East Side, for example, is perhaps the highest-status territory for home living in the country; it is large and at the same time located on the world's most expensive real estate. Status is also signaled by the unwritten law granting the right of invasion. Higher-status individuals have more of a right to invade the territory of others than vice versa. The boss of a large company, for example, can invade the territory of a junior executive by barging into her or his office, but the reverse would be unthinkable.

These general patterns are felt by many to be integral parts of human behavior. Some researchers claim that territoriality is innate and demonstrates the innate aggressiveness of humans. Others claim that territoriality is learned behavior and is culturally based. Most, however, agree that a great deal of human behavior can be understood and described as territorial, regardless of its origin or development.

Territorial Encroachment

Looking around our homes, we will probably find certain territories that different people have staked out and where invasions are cause for at least mildly defensive action. This is perhaps seen most clearly with siblings who each have (or "own") a specific chair, room, radio, and so on. Father has his chair and mother has her chair. Archie and Edith Bunker always sit in the same chairs, and great uproars occur when Archie's territory is invaded. Similarly, the rooms of the house may be divided among members of the family. The kitchen has traditionally been the mother's territory. Invasions from other family members may be tolerated but are often not welcomed, and at times they are resisted. Invasions by members not of the immediate family—from a sister-in-law, mother-in-law, or neighbor, for example—are generally resented much more.

In the classroom, where seats are not assigned, territoriality can also be observed. When a student sits in a seat that has normally been occupied by another student, the regular occupant will often become disturbed and resentful and might even say something about it being his or her seat.

We may distinguish three major types of territorial encroachment.

Violation   Violation constitutes unwarranted use of another's territory, as when we enter another's office or home without permission or when we enter a place normally restricted to the use of one group—for example, a rest room for the opposite sex.

Invasion   Invasion constitutes entering the territory of another and thereby changing the meaning of that territory. For example, if students entered a faculty meeting or if parents entered their teenagers' hangout, it would change the meaning of the meeting and of the territory.

Contamination   Contamination occurs when one renders a territory impure. For example, a person who smokes a smelly cigar may contaminate an area. A couple's home or bed may be contaminated if an unfaithful spouse uses it for an extramarital affair. Someone's obscenity may also contaminate a territory.

Reactions to Encroachment

We can react to encroachment in a number of ways. The most extreme form is *turf defense*. When the intruders cannot be tolerated, the territory is defended against them and they are expelled. Gangs defend "their" streets and neighborhoods by fighting off members of rival gangs (intruders) who enter the territory.

A less extreme form is *insulation*—the erection of some sort of barrier between ourselves and the invaders. We can do this by wearing sunglasses to avoid eye contact or by putting up fences to let others know that interpersonal interaction is not welcomed.

Linguistic collusion is another method frequently used to separate ourselves from unwanted invaders. Here we speak in a language unknown to these outsiders or perhaps we might use a professional jargon to which they are not privy. Linguistic collusion serves both to solidify those who speak that language or sublanguage and to exclude those who do not know the linguistic code being used.

Still another type of response is *withdrawal;* we can leave the territory.

Markers

Like animals, humans also mark their territory, though generally not with urine. Instead we make use of three types of markers: central, boundary, and ear markers. *Central markers* are items placed in a territory and intended to reserve it for us—for example, a drink at the bar, books on our desk, and a sweater over the chair.

Boundary markers set boundaries that divide our territory from "theirs." In the supermarket checkout line, the bar that is placed between your groceries and those of the person behind you is a boundary marker, as are the armrests separating your chair from those of the people on either side, and the molded plastic "seats" on a bus or train.

Ear markers—a term taken from the practice of branding animals on their ears—are those identifying marks that indicate your possession of a territory or object. Trademarks, initials, nameplates, and initials on a shirt or attaché case are all examples of ear markers.

TOUCH COMMUNICATION

Touch communication, also referred to as *haptics*, is perhaps the most primitive form of communication. Developmentally, touch is probably the first sense to be used; even in the womb the child is stimulated by touch. Soon after birth the child is fondled, caressed, patted, and stroked. In turn, the child explores its world through touch. In very short time, the child learns to communicate a wide variety of meanings through touch.

The Meanings of Touch

Five of the major meanings of touch, identified in a recent and extensive study by Stanley Jones and Elaine Yarbrough, are considered here.

Positive Affect

Touch may communicate positive emotions. This touching occurs mainly between intimates or others who have a relatively close relationship. "Touch is such a powerful signalling system," notes Desmond Morris, "and it's so closely related to emotional feelings we have for one another that in casual encounters it's kept to a minimum. When the relationship develops, the touching follows along with it." Among the most important of these positive emotions are support, which indicates nurturing, reassurance, or protection; appreciation, which expresses gratitude; inclusion, which suggests psychological closeness; sexual interest or intent; and affection, which expresses a generalized positive regard for the other person.

Playfulness

Touch often communicates our intention to play, either affectionately or aggressively. When affection or aggression is communicated in a playful manner, the playfulness deemphasizes the emotion and tells the other person that it is not to be taken seriously. Playful touches serve to lighten an interaction.

Control

Touch may also serve to direct the behaviors, attitudes, or feelings of the other person. Such control may communicate a number of messages. In compliance, for example, we touch the other person to communicate "move over," "hurry," "stay here," and "do it." In attention-getting, we touch the person to gain his or her attention, as if to say "look at me" or "look over here."

Touching to control may also communicate dominance. Consider, as Nancy Henley suggests in her *Body Politics*, who would touch whom—say, by putting an arm on the other person's shoulder or by putting a hand on the other person's back—in the following dyads: teacher and student, doctor and patient, master and servant, manager and worker, minister and parishioner, police officer and accused, businessperson and secretary. Most people brought up in our culture would say that the first-named person in each dyad would be more likely to touch the second-named person than the other way around. It is the higher-status person who is permitted to touch the lower-status person; in fact, it would be a breach of etiquette for the lower-status person to touch the person of higher status.

Henley further argues that in addition to indicating relative status, touching also demonstrates the assertion of male power and dominance over women. Men may, says Henley, touch women in the course of their daily routine—in the restaurant, office, and school, for example—and thus indicate their "superior status." When women touch men, on the other hand, the interpretation that it designates a female-dominant relationship is found not acceptable (to men), and so this touching is frequently explained and interpreted as a sexual invitation.

Ritual

Ritualistic touching centers on greetings and departures. Shaking hands to say "hello" or "goodbye" is perhaps the clearest example of ritualistic touching, but we might also hug, kiss, or put our arm around another's shoulder in meeting someone or in anticipating the person's departure.

Task-Relatedness

Task-related touching is associated with the performance of some function; this ranges from removing a speck of dust from another person's face to helping someone out of a car or checking someone's forehead for fever.

Touch Avoidance

Much as we have a need and desire to touch and be touched by others, we also have a tendency to avoid touch from certain people or in certain circumstances. Peter Andersen and Ken Leibowitz have investigated touch avoidance and have found some interesting relationships between it and other significant communication variables. For example, touch avoidance is positively related to communication apprehension. Those who fear oral communication also seem to score high on touch avoidance. Touch avoidance is also high with those who self-disclose little; both touch and self-disclosure are intimate forms of communication, and people who are reluctant to get close to another person by self-disclosure also seem reluctant to get close through touch. The tendency to avoid communication of one form seems to generalize to other forms.

Older people have higher touch-avoidance scores for opposite-sex persons than do younger people. Apparently, as we get older we are touched less by members of the opposite sex, and this decreased frequency of touching may lead us to avoid touching.

Males score higher on same-sex touch avoidance than do females. This accords well with our stereotypes; men avoid touching other men, but women may and do touch other women. Women, it was also found, have higher touch-avoidance scores for opposite-sex touching than do men.

Who Touches Whom Where

A great deal of research has been directed at the question of who touches whom where. Most of it has addressed two basic questions: (1) Are there gender differences? Do men and women communicate through touch in the same way? Are men and women touched in the same way? (2) Are there cultural differences? Do people in widely different cultures communicate through touch in the same way?

Gender Differences and Touch

One of the most famous studies on gender differences and touch was conducted in 1968 by Sidney M. Jourard, a summary of whose findings is presented in Figure 12.2. In the first figure, labeled "Body for mother," we have the areas and frequency with which these areas of a male college student's body were touched by his mother. The second figure records the areas and frequency with which these areas were touched by the student's father, and so on. The key within the figure indicates the percentage of students who reported being touched in these areas.

Jourard reports that touching and being touched differ little between men and women. Men touch and are touched as often and in the same places as women. The major exception to this is the touching behavior of mothers and

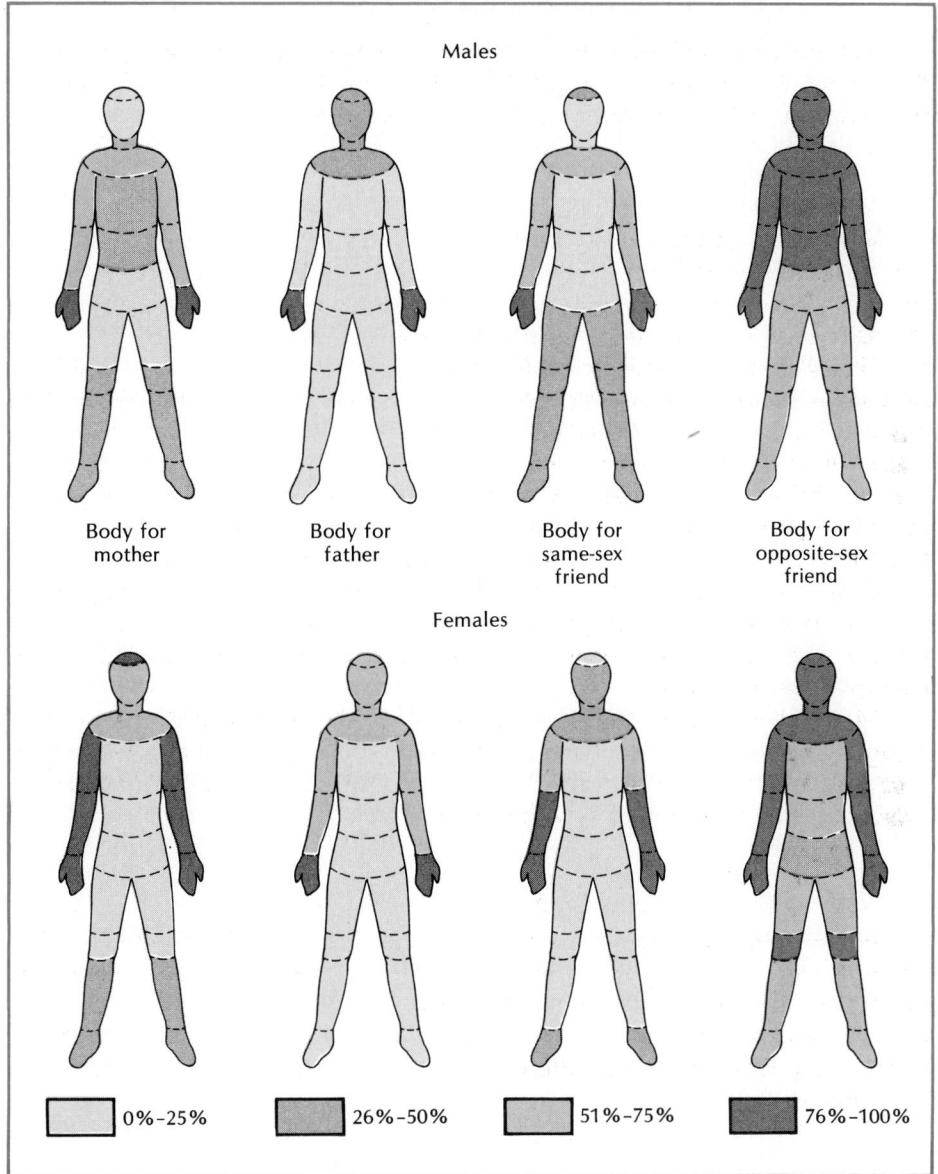

FIGURE 12.2 The amount of touching of the various parts of the body as reported by male and female college students. *Source:* S. M. Jourard, "An Exploratory Study of Body-Accessibility," *British Journal of Social and Clinical Psychology* 5 (1966): 221–231.

fathers. Mothers touch children of both sexes and of all ages a great deal more than do fathers, who in many instances go no further than touching the hands of their children. The studies that have found differences between touching behavior in men and women seem to indicate women touch more than men do. For example, women seem to touch their fathers more than men do. Also, it seems that female babies are touched more than male babies. In an investigation of the wish to be held versus the wish to hold, it was found that women report a greater desire to be held than to hold; men also report a desire to be held, but it is not as intense as that of women. This, of course, fits in quite neatly with our cultural stereotypes of men being protectors (and therefore indicating a preference for holding) and women being protected (and therefore indicating a preference for being held).

A great deal more touching is reported among opposite-sex friends than among same-sex friends. Both male and female college students report that they touch and are touched more by their opposite-sex friends than by their same-sex friends. No doubt the strong societal bias against same-sex touching accounts, at least in part, for the greater prevalence of opposite-sex touching. I suspect, however, that a great deal of touching goes on among same-sex friends but goes unreported, for at least two reasons. First, college students are often fearful that they might be thought homosexual if they admit to touching or being touched by same-sex friends, and homosexual students will often be "forced" by various pressures to play the role of the heterosexual and give even more heterosexually oriented responses than would heterosexuals themselves. Second, many people are unaware of touching same-sex partners when the touching is nonsexual; it is a behavior that is often engaged in without any conscious awareness, much as we are unaware of making slight movements with our head when we indicate a direction or of smiling when we are feeling good. Sexual touching, on the other hand, is often done with awareness—sometimes a planned awareness—and, at least in the early stages, with considerable self-consciousness.

The Jourard study was replicated 10 years later; support was found for all Jourard's earlier findings, except that in the later study both males and females reported being touched more by opposite-sex friends than in the earlier study.

Culture Differences and Touch

In a similar study, college students in Japan and in the United States were surveyed. The results, shown in Figure 12.3, present a particularly dramatic case for cross-cultural differences; students from the United States reported being touched twice as much as did students from Japan. In Japan there is a strong taboo against strangers' touching, and the Japanese are therefore especially careful to maintain sufficient distance.

Another obvious cross-cultural contrast is presented by the Middle East, where same-sex touching in public is extremely common. Men will, for example, walk with their arms around each other's shoulders—a practice that would cause many raised eyebrows in the United States. Middle Easterners, Latin Americans, and southern Europeans touch each other while talking a great deal more than do people from "noncontact cultures"—Asia and northern Europe, for example.

Even such seemingly minor nonverbal differences as these can create difficulties when members of different cultures interact. Northern Europeans or Japanese may be perceived as cold, distant, and uninvolved by southern Europeans, who in turn may be perceived as pushy, aggressive, and inappropriately intimate.

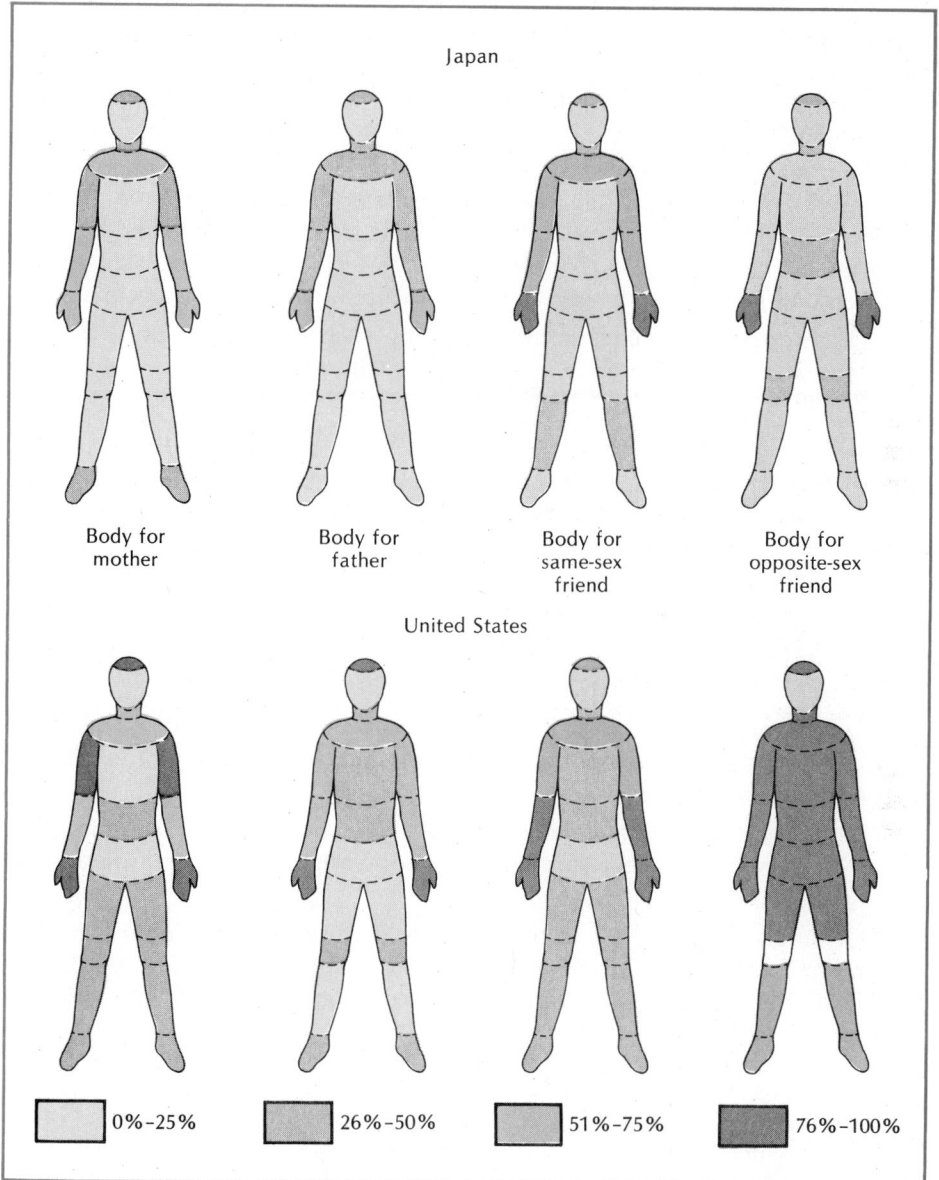

FIGURE 12.3 Areas and frequency of touching as reported by Japanese and United States college students. *Source:* Dean C. Barnlund, "Communicative Styles in Two Cultures: Japan and the United States." In A. Kendon, R. M. Harris, and M. R. Key, eds., *Organization of Behavior in Face-to-Face Interaction* (The Hague: Mouton, 1975).

SUMMARY

1. *Proxemics* refers to the communicative function of space and spatial relationships.

2. Four major proxemic distances are generally identified: (1) *intimate distance*, ranging from actual touching to 18 inches; (2) *personal distance*, ranging from 1½ to 4 feet; (3) *social distance*, ranging from 4 to 12 feet; and (3) *public distance*, ranging from 12 to more than 25 feet. These four distances correspond to four major types of relationships existing among people.

3. Our treatment of space is influenced by such factors as status, culture, context, subject matter, sex, age, and positive or negative evaluation of the other person.

4. *Territoriality* refers to one's possessive reaction to an area of space or to particular objects.

5. Territorial encroachment may take any of three major forms: violation, invasion, and contamination.

6. We may react to territorial encroachment by turf defense, insulation, linguistic collusion, and withdrawal.

7. *Markers* are devices that identify a territory as ours; these include central markers, boundary markers, and ear markers.

8. Touch communication (or haptics) may communicate a variety of meanings, the most important being positive affect, playfulness, control, ritual, and task-relatedness.

9. *Touch avoidance* refers to our desire to avoid touching and being touched by others; it has been found to be related to apprehension, self-disclosure, age, and sex.

10. Generally, research has found that women touch more and are touched more than are men. Touching patterns also vary greatly from one culture to another. Both gender and culture differences in touch behavior are learned rather than innate.

SOURCES

For spatial communication, the work of Edward T. Hall is perhaps the most well known and insightful. A discussion of proxemic dimensions is found in his "System for the Notation of Proxemic Behavior," *American Anthropologist* 65 (1963): 1003–1026. The discussion of proxemic distances comes from his *Hidden Dimension* (Garden City, N.Y.: Doubleday, 1966). Hall's first popular work on spatial communication and perhaps still one of the most famous is *The Silent Language* (Garden City, N.Y.: Doubleday, 1959). Robert Sommer also deals with spatial communication but from a somewhat different point of view. Particularly interesting is his *Personal Space: The Behavioral Basis of Design* (Englewood Cliffs, N.J.: Prentice-Hall, 1969). For research and theory on space and its influence on human interaction, see Albert Mehrabian, *Public Places and Private Spaces* (New York: Basic Books, 1976). For the classifications of territories, encroachments, and possible reactions I relied on Stanford M. Lyman and Marvin B. Scott's classic article, "Territoriality: A Neglected Sociological Dimension," *Social Problems* 15 (1967): 236–249. On markers, see Erving Goffman, *Relations in Public: Microstudies of the Public Order* (New York: Harper Colophon, 1971), and Mark L. Hickson and Don W. Stacks, *NVC: Nonverbal Communication, Studies and Applications* (Dubuque, Iowa: Brown, 1985).

For body touching, see Ashley Montague, *Touching: The Human Significance of the Skin* (New York: Harper & Row, 1971). For Jourard's studies on touching, see Sidney M. Jourard, *Disclosing Man to Himself* (New York: Van Nostrand Reinhold, 1968), and *Self-Disclosure* (New York: Wiley, 1971). Marc Hollender and Alexander Mercer conducted the study on holding, discussed in "Wish to Be Held and Wish to Hold in Men and Women," *Archives of General Psychiatry* 33 (January 1976): 49–51. On the role of touching in status and power relationships, see Nancy M. Henley, *Body Politics: Power, Sex, and Nonverbal Communication* (Englewood Cliffs, N.J.: Prentice-Hall, 1977). The discussion of the meanings of touch was drawn from Stanley E. Jones and A. Elaine Yarbrough, "A Naturalistic Study of the Meanings of Touch," *Communication Monographs* 52 (March 1985): 19–56. In addition to the five categories discussed here, Jones and Yarbrough also include "hybrid" (a combination category) and "accidental" touching. On sex differences and touching, see Stanley E. Jones, "Sex Differences in Touch Communication," *Western Journal of Speech Communication* 50 (summer 1986): 227–241. The discussion of touch avoidance was based on Peter A. Andersen and Ken Leibowitz, "The Development and Nature of the Construct Touch Avoidance," *Environmental Psychology and Nonverbal Behavior* 3 (1978): 89–106.

UNIT 13
PARALANGUAGE AND TIME

LEARNING GOALS

After completing this unit, you should be able to

1. define *paralanguage*
2. explain the role of paralanguage in each of the following: judgments about people, judgments about conversational turns, and judgments about believability
3. explain biological time and the general meanings of the physical, emotional, and intellectual cycles
4. define cultural time and distinguish among technical, formal, and informal time
5. distinguish between monochronism and polychronism, and between displaced and diffused time orientations
6. explain the concept of psychological time and distinguish among past, present, and future orientations
7. identify some of the implications of different time orientations
8. explain the relationship of time and status
9. explain the concept of appropriateness as it relates to temporal communication

PARALANGUAGE

An old exercise to increase the student's ability to express different emotions, feelings, and attitudes was to have the student say the following sentences while accenting or stressing different words: "Is this the face that launched a thousand ships?" Significant differences in meaning are easily communicated depending on where the stress is placed. Consider, for example, the following variations:

1. *Is* this the face that launched a thousand ships?
2. Is *this* the face that launched a thousand ships?
3. Is this the *face* that launched a thousand ships?
4. Is this the face that *launched* a thousand ships?
5. Is this the face that launched a *thousand ships?*

Each of the five sentences communicates something different. Each, in fact, asks a totally different question even though the words used are identical. All that distinguishes the sentences is stress, one of the aspects of what is called *paralanguage.* Paralanguage may be defined as the vocal (but nonverbal) dimension of speech. It refers to the *manner* in which something is said rather than to *what* is said.

In addition to stress or pitch, paralanguage includes such vocal characteristics as rate, volume, and rhythm, as well as the vocalizations involved in crying, whispering, moaning, belching, yawning, and yelling. A variation in any of these features communicates. The speaker who speaks quickly, for example, communicates something different from the one who speaks slowly. Even though the words might be the same, if the speed (or volume, rhythm, or pitch) differs, the meanings we receive will also differ. On the basis of paralanguage (or paralinguistic cues), we make a number of judgments.

Judgments About People

We are a diagnostically oriented people, quick to make judgments about another's personality based on various paralinguistic cues. Sometimes our judgments turn out to be correct, and sometimes not, but the number of times correct and incorrect does not seem to influence the frequency with which we make such judgments. We may, for example, conclude that those who speak extremely softly have some kind of problem; perhaps they feel inferior—they "know" that no one really wants to listen and that nothing they say is significant, so they speak softly. Others speak at an extremely loud volume, perhaps because of an overinflated ego and the belief that everyone in the world wants to hear them—that what they have to say is so valuable they cannot risk our not hearing every word. Those who speak with no variation, in a complete monotone, seem uninterested in what they are saying and encourage a similar disinterest from the listeners—if any are still around. We might perceive such people as having a lack of interest in life in general, as being rather bland individuals. All these conclusions are, at best, based on little evidence, yet this does not stop us from making them.

Among the most interesting findings on voice and personal characteristics is one showing that listeners can accurately judge the status (whether high, middle, or low) of speakers from hearing a 60-second voice sample. In fact, many listeners reported that they made their judgments in fewer than 15 seconds. It has also been found that the speakers judged to be of high status were rated as being of higher credibility than speakers rated middle and low in status.

Listeners can also judge with considerable accuracy the emotional states of speakers from just their vocal expression. In these studies the content of the speech is nonexistent (for example, emotions are communicated by reciting the alphabet or numbers) or is held constant (for example, the same sentence is used to communicate a wide variety of emotions). Some emotions, of course, are easier to identify than others. For example, while it may be easy to distinguish between hate and sympathy, it may not be so easy to distinguish between

In telephone communication we lose the information that gestures, facial expressions, and clothing communicate. How do we compensate for that loss of information? That is, what additional cues do we use in talking on the phone that we do not use in, say, face-to-face communication?

fear and anxiety. And, of course, listeners vary in their ability to decode and speakers vary in their ability to encode emotions.

Judgments About Conversational Turns

Paralinguistic cues are widely used to signal conversational turns—the changing (or maintaining) of the speaker or listener role during the conversation.

Turn-Maintaining Cues   Perhaps the most obvious use of paralinguistic cues in conversational turns is to maintain one's speaking position. Thus, the speaker may in the course of conversation pause while vocalizing *-em, -er*, and the like. These pauses ensure that no one else will jump in and take over; they announce to others that this speaker is not finished. Another type of paralinguistic cue is used to maintain one's role as listener. This would take the form of vocalizing some reinforcing or approving sound while someone else is talking. This kind of positive feedback tells the speaker to keep on going, to say more, and, perhaps most important, that this listener approves of what is being said.

Turn-Yielding Cues   One of the most important conversational functions paralinguistic cues serve is to announce that the speaker has finished and it is now someone else's turn to speak. So, for example, the speaker may at the end of a statement add some paralinguistic cue such as *eh?*, which asks the others in the conversation to speak now. Often, speakers will indicate that they have finished speaking by dropping their intonation, by a prolonged silence, or by asking some general question.

Turn-Requesting Cues   Still another function of paralinguistic cues is to indicate to the speaker that a listener would like to say something, that the listener would like to take a turn as speaker. Sometimes listeners do this by simply saying, "I would like to say something," but often it is done paralinguistically through some vocalized *-er* or *-um* that tells the speaker (at least the sensitive speaker) someone else would now like to speak. (These vocalizations are in many instances indistinguishable from those the speaker uses to maintain the speaking position.) This request to speak is also often made with facial and mouth gestures. Frequently a listener will indicate a desire to speak by opening his or her eyes and mouth wide as if to say something or just by beginning to gesture with a hand.

Turn-Denying Cues   We may also indicate our reluctance to assume the role of speaker by, for example, intoning a slurred "I don't know" or by giving the speaker some brief grunt that signals you have nothing to say. Often turn-denying is accomplished by avoiding eye contact with the speaker who wishes you to now take on the role of speaker, or by engaging in some behavior that is incompatible with speaking—for example, coughing or blowing your nose.

Judgments About Communication Effectiveness

The rate of speed at which people speak is the aspect of paralanguage that has received the most attention. It is of interest to the advertiser, the politician, and, in fact, anyone who attempts to convey information or to influence others, especially when time is limited or expensive.

Persuasiveness and Credibility   The research conducted on rate shows that in one-way communication (when one person is doing all or most of the speaking and the other person is doing all or most of the listening), those who talk fast are more persuasive and are evaluated more highly than those who talk at or below normal speeds. This finding holds true regardless of whether the speech is naturally fast or electronically speeded up (as with time-compressed speech).

In one experiment, for example, subjects were asked to listen to taped messages and then to indicate their degree of agreement with the message and their opinion of the speaker's intelligence and objectivity. Rates of 111, 140, and 191 words per minute were used. (The average speaking rate is about 130 to 150 words per minute.) Subjects agreed most with the fastest speech and least with the slowest speech. Further, they rated the fastest speaker as being the most intelligent and objective, and the slowest speaker as the least intelligent and objective. Even when the speaker was demonstrated to have something to gain personally from persuasion (as would, say, a used-car dealer), the fastest speaker rate was the more persuasive.

Comprehension   When we look at comprehension, rapid speech shows an interesting effect. Subjects who listened to speeches at different speeds had their comprehension measured by means of multiple-choice tests. For example, using 141 words per minute as the average and considering comprehension at this rate as 100 percent, it was found that when the rate was increased to 201 words per minute the comprehension was 95 percent, and when the rate was further increased to 282 words per minute (that is, double the normal rate) comprehension was still 90 percent. Even though the rates increased dramatically, the comprehension rates fell only slightly. These 5 and 10 percent losses are more than offset by the increased speed and thus make the faster rates much more efficient in communicating information. If the speech speeds are increased more than 200 percent, however, comprehension falls dramatically.

Preferences   A somewhat faster than normal speed is preferred by most listeners. For example, when subjects were able to adjust the speed at which they heard a message, they adjusted it to approximately 25 percent faster than normal speed. Similarly, persons find commercials presented at approximately 25 percent faster than normal more interesting than those presented at normal speeds, and the level of attention (indexed by the amount of electrical activity measured by electrodes attached to the subject's frontalis muscle of the forehead) is greater for fast speeds.

We need to be cautious, however, in applying this research to the field of interpersonal communication. As John MacLachlan points out, during the time the speaker is speaking, the listener is generating and framing a reply. If the speaker talks too rapidly, there may not be enough time to compose this reply, and resentment may be generated. Furthermore, the increased rate may seem so unnatural that the listener may come to focus on the speed of speech rather than the thought expressed. But with one-way communication, especially mass communication, it is clear that increased speech rates will become more and more popular. They are already used extensively in direct-selling commercials. Their popularity will, it seems, influence other forms of mass media advertising.

TEMPORAL COMMUNICATION

Temporal communication (*chronemics*) is concerned with the use of time—how we organize it, how we react to it, and the messages it communicates. We may view time from at least three perspectives: biological, cultural, and psychological.

Biological Time

Some writers have asserted that we each have a built-in biological clock and that we are greatly influenced by our biorhythms. Our biorhythms consist of three major cycles—physical, emotional, and intellectual—that greatly influence our related behaviors. Each cycle has an up-side, during which we function effectively and efficiently; a down-side, during which we function ineffectively and inefficiently; and critical days, during which we are at our absolute worst. Each cycle starts at birth, lasts a fixed number of days, and then repeats itself throughout our lives.

The Physical Cycle   The physical cycle is concerned with strength, energy, coordination, and resistance to disease; it lasts 23 days. During the up-side (the first 11½ days) we are in good health, have coordinated balance, and perform at our best athletically. During the second half of the cycle we are tired and lazy, lack coordination, have low endurance, and are generally more accident- and ailment-prone.

The Emotional Cycle   The emotional cycle is concerned with mood, optimism-pessimism, and the ability to work with others; it lasts 28 days. During the first half of the cycle we are calm, cheerful, cooperative, understanding, and creative. During the second half our emotions shift to moodiness, negativism, irritability, and hypersensitivity.

The Intellectual Cycle   The intellectual cycle is concerned with cognitive and intellectual abilities and activities; it lasts 33 days. During the first half we feel intellectually driven and efficient; we have good memory capacity and seem able to make accurate and quick judgments. During the second half our thinking capacity is diminished, our mental abilities are slow, and our memory is poor.

We do function effectively and efficiently during certain days and ineffectively and inefficiently during other days. There seems to be some evidence (though not a great deal) that these effective and ineffective days correspond to our biorhythms. Right now, however, the influence of biorhythms seems more an interesting and curious hypothesis than a well-established theory.

Cultural Time

Generally, we distinguish three types of cultural time. *Technical time* is precise, scientific time. Milliseconds and atomic years are examples of technical or scientific time. We use this time system only in the laboratory, so it seems to have little relevance to our daily lives.

Formal time refers to the manner in which a culture defines and teaches time. In our culture time is divided into seconds, minutes, hours, days, weeks, months, and years. Other cultures may use phases of the moon or the seasons to delineate time periods. We divide college courses into 50- or 75-minute periods that meet two or three times a week for a 14-week period called a semester. Eight semesters of fifteen or sixteen 50-minute periods per week equal a college education. In fact, we seem to divide almost all knowledge—at least as it appears in college courses—into units of 35 to 45 hours each. It should be clear from these examples that formal time units are arbitrary and are established for convenience by the culture.

Informal time, perhaps the most interesting in terms of communication, refers to a rather loose use of time terms—for example, *forever, immediately, soon, right away, as soon as possible.* This is the area of time that creates the most communication problems because the terms have different meanings for different people.

Monochronism and Polychronism

One of the most important distinctions made in discussions of time, and especially informal time, is that between monochronic and polychronic time orientations. Monochronic people or cultures schedule one thing at a time. Time is compartmentalized; there is a time for everything, and everything has its own time. Polychronic people or cultures, on the other hand, schedule a number of things at the same time. Thus, eating, conducting business, and taking care of home chores may all be conducted at the same time.

Displaced and Diffused Time Orientations

Another important distinction is between displaced and diffused time orientations. In a displaced time orientation, time is viewed exactly. Persons with this orientation will be exactly on time. In a diffused time orientation, time is seen as approximate rather than exact. People with this orientation are usually late for appointments because they understand, for example, a scheduled time of 8 P.M. as meaning anywhere from 7:45 to 8:15 or 8:30.

In one study, researchers LeVine and Bartlett examined the accuracy of the clocks in different cultures and found considerable variation. Clocks in Japan were the most accurate, while clocks in Indonesia were the least accurate. Clocks in England, Italy, Taiwan, and the United States fell between these two extremes in accuracy. Not surprisingly, when the speed of pedestrians in these cultures were measured, the researcher found that the Japanese walked the fastest and the Indonesians the slowest. Such differences reflect the different ways in which cultures treat time and their general attitude toward the importance of time in their everyday lives.

Psychological Time

Psychological time refers primarily to the importance we place on the past, present, or future. In a *past orientation* we accord particular reverence for the past; we relive old times and regard the old methods as the best. Events are seen as circular and recurring, so that the wisdom of yesterday is applicable also to today and tomorrow. In a *present orientation* we live in the present for the present. Present activities command attention and are engaged in not for their future rewards or their past history, but because they are happening now. In its extreme form, this orientation is hedonistic. In a *future orientation* we give primary attention to the future. We save today, work hard in college, and deny ourselves certain enjoyments and luxuries all because we are preparing for the future.

Recently, Alexander Gonzalez and Philip Zimbardo have provided us with some interesting correlations of these different time orientations. For example, the annual income of a future-oriented person is likely to be higher than that of a present-oriented person. Present orientation is strongest among the lowest-income males.

The particular time orientation that people develop depends in great part on their socioeconomic class and personal experiences. "A child with parents in unskilled and semiskilled occupations," note Gonzalez and Zimbardo, "is usually socialized in a way that promotes a present-oriented fatalism and hedonism. A child of parents who are managers, teachers or other professionals learns future-oriented values and strategies designed to promote achievement."

Present-oriented people are fatalistic and tend to see their lives as being controlled by outside forces and by others. Future-oriented people, on the other hand, see themselves as being in charge of their own lives. Gonzalez and Zimbardo note: "In an industrial, technologically based society such as ours, a present-oriented time sense dooms most people to life at the bottom of the heap. There is no place for fatalism, impulsivity or spontaneity when the marketplace is run on objectives, deadlines, budgets and quotas."

Perhaps the most important point to make here is that different time perspectives account largely for our misunderstanding other cultures and peoples. Someone from a future-oriented culture may see people from a present-oriented culture as inefficient and imprudent. Alternatively, those with a present orientation may see those with a future orientation as obsessed with efficiency and foolish for delaying life's gratifications.

Time and Status

Time is especially linked to status considerations. For example, the importance of being on time varies directly with the status of the individual we are visiting. If the person is extremely important, we had better be there on time; in fact, we had better be there early just in case he or she is able to see us before schedule. As the individual's status decreases, it is less important for us to be on time. Students, for example, must be on time for conferences with teachers, but it is more important to be on time for deans and still more important to be on time for the president of the college. Teachers, on the other hand, may be late for conferences with students but not for conferences with deans or the president. Deans, in turn, may be late for teachers but not for the president. Within any hierarchy, similar unwritten rules seem to be followed in dealing with time. This is not to imply that these "rules" are just or fair; they just exist.

Even the time of dinner and the time from the arrival of guests to eating varies on the basis of status. Among lower-status individuals, dinner is served relatively early. If there are guests, they eat soon after they arrive. For higher-status people, dinner is relatively late, and a longer period of time elapses between arrival and eating—usually the time it takes to consume two cocktails.

Time and Appropriateness

Promptness or lateness in responding to letters, returning telephone calls, acknowledging gifts, and returning invitations all communicate significant messages to others. These messages may be indexed on such scales as interest-disinterest, organized-disorganized, considerate-inconsiderate, sociable-unsociable, and so on.

Also, there are times when certain activities are considered appropriate and other times when they are considered inappropriate. Thus, it is permissible to make a social phone call during the late morning, afternoon, and early evening, but not before 8:00 or 9:00 in the morning, or during dinner time or after 11:00 at night. Similarly, in making dates, an appropriate amount of notice is customary. When that acceptable amount of time is given as notice, it communicates a recognition of the accepted standards, perhaps respect for the individual, and perhaps a certain social grace. Should any of these time conventions be violated, however, other meanings are perceived. For example, a phone call at an abnormal hour will almost surely communicate urgency of some sort; we begin to worry as we race toward the phone.

Paralanguage and time are two elements of nonverbal communication that often function below the level of conscious awareness. Nevertheless, when a speaker or listener misuses any of the unstated rules in these areas, it frequently identifies the individual as one lacking in some social communication skill. It often distinguishes the person we enjoy interacting with from the person with whom we feel uncomfortable and ill at ease. Through an understanding of the ways in which these two dimensions affect our communications, we will be less likely to break some small but socially significant rules of interpersonal interaction. At the same time, we will be better able to understand the problems generated by those who break these rules, as well as the reactions of others when such rules are broken.

SUMMARY

1. *Paralanguage* may be defined as the vocal (but nonverbal) dimension of speech; it includes rate, pitch, volume, resonance, and vocal quality as well as pauses and hesitations.

2. On the basis of paralanguage we make judgments about people, conversational turns, and believability.

3. Temporal communication (chronemics) refers to the messages communicated by our treatment of time.

4. Time may be viewed from at least three perspectives: biological, cultural, and psychological.

5. Biological time is concerned with our physiological biorhythms and their influence on our physical, emotional, and intellectual activities.

6. Cultural time is concerned with how our culture defines and teaches time, and with the difficulties created by the different meanings people have for informal time terms.

7. Psychological time is concerned with people's time orientations, whether past, present, or future.

8. The messages that time communicates are greatly influenced by status considerations and by the social rules for appropriateness and inappropriateness.

SOURCES

For a classification of and introduction to paralinguistic phenomena, see George L. Prager, "Paralanguage: A First Approximation," *Studies in Linguistics* 13 (1958): 1–12, and "The Typology of Paralanguage," *Anthropological Linguistics* 3 (1961): 17–21. Mark Knapp, *Nonverbal Behavior in Human Interaction*, 2d ed. (New York: Holt, Rinehart and Winston, 1978), provides an excellent summary of research findings. George F. Mahl and Gene Schulze likewise provide a thorough summary of the research and theory in this area. See their "Psychological Research in the Extralinguistic Area," in T. A. Seboek, A. S. Hayes, and M. C. Bateson, eds., *Approaches to Semiotics* (The Hague: Mouton, 1964). For a collection of research studies on paralanguage, see Joel R. Davitz, ed., *The Communication of Emotional Meaning* (New York: McGraw-Hill, 1964). For a thorough review of paralanguage, see Ernest Kramer, "Judgment of Personal Characteristics and Emotions from Nonverbal Properties," *Psychological Bulletin* 60 (1963): 408–420; Albert Mehrabian, *Silent Messages* (Belmont, Calif.: Wadsworth, 1971), in addition to Knapp, and Mahl and Schulze, cited above. An excellent review is provided by W. P. Robinson, *Language and Social Behavior* (Baltimore: Penguin Books, 1972).

For the research reported in relation to speech rate, persuasion, and comprehension, I relied on John MacLachlan, "What People Really Think of Fast Talkers," *Psychology Today* 13 (November 1979): 113–117.

On time see, for example, Edward Hall, *The Silent Language* (New York: Fawcett, 1959); Alexander Gonzalez and Philip G. Zimbardo, "Time in Perspective," *Psychology Today* 19 (March 1985): 20–26; and Tom Bruneau, "The Time Dimension in Intercultural Communication," in Larry A. Samovar and Richard E. Porter, eds., *Intercultural Communication: A Reader*, 4th ed. (Belmont, Calif.: Wadsworth, 1985), pp. 280–289. For the study on the accuracy of clocks, see R. LeVine and K. Bartlett, "Pace of Life, Punctuality and Coronary Heart Disease in Six Countries," *Journal of Cross-Cultural Psychology* 15 (1984): 233–255.

SKILL DEVELOPMENT SUMMARY

1. Do not draw **inferences about what a person is thinking** or feeling from isolated bits and pieces of nonverbal behaviors.

2. To make your communications more interesting and more effective, use nonverbal behaviors to accent, complement, contradict, regulate, repeat, and substitute for verbal messages—the major **functions of nonverbal communication.**

3. Remember **communicativeness;** all your behaviors and, in fact, everything about you communicates to others. Regulate these messages so as to communicate your intended messages more effectively.

4. Learn to recognize **behavioral synchrony** and use it only as a *possible* indication of agreement and/or liking.

5. Remember the **contextual nature of nonverbal communication.** View nonverbal behaviors as dependent in great part on the total context in which they appear. Be especially careful of making inferences about others without carefully considering the context.

6. Use **deception cues** only as sources for hypotheses (never conclusions) about lying.

7. Remember that **nonverbal behaviors follow certain rules** and that these rules differ from one culture to another. Differences in nonverbal behavior, therefore, need to be examined in terms of the specific cultural meanings.

8. Pay attention to **metacommunicational messages** so that the total meaning communicated may be more closely approximated.

9. As a communication receiver, be sensitive to the messages communicated by **body gestures and facial and eye movements.**

10. Remember that there are bodily movements **(micromomentary movements)** that we cannot perceive without slow-motion films, so do not assume that what is perceived represents the total nonverbal expression.

11. Use your eyes to seek feedback, to inform others to speak, to signal the nature of your relationship with others, and to compensate for increased physical distance—the major **functions of eye communication.**

12. Use **spatial distance** to signal the type of relationship you are in: intimate, personal, social, or public. Let your spatial relationships reflect your interpersonal relationships.

13. **Give others the space they need,** remembering for example, that when people are angry or disturbed, they need more space than usual.

14. Recognize that your own behaviors can be considered invasive by others, so be careful of **violating, invading, or contaminating the territories of others.**

15. Become sensitive to the **markers** (central, boundary, and ear) of others and learn to use these markers to define your own territories.

16. Become sensitive to the **touching behaviors** of others and distinguish among those touches that communicate positive affect, playfulness, control, ritual, and task-relatedness. Use touch to communicate these specific meanings.

17. Recognize that each person has a certain **touch-avoidance** tendency and that this desire for touch avoidance should be respected. Be especially sensitive to cultural and gender differences in touching preferences and in touch-avoidance tendencies.

18. Vary **paralinguistic features** (rate, pausing, quality, tempo, and volume) to communicate your intended meanings.

19. Use **paralinguistic cues** to signal your desire for turn-maintaining, turn-yielding, turn-requesting, and turn-denying.

20. Become alert to the significant **biological time cycles** (intellectual, emotional, and physical) of your own body, but be careful that you do not rely on these more than is warranted by the research evidence.

21. Learn to recognize when interpersonal difficulties may be caused by different meanings for **informal time.**

22. Learn to enjoy the **present-moment experience** but also remember that a **future orientation** is extremely important for success in a technological society.

23. Interpret **time cues** from the cultural perspective of the person with whom you are interacting rather than merely from your own perspective.

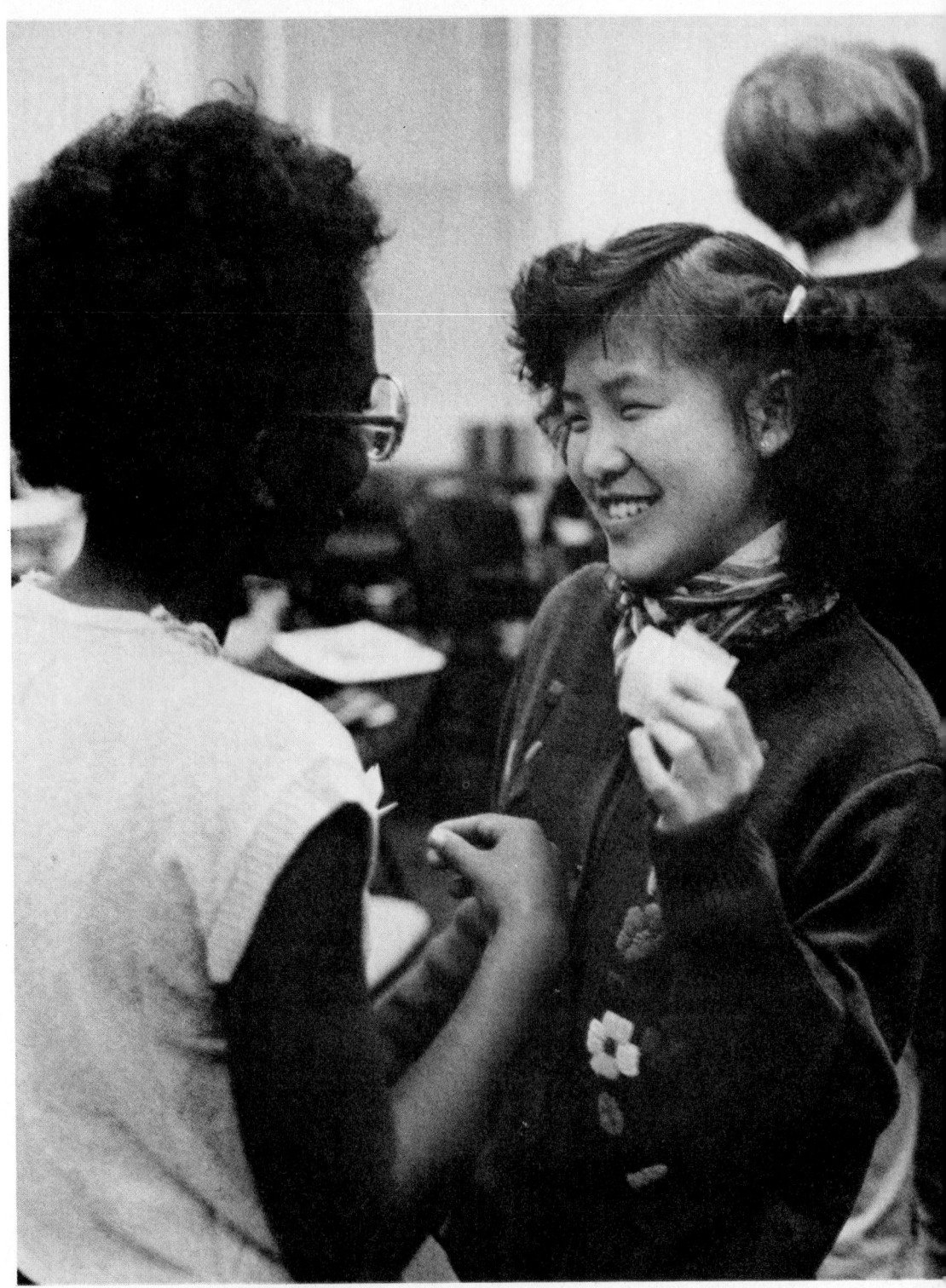

PART FOUR
INTERPERSONAL COMMUNICATION AND RELATIONSHIPS

14. PRELIMINARIES TO INTERPERSONAL COMMUNICATION AND RELATIONSHIPS: DEFINITIONS, CHARACTERISTICS, AND INTERPERSONAL ATTRACTION

15. RELATIONSHIP DEVELOPMENT AND DETERIORATION

16. IMPROVING INTERPERSONAL COMMUNICATION AND CONFLICT MANAGEMENT

In this part we deal with interpersonal communication and relationships. First, we examine the nature of these areas and the elements that make us attracted and attractive to others. Second, we look at the development and deterioration of relationships. Here we examine the reasons relationships develop and deteriorate, suggestions for initiating relationships, and the communication patterns that characterize developing and deteriorating relationships. Third, we present a variety of suggestions for increasing your own interpersonal communication and relationship effectiveness and for managing conflict.

Our major purpose in all three of these units is to provide you with the guidelines for understanding and improving your own interpersonal relationships.

UNIT 14

PRELIMINARIES TO INTERPERSONAL COMMUNICATION AND RELATIONSHIPS:
Definitions, Characteristics, and Interpersonal Attraction

LEARNING GOALS

After completing this unit, you should be able to

1. identify and explain the three approaches to defining interpersonal communication

2. explain the five-stage model of interpersonal relationships, identifying and defining the five stages and the movement among and between the stages

3. explain the concepts of breadth and depth as they relate to the development of interpersonal relationships

4. define *interpersonal attraction* and explain the five factors discussed here that account for our attraction to others

5. explain gain-loss theory and the matching hypothesis as they relate to interpersonal attraction

In this unit we focus on some preliminaries to interpersonal communication. First, we explore its nature and definition; second, we consider the nature and growth of interpersonal relationships; and third, we focus on interpersonal attraction and examine the characteristics that attract us to others and attract others to us.

INTERPERSONAL COMMUNICATION

Communication theorists define interpersonal communication in a number of different ways. Three general approaches are briefly identified here.

A Componential Definition

A componential definition explains interpersonal communication by noting its major components—here, the sending of messages by one person and the receiving of messages by another person or small group of persons, with some effect and with some opportunity for immediate feedback. These components have already been explained in Unit 1.

A Relational (Dyadic) Definition

In a relational definition, interpersonal communication is defined as communication that takes place between two persons who have a clearly established relationship. Thus, for example, interpersonal communication would include what takes place between a waiter and a customer, a son and his father, two sisters, a teacher and a student, two friends, and so on. With this definition it is almost impossible to have dyadic (two-person) communication that is not interpersonal. Not surprisingly, this definition is also referred to as the *dyadic* definition. Almost inevitably, there is some relationship between two persons. Even the stranger in the city who asks directions from a resident has a clearly defined relationship established with the resident as soon as the first message is sent. Sometimes this relational definition is extended to include small groups of persons, such as families or groups of three or four friends.

Both the componential and relational approaches define essentially the same situations as interpersonal; the componential definition emphasizes the components or elements involved in the communication act, and the relational definition emphasizes the relationship existing between the participants. Under these definitions, a vast part of our communications would be considered interpersonal. According to the next definition, only a very small number of our communications would be considered interpersonal.

A Developmental Definition

In the developmental approach, interpersonal communication is seen as the end of a progression (or development) from impersonal communication at one extreme to personal (or intimate) communication at the other. This progression signals or defines the development of interpersonal communication. I here follow communicologist Gerald Miller's analysis. Interpersonal communication is characterized by, and distinguished from, impersonal communication on the basis of at least three factors.

Psychologically Based Predictions

Interpersonal interactions are characterized by the participants' basing their predictions about each other not on the other person's membership in a specific group or culture (as would be the case in impersonal communications), but on psychological data—that is, the ways in which this person differs from the members of his or her group. In impersonal encounters we respond to each other according to the classes or groups to which we belong—for example, we respond to a particular college professor in the way we respond to college professors in general. Similarly, the college professor responds to a particular student in the way professors respond to students generally. As the relationship becomes more personal, however, both the professor and the student begin to respond to each other not as members of their groups, but as individuals; each begins to respond to the other on the basis of the individual's uniqueness. Another way of putting this would be to say that in impersonal encounters the social or cultural role of the person tells us how to interact, while in personal or interpersonal encounters the psychological role of the person tells us how to interact.

Explanatory Knowledge

Interpersonal interactions are based on *explanatory knowledge* of each other. When we know a particular person, we can predict how that person will react in a variety of situations. In interpersonal situations we can not only predict how a person will act, but we can also advance explanations for the behaviors. The college professor may in an impersonal relationship know that Pat will be five minutes late to class each Friday—that is, the professor is able to predict Pat's behavior. In an interpersonal situation, however, the professor can not only predict Pat's behavior, but can also offer explanations for the behavior—in this case, give reasons for Pat's lateness.

Personally Established Rules

In impersonal situations the rules of behavioral interaction are set down by social norms. Here, students and professors behave toward each other according to the social norms that have been established by the culture or subculture in which they are operating. However, as the relationship between a student and a professor becomes interpersonal, the social norms lose importance and no longer totally regulate the interaction. The individuals establish rules of their own. To the extent that the individuals establish rules for interacting with each other rather than using the rules set down by their society, the situation is interpersonal.

These three characteristics vary in degree. We respond to one another on the basis of psychological data *to some degree;* we base our predictions of another's behavior *to some degree* on our explanatory knowledge; and we interact on the basis of mutually established rules rather than on socially established norms *to some degree.* A developmental approach to communication implies a continuum ranging from highly impersonal to highly intimate. "Interpersonal communication" occupies a broad area of this continuum, though each person might draw its boundaries a bit differently. Therefore, although this view does not make universal distinctions concerning what is or what is not interpersonal, the three characteristics should add to our insight into interpersonal communication and how it might be distinguished from formal or impersonal communication.

Communication theorists are divided in loyalty among these three definitions, so each instructor and each text will define interpersonal communication somewhat differently. My own feeling is that interpersonal communication is best defined, in its broadest sense, to include any interaction in which there is a relationship established between or among the participants. At the same time, recognize that interpersonal communication changes as it becomes more intimate—a progression clearly explained in the developmental definition. Thus, all three definitions are helpful in explaining what interpersonal communication is and how it develops.

INTERPERSONAL RELATIONSHIPS

The nature of interpersonal relationships is explained here by identifying two essential characteristics. First, we consider the stages that interpersonal relationships go through, from initial interaction to dissolution. Second, we consider the ways in which relationships vary in breadth and depth.

Relationships Are Established in Stages

Most relationships, possibly all, are established in stages. We do not become intimate friends immediately upon meeting; we grow into an intimate relationship gradually, through a series of steps or stages. And the same is probably true with most other relationships as well. "Love at first sight" creates a problem for the stage model of relationships, so rather than argue that such love cannot occur (my own feeling is that it can and frequently does), it seems wiser to claim that the stage model of relationships characterizes *most* relationships for *most* people *most* of the time.

The five-stage model presented in Figure 14.1 seems a suitable one for describing some significant stages in the development of relationships. For each specific relationship, you might wish to modify and revise the basic model in

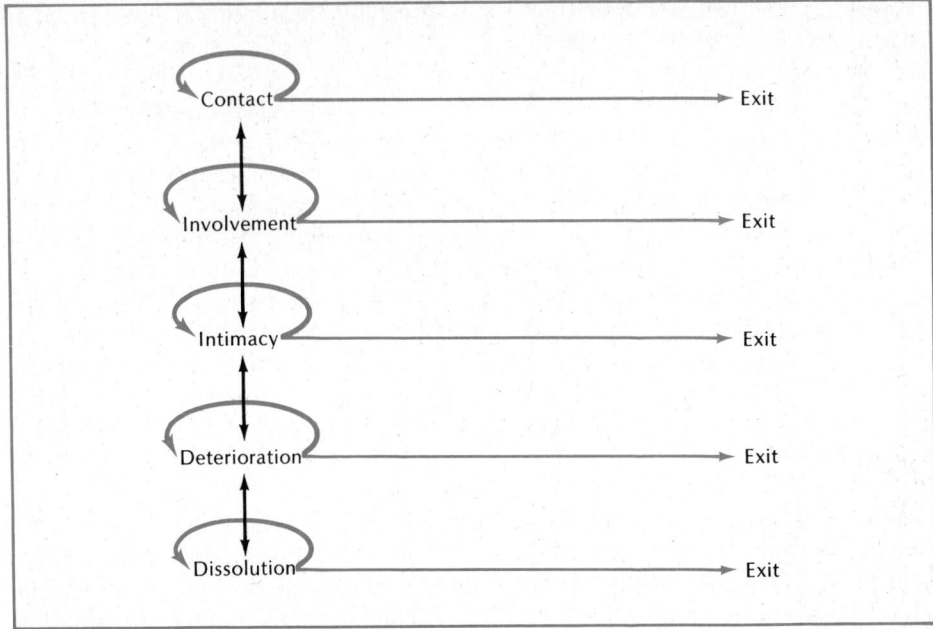

FIGURE 14.1 A five-stage relationship model.

various ways, yet as a general description of relationship development, the stages seem fairly standard.

The five stages to be identified here are *contact, involvement, intimacy, deterioration,* and *dissolution.* These stages describe relationships as they are, rather than evaluating or prescribing how relationships should be.

Contact

At the first stage we make *contact;* there is some kind of sense perception—we see, hear, and smell the person. This is the stage of saying "Hello, my name is Joe" and exchanging the basic information that is generally preliminary to any more intense involvement. According to some researchers, it is during this stage—within the first four minutes of initial interaction—that we decide whether we want to pursue the relationship. It is at this stage that physical appearance is so important, because the physical dimensions are most open to sensory inspection. Yet qualities such as friendliness, warmth, openness, and dynamism are also revealed at this stage. If we like the individual and want to pursue the relationship, we proceed to the second stage.

Involvement

The *involvement* stage is the stage of acquaintance, when we commit ourselves to getting to know the other person better and also to revealing ourselves. If this is to be a romantic relationship, then we might date at this stage; if it is to be a friendship, we might share our mutual interests—go to the movies or to some sports event together.

Intimacy

At the third stage, that of *intimacy,* we commit ourselves still further to the other person and, in fact, establish a kind of primary relationship, in which this individual becomes our best or closest friend, lover, and/or companion. This commitment may take many specific forms: marriage, helping the person or just being with him or her, or revealing our deepest secrets. The commitment will naturally vary with the relationship and the individual, but the unifying characteristic is that the commitment made is a special one, made only to a select few. This stage is reserved for very few people—sometimes just one and sometimes two, three, or perhaps four. Rarely do we have more than four intimates, except, of course, in a family situation.

Deterioration

The next two stages represent the other side of the progression, when the bonds weaken between the parties in the relationship. At the *deterioration* stage we begin to feel that this relationship may not be as important as we had previously thought. We grow further and further apart. We share less of our free time and when we are together there are awkward silences, fewer self-disclosures, and in general, a self-consciousness in our exchanges. At this stage we are not exactly sure what to call our "intimate." The person is not quite a lover or an exlover, not really a close friend but not an exfriend either. This is that awkward in-between stage of being neither here nor there. If this deterioration stage continues unaltered, we enter the stage of dissolution.

Dissolution

The *dissolution* stage is the cutting of the bonds that tie the individuals together. If the bond was marriage, the dissolution is symbolized by a divorce, although the actual relational dissolution takes the form of establishing separate and different lives away from each other. This is the stage of "goodbye"—the point at which we become exlovers, exfriends, exhusbands, exwives, and so on. Some times there is relief and relaxation—finally it is over and done with; at other times there is intense anxiety and frustration—recriminations and hostility, resentment over time ill-spent and now lost. In more materialistic terms, this is the stage when property is divided and the couple fights child custody battles. But it is also the time during which the individuals must look to the establishment of a new and different life—either alone or with another person. Some people, it is true, will continue to live psychologically with a relationship that has already been dissolved: They will frequent the old meeting places, reread old love letters, daydream about all the good times, and in general fail to extricate themselves from a relationship that has died everywhere except in their minds.

Movement Among the Stages

Figure 14.1 contains three types of arrows. The Exit arrows indicate that each stage offers the opportunity to exit the relationship. After saying "hello" we can say "goodbye" and exit. The vertical or "movement" arrows going to the next stage and back again represent our ability to move to another stage, either one that is more intense (say from involvement to intimacy) or less intense (from intimacy to deterioration). We can also go back to a previously established stage. For example, you may have established an intimate relationship with someone but did not want to maintain it at that level. At the same time, you were relatively pleased with the relationship, so it was not really deteriorating—you just wanted it to be somewhat less intense. So you might go back to the involvement stage and reestablish the relationship at that more comfortable level. Similarly, if in the stage of deterioration problems and differences are worked out, the people may reestablish themselves into an intimate relationship again.

Of course we may also skip stages, although this is probably not as common as one might think. Often people in a relationship may appear to be skipping a stage when they are merely passing through it very quickly. For example, we may see a couple skip from the initial contact to intimacy. It is not that they have bypassed involvement; instead, the involvement stage lasted for a very short time and to outsiders was not apparent. This is not to say, however, that a stage could *not* be skipped. And there is no fixed time period any stage must occupy. Stages may be extremely short or extremely long.

The "self-reflexive" arrows—the arrows that return to the beginning of the same level or stage—signify that any relationship may become stabilized at any point. We may, for example, maintain a relationship at the intimate level without the relationship's deteriorating or going back to the less intense stage of involvement. Or we might remain at the "Hello, how are you" stage—the contact stage—without getting involved any further.

Relationships Vary in Breadth and Depth

Your relationships with someone may be described in terms of the number of topics the two of you talk about and the degree of "personalness" to which you pursue these topics. The number of topics about which the parties communicate is referred to as *breadth*. The degree to which the inner personality—the core of an individual—is penetrated is referred to as *depth*.

Let us represent an individual as a circle and divide that circle into various parts. These parts represent the topics or areas of interpersonal communication, or breadth. Further, visualize the circle and its parts as consisting of concentric inner circles. These would represent the different levels of communication, or the depth (see Figure 14.2). To provide specific examples, the circles are divided into eight topic areas (identified A through H) and five levels of intimacy (represented by the concentric circles).

Note that in circle (a) only three of the topic areas are penetrated. Two are penetrated only to the first level and one is penetrated to the second level. In this type of interaction, three topic areas are talked about and they are discussed at rather superficial levels. This is the type of relationship we might have with an acquaintance. Circle (b) represents a more intense relationship, both broader (here four topics are discussed) and deeper. This is the type of relationship we might have with a friend. In circle (c) we have a still more intense relationship.

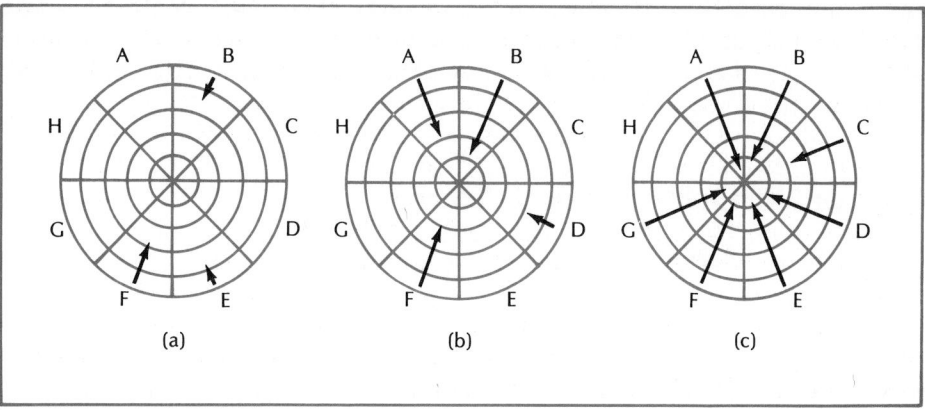

FIGURE 14.2 Social penetration with (a) acquaintance, (b) friend, and (c) intimate.

Here there is considerable breadth (seven of the eight areas are penetrated) and depth (note that most of the areas are penetrated to the deepest levels). This is the type of relationship we might have with a lover, a parent, or a sibling.

Social Penetration

All relationships—friendships, loves, families—may be profitably described in terms of the concepts of breadth and depth, which are central to the theory of *social penetration* developed by Irwin Altman and Dalmas Taylor. In its initial stage a relationship would normally be characterized by narrowness (few topics would be discussed) and shallowness (the topics discussed would be discussed only superficially). If early in a relationship topics are discussed to a depth which would normally be reserved for intimates, we would probably experience considerable discomfort. As already noted (Unit 3, "The Self in Communication"), when intimate disclosures are made early in a relationship, we feel something is wrong with the disclosing individual. As the relationship grows in intensity and intimacy, both the breadth and the depth increase and these increases are seen as comfortable, normal, and natural progressions.

Depenetration

When a relationship begins to deteriorate, the breadth and depth will, in many ways, reverse themselves—a process of *depenetration*. For example, while terminating a relationship, you might eliminate certain topics from your interpersonal interactions and at the same time discuss the remaining topics in less depth. You would, for example, reduce the level of your self-disclosures and reveal less of your innermost feelings. This reversal does not always work, of course. In some instances of relational deterioration, both the breadth and the depth of interaction increase. A good example of this is seen in the film *Making Love*. Here the relationship between Michael Ontkean and Kate Jackson is breaking up because after eight years of marriage he realizes that he is attracted to men. But during the breakup, we see a process of penetration rather than depenetration; they each reveal themselves to each other to a much greater depth and discuss more topic areas than they had previously. Usually, however, relational deterioration is characterized by a decrease in both breadth and depth.

INTERPERSONAL ATTRACTION

In developing relationships, one of the most significant and widely studied variables is that of attraction—what makes us attracted to certain people and not to others, and what makes some people attracted to us and others not so attracted. Research and theory have identified five major factors that account for our attraction to others.

How does interpersonal attractiveness influence your own communication behavior? For example, would you communicate differently if you were talking to Madonna than you would talking to a fellow student? In what ways would these communications differ? Why would these communications differ?

Attractiveness (Physical and Personality)

When we say, "I find that person attractive," we probably mean either that (1) we find that person physically attractive or (2) we find that person's personality or ways of behaving attractive. For the most part we like physically attractive people rather than physically ugly people, and we like people who possess a pleasant personality rather than an unpleasant personality.

Forming Impressions

Generally, we attribute positive characteristics to people we find attractive and negative characteristics to people we find unattractive. If people were asked to predict which qualities a stranger possessed, they would probably predict the possession of positive qualities if they thought the person attractive and negative characteristics if they thought the person unattractive. Numerous studies have supported this commonsense observation. In a Vanderbilt University study, young male psychologists who were training to be therapists responded with greater warmth and supportiveness to attractive women than to unattractive women. These soon-to-be therapists also judged that the less attractive clients would more likely discontinue therapy. Perhaps we have here wishful thinking that might develop into a self-fulfilling prophecy.

In another study, photographs of men and women varying in attractiveness were viewed by both men and women, who were then asked to assess these persons. The more attractive persons were judged to be sexually warmer and more responsive, more sensitive, kinder, more interesting, stronger, more poised, more modest, more sociable, and more outgoing; and to make more competent husbands and wives, have happier marriages, and secure more prestigious jobs. The less attractive persons were judged to make better parents.

When 400 teachers were shown report cards with identical grades but with different pictures attached, the teachers rated the report cards with the attractive students' pictures attached as having higher educational potential, higher IQs, better social relationships with peers, and parents who were more interested in their education.

Proximity

If we look around at the people we find attractive, we will probably find that they are the people who live or work close to us. This is perhaps the one finding that emerges most frequently from the research on interpersonal attraction. In one of the most famous studies, Leon Festinger, Stanley Schachter, and Kurt Back studied friendships in a student housing development. They found that the development of friendships was greatly influenced by the distance between the units in which the people lived. The closer the students' rooms were to each other, the better the chances that they would become friends. The people who became friends were those who had the greatest opportunity to interact with each other.

As might be predicted, physical distance is most important in the early stages of interaction. For example, during the first days of school, proximity (in class or in dormitories) is especially important. It decreases (but always remains significant) as the opportunity increases to interact with those farther away.

Why Proximity Works

When we attempt to discover why physical closeness influences interpersonal attraction, we can think of many reasons. We seem to have positive expectations of people and consequently want to like or be attracted to those we must find ourselves near. Proximity also allows us the opportunity to get to know the other person. We may come to like people we know because, being better able to predict their behavior, we find them less frightening to us than complete strangers.

Still another approach argues that *mere exposure* to others leads us to develop positive feelings for them. In one study, women who were supposedly participating in a taste experiment were exposed to particular people throughout the course of the experiment. The subjects were exposed to some people ten times, to others five times, to others two times, to others one time, and to others not at all. The subjects did not talk with these other people and had never seen them before this experiment. The subjects were then asked to rate each other person in terms of how much they liked him or her. The results showed that they rated highest the persons they had seen ten times, next highest those they had seen five times, and so on down the line. How can we account for these results except by mere exposure?

Of course, if our initial interaction with a person is unpleasant, repeated exposure may not increase attraction. Mere exposure seems to work when the initial interaction is favorable or neutral; in these cases exposure increases attraction. When the initial interaction is negative, however, repeated exposure may actually decrease attraction.

Connected to this "mere exposure" concept is the finding that the greater the contact between people, the less they are prejudiced against each other. For example, whites and blacks living in the same housing development become less prejudiced against each other as a result of living together and interacting.

Reinforcement

We tend to like people who reward or reinforce us. The reward or reinforcement may be social, as with compliments or praise, or it may be material, as with gifts of the suitor who eventually wins the hand of the beloved.

But reward can backfire. When overdone, reward loses its effectiveness and may even lead to negative responses. The people who reward us constantly soon become too sweet to take, and we come to discount whatever they say. Also, if the reward is to be effective, it must be perceived as genuine and not motivated by selfish concerns.

The order in which reinforcements occur and whether or not they are coupled with negative evaluations also affects their influence. Researchers investigated this issue by having subjects "overhear" conversations by others about themselves. Four conditions were established, each consisting of overhearing seven conversations. In the positive condition, all seven conversations the subjects overheard were positive. In the negative condition, all conversations were negative. In the negative-positive condition, the first three conversations were negative and the last four were positive. In the positive-negative condition, the first three conversations were positive and the last four were negative. After overhearing these conversations, the subjects were asked to indicate the extent to which they liked the "gossiping" individual on a scale ranging from -10 to $+10$. The most-liked persons were those who first spoke negatively and then positively; that is, the negative-positive condition produced the greatest amount of attraction ($+7.67$). The next most-liked persons were those in the positive condition ($+6.42$). The third most-liked were the persons in the negative condition ($+2.52$). The least-liked were the persons who first spoke positively and then negatively, the positive-negative condition ($+0.87$).

Gain-Loss Theory

Elliot Aronson has proposed that a *gain-loss theory* can account for such findings as these. Basically, the theory states that increases in rewards have greater impact than constant, invariant rewards. We like a person more if that person's liking (reward) for us increases over time than if that person constantly rewards us indiscriminately. This holds true even if the number of rewards given by the person who always likes us are greater than those given by the person whose liking for us increases over time. Conversely, decreases in rewards have a greater impact than constant punishments; we dislike the person whose rewards decrease over time more than the person who always punishes us or who never has anything good to say about us.

Intuitively this seems satisfying. We seem to have a greater attraction for the person who changes his or her mind toward us, as long as the final evaluation is positive. The person who first evaluates us positively and then negatively may well be perceived as a traitor—an ally who later deserts us—and as such is even less liked than the person who speaks consistently of us in the negative.

Rewarding Others

We also become attracted to those we reward. We come to like people for whom we do favors. Although our initial reaction might be to say that we give rewards to people because we like them—and this is certainly true—the reverse is also true. It seems that we justify going out of our way by convincing ourselves that the person is worth the effort and is a likable person. In an experiment in which subjects won money, one-third were asked to give it back as a special favor to the experimenter, one-third were asked to give it back for the psychology department's research fund, and one-third were not asked to return it at all. The subjects were later tested on how much they liked the experimenter. The subjects who gave back the money to the experimenter indicated the greatest liking for him. By liking him, the subjects justified giving back the money they had won. You may have noticed this same phenomenon in your own interactions. You have probably increased your liking for someone after buying that person an expensive present or going out of your way to do a special favor. In these and numerous similar instances, we justify our behavior by believing that the person was worth our efforts; otherwise, we would have to admit to being poor judges of character and to spending our money or our effort on people who do not deserve it.

Similarity

If people could construct their mates, the mates would look, act, and think very much like themselves. By being attractive to people like ourselves, we are in effect validating ourselves, saying to ourselves that we are worthy of being liked and are attractive. Although there are exceptions, we generally like people who are similar to us in nationality, race, ability, physical characteristics, intelligence, attitudes, and so on. We are often attracted to mirror images of ourselves.

The Matching Hypothesis

If you were to ask a group of friends, "To whom are you attracted?" they would probably name very attractive people; in fact, they would probably name the most attractive people they know. But if we were to observe these friends, we would find that they go out with and establish relationships with people who are quite similar to themselves in physical attractiveness. The *matching hypothesis* describes such behaviors: Although we may be attracted to the most physically attractive people, we date and mate with people who are similar to ourselves in physical attractiveness. In some cases, however, we notice discrepancies; we notice an old person dating a younger partner or an unattractive person with a handsome partner. In these cases, we will probably find that the less attractive partner possesses some quality that compensates for the lack of physical attractiveness. Prestige, money, intelligence, power, and various personality characteristics are obvious examples of qualities that may compensate for being less physically attractive.

Attitude Similarity

Similarity is especially important when it comes to attitudes. We are particularly attracted to people who have attitudes and preferences similar to our own. The more significant the attitude, the more important the similarity. Marriages between people with great attitude dissimilarities are more likely to end in divorce than are marriages between people who are very much alike.

Complementarity

Although many people would argue that "birds of a feather flock together," others would argue that "opposites attract." This latter approach follows the principle of complementarity.

Take, for example, the individual who is extremely dogmatic. Would this person be attracted to people who are high in dogmatism or to those who are low in dogmatism? The similarity principle predicts that this person will be attracted to those who are like him or her (that is, high in dogmatism), while the complementarity principle predicts that this person will be attracted to those who are unlike him or her (that is, low in dogmatism).

People are attracted to dissimilar others only in certain situations. For example, the submissive student may get along especially well with an aggressive teacher rather than a submissive one but may not get along with an aggressive spouse. The dominant wife may get along with a submissive husband but may not relate well to submissive colleagues.

Theodore Reik, in *A Psychologist Looks at Love,* argues that we fall in love with people who possess characteristics that we do not possess and that we actually envy. For example, the introvert who is displeased with being shy might be attracted to an extravert.

Intuition supports both complementarity and similarity, and certainly neither can be ruled out as a significant influence on interpersonal attraction. The experimental evidence, however, favors similarity. Glenn Wilson and David Nias, in *The Mystery of Love,* review evidence demonstrating that similarity in attitudes, physical attractiveness, self-esteem, race, religion, age, and social class increase attraction and therefore support the similarity theory.

Complementarity finds less experimental support. The most obvious instance of complementarity is heterosexuality; most persons are heterosexual. One interesting support for complementarity appears in the finding that when one person in a relationship is "witty," the other person is "placid." It seems so much easier being witty with a placid listener than with a competing wit—something we have probably all observed in our own interpersonal relationships.

SUMMARY

1. In a componential definition of interpersonal communication, we identify the components or elements in the interpersonal communication act.

2. In a relational or dyadic definition, interpersonal communication is defined as communication that takes place between two persons who have a clearly established relationship.

3. In a developmental definition, interpersonal communication is defined as a development or progression from impersonal communication at one extreme to personal communication at the other. Interpersonal communication is distinguished from other types in that (1) predictions are based on psychological rather than sociological data; (2) predictions are based on explanatory knowledge of each other; and (3) behaviors are based on personally established rules.

4. Relationships are established in stages. At least the following five stages should be recognized: contact, involvement, intimacy, deterioration, and dissolution.

5. Relationships vary in breadth (the number of topics talked about) and depth (the degree of "personalness" to which the topics are pursued).

6. Social penetration theory holds that as relationships develop, the breadth and depth increase. When a relationship deteriorates, the breadth and depth will often (but not always) decrease, a process referred to as depenetration.

7. Interpersonal attraction depends on at least five factors: attractiveness (physical and personality); proximity (physical closeness); reinforcement (we are attracted to those who reward us but also to those whom we reward); similarity (especially attitudinal); and complementarity.

8. Gain-loss theory holds that increases in rewards have greater impact than constant, invariant rewards; conversely, decreases in rewards have a greater impact than constant punishments.

9. The matching hypothesis holds that we mate with and date those who are about equivalent to ourselves in physical attractiveness.

SOURCES

For a comprehensive overview of interpersonal communication, see my *Interpersonal Communication Book*, 4th ed. (New York: Harper & Row, 1986), and James C. McCroskey, Virginia P. Richmond, and Roberta A. Stewart, *One on One: The Foundations of Interpersonal Communication* (Englewood Cliffs, N.J.: Prentice-Hall, 1986). On definitions of interpersonal communication, see Gerald R. Miller, "The Current State of Theory and Research in Interpersonal Communication," *Human Communication Research* 4 (winter 1978): 164–178, and Art Bochner, "On Taking Ourselves Seriously: An Analysis of Some Persistent Problems and Promising Directions in Interpersonal Research," *Human Communication Research* 4 (winter 1978): 179–191.

On models of relationship development, see my "Teaching as Relational Development," in *Communicating in College Classrooms (New Directions for Teaching and Learning)*, No. 26, June 1986 (San Francisco, Calif.: Jossey-Bass, 1986), pp. 51–60. On social penetration, see Irwin Altman and Dalmas Taylor, *Social Penetration: The Development of Interpersonal Relationships* (New York: Holt, Rinehart and Winston, 1973), and Leslie A. Baxter, "Relationship Disengagement: An Examination of the Reversal Hypothesis," *Western Journal of Speech Communication* 47 (spring 1983): 85–98.

UNIT 15
RELATIONSHIP DEVELOPMENT AND DETERIORATION

LEARNING GOALS

After completing this unit, you should be able to

1. identify and explain at least four reasons for relationship development
2. identify and explain the six stages in initiating relationships
3. identify at least six suggestions for nonverbally initiating the first encounter
4. identify at least six suggestions for verbally initiating the first encounter
5. explain the distinction between gradual and sudden deterioration and give examples of each
6. identify and explain at least five reasons for relationship deterioration
7. discuss at least five changes in communication that take place during relationship deterioration

In this unit we consider the development and deterioration of interpersonal relationships. First, we consider relationship development: its motivations and the process of and guidelines for initiating relationships. Second, we consider relationship deterioration: its nature and causes, and the changes in communication that take place during relationship deterioration.

RELATIONSHIP DEVELOPMENT

There is probably nothing as important to us as contact with another human being. So important is this contact that when it is absent for prolonged periods, depression sets in, self-doubt surfaces, and one finds it difficult to conduct even the basics of daily living. Desmond Morris, in *Intimate Behaviour,* notes that contact with other human beings is so important that our culture has established all sorts of substitutes to compensate for its occasional absence. People often visit professional contact persons such as doctors, nurses, and masseurs not because of some physical ailment, but because of the need for contact.

Each relationship is unique, and similarly, each of us pursues a relationship for unique reasons. Yet amid all this diversity, a few general principles may be offered. First, we examine some general reasons for the development of most relationships. Second, we discuss the process of initiating relationships, the stages one would go through, and some nonverbal and verbal suggestions for making the first encounter more effective.

Reasons for Relationship Development

Four general reasons for relationship development may be identified.

Lessening Loneliness

Contact with another human being helps to alleviate loneliness. At times we experience loneliness because we are physically alone, although being physically alone does not necessarily produce loneliness. At other times we are lonely because, although we may be with another person, we have a need for close contact—sometimes physical, sometimes emotional, and most often both—that is not being fulfilled.

Some people, in an attempt to alleviate loneliness, seek always to surround themselves with numerous acquaintances. Sometimes this helps; often it only serves to make the loneliness all the more real. One close relationship usually works much better. Most of us know this, and that is why we seek to establish relationships.

Securing Stimulation

Human beings need stimulation; if they are not stimulated, they withdraw, and sometimes they die. Human contact provides one of the best ways to be stimulated. We are composites of many different dimensions, and all our dimensions need stimulation. We are intellectual creatures, and so we need intellectual stimulation: We talk with people about ideas, attend classes, and argue about different interpretations of a film or novel. We thus exercise our reasoning, analytical, and interpretative abilities, and in doing so we improve, sharpen, and expand them. We are also physical creatures who need physical stimulation. We need to touch and be touched, hold and be held, and look at people and have them look at us.

Finally, we are also emotional creatures who need emotional stimulation. We need to laugh and cry, feel hope and surprise, and experience warmth and affection. We need exercise for our emotional as well as our intellectual capacities.

Acquiring Self-Knowledge

It is largely through contact with other human beings that we learn about ourselves. In the discussion of self-awareness I pointed out that we see ourselves in part through the eyes of others. If our friends see us as warm and generous, for example, we will probably also see ourselves as warm and see ourselves as warm and generous. Our self-perceptions are greatly influenced by what we believe others think of us. Contact with others enables us to see ourselves in a somewhat different way, from a somewhat different perspective.

Maximizing Pleasures, Minimizing Pains

The most general reason to establish relationships, and one that could include all the others, is that we seek human contact so that our pleasures may be maximized and our pains minimized. We need to share with others both our good fortune and our emotional or physical pain. Perhaps this latter need began in childhood, when we ran to mother so that she could kiss our wounds or tell us everything was all right. We now find it difficult to run to mother, and so we go to others, generally to friends who will provide us with the same kind of consolation mother did.

Initiating Relationships: The First Encounter

Perhaps the most difficult and yet the most important aspect of relationship development is the process of initiating relationships—meeting the person, presenting yourself, and somehow moving to another stage, which, in our earlier model, would be to exit or to progress to a stage that is somewhat more intimate. Murray Davis, in *Intimate Relations*, notes that the first encounter consists of six steps. In addition to presenting these six steps, we will consider some communication guidelines or principles that should help make the first encounter more effective.

Examine the Qualifiers   Examine the *qualifiers*—those qualities that make the individual you wish to encounter an appropriate choice. Some qualifiers are obvious, such as beauty, style of clothes, jewelry, and the like; others are hidden, such as personality, health, wealth, talent, intelligence, and the like. These qualifiers tell us something about who the person is and help us to decide if we wish to pursue this initial encounter.

Determine Clearance   Try to determine if the person is available for the type of encounter you are interested in—if dating, for example, is the person wearing a wedding ring? Does the person seem to be waiting for someone else?

Open the Encounter   Open the encounter, both nonverbally and verbally. Davis suggests that we look for two things: (1) a topic that will interest the other person (and you) and that could be drawn out of the opener, and (2) indications by the other person of a readiness to engage in a more protracted encounter. If yes/no answers are given to your questions or if eye contact is not maintained, then you have some pretty good indication that this person is not open to an extended encounter with you at this time. If, on the other hand, the person responds at length or asks you questions in return, then you have some positive feedback that says "continue."

An Integrating Topic   An integrating topic is one that will interest the other person and you and will serve to integrate or unite the two of you. Generally, such topics are found through an analysis of free information and questions and answers. Look, therefore, for *free information*—information about a person that you can see or that is dropped into the conversation. For example, a college ring or jacket, a political button, or a uniform will tell you something about the person and will suggest a possible topic of conversation. Similarly, a casual remark may include the person's occupation or area of study or sports interests—all of which can be used as take-off points for further interaction. Look and listen, therefore, for the free information that will enable you to continue the interaction and that will suggest additional communication topics. Further, ask questions (none that are too prying, of course) to discover more about this person and to communicate your interest.

Create a Favorable Impression   Display what is called a "come-on" self—that part of you that is inviting, engaging, and otherwise interesting to another person. Display a part of you that will make the other person want to continue the encounter.

Establish a Second Meeting   If you and your new acquaintance seem to be getting along, then a second meeting should be established. This may be a very general type of meeting—"Do you always eat here on Fridays?"—or a very specific type of meeting—"How about going to the beach next Saturday?"

During this first encounter, put into operation all the interpersonal communication principles you have already acquired. Here are some additional suggestions geared specifically to this first encounter. Although we distinguish between nonverbal and verbal encounters, recognize that these must be integrated into any effective encounter.

The Nonverbal Encounter

Nonverbal communication concerns all aspects of yourself that sends messages to another person. On the basis of these messages, the other person forms a quick but lasting impression of you.

1. Establish eye contact first. The eyes communicate awareness of and interest in the other person.
2. While maintaining eye contact, smile and further signal your interest in and positive response to this other person.
3. Concentrate your focus. The rest of the room should be nonverbally shut off from awareness. Be careful, however, that you do not focus so directly that you make the person uncomfortable.
4. Establish physical closeness or at least lessen the physical distance between the two of you. Approach, but not to the point of discomfort, so that your interest in making contact is obvious.
5. Maintain an open posture. Throughout this nonverbal encounter, maintain a posture that communicates a willingness to enter into interaction with the other person. Hands crossed over the chest or clutched around your stomach are exactly the kinds of posture that you want to avoid. These often signal an unwillingness to let others enter your space.
6. Respond visibly. Assuming that your nonverbal communication is returned, respond to it visibly with a smile, a head nod, or a wink.
7. Reinforce positive behaviors—what the other person does to signal interest and a reciprocal willingness to make contact. Respond positively; again, nod, smile, or somehow indicate your favorable reaction.
8. Avoid overexposure. Nonverbal communication works to establish contact or to signal interest, but it can cause problems if it is excessive or if it is not followed by more explicit communication. Consequently, if you intend to make verbal contact, do so after a relatively short time or try another time.

The Verbal Encounter

1. Introduce yourself. Try to avoid trite opening lines: Don't become identified with the line "Haven't I seen you here before?" Actually, these openers are merely types of phatic communion, but many people do not understand this, so it is probably best simply to say, "Hi, my name is Pat."
2. Focus the conversation on the other person. Get the other person talking about himself or herself; no one enjoys talking about any topic more than this one. Also, you will gain an opportunity to learn something about the person you want to get to know.
3. Exchange favors and rewards. Compliment the other person; be sincere but complimentary and positive. If you can't find anything to compliment, then you should probably reassess your interest in this person.
4. Be energetic. No one likes a lethargic, slow-moving, nondynamic person.

Demonstrate your high energy level by responding facially with appropriate affect, smiling, talking in a varied manner, being flexible with your body posture and gestures, asking questions as appropriate, and otherwise demonstrating that you are really "there."

5. Stress the positives. Positiveness contributes to a good first impression simply because we are more attracted to a positive than to a negative person.

6. Avoid negative or too intimate self-disclosures. Enter a relationship gradually and gracefully. Disclosures should come slowly and along with reciprocal disclosures. Anything too intimate or too negative early in the relationship will create a negative image. If you cannot resist self-disclosing, try to stick to the positives and to those matters that would not be considered overly intimate.

7. Establish commonalities. Seek to discover in your interaction those things you have in common with the other person—attitudes, interests, personal qualities, third parties, places, and in fact anything that will stress a connection.

RELATIONSHIP DETERIORATION

The other half of relationship development is, obviously, deterioration—the relationship's decline and possible termination. Here the nature of relationship deterioration is defined, some of its major causes are identified, and the communication changes that take place during relationship deterioration are explored.

The Nature of Relationship Deterioration

By *relational deterioration* I mean the weakening of the bonds that hold people together. At times a relationship may be weakened only mildly; it may appear normal to outsiders, but the participants can see clearly that it has weakened. The obvious extreme of relational deterioration is the termination of the relationship. In between these two extremes are an infinite number of variations. Relational deterioration, then, exists on a continuum from something a little bit less than intimacy to total separation and dissolution.

Gradual and Sudden Deterioration

The process of deterioration may be gradual or sudden. Murray Davis, in *Intimate Relations*, uses the terms *passing away* to designate gradual deterioration and *sudden death* to designate immediate or sudden deterioration. An example of passing away occurs when one of the parties develops close ties with a new intimate and this new relationship gradually pushes out the old intimate. An example of sudden death occurs when one or both of the parties break a rule that was essential to the relationship (for example, the rule of fidelity), and both realize that since the rule has been broken, the relationship cannot be sustained and, in fact, must be terminated.

Some Advantages of Breaking Up

At times a relationship may be unproductive for one or both parties, and a breakup is often the best thing that could happen. Such a termination may provide a period for the individuals to regain their independence and self-reliance. Some relationships are so absorbing that there is little time available for reflection about oneself, others, and the relationship itself. Some distance often helps.

One of the major problems with some relationships is that they prevent one or both parties from developing new relationships, becoming involved with new intimates, or developing new friends and associations. Terminating such a relationship provides the individuals with opportunities to develop these new associations and to explore different types of relationships with different types of people.

What one person finds a benefit, another may find a burden. The freedom to explore new relationships may be viewed by one person as a challenging and exciting opportunity; to another it may be threatening and frightening. And so it would be foolhardy to specify authoritatively the benefits to specific people in specific relationships. The only point I will want to make here is that deterioration need not have only negative consequences. For the most part, it is up to the individual to draw out of any decaying relationship some good, positive characteristics and some learning that can be used later on.

Some Causes of Relationship Deterioration

The causes of relationship deterioration are as numerous as the individuals involved, so we cannot pretend to treat them exhaustively here. We can, however, examine some of the major causes. We begin by looking at some of the reasons relationships are developed and seeing how changes in these factors may lead to deterioration. We can then examine additional factors that create problems for relationships and that often lead to deterioration.

Reasons for Establishing the Relationship Have Diminished

Earlier we noted some factors that are important in establishing relationships. When these are no longer operative or when they are changed drastically, the relationships may deteriorate.

Loneliness Is Not Reduced   When loneliness is no longer lessened by the relationship, or when one or both parties experience loneliness for prolonged or frequent periods, the relationship may well be on the road to decay.

Stimulation Is Weak   If relationships are established and maintained in part because they are stimulating to the individuals, then relationships will decay when that stimulation is removed or significantly lessened. This is often the case in marriages. Before marriage the couple said, "I love you," held each other's hands, hugged each other, and otherwise demonstrated their affection for each other. After some years of marriage that emotional and physical stimulation often fades. Such shows of affection were among the important reasons

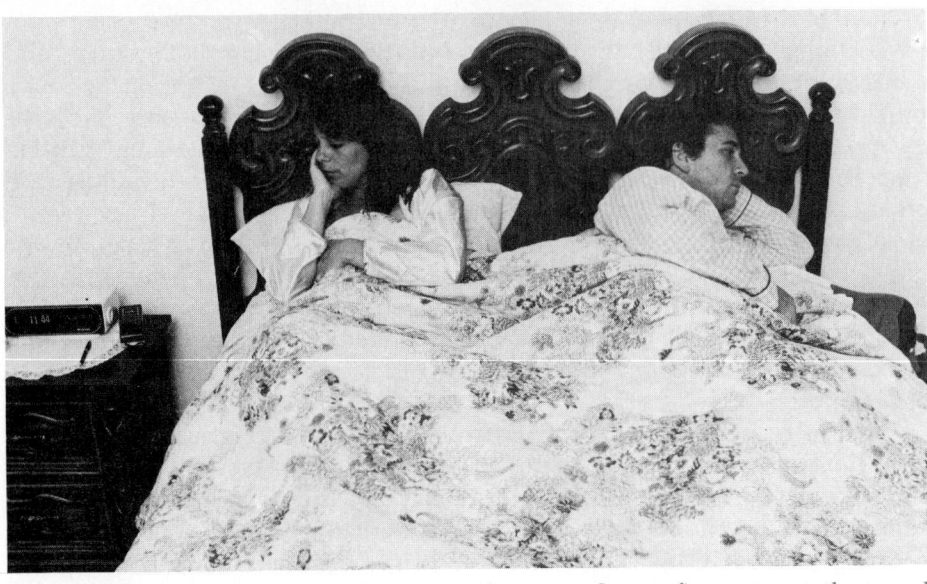

Relationships deteriorate for a wide variety of reasons. Survey five or ten students and compile a list of reasons why friendship or romantic relationships deteriorate. Are the reasons for friendship and romantic relationship deterioration similar? Different? In what ways are they similar? In what ways are they different? Do you think these reasons would be very different for a much older group? For a much younger group? Do men and women give the same or different reasons for relationship deterioration?

the relationship was established and maintained; allowing them to become just memories jeopardizes the relationship.

Self-Knowledge and Self-Growth Are Insufficient   We are complex creatures; we need constantly to learn more about ourselves and grow, and we often establish a relationship to these ends. When we cease to gain self-knowledge and to grow, the relationship is not fulfilling one of its major functions and may soon show signs of decay.

Attractiveness Has Faded   The reason most often mentioned for relational deterioration is that the initial attractiveness that brought the individuals together is gone—the pot-belly, the baldness, the sagging buttocks, the lines in the face, the extra weight, and so on all contribute to the loss of mutual attractiveness. Similarly, in long-term relationships people have a tendency to ignore or drop the social niceties they thought essential when the relationship was in its formative stages. The common courtesies—the phone call to say "I'll be late," the card on a birthday or anniversary, the flowers for no reason at all—are often forgotten or considered unimportant, and this attitude contributes to the loss of attractiveness. People who assume that physical and personality attractiveness are no longer important after 5, 10, or 20 years of a relationship are probably fooling themselves. They may be attempting to find an excuse for sloppiness, for not exercising, for not keeping to a diet, or for not being considerate. Or perhaps they are trying to convince themselves that their partners still desire them despite the physical changes. Perhaps they are right—if so, it is probably in spite of themselves.

Research tells us that men who place a great deal of emphasis on physical attractiveness are less likely to stay in a relationship a long time. Such men quit a relationship when the physical attractiveness of their partners—a major contributor to the development of their relationship—fades. Further, when relationships break up, it is the more attractive partner who leaves. There is no denying the power of attractiveness in the development of relationships and the influence of its loss in the deterioration of relationships.

Intimacy Claims

At times intimacy claims may create problems (or at least underlie some relationship conflicts). In many relationships—especially those of considerable intensity—the members make extensive intimacy claims on each other. Such claims may include, for example, expectations that the partner will sympathize and empathize, attend to self-disclosures with total absorption, or share the other's preferences with equal intensity. These intimacy claims often restrict personal freedom and take the form of possessiveness, when one member of the relationship becomes defined (functionally as well as verbally) as a part of the other person—"*my* woman," "*my* husband," "*my* child." Intense intimacy claims often put people under pressure that some find difficult to live with on a day-to-day basis. To be always responsive, always sympathetic, always loving, and always attentive is more than many people can manage.

Third-Party Relationships

Relationships are established and maintained largely because within them, pleasures are maximized and pains are minimized. When this ceases to be the case, the relationship stands little chance of survival. The reason, I think, is obvious: These needs are so great that when they are not met within the existing relationship, their satisfaction and fulfillment will be sought elsewhere. When a new relationship serves these needs better, the old relationship may deteriorate. At times the new partner may be a romantic interest (more on this under "Sex"); at other times it may be a parent or, frequently, a child. When an individual's needs for affection or attention were once supplied by the other party in the primary relationship and are now supplied by a friend or a child, the primary relationship is in for alteration and sometimes deterioration.

Relational Changes

Relational deterioration may be encouraged through various relational changes in one or both parties. *Psychological changes* such as the development of different intellectual interests or incompatible attitudes may create relational problems. *Behavioral changes* such as preoccupation with business or schooling may strain the relationship and create problems. *Status changes* may also create difficulties for a couple. In F. Scott Fitzgerald's *Tender Is the Night*, we see how status changes can create problems. Here Dick Diver, a young psychiatrist, and Nicole Warren, a wealthy and beautiful patient, fall in love. While Nicole is mentally ill and in need of Dick's care, the relationship flourishes for both; each apparently serves the needs of the other. But, as Nicole gets stronger, Dick gets weaker; the relationship changes drastically and ultimately deteriorates.

Undefined Expectations

At times conflicts seem to center on "trivial" issues such as who will do the dishes and the wash, who will cook, who will use the new car and who will use the old one. To an outsider these issues seem unimportant, but recall that in these conflicts the content is often not the true focus of the conflict; often such conflicts center on relational dimensions (see Unit 16). The fact that there are frequent conflicts over who will do the dishes may mean that the individuals have problems that go beyond the dishes and perhaps center on more significant issues, such as who is the boss or whose time is less valuable and should therefore be devoted to household chores. Often conflicts over such minor issues mask resentment and hostility concerning some general dissatisfaction or unhappiness. At times these conflicts are generated because some other more significant conflict has not been adequately resolved and the ill feeling one person feels toward the other has not yet dissipated.

Sometimes the expectations each person has of the other may be unrealistic, and when reality enters the relationship, conflict may ensue. This type of situation often occurs early in a relationship when, for example, the individuals think that they will want to spend all their time together. When it is discovered that neither one does, each resents this "lessening" of feeling in the other. The resolution of such conflicts lies not so much in meeting these expectations as in demonstrating that the original ones were unrealistic and in substituting satisfying and attainable expectations.

Sex

Few sexual relationships are free of sexual problems and differences that cannot be resolved easily and that often generate conflicts of considerable magnitude. In fact, sexual problems rank among the top three problems in almost all studies of newlyweds. When the same couples are surveyed later in their relationship, the sexual problems have not gone away; they are just talked about less. Apparently the individuals resign themselves to living with the problems. In one survey, for example, 80 percent of the respondents identified their marriages as either "very happy" or "happy," but some 90 percent of these said that they had sexual problems.

Although sexual frequency is not related to relational breakdown, sexual satisfaction is. Research clearly shows that it is the quality and not the quantity of a sexual relationship that is crucial. When the quality is poor, sexual affairs outside the primary relationship may be sought. And although there is much talk of sexual freedom within and outside primary relationships, the research is again clear: Extrarelational affairs contribute significantly to breakups for all couples, whether married or cohabiting. Interestingly enough, even "open relationships"—ones in which the individuals permit each other sexual freedom outside the primary relationship—create problems and are more likely to break up than the traditional "closed" relationship.

Work

Unhappiness with work often leads to difficulties with relationships. Recent research reported by Philip Blumstein and Pepper Schwartz demonstrates that problems at and with work cannot be separated from one's relationships. Dissatisfaction with work is often associated with relationship breakup. This is true for all types of couples. With heterosexual couples (both married and cohabiting), if the man is disturbed over the woman's job—for example, if she earns a great deal more than he does or she devotes a great deal of time to the job—the relationship is in for considerable trouble, and this is true whether the relationship is in its early stages or is a well-established one. Often the man expects the woman to work but does not reduce his expectations concerning her household responsibilities. The man becomes resentful if the woman does not fulfill these expectations, and the woman becomes resentful if she takes on both outside work and full household duties. It is a no-win situation, and the relationship suffers as a result.

Although the stability of a relationship is not hampered by the husband's doing little or no housework, it is hampered when the husband perceives that the wife is doing less than he thinks she should. Another instance of inequality in heterosexual couples concerns ambition. Women want their partners to be ambitious in their work; men who are not ambitious are less appreciated by their partners, and their relationship loses stability. However, men do not appreciate ambitious women; relationships with ambitious women are less stable than those with unambitious women. Further, it is found that the more ambitious, more work-devoted partner is the one more likely to leave the relationship.

A further work-related issue that contributes to relationship dissolution is the amount of time couples spend together. Blumstein and Schwartz observe, "Spending too much time apart is a hallmark of couples who do not stay together." If couples take separate vacations, meet with different friends, eat separately, and spend a great deal of time at work and away from home, their relationships are less likely to survive. Time spent away from each other is both a cause and an effect of relationship deterioration: The more time spent apart, the more a relationship tends to deteriorate, and as the relationship deteriorates, we feel less desire to spend time together and so look for other ways to gain satisfaction. It is a spiral that often grows until the relationship dissolves.

Financial Difficulties

In surveys of problems among couples, financial difficulties loom large. Money is perhaps the most taboo topic for couples beginning a relationship, yet it proves to be one of the major problems faced by all couples as they settle into their relationship. One-fourth to one-third of all couples rank money as their primary problem; almost all rank it as one of their major problems.

Perhaps the major reason money is so important in relationships is its close connection with power. Money brings power; this is true in business and in relationships. The person bringing in the most money wields the most power. This person has the final say on, for example, the purchase of expensive items as well as on decisions having nothing to do with money. The power that money brings quickly generalizes to nonfinancial issues as well.

The unequal earnings of men and women create further problems regardless of who earns more. In most relationships, the man earns more money than the woman. Because of this, men possess a disproportionate share of power. This creates, as Shulamith Firestone points out in *The Dialectic of Sex*, a situation in which the woman, because of her lack of power, will often turn to manipulative and underhanded tactics to get what she wants. This type of tactic also generalizes, resulting in a relationship in which dishonesty and deception are the normal modes of interpersonal interaction.

When the woman earns more than the man, the problems are different. Although our society has finally taught women to achieve in business and the professions, it has not taught men to accept this very well, and as a result the higher-earning woman is often resented by the lower-earning man. This is true for both married and cohabiting couples.

Financial difficulties often interact with other relationship dimensions to create further problems. For example, men who earn little or less than their female partners or who worry about not being good providers often avoid sex at payday, when their self-perceived inadequacy is particularly salient. This avoidance feeds back and causes other difficulties, especially when the man is not aware of why he is avoiding sexual intimacy. Often partners perceive this decreased drive as an indication that they are no longer interesting to their mates or that the mates have found someone outside the relationship. Jealousy and suspicion may quickly follow.

Money also creates problems because men and women view it differently. To men, money is power; to women, it is security and independence. To men, money is accumulated to exert power and influence; to women, money is accumulated to achieve security and reduce dependence on others. Conflicts over how the couple's money is to be spent or invested can easily result from such different perceptions.

The most general equation, as Blumstein and Schwartz observe, would be this:

Dissatisfaction with money = dissatisfaction with the relationship

This is true for married and cohabiting heterosexual couples and gay male couples but not for lesbian couples, who seem to care a great deal less about financial matters. This difference has led some researchers to speculate that concern over money and its equation with power and relational satisfaction are largely male attitudes.

Inequitable Distribution of Rewards and Costs

Generally, we stay in relationships that are rewarding, and leave relationships that are punishing. Further, we expect and desire equity in our relationships. Equitable relationships are those in which the rewards and the costs are almost equally distributed between the two individuals; each derives about equal rewards, and each pays or suffers about equal costs. When a relationship becomes inequitable—that is, when one person derives a disproportionate share of the rewards or suffers an excessive share of the costs—the relationship suffers.

Research demonstrates that when partners perceive their relationship to be equitable, they will continue to date, live together, or be married. The partners will be more content with each other and with the relationship and will derive greater satisfaction from the relationship. Sexual fulfillment and relational stability are greater in equitable relationships. When the relationship is not equitable, these benefits are not obtained and the relationship suffers and may well deteriorate.

Commitment

All our relationships are held together, in part, by our degree of commitment, and the strength of the relationship—including its resistance to possible deterioration—is often directly related to the degree of commitment of the individuals. When relationships show signs of deterioration and yet there is still a strong commitment to the relationship—a strong desire to keep the relationship together—the individuals may well surmount the obstacles and reverse the process of deterioration. When their commitment is weak and the individuals see no good reasons for staying together, relational deterioration seems to come faster and stronger.

Financial Commitment   Commitment is closely related to financial considerations. On the one hand, it is only after a couple develops a strong commitment to each other and to the relationship that they will pool their financial resources. "Failure to pool," note Blumstein and Schwartz, "often indicates that couples have not given up their independence and may never have visualized the relationship as lasting into the indefinite future." With cohabitors, who have few legal bonds, the fact that such pooling of finances comes only after a strong commitment has been made clearly illustrates this natural sequence of events. Conversely, the pooling of finances often increases the commitment of the individuals to each other and to the relationship. People may feel committed because they have invested all their money together or because they have established a business or own real estate together.

Temporal Commitment   At other times the commitment is based on time investment. People may feel that since they have lived together for these past 10 or 15 years, all that time would be lost if the relationship were terminated. College students who have dated the same person for three or four years often feel that the time investment has been so great that they might as well continue the relationship, and often allow and encourage the relationship to progress to permanency, perhaps marriage.

Emotional Commitment   Sometimes the commitment is based on emotional investment; so much emotional energy may have been spent on the relationship that the individuals find it difficult even to consider dissolving it. Or people may feel committed because they care for each other and for the relationship, and feel that for all its problems and difficulties, the relationship is more good than bad, more productive than destructive, more pleasurable than painful. This last, it seems, is the kind of commitment that will stem and perhaps reverse relational deterioration.

All these "causes" of relational deterioration are also the effects of relational deterioration. For example, just as the contextual changes may influence the deterioration of a relationship, they may also be an effect of the deterioration. Thus when things start to go sour, the individuals may remove themselves physically from one another in response to the deterioration. This physical separation in turn functions as a cause of further deterioration by driving the individuals farther apart emotionally and psychologically. Similarly, the degree of commitment that the individuals have for each other may lessen as other signs of deterioration manifest themselves. In turn, the lack of commitment may also function as a cause of deterioration in, for example, lessening the need the individuals may feel to resolve conflicts or to leave the channels of communication open.

Communication in Relationship Deterioration

Like relational development, relational deterioration involves unique and specialized communication. Here we describe and analyze some of the ways in which we communicate during relational deterioration. These communication patterns are in part a response to the deterioration; we communicate as we do because of the way we feel our relationship is deteriorating. However, these patterns are also causative; the communication patterns we employ determine largely the fate of our relationship. Seven major patterns that characterize communication during relational deterioration are considered: withdrawal, self-disclosure, supportiveness, deception, evaluative responses, request behaviors, and exchange of favors.

Withdrawal

Perhaps the easiest communication pattern to see is that of a general withdrawal. As Gerald Miller and Malcolm Parks note: "We would expect dissolution to be characterized by both a decrease in the duration of encounters and an increase in the time between encounters." Nonverbally, this withdrawal is seen in the greater space each person seems to require and the ease with which tempers and other signs of disturbance are aroused when that space is encroached upon. When people are close emotionally, they can occupy close physical quarters, but when they are growing apart, they need wider spaces. Other nonverbal signs include the failure to engage in direct eye contact, to look at each other generally, and to touch each other. All these changes seem to be part of the desire to withdraw physically from the emotional pairing.

Verbally, withdrawal is seen in a number of ways. Where once there was a great desire to talk and listen, there is now less desire—perhaps none. At times phatic communion is also severely limited since the individuals do not want any of its regular functions served. At other times, however, phatic communion (or what would appear to be phatic communion) is engaged in as an end in itself. Whereas phatic talk is usually a preliminary to serious conversation, here phatic communion is used as an alternative to or to forestall serious talk. And so people in the throes of dissolution may talk a great deal about insignificant events—the weather, a movie on television, a neighbor down the hall. By focusing on these topics, the individuals are able to avoid confronting the serious issues that might be raised if the silence were to become too unpleasant.

Withdrawal of another kind may be seen, as Mark Knapp notes, in the decrease in similarities in clothing and in the display of "intimate trophies" such as bracelets, photographs, and rings.

Self-Disclosure

Self-disclosing communications decline significantly. Self-disclosure may not be thought worth the effort if the relationship is dying. We only wish to self-disclose to people we feel close to. We may also limit our self-disclosures because we feel that the other person may not accept our disclosures—an essential assumption if disclosures are to be made in the first place.

Supportiveness

Where once supportiveness characterized the relationship, defensiveness is now more prevalent. In many deteriorating relationships, one party blames the other; neither wants to assume the blame for the failure of the relationship, and it seems difficult to believe that no one really caused the breakup. Instead, it is easier to blame the other person. The primary method available for dealing with accusations of blame is defensiveness. We want to protect our egos; we want to continue believing that we are not to blame, that it is not our fault. And perhaps we want especially to believe that we are not the cause of another person's and our own pain.

Deception

Deception increases as relationships break down. Sometimes this takes the form of clear-cut lies that may be used to avoid more arguments over staying out all night, not calling, or being seen in the wrong place with the wrong person. At other times lies may be used because of some feeling of shame; we do not want the other person to think less of us even though we fully realize that the relationship is deteriorating. Perhaps we want to save the relationship and do not want to add another obstacle. At other times, although we may wish to see the relationship terminated, we do not want to appear to be the cause of the problem. So we lie. Sometimes the deception takes the form of avoidance—the lie of omission. We talk about everything we did last night except the crux of the difficulty. Whether by omission or commission, deception runs high in relationships that are deteriorating. One of the problems with this is that deception has a way of escalating. And although we may tell ourselves that we lied to protect the other person or to avoid some greater problem (both of which may be true), we have at the same time created a climate, in our own minds and ultimately in the mind of the other person, of distrust, disbelief, and falsity rather than truthfulness.

Evaluative Responses

One of the most obvious communication changes is an increase in negative evaluation and a decrease in positive evaluation. Where once we praised the other's behaviors, talents, or ideas, we now criticize them. Often the behaviors have not changed significantly; what has changed is our way of looking at them. What was once a cute habit now becomes annoying, even repulsive. When we like someone, we seem able to tolerate almost anything; when we dislike someone and want to terminate the relationship, we seem able to tolerate very little. This negative evaluation frequently leads to outright fighting and conflict, and although conflict is not necessarily bad, in relationships that are deteriorating, the conflict is often not resolved. Neither party may care enough to go through the effort of resolving the conflict, so it resurfaces the next day or perhaps escalates into an all-out battle. Seldom does it go away. One of the characteristics of such conflicts is that a great deal of time is needed to resolve them, and the cooling-off period lasts much longer.

Request Behaviors

During relational deterioration, as William Lederer points out, there is a marked change in the types of requests made. When a relationship is deteriorating, there is a decrease in requests for pleasurable behaviors ("Will you fix me my favorite desert? The one with the whipped cream and nuts?" or "Hug me real tight"). At the same time, there is an increase in requests to stop unpleasant or negative behaviors ("Will you stop bragging about your ex-husband's money?" or "Will you stop monopolizing the phone every evening?").

Another symptom is the sometimes gradual, sometimes sudden decrease in the social niceties that accompany requests, a progression from "Would you please make me a cup of coffee, honey?" to "Get me some coffee, will you?" to "Where's my coffee?"

Exchange of Favors

Earlier we noted that one of the main reasons relationships were developed and maintained was that the rewards exceeded the costs. When a relationship deteriorates, the costs begin to exceed the rewards, until a point is reached when the individuals feel that the costs are too high (and the rewards too low), at which point the relationship is terminated. In relational deterioration there is little favor exchange; compliments, once given frequently and sincerely, are now rare. Positive stroking is minimal. Nonverbally, we avoid looking directly at the other, smile seldom, and touch, caress, and hold each other infrequently, if at all.

SUMMARY

1. Relationships develop for a variety of reasons, of which some of the most important are to lessen loneliness, to secure stimulation (intellectual, physical, and emotional), to acquire self-knowledge, and to maximize pleasures and minimize pains.

2. Six steps may be identified in initiating relationships: examining the qualifiers, determining clearance, opening the encounter, introducing an integrating topic, creating a favorable impression, and establishing a second meeting.

3. In initiating relationships, the following nonverbal behaviors are suggested: establish eye contact, signal positive response, concentrate your focus, establish proximity, maintain an open posture, respond visibly, reinforce positive behaviors, and avoid overexposure.

4. In initiating relationships, the following verbal behaviors are suggested: introduce yourself, focus the conversation on the other person, exchange favors and rewards, be energetic, stress the positives, avoid negative or too intimate self-disclosures, and establish commonalities.

5. Relationship deterioration—the weakening of the bonds holding people together—may be gradual or sudden.

6. Among the causes for relationship deterioration are diminution of the reasons for establishing the relationship, intimacy claims, third-party relationships, relational changes, undefined expectations, sex, work, financial difficulties, the inequitable distribution of rewards and costs, and a decrease in commitment.

7. Among the changes in communication that take place during relationship deterioration are general withdrawal, a decrease in self-disclosure, a decrease in supportiveness, an increase in deception, a decrease in positive and an increase in negative evaluative responses, a decrease in requests for pleasurable behaviors and an increase in requests to cease negative ones, and a decrease in the exchange of favors.

SOURCES

For relationship development, see Murray S. Davis, *Intimate Relations* (New York: Free Press, 1973), and Mark L. Knapp, *Interpersonal Communication and Human Relationships* (Boston: Allyn and Bacon, 1984). A thorough and insightful review of research in relationships is provided by Arthur Bochner, "The Functions of Human Communication in Interpersonal Bonding," in Carroll C. Arnold and John Waite Bowers, eds., *Handbook of Rhetorical and Communication Theory* (Boston: Allyn and Bacon, 1984), pp. 544–621. On approaches to studying interpersonal relationships, see Steve Duck and Robin Gilmour, eds., *Personal Relationships. 1: Studying Personal Relationships* (New York: Academic Press, 1981).

For a somewhat different approach, see Donald P. Cushman and Dudley D. Cahn, Jr., *Communication in Interpersonal Relationships* (Albany: State University of New York, 1985).

On communication and relational deterioration, see, for example, Knapp, *Interpersonal Communication and Human Relationships,* and Gerald R. Miller and Malcolm R. Parks, "Communication in Dissolving Relationships," in Steve Duck, ed., *Personal Relationships. 4: Dissolving Personal Relationships* (New York: Academic Press, 1982), pp. 127–154. Loneliness and the loneliness cycle are discussed by Carin Rubenstein and Philip Shaver, *In Search of Intimacy* (New York: Delacorte, 1982). For a thorough discussion of research and theory on loneliness, see Letitia Anne Peplau and Daniel Perlman, eds., *Loneliness: A Sourcebook of Current Theory, Research and Therapy* (New York: Wiley/Interscience, 1982). The connection between loneliness and interpersonal relationships is considered by Daniel Perlman and Letitia Anne Peplau, "Toward a Social Psychology of Loneliness," in *Personal Relationships. 3: Personal Relationships in Disorder,* ed. Steve Duck and Robin Gilmour (New York: Academic Press, 1981), pp. 31–56.

UNIT 16
IMPROVING INTERPERSONAL COMMUNICATION AND CONFLICT MANAGEMENT

LEARNING GOALS

After completing this unit, you should be able to

1. identify and define the five characteristics of effectiveness in a humanistic model of communication
2. define *stroking* and explain its relevance to the concept of positiveness
3. identify and define the five characteristics of effectiveness in a pragmatic model of communication
4. define *self-monitoring* and explain its relationship to interaction management
5. explain the assumptions of social exchange and equity theories as they relate to interpersonal communication
6. identify and define the four suggestions for interpersonal effectiveness deriving from a social exchange approach to communication
7. explain the operation of the eight unproductive methods of conflict resolution identified in this unit
8. identify and explain the five guides to effective conflict management identified in this unit

Interpersonal communication, like any form of behavior, can vary from extremely effective to extremely ineffective. No interpersonal encounter is a total failure or a total success; each could have been worse, but each could have been better. In the first part of this unit we review the characteristics of effective interpersonal communication while emphasizing that each communicative act is different and that any principle or rule must be applied judiciously, with full recognition of the uniqueness of each communication event. These characteristics of effectiveness are considered from three perspectives.

Humanism The first is the humanistic perspective, which stresses openness, empathy, supportiveness, and, in general, qualities that foster meaningful, honest, and satisfying interactions. This approach is in the tradition of humanistic psychology articulated by Abraham Maslow, Gordon Allport, Carl Rogers, and numerous others. This approach begins with the general qualities that philosophers and humanists feel define superior human relationships (for example, honesty, openness, and positiveness). From these general qualities, we then derive specific behaviors that should characterize effective interpersonal communication.

Pragmatism The second is the pragmatic or behavioral perspective, which stresses interaction management and immediacy, and in general, qualities that contribute to achieving a variety of desired goals. This approach derives from the more recent pragmatic approach to communication articulated by such writers as Paul Watzlawick, William Lederer, Don Jackson, and others. (Some of the basic axioms of this pragmatic approach were identified in Unit 2.) This approach starts from specific skills that research finds effective in interpersonal communication, then groups these specific skills into general classes of behaviors (for example, interaction management skills, other-orientation skills).

Social Exchange and Equity The third perspective is that of social exchange and equity theory. This approach is based on an economic model of rewards and costs; it assumes that a relationship is a partnership in which rewards and costs are exchanged. Some patterns of exchange prove productive and others destructive of relationships.

These approaches are not mutually exclusive, but actually complement each other. Each approach has much to recommend it; each contributes substantially to our understanding of interpersonal communication effectiveness. Each provides a clarification of qualities that, put together, will improve interpersonal communication considerably. My goal here is to provide you with a number of insights into interpersonal communication effectiveness so that you may select the guides and insights that seem most helpful in any specific situation. Put differently, my aim is to provide a readily available arsenal of communication guides and principles that will prove useful in a wide variety of communication settings.

A HUMANISTIC APPROACH TO INTERPERSONAL EFFECTIVENESS

In this humanistic (sometimes referred to metaphorically as "soft") approach to interpersonal effectiveness, five general qualities are considered: openness, empathy, supportiveness, positiveness, and equality.

Openness

The quality of *openness* refers to at least three aspects of interpersonal communication. First, effective interpersonal communicators must be open to the people with whom they interact. This does not mean that one should immediately pour out one's entire life history; interesting as that may be, it is not usually very helpful to the communication. Rather, there should be a willingness to "self-disclose," to reveal information about oneself that might normally be kept hidden, provided that such disclosures are appropriate (see Unit 3).

A second aspect of openness refers to the willingness of a communicator to react honestly to incoming stimuli. Silent, uncritical, and immovable psychiatrists may be of some help in a clinical situation, but they are generally boring conversationalists. We want people to react openly to what we say, and we have a right to expect this. Nothing seems worse than indifference; even disagreement seems more welcome, although, of course, there are destructive extremes here too. We demonstrate openness by responding spontaneously and without subterfuge to the communications and the feedback of others.

A third aspect of openness concerns the "owning" of feelings and thoughts. To be open in this sense is to acknowledge that the feelings and thoughts we express are ours and that we bear the responsibility for them; we do not attempt to shift the responsibility for our feelings to others. Arthur Bochner and Clifford Kelly put it this way: "The person who owns his feelings or ideas makes it clear that he takes responsibility for oneself and commitment to others. It is the antithesis of blaming others for the way one feels." Bochner and Kelly advise us not to say, "Isn't this group supposed to listen to people?" but rather, "I feel ignored. I don't think people in this group listen to me."

I-Messages

When we own our feelings and thoughts—when we use "I-messages"— we say in effect, "This is how *I* feel," "This is how *I* see the situation," "This is what *I* think," with the *I* always paramount. Instead of saying, "This discussion is useless," one would say something like, "*I'm* bored by this discussion," "*I* want to talk more about myself," or any other statement that includes reference to the fact that *I* am making an evaluation and not describing objective reality. By including in such statements what the general semanticists call "to me–ness," we make explicit the fact that our feelings are the result of the interaction between the outside reality and our own preconceptions, attitudes, prejudices, and the like.

Empathy

Perhaps the most difficult of all communication qualities to achieve is *empathy* for another individual. *Empathy* was created from Greek roots to translate the German word *Einfühlung,* meaning "feeling with." To empathize with someone is to feel as that person does. As Henry Backrack puts it, empathy refers to "the ability of one person to experientially 'know' what another is experiencing at any given moment, from the latter's frame of reference, through the latter's eyes." To sympathize, on the other hand, is to feel *for* the individual—to feel sorry for the person, for example. To empathize is to feel *as* the individual feels—to be in the same shoes and to feel the same feelings in the same way.

If we are able to empathize with people, we are in a better position to understand, for example, their motivations and past experiences, their present feelings and attitudes, and their hopes and expectations for the future. Empathy enables one to understand, emotionally and intellectually, what the other person is experiencing. This empathic understanding in turn better enables the individual to adjust his or her communications—what is said, how it is said, what is to be avoided, if and when silence is to be preferred, whether self-disclosures should be made, and so on. In fact, C. Truax includes one's communication ability as part of the definition of empathy. "Accurate empathy," writes Truax, from a psychotherapist's point of view, "involves both the sensitivity to current feelings and the verbal facility to communicate this understanding in a language attuned to the client's own feelings."

More difficult than defining empathy is describing or advancing ways to increase our empathic abilities. Perhaps the first step is to avoid evaluating the other person's behaviors. If we evaluate them as right or wrong, good or bad, we will see their behaviors through these labels and will overlook a great deal that might not be consistent with these labels. Therefore, resist the temptation to evaluate, judge, interpret, and criticize. It is not that these responses are "wrong," but merely that they often get in the way of understanding. Focus on understanding. Second, the more we know about a person—her or his desires, experiences, abilities, fears, and so on—the more we will be able to see what that person sees and feel as that person feels. Try to understand the reasons and motivations that contribute to making the person feel as he or she does. Even if these reasons and motivations may appear illogical or self-destructive to you, you need to understand them if you are to achieve a meaningful degree of empathy with the other person. If you have difficulty understanding the perspective of the other, ask questions, seek clarification, and encourage the person to talk. Third, try to experience what the other person is feeling from his or her point of view. Playing the other's role in your mind (or even out loud) can help you see the world a little more as the other person does.

Supportiveness

An effective interpersonal relationship is one in which there is supportiveness—a concept that owes much of its formulation to the work of Jack Gibb. Open and empathic communication cannot survive in an unsupportive atmosphere. Supportiveness is demonstrated and fostered by our being (1) descriptive rather than evaluative, (2) spontaneous rather than strategic, and (3) provisional rather than certain.

Descriptiveness

An atmosphere that is descriptive rather than evaluative leads to supportiveness. When we perceive a communication as being a request for information or a description of some event, we generally do not perceive it as threatening. We are not being challenged and have no need to defend ourselves. On the other hand, a communication that is judgmental or evaluative often leads us to become defensive, to back off, and to erect some kind of barrier between ourselves and the evaluator. This is not to imply that all evaluative communications elicit a defensive response. Positive evaluations are often responded to without defensiveness and in fact with all sorts of positive reactions. Even here, however, recall that the very fact of someone's having the power, the knowledge, or the "right" to evaluate us in any way (even if positively) may lead us to feel uneasy and perhaps defensive. Perhaps we anticipate that the next evaluation may not be so positive. In a similar way, negative evaluations do not always elicit a defensive response. The aspiring actor who wants to improve and perfect technique often welcomes negative evaluations.

Generally, however, an evaluative atmosphere leads people to become more defensive than would a descriptive atmosphere. In being descriptive, Toni Brougher, in *A Way with Words*, advises that we describe (1) what happened—"I lost the promotion," (2) how we feel—"I feel miserable and I feel I've failed," and (3) how this relates to the other person—"Would you mind if we went to the city tonight? I need to forget the job and everything about it." Further, Brougher advises us to avoid accusations or blame ("Those Martians, they always stick together; I should have stayed with my old job and not listened to your brother's lousy advice"), evaluative terms ("Didn't your sister look *horrible* in that red dress?"), and "preaching" ("Why can't you ever cook steak the way I like it?" "Why don't you learn something about word processing before you open your mouth?").

Spontaneity

A spontaneous style, as opposed to a strategic one, also helps create supportiveness. Individuals who are spontaneous in their communication and are straightforward and open about what they think are usually responded to in the same manner—straightforwardly and openly. But in some situations we feel that certain people are hiding their true feelings—that they have some hidden plan or strategy that they are attempting to implement for some unrevealed purpose. Generally, this strategic approach is resented and is responded to with defensiveness.

Provisionalism

Being provisional means having a tentative, open-minded attitude, a willingness to hear opposing points of view and to change one's position if warranted. Such provisionalism, rather than unwavering certainty, assists in creating a supportive atmosphere.

We resist people who "know everything" and who always have a definite answer to any question. Such people are set in their ways and will tolerate no differences. They have arguments ready for any possible alternative attitude or belief. After a very short time, we become defensive with such people, and we hold back our own attitudes rather than subject them to attack. But we open up with people who take a more provisional position and are willing to change their minds should reasonable arguments be presented. With such people we feel equal.

What is most important to understand is that to the extent that we act certain and closed-minded, we encourage defensive behavior in the listener. To the extent that we act in a provisional manner—with an open mind, with full recognition that we might be wrong, and with a willingness to revise our attitudes and opinions—we encourage supportiveness.

Positiveness

We communicate positiveness in interpersonal communication in at least two ways: (1) stating positive attitudes and (2) positively stroking the person with whom we interact.

Attitudes

Attitudinal positiveness in interpersonal communication refers to at least two aspects or elements. First, interpersonal communication is fostered if there is a positive regard for the self. People who feel negatively about themselves invariably communicate these feelings to others, who in turn probably develop similar negative feelings. On the other hand, people who feel positively about themselves convey this feeling about themselves to others, who in turn are likely to reflect the positive regard.

Second, a positive feeling for the general communication situation is important for effective interaction. Nothing is more unpleasant than communicating with someone who does not enjoy the exchange or does not respond favorably to the situation or context. A negative response to the situation makes one feel almost as if one is intruding, and communication seems sure to break down quickly.

Stroking

Positiveness may be further explained by reference to the concept of positive stroking. *Stroking* is a term that has crept into the general vocabulary, no doubt because of its central importance in transactional analysis and in human interaction generally. Stroking behavior acknowledges the existence, and in fact the importance, of the other person; it is the antithesis of indifference. When we stroke someone, whether positively or negatively, we are acknowledging him or her as a person and a significant human being.

Stroking may be verbal—as in saying "I like you," "I enjoy being with you," or "You're a pig"—or nonverbal as in giving a smile, a pat on the back, or a punch in the mouth. As these examples illustrate, stroking may be positive or negative. Positive stroking generally takes the form of compliments or rewards, and consists of behaviors we would normally look forward to, enjoy, and take pride in. They bolster our self-image and make us feel better. Negative strokes, on the other hand, are punishing and aversive. Some negative strokes, such as cruel remarks, hurt us emotionally or psychologically; some, such as punches in the mouth, hurt us physically.

Many interpersonal encounters are structured by one or even both participants almost solely to get positively stroked. People compliment associates, do favors, associate with generous people all in order to get stroked. Marriages and other primary relationships are often entered into because they hold the promise of frequent positive stroking. We all do these things for the same basic reasons—to be acknowledged as people and to ward off any possibility of indifference. Positive stroking leads to more effective interpersonal communication when it helps to reinforce productive and satisfying behavior patterns or, alternatively, when it functions to decrease unproductive and unsatisfying patterns.

Equality

Equality is a peculiar characteristic. In any situation, there is probably some inequality: One person will be smarter, richer, better looking, or more athletic than the other. Never are two people absolutely equal in all respects, and even identical twins are unequal in some ways. Despite this inequality, interpersonal communication is generally more effective when the atmosphere is one of equality. This does not mean that unequals cannot communicate. Certainly they can. Yet their communication, if it is to be effective, should recognize the equality of personalities; that is, there should be a tacit recognition that both parties are valuable and worthwhile human beings and that each has something important to contribute.

One of the most frequent ways we neglect the equality characteristic is in the way we ask questions. Compare these examples:

1. "When will you learn to phone for reservations? Must I do everything?"
2. "One of us should phone for reservations. Do you want me to do it, or do you want to do it?"

1. "When are you going to fix this wallpaper? It's coming down on my head!"
2. "This wallpaper is coming down on my head. How about we stay home tonight and try to fix it together?"

In each example, in sentence 1 there is no equality; one person demands compliance and the other is ordered to do something. Such questions encourage defensiveness, resentment, and hostility. They provoke arguments rather than solve problems. In sentence 2 in each example, there is equality—an explicitly stated desire to cooperate—to work together to address a specific problem. As a general rule, requests (especially courteous ones) communicate equality; demands (especially discourteous ones) communicate superiority.

In an interpersonal relationship characterized by equality, disagreement and conflict are seen as attempts to understand inevitable differences rather than as opportunities to put the other person down. Disagreements are viewed as ways of solving problems rather than of winning points, getting one's way, or proving one's superiority. Equality does not require that we accept and approve of all the verbal and nonverbal behaviors of the other person. Some behaviors are self-destructive or have negative consequences for others and should be challenged—not out of a desire to win an argument or prove a point but out of concern for the other person and for the interpersonal relationship. Equality means acceptance and approval of the person or, to use Carl Roger's terms, equality asks that we give the other person "unconditional positive regard."

A PRAGMATIC APPROACH TO INTERPERSONAL EFFECTIVENESS

A pragmatic, behavioral, or metaphorically, "hard" approach to interpersonal effectiveness, sometimes called a *competence model*, focuses on specific behaviors that a speaker or listener should use to gain his or her desired outcome. This model too offers five qualities of effectiveness: confidence, immediacy, interaction management, expressiveness, and other-orientation.

Confidence

The effective communicator has social confidence; any anxiety is not readily perceived by others. There is instead comfort with the other person and with the communication situation generally.

We all have some communication apprehension or shyness, but the effective interpersonal communicator controls it to the extent that it is not a source of discomfort and does not interfere with communication. Further, this quality also enables the speaker to deal effectively with people who are anxious, shy, or apprehensive and to make them feel more comfortable.

The socially confident communicator is relaxed, rather than rigid; flexible in voice and body, rather than locked into one or two ranges of voice or body movement; and controlled, rather than shaky or awkward.

A relaxed posture, researchers find, communicates a sense of control, status, and power. Tenseness, rigidity, and discomfort, on the other hand, signal a lack of self-control, which in turn signals general inability to control one's environment or fellow workers and an impression of being under the power and control of some outside force or other person.

Immediacy

The effective interpersonal communicator conveys a sense of immediacy, contact, and togetherness. This person communicates to others a feeling of interest, an attentive attitude, and a liking for and attraction toward the other person.

Immediacy is communicated both verbally and nonverbally. Verbally we communicate immediacy by joining ourselves to the other person with terms such as *we, our,* and *us;* by using the other person's name; by focusing on the other person's remarks; by providing relevant and immediate feedback; and, of course, by reinforcing or rewarding the other person. Nonverbally we communicate immediacy by maintaining appropriate eye contact, a physical closeness that echoes a psychological closeness, and a direct and open body posture. This involves limiting looking around at others, arranging the body to keep others out, smiling, and similar behaviors that say, "I'm interested in you."

Interaction Management

The effective communicator controls the interaction to the satisfaction of both parties. In effective interaction management, neither person feels ignored or on stage; each contributes to the total communication interchange.

Maintaining one's role as speaker or listener and passing back and forth—through appropriate eye movements, vocal expressions, and body and facial gestures—the opportunity to speak are interaction management skills. Similarly, keeping the conversation flowing and relatively fluent, without long and awkward pauses that make everyone uncomfortable, are signs of effective interaction management.

The effective interaction manager presents verbal and nonverbal messages that are consistent and reinforce each other. Contradictory signals—in which, for example, the nonverbal message contradicts the verbal message—are rarely in evidence. It is relevant to note here that women generally use more positive or pleasant nonverbal expressions than men. For example, women smile more, nod in agreement more, and more openly verbalize positive feelings. When expressing anger or power, however, many women continue using these positive nonverbal signals, which dilute the verbally expressed anger or power. The net result is that such women appear uncomfortable with strong negative emotions and expressions of power, and others are therefore less likely to believe them or feel threatened by them.

Self-Monitoring

Integrally related to interpersonal interaction management is *self-monitoring,* the manipulation of the image that we present to others in our interpersonal interactions. High self-monitors carefully adjust their behaviors on the basis of feedback from others, to produce the most desirable effect. Their interpersonal interactions are manipulated in an attempt to give the best and most effective interpersonal impression. Low self-monitors, on the other hand, are not concerned with the image they present to others. Rather, their interactions are characterized by an openness in which they communicate their thoughts and feelings with no attempt to manipulate the impressions they create. Most of us lie somewhere between the two extremes. (You may wish at this point to take the brief self-monitoring test on page 229.)

When high and low self-monitors are compared, a number of interesting differences emerge. For example, high self-monitors are more apt to take charge of a situation, are more sensitive to the deceptive techniques of others, and are better able to detect self-monitoring or impression management techniques when used by others. High self-monitors prefer to interact with low self-monitors; they prefer to live in a relatively stable world, with people who will not be able to detect their self-monitoring techniques. By interacting with low self-monitors, the high self-monitors are better able to assume positions of influence and power. High self-monitors also seem better able to present their true selves than are low self-monitors. For example, if an innocent person is charged with a crime, to use the example cited by Mark Snyder (on whose research this discussion is based), a high self-monitor would be able to present his or her innocence more effectively than would a low self-monitor.

Although these seem to be two relatively clear-cut types, we all engage in selective monitoring, depending on the situation. If we go for a job interview, we are likely to monitor our behaviors very carefully. On the other hand, if we are interacting with a group of friends, we are less likely to monitor our performance; we are more apt to express our feelings and thoughts openly without any great attempt at impression management.

A careful reading of the research and theory on self-monitoring, openness, and self-disclosure (reviewed in detail in Unit 3) supports the conclusion that our effectiveness is ordinarily increased if we are selectively self-disclosing, are selectively open, and engage in selective self-monitoring. It would seem absurd to be totally open, to disclose everything to everyone, to ignore the feedback of others, and to refuse to engage in any self-monitoring. The opposite extreme—the closed, never-disclosing individual who monitors each and every utterance—is equally absurd and should likewise be avoided.

Expressiveness

Expressiveness refers to the skill of communicating genuine involvement in the interpersonal interaction. It is playing the game instead of just watching it as a spectator. Expressiveness is similar to openness in its emphasis on involvement and includes, for example, expressing responsibility for ("owning") one's thoughts and feelings, encouraging expressiveness or openness in others, and providing feedback that is relevant and appropriate.

This quality also includes taking responsibility for both talking and listening and in this way is similar to equality. In conflict situations, expressiveness involves fighting actively and stating disagreement directly and with I-messages rather than fighting passively, withdrawing from the encounter, or attributing responsibility to others.

SELF-MONITORING TEST

These statements concern personal reactions to a number of different situations. No two statements are exactly alike, so consider each statement carefully before answering. If a statement is true or mostly true as applied to you, circle the T. If a statement is false or not usually true as applied to you, circle the F.

1. I find it hard to imitate the behavior of other people.	T	F
2. I guess I do put on a show to impress or entertain people.	T	F
3. I would probably make a good actor.	T	F
4. I sometimes appear to others to be experiencing deeper emotions than I actually am.	T	F
5. In a group of people, I am rarely the center of attention.	T	F
6. In different situations and with different people, I often act like very different persons.	T	F
7. I can argue only for ideas I already believe.	T	F
8. In order to get along and be liked, I tend to be what people expect me to be rather than who I really am.	T	F
9. I may deceive people by being friendly when I really dislike them.	T	F
10. I am always the person I appear to be.	T	F

Scoring. Give yourself one point for each of questions 1, 5, and 7 that you answered F. Give yourself one point for each of the remaining questions that you answered T. Add up your points. If you are a good judge of yourself and scored 7 or above, you are probably a high self-monitoring individual; 3 or below, you are probably a low self-monitoring individual.

Source: This test appeared in Mark Snyder, "The Many Me's of the Self-Monitor," *Psychology Today* 13 (March 1980), p. 34, and is reprinted here by permission of Mark Snyder.

We demonstrate expressiveness by using appropriate variations in vocal rate, pitch, volume, and rhythm to convey involvement and interest and by allowing our facial muscles to reflect and echo this inner involvement.

Similarly, the use of gestures (appropriate in style and frequency) communicates involvement. Using too few gestures signals disinterest, while too many may communicate discomfort, uneasiness, and awkwardness.

The monotone and motionless speaker who talks about sex, winning the lottery, and fatal illnesses all in the same tone of voice, with a static posture and an expressionless face, is the stereotype of the ineffective interaction manager.

Other-Orientation

Too often we are self-oriented; that is, we focus almost exclusively on ourselves. In interpersonal interaction, this takes the form of talking about ourselves and our experiences, interests, and desires; doing most if not all of the talking; and paying little or no attention to verbal and nonverbal feedback from the other person.

Other-orientation is the opposite of self-orientation. It refers to one's ability to adapt to the other person during the interpersonal encounter. It involves communicating attentiveness and interest in the other person and in what is being said.

We communicate our orientation toward the other nonverbally through focused eye contact, smiles, head nods, leaning toward the other person, and displaying feelings and emotions through appropriate facial expression. Verbally we show interest through such comments as "I see" and "Really," through requests for further information ("What else did you do in Vegas?"), and through expressions of empathy ("I can understand what you're going through; my parents divorced recently too").

An other-oriented communicator perceives the situation and the interaction from the viewpoint of the other person and appreciates the different ways in which this other person punctuates the sequence of events. Similarly, the other-oriented person communicates empathic understanding by echoing the feelings of the other or disclosing similar experiences or feelings. To achieve empathy, the other-oriented person listens attentively—demonstrating this attention verbally and nonverbally—and provides appropriate, immediate feedback that demonstrates in-depth understanding and sharing of thoughts and feelings.

Other-orientation demonstrates consideration and respect—for example, asking if it's all right to dump your troubles on someone before doing so, or asking if your phone call comes at an inopportune time before launching into your conversation. Other-orientation involves acknowledging others' feelings as legitimate: "I can understand why you're so angry; I would be too."

A SOCIAL EXCHANGE APPROACH TO INTERPERSONAL EFFECTIVENESS

Another model from which interpersonal effectiveness principles may be derived is that of social exchange theory. Social exchange theory claims that we develop relationships in which our rewards will be greater than our costs. We involve ourselves in relationships that will provide us with rewards—basically, those things that fulfill our needs for security, sex, social approval, financial gain, status, and so on. But rewards involve some cost or "payback." For example, in order to acquire the reward of financial gain, an individual might have to give up some degree of freedom. The cost of gaining parental approval might be entering a loveless marriage or giving up a relationship that provided other types of rewards or gains.

Using this basic economic-oriented model, the social exchange theory puts into clearer perspective our tendency to seek gain or reward while incurring the least cost (punishment or loss). If you think about your current or past relationships, you will be able to see quite clearly that the relationships you pursued and maintained have been those that provided you with reward and need fulfillment greater than the cost. Those relationships you did not pursue or that you terminated were probably those whose costs or losses exceeded the rewards; these were the relationships with more dissatisfaction than satisfaction, more unhappiness than happiness, and more problems than pleasures.

Most of us have an expectation baseline—a kind of comparison level of what we expect in a relationship. When our expectations are exceeded, we experience relationship satisfaction—as when, for example, we derive greater rewards than we had originally anticipated. When our expectations are not met, we experience relationship dissatisfaction.

Equity Theory

Equity theory builds on social exchange theory and claims that not only do we seek to establish relationships in which rewards exceed costs, but that we experience relationship satisfaction when there is an equal distribution of rewards and costs between the two persons in the relationship. That is, not only do we want our rewards to be greater than our costs, but we want our rewards to be about equal to our partner's rewards and we want our costs to be about equal to our partner's costs. The happiest couples seem to be those in which there is equality in rewards and costs, with each member deriving about the same amount of reward and each paying about the same cost. The unhappiest person—as might be predicted—is the one who both pays more costs and derives less reward than the partner.

We can easily find a number of practical guidelines for interpersonal communication effectiveness in this approach. Here are just four.

Exchange Rewards

In any relationship, there are going to be costs—financial problems, job tension, house or apartment problems, and interpersonal differences and conflicts. Offset these costs by exchanging favors or rewards—particularly "cherishing behaviors." Cherishing behaviors are those small favors that we enjoy receiving from our relational partner—the phone call to say "I love you," the card for no reason, the flowers, the tight squeeze, the specially prepared meal, and the prolonged kiss. Cherishing behaviors should be (1) specific and positive, (2) focused on the present and future rather than related to issues about which the partners have argued in the past, (3) capable of being performed daily, and (4) easily executed.

William Lederer suggests that the individuals make a list of the cherishing behaviors they each wish to receive and then exchange lists. Each person then performs the cherishing behaviors desired by the partner. At first these behaviors may seem self-conscious and awkward. In time, however, they will become a normal part of interaction and will go a long way toward offsetting the inevitable costs incurred in any relationship.

Bear Your Share of the Costs

As equity theory makes clear, we become dissatisfied when we have to bear an unfair share of the costs. Remember that our relational partner will feel the same way. When the costs seem to weight unfairly on your partner, share these to make the relationship more equitable.

Intensify the Exchange of Rewards in Times of Rising Costs

When a relationship experiences problems (that is, when the costs begin to exceed the rewards), many people will respond passively, waiting for the situation to change or allowing the relationship to deteriorate further. These passive approaches, as psychologists C. E. Rusbult and I. M. Zembrodt have recently demonstrated, solve nothing and seem to ensure that the relationship will in fact deteriorate. Instead, this is the time for an active approach and for intensifying the exchange of rewards and favors. The empathic understanding, the extra attention, and the increased touching and holding can often be used to counteract rising relationship costs.

Increase Rewards to Reduce the Attractiveness of Alternatives

When the costs of a relationship exceed the rewards, the attractiveness of alternatives (for example, some third party) increases. The grass next door looks especially green when ours is but weeds and mud. But when the rewards exceed the costs, the attractiveness of alternatives decreases. The moral is simple: If you want your competition (and we all have competition) to be decreased in attractiveness, structure the situation to increase the rewards and decrease the costs.

CONFLICT MANAGEMENT

In interpersonal conflict the principles of interpersonal effectiveness probably receive their toughest test. During interpersonal conflict we are least likely to pause, analyze the situation, and evaluate the effectiveness principles that might prove most relevant. Because of this difficulty, we here consider effective conflict management. First, we examine the often-used but unproductive conflict strategies; and second, we consider some principles for effective and productive conflict management.

Unproductive Conflict Management

Here we identify eight popular but unproductive and self-defeating conflict strategies. The major value in examining these ineffective methods is so that we will be better able to identify them in the behaviors of others and ultimately in our own behaviors as well.

Avoidance, Nonnegotiation, and Redefinition

One of the most frequently employed methods of conflict "resolution" is to avoid the conflict. Frequently this takes the form of actual physical flight: The individual may leave the scene of the conflict, fall asleep, or blast the stereo. It may also take the form of emotional or intellectual avoidance: Here the individual leaves the conflict psychologically by not dealing with any of the arguments or problems raised.

In *nonnegotiation,* a special type of avoidance, the individual refuses to discuss the conflict, or even refuses to listen to the other person's argument. At times this nonnegotiation takes the form of hammering away at one's own point of view until the other person gives in, a technique called "steamrolling."

At times the conflict or the assumed source of the conflict is redefined so that it becomes no conflict at all, as when someone says, "It was not a date—it was a business trip that we had to take together." At other times, the conflict may be redefined so that it becomes a totally different issue, as when someone says, "Your jealousy is getting out of hand; you had really better see a therapist about it. I'm not going to come home each night to your jealous tirades."

Notice that with these types of behavior, the source of the conflict is never confronted, it is just pushed aside. We can be almost certain, however, that it will surface again.

Force

Perhaps the most common unproductive method of dealing with conflict involves physical force. When confronted with a conflict, many prefer not to deal with the issues but rather to simply force their decision or way of thinking or behaving on the other by physical force. At other times, the force used is more emotional than physical. In either case, however, the issues are avoided. The individual who "wins" is the individual who exerts the most force. This is the technique of warring nations and spouses.

Unfortunately, this is also the technique used by many college couples. It has been estimated (*Time,* September 21, 1981) that the number of college love affairs involving violence is around 25 percent. Conflicts over some third person, sex, and drinking are the most frequent causes of these violent episodes. What is perhaps more interesting—and more frightening—is that nearly 30 percent of the couples involved in violent conflict took physical abuse as a sign of love. Many considered violence a normal part of their relationship. Seventy-five percent of those involved in an assault claimed that it did not harm their relationship, and more than one-third claimed that physical violence actually improved their relationship.

What conflict strategies do you find most damaging to relational growth and improvement? What conflict strategies actually help to improve a relationship? How might your own conflict strategies be improved? That is, what might you do to help eliminate damaging strategies and to strengthen productive strategies?

Minimization

Sometimes we deal with conflict by making light of it—by saying and perhaps believing that the conflict, its causes, and its consequences are really not important. We might argue that time alone will resolve it—but time does absolutely nothing. Over time *we* may do something, but time itself never acts one way or the other. Sometimes we minimize the conflict with humor and may literally laugh at the conflict. Sometimes it is obvious that our laughter is prompted by fear, embarrassment, or personal inadequacy. But in many instances the humor seems logical enough; it eases the tension and, at least for a time, makes for more effective interpersonal relations. The problem is that the laughter does nothing to get at the root of the problem. When the laughter dies, the conflict is still very much alive.

We also use minimization when we make light of the objections, anger, or irritation felt by the other person: "What are you so angry about? I'm only two hours late." When we do this, we are in effect telling the other person that his or her feelings are not legitimate or are not logical. Rather than minimize the other person's feelings, we should seek to validate them and to acknowledge their legitimacy: "You have a right to be angry; I should have called when I knew I'd be late."

Blame

Sometimes conflict is caused by the actions of one of the individuals; sometimes it is caused by clearly identifiable outside forces. Most of the time, however, it is caused by such a wide variety of factors that any attempt to single out one or two is doomed to failure. And yet, a frequently employed fight strategy is to avoid dealing with the conflict by blaming someone for it. In some instances we blame ourselves. This may be the result of a realistic appraisal of the situation, or it may be an attempt to evoke sympathy or to gain pity from the other individual. More often, however, we blame the other person. If a couple has a conflict over a child's getting into trouble with the police, for example, the parents may—instead of dealing with the conflict itself—start blaming each other for the child's troubles. As can easily be appreciated (when we are not parties to the conflict), such blaming does nothing other than temporarily relieve a degree of intrapersonal guilt.

Silencers

One of the most unfair but most popular fight strategies is the use of silencers—a wide variety of fighting techniques that literally silence the other individual. One frequently used silencer is crying. When confronted by a conflict and unable to deal with it, or when winning seems unlikely, an individual may cry and thus silence the other person. Another silencer is to feign extreme emotionalism—to yell and scream and pretend to be losing control of oneself. Still another is to develop some "physical" reaction—headaches and shortness of breath are probably the most popular. One of the major problems with such silencers is that we can never be certain that they are strategies to win the argument and not real physical reactions that have to be attended to. Regardless of what we do, the conflict remains unexamined and unresolved.

Gunnysacking

A gunnysack is a large bag, usually made of burlap. As a conflict strategy, *gunnysacking* refers to the practice of storing up grievances we may have been afraid to express at the time they were incurred. Some people can store up grievances for months and even years to keep them for the "right" time. And when that time comes, they are unloaded on the unsuspecting opponent. The immediate occasion may be relatively simple (or so it might seem at first), such as someone's coming home late without calling. Instead of arguing about this, the gunnysacker unloads all past grievances: the birthday you forgot, the time two months ago when you arrived late for an important dinner, last year when you delayed making hotel reservations until the rooms were all taken, and on and on. As can be expected, gunnysacking often begets gunnysacking, with the result that we have two persons who probably care for each other a great deal dumping their stored-up grievances on each other. The frequent result is that the original problem never gets addressed, and instead resentment and hostility escalate. The true gunnysacker, even after unloading these grievances, will put them right back in the sack to be dumped out at some later date.

Manipulation

In *manipulation* there is an avoidance of open conflict. The individual attempts to divert the conflict by being especially charming (disarming, actually) and getting the other individual into a receptive and noncombative frame of mind before disagreeing. That is, the conflict situation and the other individual are manipulated so that the manipulating individual may eventually win the battle, argument, or disagreement.

Personal Rejection

In *personal rejection* the individual withholds love and affection and seeks to win the argument by getting the other person to break down under this withdrawal. The individual acts cold and uncaring, attempting to demoralize the other person. In withdrawing affection, the individual hopes to make the other person question his or her own self-worth. Once the other is demoralized and feels less than worthy, it is relatively easy to get one's own way by simply making the restitution of love and affection contingent upon resolving the conflict in one's favor.

Effective Conflict Management

Effective conflict management is approached here by examining some of the insights provided by George Bach and Peter Wyden in their influential *Intimate Enemy*. Their simple but powerful guides to fair fighting will go a long way toward making our interpersonal conflicts more productive.

Fight Above the Belt

Much like fighters in a ring, each of us has a "belt line." When hit below it, we can be severely injured. As a result of such an injury, we and/or the relationship may never recover. When hit above the belt, however, we are able to absorb the blow. With most interpersonal relationships, we know where the belt line is to be drawn, especially in relationships of long standing. We know that, for example, to hit Pat with the inability to have children or to hit Chris with the failure to secure a permanent job would be to hit below the belt and cause all persons involved added problems. Keep your blows above the belt. Keep blows directed at areas that can be handled and absorbed by your opponent and that will not cause increased hostility and resentment.

Fight Actively

Play an active role in your interpersonal conflicts. Don't close your ears (or mind), blast the stereo, or walk out of the house during an argument. This is not to say that a cooling-off period is not at times desirable. It is to say, instead, that if conflicts are to be resolved, they need to be confronted actively by both parties.

Take Responsibility for Your Thoughts and Feelings

When you disagree with your partner or find fault with her or his behavior, take responsibility for these feelings and say, for example, "I disagree with . . . "

or "I don't like it when you . . ." instead of "Everybody thinks you're wrong about . . ." or "Chris thinks you shouldn't . . . ." Own your own thoughts and feelings and make this ownership explicit.

Be Direct and Specific

Focus your conflict on the here-and-now rather than on issues that occurred two months ago (as in gunnysacking). Similarly, focus your conflict on the person with whom you are fighting, and not on the person's mother, boss, child, or friends.

Focus your conflict on observable behaviors—on what the other person did with which you find fault or disagree. Try to avoid attributing motives to the person without any real attempt first to describe the behavior and then to understand it. Thus, if the person forgot your birthday and this disturbs you, fight about the forgetting of the birthday (the actual behavior), and try not to presuppose motives: "Well, it's obvious you just don't care about me; all you really care about is yourself! If you really cared, you could never have forgotten my birthday!"

Use Humor for Relief, Never for Ridicule

In almost any conflict situation, humor will be used. Unfortunately, most often it is used sarcastically to ridicule, make fun of, or somehow embarrass the other person. This use of humor aggravates and intensifies the conflict. When humor is used, it should provide a momentary break in the tension and not become a strategy for winning the battle or putting down the other person.

SUMMARY

1. The humanistic perspective on interpersonal effectiveness begins with the general qualities that philosophers and humanists claim should define superior human relationships.

2. The humanistic model of interpersonal effectiveness stresses five qualities: openness, empathy, supportiveness (descriptiveness, spontaneity, and provisionalism), positiveness, and equality.

3. The pragmatic (or behavioral) perspective on interpersonal effectiveness focuses on specific behaviors that a speaker or listener should use to gain his or her desired outcome.

4. The pragmatic model of interpersonal effectiveness stresses confidence, immediacy, interaction management, expressiveness, and other-orientation.

5. The social exchange and equity perspective on interpersonal effectiveness focuses on the exchange of rewards and costs and the implications of these exchange patterns for relationships.

6. The social exchange model of interpersonal effectiveness stresses the exchange of rewards (including cherishing behaviors), bearing one's share of

the costs, intensifying the exchange of rewards in times of rising costs, and increasing rewards to reduce the attractiveness of alternatives.

7. Eight unproductive conflict strategies are identified: avoidance (including nonnegotiation and redefinition), force, minimization, blame, silencers, gunnysacking, manipulation, and personal rejection.

8. Bach and Wyden, in *The Intimate Enemy,* offer a number of useful guides to fair fighting. Among these are fighting above the belt, fighting actively, taking responsibility for your thoughts and feelings, being direct, being specific, communicating clearly, and using humor for relief but never for ridicule.

SOURCES

For this unit I relied on the work of Jack Gibb, particularly his insightful "Defensive Communication," *Journal of Communication* 11 (1961): 141–148, reprinted in my *Communication: Concepts and Processes,* 3d ed. (Englewood Cliffs, N.J.: Prentice-Hall, 1981).

On empathy, see C. Truax, *A Scale for the Measurement of Accurate Empathy,* Wisconsin Psychiatric Institute Discussion Paper No. 20 (Madison, 1961). This and various other contributions to the study of empathy are discussed in Henry M. Backrack, "Empathy," *Archives of General Psychiatry* 33 (1976): 35–38. The concept of owning thoughts was taken from Arthur P. Bochner and Clifford W. Kelly, "Interpersonal Competence: Rationale, Philosophy, and Implementation of a Conceptual Framework," *Communication Education* 23 (November 1974): 279–301. Two useful works that provide interesting perspectives on interpersonal skills are Albert Ellis and Robert A. Harper, *A New Guide to Rational Living* (Hollywood, Calif.: Wilshire Books, 1975), and Toni Brougher, *A Way With Words* (Chicago, Ill.: Nelson-Hall, 1982).

On the pragmatic model of communication effectiveness, see John M. Wiemann, "Explication and Test of a Model of Communicative Competence," *Human Communication Research* 3 (1977): 195–213 and John M. Wiemann and P. Backlund, "Current Theory and Research in Communicative Competence," *Review of Educational Research* 50 (1980): 185–199; Brian H. Spitzberg and Michael L. Hecht, "A Component Model of Relational Competence," *Human Communication Research* 10 (summer 1984): 575–599, and Brian H. Spitzberg and William R. Cupach, *Interpersonal Communication Competence* (Beverly Hills, Calif.: Sage, 1984).

For social exchange theory, see, for example, J. W. Thibaut and H. H. Kelley, *The Social Psychology of Groups* (New York: Wiley, 1959), and H. H. Kelley and J. W. Thibaut, *Interpersonal Relations: A Theory of Interdependence* (New York: Wiley/Interscience, 1978). On equity theory, see Elaine Walster, G. W. Walster, and Ellen Berscheid, *Equity: Theory and Research* (Boston: Allyn and Bacon, 1978) and Elaine Hatfield and Jane Traupman, "Intimate Relationships: A Perspective from Equity Theory," in Steve Duck and Robin Gilmour, eds., *Personal Relationships. 1: Studying Personal Relationships* (New York: Academic Press, 1981), pp.

165–178. For cherishing behaviors, see William J. Lederer, *Creating a Good Relationship* (New York: Norton, 1984).

A number of excellent works in interpersonal conflict may be recommended: Alan C. Filley, *Interpersonal Conflict Resolution* (Glenview, Ill.: Scott, Foresman, 1975); Joseph P. Folger and Marshall Scott Poole, *Working Through Conflict: A Communication Perspective* (Glenview, Ill.: Scott, Foresman, 1984); and Joyce L. Hocker and William W. Wilmot, *Interpersonal Conflict*, 2d ed. (Dubuque, Iowa: Brown, 1985). George R. Bach and Peter Wyden's *The Intimate Enemy* (New York: Avon, 1968) is a popular, well-written, and insightful account of conflict and of productive and unproductive ways of fighting. On gunnysacking and other unproductive strategies (called "crazymakers" by Bach), see George R. Bach and Ronald M. Deutsch, *Stop! You're Driving Me Crazy* (New York: Berkley, 1979). John Wright, *Survival Strategies for Couples* (Buffalo, N.Y.: Prometheus, 1985), offers some useful strategies for conflict resolution.

SKILL DEVELOPMENT SUMMARY

1. **Adjust your communication patterns** on the basis of the intimacy of your relationship. Be careful, for example, of disclosing too much or too early in the relationship. Avoid touching that might be seen as too intimate or too intrusive.

2. Increase the **breadth and depth of a relationship** gradually.

3. Use **physical proximity** to increase personal attractiveness.

4. Reinforce others as a way to increase interpersonal **attractiveness** and satisfaction.

5. Be aware of the **increases in perceived attractiveness** that you will feel toward others as a result of your reinforcing behaviors.

6. Emphasize similarities as a way of **increasing interpersonal attraction.** But beware of differences—for example, in attitudes—that are significant in the development of interpersonal relationships.

7. Know your **relationship needs.** Identify the needs that lead you to seek the interpersonal relationships that you do, in order to understand and deal with these relationships more effectively.

8. In **initiating relationships,** the following steps should prove useful: examine the qualifiers, determine clearance, open the encounter, introduce an integrating topic, create a favorable impression, and establish a second meeting.

9. Use the following **nonverbal guidelines in initiating relationships:** establish eye contact, smile and further signal your interest in and your positive responses to the other person, concentrate your focus, establish physical closeness, maintain an open posture, respond visibly, reinforce positive behaviors, and avoid overexposure.

10. Use the following **verbal guidelines in initiating relationships:** introduce yourself, focus the conversation on the other person, exchange favors and rewards, be energetic, stress the positive, avoid negative or too intimate disclosures, and establish and stress commonalities.

11. Learn to recognize the following **symptoms of relational deterioration:** the reasons for the establishment of the relationship have diminished, extensive intimacy claims, third-party relationships taking over the functions normally served by the primary relationship, significant relational changes, undefined expectations, sexual difficulties, incompatible work schedules and attitudes, financial difficulties and dissatisfaction, inequitable distribution of rewards and costs, and a decrease in commitment.

12. Learn to recognize the following **communication patterns that may be symptomatic of relational deterioration:** general withdrawal, a decrease in self-disclosure, a decrease in supportiveness, an increase in deception,

an increase in negative evaluation and a decrease in positive evaluation, a decrease in requests for positive behaviors and an increase in requests to cease negative behaviors, and a decrease in the exchange of favors.

13. Practice **openness.** Be judiciously open to those with whom you interact, react openly to incoming stimuli, and own your own feelings and thoughts.

14. Use **I-messages** to indicate your willingness to own your own thoughts and feelings, and to avoid evaluative or accusatory statements.

15. Increase your **empathic abilities** by avoiding evaluating others' behaviors; by learning about others, especially their motivations; and by trying to experience what the other person is feeling from his or her point of view.

16. Express **supportiveness** by being descriptive rather than evaluative, spontaneous rather than strategic, and provisional rather than certain.

17. Communicate **positiveness**—express positive attitudes toward yourself, toward others, and toward the communication act through smiles, positive facial expressions, attentive gestures, positive verbal expressions, and the reduction and (if possible) the elimination of negative appraisals.

18. **Positively stroke others** to express acknowledgment and validation and thus encourage increased positiveness and satisfaction.

19. Express **equality** in interpersonal interaction by listening as well as speaking, by assuming that others have important contributions to make, and by seeing conflicts and disagreement as attempts to understand inevitable differences rather than as opportunities to win a fight.

20. Communicate **confidence** by exhibiting a relaxed rather than a rigid demeanor, speaking in a flexible voice, and assuming a controlled rather than an awkward body posture.

21. Express **immediacy** both verbally and nonverbally by joining yourself to the other person with terms such as *we* and *our,* using the other's name, focusing on the communications of the other, providing relevant feedback, and positively reinforcing the other.

22. **Manage the interpersonal interaction** to the satisfaction of both parties by sharing the roles of speaker and listener, avoiding long and awkward pauses, and communicating so that verbal and nonverbal messages are consistent.

23. **Self-monitor** your verbal and nonverbal behaviors as appropriate in order to communicate the desired impression.

24. Communicate **expressiveness** by being an active communicator; taking responsibility for both talking and listening; making appropriate variations in vocal rate, pitch, volume, and rhythm; using gestures that signal interest and attention; and allowing your facial muscles to reflect this involvement.

25. Practice **other-orientation.** Communicate a concern and an interest in the other person by focused eye contact, smiles, head nods, leaning toward the other, and displaying feelings and emotions through appropriate facial expressions. Demonstrate other-orientation verbally with comments such as "I see," through requests for further information, and through expressions of empathy ("I can see why you're angry").

26. Use the suggestions for interpersonal effectiveness and satisfaction found in **social exchange and equity theory:** exchange rewards (especially cherishing behaviors), bear your share of the costs, intensify the exchange of rewards in times of rising costs, and increase rewards to reduce the attractiveness of alternatives.

27. Avoid using **unproductive methods of conflict resolution,** especially avoidance (including nonnegotiation and redefinition), force, minimization, blame, silencers, gunnysacking, manipulation, and personal rejection.

28. Use the following **guides to fair fighting:** fight above the belt, fight actively, take responsibility for your thoughts and feelings, be direct and specific, and use humor for relief but never for ridicule.

PART FIVE
GROUP AND ORGANIZATIONAL COMMUNICATION

17. PRELIMINARIES TO GROUP COMMUNICATION: TYPES, PROCEDURES, AND FORMATS

18. MEMBERS AND LEADERS IN GROUP COMMUNICATION

19. ORGANIZATIONAL COMMUNICATION

20. INTERVIEWING

In this part we examine groups and group communication in a variety of contexts and from a variety of points of view. We begin by looking at what a small group is and at some of the major types of small groups in which we participate regularly, providing both an increased awareness of what these groups are and also some suggestions for making group experiences more enjoyable and productive. In the next unit we look at the roles of members and leaders in small group situations. Our major purpose in these two units is to increase our own effectiveness in group situations—as members and leaders.

In the next unit we look at communication within the organizational setting and seek to provide a broad overview of a rapidly developing area. Here we survey the nature of organizations, the types of organizational communication, the varied approaches one might take in dealing with organizations, the communication networks, and how communication flows within an organization. In the last unit of this part we examine interviewing—communication in a two-person group designed to achieve rather specific functions. Here we have two goals. The first is to provide a broad overview of interviewing—its major types, the steps involved, and the role and kinds of questions used. The second goal is to provide you with some very practical insights and strategies for dealing more effectively with interview situations.

UNIT 17
PRELIMINARIES TO GROUP COMMUNICATION:
Types, Procedures, and Formats

LEARNING GOALS

After completing this unit, you should be able to

1. define the nature of a small group
2. identify the steps that should be followed in problem-solving discussions
3. explain the four principles of brainstorming
4. identify two ways in which personal growth groups may benefit their members
5. explain one set of procedures that may be followed in consciousness-raising groups
6. explain the function of the educational or learning group and the patterns it may use
7. define and distinguish among the panel or round table, the colloquy, the symposium, and the symposium-forum

We are all members of various small groups. The family is the most obvious example, but we also may function as members of a team, a class, a collection of friends, and so on. Some of our most important and most personally satisfying communications take place within the small group context.

In this unit we first inquire into the nature of the small group and identify its characteristics. With this as a foundation, we examine four major types of small group and the procedures discussants may follow in participating in these groups. Last, we examine four popular small group formats.

THE SMALL GROUP

For our purposes, a *small group* is best defined as a relatively small collection of individuals who are related to each other by some common purpose and have some degree of organization or structure among them. Each of these characteristics needs to be explained a bit.

A small group is a collection of individuals, few enough in number that all members may communicate with relative ease as both senders and receivers. This part of the definition touches on one of the most essential aspects of the small group. Generally, a small group consists of approximately 5 to 12 people. The important point to keep in mind is that each member should be able to function as both source and receiver with relative ease. If the group gets much larger than 12 this becomes difficult.

The members of a group must be related to one another in some way. People in a movie house would not constitute a group, since there is no relationship among the various individuals. In a small group the behavior of one member is significant for all other members, whereas in "nongroups" the behavior of one member may not even be noticed by the other members.

There must be some common purpose among the members for them to constitute a group. This does not mean that all members must have exactly the same purpose in mind, but generally there must be some similarity in the reasons the individuals have for interacting.

The people must be connected by some organization or structure. Individuals not constituting a group have no such structure—the behaviors of the various individuals do not constitute any system, and there is no pattern to their behaviors. In a small group there is a pattern. At times the structure is a rigid one—as in groups operating under parliamentary procedure, wherein each comment must follow prescribed rules. At other times, the structure is very loose, as in a social gathering, dinner, or card game. Yet in both groups there is some organization and some structure: Two people do not speak at the same time, comments or questions by one member are responded to by others rather than ignored, and so on.

Another characteristic that is frequently included in definitions of the small group is proximity. It is often held that the members must be face to face for them to constitute a small group. This is usually the case. However, with teleconferencing becoming more popular, we should recognize that the characteristic of proximity is included only because it is usually, but not always, present.

The area of small group communication, then, is concerned with the interaction process that occurs within small group settings.

THE PROBLEM-SOLVING GROUP

Perhaps the type of group most familiar to us when we think of small group communication is the problem-solving group. Here we have a group of individuals meeting to solve a particular problem or to reach a decision that may be a preface to the problem solving itself.

In one sense this is the most exacting kind of group to participate in, since it requires not only a knowledge of small group communication techniques, but a thorough knowledge of the particular problem and usually a rather faithful adherence to a somewhat rigid set of procedural rules.

Steps to Successful Group Problem Solving

In a problem-solving discussion it is useful to identify approximately seven steps that should be followed (see Figure 17.1). These steps are designed to make problem solving more efficient and effective. Although some of the initial steps may at first seem unnecessary and there may be a temptation to short-circuit this process, it has been found repeatedly that this does not in fact save time; it wastes time.

Define the Problem

In many instances the nature of the problem is clearly specified, and everyone in the group knows exactly what the problem is—for example, what color the new soap package should be, or what the name of the new candy bar should be. In other instances, however, the problem may be vague, and it remains for the group to define it in concrete, unambiguous, specific terms. Thus, for example, the general problem may be poor campus communications. But such a vague and general topic is difficult to tackle in a problem-solving discussion, so it is helpful to specify the problem clearly for purposes of this discussion—for example, "How can we improve the school newspaper?"

Generally, it is best to define the problem as an open-ended question ("How can we improve the student newspaper?") rather than as a statement ("The student newspaper needs to be improved") or a yes/no question ("Does the student newspaper need improvement?"). The open-ended question allows for greater freedom of exploration and does not restrict the ways in which the problem may be approached. Further, the statement of the problem should not suggest possible solutions, as would, for example, "How can faculty supervision

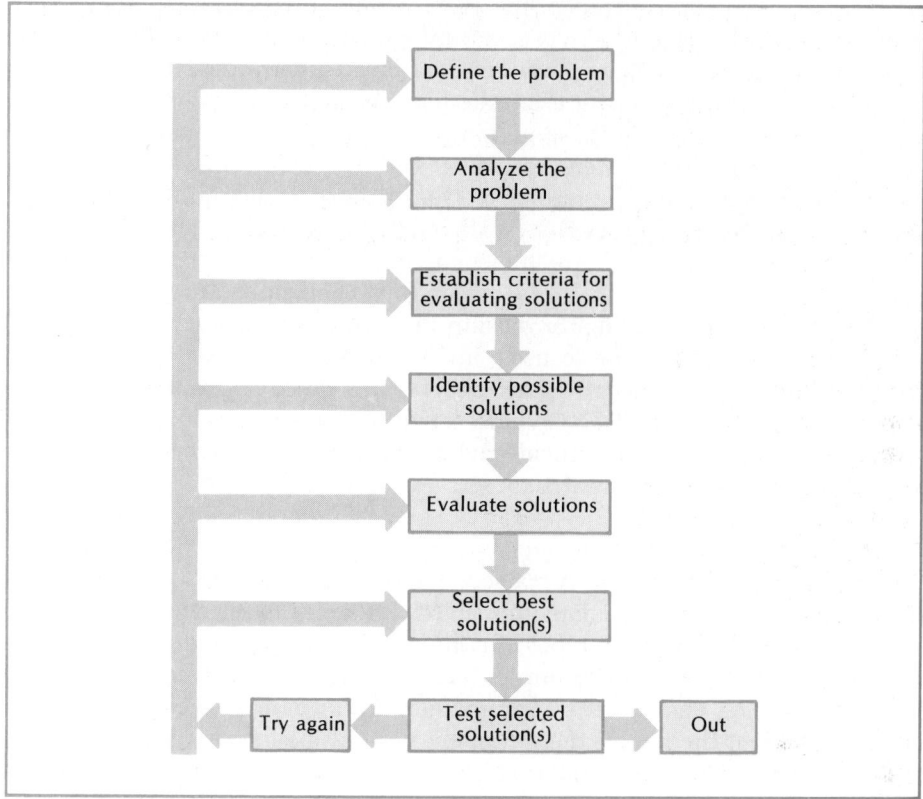

FIGURE 17.1 Steps in problem-solving discussion.

improve the student newspaper?" Here we are stating that faculty supervision is the solution to the problem rather than leaving the solutions open for the discussants to identify and evaluate.

The problem should also be limited in some way so that it identifies a manageable area for discussion. To state as a discussion problem "How can we improve the university?" seems too broad and too general for most problem-solving discussions. Rather, it would be more effective to limit the problem and to identify one subdivision of the university on which the group might focus— for example, the student newspaper, student-faculty relationships, registration, examination scheduling, or student advisory services.

Analyze the Problem

Given a general problem, we seek in this analysis stage to identify its particular dimensions. Although there are no prescribed questions to ask of all problems, appropriate questions (for most problems) seem to revolve around the following issues: (1) *Duration*—How long has the problem existed? Is it likely to continue in the future? What is the predicted course of the problem? For example, will it grow or lessen in influence? (2) *Causes*—What are the major causes of the problem? How certain may we be that these are the actual causes?

(3) *Effects*—What are the effects of the problem? How significant are they? Who is affected by this problem? How significantly are they affected? Is this problem causing other problems? How important are these other problems?

Applied to our newspaper example, the specific questions we might ask in the analysis stage might look something like this. Under *Duration*, we might ask: "How long has there been a problem with the student newspaper?" "Will the problem continue in the future?" "Does it look as though it will grow or lessen in importance?" Under *Causes*, we might ask: "What seems to be causing the newspaper problem?" "Are there specific people (an editor or a faculty adviser, for example) who might be causing the problem?" "Are there specific policies (editorial, advertising, or design) that might be causing the problem?" "How sure are we that the 'causes' are the actual causes of the problem?" Under *Effects*, we might ask: "What effects is this problem producing?" "How significant are these effects?" "Who is affected—students? alumni? faculty?" "Are there people within or outside the college community who are not benefiting as they should be from the student newspaper?

Establish Criteria for Evaluating Solutions

Before any solutions are proposed, identify the standards or criteria that will be employed in evaluating the possible solutions or in selecting one solution over another. Generally, two types of criteria need to be considered. First, there are the *practical criteria*—for example, that the solutions must not increase the budget (assuming that there is a limited amount of money to be spent on the newspaper), that the size of the newspaper cannot be increased (if this is tied to the budget), or that the number of issues per semester may not be increased. The solutions must draw only on volunteers to staff the paper regardless of their qualifications, must lead to a higher number of advertisers, must increase the readership by at least 10 percent, and so on. Second, there are the *value criteria*, which are much more difficult to identify and to determine. These might include, for example, that the newspaper must be a learning experience for all those who work on it or that it must reflect the attitudes of the board of trustees, the faculty, or the students.

After the solutions are identified, go back to these standards to make certain that the new solution meets these criteria.

Identify Possible Solutions

At this stage identify as many solutions as possible. Focus on quantity rather than quality. Brainstorming may be particularly useful at this point (see discussion of idea generation, below). Solutions to the student newspaper problem might include incorporating reviews of faculty publications; student evaluations of specific courses; reviews of restaurants in the campus area; outlines for new courses; student, faculty, and administration profiles; and employment information.

Evaluate Solutions

After all the solutions have been proposed, the members go back and evaluate each according to the criteria established for evaluating solutions. For example, to what extent does incorporating reviews of area restaurants meet the criteria for evaluating solutions? Would it increase the budget? Would it lead to an increase in advertising revenue? Each solution should be matched against the criteria for evaluating solutions.

Select the Best Solution(s)

At this stage the best solution or solutions are selected and put into operation. Thus, for example, we might incorporate in the next issue reviews of faculty publications and outlines for new courses, assuming that these two possible solutions best meet the criteria for evaluating solutions.

Test Selected Solution(s)

After the solution(s) are put into operation, test their effectiveness. We might, for example, poll student response to the new newspaper, examine the number of copies purchased (if the students buy individual copies), analyze the advertising revenue, or determine whether the readership did increase 10 percent.

If these solutions prove ineffective, go back to one of the previous stages and repeat part of the process. Often this takes the form of selecting other solutions to test, but it may involve going further back to, for example, a reanalysis of the problem, an identification of other solutions, or a restatement of criteria.

THE IDEA-GENERATION GROUP

Many small groups exist solely for the purpose of generating ideas; in these, a formula called brainstorming is often followed.

Brainstorming is a technique for bombarding a problem and generating as many ideas as possible. In this system the group members meet in two periods: The first is the brainstorming period proper, and the second is the evaluation period. The procedure is relatively simple. A problem is selected that is amenable to many possible solutions or ideas. Group members are informed of the problem to be brainstormed before the actual session, so that some prior thinking can be done. When the group meets, each person contributes as many ideas as he or she can think of. All ideas are recorded either in writing or on tape. During this idea-generating session, four general rules are followed.

No Negative Criticism Is Allowed All ideas are treated in exactly the same way; they are recorded. They are not evaluated in this phase, nor are they even discussed. Any negative criticism—whether verbal or nonverbal—is itself criticized by the leader or the members.

Quantity Is Desired The assumption made here is that the more ideas the better; somewhere in a large pile of ideas will be one or two good ones that may be used. The more ideas generated, the more effective the brainstorming session.

Combinations and Extensions Are Desired   While we may not criticize a particular idea, we may extend it or combine it in some way. The value of a particular idea may well be in the way it stimulates another member to combine or extend it.

Freewheeling Is Wanted   The wilder the idea, the better. The assumption is that it is easier and generally more profitable to tone an idea down than spice it up. A wild idea can easily be tempered, but it is not so easy to elaborate on a simple or conservative idea.

After all the ideas are generated—a period lasting no longer than 15 or 20 minutes—the entire list of ideas is evaluated. The ones that are unworkable are thrown out, while the ones that show promise are retained and evaluated. Here, of course, negative criticism is allowed.

THE PERSONAL GROWTH GROUP

Personal growth groups exist in a variety of forms and serve a variety of functions. Some groups are designed to enable members to cope with particular problems, even though the problem may be "external" to the member—for example, having an overactive child, a promiscuous spouse, or an alcoholic parent. Other groups are more clearly therapeutic and are designed to change significant aspects of one's personality or behavior.

Some Popular Personal Growth Groups

There are so many varieties of personal growth groups that a catalog of all would be impossible. Instead, a few of the more popular will be briefly identified, and the procedures used in one of these will be considered in depth.

The Encounter Group   The *encounter group* provides an interpersonal and small group atmosphere that facilitates personal growth and the ability to deal effectively with other people. One of its assumptions is that the members will be more effective psychologically and socially if they get to know themselves better (particularly their feelings, but also their failures, vices, virtues, and the like) and get to like themselves better (despite the recognized faults). Consequently, the atmosphere of the encounter group is one of acceptance and support. Freedom to express one's inner thoughts, fears, and doubts is stressed.

The Assertiveness Training Group   The *assertiveness training group* is designed to increase the ability of its members to act more assertively in a wide variety of situations.

The Consciousness-Raising Group   The *consciousness-raising group* grew out of the women's movement and was originally designed to help women cope with the problems society confronts them with and with the rapid changes in atti-

People of all ages spend a great deal of time in small group communication. What types of small groups do you find most rewarding? Least rewarding? What specific factors contribute to making your experiences rewarding or unrewarding?

tudes and behaviors taking place throughout all levels of society. The members of a consciousness-raising group all have one characteristic in common (for example, they are all women, all unwed mothers, all new fathers, or all ex-priests). It is this commonality that leads the members to join together and assist one another in dealing with themselves as well as others. Notice that in the consciousness-raising group the assumption is that similar people are best equipped to assist in one's personal growth.

How One Type of Group Works

Although each personal growth group is unique, there are enough similarities among groups to justify our describing one type of personal growth group to provide further insight into this important type of small group communication situation.

The consciousness-raising group is leaderless; all members (usually ranging from 6 to 12 in number) are equal in their control of the group and in their presumed knowledge.

Topic Selection   A topic is selected by majority vote of the group. At times this topic is drawn from a prepared list and at other times it is suggested by one of the group members. If this group is concerned with, say, women's liberation, the topics are naturally related to this general issue of women's liberation. But regardless of what topic is selected, it is always discussed from the point of view of the larger topic that brings these particular people together—in this case, women's liberation. Whether the topic is "men," "employment," or "family," it is pursued in light of the issues and problems of the liberation of women. The topics may be more completely phrased as "men and the liberated woman," "the liberated woman and employment," or "the liberated woman and the family."

Member Contributions and Feedback   After a topic is selected, a starting point is established through some random procedure. For example, a pencil might be spun, with the discussion beginning with the member at whom the pencil points. Each member speaks for up to 10 minutes about his or her feelings, experiences, and thoughts. The focus is always on oneself. No interruptions are allowed. After the member has finished, the other group members may ask questions of clarification. Challenges, arguments, and disagreements are not permitted. Should a member argue or challenge the speaker, any member of the group may call that person out of order. The feedback from other members is to be totally supportive.

After the questions of clarification have been answered, the next member speaks. The same procedure is followed until all members have spoken. After the last member has spoken, a general discussion follows, during which members may attempt to relate different aspects of their experience to the experiences of others or tell the group how they feel about certain issues. After this discussion period (usually around 20 to 60 minutes), the group disbands to meet again at a prearranged time and place.

With this procedure one's consciousness is raised by formulating and verbalizing one's thoughts on a particular topic, hearing how others feel and think about the same topic and how they have dealt with the issue involved, and formulating and answering questions of clarification.

THE EDUCATIONAL OR LEARNING GROUP

In *educational* or *learning groups,* the purpose is to acquire new information or skill through a mutual sharing of knowledge or insight. In most small group learning situations, all members have something to teach and something to learn, and the members pool their knowledge to the benefit of all.

In the educational or learning group, members may follow a variety of discussion patterns. For example, a historical topic might be developed chronologically, with the discussion progressing from the past into the present and perhaps predicting the future. Issues in developmental psychology—for example, language development in the child or physical maturity—might also be discussed chronologically. Some topics lend themselves to spatial development, wherein the discussion follows a left-to-right or a north-to-south pattern—for example, the development of the United States might take a spatial pattern going from east to west or a chronological pattern going from 1776 to the present. Other suitable patterns, depending on the nature of the topic and the needs of the discussants, might be developed in terms of causes and effects, problems and solutions, or structures and functions.

Perhaps the most popular is the topical pattern, in which the main topic is divided into subdivisions without regard for time or space considerations. A group might discuss the functions of the legal profession by itemizing each of its major functions and discussing these without regard for any additional system of ordering. The structure of a corporation might also be considered in terms of its major divisions. As can be appreciated, each of these two topics may be further systematized by, say, ordering the functions of the legal profession in terms of importance or complexity and ordering the major structures of the corporation in terms of decision-making power.

These patterns are essentially the same ones we consider under the structures of public speaking (in Part Six); they are actually patterns for organizing all sorts of communications. What is most important for the discussants and the leader to recognize is that some pattern or prearranged agenda must be developed if the discussion is to progress productively and if each of the major topics is to be given adequate time.

SMALL GROUP FORMATS

Small groups may serve their functions in a variety of formats. Among the most popular are the panel or round table, the colloquy, the symposium, and the symposium-forum.

The Panel or Round Table   In the panel or round table format, the group members arrange themselves in a circular or semicircular pattern and share the relevant information or attempt to solve the problem without any set pattern to identify who speaks when. Members contribute as they see fit.

The Colloquy   In the colloquy, members of the group are "experts" and participate in a panel or round table format, except that members of the audience are at times asked to contribute, to ask a question, or to provide some feedback.

There is also a two-panel colloquy format, with an expert panel and a lay panel. The lay panel discusses the topic but when in need of technical information, additional data, or direction, they may turn to the expert panel members to provide the needed information.

The Symposium   In the symposium, each member delivers a relatively prepared presentation, much like a public speech. All speeches are addressed to different aspects of one topic. In the symposium, the leader introduces the speakers, provides transitions from one speaker to another, and may provide periodic summaries.

The Symposium-Forum   The symposium-forum consists of two parts: The symposium part consists of prepared speeches, and the forum part consists of questions from the audience and responses by the speakers. The leader here would provide the functions noted for the symposium and in addition would moderate the question-and-answer session.

SUMMARY

1. A small group is a collection of individuals that is small enough for all members to communicate with relative ease as both senders and receivers. The members are related to each other by some common purpose and have some degree of organization or structure among them.

2. The problem-solving group attempts to solve a particular problem or at least to reach a decision that may be a preface to the problem solving itself.

3. Seven steps may be identified in the problem-solving process: define the problem, analyze the problem, establish criteria for evaluating solutions, identify possible solutions, evaluate solutions, select best solution(s), and test solution(s).

4. The idea-generation or brainstorming group attempts to generate as many ideas as possible.

5. The rules for brainstorming are these: no negative criticism is allowed, quantity is desired, combinations and extensions are desired, and free-wheeling is wanted.

6. The personal growth group attempts to enable members to deal with personal problems and to function more effectively.

7. Popular personal growth groups are the encounter group, the assertiveness training group, and the consciousness-raising group.

8. The educational or learning group attempts to acquire new information or skill through a mutual sharing of knowledge or insight.

9. Among the popular small group formats are the panel or round table, with no set pattern as to who speaks when; the colloquy, with "expert" members discussing in a panel-type format and the audience being invited to contribute or to ask questions; the symposium, with each member delivering a relatively prepared presentation, much like a public speech; and the symposium-forum, with each member delivering a talk and the audience questioning the speakers.

SOURCES

Introductions to the area of small group communication are plentiful and generally excellent. Thorough and useful overviews are provided by B. Aubrey Fisher, *Small Group Decision Making: Communication and the Group Process*, 2d ed. (New York: McGraw-Hill, 1980); Francis L. Ulschak, Leslie Nathanson, and Peter G. Gillan, *Small Group Problem Solving* (Reading, Mass.: Addison-Wesley,

1981); and Rodney W. Napier and Matti K. Gershenfeld, *Groups: Theory and Experience*, 2d ed. (Boston: Houghton Mifflin, 1981). On personal growth groups, see Charles M. Rossiter, Jr., "Defining 'Therapeutic Communication,'" *Journal of Communication* 25 (summer 1975): 127–130.

A number of interesting case studies as well as a thorough overview of small group communication are provided by John F. Cragan and David W. Wright, *Communication in Small Group Discussions: A Case Study Approach*, 2d ed. (St. Paul, Minn.: West, 1986).

UNIT 18
MEMBERS AND LEADERS IN GROUP COMMUNICATION

LEARNING GOALS

After completing this unit, you should be able to

1. identify and define the three major types of member roles
2. provide at least two examples of each of the three major types of member roles
3. define *groupthink* and identify at least five of its major symptoms
4. identify and explain at least four functions of leaders in small group communication
5. identify and define the three leadership styles
6. state at least one occasion when each of the three leadership styles would be appropriate

In this unit we consider the roles or functions of small group members and leaders. Each person may well serve all these roles throughout his or her membership in various groups. More often, however, people fall into particular roles that they fulfill in every group in which they participate whether they wish to or not, whether the roles are productive or not. By gaining insight into the various roles of both members and leaders, we will be in a better position to analyze our own small group behavior and to change it if we wish.

MEMBERS IN SMALL GROUP COMMUNICATION

In this section we present a consideration of the major roles members may serve in small group communication and offer some suggestions for more effective and enjoyable member participation.

Member Roles

Kenneth Benne and Paul Sheats in 1948 proposed a classification of the roles of members in small group communication that still seems to serve as the best overview of this important topic. Benne and Sheats divide member roles or functions into three general classes: group task roles, group building and maintenance roles, and individual roles. Each of these general functions may be served by different specific roles. These roles are, of course, frequently served by leaders as well.

Group Task Roles

Group task roles are those that enable the group to focus more specifically on the achievement of its goal or goals. In the performance of any of these roles, the individual does not act as an isolated individual, but rather as a member of a larger whole. The individual's behavior is governed by the immediate and long-range needs and goals of the group. The effective group member will generally serve a number of these functions, perhaps all of them, although often people lock into very few and very specific roles. Thus, for example, one person may almost always seek the opinions of others, another may concentrate on elaborating details, still another on evaluating, and so on. Usually, this singular focus is counterproductive; it is generally better for the roles to be spread more evenly among the members so that each may serve many group task roles.

Twelve specific roles are distinguished as group task roles. The *initiator-contributor* presents new ideas or new perspectives on old ideas. He or she may suggest new goals, a new definition of the problem, or new procedures or organizational strategies. The *information seeker* asks for facts and opinions; this person attempts to secure clarification of the issues being discussed. The *opinion seeker* attempts to discover the values underlying the group's task. The *information giver* presents facts and opinions to the group members, while the *opinion giver* presents values and opinions and attempts to spell out what the values of the group should be. The *elaborator* gives examples and tries to work out possible solutions, trying to build on what others have said.

The *coordinator* spells out relationships among ideas and suggested solutions. This person also coordinates the activities of the different members. The individual serving the *orienter* function summarizes what has been said and addresses himself or herself to the direction the group is taking as well as to the digressions of the group members. He or she attempts to provide the group members with a clear picture of where they are going. The *evaluator-critic* evaluates the group's decisions or proposed solutions. This person questions the logic or the practicality of the suggestions and thus provides the group with both positive and negative feedback on their various decisions and solutions. The *energizer* stimulates the group to greater activity, while the *procedural technician* takes care of the various mechanical duties such as distributing group materials and arranging the seating. Last, the *recorder* writes down the group's activities, suggestions, and decisions. The recorder serves as the memory of the group.

Group Building and Maintenance Roles

No individual and no group can be task-oriented in all matters at all times. The group is a unit that includes varied interpersonal relationships among its members, and these interpersonal relationships need to be built up and maintained if the group is to function effectively—if the group members are to be both satisfied and productive. When these functions are not served, group members may tire of the group quickly, become irritable when the group process gets bogged down, engage in frequent conflicts with one another, or find the small group communication process unsatisfying on a personal or social level. The group and its members need the same kind of interpersonal support that individuals need. The group building and maintenance roles serve this general function.

Group building and maintenance are broken down into seven specific roles. The *encourager* supplies members with positive reinforcement in the form of social approval or praise for its ideas. This person provides the group with understanding and acceptance. The *harmonizer* mediates the various differences between group members. The *compromiser* attempts to resolve conflict between his or her ideas and those of others. This person will offer a compromise by either changing his or her position halfway or even by giving up his or her initial position.

The *gatekeeper-expediter* keeps the channels of communication open by reinforcing the efforts of others. The gatekeeper-expediter may propose to hear from a member who has not yet spoken, or to limit the length or frequency of the contributions from the members. The *standard setter*, or *ego ideal*, sets or proposes standards pertaining to the functioning of the group or to solutions. The *group observer and commentator* keeps a record of the proceedings and uses this in the group's evaluation of itself. Last, the *follower* goes along with the members of the group. He or she passively accepts the ideas of others and functions more as an audience for the other members than as an active member. This last role is not one that is generally recommended, and yet in some instances—for example, when the group is under considerable stress or when there has been a great deal of interpersonal conflict—it may be productive and help preserve group cohesiveness.

Individual Roles

In contrast to the group task and the group building and maintenance roles—which are all productive, aid the group in achieving its goal, and are group-oriented—the roles noted here are counterproductive, hinder the group in achieving its goal, and are individual-oriented. Such roles, often termed *dysfunctional*, hinder the group's effectiveness in both productivity and personal satisfaction.

Eight specific types are identified. The *aggressor* expresses negative evaluation of the actions or feelings of the group members. The aggressor attacks the group or the problem being considered. The *blocker* provides negative feedback, is disagreeable, and opposes other members or suggestions regardless of whether he or she has reasonable grounds for doing so or not. The *recognition seeker* attempts to have attention focused on himself or herself and achieves this by boasting and talking about his or her own accomplishments rather than the task at hand. The *self-confessor* expresses his or her own feelings and personal perspectives rather than focusing on the group. The *playboy* and *playgirl* possess all the negative features we think of when we talk of playboys and playgirls. This person is cynical and jokes around without any regard for the group process.

The *dominator* tries to run the group or the group members. This person may attempt to achieve this by pulling rank, flattering members of the group, or simply acting the role of the boss. The *help seeker* expresses insecurity or confusion or deprecates himself or herself, thereby attempting to make the other members sympathetic toward him or her. Last, the *special-interest pleader* disregards the specific goals of the group and pleads the case of some special group, whether it is labor or management, students or faculty, miners or farmers, or some minority group. To this person, all problems present opportunities to plead for a special interest.

Member Participation

Here are several guidelines that will help make the participation of members in small group communication both more effective and more enjoyable. These suggestions are offered as a kind of elaboration and extension of the basic characteristics of effective interpersonal communication identified in Unit 16.

Be Group-Oriented

In the small group you are a member of a team, a member of some larger whole. Your participation is of value to the extent that it advances the goals of the group with effectiveness and with member satisfaction. The effective participant cooperates with others to achieve some mutually satisfying goal. Your task is to pool your talents, knowledge, and insight so that a solution may be arrived at that is more effective than the solution that could have been reached by any one individual. Persons who attempt to parade their intelligence or individual knowledge, for example, are personally oriented rather than group-oriented; their solo performances hinder the group.

This call for group orientation is not to be taken as a suggestion for abandoning one's individuality or giving up one's personal values or beliefs for the sake of the group. This is clearly an undesirable extreme but one seen frequently in many contemporary cults and small groups. Individuality with a group orientation is what is advocated here.

Center Conflict on Issues

Conflict in small group situations is inevitable. If some form of conflict does not occur, the group is probably irrelevant or the members are so bored that they do not care what is going on. Conflict is a natural part of the exchange of ideas; it is not something that should be feared or ignored. Recognize conflict as a natural part of the small group process, but center it on issues rather than on personalities. Conflict creates problems in small groups when it is person-centered rather than issue-centered.

When you disagree, make it clear that your disagreement is with the proposal advanced, the solution suggested, or the ideas expressed, and not with the person who expressed them. Similarly, when someone disagrees with what you say, do not take this as a personal attack, but rather as an opportunity to discuss issues from an alternative point of view.

When conflict does center on personalities, members have a responsibility to redirect that conflict to the significant issues and to get the conflicting individuals to see that the goals of the group will be better advanced if the conflict is pursued only insofar as it relates to the issues under consideration. For example, right before Chris and Pat come to blows, one might say: "Then, Chris, you disagree with Pat's proposal mainly because it ignores the needs of the handicapped, right?" and go on to suggest that perhaps the group might focus on how the proposal might be enlarged or altered to deal with the needs of the handicapped. When a more direct approach is necessary, you might say, for example: "Let's stick to the issue," "Can we get back to the proposal," or perhaps "Let's hear from a third point of view."

Be Critically Open-Minded

One of the most detrimental developments in a small group occurs when members come to the group with their minds already made up. When this happens, the small group process degenerates into a series of individual debates, each person arguing for his or her own position. Instead, each member should come to the group equipped with relevant information—facts, figures, and ideas that will be useful to the discussion—but should not have decided on the solution or conclusion they will accept. Any solutions or conclusions should be advanced with tentativeness rather than certainty. Discussants should be willing to alter their suggestions and revise them in light of the discussion.

Listen openly but critically to the comments, information, and conclusions of others. Do not come to the discussion prepared to listen openly to some people but not to others, or prepared to accept everything some people say without critically evaluating it. If we regard the information we advance with tentativeness, we should respond in kind to the information advanced by others. This is not to say that we need to ask the source and check the references of everything anyone says, but rather that uncritical acceptance is just as dangerous as closed-mindedness. Be *judiciously* open-minded and *judiciously* critical with your own contributions as well as with the contributions of others.

Ensure Understanding

Make sure that your ideas and information are understood by all participants. If something is worth saying, it is worth making it clearly understood. And so when in doubt, ask the members whether what you are saying is clear—not with "Can you understand that bit of complex reasoning?" but rather with "Is that clear?" or "Did I explain that clearly?"

Make sure too that you understand fully the contributions of the other members, especially before you take issue with them. In fact, it is often wise to preface any extended disagreement with some kind of statement such as "As I understand you, you want to exclude freshmen from playing on the football team, and if that is correct then I want to say why I think that would be a mistake." Then you would go on to state your objections. In this way you give the other person the opportunity to clarify, deny, or otherwise alter what was said and thus frequently save yourself a long argument and the group's time and energy.

Groupthink

After examining the decisions and the decision-making processes of large government organizations—the catastrophic decisions of the Bay of Pigs and Pearl Harbor, the decision processes that went into the development of the Marshall Plan, and President Kennedy's handling of the Cuban missile crisis—Irving Janis developed a theory he calls "groupthink." Groupthink, according to Janis, may be defined as "the mode of thinking that persons engage in when *concurrence seeking* becomes so dominant in a cohesive ingroup that it tends to override realistic appraisal of alternative courses of action." The term itself is meant to signal a "deterioration in mental efficiency, reality testing, and moral judgments as a result of group pressures."

Many specific behaviors of the group members may be singled out as characteristic of groupthink. One of the most significant occurs when the group limits its discussion of possible alternatives to only a small range, overlooking other possibilities. Once the group has made a decision, it does not reexamine its decisions even when there are indications of possible dangers. Little time is spent in discussing why certain initial alternatives were rejected. For example, if high cost led the group to reject a certain alternative, the group members will devote little time, if any, to the ways in which the cost may be reduced. Similarly, the group members make little effort to obtain expert information even from people within their own organization.

The group members are extremely selective in the information they consider seriously. Facts and opinions contrary to the position of the group are generally ignored, while those facts and opinions that support the position of the group are welcomed. The group members generally limit themselves to the one decision or one plan. They fail to discuss alternative decisions or plans in the event that their initial decision fails or encounters problems on the way to implementation.

The following list of symptoms should help us in recognizing the existence of groupthink in the groups we observe or in which we participate.

1. Group members think the group and its members are invulnerable to dangers.
2. Members create rationalizations to avoid dealing directly with warnings or threats.
3. Group members believe their group is moral.
4. Those opposed to the group are perceived in simplistic, stereotyped ways.
5. Group pressure is put on any member who expresses doubts or who questions the group's arguments or proposals.
6. Group members censor their own doubts.
7. Group members believe all members are in unanimous agreement, whether such agreement is stated or not.
8. Group members emerge whose function it is to guard the information that gets to other members of the group, especially when such information may create diversity of opinion.

A Group Membership Evaluation Form

Here is an evaluation form I use in my course in Small Group Communication. It should provide a convenient summary of the member's responsibilities discussed here, as well as some additional effective communication principles that should be demonstrated in small group communication encounters. This form (and the leadership evaluation form to follow) may be adapted to serve more directly and more specifically the unique group situation being observed and evaluated.

LEADERS IN SMALL GROUP COMMUNICATION

In many small group communication situations, one person may serve as leader; in others leadership may be shared by several persons. The leader may be appointed or may simply emerge during the progress of the group communication. In considering leaders and leadership, we focus on two main dimensions. First, we identify the roles or functions leaders perform and examine how leaders might best go about serving these important functions. Second, we identify the general styles leadership may take and the ways these leadership functions may be exercised.

Group Member Evaluation Form

Roles Served

Circle those roles played by the group member and *indicate the specific behaviors that led to these judgments.*

Group task roles: initiator-contributor, information seeker, opinion seeker, information giver, opinion giver, elaborator, coordinator, orienter, evaluator-critic, energizer, procedural technician, recorder

Group building and maintenance roles: encourager, harmonizer, compromiser, gatekeeper-expediter, standard setter or ego ideal, group observer and commentator, follower

Individual roles: aggressor, blocker, recognition seeker, self-confessor, playboy-playgirl, dominator, help seeker, special-interest pleader

Small Group Participation

Is group-oriented	YES!	YES	yes	?	no	NO	NO!
Centers conflict on issues	YES!	YES	yes	?	no	NO	NO!
Is critically open-minded	YES!	YES	yes	?	no	NO	NO!
Ensures understand-ing	YES!	YES	yes	?	no	NO	NO!
Listens attentively	YES!	YES	yes	?	no	NO	NO!
Is well-prepared	YES!	YES	yes	?	no	NO	NO!
Demonstrates confi-dence	YES!	YES	yes	?	no	NO	NO!
Demonstrates posi-tiveness	YES!	YES	yes	?	no	NO	NO!

Improvement Suggestions

Reflect on your recent small group interactions. What behaviors do you find particularly unproductive in small group leaders? In small group members? What behaviors do you find especially productive in leaders? In members?

Leader's Functions

In relatively formal small group situations, as when politicians plan a campaign strategy, advertisers discuss a campaign, or teachers consider educational methods, the leader has a number of specific functions.

These functions are not the exclusive property of the leader; it is more important that these functions be served than who serves them. Nevertheless, when a specific leader is appointed or exists by virtue of some position of prior agreement, these functions are generally expected to be performed by him or her. Leadership functions are performed best when they are performed unobtrusively—when they are performed in a nonobvious, natural manner. Leaders carry out six major functions.

Activate Group Interaction

In many situations, the group needs no encouragement to interact. On the other hand, many groups need some prodding and stimulation to interact. Perhaps the group is newly formed and the members feel a bit uneasy with one another. Here the leader serves an important function by stimulating the members to interact. This function also needs to be served when the individuals of a group are acting as individuals rather than as a group. In this case the leader must do something to make the members recognize that they are part of a group rather than of a subgroup or pair.

Maintain Effective Interaction

Even after the group is stimulated to group interaction, the leader should see that the members maintain effective interaction throughout the discussion and throughout the membership. Discussions have a way of dragging after the preliminaries are over and before the meat of the problem is gotten to. When this happens it is necessary for the leader to prod the group to effective interaction. Also, interaction is seldom shared by all members equally. When disproportionate participation is extreme or when members feel an unease about entering the group interaction, the leader needs to ensure that all members have an opportunity to express themselves.

Keep Members on the Track

Many individuals are egocentric and will pursue only their own interests and concerns. It is the leader's task to keep all members reasonably on track— perhaps by asking relevant questions, by interjecting internal summaries as the group goes along, or by providing suitable transitions so that the relationship of an issue just discussed to one about to be considered is made clear. In some problem-solving and educational groups, a formal agenda may be used to assist in this function.

Ensure Member Satisfaction

Members have different psychological needs and wants, and many people enter groups because of these needs and wants. Even though a group may, for example, deal with political issues, the various members may have come together for reasons that are more psychological than political or intellectual. If a group is to be effective, it must meet not only the surface purposes of the group (in this case, political), but also the underlying or psychological purposes that motivated many of the members to come together in the first place.

One sure way to ignore these needs is for the leader to insist the group members do nothing that is not directly related to the surface purposes of the group. Digressions, assuming they are not too frequent or overly long, are significant parts of the small group process, so they should be recognized as such and allowed.

Encourage Ongoing Evaluation and Improvement

All groups encounter obstacles as they attempt to solve a problem, reach a decision, or generate ideas. No group is totally effective. All groups have room for improvement. If the group is to improve, it must focus some attention on itself. Along with attempting to solve some external problem, it must attempt to solve its own internal problems as well.

Prepare Members for the Discussion

Groups form gradually and need to be eased into any discussion that is meaningful. It is the function of the leader to prepare the group members for the discussion, and this involves preparing the members for the small group interaction as well as for the discussion of a specific issue or problem.

Diverse members should not be expected to just sit down and discuss a problem without becoming familiar with each other, at least superficially. Similarly, if the members are to discuss a specific problem, it is necessary that a proper briefing take place. Perhaps materials need to be distributed to members before the actual discussion, or perhaps members need to be instructed to read certain materials or view a particular film or television show. Whatever the preparations, they should be organized and coordinated by the leader.

Leadership Styles

The functions of the leader may be served with different leadership styles. Generally, three types of leadership are distinguished: laissez-faire, democratic, and authoritarian.

Laissez-Faire Leader

The laissez-faire leader takes no initiative in directing or suggesting alternative courses of action, but rather allows the group to develop and progress on its own, even allowing it to make its own mistakes. This leader gives up or denies any real authority, and so this type may well be called a nonleadership rather than a leadership style. The laissez-faire "leader" does answer questions or provide relevant information, but only when specifically asked. This leader gives little if any reinforcement to the group members; at the same time this leader does not punish either, and so is nonthreatening.

Democratic Leader

The democratic leader provides direction, but allows the group to develop and progress the way the members wish. Group members are encouraged to determine goals and procedures. The democratic leader stimulates self-direction and self-actualization of the group members. Unlike the laissez-faire leader, the democratic leader gives members reinforcement and contributes suggestions for direction and alternative courses of action. Always, however, this leader allows the group to make its own decisions.

Authoritarian Leader

The authoritarian leader is the opposite of the laissez-faire leader. This leader determines the group policies or makes decisions without consulting or securing agreement from the members. This leader is impersonal. Communication goes to the leader and from the leader, but rarely from member to member. This leader attempts to minimize intragroup communication. In this way, the leader's role becomes even more important.

The authoritarian leader assumes the greatest responsibility for the progress of the group and wants no interference from members. This person is concerned with getting the group to accept his or her decisions. This leader often satisfies the group's psychological needs; he or she rewards and punishes the group much as a parent does. And like a parent, the leader concentrates responsibility on himself or herself.

Effectiveness and Leadership Style

A number of important studies have been conducted to examine the relative effectiveness of these various leadership styles. Ralph White and Ronald Lippett studied groups of boys led by the three different styles. They found that in the laissez-faire group, the discussion was member-centered but the boys were inefficient. In the democratic group, cohesiveness was greatest, as was member satisfaction; the work completed, however, was less than that produced by the authoritarian group, though it was judged to be of higher quality. In the authoritarian group, the boys were most productive and efficient. However, morale and satisfaction were lower than in the democratic group. Marvin Shaw found that a group led by an authoritarian leader made fewer errors, took less time, and communicated with fewer messages in solving mathematical problems than the democratic group.

Cecil Gibb, in summarizing the results of a series of studies on democratic as opposed to authoritarian leadership, notes that the authoritarian group produced "(1) a greater quantity of work, but (2) less work motivation and (3) less originality in work; (4) a greater amount of aggressiveness expressed both toward the leader and other group members; (5) more suppressed discontent; (6) more dependent and submissive behavior; (7) less friendliness in the group; and (8) less 'group mindedness.'"

Each of these leadership styles has its place, and we should not consider one style superior to the others. Each is appropriate for a different purpose. In a social group at a friend's house, any leadership other than laissez-faire would be difficult to tolerate. But as Gibb notes, when speed and efficiency are paramount, authoritarian leadership seems the most appropriate. It also seems appropriate when group members continue to show lack of motivation toward the task despite repeated democratic efforts to move them. When all members are about equal in their knowledge of the topic or when the members are very concerned with their individual rights, the democratic leader seems the most appropriate.

A Leadership Evaluation Form

Here is an evaluation form I use in Small Group Communication to evaluate the effectiveness of the group leader in serving a wide variety of roles and functions. As with the group member evaluation form, this leadership form should serve to summarize the wide variety of functions a group leader is expected to serve (some of which have been discussed in the previous unit and others of which should be self-explanatory) and at the same time to provide a useful tool for an observer/critic to use in recording reactions to leadership behaviors.

Leadership Evaluation Form

Introductory Remarks

Greets members	YES!	YES	yes	?	no	NO	NO!
Introduces topic(s)	YES!	YES	yes	?	no	NO	NO!
Introduces members	YES!	YES	yes	?	no	NO	NO!
Explains procedures	YES!	YES	yes	?	no	NO	NO!
Gets group going	YES!	YES	yes	?	no	NO	NO!

Maintenance of Interaction

Keeps members on time schedule	YES!	YES	yes	?	no	NO	NO!
Keeps to agenda	YES!	YES	yes	?	no	NO	NO!

Communication Guidance

Encourages conflict resolution	YES!	YES	yes	?	no	NO	NO!
Clarifies	YES!	YES	yes	?	no	NO	NO!
Ensures member understanding	YES!	YES	yes	?	no	NO	NO!
Involves all members	YES!	YES	yes	?	no	NO	NO!
Encourages expression of differences	YES!	YES	yes	?	no	NO	NO!
Uses transitions	YES!	YES	yes	?	no	NO	NO!
Secures relevant information	YES!	YES	yes	?	no	NO	NO!

Development of Effective Interpersonal Climate

Works for member satisfaction	YES!	YES	yes	?	no	NO	NO!
Builds open atmosphere	YES!	YES	yes	?	no	NO	NO!
Encourages supportiveness	YES!	YES	yes	?	no	NO	NO!

Ongoing Evaluation and Improvement

Encourages criticism	YES!	YES	yes	?	no	NO	NO!
Encourages process suggestions	YES!	YES	yes	?	no	NO	NO!
Accepts disagreements	YES!	YES	yes	?	no	NO	NO!
Directs group self-evaluation	YES!	YES	yes	?	no	NO	NO!
Encourages improvement suggestions	YES!	YES	yes	?	no	NO	NO!

Concluding Remarks

Summarizes	YES!	YES	yes	?	no	NO	NO!
[Involves audience]	YES!	YES	yes	?	no	NO	NO!
Closes discussion	YES!	YES	yes	?	no	NO	NO!

Improvement Suggestions

SUMMARY

1. A popular classification of the roles of members in small groups has been provided by Kenneth Benne and Paul Sheats, who offer a three-part system: group task roles, group building and maintenance roles, and individual roles.

2. Twelve group task roles are identified: initiator-contributor, information seeker, opinion seeker, information giver, opinion giver, elaborator, coordinator, orienter, evaluator-critic, energizer, procedural technician, and recorder.

3. Seven group building and maintenance roles are identified: encourager, harmonizer, compromiser, gatekeeper-expediter, standard setter or ego ideal, group observer and commentator, and follower.

4. Eight individual roles are identified: aggressor, blocker, recognition seeker, self-confessor, playboy or playgirl, dominator, help seeker, and special-interest pleader.

5. Member participation should be group-oriented, should center conflict on issues, should be critically open-minded, and should ensure understanding.

6. *Groupthink* is defined by Irving Janis as "the mode of thinking that persons engage in when *concurrence seeking* becomes so dominant in a cohesive ingroup that it tends to override realistic appraisal of alternative courses of action." The term itself is meant to signal a "deterioration in mental efficiency, reality testing, and moral judgments as a results of group pressures."

7. Among the leader's functions are these: to activate the group interaction, maintain effective interaction, keep members on the track, ensure member satisfaction, encourage ongoing evaluation and improvement, and prepare members for the discussion.

8. Three major leadership styles may be identified. The laissez-faire leader allows the group to develop and progress on its own, the democratic leader provides direction but allows the group to develop and progress as the members wish, and the authoritarian leader determines the group policies or makes decisions without consulting or securing agreement from the members.

SOURCES

On member's roles, see Kenneth D. Benne and Paul Sheats, "Functional Roles of Group Members," *Journal of Social Issues* 4 (1948): 41–49. On leadership roles, see any of the general references noted in Unit 17. For the definitional aspects of leadership, I relied on the reviews by L. F. Carter, "On Defining Leadership," in M. Sherif and M. O. Wilson, eds., *Group Relations at the Crossroads* (New York: Harper & Row, 1953), pp. 262–265, and Marvin Shaw, *Group Dynamics: The Psychology of Small Group Behaviors*, 3d ed. (New York: McGraw-Hill, 1981).

On styles of leadership, see the seminal study by Ralph White and Ronald Lippitt, *Autocracy and Democracy* (New York: Harper & Row, 1960). Also see Marvin E. Shaw, "A Comparison of Two Types of Leadership in Various Communication Nets," *Journal of Abnormal and Social Psychology* 50 (1955): 127–134, and J. F. Sargent and G. R. Miller, "Some Differences in Certain Communication Behaviors of Autocratic and Democratic Leaders," *Journal of Communication* 21 (1971): 233–252. Excellent sources on leadership are Cecil A. Gibb's "Leadership," in G. Lindsey and E. Aronson, eds., *The Handbook of Social Psychology*, 2d ed., vol. 4 (Reading, Mass.: Addison-Wesley, 1969), pp. 205–282 and Warren Bennis and Burt Nanus, *Leaders: The Strategies for Taking Charge* (New York: Harper & Row, 1985).

For groupthink, see Irving L. Janis's *Victims of Groupthink: A Psychological Study of Foreign Policy Decisions and Fiascoes*, 2d ed., rev. (Boston: Houghton Mifflin, 1983).

UNIT 19
ORGANIZATIONAL COMMUNICATION

LEARNING GOALS

After completing this unit, you should be able to

1. define an *organization*
2. define *organizational communication*
3. define the communication roles of the gatekeeper, the liaison, the opinion leader, and the cosmopolite
4. explain the essential characteristics of the four approaches to organizations discussed here: the scientific approach, the human relations approach, the systems approach, and the cultural approach
5. describe the five communication network structures: the wheel, the Y, the circle, the chain, and the all-channel
6. describe the ways in which the network structures influence communication
7. define and identify the major characteristics of upward communication, downward communication, lateral communication, serial communication, and the grapevine
8. explain the concept of information overload and its relevance to organizations and to organizational communication

n his landmark book, *The Functions of the Executive,* Chester Barnard observed: "In an exhaustive theory of organization, communication would occupy a central place, because the structure, extensiveness, and scope of organization are almost entirely determined by communication techniques." In this unit we explain this central position of communication by covering a number of interrelated topics in an area now called "organizational communication." First, we define organizations and organizational communication. Second, we explore four approaches to organizations and look specifically at the role these approaches give to communication. Third, we examine a variety of communication patterns or networks and their influence on two of the major concerns of organizations: productivity and worker satisfaction or morale. Fourth, we consider the issue of communication flow. We look at upward, downward, lateral, and serial communication and the ubiquitous grapevine and examine the causes and consequences of information overload.

ORGANIZATION AND ORGANIZATIONAL COMMUNICATION: DEFINITIONS

If we are to understand organizational communication, we first must define what an organization is and what characterizes the communication taking place within organizations.

The Organization

An *organization* may be defined as a group of individuals organized for the achievement of specific goals. The number of individuals varies greatly from one organization to another. Some have three or four members working in close contact; others have thousands of workers scattered throughout the world. What is important is that these individuals operate within a defined structure. The level of structure also varies greatly from one organization to another. Some are rigidly structured: Each person's role and position within the hierarchy is clearly defined. Others are more loosely structured: Roles may be interchanged, and hierarchical status may be unclear and relatively unimportant.

Within any organization, there are both formal and informal structures. For example, in a college there is the formal academic structure, with the president at the top, deans at the next level, department chairpersons at the next, faculty at the next, and so on. Through this structure the work of the university is accomplished. But there are also informal structures throughout the university, and in many cases these cross the various hierarchical lines. These might include, for example, the four math professors who bowl together, the sociology instructor and the dean of arts who attend AA meetings together, and the graduate assistants and junior faculty members who study together and write their early articles. These informal structures serve the human needs of the individuals and keep the workers together as a unit.

The goal of most organizations is to make money, but a variety of subordinate goals must be achieved if this ultimate goal is to be reached. Thus, for example, in order to make money, the organization must maintain an effective work force. To do this, it is necessary to have satisfied workers. To have satisfied workers, it may be necessary to have adequate parking facilities, merit bonuses, clean and safe working conditions, and so on. A nonprofit organization, on the other hand, would have as its ultimate goal something other than making money—to disseminate information, offer legal counsel for the poor, or compile statistics on various events. In these cases, the goal of making money (or of getting funded, as the expression goes) would probably be a subordinate one, necessary to achieve if these other goals are to be realized.

Each worker in each organization will naturally have different goals. The ultimate goal for most is to earn a salary, but workers, like organizations, also have subordinate goals that are usually consistent with this general goal. So workers may have such goals as to perform a job well; to get a promotion, a transfer, a raise, or a bonus; to interact with others in pleasant surroundings; to develop a network of friends; and so on.

These varied goals are often compatible—performing a job well and thus earning a promotion is likely to be consistent with the organization's goal of increasing productivity and earning more money. But sometimes these goals are incompatible—for example, workers may want raises, which means less profit for the organization. These goals of both the organization as a whole and the individual workers are achieved largely through the formal and informal communication that takes place within the organization.

The Communications

Organizational communication refers to the messages sent and received within the organization—within the organization's formal and informal groups. As the organization becomes larger and more complex, so do the communications. In a three-person organization communication is relatively simple, but in an organization of thousands it becomes a highly complex and often specialized function. In such complex organizations, even the communication roles become specialized, and each exerts considerable influence on the organization. Rogers and Rogers have identified four such crucial communication roles.

The Gatekeeper This person controls the messages that get into the system or that get to any one member of the organization. The secretary who screens phone calls or who sorts the mail serves this function every day, as does a line manager who conveys to or conceals from the workers certain information received from the executive level.

The Liaison This person connects two subgroups within the organization but does not belong to either. The liaison serves as a link between, say, students and faculty within a college organization but is neither a student nor a faculty member, perhaps being instead a counselor, coach, or dormitory director.

The Opinion Leader   This person is the one to whom others look for guidance and direction. This is the person who influences others.

The Cosmopolite   This person is the one who communicates often with many individuals from various subgroups throughout the organization.

Formal and Informal Communications

Organizational communication may be both formal and informal. The formal communications are those sanctioned by the organization itself and are organizationally oriented; they deal with the workings of the organization, with productivity, and with the various jobs done throughout the organization. The informal communications are socially sanctioned; they are oriented not to the organization itself, but to the individual members.

Although we have defined organizational communication as occurring within the organization, remember that organizations spend considerable time, energy, and money on securing information from outside and on disseminating information to other organizations or to the general public. Although these outgoing messages are organizationally motivated, they are probably best treated as examples of public, mass, or even interpersonal communication, depending on the situation.

APPROACHES TO ORGANIZATIONS

Four major approaches to organizations have been identified and are discussed here: the scientific management or classical approach, the human relations approach, the systems approach, and the cultural approach.

The Scientific Approach

This approach holds that scientific methods should be applied to organizations to increase productivity. Scientifically controlled studies will enable management to identify the ways and means for increasing productivity and ultimately profit. The scientific management approach owes much of its formulation to the theories of Frederick W. Taylor, most thoroughly presented in his *Scientific Management*, published in 1911.

In this view productivity is largely a physical and physiological problem. It is viewed in terms of the physical demands of the job and the physiological capabilities of the workers. Time-and-motion studies are perhaps the most characteristic type of research and are designed to enable the organization to reduce the time it takes to complete a specific task—to cut down the motion and to best fit the person to the task. Taylor, for example, conducted time-and-motion studies of coal shoveling, and analyzed and compared different sizes of shovels and the various tasks to be accomplished. As a result, he was able to reduce the number of workers needed to do the same work from 400–600 to 140. Under this system, workers were to be paid according to individual performance; there was a clear reward system.

Communication is viewed as the giving of orders and the explaining of procedures and operations. Only the formal structure of the organization and the formal communication system are recognized.

The Human Relations Approach

The human relations approach developed as a reaction against the exclusive concern with the physical and the exclusion of psychological and social factors in measuring organizational success. One of the principal assumptions of the human relations approach is that increases in worker satisfaction lead to increases in productivity: A happy worker is a productive worker. Management's function, therefore, is to keep the workers happy.

Since leaders establish the norms that group members follow, control of the leadership is considered one of the best ways to increase satisfaction and production. Management is to influence the leaders, who then influence the workers to be happy and hence productive. The human relations approach strongly favors the democratic leader—the leader who encourages members to participate in the running of the organization by offering suggestions, giving feedback, and sharing their problems and complaints. What is desired, in Rensis Likert's terms, is "participatory management." All members of the organization are to participate in the decisions that ultimately affect them. Communication is one of management's main tools in this endeavor. The human relations approach acknowledges the importance of the social, informal groups within the organization and gives special consideration to the interpersonal communications within these groups.

But even in this seemingly best of all possible worlds, where the communication is free and the leadership democratic, the human relations school too encountered difficulties. The major problem was that the approach was based on an invalid assumption—namely, that satisfaction and productivity were positively related. They were in some cases, but certainly not in all. As you know from your own courses, there are some classes in which you are very productive, learn a great deal, and do well, but that you simply do not enjoy. And there are others you enjoy, but from which you gain little. Yet another problem with the human relations approach is that it gives too much attention to agreement and fails to note the very real and important contribution played by conflict and competition.

The Systems Approach

The systems approach combines the best elements of the scientific and human relations approaches. It views an organization as a system in which all parts interact and in which each part influences every other part. This view is the same view we take of communication (see Unit 1). Ideally, the organization is to be viewed as an open system—open to new information, responsive to the environment, dynamic and ever-changing. A closed system, in contrast, is closed to new information, unresponsive to the environment, and static or unchanging.

The systems approach argues that both the physical and physiological factors of the scientific management approach and the social and psychological factors of the human relations approach are important, and each influences the others. All must be taken into consideration if a fully functioning organization is to be achieved.

Here too, communication is extremely important; communication is what keeps the system vital and alive. If a system is to survive and if its parts are to be coordinated and its activities synchronized, communication is essential. Communication is what relates the various parts to each other and what brings in the new ideas. The systems approach emphasizes that the organization—the whole—is more complex than the sum of all its parts, simply because the organization is the sum of its parts PLUS their interactions, and the effects of these interactions, and the effects of these effects, and so on.

The Cultural Approach

A contemporary approach to organizations holds that a corporation should be viewed as a society or a culture. Much as a social group or culture will have various norms or rules of behaviors, roles, heroes, and values, for example, so does an organization. In this approach, then, an organization is studied to identify the type of culture it is and its specific norms or values. The aim of such an analysis is to enable us to understand better the ways the organization functions and the ways in which it influences and is influenced by the members (workers) of that organizational culture.

Ultimately, this approach would enable us to identify weaknesses and suggest correctives; ways to increase worker satisfaction, productivity, and company profit; and new directions for workers and the organization.

Hypotheses or educated guesses about what will make for a successful corporation can be derived from an examination of those qualities that make for a successful social group or society. For example, heroes are important to a social group and successful corporations can sometimes create their own. If an organization can create a hero—perhaps like Henry Ford was to Ford Motors and Lee Iacocca is to Chrysler—it may succeed in developing a dominant culture (or corporation).

The corporation is here viewed as a social group or culture—often in the language of the sociologist and anthropologist—organized around a similar set of values and goals with workers who have a kind of citizenship in the corporation. Much like citizens of a country, workers contribute to the growth and prosperity of the organization but also—as members of the culture or organization—reap the benefits of this growth and prosperity. Both worker morale or satisfaction and productivity and profits, therefore, go hand-in-hand. They are not separate and isolated goals but integrally related ones.

In this view communication is not simply messages that are sent from one member to another through one or more channels (as conceived in some network analyses). Rather, communication is seen as integral to the very definition of an organization; communication, in fact, defines and constructs the organization, its structures, and its functions. The organization is not something apart from its workers and its communications; rather, the organization is created and takes its form—its very identity—from its workers and their communication interactions.

In one of the most popular books on the topic of organizations, *In Search of Excellence: Lessons from America's Best-Run Companies,* Thomas Peters and Robert Waterman make great use of this view of corporations as cultures—though they use other approaches and perspectives as well—and propose that "excellent corporations" are characterized by eight qualities. A review of these qualities should effectively round out our discussion of approaches to organizations. In reviewing these qualities, try to identify the organizational approach each derives from or supports. Excellent companies do the following:

1. *They have a bias for action.* These companies prefer action to lengthy surveys, reports, and committee meetings.
2. *They stay close to the customer.* These companies listen to their customers and try to provide the quality and service that the customers want.
3. *They encourage leaders who are autonomous and entrepreneurial.* These companies encourage "practical risk taking" and creativity in their workers.
4. *They achieve productivity through people.* These companies regard the rank and file members as the major source of productivity; sharp divisions between management and labor are discouraged.
5. *They encourage hands-on management.* In these companies management knows what is going on because management stays close to the main operations of the company, for example, visiting the stores and inspecting the plants.
6. *They stick to what they know.* These companies know the business the company is in and do not attempt to involve themselves in operations about which they are not expert.
7. *They have simple organizational structures and are lean at the top.* These companies are structured very simply, without a complicated organizational structure to create problems, and with a relatively small staff at the top of the hierarchy.
8. *They are decentralized (loose) and centralized (tight).* These companies are generally decentralized in that the workers are relatively autonomous but they are highly centralized in terms of their goals and their values, for example.

COMMUNICATION NETWORKS

Diagraming normal face-to-face communication would be relatively simple; we might diagram it as shown in Figure 19.1. But in organizations, because of their rigidly structured hierarchies, the large physical distances between people, the

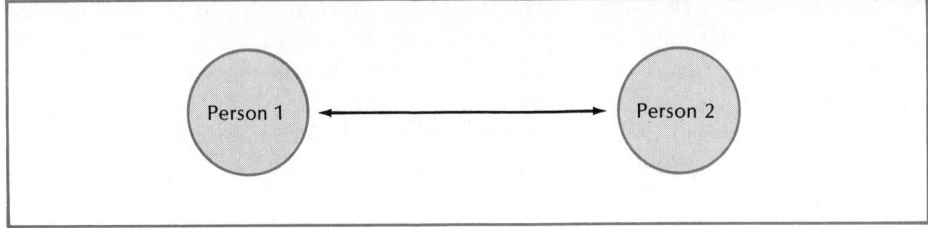

FIGURE 19.1 Face-to-face communication.

great differences in competence, and the specialized tasks that must be accomplished, a number of different networks have evolved. By a *network*, we mean the channels through which messages pass from one person to another. These networks may be viewed from two perspectives. First, small groups left to their own resources will develop communication patterns resembling these several network structures. These networks, then, represent some of the most commonly employed systems of communication channels that groups use to send messages from one person to another. Second, these networks may also be viewed as formalized structures established by an organization for communication within the company. With either perspective, recognize that these networks represent general types of group communication patterns whose counterparts, often in some modified form, can be found in most groups and in most organizations. Five major networks are examined briefly, first in terms of structure and second in terms of their actual operation within an organization.

The Network Structures

The five patterns are presented in Figure 19.2. Each contains five individuals, although they may be enlarged to incorporate more or reduced to deal with fewer than five. The arrows indicate the direction the messages may take.

The Wheel   The wheel is characterized by the centralized position of a clear leader, who is the only one who can send messages to all members and the only one who can receive messages from all members. All others are restricted to sending and receiving messages from only one other person (namely, the leader).

The Y   The Y pattern is somewhat less centralized than the wheel, but more centralized than some of the other patterns. Here there is also a clear leader (the third person from the bottom in Figure 19.2). But one other member plays a type of secondary leadership role (the second person from the bottom). This member can send and receive messages from two others, whereas the remaining three are restricted to communicating with only one other.

The Circle   The circle has no leader; here there is total equality. Each member of the circle has exactly the same authority or power to influence the group; each of the members may communicate with the two members on either side.

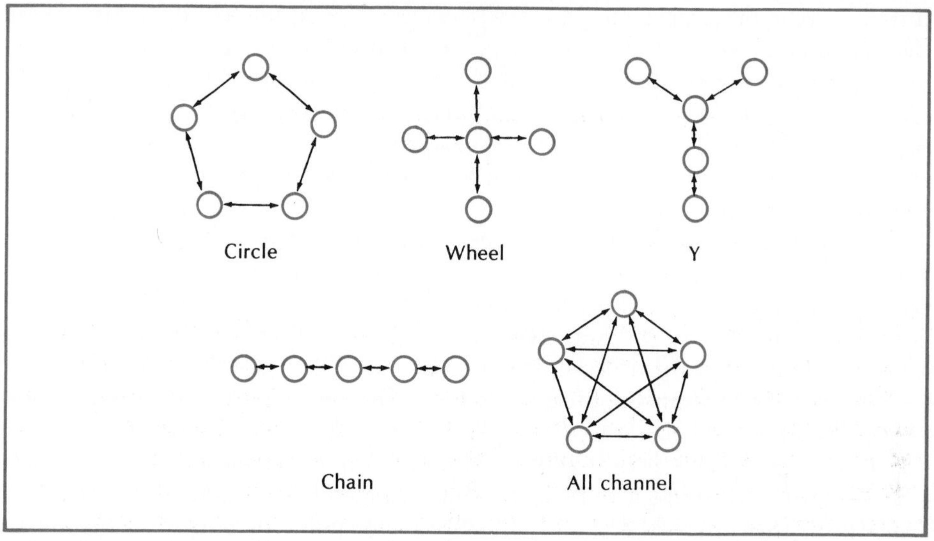

FIGURE 19.2 Five network structures.

The Chain   The chain is similar to the circle except that the end members may communicate with only one person each. There is some centrality here; the middle position is more leaderlike than any of the other positions.

The All-Channel   The all-channel or star pattern is like the circle in that all members are equal and all have exactly the same amount of power to influence others, except that each member in this pattern may communicate with any other member. This pattern allows for the greatest member participation. Note another characteristic of the all-channel group: It can be restructured into any of the other four patterns, but the other four patterns have no such flexibility. (The one exception is that the circle can be restructured into the chain.) Thus, for example, the all-channel pattern may, if conditions warrant, be changed to the wheel to gain the advantage of a central leader.

Communication through these networks occurs often but not always face-to-face. Messages may be written in informal memos or in formal letters and reports. Messages may be sent and responded to by computer. Groups may also communicate in a teleconference, wherein several members are simultaneously connected by telephone, or in a video teleconference, wherein each member can both see and hear each other member although they may be in separate offices, buildings, or cities.

Network Productivity and Morale

These networks are not good or bad in themselves; they are better viewed as useful or useless for a specific task. For example, the highly centralized patterns—the wheel and the Y—are most efficient for dealing with relatively simple and repetitive tasks, such as those in which information must be collected in one place and disseminated to others. Information overload, to be discussed later, is most likely to occur in the highly centralized groups, since all information is coming to one person. These central individuals also become gatekeepers and often prevent information from getting to the various members. Sometimes this may be due simply to information overload; at other times it may be due to the leader's evaluating the information as useless or harmful to the workings of the group.

Those in the central positions seem to have relatively high morale; they do a lot of work, have the most power, and are the most satisfied. The others in these centralized groups, however, develop relatively low morale since they do little and have little or no influence on the functioning of the group. Members of an all-channel group, in contrast, usually have high morale.

All highly centralized groups depend on the effectiveness of that one person in the central position. If that person is an effective leader-communicator, the success of the group as a whole is almost assured; conversely, if that person is ineffective, the entire group will suffer. In the all-channel pattern, however, the effectiveness of any one individual will not make or break the group; in fact, the contributions of any one individual in the all-channel pattern are relatively unimportant.

But even the relationship between morale and participation or power may be oversimplified. Although, for example, it has been found that morale is high when participation is high, as in the all-channel group, this group is inefficient in dealing with relatively simple and repetitive tasks. This inefficiency may well lead to a decline in morale, since few people want to be associated with an inefficient organization. Here, by the way, is a good example of the value of the systems view: all elements (here morale and efficiency) interact; they are not separate and distinct parts, but rather interrelated aspects of the same whole.

Some groups seem to adapt well to change, whereas others do not. Groups in the wheel pattern, for example, seem to have difficulty adapting to changing tasks and changing conditions. But when the pattern is the circle, where everyone is equal, the group seems to adapt well. It accepts new ideas much more readily. Yet its relative inefficiency in terms of time makes it a poor choice for dealing with simple, repetitive tasks.

COMMUNICATION FLOW IN ORGANIZATIONS

It is useful to discuss communication in organizations in terms of the direction in which it flows. Upward and downward (also called vertical) communication, lateral communication, and serial (also called horizontal) communication are perhaps the most important. In addition, we will look at the grapevine and at some of the causes and effects of information overload.

Upward Communication

Upward communication refers to messages sent from the lower levels of the hierarchy to the upper levels—for example, line worker to manager, faculty member to dean. The type of information communicated is usually concerned with (1) job-related activities—that is, what is going on on the job, what was accomplished, what remains to be done, and similar issues; (2) job-related problems and unresolved questions; (3) ideas for change and suggestions for improvement; and (4) job-related feelings about the organization, about the work, about other workers, and similar issues.

Upward communication is vital to the maintenance and growth of the organization. It gives management the necessary feedback on worker morale and possible sources of dissatisfaction. It gives subordinates a sense of belonging to and being a part of the organization. And it provides management with the opportunity to learn of new ideas, which often originate from line workers.

Problems with Upward Communication

Despite its importance to the organization, upward communication is extremely difficult to handle. One problem is that messages traveling up the ladder are often messages higher-ups want to hear. Workers are often reluctant to send up a negative message for fear that they will be viewed as troublemakers. Workers may send only positive messages and thus prevent management from obtaining an accurate view of what is going on. Often the messages that are sent up, especially those concerning worker dissatisfaction, are not heard or responded to by management because of its preoccupation with productivity or because it does not know how to deal with such problems. When these messages are ignored, workers feel there is no point to sending them. Then dissatisfactions fester and become major problems.

Sometimes the messages never get through: Gatekeepers may be so rigid that certain types of messages are automatically rerouted. When the issues concern clarification of job assignments, many workers prefer to go to other workers rather than to management for fear that they will be thought incompetent. Students will often do the same thing. Rather than ask the teacher to clarify something, they will frequently ask other students who probably do not understand the issues any better.

Still another problem is that management, preoccupied with sending messages down the ladder, may have lost some capacity for receiving messages. Managers are so used to serving as sources for messages that they become poor listeners. Workers easily sense this and, quite logically, don't waste their time on upward communication. One further barrier is the purely physical one; management is frequently physically separated from the workers. Usually management offices are on other floors of the building, and not infrequently they are in other cities. It becomes difficult in such situations to go to management with a work-related problem that needs immediate attention.

Downward Communication

Downward communication refers to messages sent from the higher levels of the hierarchy to the lower levels—for example, messages sent by managers to workers, or from deans to faculty members. Perhaps the most obvious example of downward communication is the giving of orders: "Type this in duplicate," "Send these crates out by noon," "Design and write the advertisement," and so on. Along with these order-giving messages are the accompanying explanations of procedures, goals, and the like. Managers are also responsible for giving appraisals of workers and for motivating them, all in the name of productivity and for the good of the organization as a whole.

Problems with Downward Communication

Management and labor often speak different languages, and many managers simply do not know how to make their messages understandable to workers. Most managers, for example, have more education and a greater command of the technical language of the business; these differences can create communication problems. Today we also see a large number of workers in factories, auto plants, and the like who speak English very poorly or not at all. Many managers cannot speak the native language of the workers, so communication becomes nearly impossible.

In both upward and downward communication, management controls the communication system. The managers have the time, the expertise, and the facilities to improve the communication that takes places in an organization. And it seems logical to assign the responsibility for an effective communication system to management. This is not to say that the workers or lower levels are absolved of their responsibility; effective communication is a two-way process. Nevertheless, management bears the larger responsibility for establishing and maintaining an effective and efficient internal communication system.

Lateral Communication

Lateral communication refers to messages sent by equals to equals—manager to manager, worker to worker, and faculty member to faculty member. Such messages may move within the same subdivision or department of the organization or across divisions. Lateral communication may refer to the communication that takes place between two history professors at Illinois State University as well as that which takes place between the psychologist at Ohio State and the communicologist at Kent State.

Lateral communication facilitates the sharing of insights, methods, and problems and thus enables the organization to avoid some problems and to solve others. Lateral communication also facilitates worker satisfaction and builds morale. Good relationships and meaningful communication between workers are among the main sources of worker satisfaction. More generally, lateral communication serves the purpose of coordinating the various activities of the organization and enabling the various divisions to pool insights and expertise.

Problems with Lateral Communication

One obvious problem with lateral communication is the specialized languages that divisions of an organization may develop. Such languages are often unintelligible to receivers. To communicate with the psychologist, for example, it is essential to speak the language of psychology—to know the meaning of such terms as *reinforcement schedules, egoism, catharsis, STM,* and *free association.* Not everyone does. And as specialization increases in every field, it becomes increasingly difficult for the behavioral psychologist to understand the clinical psychologist and, even within clinical psychology, for the Freudian to understand the Jungian.

Another problem is the tendency of workers in a specialized organization to view their area as the one crucial to the health and success of the company. Within a university, we see this clearly: Each faculty member sees her or his department as being, if not the most important, certainly one of the most important for the education of the student. This prevents us from seeing the value in the work of others and often precludes a meaningful exchange of ideas.

Another barrier is that while effective lateral communication is a sharing and pooling of insights and resources, we live in a competitive society and work in competitive organizations. If there is only one promotion available and that promotion is to be made on the basis of quality of work accomplished, it really does not benefit workers to share their best insights with those who may, because of these added insights, secure that one promotion.

Serial Communication

Serial communication refers to messages sent along a chain of people. We see this kind of communication all around us; we hear something and tell a friend, who then tells another friend, who then tells someone else, and so on. In an organization, this is how rumors spread; generally, the system works quickly and efficiently.

Problems with Serial Communication

Gordon Allport and Leo Postman, in the influential study of rumor, found that three distortions interfered with effective and efficient serial communication: leveling, sharpening, and assimilation. In *leveling*, the number of details is reduced; some are omitted entirely, and some lose their complexity. In leveling, we reduce the original message to a more simplified form that is more easily transmitted to the next person.

At the same time that details become omitted in leveling, other details become crystallized and heightened in a process called *sharpening*. One or two aspects of the message that may be particularly relevant to you become highlighted, emphasized, and perhaps embellished.

Assimilation refers to the tendency to rework messages that we receive in terms of our own attitudes, prejudices, needs, and values. Thus, for example, if we had an extremely negative attitude toward management and we received a message that was ambiguous in its evaluation of management, we might not perceive the ambiguity. We might instead assimilate this message into our own value system and see a negative evaluation. In passing this message on to others, it is the negative evaluation that is transmitted. The next person receiving the message knows nothing of the original ambiguity, but learns only the now explicit negative evaluation.

Organizational communication is one of the fastest growing areas in the broad field of communication. Reflect on the organizations in which you have participated and identify the common communication problems you have witnessed. How might you apply some of the principles discussed in this text and in this course to solve these common problems? Put differently, what recommendations would you make to the organization's members for improving their communications?

The Grapevine

The types of communication discussed so far follow the formal structure of the organization. If we had an organizational chart, we would be able to plot the flow of messages along clearly established lines, whether upward, downward, or across. Grapevine messages—a type of serial communication but having some additional properties that merit its separate consideration—do not follow such formal lines; rather, they seem to have a life of their own and travel many routes. Often it is difficult to discover the source of the original message, which is why it is so difficult to ascertain the truth or falsity of grapevine information.

The term *grapevine* seems to have originated during the Civil War, when telegraph wires were hung from tree to tree and resembled grapevines. Messages that travel through no organized structure also resemble the physical grapevine, with its unpredictable pattern of branches. The grapevine, according to organizational theorist Keith Davis, seems most likely to be used when (1) there is great upheaval or change within the organization; (2) the information is new—no one likes to spread old and well-known information; (3) face-to-face communication is physically easy; and (4) workers "cluster in clique-groups along the vine." The grapevine is most active immediately after the happening that is to be communicated and is most likely to be activated when the news concerns one's intimates, friends, and associates. We seem less concerned with grapevine information when it concerns those about whom we know or care little.

Although the grapevine is part of every large organization's informal communications, it is not used as frequently as folklore would have us believe, according to John Baird. It is unlikely to grow in climates that are stable and comfortable; change and ambiguity nourish the grapevine. Even more surprising than its relative infrequency of usage, however, is its reported accuracy. Keith Davis, for example, found that 75 to 95 percent of grapevine information is correct. Even though many details are omitted, the stories are basically true.

Although many managers may view the grapevine as a great inconvenience and would, if they could, wish it out of existence, it actually serves some useful purposes. Keith Davis observes: "A lively grapevine reflects the deep psychological need of people to talk about their jobs and their company as a central life interest. Without it, the company would literally be sick." Its speed and accuracy make it an ideal medium to carry a great deal of the social communications that so effectively bind together workers in an organization.

Information Overload

Today, with the explosion of technology, information overload is becoming one of our greatest problems. Information is being generated at such a rapid rate that it is becoming extremely difficult (actually, impossible) to keep up with all that is relevant to one's job. Invariably, each person must select certain information to attend to and other information to omit.

Information is so easily and quickly generated and disseminated throughout an organization that we often forget that it still takes time to digest the information and to make use of it in a meaningful way. The junk mail that seems to grow every day is a perfect example of the results of the technological advances that make this sending of information so easy, quick, and inexpensive. Now what we need is the corresponding technology to enable us to read and use the information just as quickly.

Another major cause of overload is that many organizational managers disseminate information as a substitute for doing something about a problem or issue. A department head confronted with a problem may choose to write a memo on the problem and distribute it to all workers. The manager has thus bought time, but has also added to the information overload. Action on the problem can now be delayed until responses from the workers or other managers are received—until they can digest, think about, and respond to the memo.

Information overload has probably crept into all organizations of any size. And of course this is the major reason why so many organizations have computerized their operations; putting everything on computer is a relatively easy and efficient way to deal with vast amounts of information. But putting it on computer isn't the whole answer; some human being must still do something about the information—at least usually. And under conditions of information overload, errors are more likely simply because the person cannot devote the needed time to any one item. The more rushed we are, the more likely we are to make mistakes. There are also likely to be great delays between the sending of the message and the taking of the required action. And delays are inefficient and costly to an organization.

SUMMARY

1. An organization may be defined as a group of individuals organized for the achievement of specific goals.

2. *Organizational communication* refers to the messages sent and received within the organization, within both its formally structured and informally established groups.

3. The *gatekeeper* controls the messages that get into the organizational system or that get to any one member of the organization.

4. The *liaison* connects two subgroups within the organization but does not belong to either.

5. The *opinion leader* is looked to for guidance and direction, and influences other members of the group.

6. The *cosmopolite* communicates often with many individuals from various subgroups throughout the organization.

7. Four major approaches to organizations have been identified: The *scientific management* or classical approach holds that scientific methods should be applied to organizations to increase productivity; the *human relations approach* holds that increases in worker satisfaction lead to increases in productivity; the *systems approach* combines the best elements of the scientific and human relations approaches, and emphasizes the fact that an organization is a system in which all parts interact and in which each part influences every other part; and the *cultural approach* suggests that we view organizations as cultures.

8. *Communication networks* refer to the channels that messages pass through from one person to another. They may be viewed both as the communication patterns that develop when small groups are left to their own resources, as well as the formalized structures that are established by an organization for communication within the company.

9. *Upward communication* refers to messages sent from the lower levels of the hierarchy to the upper levels.

10. *Downward communication* refers to messages sent from the higher levels of the hierarchy to the lower levels.

11. *Lateral communication* refers to messages sent by equals to equals.

12. *Serial communication* refers to messages sent along a chain of people.

13. The *grapevine* refers to the informal channels that messages pass through in an organization and that are especially likely to be used when there is great upheaval or change within the organization, the information is new,

face-to-face communication is physically easy, and workers are grouped into cliques along the vine.

14. *Information overload* refers to the situation in which the information sent to any person exceeds that person's capacity to process it.

SOURCES

The area of organizational communication is one of the fastest-growing within the entire field of communication, and the literature is extensive. One of the most useful sources for the preparation of this unit was John E. Baird, Jr., *The Dynamics of Organizational Communication* (New York: Harper & Row, 1977). Also useful were Ernest G. Bormann, William S. Howell, Ralph G. Nichols, and George L. Shapiro, *Interpersonal Communication in the Modern Organization*, 2d ed. (Englewood Cliffs, N.J.: Prentice-Hall, 1982), and Richard K. Allen, *Organizational Management Through Communication* (New York: Harper & Row, 1977). For the different approaches to organizations and the communication roles in organizations, see Everett Rogers and Rekha Agarwala-Rogers, *Communication in Organizations* (New York: Free Press, 1976), Marshall Sashkin and William C. Morris, *Organizational Behavior: Concepts and Experiences* (Reston, Va.: Reston Publishing [Prentice-Hall], 1984), and Gary L. Krebs, *Organizational Communication* (New York: Longman, 1986). For a recent and insightful analysis of organizational communication, see Linda Putnam and M. Pacanowsky, eds., *Communication and Organizations: An Interpretive Approach* (Beverly Hills, Calif.: Sage, 1983). For an excellent introduction to organizations that emphasizes communication, see Stan Kossen, *The Human Side of Organizations*, 3d ed. (New York: Harper & Row, 1983). Perhaps the most comprehensive introduction is provided by Gerald Goldhaber, *Organizational Communication*, 4th ed. (Dubuque, Iowa: Wm. C. Brown, 1986).

UNIT 20
INTERVIEWING

LEARNING GOALS

After completing this unit, you should be able to

1. define *interviewing*
2. explain the major characteristics of the following types of interview: the informative interview, the persuasive interview, the appraisal interview, the exit interview, the employment interview, and the counseling interview
3. identify and explain at least three principles you should follow in preparing for the interview
4. identify and explain at least three principles you should follow during the interview transaction
5. identify and explain the two procedures you should follow after the interview has been concluded
6. identify at least three types of questions that are unlawful to ask and explain how you would deal with such questions

- A salesperson attempts to sell a client a new car.
- A teacher talks with a student about the reasons for the student's having failed the course.
- A counselor talks with a family about their communication problems.
- A recent graduate applies to IBM for a job in the product development division.
- A building owner talks with a potential apartment renter.
- A priest talks with a parishioner about marital problems.
- A lawyer examines a witness during a trial.
- A theatrical agent talks with a potential client.
- A client discusses some of the qualities desired in a potential mate with a dating service employee.
- A boss talks with an employee about some of the reasons for terminating the contract.

Each of these communication situations constitutes an interview, the subject of this unit.

INTERVIEWING DEFINED

Interviewing is a particular form of interpersonal communication in which two persons interact largely through a question-and-answer format for the purpose of achieving specific goals. Interviews *usually* involve two persons; some, however, take place among more people. At conventions, for example, where many people apply for the few available jobs, interviewers often interview several persons at once. The idea is to present the general nature of the job, to answer some of the more common questions, to learn something about the candidates, and perhaps to pare the numbers down. Similarly, therapy situations, although normally involving only two persons, frequently involve entire families, groups of co-workers, or other related individuals. Nevertheless, the two-person interview is certainly the most common and is the one we will be referring to throughout this unit.

The interview is distinctly different from other forms of communication because it proceeds through questions and answers. The content of the interview is guided and, in fact, rigidly structured on the basis of the specific questions asked and the answers given. Both parties in the interview ask and answer questions, but most often the interviewer asks the questions and the interviewee answers them.

The interview has specific goals. The achievement of these goals constitutes the reason for the interview, and they guide and structure the interview in terms of both content and format. In an employment interview, for example, the goal for the interviewer is to find an applicant who can fulfill the tasks of the position, and the interviewee's goal is to get the job, if it seems desirable. These goals guide the behaviors of both parties, are relatively specific, and are usually clear to both parties.

KINDS OF INTERVIEWS

The various types of interviews are often distinguished on the basis of the goals of interviewer and interviewee. Some of the most important are considered here.

The Information Interview

In the information interview, the interviewer attempts to learn something about the interviewee and asks the interviewee, usually a person of some reputation and accomplishment, a series of questions designed to elicit his or her views, beliefs, insights, perspectives, predictions, life history, and so on. Examples of the information interview are those published in such popular magazines as *Psychology Today* and *Playboy;* the TV interviews conducted by Johnny Carson, Ted Koppel, and Barbara Walters; and the interviews conducted by a lawyer during a trial. All are designed to elicit specific information from someone who supposedly knows something others do not know.

The Persuasive Interview

In the persuasive interview the goal is to change an individual's attitude or behavior. The persuader may either ask questions that will lead the persuadee to the desired conclusion or answer questions in a persuasive way. For example, if you go into a showroom to buy a new car, you interview the salesperson whose goal is to get you to buy a particular car. He or she attempts to accomplish this by answering your questions persuasively. You ask about mileage, safety features, and finance terms; the salesperson discourses eloquently on the superiority of this car above all others.

All interviews contain elements of both information and persuasion. When, for example, a guest appears on "The Tonight Show" and talks about a new movie, television show, or record album, information is communicated, but there is also persuasion. In fact, the performer is interviewed primarily to persuade the audience to see the movie or television show or to buy the record album. Informing and persuading are the two major functions of communication, and there is probably no type of communication that does not in part serve one or both functions. The interview is no exception.

The Appraisal Interview

In the appraisal or evaluation interview, the interviewee's performance is assessed by management or more experienced colleagues. The general aim is to discover what the interviewee is doing well (and to praise this), and what he or she is not doing well and why (and to correct this). You may discover from time to time that an unidentified faculty member is observing your class. Actually this observer is probably watching your instructor as part of an appraisal interview. It is a means of gathering preliminary information (in this case, on your instructor's teaching) that will later be used to assess and evaluate your instructor's total performance. These interviews are particularly important in providing a means for the new member of an organization to find out what the rules of the game are and how they can be played more effectively. It is a way for the new member to see how his or her performance matches up with the expectations of management or of those making promotion and firing decisions.

The Exit Interview

Another type of interview, reportedly used by some 80 percent of companies in the United States, is the exit interview. When an employee leaves the company voluntarily, it is important for the company to know why. All organizations compete in one way or another for superior workers, and if an organization is losing its workers, it must discover why, to prevent others from leaving as well.

The money it costs to train an employee is considerable, so most companies prefer to retain their effective workers rather than lose them and have to spend time and money to train someone else. There is also the danger that the exiting employee will take along company secrets, contacts, and plans that may be used by rival firms. Another function of this interview is to provide a way of making the exit as pleasant and as efficient as possible for both employee and employer.

The Employment Interview

Perhaps of most concern to college students is the employment interview. Here you are (or will soon be) in the position of looking for a job. Interviewers from various companies will attempt to interest superior students in entering their firms. Your task, once you have determined that you want the job, is to convince them that you are one of these superior students and that they should offer you a position. In such an employment interview, a great deal of information and attempts at persuasion will be exchanged. The interviewer will learn about you, your interests, your talents—and, if the interviewer is clever, some of your weaknesses and liabilities. You will be informed about the nature of the company, its benefits, its advantages—and, if you are clever, some of its disadvantages and problems.

If the interviewer thinks highly of you, he or she will attempt to persuade you to look no further than the XYZ Company: This is the company in which you can build your fame and fortune. If you think highly of the company, you will attempt to persuade the interviewer to look no further than you: You are exactly what this company needs, and in you the company has found an exceptional worker.

The Counseling Interview

Another popular type of interview is that designed to provide guidance. Usually this type of interview is conducted by someone trained in psychology,

At one time or another we all participate in an interview situation. How will interviewing figure into your professional life? What skills discussed throughout this text would you find particularly helpful in interviewing situations?

guidance, education, communication, or some other field concerned with personal and interpersonal adjustment. The goal here is to help the individual deal more effectively with problems; to work more effectively; to get along better with friends, relatives, children, or lovers; and to cope more realistically and effectively with day-to-day living. Like the employment interview, this interview contains elements of both information and persuasion. For the interview to be of any value, the guidance counselor (the interviewer) must learn a considerable amount about the person—habits, problems, self-perceptions, goals, and so on. With this information, the counselor then attempts to persuade the person to alter certain aspects of his or her thinking and/or behaving. The counselor may attempt to persuade you, for example, to listen more attentively when your spouse argues, to devote more time and energy to your classwork, to avoid seeing people who might have a disturbing influence on you, and so on.

THE INTERVIEW SEQUENCE

The interview sequence might, for convenience, be divided into three main periods: a preparatory period, in which the individual prepares for the interview; the interview proper; and the postinterview period, in which the person reflects on and follows up on the interview. Each of these periods is explained with a view to providing you with some specific suggestions to make the interview work more effectively for you.

Before the Interview

The preinterview period has no clear beginning. If, for example, you are to be interviewed for an accounting job, your preparation might logically be said to have begun when you enrolled as an accounting major or when you entered college. For our purposes, however, the preinterview period may be said to start at the time you begin specific preparation for a specific interview. In this preinterview period, you should: prepare yourself intellectually, attitudinally, and physically; establish your objectives; and prepare answers to predicted questions.

Prepare Yourself

This is perhaps the most difficult aspect of the entire interview process, and it is probably the step that is most often overlooked. Preparation (or lack of it) causes considerable trouble.

Intellectual Preparation At the most obvious level, prepare yourself intellectually; educate yourself as much as possible about relevant topics. Learn something about the company and its specific product or products. If possible, learn something about the person who will interview you. I have frequently interviewed candidates for teaching positions. When asked what they would like to teach, many had no idea of the courses we offered. They had no idea of the people who were already teaching in our department and therefore could not build a case for themselves as unique contributors to the department. When this happens, the interviewer may legitimately conclude that too little thought and preparation went into this particular interview.

Attitudinal Preparation Many interviewees go into the interview with the idea that it is a contest or a competitive bout. They assume that they will have to fight to prove they are worthy of the position, or whatever is at stake. If you are applying for a job, both you and the company want something: You want a job that will meet your needs, and the company wants an employee who will meet its needs. In short, you each want something that perhaps the other has. So the interview should not be thought of as a contest; both interviewer and interviewee stand to gain something from the experience. View the interview as an opportunity to engage in a joint effort to gain something beneficial to both. If you do go into the interview in this cooperative frame of mind, you are much less likely to become defensive in your communications, which in turn will help make you more appealing as a potential colleague.

Physical Preparation Physical preparation is always difficult to give advice about, especially because the type of physical preparation that will be helpful in one situation will not matter much in another. And yet we do know that a great number of jobs are won or lost on the basis of physical appearance alone, so considerable attention should be given to the physical dimensions of the interview. Dress in a manner that shows that you care enough about the interview to make a good impression. At the same time, your dress should be comfortable. It should not make you strain at the collar each second. To avoid extremes is perhaps the most specific advice that can be given. If in doubt, it is probably best to err on the side of formality: Wear the tie, high heels, or dress.

Bring with you the appropriate materials, whatever they may be. At the very least bring a pen and some paper so that you can take down any information the interviewer may wish to give you—an address or the title of a reference book to consult, for example. It is not necessary to appear with a clipboard, notebook, and a handful of pens and pencils. In fact, don't. Keep a pen and a small pad handy. Also, bring an extra copy or two of your résumé and, if appropriate, a business card. If you are applying for a job in an area where you have worked before, you might bring samples of your previous work.

The importance of the résumé should be stressed here. The résumé is a summary of essential data on your experience, goals, and abilities. Often, a job applicant first submits a résumé. If it is thought interesting by the employer, the candidate is asked in for an interview. Because of the importance of the résumé and its close association with the interview, I have provided a sample résumé and some guidelines to assist you in preparing your own (see pp. 298–300).

Establish Objectives

All interviews have specific primary objectives. As part of your preparation, fix these objectives firmly in mind and use them as guides to the remainder of your preparation, and also to your behavior during and even after the interview. Many interviews also have secondary objectives; these too should be established and should figure in your preparation and behaviors. For example, you may enter an interview with the primary objective of getting the particular job offered. But there may also be secondary objectives, such as learning to relax during an interview or making enough of an impression so that you are asked back for a second, more extensive interview.

After establishing these primary and secondary objectives clearly in your own mind, relate your preparation to these objectives. For example, in considering how to dress, what to learn about the specific company, and what questions to ask during the interview, ask yourself how your objectives might help you answer these questions.

Prepare Answers and Questions

If the interview is at all important to you, you will probably think about it for some time. In fact, you will probably devote a considerable amount of worry time to it. While this is often inevitable, part of that time might more profitably be directed to rehearsing the predicted course of the interview and predicting the questions that will be asked and the answers you will most likely give.

Some questions are obvious. Think about these inevitable questions and how you will answer them. Other questions might not seem so obvious at first, but if you think sufficiently about the specific interview, you may be able to predict at least some of them. If you accurately predict the questions that will be asked you will be that much ahead, because you will have had the time to think of intelligent answers. But even if you do not succeed in predicting any of the questions, the rehearsal of the interview process will have the beneficial effect of helping you to relax once you get into the interview.

Even though the interviewer will ask most of the questions and you will be answering most of the time, in any interview both parties ask and both answer at least some questions. In addition to rehearsing some answers to predicted questions, fix firmly in mind the questions you want to ask the interviewer and the ways in which you will respond to any of the predicted answers he or she may give.

During the Interview

After the preparations, you are ready for the interview proper. Several suggestions may guide you through this sometimes difficult procedure.

Make an Effective Presentation of Self

The first step is to present yourself—an aspect of the interview process that many persons claim is the most important part of the entire procedure. If you fail here and make a bad initial impression, it will be difficult to salvage the rest of the interview. So devote special care to the way in which you present yourself.

Arrive on time, which in interview situations generally means five to ten minutes early. This is advisable since the interviewer may be running ahead of schedule and your being there early would be appreciated; it will also allow you time to relax, to get accustomed to the general surroundings, and perhaps to fill out any forms that may be required; and it gives you a cushion should something delay you on the way. But do not arrive at the office *too* early and certainly do not arrive late. If you arrive late to the interview, the interviewer may reasonably conclude that you are not interested in the job and/or that you are not responsible or organized.

Establish a Relationship with the Interviewer

At the very beginning of the interview, try to establish some interpersonal relationship with the interviewer. Try to make the interviewer, who sees perhaps 10 or 20 people in one day, see you as unique and different from everyone else. Having said this, I must add that this advice does not mean "at all costs." Do not be outrageous just to be remembered; while you may be remembered, it will be as someone to avoid.

Be sure you know the name of the company, the job title, and the interviewer's name. Although you will have much on your mind when you go into the interview, the interviewer's name is not one of the things you can afford to forget (or mispronounce).

1

Chris Smith
166 Josen Road
Accord, New York 10009
(914) 555–3379

2   Career Goals
To secure position with film company; to work on
documentaries as script writer, director, cameraperson

3   Education
B.A., University of Montana, 1988 [expected]
Major: Communication arts and sciences, with emphasis in mass
media production
Minor: English, with emphasis on writing

4   Work Experience
1982–1986:   studio engineer, Radio-Television-Film Studio, University
of Montana
1980–1982:   reporter on student newspaper, with emphasis on sports
articles

5   Special Competencies
Language: speaking and writing knowledge of Spanish
Media production: ability to operate Show Pro systems, create mediated slide shows, edit television scripts, direct video produc-
tions, manage sound studio

6   References
The following persons have agreed to provide references on
request:

Dr. Jack Sprat (major advisor)
Department of Communication
University of Montana
Missoula, Montana 59801

Professor Mary Contrari (script
writing instructor)
Department of English
University of Montana
Missoula, Montana 59801

Dr. Pat Pendleton
Office of the Dean of Students
University of Montana
Missoula, Montana 59801

1. Your name, address, and phone number are generally put at the top of the résumé to ensure ease in locating your résumé. It may be placed to the right if you prefer.

2. For most people just getting out of college, career goals are usually tentative and somewhat general. Only after considerable experience does one narrow one's focus to a particular aspect of a field. And so although this career goal description may seem a bit general, it is probably more realistic than those that list, say, "script writer" or "sound engineer." Of course, if you do have more limited career goals, put them down. In setting your career goals, do not indicate that you will take just anything; you should not appear so desperate that no matter what is offered you will take it. Although you may sometimes feel that any job will do, I think it is generally ineffective to put this feeling down on paper. At the other extreme, do not be so specific or so demanding that you give the impression that whatever is offered, you will not be satisfied.

3. It will be helpful to potential employers if you give a bit more information than simply your educational degree. Even the major department in which you earned your degree might be too vague: For example, in a communication arts and sciences department you could have concentrated on speech pathology, speech science, audiology, public communication, journalism, interpersonal communication, mass media theory, media production, film criticism, and so on. The same is true for many other departments as well, so identify your emphasis. If you earned honors or awards, list these if they are relevant to your educational experience or to your job experience— being on the Dean's List, receiving departmental honors, or winning any awards for working in your field. If the awards are primarily educational (for example, Dean's List), put them under the *Education* heading. If they are job-related, then put them under the *Work Experience* heading.

4. Work experience is generally listed in chronological order, beginning with the latest position and working back. Depending on your work experience, you may have a great deal to write and hence will have to pare it down, or you may have little or nothing to write and so you will want to search through your history for some relevant experience. The example given here focuses simply on work experience during college that is particularly relevant to the position being sought. This reflects my own preference to simply put down what is relevant to your career goals and to demonstrating your competence for the job being sought and to eliminate the rest. Do not pad the résumé. Do not insult the intelligence and insight of your potential employer by itemizing things that have little or no relevance to the position you are seeking.

5. The section on special competencies is an often-overlooked area, but one where college students and recent graduates actually have a great deal to say. Many, for example, have some foreign language ability: If you do, put it down, since it is often relevant. You have also acquired a great number of competencies in classes. For example, if you took accounting, statistics, or computer science courses, you may have acquired such competencies as

keeping profit-and-loss statements, analyzing statistical data, and programming selected computers.

6. References may be handled in a number of different ways. Here, the specific names of people the potential employer may write to are listed. Sometimes phone numbers are included. If your school maintains personnel files on its students, you may simply note that references may be obtained by writing to the relevant department. (Be sure you keep your file up to date.) Still another way is simply to note that references will be furnished on request. If the employer is interested enough to ask for the references, he or she will let you know and you in turn will contact the people who have agreed to write references for you. It is sometimes helpful to identify briefly the relationship between you and the person named as reference. The brief identifying phrases used here—script writing instructor, major advisor—are sufficient in most cases. Three references are generally considered enough. Note that the people listed here would have knowledge relevant to the job sought.

7. Give special care to the form of your résumé. Typographical errors, incorrect spelling, poorly spaced headings and entries, and generally sloppy work will not produce the effect you want. Make sure your résumé gives the impression you want to give. It is the first sample of your work the employer sees; if it is going to be read, it has to look worth the time.

In presenting yourself, be sure that you do not err on the side of too much casualness or too much informality. When there is doubt, act on the side of increased formality. Slouching back in the chair, smoking, and gum or candy chewing are obvious behaviors to avoid when you are trying to impress an interviewer.

Demonstrate Effective Interpersonal Communication

Throughout the interview, be certain that you demonstrate the skills of interpersonal communication that are spelled out in this book and emphasized in this course. The interview is the ideal place to put into practice all the skills you have learned. Here, a few particularly important skills are noted.

Be Responsive to Feedback   Be especially alert to feedback from the interviewer. Take note of the small movements that tell you he or she has heard enough and those movements that say "What else?" Distinguish between the nod that says "I'm listening" and the nod that says "I agree." Concentrate on the interviewer and not merely on yourself. So many people get so wrapped up in themselves—their own nervousness and anxiety, for example—that they forget this is two-way communication. If you are unsure of something, ask for clarification. It is better to ask for clarification than to give inappropriate and potentially damaging responses.

Treat Everything as Important   Remember that in the interview, everything the interviewer says is important; otherwise, it would not be said. The interviewer, for example, may interject something about art, theater, or music that you may take to be irrelevant. "What does this have to do with accounting?" you might say to yourself. And yet the interviewer may be using this question as a way of investigating your ability to get along well with other persons in the organization who are perhaps interested in theater, art, or music. The intention may also be to see how well-rounded you are. So treat all questions as important even if they may not seem so at the time.

Avoid Defensiveness   When an interviewer asks a question, assume that the question is asked to determine your suitability for the position and is not a personal attack. Some interviewers are not terribly effective in asking questions and often ask them in ways that sound like personal attacks. In some cases they might be, but most often they are not. The interviewer does not know you and probably has little desire to insult you in any way. So treat without defensiveness questions such as "Do you think you could really do this job?" "You have no experience with this type of product—are you sure you could handle it?" or "What makes you think that we should hire you?"

Admittedly, these questions could be asked more effectively and more courteously, but when they are not, it is best to answer them with the assumption that they are merely attempts to evaluate you as a candidate for the position. Another way in which defensiveness is often demonstrated is when interviewees evaluate rather than answer the questions. When the interviewer asks a question, answer it without worrying about the relevance or the effectiveness of the question; concern yourself with the effectiveness of your answers instead. There is one important exception to this general rule, and that is when the interviewer asks you questions that are unlawful (see the section below on "Lawful and Unlawful Questions").

Be Positive   One of the principles of effective interpersonal communication is positiveness, a feature that should be noted here for its particular relevance to interviewing. In interviewing, this refers to being positive about the potential job, about the company, about the interview situation, and particularly about employment in general. This last area is one where many interviewees err; they criticize their previous employers, job, and company. Their aim, I guess, is to contrast the previous position with the present one, but the interviewer sees a complainer—a person who will soon be sitting in another interview, criticizing this company. The interviewer may well see, rightly or wrongly, a malcontent. So, demonstrate positiveness.

Demonstrate Competence and Self-Esteem
Steer a clear course between appearing overly confident and cocky (the "I know everything" type of response) and insecure (the "I'm not sure I could do this job" type of response). The interviewer wants to hire a competent and self-confident individual; the company probably has enough of the other kind. So, throughout the interview demonstrate that you have the relevant knowledge (but that you could certainly learn more), that you are self-confident (but not overly so), and that you have a positive image of yourself (but not that you are blind to your faults or that you cannot improve).

If you think you are not competent, that you lack the requisite knowledge, that you lack self-confidence and have a low self-image, you can be fairly certain the interviewer will agree with you. During the interview, play up your good points; emphasize and accent your best features.

Recognize too that competence for a job goes beyond a knowledge of the specific workings of a particular product or machine. Employment competence also consists of such qualities as sincerity, enthusiasm, diligence, interest, and the like. Demonstrate these qualities in interviewing, as in all interpersonal interactions.

After the Interview

Even after the interview, you still have work to do.

Mentally Review the Interview

By reviewing the interview, you will fix it firmly in your mind. Go over what happened—what questions were asked and what answers were given. Review any especially important information the interviewer gave. Write down any significant information. (The pen and paper you took to the interview will come in handy now, since it is best to write down what happened as soon after you leave the interview as possible.) Ask yourself what you could have done more effectively and what you did do effectively that you could repeat in other interviews. That is, analyze your strengths and your weaknesses as they are evidenced in the interview, and consider how you might correct your weaknesses and capitalize on your strengths.

Follow Up

In most cases, follow up an interview with a thank-you note to the interviewer. In this brief, professional letter, thank the interviewer for his or her time and consideration, reiterate your interest in the company, and perhaps add that you hope to hear from him or her soon.

This letter provides you with an opportunity to resell yourself—to reiterate those qualities you possess and wish to emphasize, but may have been too modest to discuss at the time. It will help to make you stand out in the mind of the interviewer, since not many interviewees write letters of thanks. It will help to remind the interviewer of your interview and perhaps fix it in mind a bit more firmly. It will also help to convince the interviewer that you are still interested in the position. It is a kind of pat on the back to the interviewer and it says, in effect, that the interview was an effective one. Finally, the letter will help to further demonstrate your sophistication in the employment world. A short letter that serves all these functions seems surely worth the small effort required.

LAWFUL AND UNLAWFUL QUESTIONS

The federal government, although not expressly outlawing certain questions, has, through the Equal Employment Opportunity Commission, noted that questions concerning race, religion, and national origin—except under rare circumstances—are irrelevant to the candidate's ability to function effectively on the job. Hence, interview questions focusing on these areas serve no useful and ethical function.

The various state laws are more explicit on questions that may or may not be asked during employment interviews. H. Anthony Medley, in his *Sweaty Palms: The Neglected Art of Being Interviewed*, discusses some of these areas and provides a number of specific illustrations. I follow his insights here. If you wish additional guidance for a particular state, contact your state office of employment or the Equal Employment Opportunity Commission.

Some of the more important areas in which unlawful questions are frequently asked concern age, marital status, race, religion, nationality, citizenship, and physical condition. For example, in California and New York it is legal to ask applicants whether they meet the legal age requirements for the job and could provide proof of that, but it is unlawful to ask about their age. In both California and New York it is unlawful to ask about a person's marital status, although an interviewer may ask you to identify your close relative, or guardian if you are a minor, or any relative who currently works for the same company.

Questions concerning the applicant's race, religion, and country of national origin are unlawful in many states, as are questions that get at this same information in oblique ways. Thus, for example, the interviewer may ask applicants what languages they are fluent in but may not ask about their native language, what language is spoken at home, or what language their parents speak. Such questions may simply be a back road to getting at the individual's nationality, race, and, in some cases, religion. The interviewer may not ask candidates whether they or their parents are citizens, but the interviewer may ask whether candidates are in this country legally. The interviewer may inquire into the candidate's physical condition insofar as the job is concerned—for example, "Do you have any physical problems that might prevent you from fulfilling your responsibilities at this job?"—but the interviewer may not ask if the candidate has any physical disabilities.

These are merely examples, and since the regulations vary from one state to another, you should investigate those governing your particular state. Once you have discovered what questions are unlawful, consider how to deal with them if they come up during an interview.

Possible Strategies

Your first strategy should be to deal with such questions by answering the part you do not object to and omitting any information you do not want to give. For example, if you are asked the unlawful question concerning what language is spoken at home, you may respond with a statement such as "I have some language facility in German and Italian," without specifying a direct answer to the question. If you are asked to list all the organizations of which you are a member (an unlawful question in many states, since it is often a way of getting at political affiliation, religion, nationality, and various other areas), you might respond by saying something like: "The only organizations I belong to that are relevant to this job are the International Communication Association and the Speech Communication Association."

This type of response, I think, is preferable to the one that immediately tells the interviewer he or she is asking an unlawful question. In many cases, the interviewer may not even be aware of the legality of various questions and may have no intention of attempting to get at information you are not obliged to give. It is easy to conceive of situations in which the interviewer, for example, recognizes the nationality of your last name and wants to mention that he or she is also of the same nationality. If you immediately take issue with the question, you will be creating problems where none really exist.

On the other hand, do recognize that in many employment interviews, the unwritten intention is to keep certain people out, whether it is people who are older or those of a particular marital status, sexual orientation, nationality, religion, and so on. If you are confronted by questions that are unlawful and that you do not want to answer, and if the gentle method described above does not work and your interviewer persists—saying, for example, "Is German the language spoken at home?" or "What other organizations have you belonged to?"—you might counter by saying that such information is irrelevant to the interview and to the position you are seeking. Again, be courteous but firm. Say something like "This position does not call for any particular language skill and so it does not matter what language is spoken in my home," or "The organizations I mentioned are the only relevant ones; whatever other organizations I belong to will certainly not interfere with my ability to perform at this job." If the interviewer still persists—and I doubt that many would after these rather clear and direct responses—you might note that these questions are unlawful and that you are not going to answer them.

SUMMARY

1. *Interviewing* is that form of interpersonal communication in which two persons interact largely through a question-and-answer format for the purpose of achieving rather specific goals.

2. Six types of interviewing may be distinguished: (1) the information interview attempts to learn something about the interviewee, (2) the persuasive interview is designed to change an individual's attitudes or behaviors, (3) the appraisal interview is designed to assess an interviewee's performance at a particular task, (4) the exit interview is designed to discover why a worker is leaving the company, (5) the employment interview attempts to assess the suitability of a prospective employee for a particular position, and (6) the counseling interview is designed to provide guidance.

3. Before the interview, interviewees should prepare themselves intellectually, attitudinally, and physically for the interview; should establish their objectives; and should prepare answers to predicted questions.

4. During the interview, interviewees should make an effective presentation of self, establish a relationship with the interviewer, demonstrate effective

interpersonal communication skills, and demonstrate competence and self-esteem.

5. After the interview, interviewees should mentally review the interview and follow up the interview with a brief letter.

6. Interviewees should familiarize themselves with questions that may be unlawful in their states and develop strategies for dealing with these questions.

SOURCES

There are a number of excellent sources on interviewing that you may consult for additional theory, research, and practical suggestions. Thorough reviews of interviewing, covering the theoretical bases, some of the research findings, and some practical suggestions, are Charles J. Stewart and William B. Cash, Jr., *Interviewing: Principles and Practices*, 4th ed. (Dubuque, Iowa: Brown, 1984) and Cal W. Downs, G. Paul Smeyak, and Ernest Martin, *Professional Interviewing* (New York: Harper & Row, 1980). An excellent practical introduction, written entirely from the point of view of the person being interviewed, is H. Anthony Medley, *Sweaty Palms: The Neglected Art of Being Interviewed* (Belmont, Calif.: Wadsworth Lifetime Learning Publications, 1978). A thorough text with numerous practical exercises is Joseph P. Zima, *Interviewing: Key to Effective Management* (Chicago, Ill.: Science Research Associates, Inc., 1983). Michael Z. Sincoff and Robert S. Goyer, *Interviewing* (New York: Macmillan, 1984), cover the various types of interviews (emphasizing the employment interview) and the legal aspects of employment interviewing.

SKILL DEVELOPMENT SUMMARY

1. In **group problem solving,** follow these seven steps: define the problem, analyze the problem, establish criteria for evaluating solutions, identify possible solutions, evaluate solutions, select the best solution, and test the selected solution.

2. For generating ideas, try **brainstorming** and follow its four general rules: no negative criticism is allowed, quantity is desired, combinations and extensions are desired, and freewheeling is wanted.

3. For getting to know each other and for sharing ideas, insights, and experiences, try a **consciousness raising experience.** Remember that this group is a totally supportive one.

4. For sharing information, try the **educational or learning group.** Use one of the patterns identified in depth in the discussion of organization for the public speech (Unit 22).

5. Select a **small group format** that best meets the needs of your specific group—for example, panel or round table, colloquy, symposium, or symposium-forum.

6. Be careful to avoid playing one of the popular but dysfunctional **individual roles** in a small group: aggressor, blocker, recognition seeker, self-confessor, playboy-playgirl, dominator, help seeker, or special interest pleader.

7. In **participating in a small group,** be group- rather than individually oriented, center conflict on issues rather than on personalities, be critically open-minded, and make sure that your meanings and the meanings of others are clearly understood.

8. Beware of **groupthink.** Identify the major groupthink symptoms: being invulnerable to dangers, rationalizing to avoid dealing with warnings, believing in the group's morality, perceiving the opposition in simplistic ways, pressuring members who express doubts, censoring your own doubts, believing in the members' unanimous agreement, and preventing certain information from getting to other group members.

9. As a **small group leader,** activate group interaction, maintain effective interaction throughout the discussion, keep members on the track, ensure member satisfaction, encourage ongoing evaluation and improvement, and prepare members for the discussion as necessary.

10. Learn to recognize and function in the different **styles of leadership,** especially the laissez-faire, democratic, and authoritarian leadership styles.

11. Adjust the communication patterns in an organizational group so that they are most effective in accomplishing the desired goals. Make use of,

for example, the **network structures** of the wheel, the Y, the circle, the chain, and the all-channel, remembering that each network has different effects on productivity and morale.

12. Become sensitive to the problems associated with **upward communication** and try to eliminate such barriers as sending only positive messages, gatekeepers preventing important messages from getting through, and management's difficulty in dealing with upward communications.

13. In dealing with **downward communication,** look for problems that are not verbalized and learn the language of groups you will deal with or represent.

14. Be careful to avoid the common problems associated with **lateral communication.** Learn the relevant specialized languages and the importance of areas other than your own to the well-being of the organization.

15. Recognize and combat the popular distortions interfering with **serial communication** or rumor: leveling, sharpening, and assimilation.

16. Avoid the tendency toward **information overload;** avoid presenting others with information beyond their processing capacity.

17. **Before the interview,** prepare yourself intellectually, attitudinally, and physically; establish your objectives as clearly as you can; and prepare answers to predicted questions.

18. **During the interview,** make an effective presentation of self; establish a relationship with the interviewer; demonstrate effective interpersonal communication (be responsive to feedback, treat everything as important, avoid defensiveness, and be positive); and demonstrate competence and self-esteem.

19. **After the interview,** mentally review the interview to analyze your strengths and weaknesses; follow up with a letter of continued interest and appreciation for the interview.

20. Learn what questions are unlawful to ask in your state and develop appropriate strategies for dealing with such **unlawful questions.**

PART SIX
PUBLIC
COMMUNICATION

21. PRELIMINARIES TO PUBLIC COMMUNICATION: STEPS IN SPEECH PREPARATION (IN BRIEF) AND SPEAKER APPREHENSION

22. ORGANIZING THE PUBLIC SPEECH

23. STYLE AND LANGUAGE IN THE PUBLIC SPEECH

24. DELIVERY IN PUBLIC SPEAKING

25. THE INFORMATIVE SPEECH

26. THE PERSUASIVE SPEECH

In this part we cover public speaking. An overview of the entire public speaking preparation process and apprehension are covered in the first unit, Unit 21. Unit 22 is devoted to organizing the body of the speech and includes discussions of the thesis, the generation of main ideas, transitions and internal summaries, the major thought patterns for organizing your main propositions, introductions, conclusions, and preparation and delivery outlines. Unit 23 is devoted to style and language, and provides specific guidance for achieving effective oral style in word choice and in sentence construction. Unit 24 is devoted to delivery—to the effective use of the voice and bodily action. In Unit 25 we consider the informative speech—its major types and purposes, the principles for communicating information, and the supporting materials that may be used in informative speeches. Unit 26 is devoted to the persuasive speech. Here we consider the nature of attitude, belief, and behavior; the major types of persuasive speeches; the major principles of persuasion; and the three types of proof: argument or logical proof, psychological appeals, and credibility or ethical proof.

After completing this part, you should be able to prepare and deliver a wide variety of effective public speeches.

UNIT 21
PRELIMINARIES TO PUBLIC COMMUNICATION:

Steps in Speech Preparation (in Brief) and Speaker Apprehension

LEARNING GOALS

After completing this unit, you should be able to

1. define *public speaking*
2. identify the two major types of speeches
3. identify and explain the variables that should be investigated in audience analysis
4. define *thesis* and explain its function in the public speech
5. identify three organizational patterns and give examples of the kinds of speeches that would be suited to each organizational pattern
6. identify at least three qualities that should characterize the style of the public speech
7. identify three functions of the conclusion
8. identify two functions of the introduction
9. define *speaker apprehension*
10. explain at least three principles or guidelines for dealing with speaker apprehension

Public speaking may be defined as that form of communication in which a speaker addresses a relatively large audience with a relatively continuous discourse, usually in a face-to-face situation: a student delivers a report to a political science class, a teacher lectures on the structure of DNA, a minister preaches a sermon, and a politician delivers a campaign speech. These and thousands of similar examples are public speaking situations.

This elementary definition will be expanded in our discussion of the steps involved in preparing a public speech.

PREPARING THE PUBLIC SPEECH: A CAPSULE SUMMARY

Eight steps necessary to prepare an effective public speech are presented here. The steps are presented in a linear fashion (one after the other), but the process of constructing a public speech often does not follow such a logical and linear sequence. That is, you will probably not progress simply from step 1 to 2, and so forth, to 8. Instead, your progression might go more like this: step 1 to step 2, back again to step 1, to step 3, back again to step 2, and so on. For example, after selecting your subject and purpose (step 1), you may progress to step 2 and analyze your audience. On the basis of this analysis, however, you may wish to go back and modify your subject, your purpose, or both. Similarly, after you research the topic (step 3), you may find that you need additional information on your audience and should go back to step 2.

We present these eight steps in highly abbreviated form to give you an overview of the entire speech preparation process. In the following units we elaborate on these steps and provide numerous examples to further clarify the process.

Select the Subject and Purpose

The first step in preparing a public speech is to select the subject on which you will speak, and the general and specific purposes you hope to achieve.

The Subject

Select a topic that is worthwhile and will prove relevant and interesting both to the audience and, of course, to you. After all, you will invest a great deal of time and energy in studying and organizing the topic, and you should derive something of value from the topic itself as well as from the application of public speaking principles.

If your initial speech is to be a persuasive one, it would be best to select a topic about which both you and the audience agree, and to attempt to strengthen rather than to change their existing attitudes. Or you might select a topic about which the audience is relatively neutral, and attempt to persuade them to feel either positively or negatively, as you think best. (See Table 21.1 for topic suggestions.)

Be certain to limit and narrow your topic to manageable proportions. Do not try to cover too much: It would be much better to cover a limited aspect of a topic in depth than to attempt to cover a broad topic superficially.

The Purpose

Here we focus on the two universally recognized purposes of speeches: to inform and to persuade.

The informative speech is designed to create understanding—to clarify, enlighten, correct misunderstandings, demonstrate how something works, or explain how something is structured. In this type of speech we rely most heavily on materials that amplify—examples, illustrations, definitions, testimony, visual aids, and the like.

The persuasive speech, on the other hand, is designed to influence attitudes or behaviors—to strengthen existing attitudes or change the beliefs of the audience, or to motivate behavior or redirect the way in which audience members act. In this type of speech we rely most heavily on materials that offer proof—evidence, argument, and psychological appeals, for example. Any persuasive speech is in part an informative speech and as such contains materials that amplify, illustrate, define, and so on. It would probably be impossible to persuade an audience of something without informing them as well. But in its concern with strengthening or changing attitudes and behaviors, the persuasive speech must go beyond amplification to the use of evidence, argument, motivational appeals, and the like.

Narrowing the Purpose

Whether you intend to inform or persuade, you must narrow your specific purpose. If your specific purpose is narrow enough, you can go into some depth on those aspects of the topic you do choose to cover. The audience benefits most from a speech that covers a small area in some depth.

Select a few main issues within the topic and illustrate, explain, describe, and support them in a variety of ways. Thus, for example, do not attempt to inform the audience about the causes of war; instead, focus on the causes of a specific war or one cause as it appeared in several wars. Do not attempt to inform the audience about the nature of drugs; instead, select one drug and explain, perhaps, its structure and its function.

If your general purpose is *to persuade*, be especially careful to narrow your purpose to manageable proportions. Thus, if the audience is adamantly opposed to abortion, it would be foolish to attempt in a three-minute speech to get them to vote in favor of abortion legislation. Instead, you might attempt to persuade them that others have the right to abortion and that it is against values they themselves hold to prevent others from seeking abortion. Or you might only attempt to get them to see there is some validity to the antiabortion position. Persuasion is a most difficult and complex process; small gains are in many instances all you can expect from a relatively short speech.

Analyze the Audience

If you are to inform or persuade your audience, you must know them. Who are they? What do they already know? What would they want to know more about? What special competencies do they have? What opinions, attitudes, and beliefs do they have? Where do they stand on the issues you wish to address? What needs do they have? Specifically, you might wish to focus on some of the following variables, asking yourself about the implications of each for your subject, purpose, and method of construction and presentation.

Age What is the general age of the audience? How wide is the range? Are there different age groups that will have to be addressed differently? Does the age of the audience impose any limitations on the topics? On the language that will be used? On the examples and illustrations to be selected?

Sex What is the predominant sex of the audience? Do men and women view the topic differently? If so, how? Do men and women have different backgrounds, experiences, and knowledge about the topic? How will this influence the way in which the topic is developed?

Cultural and Subcultural Factors How does the audience break down in terms of ethnic and racial background? What implications are there for the topic? For the purpose? For the method of development? Do the experiences, back-

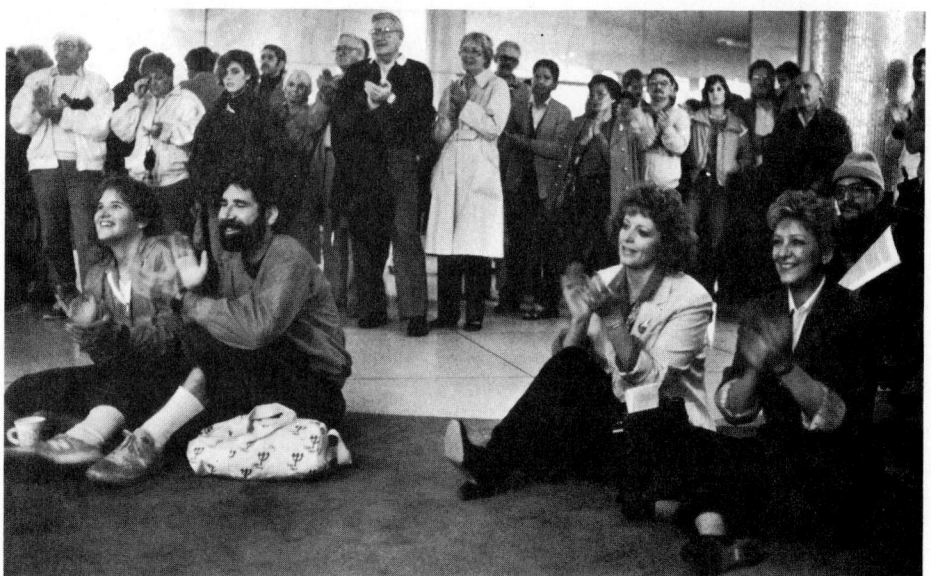

Perhaps the most important but most often neglected element in public speaking is the audience. Unlike the written composition which is often written for a vague and ill-defined audience, the public speech, with perhaps rare exceptions, is conceived for and delivered to a specific audience. In what ways does the audience influence the speech? What audience factors do you feel should be given special attention by the public speaker?

TABLE 21.1 SOME TOPICS FOR PUBLIC SPEAKING

Art/Music/Theater Topics

Abstract art: meaning of; and emotion; leading artists; Kandinsky; Léger; Mondrian; Picasso; Pollock; contributions of movement; values of

Entertainment: industry; benefits; abuses; tax; functions of; and communication

Movies: censorship; famous; making; producing; directing; acting in; history of; economics of; career training; and communication

Music: festivals; forms; instruments; composition; styles; drama; opera; rock; punk; disco; country-western; popular; symphonic; new wave

Theater: Greek, Roman; commedia dell'arte; American; British; Eastern; Italian; French; performers; styles of; and television; and film; Broadway; and critics

Biological-Physiological Topics

Anesthesia: nature of; types of; uses of; development of; dangers of

Biological: clock; control; warfare; rhythm; sciences

Biorhythm: nature of; predictions from; life cycles; charting

Brain: -washing; damage; genius; intelligence; aphasia

Diseases: major diseases of college students; prevention; detection; treatment

Food: health; preservatives; additives; red dye; and allergies; preparation

Medicine: preventive; forensic; and health insurance; history of; and poisoning

Nutrition: nature of; functions of food; essential requirements; animal; human; and starvation; and diet; vitamins

Transplants: nature of; rejection; donor selection; legal aspects; ethical aspects; religious aspects; future of; advances in

Communication Topics

Advertising: techniques; expenditures; ethical; unethical; subliminal; leading agencies

Freedom of speech: laws protecting; and Constitution; significance of; abuses of; and censorship; and economics

Languages: artificial; sign; natural; learning of; loss of; pathologies of; sociology of; psychology of; international

Media: forms of; contributions of; abuses; regulation of; popularity of; influences of; and violence; and censorship; Nielsen ratings

Television: development of; history of; workings of; satellite; cable; commercials; propaganda; and leisure time; programming; economics

Translation: computer; missionary impetus; problems in; history of

Writing: styles; forms of; calligraphy; graphology; development of; and speech

Economic Topics

Business: cycles; associations; law; in performing arts; finance

Capitalism: nature of; economics of; development of; depression and inflation

Corporation: law; business; nature of; history; growth of the

Inflation: and deflation; causes of; effects of; types of

Investment: stocks; gold; real estate; art; restrictions on; bank; allowance

Taxation: alcohol; cigarette; history of; purposes of; historical methods of; types of

Treasury Department: monetary system; origin; functions of; and counterfeiting

Wealth: economic; distribution of; primitive economic systems; contemporary view

TABLE 21.1 SOME TOPICS FOR PUBLIC SPEAKING (continued)

Philosophical Topics

Empiricism: radical; nature of; doctrines; opposition to
Existentialism; meaning of; and choice; history of; leaders in; movement
Occultism: theories of; practices; rituals; astrology; theosophy; witchcraft; divination
Phenomenology: characteristics of; principles of; growth of; development of
Relativism: philosophy; ethical; meaning of; leaders of; influence
Religion: different religions; leaders in; influence of; beliefs and agnosticism
Witchcraft: meaning of; white and black; and magic; structure of; functions of; theories of; in primitive societies; in contemporary societies
Zen: meaning of; principles of; historical development of; contemporary interest in; teachings of; influence of

Political Topics

Amnesty: in draft evasion; in criminal law; and pardons; in Vietnam War
Communism: development of; theories of; religion and; ideologies
Government: federal; state; city; powers of; abuses of; types of; democracy; socialism; communism
Imperialism: nature of; economics of; problems with; practices; history
Nationalism: nature of; history of; philosophy of; chauvinism; self-determination
Supreme Court: judicial review; decisions; makeup of; chief justices; jurisdiction
United Natons (UN): development of; functions of; agencies; and League of Nations; structure of; veto powers; Security Council
War: conduct of; financing; destruction by; causes of; debts; games; casualties

Psychological Topics

Aggression: aggressive behavior in animals; in human beings; as innate; as learned
Alcohol: alcoholism; nature of; Alcoholics Anonymous; Al Anon; physical effects of; among the young; treatment of alcoholism
Autism: nature of; treatment for; symptoms; causes
Depression: nature of; and suicide; among college students; dealing with
Guilt: causes of; symptoms of; dealing with; effects of; and suicide; and religion
Intelligence: quotient; tests; theories of; cultural differences; measuring
Love: nature of; theories of; romantic; family; and hate; and interpersonal relationships; of self; and materialism
Personality: development of; measurement of; theories of; disorders

Sociological Topics

Cities: problems of; population patterns; and crime; movement into and out of
Crime: prevention; types of; and law; and punishment
Divorce: rate; throughout world; causes of; advantages of; disadvantages of; proceedings; traumas associated with
Ethnicity: meaning of; and prejudice; theories of; and culture
Feminism: meaning of; implications of; changing concepts of; and chauvinism
Gay: rights; life-style; laws against; prejudice against; and religion; and lesbian; statistics; relationships
Prison: reform; systems; security; routine; effect on crime; personality; behavior
Racism: nature of; self-hatred; genetic theory; human rights; education; religious
Suicide: causes; among college students; laws regulating; methods; aiding the suicide of another; philosophical implications; and religion

grounds, and knowledge of these groups differ so that adjustments must be made in the way the speech is constructed? Will the audience identify with you or see you as an outsider—as one outside their own cultural or subcultural group? What are the implications of this?

Occupation, Income, and Status   What are the main occupations of the audience? How might this influence your speech? Does the income of the audience have any implications for the subject chosen, or the way in which it will be developed? What about the general status of the audience members? Might this influence the speech in any way?

Religion and Religiousness   What is the dominant religious affiliation of the audience? What are the implications of this for the speech? What is the strength of their belief? How might this relate to the speech topic?

Other Factors   What other factors will influence the way in which your speech is prepared and presented? Is marital status relevant? Does the audience have special interests that might be noted in the speech?

Occasion   Is it a special occasion? Does it impose any restrictions on what may be considered appropriate? Are there any implications for the way in which the speech is prepared or presented?

Context   Will the context influence what you discuss or the way in which your speech is presented? Will the context impose any restrictions? Are there appropriate facilities for showing slides? Is there a blackboard? Is there adequate light? Are there enough seats? Is there a podium? Is a microphone necessary?

Research the Topic

If the speech is to be worthwhile and if you and the audience are to profit from it, you must research the topic. First read some general source—an encyclopedia article or a general article in a journal or magazine. You might pursue some of the references in the article or seek a book or two on the topic. You might also consult one or more of the guides to periodical literature for recent articles in journals, magazines, and newspapers. For some topics, you might want to consult individuals—professors, politicians, physicians, or any person or group with specialized information of value to the development of your speech (see Table 21.2 for some helpful research sources).

Formulate Your Thesis and Identify the Major Propositions

The thesis of your speech is simply the main assertion; it is the essence and core of what you want your audience to derive from your speech. If your speech is an informative one, then your thesis is the main idea you want your audience to understand—for example, *Human blood consists of four major elements,* or *Speeches may be delivered in four general ways.* If your speech is to be a persuasive one, your thesis is your main or most general proposition that you wish your audience to accept, to believe in, or to follow—for example, *We should buy brand X,* or *We should contribute to the college athletic fund.*

Once the thesis statement is formulated, you should—as would an audience—ask questions about the thesis to identify its major components. In an informative speech, the questions that seem most relevant are *what?* or *how?* So, to the thesis *Human blood consists of four major elements,* the logical question seems to be: *What are they?* To the thesis *Speeches may be delivered in four general ways,* the logical question seems to be: *How?* or *What are they?* In answering these questions, you identify the major propositions you will cover in your speech. The answer to the question *What are the major elements of the blood?* in the form of a brief public speech outline, would look something like this:

Thesis: There are four major elements in human blood. (What are they?)

  I. Plasma
 II. Red blood cells (erythrocytes)
III. White blood cells (leukocytes)
 IV. Platelets (thrombocytes)

In the persuasive speech, the questions an audience would ask would more often be of the *why* type. If your thesis is *We should buy brand X,* then the inevitable question is *Why should we buy brand X?* Your answers to this question will then enable you to identify the major parts of the speech, and might look something like this:

Thesis: We should buy brand X. (Why should we buy brand X?)

  I. Brand X lasts longer.
 II. Brand X is cheaper.
III. Brand X does a better job.

Support the Major Propositions

Now that you have identified your thesis and your major propositions, you must support each of them. Devote attention to telling the audience what it needs to know about plasma and white blood cells, or convince them that brand X does in fact last longer and that it does a better job.

In the informative speech, your support primarily amplifies—describes, illustrates, defines, exemplifies—the various concepts being discussed. You want the "elements of human blood" to come alive to the audience, to stand out as real, significant, and relevant. Amplification accomplishes this. Specifically, you might use examples, illustrations, and the testimony of various authorities or eyewitnesses to reconstruct an event—for example, a crime of some sort. Definitions especially make the audience conversant with what you are talking about and breathe life into concepts that may otherwise be too abstract or vague. Statistics and summary figures that explain various trends are essential for certain topics. Audiovisual aids—charts, maps, objects, slides, films, tapes, records, and so on—will illustrate normally vague concepts.

TABLE 21.2 SOME RESEARCH SOURCES

The Catalog

The *card catalog* contains cards of three types: title, subject, and author cards. Each card also contains such information as the number of pages in the book; whether or not the book has illustrations, bibliographies, and index; the date of publication; the publisher; and, of course, the identifying number, which tells you where the book can be found in your library. In some libraries, the card catalog has been replaced by books or by computers. The basic information and types of entries noted for the card catalog can usually be found in these other types of catalog as well.

The Vertical File

The *vertical file*, sometimes called the "information file," contains clippings from newspapers and magazines, pamphlets, and other materials such as photographs and letters, organized by topic and arranged in files.

Encyclopedias

Encyclopaedia Britannica: 30 volumes; the most comprehensive and authoritative of all encyclopedias.
Collier's Encyclopedia: 24 volumes; distinguished by its illustrations and clarity of style.
Encyclopedia Americana: 30 volumes; especially useful for American topics.
Columbia Encyclopedia and *Random House Encyclopedia:* Useful one-volume encyclopedias.
The New Catholic Encyclopedia, Encyclopaedia Judaica, Encyclopedia of Islam, Encyclopedia of Buddhism, McGraw-Hill Encyclopedia of Science and Technology, International Encyclopedia of the Social Sciences: As their titles imply, these are more specialized works and are representative of the wide variety of available encyclopedias.

Biographical Material

Biography Index contains an index to biographies appearing in numerous and different sources.
Dictionary of National Biography (DNB) contains articles on famous dead British men and women as does its short edition, *Concise Dictionary of National Biography.*
Dictionary of American Biography (DAB) contains articles on famous dead Americans as does its short edition, *The Concise Dictionary of American Biography.*
Dictionary of Canadian Biography (DCB) contains articles on those who have contributed significantly to Canada.
Current Biography contains articles on living individuals, most with photographs.
Directory of American Scholars, International Who's Who, Who's Who in America, Who's Who (primarily British), *Dictionary of Scientific Biography,* and *American Men and Women of Science* are more specialized and are representative of the numerous biographical sources available.

Newspaper, Magazine, and Journal Indexes

The New York Times Index, published since 1913, indexes *New York Times* articles of all sorts.
Reader's Guide to Periodical Literature, published from 1900, indexes over 100 different popular magazines.
Education Index covers articles from journals and magazines relevant to education.
The Catholic Periodical and Literature Index, The Social Science and Humanities Index, Business Periodicals Index, Art Index, and *Applied Science and Technology Index* are more specialized indexes.
Psychological Abstracts, Sociological Abstracts, Language and Language Behavior Abstracts, and *Communication Abstracts* contain brief summaries of articles in these areas of study.

TABLE 21.2 SOME RESEARCH SOURCES (continued)

Almanacs

The World Almanac & Book of Facts, published since 1868, is the most popular and probably the best of the numerous almanacs, which contain information on the arts, science, governments, population, geography, religion, and just about every conceivable topic.

Information Please Almanac, Reader's Digest Almanac and Yearbook, and *The New York Times Encyclopedia Almanac* are similar in style and purpose to *The World Almanac & Book of Facts.*

Whitaker's Almanac focuses on Great Britain, and *Canadian Almanac and Directory* focuses on things Canadian.

Statistical Abstracts of the United States summarizes all types of facts and figures.

In a persuasive speech your support is proof—material that offers evidence, argument, and motivational appeal and that establishes the credibility and reputation of the speaker. If you want to persuade the audience that brand X should be their choice and if you are going to accomplish this in part by demonstrating that brand X is cheaper, you must give them good reasons for believing this to be true. You might, for example, compare the price of brand X with those of five or six other brands and/or you might demonstrate that the same amount of brand X will do twice the work of other brands selling at the same price.

Generally, we support our propositions with reasoning from specific instances, from general principles, from analogy, and from causes and effects. These may be thought of as logical support. Also, we support our position through the use of motivational appeals—to the audience's desire for status, financial gain, or increased self-esteem. We also add persuasive force to our propositions through our own personal reputation or credibility. If the audience members see us as competent, highly moral, and charismatic, they are more likely to believe what we say.

Organize the Speech Materials

The materials must be organized if the audience is to understand and retain them. Here we consider just three patterns you might use for organizing the body of the speech. The following unit will go into greater depth on these and other organizational patterns.

Problem-Solution Pattern

One popular pattern of organization is to present the main ideas in terms of problem and solution. The speech is divided into two basic parts: One part deals with the problem and the other with the solution. Generally the problem is presented first and the solution second, but under certain conditions the solution may be more appropriately presented first.

Let us say you are attempting to persuade an audience that teachers should be given higher salaries and increased benefits. Here a problem-solution pattern might be appropriate. We might, for example, discuss in the first part of the speech some of the problems confronting contemporary education, such as the fact that industry lures away the most highly qualified graduates of the leading universities, that many excellent teachers leave the field after two or three years, and that teaching is currently a low-status occupation in the minds of many undergraduates. In the second part of the speech we might consider the possible solutions—namely, that salaries for teachers must be made competitive with salaries offered by private industry, that the benefits teachers receive must be made at least as attractive as those offered by industry, and that steps must be taken to raise the status of the teaching profession.

The speech might look something like this in outline form:

I. There are three major problems confronting contemporary education.
   A. Industry lures away the most qualified graduates.
   B. Numerous excellent teachers leave the field after two or three years.
   C. Teaching is currently a low-status occupation.
II. There are two major solutions to these problems.
   A. Salaries for teachers must be increased.
   B. Benefits for teachers must be made more attractive.
   C. The status of the teaching profession must be raised.

Temporal Pattern

Organizing the major issues on the basis of some temporal relationship is another popular pattern. Generally, when this pattern is used the speech is organized into two or three major parts, beginning with the past and working up to the present or the future, or beginning with the present or the future and working back to the past. A speech on the development of speech and language in the child might be organized in a temporal pattern:

I. Babbling is the first stage.
II. Lallation is the second stage.
III. Echolalia is the third stage.
IV. Communication is the fourth stage.

Here each of the events is considered in temporal sequence beginning with the earliest stage and working up to the final stage—in this case, the stage of true communication.

Most historical topics lend themselves to organization by temporal patterning. The events leading up to the Civil War, the steps toward a college education, the history of writing, and the like will all yield to temporal patterning.

Topical Pattern

Perhaps the most popular pattern of organization is the topical pattern, which divides the speech into the major topics. This pattern should not be regarded as a catch-all for topics that do not seem to fit into any of the other patterns, but rather as one appropriate to the particular subject. For example, the topical pattern is an obvious one for organizing a speech on the powers of the government. Here the divisions are clear:

I. The legislative branch is controlled by Congress.
II. The executive branch is controlled by the president.
III. The judicial branch is controlled by the courts.

A speech on important cities in the world could be organized into a topical pattern, as well as speeches on problems facing the college graduate, great works of literature, the world's major religions, and the like. Each of these topics would have several subtopics or divisions of approximately equal importance.

Wording the Speech

In wording the speech put your main ideas as well as your supporting materials into language that will be readily understood by your audience. The audience will hear your speech only once. Consequently, make what you are saying instantly intelligible. Do not speak down to your audience, but make your ideas—even complex ones—easy to understand in one hearing.

Use words that are simple rather than complex, and concrete rather than abstract. Use personal and informal rather than impersonal and formal language. Use simple and active rather than complex and passive sentences. Be careful that you do not offend members of your audience. Remember that not all doctors are men and not all secretaries are women; not all persons are married or want to be. Not all persons love parents, dogs, and children. The hypothetical person does not have to be male.

In wording the persuasive speech, phrase your main assertions in a convincing manner. Be forceful. If the audience you are addressing is hostile or holds a position very different from yours, your wording might be more conciliatory. If you wish to strengthen the position of an already favorable audience, you might be more direct at the start. In Unit 23 we offer numerous specific suggestions for wording the speech.

Construct the Conclusion and the Introduction

A speech, like an essay or any written composition, needs an introduction, a body, and a conclusion. In a previous step, the body was organized. Here are some suggestions on the conclusion and the introduction. In contrast to the order in which they will be presented, the conclusion should be constructed first and the introduction last.

Conclusions

The conclusion is extremely important, since it is frequently the part the audience will remember most clearly. It is the conclusion that will in many cases determine what image of you is left in the minds of the audience.

The conclusion has two main functions. First, it should summarize the essentials of the speech, perhaps your major propositions or perhaps just your central idea or thesis. Second, it should provide closure and wrap up your speech in some neat and crisp manner.

Introductions

The introduction to a speech, like the first day of a class or the first date, is especially important because it sets the tone for what is to follow. It should put the audience into a receptive frame of mind and build up a positive attitude toward the speech and the speaker.

The introduction to a speech, although obviously delivered first, should be constructed only after the entire speech, including the conclusion, has been written. In this way you will be in a position to see the entire speech and will be better able to determine those elements that should go into introducing this speech. If the speech were not completed first, you would be constructing an introduction to a speech you were not very sure of. The same advice pertains to written compositions; the introductions should always be constructed last.

The introduction should serve two major functions. First, it should gain the audience's attention. Do this by stressing the importance of the topic, telling an interesting story, citing some little-known fact or statistic, or using any of the numerous and appropriate attention-gaining devices discussed in the following unit.

Second, it should orient the audience and give them a brief preview of what you will cover in the body of your speech.

SPEAKER APPREHENSION

Of all the speaker-related variables, speaker apprehension (or "stage fright") is perhaps the most salient from the point of view of the speaker. James Mc-Croskey and Lawrence Wheeless, in their excellent *Introduction to Human Communication*, note that "communication apprehension is probably the most common handicap that is suffered by people in contemporary American society." According to a nationwide survey conducted by Bruskin Associates, speaking in public was ranked as the number one fear of adult men and women. According to surveys of college students noted by McCroskey and Wheeless, between 10 and 20 percent suffer "severe, debilitating communication apprehension," while another 20 percent suffer "from communication apprehension to a degree substantial enough to interfere to some extent with their normal functioning."

Apprehension: Is It Normal? Is It Harmful?

Speaker apprehension is normal. Everyone experiences some degree of fear during the relatively formal public speaking situation in which you are the sole focus. Public speaking is perhaps the most anxiety-provoking communication situation; experiencing fear or anxiety is, therefore, not strange or unique. I have experienced speaker apprehension and, in fact, still do in a variety of situations. In most cases, I think, it actually helps me: It leads me to prepare my lectures very thoroughly and to rehearse a great deal, and it keeps me alert and energized throughout the speaking transaction. Once you recognize—on a gut level—that you are not unique in experiencing speaker apprehension, you will have taken a most important first step in managing your own apprehension.

Apprehension is not necessarily detrimental. As noted, fear can energize us and may even get us to work a little more to produce a better speech. The apprehension symptoms most speakers experience cannot be seen by the audience. Even though you may think the audience can feel your heart beat faster and faster, they cannot. They cannot see your knees tremble and they cannot feel your dry throat—at least not most of the time.

Dealing with Speaking Apprehension

Here are a few suggestions that should prove helpful in dealing with and controlling speaker apprehension.

Prepare and Practice Thoroughly   Inadequate preparation—not having rehearsed the speech enough, for example, or not having researched it thoroughly and fearing questions you cannot answer—is reasonable cause for anxiety. Much of the fear we experience is a fear of failure. Adequate and even extra preparation will lessen the possibility of failure and the accompanying apprehension.

Familiarize yourself with the actual public speaking context. Try, for example, to rehearse in the room in which you will give your speech, or stand in the front of the room before the actual presentation, as if you were giving your speech. You will thus acquaint yourself with the context, and this will ease your apprehension.

Gain Experience   Experience will help normal or moderate degrees of apprehension a great deal. Experience will show that a public speech can be effective despite these fears and anxieties, that the resultant feelings of accomplishment are most rewarding, and that public speaking can be intellectually rewarding as well as enjoyable. The situation is similar to learning to drive a car or ski down a mountain: With experience the initial fears and anxieties give way to feelings of control, comfort, and pleasure.

Put Apprehension in Perspective   Maintain realistic expectations for yourself and your audience. You do not have to be the best in the class or even as good as the person sitting next to you. You should be the best you can—whatever that is. Compete with yourself. Your second speech does not have to be better than the speech of your friend or of the previous speaker, but it should be better than your own first one.

Your audience does not expect perfection, either. Your classmates are not there to cut you down but to help you become a more effective public speaker, as you are there to help them become more effective public speakers. In fact, recent research indicates that apprehension increases when we feel that the audience's expectations are very high and decreases when we perceive their expectations to be lower. "According to the rationale developed here," notes Joe Ayres, "students' fear arises out of the feeling [that] they are unable to meet audience expectations—when they find out the audience is not as difficult to please as they had thought, their fear subsides because they perceive themselves as better able to meet these lower expectations."

So put apprehension in perspective. Let your apprehension motivate you to produce a more thoroughly prepared and rehearsed speech, but do not let it debilitate you or upset you to the point of interfering with your other activities.

Use Physical Activity and Deep Breathing Apprehension is generally eased or lessened by physical activity—by gross bodily movements as well as by the small movements of the hands, face, and head. If you are apprehensive, you might work into your speech some writing on the chalkboard or some demonstration that requires considerable movement. You could use a visual aid: Manipulating the aid or showing slides temporarily diverts attention from you and allows you to expend your excess energy. Do not, however, walk around for the sake of walking around, and do not use a visual aid just so that you can move about. Integrate such activities into your speech.

Deep breathing relaxes the body. By breathing deeply a few times before getting up to speak, you will feel your body relax and you will overcome your initial fear of getting out of your seat and walking to the front of the room. If you find yourself getting a bit more nervous than you want during your actual speech, again try breathing deeply.

SUMMARY

1. The preparation of a public speech involves following eight steps: select the subject and purpose, analyze the audience, research the topic, formulate the thesis and identify the major propositions, support the major propositions, organize the speech materials, word the speech, and construct the conclusion and the introduction.

2. Speech topics should deal with significant issues and should prove relevant and interesting to the audience and to the speaker. Subjects and purposes should be limited in scope.

3. In analyzing the audience, consider such factors as age; sex; cultural and subcultural factors; occupation, income, and status; and religion and religiousness. Also, consider the occasion and the specific context in which the speech is to take place.

4. Research the topic, beginning with general sources and gradually exploring more specific and more specialized sources.

5. Formulate the thesis of the speech, the main assertion, or the essence or core of what you want the audience to derive from the speech. On the basis of this thesis, develop your major propositions by asking relevant questions about the thesis.

6. Support the major propositions with a variety of relevant and interesting forms of amplification and evidence.

7. Organize the speech materials into a clear and easily identifiable thought pattern, for example, problem-solution, temporal, or topical.

8. Word the speech using language that is simple to understand on first hearing, personal, and informal.

9. Construct the conclusion to summarize your main ideas and to provide closure to the speech. Construct the introduction to gain the attention of the audience and to orient them as to what will follow.

10. Speaker apprehension refers to one's fear of communication and is most prevalent in public speaking situations.

11. In dealing with speaker apprehension, follow these suggestions: prepare and practice thoroughly, gain experience, put apprehension in perspective, and use physical activity and deep breathing to help relax the body.

SOURCES

Most contemporary texts on public speaking cover the various steps in the preparation of informative and persuasive speeches. These same steps are considered in greater detail in my *Elements of Public Speaking*, 3d ed. (New York: Harper & Row, 1987). Also recommended are James C. McCroskey, *An Introduction to Rhetorical Communication*, 4th ed. (Englewood Cliffs, N.J.: Prentice-Hall, 1982), and Douglas Ehninger, Bruce E. Gronbeck, and Alan H. Monroe, *Principles of Speech Communication*, 9th ed. (Chicago, Ill.: Scott, Foresman, 1984). An excellent sourcebook for public speaking principles is Jo Sprague and Douglas Stuart, *The Speaker's Handbook* (San Diego, Calif.: Harcourt Brace Jovanovich, 1984). Additional types of speeches—for example, the special occasion speech—are considered in most public speaking texts, such as those cited above. Much has been written on dealing with speaker apprehension. See, for example, Blaine Goss, M. Thompson, and S. Olds, "Behavioral Support for Systematic Desensitization for Communication Apprehension," *Human Communication Research* 4 (1978): 158–163; and Arden K. Watson and Carley H. Dodd, "Alleviating Communication Apprehension through Rational Emotive Therapy: A Comparative Evaluation," *Communication Education* 33 (July 1984): 257–266. For the research on apprehension and expectations, see Joe Ayres, "Perceptions of Speaking Ability: An Explanation of Stage Fright," *Communication Education* 35 (July 1986): 275–287.

UNIT 22
ORGANIZING THE PUBLIC SPEECH

LEARNING GOALS

After completing this unit, you should be able to

1. define the *thesis*
2. explain how the thesis statement can be used to generate main ideas
3. explain the process by which propositions are generated and refined into the major assertions of your speech
4. define *transitions* and *internal summaries* and explain their major functions
5. explain the spatial, cause-effect, and motivated sequence patterns for organizing speeches
6. identify the two major functions of the introduction and the specific means by which these functions may be served
7. identify at least three common faults that should be avoided in introductions
8. identify the two major functions of the conclusion and the specific means by which these functions may be served
9. identify at least three common faults that should be avoided in conclusions
10. explain the suggestions offered for "before the introduction" and "after the conclusion"
11. explain the processes involved in constructing the speech outline
12. identify the four suggestions on the "mechanics" of outlining
13. explain the nature of the delivery outline and how it differs from the preparation outline

In this consideration of organization we focus on the thesis, the propositions or main assertions, transitions and internal summaries, thought patterns for organizing the main assertions, introductions, conclusions, and outlining.

THE THESIS (YOUR MAIN ASSERTION)

The first step in the development and organization of any public speech is to write out the thesis statement.

The thesis is your main assertion—what you want the audience to absorb from your speech. The thesis of Lincoln's Second Inaugural Address was that Northerners and Southerners should now work together for the good of the entire country. The thesis of the "Rocky" movies was that the underdog can win.

Let us say, for example, that you are planning to deliver a speech in favor of Senator Farrington. Your thesis statement might be something like this: "Farrington's candidacy should be supported." This is what you want your audience to believe as a result of your speech. In an informative speech the thesis statement would focus on what you want your audience to learn as a result of your speech. For example, if you were to speak on the topic of jealousy, one suitable thesis might be: "There are two main theories to account for jealousy."

Limit the thesis statement to one central idea, focus, or purpose. Statements such as "We should support Farrington and the entire Democratic party" contain not one but two basic ideas.

Using Thesis Statements to Generate Main Ideas

Use your thesis statement to help generate your main ideas. Once you have phrased the thesis statement, the main divisions of your speech are readily suggested. Let us take an example: "The Hart bill will provide the needed services for senior citizens." Once stated in this form, the obvious question to address in preparing a speech with this thesis is: *What are they?* The answer to this question suggests the main parts of your speech—for example, health, food, shelter, and recreational services. These four areas then become the four main points of your speech. An outline of the main ideas would look something like this:

   I. The Hart bill provides needed health services.
  II. The Hart bill provides needed food services.
 III. The Hart bill provides needed shelter services.
 IV. The Hart bill provides needed recreational services.

THE PROPOSITIONS (YOUR MAIN POINTS)

In discussing the thesis, we mentioned how you can develop your main points or propositions by asking strategic questions. Let us look in greater depth at the process of identifying your main points.

Let us say you are giving a speech to a group of high school students on the values of a college education. Your thesis is *A college education is valuable.* You then ask, "Why is it valuable?" and from this question attempt to generate your major propositions. Your first step might be to brainstorm this question and identify as many answers as you can. Don't evaluate them now; just try to generate as many ideas as possible. A college education is valuable because

1. It will enable us to get a job.
2. It will increase our potential to earn a good salary.
3. It will give us greater job mobility.
4. It will enable us to secure more creative work.
5. It will enable us to appreciate the arts more fully.
6. It will enable us to understand an extremely complex world.
7. It will help us to understand different cultures.
8. It will help us to avoid taking a regular job for a few years.
9. It will enable us to meet lots of people and make friends.
10. It will enable us to increase personal effectiveness.

Of course, we can go on and on, but for purposes of illustration, let us stop at this point. We have 10 possible main points. Surely, these are too many to cover in a relatively short speech. Further, not all 10 are equally valuable or relevant to your audience. Look over the list and see what can be done with it to make it shorter and more meaningful. Here are some suggestions:

Eliminate Those Points That Seem Least Important to Your Thesis

You might want to eliminate, let us say, number 8 since this seems least consistent with your intended emphasis on the positive values of college.

Combine Those Points That Have a Common Focus

Notice, for example, that the first four points all center on the values of college in terms of jobs. You might, therefore, consider grouping these four items together under a general heading:

A college education will enable you to secure a better job.

This might be one of your major propositions. You can then develop this proposition by defining just what you mean by "better job" and in the process might use some of the other ideas you generated in your brainstorming session. This main point or proposition and its elaboration might look something like this:

I. A college education will enable you to secure a better job.
   A. College graduates earn higher salaries.
   B. College graduates enter more creative jobs.
   C. College graduates have greater job mobility.

Note that A, B, and C are all aspects or subdivisions of "a better job."

Select Points That Are Most Relevant to Your Audience

Ask yourself what the audience will be most interested in. On this basis you might want to eliminate numbers 5 and 7 on the assumption that your audience, high school students, will not see learning about the arts or different cultures to be particularly exciting or valuable. Further, on this criterion of relevance, we might conclude that high school students would be most interested in the idea of increasing personal abilities, so we might select this point for inclusion as our second major proposition:

II. A college education will enable us to increase our personal effectiveness.

Much as we developed the subordinate points in our first proposition by defining more clearly what we meant by a "good job," we might follow the same process by defining what we mean by "personal effectiveness":

II. A college education will enable us to increase our personal effectiveness.
   A. A college education will enable us to increase our ability to communicate.
   B. A college education will enable us to learn the skills for learning how to learn.
   C. A college education will enable us to acquire coping skills.

We can then follow the same procedure we used to generate these subordinate points (A, B, and C) to develop the subheadings of A, B, and C. For example, A might be divided into two major subheads:

A. A college education will improve our ability to communicate.
   1. A college education teaches us writing skills.
   2. A college education teaches us speech skills.

Points B and C would be developed in essentially the same way; we would seek, for example, to more clearly define in B what we mean by "learning how to learn" and, in C, what we mean by "coping skills."

As you can see there is nothing magical or mysterious about this process of developing your main points. In fact, it is quite simple once a few basic principles are understood.

Some Added Guidelines

Now that the general process of identifying and developing your main points is understood, here are a few additional guidelines that should prove useful.

Use Two, Three, or Four Main Points at the Most   Remember that our aim in a speech is not to cover every aspect of a topic but only selected parts. Further, we want to make sure that we have enough time to amplify and support the points we do present. With too many propositions this becomes impossible. Also, we want to be careful that we don't overload the channels.

Phrase Your Propositions in Parallel Style   Use similar language in wording your major propositions.

NOT THIS:

   Mass Media Functions
  I. The media entertain.
 II. The media function to inform their audiences.
III. Creating ties of union is a major media function.
IV. The conferral of status is a function of all media.

THIS:

   Mass Media Functions
  I. The media entertain.
 II. The media inform.
III. The media create ties of union.
IV. The media confer status.

Develop Your Main Points So That They Are Separate and Discrete   Do not allow your main points to overlap.

NOT THIS:

  I. Color and style are important in clothing selection.

THIS:

  I. Color is important in clothing selection.
 II. Style is important in clothing selection.

TRANSITIONS AND INTERNAL SUMMARIES

Connect the parts of your speech to each other so that their relationships are clear to you *and* to the audience, which hears the speech but *once*. Transitions and internal summaries will enable the audience to more effectively and efficiently understand your speech.

Transitions

Transitions are words, phrases, or sentences used to connect the various parts of your speech, and to provide the audience with guideposts that help them follow the development of your thoughts and arguments. Incorporate transitions between the introduction and the body of the speech and between the body and the conclusion. Also, use transitions between one main point and the next.

Here are some examples of transitional expressions you should find useful:

- My next point . . .
- A second example (argument, fact) . . .
- By way of introduction . . .
- If you want further evidence, consider . . .
- First, . . , Second, . . .
- Furthermore, . . .
- But, as we will see . . .
- So, as you can see . . .
- Given this situation, what should we do?
- How, then, can we deal with these three problems?
- It follows, then, that . . .
- Not only should we . . . , but we should also . . .
- Now that we understand the basic structure of X, let us look into its basic functions.
- In contrast, consider . . .
- The other side of the issue is this: . . .

Internal Summaries

An *internal summary* is a statement summarizing what you have already discussed; it is a statement that usually summarizes some major subdivision of your speech. Incorporate a number of internal summaries into your speech— perhaps working them into the transitions connecting, say, the major arguments or issues.

An internal summary that is also a transition might look something like this:

The three arguments advanced here were (1) . . . , (2) . . . , (3) . . . . Now, what can we do about them? I think we can do two things. First, . . .

Another example:

Inadequate recreational facilities, parental ignorance, and lack of adequate role models seem to be the major problems faced by Tryskillion youngsters. Each of these, however, can be remedied and even eliminated. Here is what we can do.

Note that these brief passages remind the listeners of what they have just heard and preview for them what they will now hear. The clear connection in their minds will fill in any gaps that may have been created through inattention, noise, and the like.

THOUGHT PATTERNS FOR ORGANIZING MAIN ASSERTIONS

In the previous unit, we considered three thought patterns for organizing your main assertions: the problem-solution pattern, the temporal pattern, and the topical pattern. Here we focus on several additional patterns—namely, the spatial, cause-effect, and motivated-sequence patterns.

Spatial Pattern

Similar to temporal patterning is patterning that organizes the main points of a speech on the basis of space. Physical objects generally fit well into organization by spatial patterning. For example, in a speech on places to visit in southern Europe, you might go from west to east, considering the countries to visit and, within these countries, the cities:

I. Your first stop is Portugal.
II. Your second stop is Spain.

Of all the public speaking principles perhaps the most difficult is organization. Listen to a lecture in one of your classes and comment on the organization the instructor has used. Was it effective? Ineffective? How might it have been improved?

III. Your third stop is Italy.
IV. Your fourth stop is Greece.

Similarly, the structure of a hospital, school, skyscraper, or a dinosaur might be appropriately described using a spatial pattern of organization.

Cause-Effect/Effect-Cause Pattern

Similar to the problem-solution pattern of organization is the cause-effect or effect-cause pattern. Here you divide the speech into two major sections—causes and effects. For example, a speech on the reasons for highway accidents or birth defects might yield to a cause-effect pattern, in which you first consider, say, the causes of highway accidents or birth defects and then some of the effects—the number of deaths, the number of accidents, and so on.

A speech on high blood pressure, designed to spell out some of the causes and effects, might look like this:

  I. There are three main causes of high blood pressure.
     A. High salt intake increases blood pressure.
     B. Excess weight increases blood pressure.
     C. Anxiety increases blood pressure.
 II. There are three major effects of high blood pressure.
     A. Nervousness increases.
     B. Heart rate increases.
     C. Shortness of breath increases.

The Motivated Sequence

Developed by Alan H. Monroe in the 1930s and widely used in all sorts of oral and written communications, the *motivated sequence* is a pattern of arranging your information so as to motivate your audience to respond positively to your purpose. In fact, it may be reasonably argued that all effective communications follow this basic pattern, whether it is called the motivated sequence or given some other name. In the motivated sequence there are five steps: attention, need, satisfaction, visualization, and action.

Attention

The function of this step is to make the audience give you their undivided attention. If you execute this step effectively, your audience should be anxious and ready to hear what you have to say. You can gain audience attention through a variety of means (more fully identified and exemplified in our discussion of the introduction presented below [pp. 335–337]).

Need

Here you would demonstrate that a need exists. The audience should feel that something has to be learned or be done because of this demonstrated need. Monroe suggests that need be established in four parts:

1. State the need or problem as it exists or will exist.
2. Illustrate the need with specific examples.
3. Further support the existence of the need with additional illustrations, statistics, testimony, and other forms of support identified in Units 25 and 26.
4. Point to how this need affects your specific listeners—for example, how it affects their financial status, career goals, or individual happiness.

Satisfaction

Here you would present the "answer" or the "solution" to satisfying the need that you demonstrated existed in step 2. The audience should believe that what you are informing them about or persuading them to do will properly and effectively satisfy the need. Here you would answer the question "How will the need be satisfied by what I am asking the audience to learn, believe, or do?" This satisfaction step would usually involve

1. A clear statement (with examples and illustrations if necessary) of what you want the audience to learn, believe, or do.
2. A statement of how or why what you are asking them to learn, believe, or do will lead to satisfying the need identified in step 2.

Visualization

Visualization intensifies the audience's feelings or beliefs. It takes the audience beyond the present time and place and enables them to imagine the situation as it would be if the need were satisfied as suggested in step 3. There are two basic ways of doing this:

1. Demonstrate the positive benefits to be derived if this advocated proposal is put into operation.
2. Demonstrate the negative consequences that will occur if your plan is not put into operation.

Of course, you could combine these two methods and demonstrate both the positive benefits of your plan and the negative consequences of the existing plan or of some alternative plan.

Action

Tell the audience what they should do to ensure that the need (as demonstrated in step 2) is satisfied (as stated in step 3). Here you want to move the audience in a particular direction, for example, to speak in favor of X or against Y, to attend the next student government meeting, to contribute free time to a specific political candidate, and so on. You can accomplish this step by stating exactly what the audience members should do, using an emotional appeal, or providing the audience with general guidelines for future action. These and other methods of concluding and motivating an audience are covered in depth below and in Unit 26.

Here is a much-abbreviated example of how these five steps would look in a speech designed to inform an audience about the workings of home computers.

- *Attention:* By the time we graduate, there will be more home computers than automobiles.
- *Need:* Much as it is now impossible to get around without a car, it will be impossible to get around the enormous amount of information without a home computer.
- *Satisfaction:* Learning a few basic principles of home computers will enable us to process our work more efficiently, in less time, and more enjoyably.
- *Visualization:* With these basic principles firmly in mind (and a home computer), you'll be able to stay at home and do the library research for your next speech by just punching in the correct code.
- *Action:* These few principles should be supplemented by further study. Probably the best way to further your study is to enroll in a computer course. Such a course . . . . Another useful way is to read the brief paperback, *The Home Computer for the College Student.*

Notice that an informative speech could have stopped after the satisfaction step because the speaker would have accomplished the goal of informing the audience about some principles of home computers. In some cases, though, you may feel it helpful to complete the steps to emphasize your point in detail.

In a persuasive speech, on the other hand, you must go at least as far as visualization (if your purpose is limited to strengthening or changing attitudes or beliefs) or to the action step (if you are attempting to motivate behavior).

INTRODUCTIONS

The introduction to a speech, although delivered first, should be constructed last. In this way you will be able to see the entire speech before you and will be better able to determine which elements should and should not go into introducing the now-completed speech.

In the previous unit, we identified two major functions of the introduction: to gain attention and to orient the audience as to what is to follow. Here we spell out the specific methods for accomplishing these goals.

Gain Attention

The introduction must gain the attention of the audience and focus it on your speech topic. Of course, you must also maintain that attention throughout the speech, so what is said here also applies to other parts of the speech.

Ask a Question Questions are effective because they not only represent a change from the normal statements but also involve the audience; they tell the audience that you are talking directly to them and that you care about their responses.

Make Reference to Audience Members   This generally makes members perk up and pay attention because you are involving them directly in your talk.

Make Reference to Recent Happenings   This helps to secure attention because the audience, being familiar with such events, will want to see how you are going to approach them.

Use Humor   A clever and appropriate joke or anecdote is always useful in holding attention. But avoid this method if there is any doubt that your story will in fact prove humorous.

Use an Illustration or Dramatic Story   Much as people are drawn to "Dynasty" and "Dallas," so are we drawn to illustrations and stories about people. Use such stories to secure audience attention in the introduction as well as throughout your speech.

Use Audiovisual Aids   These will engage attention because they are new and different. Specific examples of appropriate audiovisual aids are provided in Unit 25, "The Informative Speech."

Orient the Audience

The introduction should orient the audience in some way. This orientation or preview will help the audience to follow your thoughts more closely. The orientation may be covered in several ways.

Give the Audience a General Idea of Your Subject   Statements such as "Tonight I want to discuss the proposed tax revision," "I'm going to focus on gender differences in communication," or "I will cover the pros and cons of the new Brommel proposal for dealing with atomic waste" are examples of general orientations.

Give a Detailed Preview of Your Main Propositions   In this method you would identify the propositions you will discuss in your speech—for example, "In this brief talk I will cover four major attractions of New York City: the night life, theater, restaurants, and museums.
James Kelley provides a detailed preview in this way:

> I would like to deal with four questions that I am constantly asked about computers in the schools. First, are we truly in a computer revolution? Second, are schools addressing the computer issue? Third, exactly how are schools using computers? And fourth, where do you and I fit into all of this?

Identify Your Goal or the Objectives You Hope to Achieve   A librarian addressing my public speaking class last year oriented the audience by stating objectives in this way:

Pay attention for the next few minutes and you'll be able to locate anything we have in the library through the use of the new touch-screen computer access system.

Some Common Faults with Introductions

The introduction is perhaps the most important single part of the speech; your listeners will form an impression of you based largely on your introduction and will respond to you according to the way they felt about the introduction. Avoid the common faults that many beginning speakers make:

Don't Apologize   A common fault is to apologize for *something*. Generally, don't do it. Your inadequacies—whatever they are—will be clear enough to any discerning listener; do not point them out specifically. You do not have to say, "I am not an expert on this topic" or "I didn't do as much reading on it as I should have." And *never* start a speech with "I'm not very good at giving public speeches."

Don't Make Hollow Promises   A related fault is to promise to deliver something that you will not in fact deliver. The speaker who promises to tell you how to solve your love life, how to make a fortune in the stock market, or how to be the most popular person on campus and fails to deliver such insights quickly loses credibility.

Don't Rely on Gimmicks   Avoid gimmicks that gain attention but are irrelevant to the nature of the speech or inconsistent with the treatment to be given the topic. Thus, for example, to slam a book on the desk, yell obscenities, or otherwise jar the audience into attention usually accomplishes this very limited goal. But when such actions are out of place, the audience sees such actions for what they are—gimmicks and tricks that have fooled them into paying attention. Such actions are resented and will set up barriers between you and your listeners.

Don't Preface Your Introduction   Do not preface your speech with such common but ineffective statements such as:

I'm really nervous, but here goes.

Before I begin my talk, I want to say . . . .

I hope I can remember everything I want to say.

CONCLUSIONS

The conclusion is especially important, since it is often the part of the speech that the audience remembers most clearly. It is the conclusion that in many cases determines what image of you is left in the minds of the audience. Devote special care to this brief but crucial part of your speech. Two major functions of the conclusion are identified here.

Summarize

You may summarize your speech in a variety of ways.

Restate Your Thesis or Objectives   In this type of brief summary, you restate the essential thrust of your speech—your thesis or perhaps the objectives you hoped to achieve.

Restate the Importance of the Topic or Thesis   Tell the audience again why your topic or thesis is so important. Walter Light used this type of conclusion:

> If we do not move to restore our universities and improve the educational infra-structure in Canada, we will be unilaterally withdrawing from the future. We will be condemning ourselves to the economic vassaldom of those who do perceive education and brains as the only real resource and, in fact, the ultimate resource of any nation.

Restate Your Major Propositions   Here you would simply reiterate your two, three, or four major propositions.

Provide Closure

The second function of the conclusion is to provide some kind of closure—to give the speech a crisp and definite end. The audience should not be left hanging on, wondering whether or not you have finished. Closure may be achieved through a variety of methods.

Use a Quotation   Using a quotation that summarizes your thesis or provides an interesting perspective on your point of view will often provide effective closure.

Refer to Subsequent Events   John Silber, in a speech on higher education, uses this type of conclusion most effectively:

> Each of these three issues has relevance not only for Americans but for any country seriously concerned about higher education and its relation to democracy. They are not the only issues of importance I have raised today, but they form a basis for further discussion. I am looking forward to a fruitful exchange of ideas in the panels that will follow.

Pose a Challenge or Question   You may wish to end your speech with a provocative question for the audience to ponder or a challenge to consider. Here, for example, R. G. P. Styles concludes his speech by posing a question and answering it:

What does that mean for Canada? Weighed in the global balance, as well as our trade balance, we have a working partnership with what is still the most powerful nation on earth. It's imperative that we maintain it and (with our, at times, somewhat different points of view) vital that we continue to work hard at explaining our interests, so that for both of us the best possible results are achieved.

Refer Back to the Introduction   Sometimes it is possible to refer back to the introduction. For example, Win Borden, in a commencement address, noted in his introduction that he could not remember what his own commencement speaker said at his graduation. He then concluded his speech as follows:

People are always watching you, learning from you, and looking to you for inspiration. In other words, it is important how you play the game of life. If, sometime in the future, someone asks you to remember what was significant about your commencement speech, I hope that you will tell them you remember that. It is important how you play the game of life.

Some Common Faults with Conclusions

Beginning speakers often fall into various common faults with conclusions, as with any part of the speech. Highlighting them here may help alert you to them and perhaps make it easier to avoid them.

Don't Apologize   Do not apologize for any manifested inadequacies. Actually, apologies are not always ineffective; handled well, they may help to interject a needed note of modesty. In most cases, however, it is best not to apologize.

Don't Introduce New Material   You may, of course, give new expression to ideas covered in the body of the speech but do not introduce new material in your conclusion. Instead use your conclusion to reinforce what you have already said in your discussion and to summarize your essential points.

Don't Drag Out the Conclusion   End crisply and just once. Beginning speakers will often preface each statement of their conclusion with terms that lead the audience to think that this is the last statement. Expressions such as "in summary" or "in conclusion" or "therefore" and similar ones will often lead the audience to expect an ending. When you are ready to end, end: Do not linger at the door.

BEFORE THE INTRODUCTION AND AFTER THE CONCLUSION

Although it is convenient to consider your speech beginning when you begin your introduction, it actually begins as soon as the audience focuses on you as a speaker. Similarly, your speech does not end after your have spoken the last sentence of your conclusion: It ends only after the audience directs its focus away from you to another speaker or another project. Here are a few suggestions for dealing with the speech before the introduction and after the conclusion.

Before the Introduction

Display enthusiasm when you get up from your seat and walk to your speaking position. Display no signs of discomfort or displeasure. No one wants to listen to a speaker who is obviously not enjoying the experience. Stand in front of the audience with a sense of control.

Do not start your speech as soon as you get up from your seat or even as soon as you get to the front. Survey your audience; engage their attention. Pause briefly, then begin your speech.

After the Conclusion

If there is a question period following your speech and you are in charge of this, pause after you have completed your conclusion and ask the audience members whether they have any questions. If there is a chairperson who will recognize audience members having questions, pause after your conclusion, and then nonverbally indicate to the chairperson that you are ready to entertain questions.

If there are no questions, pause after the last statement of your conclusion. Continue maintaining eye contact with the audience for a second or two and then walk (do not run) to your seat. Once you sit down, show no signs of relief—do not sigh or in any other way indicate that you are relieved or pleased that the experience is over. Focus your attention on the chairperson, the next speaker, or on whatever activity is taking place.

CONSTRUCTING THE OUTLINE

After you have completed your research and have mapped out an organizational plan for your speech, put this plan or blueprint on paper—that is, construct an outline of your speech. In constructing your outline, follow these guidelines.

Preface the Outline with Identifying Data

Before you begin the outline proper, identify the general and specific purposes as well as your thesis. This prefatory material would look something like this:

General purpose: To inform my audience of the functions of the media

Specific purpose: To inform my audience of four major functions of the mass media: to entertain, inform, create ties of union, and confer status

Thesis: The mass media serve a number of functions.

These identifying data are not part of your speech proper; they are not, for example, mentioned in the delivery of the speech. Rather, they are guides to the preparation of the speech and the outline. They are like road signs to keep you going in the right direction and to signal you when you have gone off course.

Outline the Introduction, Body, and Conclusion as Separate Units

These three parts of the speech, although intimately connected, should be labeled separately and should be kept distinct in your outline. Like the identifying data above, these labels are not addressed to the audience but rather provide further guides to your preparation.

Your introduction should gain attention and orient the audience. The body of your speech should contain the major propositions and the materials necessary for amplification and support. The conclusion should summarize and provide crisp closure. By keeping these three parts separate, you will be able to see at a glance whether they do in fact serve the functions you want them to serve.

Insert Transitions and Internal Summaries

Insert [using square brackets] transitions

1. between the introduction and the body
2. between the body and the conclusion
3. between the major propositions of the body
4. wherever else they might be needed

Insert your internal summaries (if these are not integrated with your transitions) wherever you feel they will help the audience to understand and remember your ideas.

Append a List of References

Some instructors require that you append a list of references to your speeches. If this is requested, then do so at the end of the outline or on a separate page. Some instructors require that only sources cited in the speech be included in the list of references, while others require that the full list of sources consulted—those mentioned in the speech as well as those not mentioned—be provided.

Whatever the specific requirements, remember that these sources will prove most effective with your audience if you carefully integrate them into the speech. It will count for little if you consulted the latest works by the greatest authorities but never mention this to your audience. So, when appropriate, weave into your speech the source material you have consulted. In your outline, refer to the source material by author's name, publication date, and page number in parentheses and then provide the complete citation in your list of references. For example:

> The bellwether states are California, Florida, Washington, Colorado, and Connecticut (Naisbitt, 1984, p. xxvii).

The reference list would then include, among others, the following citation:

> Naisbitt, John. *Megatrends: Ten New Directions Transforming Our Lives*. New York: Warner, 1984.

In your actual speech it might prove more effective to include the source with your statement:

> According to John Naisbitt, author of the nationwide bestseller, *Megatrends*, the bellwether states are California, Florida, Washington, Colorado, and Connecticut.

Regardless of what specific system is required (do find out before you prepare your outline), make certain to include all sources of information, not only written materials. Personal interviews, information derived from course lectures, and data learned from television should all be included in your list of references.

SOME MECHANICS OF OUTLINING

Assuming that the outline you construct for your early speeches will be relatively complete, here are a few guidelines concerning the mechanics—the technical aspects—of outlining.

Use a Consistent Set of Symbols

The following is the standard, accepted sequence of symbols for outlining:

I.
  A.
    1.
      a.
        (1)
          (a)

Begin the introduction, the body, and the conclusion with Roman numeral I. That is, each of the three major parts should be treated as a complete unit.

NOT THIS:

    Introduction
  I. _____
  II. _____
    Body
 III. _____
 IV. _____
  V. _____
    Conclusion
 VI. _____
VII.

THIS:

    Introduction
  I. _____
  II. _____
    Body
  I. _____
  II. _____
 III. _____
    Conclusion
  I. _____
  II. _____

Use Visual Aspects to Reflect and Reinforce the Organizational Pattern

Use proper and clear indentation. This will help to set off visually coordinate and subordinate relationships.

NOT THIS:

I. Television caters to the lowest possible intelligence.
  A. Situation comedies
    1. "Growing Pains"

THIS:

I. Television caters to the lowest possible intelligence.
  A. Situation comedies illustrate this.
    1. "Growing Pains" illustrates this.
    2. "Benson" illustrates this.
    3. "Who's the Boss?" illustrates this.

  B. Soap operas illustrate this.
    1. "As the World Turns" illustrates this.
    2. "General Hospital" illustrates this.
    3. "Young and the Restless" illustrates this.

Use One Discrete Idea per Symbol

If the outline is to reflect the organizational pattern among the various items of information, use just one discrete idea per symbol. Compound sentences are sure giveaways that you have not limited each item to one single idea. Also, be sure that each item is discrete, that is—that it does not overlap with any other item.

NOT THIS:

 I. Education might be improved if teachers were better trained and if students were better motivated.

THIS:

 I. Education would be improved if teachers were better trained.
 II. Education would be improved if students were better motivated.

Note that in THIS, items I and II are single ideas but in NOT THIS they are combined.

Use Complete Declarative Sentences

Phrase your ideas in the outline in complete declarative sentences rather than as questions or phrases. This will further assist you in examining the essential relationships. It is much easier, for example, to see if one item of information supports another when both are phrased in the declarative mode. If one is a question and one is a statement, this will be more difficult.

NOT THIS:

 I. Who should raise children?
 II. Should the state raise children?
  A. Equality for children
  B. Parents will be released for work.

THIS:

 I. Children should be raised by the state.
  A. All children will be treated equally.
  B. Parents will be released to work.

Note that in THIS, all items are phrased as complete declarative sentences, so their relationship is brought out clearly. In NOT THIS, on the other hand, a mixture of question, sentence, and phrase obscures the relationship.

THE DELIVERY OUTLINE

Now that you have constructed what is called a preparation outline, you need to construct a delivery outline, which will assist you in the actual delivery of the speech. Do *not* use your preparation outline to deliver the speech. If you do, you will have a tendency to read from the outline and to in effect verbalize a written outline—obviously, not a very effective way to give a speech. Instead, construct a brief delivery outline to assist rather than hinder your delivery of the speech. Here are some guidelines in preparing this delivery outline.

Be Brief

This outline should assist you in communicating your ideas to your audience. It should not and must not stand in the way of speaker-audience contact. Therefore, it should be brief. Do not use full sentences; instead, use key words that will trigger in your mind the ideas you wish to discuss with your audience. Follow, too, the principles noted for the construction of the preparation outline: (1) use a consistent set of symbols—the same ones you used in your preparation outline—and (2) use the visual aspects to reflect and reinforce the organizational pattern. Try to limit yourself to one side of one sheet of paper.

Be Clear

Be sure that you can see the outline while you are speaking. Do not make your writing so small that you will have to squint to read it. On the other hand, do not make it so large that you will need reams of paper to deliver a five-minute speech. Use different colors of ink, underlining, and whatever other symbols or system will help you communicate your ideas to your audience most effectively.

Be Delivery-Minded

This is your outline: It is constructed to help you deliver your speech most effectively. Therefore, include in this outline any guides to delivery you might wish to remember while you are speaking. For example, you might note in the outline when you will use your visual aid and when you will remove it. A simple "Show VA" or "Remove VA" should suffice.

You might also wish to note some speaking cues, such as "slow down" when reading a poetry excerpt, for example, or "pause" when an extended pause might help.

Rehearse Your Speech with This Outline

In your rehearsals, use this outline and this outline only. Do not rehearse with your full-sentence outline. This is simply a specific application of the general rule: Make rehearsals as close to the real thing as possible.

SUMMARY

1. The thesis is the main assertion of the speech, the main idea that you want your audience to retain.

2. Thesis statements are useful for generating main ideas and for suggesting organizational patterns.

3. After generating your main points or propositions: eliminate those that seem least important to your thesis, combine those points that have a common focus, select points that are most relevant to your audience, use no more than four main points, and phrase your propositions in parallel style.

4. Use transitions (words, phrases, or sentences that connect the various parts of your speech) and internal summaries liberally.

5. Arrange your main propositions into some relevant thought pattern, for example, problem-solution, temporal, topical, spatial, cause-effect, or the motivated sequence.

6. The motivated sequence pattern contains five steps: attention, need, satisfaction, visualization, and action. Informative speeches need only use the first three steps but may use all five; persuasive speeches must use at least the first four but frequently include all five steps.

7. Introductions should gain the attention of the audience and orient them as to what will follow.

8. Attention may be gained through a variety of methods—for example, asking a question, making reference to audience members, making reference to recent happenings, using humor, using an illustration or dramatic story, or using audiovisual aids.

9. Audience orientation may be achieved by giving the audience a general idea of your subject, giving a detailed preview of your major propositions, or identifying your goals or objectives.

10. Among the common faults with introductions are apologizing, making hollow promises, relying on gimmicks, and prefacing the introduction.

11. The conclusion of the speech should summarize the speech and provide closure.

12. Summaries may be of varied types: restatement of the thesis or objective, the importance of the topic, or your major propositions.

13. Closure may be achieved by using a quotation, referring to subsequent

events, posing a challenge or question to the audience, or referring back to the introduction.

14. Some of the more common faults with conclusions are apologizing, introducing new material, and dragging out the conclusion.

15. Your speech begins not with your introduction but when the audience focuses on you as a speaker. Your speech ends not with the last line of your conclusion but when the audience refocuses their attention on another speaker or another activity.

16. Before your introduction, display enthusiasm with no signs of discomfort, stand in front of the audience with a sense of control, pause, engage their attention, and then begin.

17. After the conclusion, pause, continue to maintain eye contact, and then walk confidently back to your seat. If there are questions to follow your speech, pause after your conclusion and then indicate to the chairperson that you are ready to entertain questions, or ask the audience if anyone has any questions.

18. In constructing the speech outline, follow these steps: preface the outline with identifying data; outline the introduction, body, and conclusion as separate units; insert transitions and internal summaries, and append a list of references (if required).

19. Follow these mechanics of outlining: use a consistent set of symbols; use visual aspects to reflect and reinforce the organizational pattern; use one discrete idea per symbol; and use complete declarative sentences.

SOURCES

On thesis statements, see Frank J. D'Angelo, *Process and Thought in Composition,* 2d ed. (Cambridge, Mass.: Winthrop, 1980). I relied in part on D'Angelo and on the insights of and research evidence presented by Bert E. Bradley, *Fundamentals of Speech Communication: The Credibility of Ideas* (Dubuque, Iowa: Brown, 1974). The remaining general principles of organization are covered in just about every text in public speaking. Organizational patterns for the body of the speech are considered in all of the works cited in the previous unit. On the effects of organization, see, for example, Richard F. Whitman and John H. Timmis, "The Influence of Verbal Organizational Structure and Verbal Organizing Skills on Select Measures of Learning," *Human Communication Research* 1 (summer 1975): 293–301. For the motivational sequence, use Douglas Ehninger, Bruce E. Gronbeck, Ray E. McKerrow, and Alan H. Monroe, *Principles and Types of Speech Communication,* 10th ed. (Glenview, Ill.: Scott, Foresman, 1986). On outlining, see the works cited above. A useful workbook is Stephen D. Boyd and Mary Ann Renz, *Organization and Outlining: A Workbook for Students in a Basic Speech Course* (New York: Macmillan, 1985).

On introductions and conclusions see Douglas Ehninger, Bruce E. Gronbeck, Ray E. McKerrow, and Alan H. Monroe, *Principles and Types of Speech Communication*, 10th ed. (Glenview, Ill.: Scott, Foresman, 1986); Michael Osborn, *Speaking in Public* (Boston, Mass.: Houghton Mifflin, 1982); and Joe Ayres and Janice Miller, *Effective Public Speaking*, 2d ed. (Dubuque, Iowa: Wm. C. Brown, 1986). Additional examples and complete references to speeches may be found in Joseph A. DeVito, *The Elements of Public Speaking*, 3d ed. (New York: Harper & Row, 1987).

UNIT 23
STYLE AND LANGUAGE IN THE PUBLIC SPEECH

LEARNING GOALS

After completing this unit, you should be able to

1. define *oral style* and distinguish it from written style
2. define the five qualities of effective style that should govern word choice in public speaking
3. identify at least five specific suggestions for achieving greater clarity of style
4. identify at least three specific suggestions for achieving vividness, appropriateness, personalness, and forcefulness in public speaking style
5. define, distinguish among, and provide examples of the parallel, antithetical, and periodic sentence types

In this unit we cover style and language in public speaking. We do this in three parts. First, we consider oral style—that particular style that seems best to characterize the style of the effective public speech. Second, we focus on word choice—how to select the best words to communicate your meaning and accomplish your public speaking purpose, whether this be to inform or to persuade. Third, we consider sentence construction and suggest several effective ways of phrasing sentences.

ORAL STYLE

"Oral style" is a quality of spoken language that clearly differentiates it from written language. You do not speak as you write. The words and grammatical constructions you use differ depending on whether you are speaking or writing. The major explanation for this difference is that you compose speech instantly; you select your words and construct your sentences as you think your thoughts, with very little time in between the thought and the utterance. When you write, however, you compose your thoughts after considerable reflection and even then often rewrite and edit as you go along. Another explanation for the difference, from the point of view of the listener, is that the listener hears a speech only once and it must therefore be made instantly intelligible. The reader can reread an essay, look up an unfamiliar word, and otherwise spend a great deal of time understanding the meaning of the written communication. The listener, however, is forced to move at the pace of the speaker. Temporary attention lapses may force the reader to reread a sentence or paragraph, but such lapses can never be made up by the listener.

Thus, the two forms of communication differ in how they are produced and how they are received. These differences lead speakers and writers to compose differently. At the same time, the differences in reception demand that speakers and writers employ different rules or principles to guide them in composing messages for their particular mode of expression and reception.

On a purely descriptive level, spoken language differs from written language in a number of important ways. Generally, spoken language consists of shorter, simpler, and more familiar words than does written language. There is a great deal more qualification in speech than in writing. For example, speakers will make greater use of such expressions as *although, however, perhaps,* and the like. Writers probably edit out such expressions before their work is published and read. Spoken language also contains a greater number of self-reference terms (terms that refer to the speaker himself or herself) and a greater number of "allness" terms (for example, *all, none, every, always, never*). Spoken language contains more concrete terms; written language contains more abstract terms.

Spoken language also contains more pseudo-quantifying terms (for example, *many, much, very, lots*) and more terms indicative of consciousness of projection—terms that incorporate the speaker as part of the observation (for example, *it seems to me that . . .* or *as I see it . . .*). Further, spoken language contains more verbs and adverbs, whereas writing contains more nouns and adjectives.

In large part, this spoken style needs to be retained in the public speech. But since the public speech is composed much as is a written essay—with considerable thought, deliberation, editing, and restyling—special consideration must be given to retain and polish the style that seems most appropriate to the spoken mode and that is most effective in communicating meaning to listeners.

The specific suggestions presented in this unit are designed to guide you in styling a speech that will retain the best of the oral style while maintaining comprehension and persuasion.

Here, we identify specific suggestions for improving your speech style. We cover this in two parts. First, we offer specific suggestions for selecting words to achieve an effective speech style. Second, we offer specific suggestions for styling sentences to give them greater clarity and force.

WORD CHOICE

Choose carefully the words you use in your public speeches. Choose words to achieve clarity, vividness, appropriateness, personalness, and forcefulness.

Clarity

Clarity in speaking style should be the primary goal of the public speaker. Here are some guidelines to help you make your speech clear.

Be Economical

Don't waste words. Two of the most important ways to achieve economy is to avoid redundancies and to avoid meaningless words. Notice the redundancy in the following expressions:

very unique

at 9 A.M. *in the morning*

we *first* began the discussion

the full *and complete* report

I *myself personally*

blue *in color*

*over*exaggerate

written *down*

you, *members of the audience*

clearly unambiguous

about *approximately* nine inches *or so*

cash *money*

By eliminating the italicized terms we get rid of unnecessary words and move closer to a more economical and clearer style.

Similarly, eliminate meaningless phrases such as:

the amount of $10 was paid

conduct a study *on* the increasing divorce rate

Rework meaningless phrases into more economical and more direct expressions: instead of saying "would seem to indicate," say "indicates"; instead of saying "the function of this plug . . . ," say "this plug . . . ," instead of saying "for the reason that," say "because."

Use Specific Terms and Numbers
Picture these terms:

- living thing
- animal
- dog
- poodle

Notice that as we get more and more specific, we get a clearer and more detailed picture. Be specific, so that your audience will be able to see what you want them to see. Don't say *car* when you want them to picture a limousine, and don't say *movie* when you want them to think of *Raiders of the Lost Ark.*

The same is true of numbers: Don't say "earned a good salary" if you mean "earned $90,000 a year," don't say "taxes will go up" when you mean "taxes will increase 22 percent," and don't say "their defense budget was enormous" when you mean "the defense budget was $17 billion."

Use Guide Phrases
It is difficult work to listen to a public speech. Assist the listeners by using guide phrases to help them see that you are moving from one idea to another and from one piece of evidence to another. Use phrases such as "now that we have seen how . . . ," "let us consider how . . . ," and "my next argument . . ."

Terms such as *first, second, and also, although,* and *however* also help the audience to follow your line of thinking.

Use Short, Familiar, and High-Frequency Terms
Generally, favor the short word over the long one, the familiar term over the unfamiliar term, and the high-frequency (more commonly used) term over the low-frequency term. Here are a few examples:

Poor choices   *Better choices*
innocuous   harmless
elucidate   clarify
utilize   use
ascertain   find out
erstwhile   former
eschew   avoid
expenditure   cost, expense

Use Repetition, Restatement, and Internal Summaries

Repetition (repeating something in exactly the same way), restatement (rephrasing an idea or statement), and internal summaries (summaries or reviews of subsections of your speech) all help the listeners to follow what you are saying.

Vividness

Select words to help you make your ideas vivid and come alive in the minds of your listeners.

Use Active Verbs

Favor verbs that communicate activity rather than passivity. Generally, the verb *to be*, in all its forms—*is, are, was, were, will be,* and so forth—is relatively inactive. Try replacing such forms with verbs of action. Instead of saying "The senator was in the middle of the crowd," say "The senator stood in the middle of the crowd." Instead of saying "The report was on the President's desk for three days," try "The report rested (or languished) on the President's desk for three days." Instead of saying "Management will be here tomorrow," consider "Management will descend on us (or jets in) tomorrow."

Use Strong Verbs

The verb is the strongest part of your sentence. Choose verbs carefully, so that they accomplish lots of work. Instead of saying "He walked through the forest," consider such terms as *wandered, prowled, rambled, roamed,* and ask whether one of these might not better suit your intended meaning. Consult a thesaurus for any verb you suspect might be weak. A good guide to identifying weak verbs is to look at your use of adverbs. If you are using lots of adverbs, it is likely that you are using adverbs to modify weak verbs. Consider eliminating the adverbs and substituting stronger verbs.

Use Figures of Speech

One of the best ways to achieve vividness is to make use of the figures of speech and stylistic devices that have been a part of rhetoric since ancient times. Here are a few of the many figures of speech you might use:

■ *Alliteration*—repetition of the same initial sound in two or more words: "fifty famous flavors"

- *Antithesis*—presentation of contrary ideas in parallel form: "Wealth makes the marriage; want of it makes the divorce"
- *Climax*—the arrangement of individual phrases or sentences in ascending order of forcefulness: "As a child he lied; as a youth he stole; as a man he killed"
- *Hyperbole*—the use of extreme exaggeration: "your obedient and humble servant" or "I'm so hungry I could eat a cow"
- *Irony*—the use of a word or sentence whose literal meaning is the opposite of that intended: a teacher handing back failing examinations might say (using irony), "So pleased to see how many of you studied so hard"
- *Metaphor*—the comparison of two unlike things: "She's a lion when she wakes up" or "He's a real bulldozer"
- *Metonymy*—the substitution of a name for a title with which it is closely associated: "City Hall issued the following news release" where *City Hall* is used instead of *the mayor* or *the city council;* or "She will suffer the wrath of the crown" where *crown* is used instead of *king* or *government*
- *Personification*—the attribution of human characteristics to inanimate objects: "This room cries for activity" or "My car is tired and wants a drink"
- *Rhetorical question*—a question used to make a statement or produce some desired effect rather than to secure an answer, since the answer to the question is usually obvious: "Do you want to be popular?" or "Do you want to get well?"
- *Simile*—the comparison of two unlike objects using the words *like* or *as:* "He takes charge like a bull" or "The teacher is as gentle as a lamb"

Use Imagery

Appeal to the audience's senses, especially their visual, auditory, and tactual senses. Make them see, hear, and feel what you are talking about.

Visual Imagery   In describing people or objects create images that the audience can see. When appropriate, describe such visual qualities as height, weight, color, size, shape, length, and contour. Let your audience see the sweat pouring down the faces of the coal miners, and the short overweight executive in a pinstriped suit smoking an enormous cigar.

Auditory Imagery   Appeal to the audience's sense of hearing by using terms that describe sounds. Let listeners hear the car *screeching*, the wind *whistling*, the bells *chiming*, and the angry professor *roaring*.

Tactile Imagery   Use terms referring to temperature, texture, and touch to create tactile imagery. Let listeners feel the cool water running over their bodies, the hot desert sand beneath their feet, the punch of the fighter, the smooth skin of the newborn baby, the clothing as rough as sandpaper, and the soft caress of a lover.

Appropriateness

We noted in the previous unit that your language should be appropriate to you as the speaker, to your audience, to the occasion, and to the speech topic. Here are some general guidelines to help you achieve this quality.

Speak on the Appropriate Level of Formality-Informality

Although public speaking usually takes place in a relatively formal situation, the language that seems to work best is a style that is somewhat less formal than the style of, say, the written essay. One way to achieve an informal style is to use contractions: *don't* instead of *do not*, *I'll* instead of *I shall*, and *wouldn't* instead of *would not*. Contractions give a public speech the sound and rhythm of conversation—a quality to which listeners generally react favorably.

Avoid "written-style" expressions such as "the former" or "the latter" as well as such expressions as "the argument presented above." These make listeners feel you are reading to them rather than talking with them.

Use personal pronouns instead of impersonal expressions. Say "I found" instead of "it has been found" or "I will present three arguments" instead of "Three arguments will be presented."

Avoid Unfamiliar (and Hence, Inappropriate) Foreign and Technical Terms, Jargon, and Acronyms

Be especially careful to avoid using terms the audience does not know. Avoid foreign and technical terms unless you are certain the audience is familiar with them. Similarly, avoid jargon (the technical vocabulary of a specialized field) unless you are sure its meaning is clear to your listeners. Some acronyms (NATO, UN, NOW, and CORE) are probably familiar to most audiences, but most are not. When you wish to use any of these word types, fully explain their meaning.

Avoid Slang and Vulgar Expressions

Be careful that you do not offend your audience with language that embarrasses them or makes them think that you have little respect for them. Although your listeners may themselves use such expressions, they generally resent their use by public speakers.

Avoid Offensive Terms and Expressions

Avoid terms that might be interpreted as sexist or racist. Do not use the masculine pronoun to refer to the hypothetical person; that is, *he* or *him* should not be used generically. Change your sentences around so that the plural *they* or *them* can be used, or say *he and she* or *her and him*. Do not refer to professions or positions by masculine names: Avoid such expressions as *chairman*, *policeman*, and *repairman* when applied to both sexes. Substitute *chair* or *chairperson*, *police officer*, and *repairperson*. Similarly, avoid the use of *man* when referring to the human race. *Human* serves just as well and is more descriptive.

Alternatively, terms that were at one time used to refer to a woman in a

Probably nowhere is the importance of language style more obvious and more influential than in the media. Oprah Winfrey has become popular, in part at least, because of her unique style in presenting information, in asking questions, and in relating to her audience. What media personality do you find to have a unique and appealing style? What characterizes this person's style? What media personality do you feel has a style you find unpleasant?

specific position (normally originating from a masculine form) should be avoided; for example, *poetess, Negress, Jewess, heroine,* and *actress.* Don't imply that the hypothetical doctor or lawyer is male by modifying such terms with sex identifiers such as "woman doctor" or "female lawyer."

The same equality that should be shown to women should be shown to members of different races, nationalities, religions, and affectional orientations. Avoid referring to such groups with terms that carry negative connotations, or picturing members of these groups in stereotypical and negative ways. Avoid slighting members of minority groups; include references to minority groups in your examples and show minority members in your illustrations.

Personalness

Audiences seem to favor speakers who speak in a personal rather than an impersonal style—who speak with them rather than at them.

Use Personal Pronouns, Especially Self-Referential Ones

Say *I, me, he, she,* and *you.* Avoid such expressions as the impersonal *one* (as in, for example, "One is led to believe . . ."), "this speaker," or "you, the listeners." These expressions generally distance the audience and create barriers rather than bridges.

Use Questions Directed to Audience

Ask the audience questions to involve them. In a small audience, you might even briefly entertain responses. In larger audiences, you might ask the question, pause to allow the audience time to consider what their responses would be, and then move on. When you direct questions to your listeners, they feel part of a public speaking transaction.

Create Immediacy

Immediacy is a connectedness, a relatedness, and a oneness with one's listeners. Immediacy is the opposite of disconnectedness and separateness. Create this sense of immediacy by using the "you approach." Say "you'll enjoy reading . . ." instead of "everyone will enjoy reading . . ."

Refer directly to commonalities between you and the audience—for example, "We are all children of immigrants" and "We all want to see our team in the playoffs." Refer also to shared experiences and goals—for example, "We all want and need a more responsive PTA." Finally, recognize audience feedback and refer to it in your speech—for example, "I can see from your expressions that we're all here for the same reason."

Forcefulness

If you wish to achieve your purpose, whether it be informative or persuasive, then you have to direct the audience's attention, thoughts, and feelings with forceful language.

Eliminate Weakeners

Blue-pencil phrases that weaken the strength of your sentences. Note that in the following examples, the italicized phrases serve only to weaken the strength of the sentences; eliminate such weakeners.

It seems to me that Mike Swazey is the best candidate for the job.

I'm not sure about this but my research shows that movie attendance has declined in the last several years.

Further, rewrite sentences to make them more forceful, eliminating those phrases that water down your meaning. Instead of saying "There are lots of things we can do to help," say "We can do lots of things to help"; instead of saying "I'm sorry to be so graphic but Senator Bingsley's proposal . . . ," say "We need to be graphic. Senator Bingsley's proposal . . ."; instead of saying "It should be observed in this connection that, all things considered, money is not productive of happiness," say "Money doesn't bring happiness."

Avoid Bromides and Clichés

Bromides are sentences that are trite and worn out by constant usage: "Honesty is the best policy," "If I can't do it well, I won't do it at all," and "I don't understand modern art, but I know what I like." When we hear bromides, we recognize them as unoriginal and uninspired.

Clichés are overused phrases that have lost their novelty and part of their meaning, and that call attention to themselves because of their overuse. Here are some cliches to avoid:

- in this day and age
- sweet as sugar
- happy as a lark
- tell it like it is
- free as a bird
- no sooner said than done
- to all intents and purposes
- it goes without saying
- few and far between
- from the ridiculous to the sublime

Vary Intensity as Appropriate

Much as you can raise your voice in terms of intensity, you can also phrase your ideas with different degrees of stylistic intensity. You can, for example, refer to an action by an individual as "failing to support our position" or as "stabbing us in the back." You can say that a new proposal will "endanger our goals" or "destroy us completely." You can refer to a child's behavior as "playful," "creative," or "destructive" and describe that child as "pretty" or as "beautiful." The point here is that language may be varied to express different degrees of intensity—from mild through neutral to extremely intense.

A specific example of the influence of intensity of language should convince you that words must be carefully chosen if they are to have the desired effect, and that intensity is one of the language variables that must be considered in selecting your words. In one study subjects were individually shown the same film of two cars crashing into each other. The difference lay in the words used to describe the "crash." After viewing the film the subjects were asked to estimate how fast the two cars were going when they "smashed," "collided," "bumped," "hit," or "contacted." As expected, the estimated speeds differed depending on the single word used to describe the accident. The results are presented in Table 23.1. Note, for example, that the difference between "smashed" and "contacted" resulted in a difference of nine miles in estimated

TABLE 23.1 LANGUAGE INTENSITY AND PERCEPTION

Descriptive Word	Mean Estimated Speed
Smashed	40.8
Collided	39.3
Bumped	38.1
Hit	34.0
Contacted	31.8

speed, and the difference between "smashed" and "hit" resulted in a difference of almost seven miles in estimated speed.

Perhaps even more interesting is the finding that when the groups who saw the film in which the cars were described as having "hit" or "smashed" were retested and asked if there was any broken glass, differences again emerged. Although there was no broken glass in the actual film, 14 percent of those who saw the film described with the word "hit" reported the presence of broken glass, while 32 percent of those who saw the film described with "smash" reported seeing broken glass. As is clear from the results of this study (and numerous others might have been included as well), the intensity of the language used influences the meaning of what is "seen" and what is "remembered."

SENTENCE CONSTRUCTION

Not only must careful attention be given to word selection, but effective public speaking style requires similar attention to the construction of sentences. Here are some guidelines.

Favor Short over Long Sentences

Short sentences are more forceful and economical. They are easier to comprehend. They are easier to remember. Listeners do not have the time or inclination to unravel long and complex sentences. Help them to listen more efficiently: Use short rather than long sentences.

Favor Direct over Indirect Sentences

Direct sentences are more easily understood and more forceful. Instead of saying "I want to tell you of the three main reasons we should not adopt Program A," say "We should not adopt Program A. There are three main reasons."

Favor Active over Passive Sentences

Active sentences are easier to understand. They also make your speech seem livelier and more vivid. Instead of saying "The lower court's original decision was reversed by the Supreme Court," say "The Supreme Court reversed the lower court's decision." Instead of saying "The proposal was favored by management," say "Management favored the proposal."

Favor Positive over Negative Sentences

Positive sentences are easier to comprehend and to remember. Notice how sentences (A) and (C) are easier to understand than sentences (B) and (D).

(A) The committee rejected the proposal.
(B) The committee did not accept the proposal.

(C) This committee works outside the normal company hierarchy.
(D) This committee does not work within the normal company hierarchy.

Vary the Type and Length of Sentences

The advice to use short, direct, active, and positive sentences is valid most of the time. Too many sentences of the same type or length, though, will make your speech sound boring. Use variety while following (generally) the advice given above.

Here are a few special types of sentences that should prove useful, especially for adding variety, vividness, and forcefulness to your speech.

Parallel Sentences   Phrase your ideas in parallel (similar and matching) style for ease of comprehension and memory. Note the parallelism in (A) and (C) and its absence in (B) and (D).

(A) The professor prepared the lecture, graded the examination, and read the notices.
(B) The professor prepared the lecture, the examination was graded, and he read the notices.

(C) Love needs two people to flourish. Jealousy needs but one.
(D) Love needs two people. Just one can create jealousy.

Antithetical Sentences   Antithetical sentences juxtapose contrasting ideas in parallel fashion. John Kennedy used antithetical sentences when he said: "If a free society cannot help the many who are poor, it cannot save the few who are rich." In his Inaugural, Kennedy phrased one of his most often-quoted lines in antithetical structure: "Ask not what your country can do for you; ask what you can do for your country."

Periodic Sentences   In periodic sentences, the key word is reserved for the end and the sentence is not in fact grammatically complete until the last word: "Looking longingly into his eyes, the old woman fainted."

SUMMARY

1.   The generally preferred style in public speaking is oral style, which, compared with written style, contains shorter, simpler, and more familiar words; greater qualification; more self-referential, allness, concrete, and pseudo-quantifying terms; more terms indicative of consciousness of projection; and more verbs and adverbs.

2.   Clarity may be best achieved by being economical and specific; using guide phrases; using short, familiar, and high-frequency terms; and using repetition, restatement, and internal summaries.

3.   Vividness may be best achieved by using active verbs, strong verbs, figures of speech, and imagery (especially visual, auditory, and tactile imagery).

4.   Appropriateness may be best achieved by speaking on a suitable level of formality-informality, and by avoiding unfamiliar, foreign, and technical

terms, jargon, acronyms, slang and vulgar terms, and offensive expressions.

5. Personalness may be best achieved by using personal pronouns, asking questions, and creating immediacy.

6. Forcefulness may be best achieved by eliminating weakeners, avoiding bromides and clichés, and varying intensity as appropriate.

7. In constructing sentences for public speeches, favor short, direct, active, and positively phrased sentences.

8. Vary the type and length of sentences, making use of such constructions as parallel, antithetical, and periodic sentences.

SOURCES

Style is most thoroughly covered in Jane Blankenship, *A Sense of Style: An Introduction to Style for the Public Speaker* (Belmont, Calif.: Dickenson, 1968).

For the stylistic suggestions, I relied heavily on the findings of experimental research as far as was possible, particularly on my "Some Psycholinguistic Aspects of Active and Passive Sentences," *Quarterly Journal of Speech* 55 (December 1969): 401–406; "Comprehension Factors in Oral and Written Discourse of Skilled Communicators," *Communication Monographs* 32 (June 1965): 124–128; and "Relative Ease in Comprehending Yes/No Questions," in *Rhetoric and Communication*, Jane Blankenship and Herman G. Stelzner, eds. (Urbana: University of Illinois Press, 1976), pp. 143–154. Also see Herbert Clark, "The Power of Positive Speaking," *Psychology Today* 8 (September 1974): 102, 108–111. Although the language of the speech differs significantly from the language of the written composition, many of the suggestions for clarity are similar and, consequently, the more numerous works on written style may be consulted. I would recommend the classic William Strunk, Jr., and E. B. White, *The Elements of Style*, 3d ed. (New York: Macmillan, 1979), and Michael Lipman and Russell Joyner, *How to Write Clearly: Guidelines and Exercises for Clear Writing* (San Francisco: International Society for General Semantics, 1979). For a review of the literature on some of the ways in which language varies, see James J. Bradac, John Waite Bowers, and John A. Courtright, "Three Language Variables in Communication Research: Intensity, Immediacy, and Diversity," *Human Communication Research* 5 (Spring 1979): 256–269. On some of the changes in sexist language, see Barbara Bate, "Nonsexist Language Use in Transition," *Journal of Communication* 28 (winter 1978): 139–149, and the excellent articles in Barrie Thorne, Cheris Kramarae, and Nancy Henley, eds. *Language, Gender and Society* (Rowley, Mass.: Newbury House Publishers, 1983).

UNIT 24
DELIVERY IN
PUBLIC SPEAKING

LEARNING GOALS

After completing this unit, you should be able to

1. define the four general methods of delivery in public speaking
2. define volume, rate, pitch, and quality, and the problems associated with each
3. distinguish between articulation and pronunciation
4. identify and give examples of the three major articulation problems
5. identify and give examples of the two major pronunciation problems
6. distinguish between and give examples of filled and unfilled pauses
7. indicate at least four instances when pauses may be of value to the public speaker
8. explain the general guidelines that should govern the public speaker's use of eye contact, facial expression, gestures, movement, and proxemics
9. identify the four guidelines presented for using notes during the delivery of the speech
10. explain the major goals of public speaking rehearsal and the specific suggestions offered for rehearsal

In this unit we concentrate on improving delivery. More specifically, we consider first the general methods of delivery. Second, we consider how the voice may be more effectively used and how some of the major voice problems may be avoided. Third, we focus on bodily action, considering a variety of ways in which you may use your body to complement and reinforce your message. Fourth, we offer some suggestions for using notes effectively. Fifth, we present some suggestions for rehearsing your speech.

METHODS OF DELIVERY

Speakers vary widely in their methods of delivery. Some speak "off-the-cuff," with no apparent preparation; others read their speeches from manuscript. Some memorize their speeches word for word; others construct a detailed outline and actualize the speech itself at the moment of delivery. Four general methods of delivery may be distinguished: impromptu, manuscript, memorized, and extemporaneous.

The Impromptu Method of Delivery

The impromptu method of delivery involves speaking without any specific preparation for the speech. You and the topic meet for the first time, and immediately the speech begins.

On some occasions, impromptu speaking cannot be avoided. In a classroom, after someone has spoken, you might be asked to comment on the speaker and the speech you just heard and, in effect, give an impromptu speech of evaluation. When asking or answering questions in an interview situation, you are giving impromptu speeches, albeit extremely short ones. At meetings, those with particular expertise are often called upon to give an impromptu comment on various issues. Impromptu speaking, when it cannot be avoided, can be greatly improved by cultivating public speaking ability in general. The more proficient a speaker you are, the better you will be able to function impromptu.

The Manuscript Method of Delivery

In the manuscript method, the entire written speech is read to the audience. For example, when exact timing and wording are required, the manuscript method is the safest to use. It could be disastrous if a political leader did not speak from manuscript on sensitive issues: An ambiguous word, phrase, or sentence that proved insulting, belligerent, or conciliatory could cause serious problems. With a manuscript speech, an in-depth analysis of style, content, organization, and all other elements of the speech can be undertaken. In fact, the great advantage of the manuscript speech is that an entire staff of speech experts and advisers can review it and offer suggestions as to potential problems, how to resolve them, and so on. Manuscript delivery allows you to say exactly—*word for word*—what you and perhaps a host of speech writers and advisers wish to say

The Memorized Method of Delivery

Like the manuscript method, the memorized method is used when exact timing and exact wording are crucial—in politically sensitive cases or when media impose severe restrictions. The memorized method involves writing out the speech word for word and committing it to memory. The speech is then usually "acted out."

The Extemporaneous Method of Delivery

Extemporaneous delivery involves thorough preparation, memorizing the main ideas and the order in which they will appear, and perhaps memorizing the first and last few sentences of the speech. There is, however, no commitment to exact wording. This is the method of delivery we recommend you use in your public speeches.

Advantages

The extemporaneous method is useful in most speaking situations when exact timing and wording are not required. Good lecturing by college teachers uses the extemporaneous method; they have prepared thoroughly, have the organization clearly in mind, and know what they want to say and in what order they want to say it. But they have given no commitment to exact wording.

This method allows for great flexibility to feedback. Should a point need clarification, you can elaborate on it when it will be most effective. With this method it is easy to be natural, because you are being yourself. It is the method that comes closest to conversation or, as some theorists have put it, "enlarged" conversation. With the extemporaneous method, you may move about and interact with the audience.

Disadvantages

The major disadvantage is that you may stumble and grope for words. If the speech has been rehearsed a number of times, however, this is not likely to happen. Another disadvantage is that you cannot give the precise attention to style that you can give the speech in the manuscript and memorized methods. And yet, this disadvantage too can be circumvented by memorizing those phrases you want to word exactly. Nothing in the extemporaneous method would preclude your committing to memory selected phrases, sentences, or quotations.

Guidelines for Speaking Extemporaneously

Having stated a clear preference for the extemporaneous method, I do suggest that you memorize three parts of such a speech: (1) your opening lines—perhaps the first two or three sentences; (2) the major propositions and the order in which they will be presented; and (3) your closing lines—perhaps the last two or three sentences of the speech. First, the opening and closing lines should be memorized so that you can focus complete attention on the audience and best feel the interaction with them. Memorizing these parts will put you more at ease. You will feel more in control of the situation, once you know exactly what you will say in opening and in closing the speech. Second, memorize the main ideas in their order of presentation so that you will feel in control of the speech and the speech-making situation and will not have to refer to notes when making your main points. After all, if you expect your audience to remember these points, surely you should remember them as well.

VOICE

Six dimensions of voice may be distinguished: volume, rate, pitch, quality, articulation and pronunciation, and pauses. Your manipulation of these elements will enable you to control your voice to maximum advantage.

Volume

Volume refers to the relative intensity of the voice. Loudness, which is often equated with volume, refers to the perception of that relative intensity. In an adequately controlled voice, volume will vary according to the distance between speaker and listener, the amount of competing noise, the acoustics of the room, and the emphasis the speaker wishes to give a particular concept or idea.

Problems with Volume

The problems with volume are easy to identify though they are difficult to recognize in ourselves. One obvious problem is an overly soft voice. When speakers speak so low that listeners have to strain to hear, listeners will soon tire since this requires a great expenditure of energy. On the other hand, an overly loud voice will prove disturbing because it intrudes on our psychological space more than we are willing to tolerate. It feels as if someone is sitting too close or is leaning all over us. An overly loud voice is especially disturbing if the voice is also unpleasant.

Perhaps the most common problem is that speakers—particularly the extremely nervous—do not vary vocal volume enough. But an equally important problem is a volume pattern that varies in a pattern that—after a very short time—becomes totally predictable.

Fading away at the ends of sentences is particularly disturbing. Here the speaker uses a volume that is appropriate, but ends sentences (particularly long sentences) with the last few words delivered in an extremely low and often garbled manner. Be particularly careful when finishing sentences; they must be heard by the audience at an appropriate volume.

Not all problems of volume can be so readily improved. For example, some volume difficulties may be caused by deep-seated problems requiring professional help. For example, inadequate volume brought about by extreme shyness, self-consciousness, or some sense of personal inadequacy will not be solved by a course in public speaking. These issues might be identified here, but professional help may be needed. Hearing loss also creates volume difficulties. The hearing-impaired often speak at a volume that seems inappropriate to others. This is usually excessive volume, but there are also hearing losses that lead to an inappropriately low speaking volume.

Rate

Rate refers to the speed with which you speak and is normally measured in the number of words or syllables spoken per unit of time, usually a minute. Approximately 140 to 160 words per minute seems average for speaking as well as for reading aloud.

Problems with Rate

The problems of rate are speaking too fast or too slow or with too little variation. If you talk too fast, you deprive your listeners of sufficient time to comprehend, digest, think about, and perhaps internalize what you are saying. If the rate is extreme, the listeners will simply not be willing to spend the time and energy needed to understand the speech.

A rate that is too slow allows the listeners' minds to wander to more personal matters or more immediate matters—to their recent date, their next examination, and a host of matters totally unrelated to the speech. Be careful, therefore, not to bore the audience and yet not to give them information at a pace that is too rapid to absorb. Strike a happy medium—a pace that engages the listeners and allows them time for reflection without boring them.

Like volume, rate variations may be underemployed or totally absent. If you speak at the same rate throughout the entire speech, you are not making use of one of your most important vocal characteristics. Rate variations should be used to add emphasis and variety—to call a listener's attention to certain points. If you speak of the dull routine of an assembly line worker in a pace that is rapid and varied, and of the wonder of a circus in a pace with absolutely no variation, you are clearly misusing this most important vocal dimension. Again, if you are conscious of what you are saying and if you are interested in communicating with an audience, your rate variations should flow naturally and effectively.

Pitch

Pitch refers to the relative highness or lowness of the voice as perceived by the listener. More technically, pitch is created by the rate at which your vocal folds vibrate. If they vibrate rapidly, the voice is perceived as having a high pitch; if they vibrate slowly, the voice is perceived as having a low pitch.

Changes in pitch often signal changes in the meanings of many sentences, the most obvious being the difference between a statement and a question. Thus, the difference between the declarative sentence "So this is the creep you want me to meet" and the question "So this is the creep you want me to meet?" is inflection or pitch. This point, of course, is obvious. But note also that, depending on where the inflectional change is put, the meaning of the sentence changes drastically. Consider the following sentences, where the higher pitch is symbolized by italics. They are all questions, but they all ask different questions.

- Is *this* the creep you want me to meet?
- Is this the *creep* you want me to meet?
- Is this the creep you want *me* to meet?
- Is this the creep you want me to *meet?*

Problems with Pitch

The obvious problems of pitch are levels that are too high, too low, and too patterned. Neither of the first two problems is common in speakers with otherwise normal voices. If you sense that you are speaking at a pitch that is too high or too low, speak with your instructor and have the matter looked into.

A pitch pattern that is too predictable or monotonous may be corrected with some practice. Pitch changes should come naturally from the sense of what is being said. Normally, you do not have to wonder whether the last sentence was a statement or a question; it is signaled in the words used as well as in the pitch. Similarly, since each sentence is somewhat different from every other sentence, there should be a normal variation—a variation that results not from some predetermined pattern but rather from the meanings you wish to convey to the audience.

Quality

Quality is unlike volume, rate, and pitch in that it does not have a clear physiological dimension and cannot be measured as can the others. Rather, *quality* is a general characteristic of the voice that refers to a variety of factors by which one voice is distinguished from another. Quality refers to such characteristics as nasality-denasality, breathiness, and hoarseness, as well as a number of other factors.

Nasality-Denasality

Excessive nasality means that you speak through your nose—a quality that most persons find unattractive and difficult to listen to. If you put your hand under your nose and you can feel the air being expelled as you speak, it is a good bet that you have too much nasality. In English there are only a few sounds that are normally made with nasal resonance—*m, n,* and *ng.* Some speakers however, pronounce many of the sounds with extreme nasal resonance. Becoming conscious of the difference in nasal and nonnasal (or oral) resonance will often enable you to make the correction almost automatically. The opposite side of the problem is denasality—a condition that at times is often confused with nasality, but is actually its opposite; it is the absence of nasality. You can easily experience this by holding your nose as you speak; you will sound as if you have a bad cold. Again, it produces an unpleasant voice to listen to. An unusual degree of tenseness often produces denasality; once the speaker learns to relax, some of this denasality will be eliminated.

If you have excessive nasality or denasality and it is evidenced in formal as well as informal and tense as well as relaxed encounters, consult a physician to explore the possibility of a deviated septum or some other physiological problem.

Breathiness

Another problem of quality is breathiness. To appreciate the meaning of this concept, say a few sentences aloud normally and then speak these same sentences in a whisper. In both situations hold your hand in front of your mouth. You will find that the whispered sentences produce a great deal more breath than the normally spoken sentences. In some people, however, the excessive breathiness characteristic of whispering also characterizes normal speaking. This problem is caused when the vocal folds are not brought together and excessive air escapes while speaking.

Some speakers use breathiness on the assumption that this is sexy. Marilyn Monroe and contemporary imitators did a great deal to make the breathy voice popular. Although this type of voice may be attractive in certain situations and in moderation, it frequently results in fatigue because it takes a great deal of energy to speak for any length of time with a breathy voice. In the extreme, using excessive breath may swell and "thicken" the vocal cords and require professional help to correct.

Hoarseness

A third problem is hoarseness, a condition you are probably familiar with from having had a sore throat. It appears as a huskiness—a noise-filled voice. When the tissues of the vocal mechanism get swollen—as they do when infected—the vocal folds cannot vibrate as smoothly as they normally do. The result is hoarseness. In men, it is mistaken as a sign of roughness, masculinity, and general toughness. Gangsters are traditionally represented in the media with hoarse voices.

Perhaps the major difficulty with hoarseness is impaired intelligibility. A hoarse voice also tires fast; frequent rest periods are necessary and long discourses, such as public speeches, are exhausting.

Articulation and Pronunciation

Articulation and pronunciation are similar in that they both refer to enunciation—the way in which sounds and words are produced—but they differ in a more technical sense. *Articulation* refers to the physiological movements of the speech organs as they modify and interrupt the air stream emitted from the lungs. Different sounds are produced by different movements of these speech organs (for example, the tongue, lips, teeth, palate, and vocal cords). *Pronunciation* refers to the production of syllables or words according to some accepted standard, generally identified in any good dictionary.

Our concern here, however, is not with the technical distinctions between these two terms but with some of the most common problems associated with faulty articulation and pronunciation.

Articulation Problems

Three general articulation problems may be identified: omission, substitution, and addition, of sounds or syllables.

Errors of Omission   Omitting sounds or even syllables is one of the major articulation problems, but it can be easily overcome. Here are some examples:

gov-a-ment	instead of	gov-ern-ment
hi-stry	instead of	hi-story
wanna	instead of	want to
fishin	instead of	fishing
studyin	instead of	studying
ax	instead of	asks

Errors of Substitution   Substituting an incorrect sound for the correct one is another easily corrected problem. Among the most popular are substituting *d* for *t*, and *d* for *th*. Here are a few examples:

wader	instead of	waiter
dese	instead of	these
ax	instead of	ask
undoubtebly	instead of	undoubtedly
bedder	instead of	better
ekcetera	instead of	etcetera

Errors of Addition   Here, sounds are added where they do not belong:

athalete	instead of	athlete
Americker	instead of	America
idear	instead of	idea
filim	instead of	film
lore	instead of	law

As these examples demonstrate, such articulatory problems are relatively easy to correct by becoming conscious of our own articulation patterns, listening carefully to the articulation of prominent speakers (for example, broadcasters), and practicing the correct patterns.

Pronunciation Problems

Among the most popular pronunciation problems are accenting the wrong syllable and pronouncing sounds that should remain silent.

Errors of Accent   Numerous terms are frequently accented incorrectly. Here are some popular examples:

New Orleáns	instead of	New Órleans
ínsurance	instead of	insúrance
orátor	instead of	órator

Errors of Pronouncing Silent Sounds   In many terms, the acceptable pronunciation is to *not* pronounce certain sounds, as in the following examples:

offten	instead of	offen	for	often
homage	instead of	omage	for	homage
Illinois	instead of	Illinoi	for	Illinois

The best way to deal with pronunciation problems is to look up in a good dictionary any words whose pronunciation you are not sure of. Learn to read the pronunciation key for your dictionary, and make it a practice to look up words you hear that seem incorrectly pronounced or that you wish to use yourself but are not sure how to pronounce.

Pauses

Pauses come in two basic types: filled and unfilled. *Filled pauses* are pauses in the stream of speech that are filled with vocalizations such as *er, um, ah,* and the like. Even expressions such as *well* and *you know,* when used without any apparent referent, would be considered filled pauses. Eliminate these from your speech behavior in general and from your public speaking behavior in particular. They make the speaker appear hesitant, unprepared, and unsure—judgments that will hinder your credibility and general persuasiveness.

Unfilled pauses are silences interjected into the normally fluent stream of speech. Unfilled pauses can be especially effective if used correctly. Here are just a few examples of places where unfilled pauses—silences of a few seconds—can be used effectively in public speaking.

Pause at Transitional Points   This will help signal that you are moving from one part of the speech to another or from one idea to another, and will help the audience separate the main issues you are discussing.

Pause at the End of an Important Assertion   This will allow the audience time to think about the significance of what you have said.

Pause After Asking a Rhetorical Question   This will provide the necessary time for the audience to think of how they would answer the question.

Pause Before an Important Idea   This will help signal that what comes next is especially significant.

BODILY ACTION

The body is an integral instrument in the public speaking transaction: You speak with your body as well as with your mouth. The total effect of the speech is determined not only by what you say but also by the way you present yourself—by the movements, gestures, and facial expressions.

The five dimensions of bodily action that have special relevance to the public speaking situation are eye contact, facial expression, gestures, movement, and proxemics. Each of these is discussed here—its nature, its major problems, and how it may be used to increase your effectiveness as a public speaker.

Eye Contact

Perhaps the most important single aspect of bodily communication is eye contact. The two major problems with eye contact are insufficient eye contact and eye contact that is not spread fairly over the entire audience. If you do not maintain enough eye contact, you will appear distant, unconcerned, and less trustworthy than you would if you looked directly at the audience. Audience feedback will be impossible to secure without eye contact.

Maintain eye contact with the entire audience. Involve all listeners in the public speaking transaction. Communicate equally with the members on the left and on the right, in both the back and the front.

Facial Expression

Facial expressions are especially important in communicating emotions. Nonverbal researchers refer to these as *affect displays*. Such expressions show emotion; they demonstrate anger, fear, boredom, excitement, doubt, and a host of other emotions that most persons display quite naturally.

If you feel committed to what you are saying, believe in what you want your audience to believe, and are concerned with communicating these ideas and feelings to your audience, then your meanings will probably be appropriately displayed in your facial expressions.

Nervousness and anxiety may at times interfere and prevent you from relaxing sufficiently to allow your emotions to come through. But with time and practice, you will relax and the emotions you are feeling will be appropriately displayed.

Gestures

Most gestures fall into the class of nonverbal behaviors called *illustrators*—those behaviors that quite literally illustrate the verbal messages. For example, in saying "Come here," there will be movements of the head, of the hands and arms, and of the entire body that motion the listener in your direction. Your body as well as your verbal messages say "Come here."

The best bodily action is spontaneous and natural to the speaker, the audience, and the speech. If you are relaxed and comfortable with yourself and with the audience, natural bodily action will be generated without any conscious and studied attention.

Movement

Movement refers here to gross bodily movements. It generally helps to move around a bit; it keeps both the audience and you more alert. Naturally, this is impossible when speaking from a stationary microphone or when movement is otherwise restricted. Yet here too, you can give the illusion of movement by stepping back or forward or flexing the upper torso so that it appears that you are moving a great deal more than you in fact are.

Three problems to be avoided are too little, too much, and too patterned movement. With too little movement, you may appear strapped to the podium, perhaps even afraid of the audience or not sufficiently interested in the situation to involve yourself fully. With too much movement, the audience begins to concentrate on the movement itself, wondering where you will wind up next. With too patterned movement—as with all nonverbal aspects—the audience becomes bored; too steady and predictable a rhythm becomes tiring very quickly. The audience will often view you as nonspontaneous and uninvolved.

Use gross movements to emphasize transitions and to emphasize the introduction of a new and important assertion. Thus, when making a transition, you might take a step forward to signal that something new is coming; similarly, this type of movement may signal the introduction of an important assumption, bit of evidence, or closely reasoned argument.

Proxemics

Proxemics refers to that area of nonverbal communication concerned with space. It encompasses such topics as the space you require, expect, or demand while interacting with others—some need a great deal of space, while others prefer to interact at close range. The way in which you lay out space in your home, the possessiveness you have to various territories, the use of space to signal status relationships (the larger, higher up, and closer one's office is to the boss, the higher one's status), and even the ways in which cities and towns are constructed all represent proxemic communications.

In public speaking the space between you and the listeners is often a crucial factor. If you stand too close to the audience, they may feel uncomfortable, as if they are being looked over too closely and their personal space is being violated. If you stand too far away from the audience, you might be perceived as uninvolved, uninterested, and uncomfortable with the entire public speaking transaction. These perceptions of "too close" and "too far" by the audience may in reality involve distances that are actually extremely small. Thus, if you are in front of the class in a normal classroom, you might have perhaps six feet to use. Moving a foot back or forward might well give the impression of too far or too close.

USING NOTES

For speeches it may be helpful to use notes. A few simple guidelines may help you avoid some of the common errors made in using notes.

Keep Your Notes to a Minimum

As a general rule, the fewer notes you take with you the better off you will be. The reason so many speakers bring notes with them is that they want to avoid the face-to-face interaction required. But with experience, you should find this face-to-face interaction the best part of the public speaking experience. Do not bring with you the entire speech outline; you may be tempted to rely on it and hence not speaking directly to the audience. Instead, compose a delivery outline (pp. 345–346), using only key words, and bring this to the lectern with you. One side of a 3-by-5 index card, or at most an 8½-by-11 page, should be sufficient for most speeches. This will relieve anxiety over the possibility of your forgetting your speech but will not be extensive enough to prevent meaningful speaker-audience interaction.

Know Your Notes Intimately

Rehearse at least twice with the same notes that you will take with you to the speaker's stand.

Use Your Notes with "Open Subtlety"

Do not make them more obvious then necessary, but at the same time don't try to hide them from the audience. On the one hand, do not gesture with your notes and, on the other, do not turn away from the audience to steal a glance at them either. Use them openly and honestly but gracefully, with "open subtlety."

Do Not Allow Your Notes to Prevent You from Speaking Directly to Your Audience

When referring to your notes, pause to read what has to be read, then regain eye contact with the audience and continue your speech. Do not read from your notes, just take cues from them. Exceptions to this are an extensive quotation or complex set of statistics that must of necessity be read. Then, almost immediately, resume direct eye contact with the audience.

REHEARSAL: PRACTICING AND IMPROVING DELIVERY

Effective public speaking delivery does not come naturally; it takes practice. Learn now how to use your practice time most effectively and efficiently.

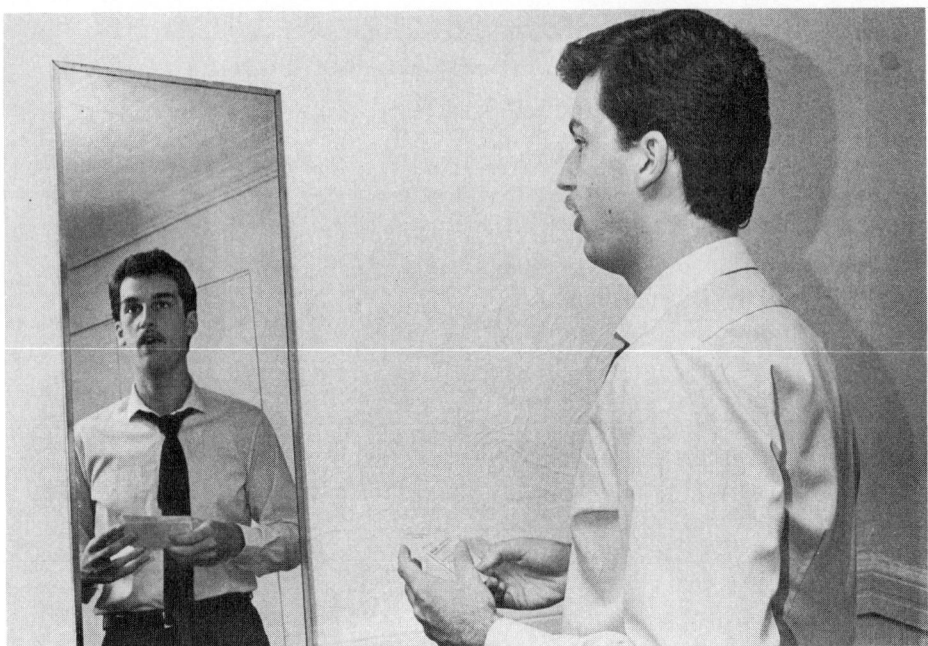

Here a public speaker practices his speech in a mirror, an extremely useful but unfortunately too-little used technique. Try practicing your own speech in front of a full length mirror. What insights does this give you into your public speaking performance?

Goals of Rehearsal

The goal or objective of your practice is to develop a delivery that will help you achieve the purposes of your speech, whether to inform, persuade, or serve any of the numerous specialized functions of public speaking. In addition, practice will enable you to see how the speech will flow as a whole, make changes and improvements as necessary, learn the speech effectively, and determine how best to present it to your audience. More specifically, your delivery goals should include at least the following:

1. timing your speech so that you use the time alotted to you but do not run over your assigned time
2. perfecting your volume, rate, pitch, and quality so that these work for rather than against you
3. checking your articulation and pronunciation to eliminate any possible errors
4. incorporating pauses and other delivery notes at appropriate places
5. perfecting your bodily action—your eye contact, facial expression, gestures, movements, and proxemic behaviors

Rehearsal Procedures

The following procedures should assist you in using your time most effectively.

Rehearse Speech as a Whole

Rehearse the speech from beginning to end. Do not rehearse in parts; rehearse the speech from getting out of your seat through the introduction, body, and conclusion, to returning to your seat. Be sure to rehearse the speech with all its examples, illustrations, and visual aids if there are any; this will enable you to connect the parts of the speech into a whole and to see how they interact with each other.

Time the Speech

Time the speech during each rehearsal. Make any necessary adjustments on the basis of this timing.

Approximate Actual Speech Situation

Rehearse the speech under conditions as close as possible to the conditions under which you will deliver the speech. If possible, rehearse the speech in the room where you will present it. If this is impossible, try to simulate the actual conditions as best you can—in your living room or even bathroom if necessary. Rehearse the speech in front of a few supportive listeners; it is always helpful, especially for your beginning speeches, for your listeners to be supportive rather than overly critical. Merely having listeners present during your rehearsal will further simulate the actual conditions. A most useful procedure is for three or four students in the class to get together in an empty classroom, where you can each serve as speaker and listener.

See Yourself as a Speaker

Rehearse the speech (if not the first time, at least during the second or third rehearsal) in front of a full-length mirror so you can see yourself as you will appear to the audience. This will be extremely difficult at first, and you may have to force yourself to watch your reflection. After a few attempts, however, you will begin to see the value of this experience. While in front of the mirror, practice your eye contact, movements, and gestures.

Incorporate Changes and Delivery Notes

Make any changes in the speech that seem appropriate between rehearsals. Do not interrupt your rehearsal to make notes or changes; otherwise, you may never experience the entire speech from beginning to end. While making these changes, note too any words whose pronunciation or articulation you wish to check, and insert pause notations, "slow down" warnings, and other delivery suggestions into your outline. An especially useful technique is to tape record your speech so that you will hear exactly what your listeners will hear. Further, you will be better able to hear your volume, rate, pitch, quality, articulation and pronunciation, and pauses, and will thus be in a better position to improve these qualities.

Rehearse Often

Rehearse the speech as often as seems necessary. Here are two useful guides: (1) Rehearse the speech at least three or four times—less than this is sure to be too little; and (2) rehearse the speech as long as your rehearsals result in improvements in the speech or its delivery.

SUMMARY

1. There are four general delivery methods that may be used by public speakers: impromptu, manuscript, memorized, and extemporaneous.

2. The impromptu method involves speaking without any specific preparation for the speech.

3. The manuscript method involves writing out the entire speech and reading it to the audience.

4. The memorized method involves writing out the entire speech, committing it to memory, and reciting it to the audience.

5. The extemporaneous method involves thorough preparation, and memorizing the main ideas and the order in which they will appear, but no commitment to exact wording.

6. The extemporaneous method is preferred, since it allows for great flexibility to feedback, appears natural (coming closest to conversation), and provides for maximum speaker-audience interaction.

7. Volume (the relative intensity of the voice) should be adjusted on the basis of the distance between you and your audience, the amount of competing noise, the acoustics of the room, and the emphasis you wish to give certain ideas. Be especially careful to avoid speaking overly softly or overly loudly, using an unvaried volume level, and fading away at the ends of sentences.

8. Rate (the pace of speech) should be adjusted on the basis of time constraints, the content of the speech, and the listening conditions. Be careful to avoid too rapid or too slow a rate, too little variation, and too predictable a rate pattern.

9. Pitch (the relative highness or lowness of the voice) should be adjusted on the basis of the meanings you wish to communicate. Be careful to avoid an overly high or overly low pitch, and a pitch pattern that is monotonous or predictable.

10. Avoid inappropriate vocal qualities such as nasality (too much nasal resonance), denasality (too little nasal resonance), breathiness (too much breath during speech), and hoarseness (husky, noisy speech). Seek professional help if any of these conditions persist or cause physical or psychological discomfort.

11. Avoid the major problems of articulation and pronunciation: errors of omission, substitution, addition, accent, and pronouncing silent sounds.

12. Use pauses to signal a transition between the major parts of the speech, to allow the audience time to think, to allow the audience to ponder a rhetorical question, and to signal the approach of a particularly important idea.

13. Effective bodily action involves maintaining eye contact with your entire audience, allowing your facial expressions to convey your feelings, gesturing naturally (neither too much nor too little), moving around a bit, and positioning yourself neither too close nor too far from your audience.

14. Use rehearsal to time your speech; perfect your volume, rate, pitch, and quality; check your articulation and pronunciation; incorporate pauses and other delivery notes; and perfect your bodily action.

15. In your rehearsal do the following: rehearse the speech as a whole, time the speech at each rehearsal, approximate the actual speech situation as much as possible, see yourself as a public speaker, incorporate changes and delivery notes, and rehearse often.

SOURCES

On voice, see Joseph A. DeVito, Jill Giattino, and T. D. Schon, *Articulation and Voice: Effective Communication* (Indianapolis: Bobbs-Merrill, 1975); Mardel Ogilvie and Norma S. Rees, *Communication Skills: Voice and Pronunciation* (New York: McGraw-Hill, 1969); and Robert King and Eleanor DiMichael, *Articulation and Voice: Improving Oral Communication* (New York: Macmillan, 1978).

For any substantial insight into nonverbal communication, see the specialized works in this area. I would particularly recommend the following: Mark Knapp, *Nonverbal Communication in Human Interaction,* 2d ed. (New York: Holt, Rinehart and Winston, 1978), and Loretta A. Malandro and Larry Barker, *Nonverbal Communication* (Reading, Mass.: Addison-Wesley, 1983).

For the discussion on using notes, I relied heavily on the excellent treatment by James C. McCroskey, *An Introduction to Rhetorical Communication,* 4th ed. (Englewood Cliffs, N.J.: Prentice-Hall, 1982). A more extensive treatment is provided by Judi Kesselman-Turkel and Franklynn Peterson, *Note-Taking Made Easy* (Chicago: Contemporary Books, 1982).

UNIT 25
THE INFORMATIVE SPEECH

LEARNING GOALS

After completing this unit, you should be able to

1. identify and explain the three major types of informative speeches and their major subdivisions
2. define and distinguish between the general and the specific purpose
3. identify and explain at least three principles of informative speaking
4. explain the nature of examples and illustrations in the informative speech and the two tests that should be applied
5. explain the nature of testimony in the informative speech and the three tests that should be applied
6. explain the nature of definition in the informative speech and the two tests that should be applied
7. explain the nature of audiovisual aids in the informative speech, identify at least seven types of such aids, and identify the four tests that should be applied

In this unit we focus on the informative speech. First, we identify the types and purposes of informative speeches. Second, we discuss the general principles of informative speaking that should be observed in all speeches but especially in speeches designed to communicate information. Third, we identify the major types of supporting materials that can be used in informative speeches, and the appropriate tests to apply for establishing their suitability.

GENERAL TYPES AND PURPOSES

Three types of informative speech and two levels of purpose are discussed in this section.

At the most general level, the informative speech can concentrate on such aspects as description, definition, and demonstration.

Speeches of Description

In speeches of description, the speaker is concerned with describing a process or procedure, an event, or an object or person. Here are some examples:

Describing a Process or Procedure

- how a newspaper is printed
- the process of buying a house
- purchasing stock
- how a child acquires language
- how to read a textbook

Describing an Event

- Gloria: the hurricane of the 1980s
- Mussolini's downfall
- organizing a body-building contest
- putting together the St. Patrick's Day Parade
- Castro's takeover of Cuba

Describing an Object or Person

- the contributions of Thomas Edison
- the parts of a telephone
- the layout of Philadelphia
- the hierarchy of a corporation
- the components of a computer system

Speeches of Definition

In the speech of definition you may focus on defining a term, a system or theory, or the similarities and/or differences among terms or systems. It may be a subject new to the audience or one familiar to them but presented in a new and different way. Here are some examples:

Defining a Term

- constructivism
- love
- censorship
- born-again Christianity
- shyness

Defining a System or Theory

- behaviorism
- the components of a generative grammar
- Confucianism: its major beliefs
- the play theory of mass communication

Defining Similar and Dissimilar Terms or Systems

- Communism and socialism: some similarities and differences
- What do Catholics and Protestants have in common?
- Psychology and sociology: three major differences
- Love and hate: their similarities
- Upward and downward communication: similarities and differences

Speeches of Demonstration

In the speech of demonstration, the speaker explains how to do something or how something operates. Here are some examples:

Demonstrating How to Do Something

- giving mouth-to-mouth resuscitation
- how to balance a checkbook
- how to drive defensively
- how to mix colors
- how to develop your body

Demonstrating How Something Operates

- how the body maintains homeostasis
- the workings of a thermostat
- how a heart-bypass operation is performed

SPECIFIC PURPOSES

On a more specific level we may look at the informative speech in terms of the specific items of information (the main points) that you want your audience to understand or learn. Here are a few examples of specific purposes and the possible main heads that might constitute the body of the speech. Further, we also include the thesis and the question to be asked of the thesis to illustrate further how this thesis statement helps to identify the main points of your speech.

Speeches of Description

In this example, the speaker describes the four steps in reading a textbook. Each main point covers one of the major steps. The thought pattern followed here is a temporal one; the main points are discussed in the order they would normally follow.

Specific purpose: to describe the four steps in reading a textbook

Thesis: You can increase your textbook-reading effectiveness. [*How can we increase our textbook-reading effectiveness?*]

I. Preview the text.
II. Read for understanding.
III. Read for retention.
IV. Review the text.

Speeches of Definition

In this example of lying, the speaker selects three major types of lying for discussion and arranges these in a simple topical pattern.

Specific purpose: to define lying by explaining the three major types of lying: concealment, falsification, and misdirection

Thesis: There are three major kinds of lying. [*What are the three major kinds of lying?*]

I. Concealment is the process of hiding the truth.
II. Falsification is the process of presenting false information as if it were true.
III. Misdirection is the process of acknowledging a feeling but misidentifying its cause.

Speeches of Demonstration

In this example, the speaker identifies and demonstrates how to listen actively.

Specific purpose: to demonstrate three techniques of active listening

Thesis: We can learn active listening. [*How can we learn active listening?*]

I. Paraphrase the speaker's meaning.
II. Express understanding of the speaker's feelings.
III. Ask questions.

PRINCIPLES OF INFORMATIVE SPEAKING

Technically, "information" is something that the receiver does not already know. A speech devoted to what listeners already know is not an informative speech. In preparing and presenting the informative speech, you need to communicate something *new* to your receivers. It may be a new way of looking at old things or an old way of looking at new things; it may be a theory not previously heard of or a familiar one not fully understood; it may describe events that the audience is unaware of or has misconceptions about. The following principles should refine your informative speech-making skills.

Limit the Amount of Information

There is a limit to the amount of information that a listener can take in at one time. Beginning speakers tend to present a great deal of information and, when they are limited to, say, five or six minutes, that information is so tightly packed that it is impossible for anyone to understand and retain more than a very small part of it. Limit the amount of information that you communicate and instead expand its presentation. It is better to present two new items of information and explain these with examples, illustrations, descriptions, and the like than to present five new items without this needed amplification.

Stress Relevance and Usefulness

Information is best attended to and retained when it is perceived as relevant and useful to some need, want, or goal. You may attend to, retain, and internalize the stages in the development of language in children simply because you will be tested on the information and you want to earn a high grade. Or, you learn what ways to invest your money because it will help you achieve financial security and independence. The implication should be obvious: If you want the audience to listen to your speech, you must make that information relevant to their needs, wants, or goals. Throughout the speech, make sure that the audience knows that the information is relevant and useful to them.

Present Information at the Appropriate Level

Information is best received and retained when it is presented on an appropriate level. Steer a middle course between being too simple, thus boring

Examples of informative speaking can be found in most college classrooms. What principles of informative speaking do you see most frequently violated? What advice would you give future teachers that might help them to become more effective public speakers?

or insulting the audience, and being too sophisticated, thus confusing the audience. Having mastered an entire body of material and having researched and analyzed it for a period of time, take care not to assume that the material is simple and that the listeners will therefore be able to grasp on first hearing what you have taken a week or two to learn. Be especially careful of information that may be too technical or specialized.

A useful rule to follow in this connection is this: Never overestimate an audience's knowledge but never underestimate their intelligence.

Relate New Information to Old

We learn information more easily and retain it longer when it is related in some way to what we already know. If you want to describe what something looks or tastes like to someone who has never seen or eaten it, compare it to something familiar. In explaining the *jicama*, the Mexican potato, you might say, for example, that it looks like a brown-skinned turnip with white inside and that it tastes something like crispy water chestnuts. As a general rule, relate the new to the old, the unfamiliar to the familiar, the unseen to the seen, the untasted to the tasted. In this way the audience will be able to imagine more clearly what they have never seen or experienced before.

AMPLIFYING MATERIALS IN INFORMATIVE SPEECHES

Once you have your specific speech purpose clearly in mind and your main points identified, devote your attention to supporting or amplifying materials. These materials will enable you to develop each point, proposition, and topic so that the audience will understand it more easily. For the informative speech, we concentrate on materials that amplify, explain, and make vivid: examples and illustrations, testimony, definitions, and audiovisual aids.

Examples and Illustrations

Examples and illustrations are specific instances that are explained in varying degrees of detail. A relatively brief specific instance is referred to as an *example;* a longer and more detailed example told in narrative or story form is referred to as an *illustration.*

Examples and illustrations are particularly useful when you wish to make concrete an abstract concept or idea. For example, it is difficult for the audience to see exactly what you mean by such abstract concepts as "persecution," "denial of freedom," "friendship," and "love" unless you provide specific examples and illustrations of what you mean. Your examples and illustrations also encourage the listeners to share your pictures of these concepts rather than to fill in their own definition of *love, friendship,* and so on.

Examples and illustrations also make an idea live—vivid and real—in the minds of the listeners. To talk in general terms about starvation in various parts of the world might have some effect on the listeners, but one specific example or illustration of a 6-year-old girl who roams the streets eating garbage and being thankful for finding moldy and decaying bread would make the entire idea of starvation more vivid and real. In explaining friendship, you might tell a story about the way in which a particular friend acted, or, in describing love, the way in which you love or are loved.

Examples and illustrations may be real and factual on the one hand or hypothetical and imagined on the other. Thus, in explaining friendship, you might tell the story of the behavior of an actual friend (and thus have a real or factual example or illustration) or you might formulate a kind of composite of an ideal friend and describe how this person would act in such-and-such a situation (and thus have a hypothetical or imagined example or illustration). Both types are useful; both types are effective.

David Rockefeller uses a particularly effective real example to illustrate how charitable contributions can be made in creative ways.

One of the most fascinating ventures along these lines has been the actor Paul Newman's venture into salad oil. Some three years ago—as a lark—he and a friend started a company to market his home-made salad oil and other products such as 'Newman's own industrial strength Venetian spaghetti sauce,' and then donate any profits to charity. Last year the company netted some $1.19 million which it gave to support 80 different nonprofit groups!

A couple of questions concerning the use of the example and the illustration are relevant to the speaker (and to the listener and critic as well).

Is the Example or Illustration Typical or Representative? Generally, use an example that is representative of the class of objects you are speaking about. At times you may want to draw an example or illustration that is purposely far-fetched, perhaps for humorous purposes or perhaps to show the inadequacies of an alternative point of view. The important point, I think, is that the speaker and the audience see the example and the illustration in the same way. If the speaker assumes that the example is typical and logical and the audience assumes that it is a caricature, it will prove ineffective and backfire.

Is the Example Relevant? Use examples that relate directly to the proposition you wish to explain. Leave out irrelevant examples, however interesting or entertaining. Be certain too that the audience sees the relevance.

When you are using examples to support the validity of a proposition rather than simply to explain it, you should apply the tests explained further in Unit 26 for using the example or specific instance as evidence: (1) Were enough specific instances examined? (2) Were the specific instances examined representative? (3) Were there significant exceptions?

Testimony

Testimony refers to the opinions of experts or the accounts of witnesses to amplify your propositions and thus to add some note of authority to your speech. Testimony may, therefore, be used in either of two ways. First, you might be concerned with the opinions, beliefs, predictions, or values of some authority or expert. You might, for example, be interested in stating an economist's predictions concerning inflation and depression, an art critic's evaluation of a painting or art movement, a media analyst's opinion of television commercials, and so on. In the following excerpt, for instance, U.S. Congresswoman Shirley Chisholm addresses the Independent Black Women's Caucus of New York City and uses the testimony of noted psychologist Rollo May to bolster her argument that black women must assume political power rather than wait for it to be given to them.

> As Rollo May has put it: "Power cannot, strictly speaking, be given to another, for then the recipient still owes it to the giver. It must in some sense be assumed, taken, asserted, for unless it can be held against opposition, it is not power and will never be experienced as real on the part of the recipient." And those of us in this room know all too well that whatever is given to us is almost always a trap.

Second, you might be interested in an individual as a witness (in the broad sense) to some event or situation. You might, for example, be concerned with the individual who saw a particular accident, the person who spent two years in a maximum-security prison, or the Trappist monk who lived for 10 years under a vow of total silence.

Testimony may be presented to the audience in the form of direct quotations or in the form of paraphrase, in which you put into your own words what the expert or witness said. Quotations are often useful but at times they become cumbersome; often they are not directly related to the point you are trying to make and their relevance gets lost. If the quotation is in technical language that members of the audience will not understand, it then becomes necessary to interject definitions as you go along. Therefore, unless the quotation is relatively short, reasonably comprehensible to the audience, and directly related to the point you are trying to make, use your own words, noting that the ideas are borrowed from your authority or source.

As a speaker concerned with using testimony for amplification (and as a listener or critic concerned with analyzing testimony), ask the following questions.

Is the Testimony Presented Fairly?   In using the testimony of others, present it fairly. If there are qualifications made by the expert, these must be included in the speech. Do not extract bits and pieces that best support your argument and imply that these ideas belong to such-and-such an authority. If you present the ideas of an authority, present them as that authority would want.

Is the Person an Authority on This Subject?   Authorities, especially today, reign over very small territories. Doctors, professors, and lawyers—to name just a few authorities—are actually experts in very small bodies of knowledge. A doctor may be an expert on the thyroid gland but may know relatively little about skin, muscles, or blood. A university professor of history might know a great deal about the Renaissance but no more than a high school history teacher or a college history major about American history. When an authority is used, be certain that the person is in fact an authority on the *specific* subject.

Is the Person Unbiased?   This question should be asked of both expert and witness accounts. Try to discover if there are any biases in the sources being cited. The real estate salesperson who tells you to "Buy! Buy! Buy!" and the diamond seller who tells you "Diamonds are the best investment in the world" obviously have something to gain and are biased. To the degree that the source is biased, suspect the validity and usefulness of the testimony. This does not mean that normally biased sources cannot provide unbiased testimony; surely they can. It means merely that once a bias has been detected, be on the lookout for how this bias *might* figure into this particular bit of testimony.

Definition

A *definition* is a statement of the meaning or significance of a concept or term. Definitions are useful when you wish to explain difficult or unfamiliar concepts or when you wish to make a concept more vivid or forceful. Some modes of definition most useful for supporting a point are noted here.

Definition by Etymology

In attempting to define the word *communication*, you might note that it comes from the Latin *communis* meaning "common"; in "communicating" you seek to establish a commonness, a sameness, and a similarity with another individual. And *woman* comes from the Anglo-Saxon *wifman*, which meant literally a "wife man" when the word *man* applied to both sexes. Through phonetic change, *wifman* became woman. Most of the larger dictionaries and, of course, etymological dictionaries will help you determine etymological definitions.

Definition by Authority

You might, for example, define *lateral thinking* by authority and say that Edward deBono, who developed lateral thinking in 1966, has noted that "lateral thinking involves moving sideways to look at things in a different way. Instead of fixing on one particular approach and then working forward from that the lateral thinker tries to find other approaches." Or you might use the authority of the cynic and satirist Ambrose Bierce and define *love* as nothing but "a temporary insanity curable by marriage" and *friendship* as "a ship big enough to carry two in fair weather, but only one in foul."

Definition by Operations

An operational definition is perhaps the most important method of definition. Here you define a concept by indicating the operations one would go through in constructing the object. Thus, for example, to operationally define a chocolate cake you would provide the recipe. The operational definition of stuttering would include an account of how the act of stuttering is performed and by what procedures stuttering might be observed.

Definition by Negation

You might also define a term by noting what that term is not—that is, defining by negation. "A wife," you might say, "is not a cook, a cleaning person, a baby-sitter, a seamstress, a sex partner. A wife is . . . ." "A teacher," you might say, "is not someone who tells you what you should know but rather one who . . . ."

Definition by Direct Symbolization

You might also define a term by direct symbolization—that is, by showing the actual thing or, if that is not possible, by showing a picture or model of it. This, as can be appreciated, is perhaps the best method for defining observables but would obviously not work with abstract concepts, such as friendship and love, or things that are impossible to perceive, such as molecules, infrared rays, and so on.

Earl G. Graves, in his speech "Leadership Challenges in the Private Sector," uses a number of these modes to define the ingredients of leadership. Notice also in this excerpt how Graves establishes his own credibility (see Unit 26) with references to his acquaintance with Robert Kennedy and Martin Luther King.

> What makes a real leader? Is it a tremendous amount of personal energy? Ambition? Experience? The skill of communication with, as some would say, manipulation of others? Brains? Hard work? Is the best motivated executive the one most likely to succeed? What about charisma? Does it come at birth? Is it forged through adversity?
>
> We all know leaders by their definition are people who move others. But what makes a leader? Power alone? Great amounts of money? The opportunity of influencing public opinion? Or is it a combination of all these factors and forces within a person?
>
> I have had the rare and good fortune in my life to have been personally touched and moved by men whose lives rewrote our definitions of leadership in this generation. As an administrative assistant to the late Senator Robert Kennedy and a friend of the Rev. Martin Luther King, Jr. . . . I have seen, felt and followed this intensity of genius and faith; compassion and conviction which moved millions and changed the course of history.
>
> Every human being is so different, yet I can say that the common gift shared by King and Kennedy is the same gift which my father gave me when I was growing up. The gift which has motivated every great leader in history is simply the all-out pursuit of excellence.
>
> That is the foundation of leadership which each of you possesses. The measure of success you achieve in your careers will reflect how much excellence you gain in your lives.

In using definitions ask the following questions.

Does the Definition Clarify and Add to the Understanding of the Audience? If the purpose of the definition is to clarify, then it must do just that. This would be too obvious to mention except for the fact that so many speakers, perhaps for want of something to say, define terms that do not need extended definitions or use definitions that do not clarify, and that, in fact, complicate an already complex concept.

Is Your Authority Credible and Known to Your Audience? When you use an authority to define a term, the audience should know who the authority is and should be told the reason for the individual's expertise.

Audiovisual Aids

Audiovisual aids are auditory and visual means used to amplify the speaker's verbal message. To aid comprehension and to make ideas vivid and easy to remember, few forms of amplifying material serve as well as the audiovisual aid. A few of the more popular and useful are identified here.

The Actual Object

If you are speaking on the care and feeding of elephants, it would be difficult to bring the actual thing to class. On the other hand, if you were talking about the workings of a computer, a lie detector, or certain kinds of tropical fish, it might be possible to use these as visual aids. As a general rule (to which there are many exceptions), the best audiovisual aid is the object itself; bring it to your speech if you can.

Models

Models—replicas of the actual object—are useful when explaining complex structures such as the hearing mechanism, the vocal apparatus, or the brain. These models help to clarify for the audience the size of the various structures, their position, and how they interact with each other.

The Chalkboard

The chalkboard is useful because of its ease of use and general availability. All classrooms have such a board and you have all seen them used by teachers with greater or lesser effect; in some way, you have all had some "experience" with them. The chalkboard may be effectively used to record key terms or important definitions, or even to outline the main structure of your speech.

Charts, Graphs, and Diagrams

These "graphics" are useful in conveying a variety of types of information. Organizational charts show clearly how an organization is structured and what the relationships are among the individuals. Flow charts are excellent for illustrating various processes such as the production of a widget, from solid disc to completed, polished, and packaged widget. Bar graphs and line graphs are useful for showing differences among elements over time.

Maps

Maps are useful for showing geographical elements as well as changes throughout history, population density, immigration patterns, economic conditions, the location of various resources, and hundreds of other issues you may wish to develop in your speeches.

People

Oddly enough, people can function effectively as "audiovisual aids." To demonstrate the muscles of the body, for example, a well-built weight-lifter is an ideal visual aid. Also, to demonstrate different voice patterns, skin complexions, or hairstyles, people are most appropriate. Aside from the obvious assistance they provide in demonstrating their muscles or voice qualities, they help to secure and maintain the attention and interest of the audience.

Slides

Slides are useful for showing various scenes or graphics that you cannot describe in words. The great advantages of slides are their visual appeal (and hence their attention-getting value) and their ease of preparation and use. Again, most departments of communication have slide projectors, so availability should not cause any difficulty. When planning to use slides, allow yourself sufficient time for shooting, developing, and organizing them. To plan a speech using slides only to find that on the day you are scheduled to speak the slides are still at the processing lab is not a pleasant prospect, so plan ahead.

Films, Filmstrips, and Videotapes

I use a variety of films to illustrate some of the breakdowns in interpersonal communication, the techniques for and the progress made in teaching animals to communicate, and various other topics. Filmstrips are also useful because they enable you to regulate timing more closely. Thus, if during a lecture there are a number of questions, you can easily stop the filmstrip to address these issues, whereas with a film it is a bit more cumbersome. Although it is a great deal to undertake, you might consider making your own videotape to illustrate your talk. But remember, a bad film is a bad audiovisual aid and it detracts rather than adds to the effectiveness of your speech.

Pictures

Assuming that you do not have films or slides, the next best visual aid is a picture. There are, however, many hazards involved in using this type of aid, so I recommend its use with reservations. If the picture is large enough for all members of the audience to see clearly (say, poster size), if it clearly illustrates what you want to illustrate, and if it is mounted on cardboard, then use it. Otherwise, do not. Do not pass pictures around the room: This only functions to draw attention away from what you are saying. Listeners will look for the pictures to get to them and will invariably miss a great deal of your speech in the interim.

Records and Tapes

To deliver a speech about music and not provide the audience with samples would seem strange, and very likely the audience's attention would be diverted from what you are saying to why you have not provided the actual music. But records and tapes can be useful for many other types of speech as well. A speech on advertising would be greatly helped, for example, by having actual samples of advertising as it is played on radio or television. A tape of such examples would go a long way to help clarify exactly what you are talking about and would also serve to break up the oral presentation most effectively.

In using audiovisual aids ask yourself the following questions.

Is the Aid Relevant?   It may be attractive, well designed, and easy to read, and may possess all the features one could hope for in an audiovisual aid, but if it is not relevant to the topic, it would be better left at home.

Does the Aid Reinforce the Message?   All messages sent to listeners should reinforce each other. The same is true of audiovisual aids. They must reinforce both verbal and nonverbal messages. Audiovisual aids are not something apart from the speech; they are an integral part of the speech as a whole.

Is the Message of the Aid Evident?   If it is not clear, it obviously serves no purpose. In fact, it will significantly detract from the effect of the speech, since the listeners will devote attention to trying to decipher what the aid conveys and will lose part of what you are saying in the speech. Two guidelines should govern clarity: First, the aid should be legible; it should be easy to read. Second, it should be simple enough to comprehend without difficulty. You don't want listeners spending inordinate amounts of time trying to see what the different colors or the double arrows mean. Whatever is important should be explained in the speech; and the aid should clarify and add vividness to your speech.

Is the Aid Appealing? Like people, audiovisual aids work best when they are appealing. Sloppy, poorly designed, and dirty visual aids will detract from the purpose they are intended to serve. Visual aids should be attractive enough to engage the attention of the audience, but not so attractive that they engage the attention of the audience to the point of distraction. The well-developed, almost-nude body may be effective in selling underwear, but such gimmicks probably detract if your object is to explain the profit-and-loss statement of Exxon.

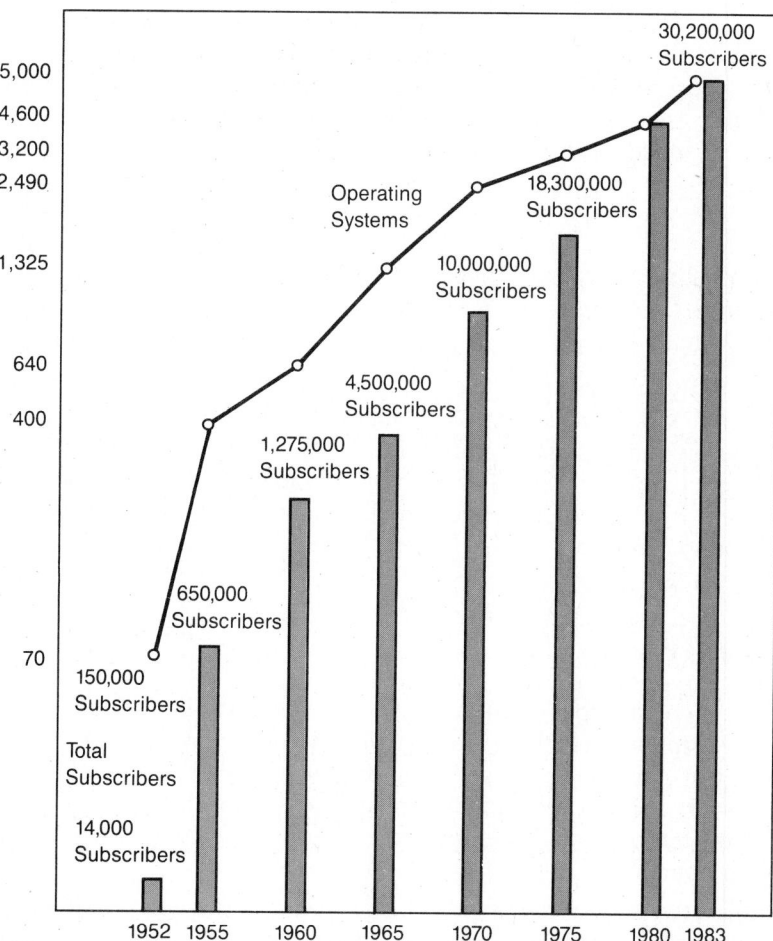

FIGURE 25.1 Growth of the cable television industry in the United States as of January of each year. (*Source:* Warren K. Agee, Phillip H. Ault, and Edwin Emery, *Introduction to Mass Communications*, 8th ed., New York: Harper & Row, 1985, p. 251.)

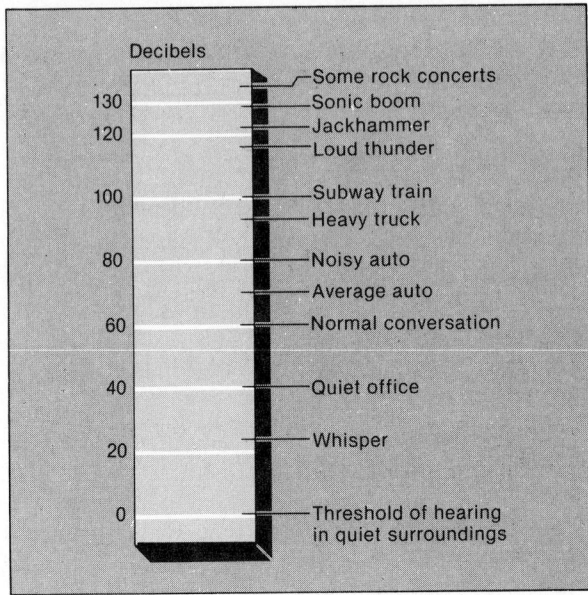

FIGURE 25.2 A scale of decibels showing values of familiar sounds for comparison. (*Source:* James Hassett, *Psychology in Perspective*, New York: Harper & Row, 1984, p. 137. Reprinted by permission of Harper & Row, Publishers, Inc.)

Figures 25.1 and 25.2 are examples of visual aids. They were professionally prepared, but your own visual aids need not be. Nevertheless, it is a good idea to make your visuals of as high a quality as your verbal presentation. Notice how effectively these visuals communicate. The bar graph in Figure 25.1 shows graphically the rapid and great growth of the cable television industry over the last few decades. Figure 25.2 effectively illustrates the decibel values of various familiar sounds and how these different sounds compare with each other.

SUMMARY

1. Three general types of informative speeches may be identified: speeches of description, which describe a process or procedure, an event, or an object or person); speeches of definition, which define a term, a system or theory, or similar and dissimilar terms of systems; and speeches of demonstration, which demonstrate how to do something or how something operates.

2. Informative speeches may also be viewed in terms of specific purposes—the specific items of information (the main points) that you want your audience to understand or learn.

3. In preparing informative speeches, observe the following principles of informative speaking: limit the amount of information, stress the relevance and usefulness of the information, present information at the appropriate level for your audience, and relate new information to information that the audience already knows.

4. Examples and illustrations are specific instances that are explained in varying degrees of detail. A relatively brief specific instance is an example; a longer and more detailed example told in story form is an illustration.

5. In using examples and illustrations, be sure that they are typical or representative, and relevant to your specific proposition.

6. Testimony refers to the opinions of experts or witnesses that are used to amplify your propositions.

7. In using testimony be sure that it is presented fairly, that the person is actually an authority on the specific subject, and that the person is unbiased.

8. Definitions are statements of the meaning or significance of a concept or term. Suitable definitions are made by etymology, authority, operations, negation, and direct symbolization.

9. In using definitions, be sure that they do clarify and add to the understanding of the audience, and that any authority is credible and known to your audience.

10. Audiovisual aids are auditory and visual means used to amplify the speaker's verbal message. Among the many types of audiovisual aids are the actual object; models; the chalkboard; charts, graphs, and diagrams; maps; people; slides, films, filmstrips, and videotapes; pictures; and records and tapes.

11. In using audiovisual aids be sure that the aid is relevant to your message, that it reinforces the message, that the message communicated by the aid is evident, and that the aid is appealing.

SOURCES

On types of speeches, see my *Elements of Public Speaking,* 3d ed. (New York: Harper & Row, 1987), or Douglas Ehninger, Bruce E. Gronbeck, Ray E. McKerrow, and Alan H. Monroe *Principles and Types of Speech Communication,* 10th ed. (Glenview, Ill.: Scott, Foresman, 1986), as well as the references cited in Unit 21. For a general introduction to information processing, see Blaine Goss, *Processing Communication* (Belmont, Calif.: Wadsworth, 1982). More advanced treatments are available in, for example, David H. Dodd and Raymond M. White, Jr., *Cognition: Mental Structures and Processes* (Boston: Allyn and Bacon, 1980), and Michael G. Wessells, *Cognitive Psychology* (New York: Harper & Row, 1982).

UNIT 26
THE PERSUASIVE SPEECH

LEARNING GOALS

After completing this unit, you should be able to

1. define *attitude, belief,* and *behavior* as used in persuasion
2. identify and explain the three major types of persuasive speeches
3. explain the operation of the following principles of persuasive speaking: attractiveness, selective exposure, audience participation, inoculation, and magnitude of change
4. explain the nature of argument and reasoning in persuasive speaking
5. explain the three general tests for reasoning
6. explain the nature of literal and figurative analogies as forms of reasoning and identify the two major tests for reasoning from analogy
7. explain the nature of cause-effect reasoning and identify the three major tests for reasoning with causes and effects
8. explain the nature of reasoning from sign and identify the three tests for reasoning from signs
9. explain the nature of reasoning from specific instances to generalizations, and identify the three tests for reasoning from specific instances to generalizations
10. define and explain the operation of the following motivational appeals: fear; power, control, and influence; self-esteem and approval; achievement; financial gain; and status
11. define *speaker credibility* and its three main dimensions
12. explain four ways the speaker can establish competence, good character, and charisma
13. identify the three general guidelines for establishing credibility

In this unit we consider the persuasive speech. First, we define some preliminary terms (attitude, belief, and behavior) as they are used in persuasion. Second, we consider the types and purposes of persuasive speeches and the ways to develop the specific propositions that you wish your audience to accept. Third, we examine selected principles of persuasion and indicate how these might be used in developing persuasive speeches. Fourth, we consider the role and types of arguments (or logical appeals) in persuasion. Fifth, we consider the psychological or motivational appeals. Sixth, we discuss the ways and means for establishing credibility.

The vast majority of speeches are designed to persuade the listener. The speeches of politicians, advertisers, and religious leaders are perhaps the clearest examples of persuasive messages. But, as will be made clear throughout this unit, persuasion is all around us, all the time.

ATTITUDES, BELIEFS, AND BEHAVIORS

Persuasive speeches are concerned with strengthening or changing attitudes or beliefs, or with motivating behavior. As a preface to discussing the types of speeches, we need first to define the following key terms.

Attitudes

We may think of an attitude as a tendency or predisposition to behave in a certain way. Thus, if we have a favorable attitude toward chemistry, we would be more apt to elect chemistry courses, to read about chemistry, to talk about chemistry, and to conduct chemistry experiments. If we have an unfavorable attitude toward chemistry, we would avoid chemistry courses, not read about chemistry, and so on.

"Attitude" is a hypothetical construct; it is a psychological fiction created to simplify our explanations of behaviors and behavioral tendencies. We cannot observe a person's attitude in the same way that we can observe a person's aggressive behaviors, for example. Instead, we infer the existence of certain attitudes from observing the individual's behaviors. If, for example, an individual speaks against censorship, reads everything that criticizes censorship, and writes articles denouncing censorship, we infer that this person has a negative attitude toward censorship. Note that we have not observed the "negative attitude"; rather, we have observed specific behaviors that we assume are attributable to the negative attitude.

Belief

A belief is an intellectual conviction in the existence or reality of some phenomenon or in the truth of some proposition. Thus we may have the belief that there is justice in the world or that there is life after death. We may believe that democracy (or socialism or communism) is the preferred system of government, or that children should be seen and not heard.

Behavior

Both attitudes and beliefs are unobservable, but when we speak of "behavior" in persuasion, we mean overt, observable behaviors. This is not to deny that there are behaviors that take place "inside the skin" but merely to say that we focus on behaviors that can be seen, confirmed, and validated by the observations of others.

TYPES AND PURPOSES OF PERSUASIVE SPEAKING

With these definitions clearly in mind, we can now identify the major types of persuasive speeches as (1) speeches to strengthen attitudes or beliefs, (2) speeches to change existing attitudes or beliefs, and (3) speeches designed to actuate or to move to action.

Speeches to Strengthen Attitudes or Beliefs

Speeches designed to strengthen existing attitudes or beliefs are heard frequently. Much religious and political speaking is addressed to strengthening attitudes and beliefs. People who expose themselves to religious speeches are usually those who already believe, and as a result the messages are addressed to strengthening attitudes and beliefs.

Speeches to Change Attitudes or Beliefs

Speeches designed to change attitudes or beliefs are much more difficult to construct and require a great deal more effort. Most people resist change, and any speaker who attempts to get people to change their beliefs or attitudes is clearly fighting an uphill (but not impossible) battle.

Speeches designed to strengthen or otherwise change attitudes or beliefs come in many forms. Depending on the initial position of the audience, the following examples may be viewed as topics for speeches to strengthen or change attitudes or beliefs.

- marijuana should be legalized
- general education requirements should be abolished
- television shows are mindless
- records should be rated for excessive sex and violence
- Puerto Rico should become the fifty-first state

Speeches to Actuate

Speeches designed to move the audience to action or to engage in some specific behavior are referred to as speeches to actuate. The persuasive speech addressed to motivating a specific behavior may focus on just about any behavior imaginable. Here are some examples:

- vote for Smith
- give money to the American Cancer Society
- buy a ticket to the football game
- listen to "20/20"
- take a course in computer science

Specific Purposes

On a more specific level, we may look at the persuasive speech in terms of the specific purpose and propositions you wish your audience to accept. Here are a few examples of specific purposes and the main propositions that might constitute the body of the speech. As with the informative speech examples, we also include here the thesis and the question to be asked of the thesis to illustrate further how this thesis statement helps to identify the main points of your speech.

Speeches to Strengthen or Change an Attitude or Belief

In this example, the speaker uses a problem-solution organizational pattern, first presenting the problems created by cigarette smoking and second, the solution.

Specific purpose: to persuade my audience that cigarette advertising should be banned from all media

Thesis: Cigarette advertising should be abolished. [*Why should it be abolished?*]

I. Cigarette smoking is a national problem.
   A. Cigarette smoking causes lung cancer.
   B. Cigarette smoking pollutes the air.
   C. Cigarette smoking creates litter problems.
II. Cigarette smoking would be lessened if advertisements were prohibited.
   A. Fewer people would start to smoke.
   B. Smokers would smoke less.

Speeches to Actuate

Although many speeches are designed specifically to change attitudes or beliefs, we are ultimately concerned with behavior—specifically, with changes in behavior. We assume that if we change attitudes and beliefs, we will have changed perhaps not the actual behaviors but at least the likelihood or probability of certain behaviors.

Here is a speech on managing time more effectively. It asks for a change in the way most people approach tasks and accordingly, presents a particularly difficult purpose to achieve. It uses a temporal thought pattern, identifying the steps to effective time management in the order in which they should be taken.

Specific purpose: to persuade my audience to manage their time more effectively by following four basic steps

Thesis: Time management can be made more effective. [*How can time management be made more effective?* or *What can we do to make time management more effective?*]

I. Make a daily "to do" list.
II. Categorized the tasks into three groups.
   A. A-items are the most essential.
   B. B-items are of moderate importance.
   C. C-items are of least importance.
III. Work systematically through the list from A, through B, to C.
IV. Reward yourself after completing each work unit.

PRINCIPLES OF PERSUASION

Thousands of articles and books—crammed with theories, descriptions, observations, and experimental tests—have been written about persuasion. Offered here is only a very small sampling of the principles of persuasion, with the objective of getting you started on your first speeches.

The Attractiveness Principle

A speaker will be more persuasive if he or she is perceived as attractive and well liked. This is a crucial characteristic that many persuasion texts omit entirely, perhaps for fear of offending. But this principle emerges from both the scientific study and the casual observation of persuasion with amazing consistency and cannot be avoided. The more attractive (physically and in personality) the speaker, the better the chance of being successful in persuasion.

The Selective Exposure Principle

Audiences generally follow the "law of selective exposure." It has at least two parts: (1) that listeners will actively seek out information to support their opinions, beliefs, values, decisions, behaviors, and the like; and (2) that listeners will actively avoid information that contradicts their existing opinions, beliefs, attitudes, values, behaviors, and so on. A few qualifications to this "law" are interesting to note. For example, if a person is very sure that the opinions and attitudes held are logical, valid, and productive, then this person may not bother to seek out the support of others or may not actively avoid nonsupportive messages. Selective exposure is exercised most often when confidence in one's opinions and beliefs is weak.

Some Implications

This principle of selective exposure suggests a number of implications for the speaker. For example, if you are attempting to persuade an audience that holds very different attitudes from your own, anticipate that selective exposure will be operating and proceed inductively; that is, hold back on your main purpose until they have assimilated some of your evidence and argument, and only then relate it to your main (and initially contrary) proposition. Another implication is that you must be thoroughly knowledgeable about the attitudes of your audience if you are to succeed in making the necessary adjustments and adaptations.

Still another implication is that if you have been successful in weakening the confidence of the listeners in their initial position, they will seek out other sources of information to restore that confidence. In many instances they will seek out the very information that will contradict what you have been persuading them to accept. Thus, at the end of your speech, it may appear that you have been successful. But you may find that the additional information exposure subsequent to the speech convinces the listeners even more firmly of their initial position. In this instance it is necessary to reinforce your point of view repeatedly—as advertisers do—or to somehow make the audience feel comfortable with their new attitudes and beliefs.

The Audience Participation Principle

Persuasion is greatest when the audience participates actively. In experimental tests, for example, the same speech is delivered to different audiences. The attitudes of one audience are measured before and after the speech, the difference being a measure of the speech's effectiveness. The attitudes of another group are measured before and after the speech, but they are also asked, for example, to paraphrase or summarize the various arguments of the speaker. It is consistently found that those listeners who participated actively (as when paraphrasing or summarizing) were more persuaded than those who passively received the message. Demagogues and propagandists who succeed in arousing huge crowds often have the crowds chant slogans, repeat catch phrases, and otherwise participate actively in the persuasive experience.

The Inoculation Principle

The principle of inoculation may be explained with the biological analogy on which it is based. Suppose you lived in a germ-free environment. Upon leaving this germ-free environment and upon exposure to germs, you will be particularly susceptible to infection because your body has not built up an immunity—it has no resistance. Resistance (the ability to fight off germs) might be achieved by the body, if not naturally, then through some form of inoculation. You could, for example, be injected with a weakened dose of the germ so that your body would begin the fight by building up antibodies that create an "immunity" to this type of infection. Your body, then, because of its production of antibodies, would be able to fight off even powerful doses of this germ.

The situation in persuasion is similar to this biological process. Some of our attitudes and beliefs have existed in a "germ-free" environment, where they have never been attacked or challenged. For example, many of us have

lived in an environment in which the values of a democratic form of government, the importance of education, and the traditional family structure have
not been challenged. Consequently, we have not been "immunized" against
attacks on these values and beliefs. We have no counterarguments (antibodies)
prepared to fight off these attacks on our beliefs. So, if someone were to come
along with strong arguments against these beliefs, we might be easily persuaded.

Contrast these "germ-free" beliefs with issues that have been attacked and
for which we have a ready arsenal of counterarguments: Our attitudes on the
draft, nuclear weapons, college athletics, and thousands of other issues have
been challenged in the press, on television, and in our interpersonal interactions. As a result of this exposure, we have counterarguments ready for any
attacks on our beliefs concerning these issues. We have been inoculated and
immunized against attacks, should someone attempt to change our attitudes or
beliefs.

Some Implications

The major implications of the inoculation principle for persuasion should
be clear. First, if you are addressing an inoculated audience, take into consideration that they have a ready arsenal of counterarguments to fight your persuasive assault. Be prepared, therefore, to achieve only small gains; don't try
to reverse totally the beliefs of a well-inoculated audience.

Second, if you are trying to persuade an uninoculated audience, your task
is much simpler in that you do not have to penetrate a fully developed immunization shield. Do recognize, however, that even when an audience has
not immunized itself, they take certain beliefs to be self-evident and may well
tune out any attacks on such cherished beliefs or values. Proceed slowly and
be content with small gains. Again, an inductive approach would suit your
purposes better here. Attacking cherished beliefs directly creates impenetrable
resistance; instead, build your case by first presenting your arguments and
evidence, and gradually work up to your conclusion.

Third, if you attempt to strengthen an audience's belief, give them the
antibodies they will need if they come under attack. Consider raising counterarguments to this belief and then demolishing them. Much as the injection of
a small amount of a germ will enable the body to build an immunization system,
presenting counterarguments and then refuting them will enable the listeners
to effectively immunize themselves against future attacks on these values and
beliefs. This procedure has been found to confer greater and longer-lasting
resistance to strong attacks than merely providing the audience with an arsenal
of supporting arguments.

The Magnitude of Change Principle

One of the most obvious principles of persuasion that many speakers
nevertheless ignore is this: The greater and more important the change desired
by the speaker, the more difficult its achievement will be. The reason for this

is simple: We normally demand a greater number of reasons and much more evidence before we make important decisions—career changes, moving our families to another state, or investing our life savings in certain stocks. On the other hand, we may be more easily persuaded (and demand less evidence) on relatively minor issues—whether to take "History of Television" rather than "History of Film," or to give to the United Heart Fund instead of the American Heart Fund.

Generally, people change gradually, in small degrees over a long period of time. And although there are cases of sudden conversions, this general principle seems to be valid more often than not. Persuasion, therefore, is most effective when it strives for small changes and works over a considerable period of time. Persuasion that attempts to convince the audience to change their attitudes radically or to engage in behaviors to which they are initially opposed will frequently backfire on the speaker. During this type of situation, the audience will frequently tune out the speaker, closing its ears to even the best and most logical arguments.

ARGUMENTS IN PERSUASIVE SPEECHES

An *argument* is a reason or series of reasons that lead to or support a conclusion. *Evidence* together with the *conclusion* that the evidence supports equal an argument. *Reasoning* is the process of formulating conclusions on the basis of evidence.

When you argue a point in a public speech, attempt to demonstrate the usefulness of a particular way of looking at something, or postulate some general principle, you are attempting to prove something to the listeners. That is, your function is a rhetorical one in the sense that you hope to prove the proposition, not in any objective sense but rather in the minds of the listeners. In the vast majority of cases, the issues cannot be proven in any objective sense. Rather, you seek, as a speaker, to establish the probability of your conclusions in the minds of the listeners. Thus, the process is in part a *logical* one of demonstrating the postulated relationship, and also a *psychological* one of convincing or persuading the listeners to accept the conclusions as you have drawn them. Throughout this discussion this dual function should be kept in mind.

What is said here is applicable to the speaker in constructing the speech, to the listener in receiving and responding to the speech, and to the speech critic or analyst in analyzing and evaluating the speech. A poorly reasoned argument, inadequate evidence, and stereotypical thinking, for example, must be avoided by the speaker, recognized and responded to by the listener, and negatively evaluated by the critic.

Before getting to the specific forms of argument or reasoning, some general tests of support applicable to all forms of argument should be stated. These general tests (and, in fact, all the tests of adequacy) are stated as questions so that you may use them to evaluate various sources of evidence and thus more easily test the adequacy of your argument and the validity of the information you use to support your argument.

Is the Support Recent?

We live in a world of rapid change; what was true 10 years ago is not necessarily true today. Therefore, it is particularly important that your supporting materials be as recent as possible. Recency alone, obviously, does not make an effective argument. Yet, other things being equal, the more recent the evidence and support the better.

Is There Corroborative Support?

Very few conditions in this world are simple; most issues are complex. Consequently, in reasoning about any issue, support the proposition from different sources and perspectives. That is, in supporting a thesis, gather evidence and argument from numerous and diverse sources all pointing to the same conclusion. This will not only help you convince listeners that the conclusion is valid, but will add generally to your credibility.

Are the Sources Unbiased?

We each see the world through our own individual filters; we do not see the world objectively, but instead we see it through our prejudices, biases, preconceptions, and stereotypes. Others see the world through their filters; no one is objective.

Consequently, in evaluating evidence, establish how biased the sources are and in what direction they are biased. Do not treat a tobacco company report on the connection between smoking and lung cancer with the same credibility as a report by some impartial medical research institute. Question research conducted and disseminated by any special interest group. As a speaker and as a listener, be particularly careful to recognize bias in your sources. It is always legitimate to ask: "To what extent might this source be biased? Might this source have a special interest that leads her or him to offer this evidence?"

Reasoning from Analogy

In reasoning from analogy, you compare like things and conclude that since they are alike in so many respects they are also alike in some heretofore unknown or unexamined respect. Analogies may be literal or figurative. In a *literal analogy* the items being compared are from the same class—cars, people, countries, cities, or whatever. For example, in a literal analogy we might argue that (1) New York, Philadelphia, London, and Paris are like Los Angeles in all essential respects—they are all large in area and all have a few million people; (2) these cities have all profited from low-cost subway transportation; (3) therefore, Los Angeles would also profit from the construction of a subway system. Here, then, we have taken a number of like items belonging to the same class (large cities), have pointed out a number of similarities (area, population), and have then reasoned that the similarity would also apply to the unexamined item (the subway system).

In a *figurative analogy,* the items compared are from different classes. These analogies are more useful for amplification than for reasoning. A figurative analogy might compare, for example, children with birds: We would note that, as birds are free to roam all over the world, children need to be free to roam all over their new and unexplored universe.

In testing the adequacy of an analogy—here of literal analogies—two general questions need to be asked.

Are the Two Cases Being Compared Alike in Essential Respects? In the example of the subway system in the various large cities, one significant and essential difference was not noted: The population of Los Angeles covers a wider geographical area than that of the other cities and is not as centralized as, say, New York or Philadelphia. Consequently, the subway would have to cover an area much greater than in other cities. Construction costs and operating expenses would be greater, and high fares would jeopardize its low-cost transportation functions.

Do the Differences Make a Difference? In any analogy, regardless of how literal it is, the items being compared will be different. No two things are the same; every item is unique. But in reasoning with analogies you need to ask whether the differences make a difference. Obviously, not all differences make a fundamental difference. The geographical spread of the various cities, however, is a substantial difference as far as subways are concerned.

Reasoning from Causes and Effects

In reasoning from causes and effects, you may go in either of two directions. You may reason from cause to effect (from observed cause to unobserved effect) or from effect to cause (from observed effect to unobserved cause).

Causal reasoning would go something like this. You would argue, for example, that X results from Y; and since X is undesirable, Y should be eliminated. With actual events substituted, you would have something like this: Cancer (X) results from smoking (Y); and since cancer is bad, smoking should be eliminated. Alternatively, of course, you might argue that X results from Y; and since X is desirable, Y should be encouraged. For example, general self-confidence (X) results from positively reinforcing experiences (Y); therefore, to encourage the development of self-confidence, foster positively reinforcing experiences.

In testing reasoning from cause to effect or from effect to cause, ask the following questions.

Might Other Causes Be Producing the Observed Effect? If you observe a particular effect (say, high crime or student apathy), you need to ask whether causes other than the one you are postulating might be producing these effects. Thus, you might postulate that poverty leads to high crime, but there might be other factors actually causing the high crime rate. Or poverty might be one cause, but it might not be the most important cause. Therefore, explore the possibility of other causes producing the observed effects.

Is the Causation in the Direction Postulated?   If two things occur together, it is often difficult to determine which is the cause and which is the effect. For example, a lack of interpersonal intimacy and a lack of self-confidence often seem to go together. The person who lacks self-confidence seldom has intimate relationships with others. But which is the cause and which is the effect? It might be that the lack of intimacy creates or "causes" low self-confidence, but it may also be that low self-confidence leads to or "causes" a lack of intimacy. Of course, it might also be that some other previously unexamined cause (a history of negative criticism, gross ugliness, obvious stupidity) might be producing both the lack of intimacy and the low self-confidence.

Is There Evidence for a Causal Rather than Merely a Temporal Relationship? Two things might vary together, but they may not be related in a cause-effect relationship. One often-cited and particularly vivid example is the cock crowing and the sun rising. The cock crows and the sun comes up, but no one would argue that the cock's crowing causes the sun to rise. Divorce frequently results after repeated instances of infidelity, but infidelity itself may not be the cause of the divorce. Rather, some other factor may be leading to both infidelity and divorce. Thus, even though infidelity may precede divorce, it may not be the cause of it. When you assume that a temporal relationship implies a causal relationship, you are committing a fallacy of reasoning called *post hoc ergo propter hoc* ("after this, because of this"), or, for short, the *post hoc* fallacy.

Reasoning from Sign

Some years ago I went to my doctor because of some minor skin irritation. Instead of looking at my skin, the doctor focused on my throat, noticed that it was enlarged, felt around a bit, and began asking me a number of questions. Did I tire easily? Yes. Did I drink lots of liquid? Yes. Did I always feel thirsty? Yes. Did I eat a great deal without gaining any weight? Yes. She then had me stretch out my hand and try to hold it steady. I couldn't do it. Last, she took a close look at my eyes and asked whether I noticed that they had expanded. I hadn't been aware of it, but when it was pointed out I could see that my eyes had expanded a great deal. These indicators were signs of a particular illness. Based on these signs, she made the preliminary diagnosis that I had a hyperthyroid condition. The results from blood and other tests confirmed the preliminary diagnosis. I was promptly treated and the thyroid condition was corrected.

Medical diagnosis is a good example of *reasoning by sign*. The general procedure is simple. If a sign and an object, event, or condition are repeatedly or frequently paired, the presence of the sign is taken as evidence or proof of the presence of the object, event, or condition. Thus, the tiredness, extreme thirst, and overeating were taken as signs of hyperthyroidism since they frequently accompany the condition. When these signs (or symptoms) disappeared after treatment with radioactive iodine, it was taken as a sign that the thyroid disease had been arrested. Further tests confirmed this as well.

In reasoning from sign ask these questions.

Do the Signs Necessitate the Conclusion Drawn?   Given the extreme thirst, the overeating, and the like, how certain may one be of the "hyperthyroid" conclusion? With most medical and legal matters we can never be absolutely certain, but we can be certain beyond reasonable doubt.

Are There Other Signs That Point to the Same Conclusion?   In the thyroid example, the extreme thirst could have been brought on by any number of factors. Similarly, the swollen throat and the overeating could have been attributed to other causes. Yet, taken together they seemed to point to only one reasonable diagnosis that was later confirmed with additional and more sophisticated signs in the form of blood tests and thyroid scans. Generally, the more signs that point toward the conclusion, the more confidence you can have that it is valid.

Are There Contradictory Signs?   Are there signs pointing toward contradictory conclusions? If, for example, "Higgins" had a motive and a history of violence (signs that would support the conclusion that Higgins was the murderer), but if Higgins also had an alibi for the time of the murder (a sign pointing to the conclusion of innocence), the conclusion of guilt would have to be reconsidered or discarded.

Reasoning from Specific Instances and Generalizations

In reasoning from specific instances, you examine several specific instances and then conclude something about the whole. This form of reasoning is particularly useful when you want to develop a general principle or conclusion but cannot examine the whole. You sample a few communication courses and conclude something about communication courses in general; you visit several Scandinavian cities and conclude something about the whole of Scandinavia. This same general process operates in dealing with one person. You see, for example, a particular person in several situations and conclude something about the person's behavior in general. You date a person a few times, or maybe even for a period of several months, and on that basis draw a general conclusion about the suitability of that person as a spouse.

Apply these tests in reasoning from specific instances.

Were Enough Specific Instances Examined?   Obviously there will be a limit to the number of specific instances you can examine; your time, energy, and resources are limited. Yet, it is important that enough instances be examined to justify your conclusion. Exactly what is enough will vary from one situation to another. Two general guidelines might prove helpful in determining how much is enough. First, the larger the group you wish to be covered by your conclusion, the greater the number of specific instances you must examine. Second, the greater the diversity of items in the class, the more specific instances you will have to examine. If you wish to draw conclusions about a class of 75 million Martians, you will have to examine a considerable number of Martians before drawing any valid conclusions. On the other hand, if you are attempting to draw a conclusion about a bushel of apples, sampling a few would seem sufficient.

Were the Specific Instances Examined Representative?   Specific instances must be representative. If you wish to draw conclusions about the entire class, examine specific instances coming from all areas or subclasses within the major class. If you wanted to draw conclusions about the student body of your school, you could not simply examine communication majors, physics majors, or art majors. Rather, you would have to examine a representative sample. All significant parts of the whole must be examined in some way.

Are There Significant Exceptions?   When you examine specific instances and attempt to draw a conclusion about the whole, take into consideration the exceptions. Thus, if you examine a number of Venusians and discover that 70 percent have an I.Q. of less than 80, you might be tempted to draw the conclusion that Venusians are stupid. But what about the 30 percent who have an I.Q. of over 140? These are significant exceptions that must be taken into account when drawing your conclusion and would necessitate qualifying your conclusion in significant ways.

PSYCHOLOGICAL APPEALS IN PERSUASIVE SPEECHES

Psychological appeals are directed at an individual's needs and desires. Although psychological appeals are never totally separate from rational appeals—appeals directed to one's reasoning and logic—they are considered separately here. We are primarily concerned here with motives—with those forces that energize, move, or motivate a person to develop, change, or strengthen particular attitudes or ways of behaving. For example, one motive might be the desire for status; this motive might then move the individual to develop certain attitudes about appropriate and inappropriate occupations, the importance or unimportance of saving and investing money, and so on. It may move this person to behave in certain ways—to buy Gucci shoes, a Rolex watch, and a Tiffany diamond. It should be clear from these examples that this same status motive may motivate different persons in different ways. Thus, the status motive may lead one person to enter the poorly paid but respected occupation of nursing, and another to enter the well-paid but often disparaged real estate or diamond business. Here are just a few of the motives to which appeals may be made.

Fear

We are motivated in great part by a desire to escape from fear. We fear the loss of those things we desire; we fear the loss of money, family, friends, love, attractiveness, health, job, and in fact, just about everything we now have and value. We also fear punishment, rejection, and failure. We fear the unknown, the uncertain, and the unpredictable.

The use of fear in persuasion has been studied extensively, and the results seem to indicate that moderate amounts of fear probably work best. With low levels of fear, the audience is not motivated sufficiently to act, and with high levels of fear they become too frightened to consider the speech at all and simply tune the speaker out.

Here, for example, Caspar W. Weinberger, United States Secretary of Defense, appeals to the audience's desire for safety, security, and freedom from fear:

> Clearly, our modernization program transmitted an unmistakable signal of America's commitment to defense of the free world. And that signal has been received. The United States is more secure than it was during the 1970s; the world is more stable, less threatened by Soviet adventurism. And, as the Soviets perceived an America determined to defend the free world, they are beginning to see value in negotiation.

Power, Control, and Influence

We want power, control, and influence. First, we want power over ourselves; we want to be in control of our own destinies. We want to be responsible for our own successes and, to a lesser extent, for our own failures. As Emerson put it, "Can anything be so elegant as to have few wants, and to serve them one's self?"

We also want control over other persons. We want to be influential. We want to be opinion leaders. We want others to come to us for advice, guidance, and instructions. (I think this is why the role of teacher is so appealing to so many people.) Similarly, we want to have control over events and things in the world; we want to control our environment. Practically every communication book designed for the popular market (that is, a non-textbook) emphasizes how the knowledge of communication will enable you to achieve power, control, and influence—whether in sales, work, or love. Listeners will be motivated when they can see their power, control, and influence increase as a result of their learning what the speaker has to say, or believing or acting as the speaker suggests.

Self-Esteem and Approval

"In his private heart," wrote Mark Twain, "no man much respects himself." And perhaps because of this, we need to have a positive self-image and to see ourselves in the best possible light. We want to see ourselves as self-confident, worthy, and contributing human beings. Inspirational speeches, of the "you are the greatest" type, never seem to lack receptive and suggestive audiences.

Self-esteem is, at least in part, attained through gaining the approval of others. College students, it seems, are especially concerned with peer approval, but also want approval from family, teachers, elders, and even children. Somehow the approval of others makes us feel positive about ourselves. If we are approved of by others, we assume that we must deserve such approval. Approval from others also ensures our attainment of a number of related goals. For example, if we have peer approval, we probably also have influence. If we have approval, we will likely have status. In relating your propositions to the audience's desire for approval, avoid being too blatant and obvious: Few people want to be told that they need or desire approval.

Achievement

We want to achieve in whatever we do. As students you want to be successful; as a teacher and writer I too want to be successful. We want to achieve as friends, parents, and lovers. This is why we read books and listen to speeches that purport to tell us how to be better achievers. We also want others to recognize our achievements as real and valuable. "Being successful in my work" was noted as "extremely important" by 63 percent of entering college students. In using the achievement motive, be explicit in stating how your speech, ideas, and recommendations will contribute to the listeners' achievements. If you tell the listeners how they can learn to increase their potential, earn better grades, secure more prestigious jobs, and become more popular with friends, you will have a highly motivated audience.

In a speech on the values of networking, Peter B. Stark appeals to the achievement motive of his audience and in the process effectively establishes his credibility:

> Networking is the most powerful success tool to get you where you want to go. To be honest, networking is one of the greatest assets I have ever owned.
> At the age of 21, I was the Executive Assistant to the President of a 25-million dollar company. An unadvertised position I had gained through a management consultant I had met in Toastmasters International.
> At the age of 23, I was the Director of Marketing for the local Caterpillar Tractor Dealer, a 100-million dollar company. Another unadvertised position, I received through a community contact. And, at the age of 25, I had enough contacts to open Photomation West, a printing and advertising firm.

Financial Gain

"Money," said George Bernard Shaw, "is the most important thing in the world. It represents health, strength, honor, generosity, and beauty as conspicuously as the want of it represents illness, weakness, disgrace, meanness, and ugliness. Not the least of its virtues is that it destroys base people as certainly as it fortifies and dignifies noble people." To some extent I suspect we are all motivated by the desire for financial gain—for what it can buy and for what it can do. We may be concerned with buying necessities, luxuries, or perhaps most important, time—time to do the things we all want to do and not be tied to the pedestrian and the mundane, such as ironing, washing, typing, painting, and so on. Advertisers know this motive well and frequently get persons interested in their messages by using such key words as SALE, 50% OFF, SAVE NOW, and the like. All of these are appeals to the desire for money. Concern for lower taxes, higher salaries, and fringe benefits are all related to the money motive. Show the audience that what you are saying or advocating will make them money, and they will listen with considerable interest, much as they read the current get-rich-quick books that are flooding the bookstores.

In a speech designed to motivate the audience to take action against certain proposed budget cuts, Cyril F. Brickfield appeals to the financial motive of his senior citizen audience:

> Congress is now considering freezing Social Security COLA's. Congress is willing to force more than a half million of us into poverty. But the defense budget is exempt from any freeze.
> Ladies and gentlemen, let me ask you, is it *fair* that older Americans must lose their inflation protection while the Pentagon doesn't?

Status

One motive that accounts for a great deal of our behavior—too much, some would argue—is our desire for status. In our society, status is mainly measured by an individual's occupation and wealth. Often job and money are positively related; at other times they are not. Nevertheless, in most estimates of status, the two are significant. But we might mention other kinds of status. For example, there is that status that comes from competence on the athletic field, from excelling in the classroom, or from superiority on the dance floor. To be most effective, link your propositions with your specific audience's desire for status. Beginning college students give considerable attention to their future jobs but rank interest and the utilization of skills and abilities as more important than other qualities we normally think of as being part of status. For example, in a recent survey, 17,000 students were asked what would make for future job satisfaction. Of those qualities listed as "very important," 93 percent noted "interesting to do" and 74 percent noted "uses skills and abilities." On the side normally considered as qualities of status, a "chance to earn a good deal of money" was noted by 47 percent, "a job most people look up to, respect" by 37 percent, and "high status, prestige" by 36 percent. I suspect that these percentages change considerably with age, giving greater importance to status in the form of financial gain and societal approval.

CREDIBILITY APPEALS IN PERSUASIVE SPEECHES

Speaker credibility is the quality of persuasiveness that depends on the audience's perception of the character of the speaker. Note that I say *audience's perception of the character of the speaker*, rather than simply *the character of the speaker*. Credibility is something a listener or receiver perceives a speaker to have; it is not something the speaker has or does not have in any objective sense. In reality the speaker may be a stupid, immoral person, but if perceived by the audience as intelligent and moral, then that speaker is said to have high credibility and will, research tells us, be believable.

Much contemporary research has been directed at the question of what makes a person believable. It is a question of vital concern to many. Advertisers are interested because it relates directly to the effectiveness or ineffectiveness of their ad campaigns. Is James Garner an effective spokesperson for Mazda? Is Bill Cosby an effective spokesperson for Jell-O? Credibility is important to

Lee Iacocca is one of the most effective persuasive speakers in the country today. What qualities does Iacocca have that make him an effective spokesperson?

the politician, since it determines in great part how people vote. It influences education, since the students' perceptions of teacher credibility will determine, in part, the degree of influence teachers have on a class. There seem, in fact, to be no communication encounters that will not be influenced by considerations of credibility.

Pooling the results of the numerous research efforts, we can identify three major characteristics or components of credibility: competence, or the knowledge and expertise the speaker is seen to possess; character, or the speaker's intentions and concern for the audience; and charisma, or the personality and dynamism of the speaker. Each of these three characteristics and the ways in which a speaker may more effectively demonstrate them will be considered in depth. But before going into these characteristics, we need to consider briefly how credibility impressions are formed.

Forming Credibility Impressions

We form a credibility impression of a speaker on the basis of the reputation the speaker has (in our minds) and how that reputation interacts with what the speaker does during the public speaking situation. Most consider a person's history, weighing it heavily in the total evaluation, and combine the information with the more immediate information derived from present interactions. Information from these two sources—from history and from present interactions—interacts, and the audience forms an assessment of your credibility.

There are, then, three types of credibility. *Initial credibility* is based on the speaker's reputation and what we know of the speaker's history. *Derived credibility* is the impression an audience gets on the basis of what the speaker says during the speech. *Terminal credibility* is the final assessment of credibility that results from the interaction between the initial and derived credibility.

Increasing Credibility

As a public speaker, part of your task is to make your audience see you as a credible, believable, spokesperson. Here I suggest some of the ways in which you may attempt to convey a favorable impression on your competence, character, and charisma.

Competence

Competence refers to the knowledge and expertise a speaker is thought to possess. The more knowledge and expertise the audience sees the speaker as possessing, the more likely it is that the speaker will be believed. The teacher, for example, is believed to the extent that he or she is thought knowledgeable and expert in the subject. Similarly, the textbook writer is thought credible to the extent that he or she is thought to know the material and to have the ability to communicate this knowledge in written form.

Competence is logically subject-specific. A person may be competent in one subject and totally incompetent in another. Your political science instructor, for example, may be quite competent in politics but quite incompetent in mathematics or chemistry. Often, however, people do not make this distinction. A person who is thought competent in politics will often be thought competent in general, and will thus be perceived as credible when talking on matters other than politics. This phenomenon is referred to as the *halo effect:* The perception of competence is generalized to all areas, and competence is seen as a general trait of the individual. This halo effect also has a counterpart—a *reverse halo effect*. Here the person who is seen as incompetent in, say, mathematics is perceived to be similarly incompetent in other areas as well. As a critic or analyst of public speaking, be particularly sensitive to competence being subject-specific and to the operation of both the halo and the reverse halo effects.

As a public speaker, demonstrate your competence to your listeners to make them aware of your knowledge and expertise. There are a number of methods you can use.

1. *Tell the Audience of Any Special Experiences or Training That Qualify You to Speak on This Specific Topic.* If you are speaking on communal living and you have lived on a commune yourself, include this in your speech.

Tell the audience of unique and personal experiences, when these contribute to your knowledge and expertise.

2. *Cite a Variety of Research Sources.* Make it clear to your audience that you have thoroughly researched the topic by citing the books you have read, the persons you have interviewed, the articles you have consulted, and so on. Spread these throughout the speech.

3. *Stress the Particular Competencies of Your Sources if Your Audience Is Not Aware of Them.* Thus, for example, instead of saying simply "Senator Smith thinks . . . ," establish the senator's credibility by saying, for example, "Senator Smith, who headed the finance committee for three years and who was formerly a professor of economics at MIT, thinks . . . ." In this way it becomes clear to the audience that you have chosen your sources carefully and with a new view toward providing the most authoritative sources possible.

4. *Demonstrate Your Command of the Language.* Your use of language and your voice will greatly influence the audience's perception of your credibility. Be especially careful to learn the correct pronunciations of terms or names about which you may be in doubt, and make certain that any potential grammatical errors are avoided.

5. *Do Not Needlessly Call Attention to Your Inadequacies as a Spokesperson or to Any Gaps in Your Knowledge.* No one can know everything, and your audience does not expect you to be the exception. But it is not necessary to remind them. Stress your competence, not your inadequacies.

Character

We will perceive a speaker as credible if we perceive that speaker as having what Aristotle referred to as a high moral *character*. Here we would be concerned with the individual's honesty and basic nature. We would want to know whether we could trust that person. A speaker who can be trusted is apt to be believed; a speaker who cannot be trusted is apt not to be believed. An individual's motives or *intentions* are particularly relevant in determining character. The salesperson who says all the right things about a product is often doubted because his or her intentions are perceived as selfish; credibility is therefore low. The salesperson is less believable than a consumer advocate who evaluates a product with no motives of personal gain. Of course, it is extremely difficult to judge when individuals are concerned with our good or with theirs, but when we can make the distinction, it greatly influences our perception of a person's character.

As a speaker, demonstrate those qualities of character that will increase your credibility. A few suggestions may be added to those noted for demonstrating competence.

6. *Stress Your Fairness.* If you are delivering a persuasive speech, stress that you have examined both sides of the issue (if, indeed, you have). If you are presenting both sides, make it clear that your presentation is an accurate and fair one. Be particularly careful not to omit any argument listeners may have already thought of; such an omission would be a sure

sign that your presentation is not a fair and balanced one. Make clear to the audience that you would not advocate a position if it were not the conclusion derived from an honest and fair evaluation of the various alternatives.

7. *Stress Your Concern for Enduring Values.* Speakers who appear to be concerned with small and insignificant issues are generally seen as less credible than speakers who demonstrate a concern and a commitment to lasting truths and general principles. Thus, in your speech make clear to the audience that your position and thesis are related to higher values—and, of course, show exactly how this is true.

8. *Stress Your Similarity with the Audience, Particularly Your Beliefs, Attitudes, Values, and Goals.* Generally, we perceive as believable those who are like ourselves, especially in basic values. The more people hold attitudes, beliefs, goals, and ambitions similar to our own, the more likely it is that they will be perceived as credible. Closely related to this is the issue of "common ground." When people align themselves with what we align ourselves with, they establish common ground with us and are generally perceived as more believable than people who do not establish this common ground.

9. *Make it Clear to Listeners That You Are Interested in Their Welfare Rather than Simply Seeking Self-gain.* If listeners feel you are out for yourself, they will justifiably downgrade your credibility. Make clear that their interests are foremost in your mind.

Charisma

Charisma is best viewed as a composite of personality and dynamism as seen by an audience. Generally, we perceive as credible or believable speakers we like rather than speakers we do not like. And, it seems, we like speakers who have what we commonly call a "pleasing personality." We believe speakers who are friendly and pleasant rather than speakers who are unfriendly and unpleasant. Similarly, we seem to favor the dynamic over the hesitant, nonassertive speaker. Generally, the shy, introverted, soft-spoken individual is perceived as less credible than the extroverted and forceful individual.

10. *Demonstrate a Positive Orientation to the Public Speaking Situation and to the Entire Speaker-Audience Encounter.* We seem to like listening to positive rather than negative people, so it will help if you accentuate the positive and eliminate the negative, as the old song had it. Positive and forward-looking people are seen as more credible than negative and backward-looking people. Perhaps, we reason, they have gotten themselves together and so are in a better position to know what is right and what is wrong. We would be leery of accepting marital advice from an unhappily married couple, perhaps for a similar reason. If they cannot solve their own problems, we reasonably doubt their ability to help us.

11. *Demonstrate Assertiveness.* Show the audience you are a person who will stand up for your rights and will not back off simply because the odds may be against you or because you are outnumbered.

12. *Be Enthusiastic.* The lethargic speaker who somehow plods through the speech is the very opposite of the charismatic speaker. Try viewing a film of Jesse Jackson or Billy Graham speaking; they are totally absorbed with the speech and with the audience. They provide excellent examples of the enthusiasm that makes speakers charismatic.

13. *Be Emphatic.* Use language that is emphatic rather than colorless and indecisive. Use gestures that are clear and decisive rather than random and hesitant. Emphatic speakers demonstrate commitment to the position advocated, and the audience will be much more likely to agree with speakers who themselves are convinced of the proposition.

General Guidelines

In addition to these suggestions, three additional general guidelines will assist you in putting these suggestions into operation most effectively.

14. *Develop or Strengthen These Characteristics as a Person as Well as a Speaker.* Enhance your competence, character, and charisma. I know that this is easy to say, but extremely difficult to put into practice. Nevertheless, it is important to have these as goals, for their development is the best insurance that they will function to make you credible in public speaking situations as well as in everyday interactions.

15. *Demonstrate Your Possession of the Three Components of Credibility, Especially in the Introduction (Whether You Introduce Your Own Speech or Whether Someone Else Does It), as Well as Throughout the Speech.* If you have a broad knowledge of the topic or first-hand experience, tell the audience of this knowledge and experience as early as possible. If there is some sort of formal introduction to your speech, you may have some important references integrated into this introduction to help establish your credibility. Thus, for example, if you are to speak on living under wartime conditions, the audience should know that you have in fact lived under these conditions and you should supply the person introducing you with the pertinent data.

16. *Use a Variety of Methods to Establish Your Credibility.* Do not rely on one or even two or three methods to build your credibility. Use a number of different methods, and be sure to give consideration to all three components of credibility: competence, character, and charisma.

SUMMARY

1. *Attitude* refers to a tendency or predisposition to behave in a certain way.

2. *Belief* refers to an intellectual conviction in the existence or reality of some phenomenon or in the truth of some proposition.

3. The major types of persuasive speech are those that attempt to strengthen attitudes or beliefs, to change existing attitudes or beliefs, and to actuate or move the listeners to action.

4. The attractiveness principle holds that a speaker will be more persuasive if he or she is perceived as attractive and well liked.

5. The selective exposure principle holds that listeners will actively seek out information that supports their opinions, beliefs, values, and behaviors, and that listeners will actively avoid information that contradicts their existing opinions, beliefs, values, and behaviors.

6. The audience participation principle holds that persuasion is greatest when the audience participates actively.

7. The inoculation principle holds that attitudes will be more resistant to change when the listener has been "immunized"—when the listener has developed counterarguments to defend existing beliefs and to ward off arguments that go against them.

8. The magnitude of change principle holds that the greater and more important the change desired by the speaker, the more difficult its achievement will be.

9. *Argument* refers to a reason or series of reasons that lead to or support a conclusion. *Evidence* plus the conclusion that the evidence supports equal an argument.

10. Three general tests of argument or reasoning should be applied: the support should be recent; there should be corroborative support, and the sources should be unbiased.

11. In reasoning from analogy, we compare like things and conclude that since they are alike in so many respects, they are also alike in some heretofore unknown or unexamined respect. Analogies may be literal or figurative.

12. In reasoning from analogy, we should ask two questions: (1) Are the two cases being compared alike in essential respects? (2) Do the differences make a difference?

13. In reasoning from causes and effects, we may go in either of two directions: We can reason from known or observed cause to unobserved effect, or from observed or known effect to some unobserved cause.

14. In causal reasoning, we should ask three questions: (1) Might other causes be producing the observed effect? (2) Is the causation in the direction postulated? (3) Is there evidence for a causal rather than merely a temporal relationship?

15. In reasoning from sign, we reason that if a sign and an object, event, or condition are repeatedly or frequently paired, the presence of the sign is taken as evidence or proof of the presence of the object, event, or condition.

16. In reasoning from sign, we should ask three questions: (1) Do the signs necessitate the conclusion drawn? (2) Are there other signs that point to the same conclusion? (3) Are there contradictory signs?

17. In reasoning from specific instances to a generalization, we examine several specific instances and then conclude something about the whole.

18. In testing reasoning from specific instances to a generalization, we should ask three questions: (1) Were enough specific instances examined? (2) Were the specific instances examined representative? (3) Are there significant exceptions?

19. Psychological or motivational appeals are those appeals directed at an individual's needs and desires. A wide variety of motivations may be appealed to by the persuasive speaker: fear; power, control, and influence; self-esteem and approval; achievement; financial gain; and status.

20. *Credibility* refers to that quality of persuasiveness that depends on the audience's perception of the character of the speaker. Three types of credibility are normally identified: *initial credibility* is based on the speaker's reputation and what we know of the speaker's history, *derived credibility* is the impression an audience gets on the basis of what the speaker says during the speech, and *terminal credibility* is the final assessment of credibility that results from the interaction between the initial and derived credibility.

21. Three dimensions of credibility are normally distinguished: *competence* refers to the knowledge and expertise that a speaker is thought to possess; *character* refers to the speaker's honesty, moral character, and basic nature; and *charisma* refers to a composite of personality and dynamism as seen by an audience.

SOURCES

There are numerous and excellent works on persuasive speaking that will prove useful to you. A review article on inoculation by William J. McGuire, who has done most of the theorizing and research on this principle, may be found in "Inducing Resistance to Persuasion: Some Contemporary Approaches," in Leonard Berkowitz, ed., *Advances in Experimental Social Psychology,* vol. 1 (New York: Academic Press, 1964), pp. 191–229. A comprehensive overview is provided by Mary John Smith, *Persuasion and Human Action: A Review and Critique of Social Influence Theories* (Belmont, Calif.: Wadsworth, 1982).

Most public speaking texts fail to do justice to argument and evidence in speech making; it is best to consult works in argumentation and logic. I recommend the following: Craig R. Smith and David M. Hunsaker, *The Bases of Arguments: Ideas in Conflict* (Indianapolis: Bobbs-Merrill, 1972); Abne M. Eisenberg and Joseph A. Ilardo, *Argument: A Guide to Formal and Informal Debate,* 2d ed. (Englewood Cliffs, N.J.: Prentice-Hall, 1980); and Michael A. Gilbert, *How to Win an Argument* (New York: McGraw-Hill, 1979). Perhaps the best single source is Stephen Toulmin, Richard Rieke, and Allan Janik, *An Introduction to Reasoning* (New York: Macmillan, 1979).

SKILL DEVELOPMENT SUMMARY

1. In **preparing a public speech** follow these steps: select your subject and (narrow) purpose, analyze your audience, research your topic, formulate your thesis and identify the major propositions, support the major propositions with amplifying and supporting materials, organize the body of the speech in a coherent thought pattern, word the speech so that it is instantly intelligible, and construct the conclusion and the introduction.

2. In dealing with **speaker apprehension** follow these simple rules: prepare and practice thoroughly, gain as much experience as possible, put apprehension in perspective, and use physical activity and deep breathing to relax yourself.

3. After selecting your **thesis** (your main assertion), expand this thesis by asking strategic questions and in this way develop your main ideas or propositions.

4. After generating your possible **major propositions,** examine the list and eliminate those points that seem least important to your thesis, combine those points that have a common focus, and select points that are most relevant to your audience. Remember too, to use two, three, or four main points at the most; phrase your propositions in parallel style; and develop your main points so that they are separate and discrete.

5. Use **transitions** to connect the major parts of your speech and to provide the audience with guideposts that will help them follow the development of your thoughts and arguments.

6. Use **internal summaries** to remind listeners of what they have just heard and to reinforce your major ideas.

7. In organizing the main points in the body of the speech, select a **thought pattern** that is appropriate to the subject matter—for example, problem-solution, temporal, topical, spatial, cause-effect, or the motivated sequence.

8. Develop an **introduction** to your speech that gains attention and orients the audience as to what is to follow.

9. Gain the **attention** of the audience in your introduction (and be sure to maintain it throughout your speech) by such techniques as asking questions, making reference to audience members, making reference to recent happenings, using humor, using an illustration or dramatic story, and using audiovisual aids.

10. **Orient your audience** by giving the audience a general idea of your subject, giving a detailed preview of your main propositions, or identifying your goal or the objectives you hope to achieve.

11. Be sure to avoid the **common faults with introductions:** don't apologize, don't make hollow promises, don't rely on gimmicks, and don't preface your introduction.

12. Develop a **conclusion** that summarizes your speech and provides closure.

13. **Summarize your speech** by restating your thesis or objectives, restating the importance of the topic or thesis, or restating your major propositions.

14. **Provide closure** by using a quotation, referring to subsequent events, posing a challenge or question, or referring back to the introduction.

15. Be sure to avoid the **common problems with conclusions:** don't apologize, don't introduce new material, and don't drag out the conclusion.

16. To your **preparation outline,** preface statements of your general and specific purposes and your thesis. Outline the introduction, body, and conclusion as separate units. Insert transitions and internal summaries.

17. In **constructing your outline,** use a consistent set of symbols, use visual aspects to reflect and reinforce the organizational pattern, use one discrete idea per symbol, and use complete declarative sentences.

18. Construct a **delivery outline** for use in the actual presentation of the speech to your audience. This outline should be brief, clear, and delivery-oriented. Rehearse with this outline, not with the more detailed preparation outline.

19. **Word your speech** so that it is (1) clear—be economical; use specific terms and numbers; use guide phrases; use short, familiar, and high-frequency terms; and use repetition, restatement, and internal summaries; (2) vivid—use active verbs, strong verbs, figures of speech, and imagery; (3) appropriate—speak on the proper level of formality-informality; avoid unfamiliar terms; and avoid slang, vulgar, and offensive expressions; (4) personal—use personal pronouns, questions directed to the audience, and immediacy expressions; and (5) forceful—eliminate weakeners; avoid bromides and clichés; and vary intensity as appropriate.

20. Construct **sentences** that are short rather than long, direct rather than indirect, active rather than passive, and positive rather than negative. In addition, try to vary the type and length of sentences. Include sentences that are parallel, antithetical, and periodic to give your speech variety.

21. In general, use the **extemporaneous method of delivery.**

22. Adjust your **vocal volume** on the basis of the distance between you and the audience, the amount of competing noise, the acoustics of the room, and the emphasis you wish to give your ideas. Be careful to avoid overly soft, overly loud, or unvaried volume levels.

23. Adjust your **vocal rate** on the basis of time constraints, the content of your speech, and the specific listening conditions. Be careful to avoid too slow, too rapid, or too unvaried or predictable a rate pattern.

24. Adjust your **vocal pitch** on the basis of the meanings you wish to communicate. Be careful to avoid too high, too low, or too monotonous a pitch pattern.

25. Avoid excessive **nasality, denasality, breathiness,** and **hoarseness.**

26. Be careful to avoid the **articulation and pronunciation errors** of omission, substitution, addition, accent, and pronouncing sounds that should be silent.

27. Use **pauses** to signal transitions between parts of your speech, to allow listeners time to think, and to signal the approach of a significant idea.

28. During your **speech delivery,** maintain eye contact with the entire audience, allow your facial expressions to convey your feelings, gesture naturally, incorporate some general body movement, and position yourself at an appropriate and comfortable distance from your listeners.

29. **Rehearse your speech** often, perfect your vocal and bodily delivery, rehearse the speech as a whole, time the speech at each rehearsal, approximate the specific speech situation as much as possible, see and think of yourself as a public speaker, and incorporate any delivery notes that may be of value during the actual speech presentation.

30. In your informative speeches, follow these **principles of informative speaking:** limit the amount of information, stress the relevance and usefulness of this information to the audience, present information at the appropriate level of sophistication, and relate any new information to what the audience already knows.

31. In your informative speeches, select a variety of **amplifying materials:** examples and illustrations that are representative and relevant; testimony that is fair, authoritative, and unbiased; definitions that clarify difficult concepts and are advanced by credible authorities; and audiovisual aids that are relevant, reinforcing of the message, easily evident to the audience, and appealing.

32. In your persuasive speeches, apply (where relevant) these **principles of persuasion:** attractiveness, selective exposure, audience participation, inoculation, and magnitude of change.

33. In your persuasive speeches, use **logical appeals** that are recent, that have corroborative support, and that are from unbiased sources. Use reasoning from analogy, when the items compared are alike in essential respects and the differences do not make a difference; from causes and effects, when other causes are not operating, the causation is in the direction postulated, and there is evidence for a causal rather than merely a temporal connection; from sign, when the signs necessitate the conclusion drawn, other signs do not point to the same conclusion, and there are no contradictory signs; and from specific instances to generalizations, when enough representative specific instances are examined, and there are no significant exceptions.

34. To motivate your audience—use **psychological appeals**—for example, fear; individuality and conformity; power, control, and influence; self-esteem and approval; achievement; financial gain; and status.

35. Establish your **competence** by telling the audience of any relevant special experiences or training, citing a variety of research sources, stressing the competencies of your sources, demonstrating your command of the language, and not calling attention to any inadequacies.

36. Establish your good **character** by stressing your fairness, concern for enduring values, similarity to the audience (especially attitudinal), and interest in their welfare.

37. Establish your **personality and dynamism (charisma)** by demonstrating a positive orientation to the situation and by being assertive, enthusiastic, and emphatic.

38. In establishing your **credibility,** pay attention to these general guidelines: develop the characteristics of competence, character, and charisma as a person and as a public speaker; demonstrate your possession of the components of credibility especially in your introduction but also throughout the speech; and use a variety of methods for establishing credibility rather than relying on just one, two, or three.

PART SEVEN
INTERCULTURAL
COMMUNICATION

27. PRELIMINARIES TO INTERCULTURAL COMMUNICATION: IMPORTANCE, DIFFICULTIES, AND FORMS

28. INTERCULTURAL COMMUNICATION: BARRIERS AND GATEWAYS

In this part of the text, we explore intercultural communication. In the first of these units, "Preliminaries," we consider the importance of intercultural communication, the difficulties involved in studying it, and its nature and forms. In the second, we consider the foundation of much of intercultural communication—namely, language and communication relativity—and then explore the major barriers and gateways to effective intercultural interaction.

We cover intercultural communication in only two units not because it is an unimportant area of communication, but rather because we have already covered much of the relevant material, especially in Unit 9, "Social Aspects of Language and Verbal Interaction," and throughout our discussion of nonverbal communication.

UNIT 27
PRELIMINARIES TO INTERCULTURAL COMMUNICATION:
Importance, Difficulties, and Forms

LEARNING GOALS

After completing this unit, you should be able to

1. explain the operation of at least four factors accounting for the importance of intercultural communication
2. define *ethnocentrism* and explain its role in the study of intercultural communication
3. distinguish between mindful and mindless states, and explain their relevance to the study of intercultural communication
4. define *culture* and *enculturation*
5. define *intercultural communication* and explain the model of intercultural communication presented in this unit
6. explain the relevance of subcultures to intercultural communication
7. identify at least six specific forms of intercultural communication

Here we explore some of the preliminaries to intercultural communication: its importance, the difficulties involved in studying it, and its nature and scope. As a preface to this discussion, consider the following cases.

AN EXCURSION INTO INTERCULTURAL COMMUNICATION

In each of the following 10 cases, something went wrong. What was it? Try to identify, perhaps with a group of friends, at least one possible explanation for the absence of effective communication in each situation. (Following custom, the term *American* designates a person from the United States, although technically all persons from North and South America are "Americans." Most, however, prefer to be designated more specifically by their country of origin— for example, *Canadian, Argentinian, Mexican,* and so on—and most persons from the United States prefer to be referred to as *American.*)

1. An American invites a Filipino co-worker to dinner. The Filipino politely refuses. The American is hurt and feels that the Filipino does not want to be friendly. The Filipino is hurt and concludes that the invitation was not extended sincerely.
2. A young American girl is talking with an older Indonesian man. She communicates as if she were talking with an American man. After a brief interchange, the Indonesian leaves, thinking the girl was disrespectful.
3. An American and an Arab are talking in an open yard. After a brief discussion the American concludes that the Arab was pushy and overly familiar; the Arab concludes that the American was cold and "standoffish."
4. An American and a Moslem are having dinner. The American, being left-handed, eats and drinks with his left hand. When another dinner is proposed the Moslem refuses; the American, the Moslem thinks, is obscene.
5. An American and a Latin American are having dinner in a Latin American restaurant. The American raises his hand and tries to catch the waiter's eye, to no avail. The Latin American hits the water glass with a fork. The waiter comes to take the order. The Latin American concludes that the American is shy and unassertive. The American concludes that the Latin American is rude and overly aggressive.
6. An American couple living in Europe invites another couple (co-workers) to dinner at their home. All goes well. Several weeks later the European couple invites the American couple to dinner but at a local restaurant. The American couple feels somewhat insulted, concluding that the European couple did not wish to share the intimacy of their home and that they therefore did not really want to become friends.

7. An American teacher gives a lecture in Beijing to a group of Chinese college students. The students listen politely but make no comments and ask no questions. The teacher concludes that her lecture was uninteresting. A colleague consoles her by saying that the students didn't understand her lecture and suggests that on future occasions she attempt to simplify some of the more complex material.

8. A college student has just heard the news that her favorite uncle has died. She bites her lip, pulls herself up, and politely excuses herself from the group of foreign students with whom she was having dinner. The Russian thinks: "How unfriendly." The Italian thinks: "How insincere." The Brazilian thinks: "How unconcerned." The fellow American thinks: "How brave."

9. An Arabian college student leaves the windows of his dormitory room open and blasts his stereo. The American students overhearing the stereo can't understand how this normally polite and considerate student could suddenly act so inconsiderate.

10. A politician is scheduled to give a 20-minute speech on economic trends. He speaks for exactly 20 minutes. The American listeners conclude that the speaker had prepared well and was considerate of his audience. The Latin American listeners conclude that the speaker was not really interested in his topic or his audience.

The "answers"—actually, the *possible* answers, since we can only guess at what went wrong here—are presented in the accompanying box.

The purpose of this little excursion, which I drew in large part from J. Vernon Jensen's insightful discussion, was to illustrate the wide variety of issues involved in intercultural communication and the numerous potential obstacles to which we need be alerted.

THE IMPORTANCE OF INTERCULTURAL COMMUNICATION

A number of factors have combined to produce a situation in which intercultural communication is today more important and more vital than at any other point in history.

Mobility

The mobility of people throughout the world is at its height. Travel from one country to another and from one continent to another, once reserved for the very rich but now relatively commonplace, is at an all-time high. People now travel frequently to other countries and other cultures for the pleasure of exploring new lands and different people and for the economic opportunities that may exist in other parts of the world. Our interpersonal relationships are becoming increasingly intercultural.

"Answers" to the Intercultural Excursion

1. A Filipino expects to be invited a number of times before accepting a dinner invitation. When an invitation is given only once it is viewed as insincere.
2. The young girl might have maintained eye contact, which to an Indonesian would be considered disrespectful.
3. Arabs generally maintain shorter distances in their interpersonal interactions than do Americans. As a result, the Arab is often considered overly forward, while the American is considered cold.
4. To the Moslem the left hand is not used for eating or for shaking hands. Rather, it is used to clean oneself after excretory functions, so using the left hand to eat or to shake hands is considered insulting and obscene.
5. Calling the waiter by hitting a glass with a utensil is a common and expected custom among many Latin Americans.
6. Many Europeans who live in small apartments feel that it is more courteous to entertain in a restaurant. This difference is probably exaggerated by the reputation many Americans have of being wealthy and of expecting to be entertained "in style."
7. Chinese students generally do not ask questions; to do so would imply that the teacher has not been clear or that they do not know what they should know. Their silence does not at all reflect on the clarity of the professor's lecture or on their interest in the lecture.
8. To Americans it is a sign of bravery to endure pain (physical or emotional) in silence and without any outward show of emotion. To members of other groups, such silence is often interpreted to mean that the individual does not consider them friends who can share such sorrow. To members of these groups, people are expected to reveal to friends how they feel.
9. In some parts of the world, radios and stereos are relatively rare and those who have such equipment often share it with others by playing it overly loud and opening the windows so that others may also enjoy the music. In the United States, where just about everyone can have access to radios and stereos, this behavior is considered inconsiderate and rude.
10. Americans are extremely time conscious. A 20-minute speech should last 20 minutes. If it does not, it is a sign that the speaker has not prepared adequately or recognized the time restraints of the audience. To many Latin Americans, speakers build up steam with time: The longer a speaker speaks, the more involved, interested in the topic and audience, and interesting he or she is seen to be.

Economic Interdependence

Today, the United States and, in fact, most countries are economically dependent on other countries. At one time, not too long ago, our economic life was bound up with that of European nations whose culture was in many ways similar to ours. Today, however, for much of our trade and especially for technological equipment we have turned to the Orient—Japan, Korea, Vietnam, and China—where cultures are drastically different from ours. Our economic lives greatly depend on our ability to communicate effectively across different cultures.

Communication Technology

The rapid increase in communication technology has brought foreign and sometimes strange cultures right into our living rooms. From the television series "Shogun" we learned a great deal about Japanese customs and history. From "The Immigrants" we learned about the many cultures that passed through Ellis Island on their way to a new life in the United States. News from foreign lands is commonplace, and we expect to see nightly—in vivid color— what is going on in countries remote in space and sometimes even in time. And, of course, we can—as competing phone companies remind us repeatedly—dial direct to just about anywhere in the world. Technology has made intercultural communication easy, practical, and inevitable.

Immigration Patterns

A walk through just about any major city in the United States will convince even the most skeptical that we are still a nation of immigrants. The immigrants coming to the United States today speak various languages, eat various foods, practice various religions, and approach work and interpersonal relationships in quite varied ways. Whether we are long-time residents or newly arrived immigrants, we are today living, going to school, and working with people who are very different from us. Our day-to-day experiences are becoming increasingly intercultural.

Political Well-Being

Today our political well-being greatly depends on that of other cultures. Political unrest in almost any part of the world—South Africa, Poland, and the Middle East, to take just a few examples—affects our own security. Small and previously powerless nations now have nuclear capabilities and consequently are now significant political forces. Intercultural communication and understanding seem now more crucial than ever.

THE DIFFICULTY IN STUDYING INTERCULTURAL COMMUNICATION

Intercultural communication is a difficult area to study and research. Two major difficulties may be identified as a way of further illustrating the uniqueness of this field.

Ethnocentrism is a particularly difficult barrier to overcome in intercultural communication. Examine your own ethnocentrism as objectively as possible. How does your ethnocentrism influence your communications with members from other cultures?

Ethnocentrism

One difficulty in studying intercultural communication is our tendency to see others and their behaviors through our own cultural filters, often as distortions of our own behaviors. Often this tendency may be described as *ethnocentrism*—the tendency to evaluate the values, beliefs, and behaviors of one's own culture as being more positive, superior, logical, and natural than those of other cultures. We need to see both ourselves and others as different but equal, with neither being inferior or superior.

Sexism and heterosexism are close relatives to ethnocentrism. Consider, for example, one of the most common sexist examples, the tendency to define maleness as the norm and femaleness as the deviation from this norm. Under this "illogic," a male who belongs to Actor's Equity and who studies at Actor's Studio is referred to as an *actor*. But a woman who belongs to the same group and who studies at the same place is an *actress*—a deviation from the norm, *actor*. The same sexist convention created the now rarely used *poetess* and *Jewess*, and still governs the use of *man* to refer to all human beings, both men and women.

This situation parallels the heterosexist tendency to specify "gayness" and "lesbianism." We do not, for example, speak of a "heterosexual teacher" or a "straight doctor," because we assume the norm of heterosexuality. Instead, we qualify the terms only when the person referred to is not a member of what is considered the norm, and so we say "gay teacher" and "lesbian doctor."

The subtle messages that ethnocentric, sexist, and heterosexist language (and thinking) communicate and the barriers to the understanding and appreciation of cultural differences can hardly be overestimated.

Mindlessness and Mindfulness

A second difficulty may be appreciated by considering the distinction that psychologist Ellen Langer draws between mindless and mindful states. According to Langer, when we are in a mindless state, we operate with a number of assumptions that would not normally pass intellectual scrutiny. For example, we know that cancer is not contagious and yet we often avoid touching cancer patients. We know that blind people do not have hearing problems and yet we sometimes use a louder voice when talking to the blind. Similar unrealistic behaviors were explored by Wheeler, Farina, and Stern who found that approximately one-third of participating college students indicated that they would not go swimming in a pool used by mental patients and that they would wash their hands after touching a mental patient. When the discrepancies between available evidence and our behavioral tendencies are pointed out and our mindful state is awakened, we realize that these behaviors are not terribly logical or realistic.

When we deal with people from other cultures we are often in our mindless state and we therefore function "non-rationally," in many ways. When our mindful state is awakened, as it is in academic discussions such as this one, we quickly resort to a more logical and rational mode of thinking, and we recognize that other people and other cultural systems are different but not inferior or superior to ours. Thus, the barriers and gateways to be discussed in the next unit may appear quite logical to our mindful states but they are frequently ignored in our mindless states.

THE NATURE OF INTERCULTURAL COMMUNICATION

In order to define the nature and scope of intercultural communication, we need to inquire first into the nature of culture. We may define *culture* as the relatively specialized life-style of a group of people—consisting of their values, beliefs, artifacts, ways of behaving, and ways of communicating—that is passed on from one generation to the next. Included in culture would be all that members of a social group have produced and developed—their language, modes of thinking, art, laws, and religion.

The process by which culture is transmitted from one generation to another is referred to as *enculturation*. We learn culture; we do not inherit it. It is transmitted through learning, not through genes. Our parents, peer group,

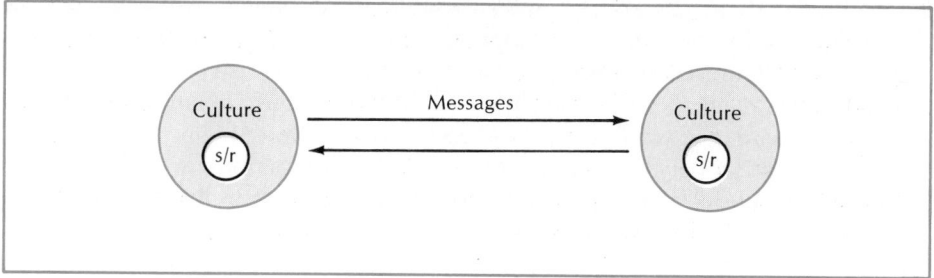

FIGURE 27.1 A model of intercultural communication.

schools, religious institutions, and government agencies are the main teachers of culture; enculturation takes place through these groups. If you think about your own patterns of behavior or your values or beliefs, you will probably find that they can be traced through learning from one of these groups.

Intercultural communication, then, refers simply to communication that takes place between persons of different cultures—between persons who have different cultural beliefs, values, or ways of behaving.

We may further explain this concept with reference to the model presented in Figure 27.1. The larger circles represent the culture of the individual communicator who is in turn symbolized by the smaller circle (source/receiver). Note the following corollaries of this model:

1. Each communicator is a member of a different culture. In some instances the cultural differences are relatively slight—say, between persons from Canada and the United States. In other instances the cultural differences are great—say, between persons from Borneo and Germany, or between persons from rural China and industrialized England.
2. All messages are sent out of a specific and unique cultural context, and that context influences their content and form. We communicate as we do largely as a result of our culture; it influences every aspect of our communication experience.
3. All messages are received through the filters imposed by a specific and unique cultural context that influences what is received (that is, the content) and how it is received (that is, the form). For example, some cultures rely heavily on television or newspapers and trust them implicitly. Other rely on face-to-face interpersonal interactions, distrusting any of the mass communication systems.

Subcultures

Earlier (in Unit 9) we discussed subcultures and noted that these were smaller groups living and interacting within the larger majority or dominant culture. We also noted that these subcultures frequently develop their own communication systems to increase communication efficiency, to enable members to identify each other, to ensure communication privacy, and to impress and confuse others. We approached subcultures and sublanguages as a way of furthering our understanding of language, and to that end we focused particularly on communication within the subculture.

Here, we need to place the topic of subcultures and sublanguages within this intercultural context. Communication between different subcultures as well as communication between a subculture and the dominant or majority culture would be considered "intercultural communication." Communications between heterosexuals and homosexuals, between born-again Christians and atheists, between the rich and the poor, between the young and the old, and even between the sexes represent just a few of the many subcultural connections that might be identified and that have now assumed increasing importance as subcultural groups demand and receive recognition and equality.

Our daily lives, school systems, work environments, and town layouts all combine to make communication interaction with people from other subcultures inevitable and essential. As a bonus, such communication can also be personally rewarding in providing us with new and significant insights into our own behaviors and customs and in enlarging our own world view.

The Forms of Intercultural Communication

The model of intercultural communication presented in Figure 27.1 may just as logically be a model of communication between different subcultures or between a variety of other groups. In summary, the following types of communication may all be considered "intercultural" and, more importantly, subject to the same barriers and gateways to effective communication identified in the following unit.

1. Communication between cultures—for example, between Chinese and Portuguese, or between French and Norwegian. (The term *intercultural* is used broadly to refer to all forms of communication among persons from different groups as well as to the more narrowly defined area of communication between different cultures.)
2. Communication between races (sometimes referred to as *interracial communication*)—for example, between blacks and whites.
3. Communication between ethnic groups (sometimes referred to as *interethnic communication*)—for example, between Italian-Americans and German-Americans.
4. Communication between religions—for example, between Roman Catholics and Episcopalians, or between Moslems and Jews.
5. Communication between nations (sometimes referred to as *international communication*)—for example, between the United States and Mexico, or between France and Italy.
6. Communication between subcultures—for example, between doctors and lawyers, or between the blind and the hard of hearing.
7. Communication between a subculture and the dominant culture—for example, between homosexuals and heterosexuals, or between senior citizens and the not-yet seniors.
8. Communication between the sexes—between men and women.

The term *cross-cultural* is often used interchangeably with the term *intercultural communication*. However, there is good reason for distinguishing between the two. Intercultural theorists William Gudykunst and Young Kim explain the distinction by noting that "the term cross-cultural implies a comparison of some phenomena across cultures." For example, if we were to study self-disclosure within two different cultures—say, Germany and Japan—we would be examining cross-cultural communication. On the other hand, if we were to study how Germans and Japanese communicate with each other, we would be examining intercultural communication.

Because our ways of communicating are largely culturally determined, persons from different cultures will communicate differently. We need to take special care to see that the cultural differences do not prevent meaningful interaction, but instead serve as sources for enriching our communication experiences. If we are to communicate effectively, we need to understand and appreciate these differences, as well as the common barriers and effectiveness principles for communication between different cultures—the topic of the following unit.

SUMMARY

1. Intercultural communication has become increasingly important because of increased mobility of people throughout the world, the economic interdependence of most countries, advances in communication technology, changing immigration patterns, and the political necessity to understand different cultures.

2. *Ethnocentrism* refers to the tendency to evaluate other cultures negatively and our own culture positively. The practice of ethnocentrism is one of the major reasons that effective intercultural communication is so difficult to study and to achieve.

3. Distinguishing between states of mindfulness (in which we are aware of the logic that governs behaviors) and mindlessness (in which we are unaware of this logic) is helpful in understanding why intercultural communication may seem quite simple on the surface but may be extremely difficult in actual practice.

4. *Culture* may be defined as the relatively specialized life-style of a group of people—consisting of their values, beliefs, artifacts, ways of behaving, and ways of communicating—that is passed on from one generation to the next.

5. The process by which culture is transmitted from one generation to another is referred to as *enculturation*.

6. Culture influences the messages we send and how we send them and the messages we receive and how we receive them. Communication rules and customs are culturally determined.

7. Communication between different subcultures as well as that between a subculture and the majority or dominant culture are also examples of intercultural communication.

8. Intercultural communication encompasses a broad range of communication and includes (in addition to the subcultural examples given above) at least the following: communication between cultures, between races, between ethnic groups, between religions, and between nations.

SOURCES

The area of intercultural communication is a fast-growing one and the literature is extensive. Three excellent introductory works are Larry A. Samovar, Richard E. Porter, and Nemi C. Jain, *Understanding Intercultural Communication* (Belmont, Calif.: Wadsworth, 1981); Carley H. Dodd, *Dynamics of Intercultural Communication*, 2d ed. (Dubuque, Iowa: Wm. C. Brown, 1987); and William B. Gudykunst and Young Yun Kim, *Communicating with Strangers: An Approach to Intercultural Communication* (New York: Random House, 1984). An up-to-date collection of readings will also prove helpful in surveying this area: Larry A. Samovar and Richard E. Porter, eds., *Intercultural Communication: A Reader*, 4th ed. (Belmont, Calif.: Wadsworth, 1985). The examples I used to open this unit were drawn in large part from J. Vernon Jensen's excellent "Perspective on Nonverbal Intercultural Communication," in *Intercultural Communication: A Reader*, pp. 256–272. On mindfulness and mindlessness, see Ellen J. Langer, "Rethinking the Role of Thought in Social Interaction," in J. H. Harvey, W. J. Ickes, and R. F. Kidd, eds., *New Directions in Attribution Research*, vol. 2 (Hillsdale, N.J.: Lawrence Erlbaum, 1978), pp. 35–58, and "Minding Matters: The Consequences of Mindlessness/Mindfulness," in Leonard Berkowitz, ed., *Advances in Experimental Social Psychology* (New York: Academic Press, in press). For the research cited and additional experimental evidence for concepts of mindlessness and mindfulness, see Edward E. Jones, Amerigo Farina, Albert H. Hastorf, Hazel Markus, Dale T. Miller, and Robert A. Scott, *Social Stigma: The Psychology of Marked Relationships* (New York: W. H. Freeman and Co., 1984). On sexist language, see, for example, Barrie Thorne, Cheris Kramarae, and Nancy Henley, eds., *Language, Gender and Society* (Rowley, Mass.: Newbury House Publishers, 1983), and James W. Chesebro, ed., *Gayspeak* (New York: Pilgrim Press, 1981).

UNIT 28
INTERCULTURAL COMMUNICATION:
Barriers and Gateways

LEARNING GOALS

After completing this unit, you should be able to

1. define *language relativity*
2. provide at least two examples of some semantic aspects and of some structural aspects of language relativity
3. identify at least three implications of language, communication, and cultural relativity for the study of human communication
4. identify and explain the operation of at least five barriers to intercultural communication
5. define *culture shock* and explain how this may function as a communication barrier
6. explain how the characteristics of effective interpersonal communication apply to intercultural communication

In this consideration of intercultural communication, we explore three major topics. First, we examine the foundation for much intercultural communication research and theory—namely, the relationships of language and cultural relativity; here, we consider differences among languages and the implications of these differences. Second, we examine some of the most common and potent barriers to intercultural communication and understanding. Third, we propose some guidelines (*gateways*) for making our own intercultural communication more effective and satisfying.

LANGUAGE AND CULTURAL RELATIVITY

In George Orwell's *1984*, a futuristic novel set in Oceania in the year 1984, the average citizen is a rather helpless creature, forbidden to love or even to think thoughts contrary to those of the party. Everywhere, the telescreen is watching, and everywhere there are posters depicting Big Brother, with the caption "Big Brother Is Watching You." There were three slogans of the party, and together these give us a first glimpse of the role of language in *1984*:

WAR IS PEACE

FREEDOM IS SLAVERY

IGNORANCE IS STRENGTH

The aspect of the novel particularly relevant to intercultural communication deals with "Newspeak"—a newly developed language that is expected to replace English by the year 2050. Already in 1984 people are speaking this new language, newspapers are using it, and books are being written and rewritten in Newspeak. The aim of Newspeak and the very reason for its creation were to control thought. Eliminating the words for concepts and ideas that were contrary to the party line, it was assumed, would eliminate the thoughts themselves.

The general idea that language influences thought and ultimately behavior got its strongest expression from linguistic anthropologists. In the late 1920s and throughout the 1930s, the view was formulated that the characteristics of language influence our cognitive processes. And since the languages of the world differ greatly in regard to their semantic and structural characteristics, it seemed logical to argue that people speaking widely different languages would also differ in how they viewed and thought about the world. This view of language generated a great deal of interest among linguists, anthropologists, psychologists, sociologists, and communicologists. The theory itself is referred to by different labels: *linguistic relativity*, *Whorfian hypothesis*, and *Sapir-Whorf hypothesis*. The latter two come from the people who are most closely associated with the formulation of the hypothesis—Benjamin Lee Whorf and Edward Sapir.

In his famous *Language* (1929), Edward Sapir wrote:

> The "real world" is to a large extent unconsciously built up on the language habits of the group. The worlds in which different societies live are distinct worlds, not merely the same world with different labels attached. We see and hear and otherwise experience very largely as we do because the language habits of our community predispose certain choices of interpretation.

Whorf, who gave the linguistic relativity hypothesis its strongest statement, noted:

> The background linguistic system (in other words, the grammar) of each language is not merely a reproducing instrument for voicing ideas but rather is itself the shaper of ideas, the program and guide for the individual's mental activity, for his analysis of impressions, for his synthesis of his mental stock in trade. . . . We dissect nature along lines laid down by our native languages. The categories and types that we isolate from the world of phenomena we do not find there because they stare every observer in the face; on the contrary, the world is presented in a kaleidoscopic flux of impressions which has to be organized by our minds—and this means largely by the linguistic systems in our minds.

In examining this hypothesis we first look at some of the semantic aspects, and second at some of the structural aspects of language relativity.

Some Semantic Aspects of Language Relativity

A great deal of anecdotal evidence has been assembled on the relationship between the semantics of a language and the way in which the speakers of that language see the world or behave.

Words, Perception, and Thought

Perhaps the most famous examples of such evidence refer to the fact that in Eskimo there are many words for *snow*, whereas in English there is only one. In Arabic there are many words for different types of horses, whereas in English there are just a few. The Trobrian Islanders have numerous terms for yams at the various stages of their development, whereas speakers of English have but one term. Conversely, in English we have three words for what the Hopi Indian denotes with one word: we distinguish *plane*, *fly* (the insect), and *pilot*, but in Hopi all three of these nouns are denoted by *Masa'ytaka*. The Hopi distinguish *pahe* (running water, as in the ocean or from a waterfall or fountain) from *keyi* (still water in a glass or bowl), whereas we make no such distinction in English.

One of the most interesting examples is the way in which the Eskimo language classifies the different kinds of seals. In Eskimo one category of nouns denotes a young spotted seal, a female harbor seal, and a swimming male ribbon seal. The giant bearded seal, although belonging to the same mammalian classification as the former seals, is not in the same language category. The reason is that the division in the Eskimo language is not based on the anatomy of the seal but rather on the hunting practices of the people. The three seals of the same linguistic category can all be hunted and killed by a single hunter; they therefore form one group. But the giant bearded seal can be killed only by a group of hunters and so is put into a different language category.

Words and Behavior

In an attempt to explore the extent to which words influence what we see and how we behave, a study conducted some years ago by John Carroll may be used as an illustration. Carroll's study focused on speakers of Hopi and English. Groups of three pictures each were shown to speakers of Hopi and to speakers of English; all the subjects were required to do was to group the two pictures that seemed to go best together. It was hypothesized that the Hopi and the English speakers would group the pictures differently because of differences in their languages. For example, of the three pictures in Figure 28.1, the English speakers grouped a and c or b and c together but the Hopi grouped a and b together. The reason offered is that in Hopi, the word *leluwi* means "to apply or spread over a surface" and this encompasses pictures a and b, whereas in English the word *painting* covers both b and c, and *decorating* covers both a and c.

Of the three pictures in Figure 28.2, the Hopi grouped a and b together because the actions depicted here are covered by the related terms *wehekna* (spilling a liquid) and *wa:hokna* (spilling a nonliquid). The word *dropping*, however (picture c), is denoted by a totally unrelated term, *po:sna*. English speakers grouped b and c most often because these were both covered by the term *accidental*.

Evaluating the Evidence

Such evidence—and numerous other examples could be given—has been used to argue that the vocabulary of our language determines in part the world we see and the world to which we respond. It does seem reasonable to conclude that by looking at the vocabulary of a language we can tell something about what is important to the speakers of the language. If there are many words for snow in Eskimo and for yams among the Trobrian Islanders, then it seems

FIGURE 28.1 Grouping experiment I.

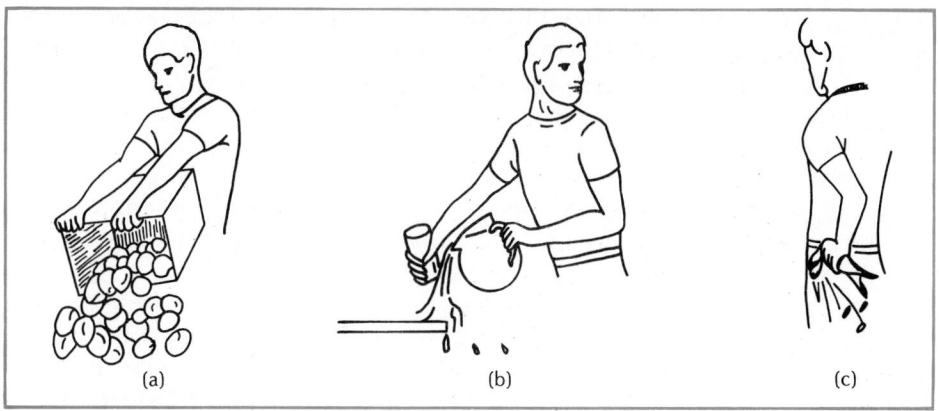

(a)   (b)   (c)

FIGURE 28.2 Grouping experiment II.

logical to argue that snow and yams are important to these particular cultures. Similarly, the vocabulary of a language may well focus our attention on certain aspects of reality rather than on others. And so the distinction between spilling and dropping in Hopi and between accidental and nonaccidental dropping in English may well direct our attention to specific facets of the world.

What seems equally clear, however, is that these differences may be learned relatively easily. That is, if we cared enough about yams we would soon learn the various distinctions and would in all likelihood notice whatever the Trobrian Islanders notice.

Some Structural Aspects of Language Relativity

The more convincing (if not the more interesting) examples of linguistic relativity center on the grammar rather than the vocabulary of the different languages.

Grammar, Perception, and Thought

For example, in English we make distinctions on the basis of tense; we distinguish present from past and future. This is the extent of our distinctions in terms of verbs. But in Hopi, distinctions are made in terms of the validity of a statement. A statement of fact from immediate observation is distinguished from a statement of fact from memory, and both are distinguished from a statement of expectation and a statement of a general law. Whorf argued that the absence of tenses as we know them in Hopi was consistent with their timeless and ahistorical view of the world; past, present, and future all belong to a continuous span of time wherein sharp divisions are unnecessary. Hopi therefore distinguish the duration of events and their certainty rather than the specific time at which they occurred. Note how differently we treat time in English. We can *waste* time or *save* it; we can *buy* time and *sell* time. We keep records, diaries, accounts, and histories. We develop elaborate schedules to keep us on time and it is imperative not only that the show go on but that it go on on time. The Hopi do not measure time in the same way. For the Hopi it is more important to be concerned with the proper sequence of events rather than the time in which the events took place. An English-speaker building a house would attempt to get the house built as soon as possible, but the Hopi would not rush and might well take years to build the house without any apparent frustration about losing time. What is most important to the Hopi is that the sequence of events occurs in the right order.

It has also been proposed that English is an inductive language, wherein the noun is preceded by the various adjectives. French and many of the Romance languages, on the other hand, are deductive—the noun comes first and is followed by the various adjectives. This difference has been related by Edmund Glenn to the differences in the English and French way of looking at the world. The English legal system is largely inductive: A series of precedents culminate in a general law. The French legal system on the other hand is largely deductive: A general rule comes first and is used to deduce the various specific applications. Similarly, Glenn notes the French have more concern for broad philosophical issues, whereas the English and Americans have more concern for details.

One of the most interesting examples of differing world views has been supplied by Peter Farb. Japanese women who married Americans were interviewed at different times—at times in English and at times in Japanese. During these interviews a few of the same questions were asked in both languages. The women were, for example, asked to complete different sentences. The responses they gave varied depending on the language in which they were interviewed. For example, when asked to complete the sentence "When my wishes conflict with my family's . . ." they answered in English "I do what I want" but they answered in Japanese "It is a time of great unhappiness." The sentence "I will probably become . . ." was answered in English with "a teacher" but in Japanese with "a housewife." The sentence "Real friends should . . ." was completed in English with "be very frank" but in Japanese it was answered with "help each other."

Grammar and Behavior

In a study very similar in design to that reported by John Carroll, Joseph Casagrande compared the grouping responses of Navaho and English children. In Navaho it is necessary to include some reference in the stem of the verb to the form of the object being considered. For example, if I ask someone to hand me an object in Navaho, I must distinguish the form of the object and say *sanleh* if it is a long flexible object like a piece of string, *santiih* if it is a long rigid object, and *sanilcoos* if it is a flat, flexible object such as a piece of paper. Because of this grammatical feature, it was hypothesized that Navaho children would group objects on the basis of form whereas English children—as has been shown repeatedly—would group objects on the basis of color. The children were presented with two objects and were asked to select the object that best went with a third object. For example, the children were presented with a yellow rope and a blue stick and were asked to select the one that best went with a blue rope. Navaho children grouped the two ropes together but English children grouped the two blue objects together.

Evaluating the Evidence

Such differences do not seem particularly great and would seem able to be easily changed if there were such a need. That is, from the purely linguistic point of view, the similarities among languages seem to far outweigh the differences. And in terms of perception and behavior it seems that there are even greater similarities. The differences in language and, concomitantly, in perception and behavior seem largely differences in ease of reference rather than in the ability or inability to express certain ideas or thoughts. So while we may conclude that differences among languages do not make for insurmountable problems, they do present us with a sufficient number of examples to sensitize us to some of the possible problems that may arise. And perhaps this increased sensitivity will help us to eventually avoid misunderstandings brought about by language differences.

Implications for Human Communication

Although many implications can be deduced from the research and theory in language and cultural relativity, only four are identified here.

First, the language we speak helps to structure what we see and how we see it. The language does not prevent us from seeing anything, nor does it force us to see other things; however, it does make easier our seeing certain things and overlooking other things. As a result, people speaking widely differing languages will *tend* to see the world somewhat differently.

Second, translations—especially of isolated words but also of sentences and of entire dialogues or speeches—only approximate similarity of meaning. Because the meanings of most terms are so interwoven with one's culture, it is impossible to obtain exact translation equivalents. Even if the denotative meanings were capable of being duplicated, the connotative meanings could never be. For example, consider the meaning of the term *wife* in the United States and, say, in the Moslem world. Denotatively we may arrive at a similar referent, but when it comes to connotative meaning the differences would be great.

Third, languages reflect the culture of which they are a part. The more widely different the cultures, the greater the language differences. Thus, it will be a great deal easier for persons from Italy and Spain to eventually communicate effectively than it would be for persons from China and Saudia Arabia.

The most general and most important implication that can be drawn from this research and theory on language and cultural relativity is that differences among languages do not make for terribly significant differences in perception, thought, and behavior. The differences that do occur and the problems and difficulties we have in intercultural communication are due, it seems, not to differences in the languages we speak but to the way in which we use or fail to use some basic communication principles. Our attention, then, needs to be directed to examining both the obstacles or barriers and the gateways to effective intercultural communication.

BARRIERS TO INTERCULTURAL COMMUNICATION

Murphy's law, "If anything can go wrong, it will," is especially applicable to intercultural communication, perhaps the most delicate and sensitive area of communication. Knowing some of the more prevalent barriers may help us to avoid them or at least to counteract their effects. Intercultural communication is, of course, subject to all the same barriers and problems as are other forms of communication; these have been discussed throughout this volume. Here we cover the barriers that are unique to the intercultural communication encounter.

Barrier One: Ignoring Differences Between Yourself and the Culturally Different

Perhaps the most prevalent barrier occurs when we assume similarities and ignore differences. This is especially true, it seems, in the area of values, attitudes, and beliefs. We can easily see and accept different hairstyles, clothing, and foods, but when it comes to basic values and beliefs, we seem to assume that deep down we are really all very similar. We aren't. When we assume similarities and ignore differences, we implicitly communicate to others that our ways are the right ways, and further, that their ways are not important enough to worry about and to take into consideration.

Barrier Two: Ignoring Differences Among the Culturally Different Group

Within every cultural group there are wide and important differences. Just as all Americans are not alike, neither are all Indonesians, Greeks, Mexicans, and so on. When we ignore these differences we are guilty of stereotyping—of assuming that all persons covered by the same label (in this case a national or racial label) are the same.

As any group gets larger, their characteristics approach the familiar bell-shaped curve, in which most individuals cluster around the middle but significant numbers fall at both the low and the high ends.

Another way of visualizing and keeping these important variations and differences in mind is to recognize that within each culture there are numerous subcultures, and these subcultures differ greatly from each other and from the majority culture. Further, the subculture in one culture may have more in common with that same subculture in another culture than it does with its own culture.

Barrier Three: Ignoring Meaning Differences in Verbal and Nonverbal Messages

Earlier, we pointed out that meaning does not exist in the words used but in the person using the words. We need to be especially sensitive to this simple principle when it comes to intercultural communication. Consider, for example, the differences in meaning that seem to exist for such words as *woman* to an American and a Moslem, *religion* to an Italian and a Russian, and *dinner* to a Chinese rice farmer and a Wall Street executive. Thus, even though the same word is used, its connotative meanings will vary greatly depending in large part on the listeners' cultural definitions.

When it comes to nonverbal messages, the potential differences seem even greater. Thus, the over-the-head clasped hands that signify victory to an American may signify friendship to a Russian. To an American, holding up two fingers to make a V signifies victory, but to certain South Americans, it is an obscene gesture that corresponds to our extended middle finger.

Barrier Four: Violating the Cultural Rules and Customs That Regulate the Content and Flow of Communication

Each culture has its own rules for communicating. These rules identify what is thought appropriate and what is thought inappropriate. Thus, for example, in our culture we would call the person we wish to date three or four days in advance; in other cultures we might be expected to call the parents weeks or even months in advance. In our culture we say, as a kind of general friendly gesture, "come over and pay us a visit"; to members of other cultures, this comment is sufficient for the listeners to actually come and visit at their convenience.

In some cultures, respect is shown by avoiding direct eye contact with the person to whom one is speaking; in other cultures this same eye avoidance would signal disinterest. In some cultures men walk arm-in-arm; in other cultures this would be considered inappropriate.

Barrier Five: Evaluating Differences Negatively

Even when we perceive the differences between cultures and within any given culture, we still have to be careful that we do not evaluate these differences negatively—that we do not fall into the trap of ethnocentric thinking. When we use such thinking, we put the other person on the defensive and create a relationship in which we are superior (thus being in the position of evaluators) and they are inferior (thus being in the position of being evaluated).

Cultural variations, by definition, are learned behaviors that have simply been passed down from one generation to another. They are not natural or innate behaviors. Consequently, these culturally determined behaviors should be viewed nonevaluatively, as different but equal.

Culture shock is one of the less frequently mentioned barriers to intercultural communication. Have you ever experienced culture shock? What effects did it have on you and on your interactions with others? How might culture shock interfere with intercultural communication?

Barrier Six: Culture Shock

Culture shock refers to the psychological reaction one experiences at being placed in a culture very different from one's own or from what one is used to. Although culture shock is normal and is experienced by most people entering a new and different culture, it is often extremely unpleasant and frustrating. Part of this unpleasantness and frustration results from the feelings of alienation, conspicuousness, and difference from everyone else. When we experience culture shock and lack knowledge concerning the rules and customs of this other society, we cannot communicate effectively and are apt to blunder frequently and seriously.

The person experiencing culture shock may not know some very basic things:

- how to ask someone for a favor or pay someone a compliment
- how to extend or accept an invitation for dinner
- how to treat time, how early or how late to arrive for an appointment, or how long to stay
- how to distinguish seriousness from playfulness, and politeness from indifference

- how to dress for an informal, formal, or business function
- how to order a meal in a restaurant, how to order what will prove agreeable, or how to summon a waiter

Anthropologist Kalervo Oberg, who first used the term *culture shock,* notes that it actually occurs in stages. These stages, incidentally, seem useful for examining many encounters with the new and the different—for example, going away to college, getting married, or joining the military.

Stage One: The Honeymoon   At first there is fascination, even enchantment, with the new culture and its people. Cordiality and friendship characterize these early and superficial relationships. Many tourists remain at this stage because their stay in foreign countries is usually so brief.

Stage Two: The Crisis   Here, the vast differences between one's own culture and the new one create problems, and feelings of frustration and inadequacy come to the fore. This is the stage at which we experience the actual shock of the new culture.

Stage Three: The Recovery   During this period we acquire the skills necessary to function effectively; we learn the language and ways of the new culture, and our feelings of inadequacy subside.

Stage Four: The Adjustment   At this final stage we adjust to and come to enjoy the new culture and the new experiences. Although we may experience periodic difficulties and strains, the experience as a whole is a pleasant one.

Culture shock may also be experienced when people, after living in a foreign culture for a considerable period, return to their original culture. For example, Peace Corps volunteers who have worked in a rural and economically deprived area and then return to Manhattan, Beverly Hills, or Las Vegas, or sailors who have served for a long period aboard ship and then return to an isolated farming community would also experience a kind of culture shock. In these cases, however, the recovery period would usually be shorter and the sense of inadequacy and frustration a great deal less.

GATEWAYS TO INTERCULTURAL COMMUNICATION

All that has been said throughout this book is applicable to intercultural communication and so, in a sense, all the principles or guidelines for effective intercultural communication have already been identified. I take this opportunity, however, to reiterate these suggestions within the context of intercultural communication.

Avoiding Barriers

Perhaps the first step in identifying the gateways or guidelines to intercultural communication is to note that the barriers just identified need to be avoided. Phrased as guidelines, these suggestions are

1. Recognize the differences between yourself and the culturally different person. When in doubt, ask questions; avoid assuming similarities. At the same time, however, do recognize the value of seeking out similarities and emphasizing these points of contact.
2. Recognize that differences exist within any group. Do not stereotype, overgeneralize, or assume that differences within a group are not important.
3. Remember that meaning is in the person and not in the words or in the gestures used. Check your meanings with those of the other person to make sure that any assumed similarity (or difference) in meaning really exists.
4. Be aware of the cultural rules operating in any intercultural communication context. Become sensitive to the rules that the other person is following. Be careful not to assume that your rules are the only valid or logical ones. When in doubt, ask.
5. Avoid negative evaluation of cultural differences, both verbally and nonverbally. See cultural customs and rules (your own as well as those of others) as arbitrary and convenient rather than as natural and logical.
6. Guard against culture shock by learning as much as possible about the culture you will enter, by reading, talking with natives and those who have had experience in the culture, and viewing films.

Employing the Principles of Effective Interpersonal Interaction

In Unit 16 we noted the characteristics of effective interpersonal interaction derived from a humanistic model and those derived from a pragmatic model. These 10 characteristics are especially significant in intercultural communication and may be profitably considered within the cultural context. You may wish to review Unit 16 to fix these characteristics more clearly in mind before reading on.

Openness   Be open to the differences existing among people. Be especially open to the different values, beliefs, and attitudes, as well as ways of behaving. This does not mean that you have to adopt these ways or that you have to see them as suitable for you, but only that you recognize that people are different.

Empathy   Put yourself into the position of the person from another culture and try to see the world from this different perspective. This practice will not only enable you to communicate more effectively with the culturally different, it will also enable you to get a unique and different perspective on your own culture. And let the person know that you do feel as he or she is feeling with facial expressions, an attentive and interested body posture, and understanding and agreement responses.

Supportiveness Be descriptive rather than evaluative, spontaneous rather than strategic, and provisional rather than certain.

Positiveness Communicate positive regard to others. This is especially important in an intercultural setting because there are so many unknowns and the ability to predict what the other person is thinking and feeling is low. Therefore, put the other person at ease by a communication of positive regard.

Equality Citizens of highly industrialized countries (and especially Americans) have the reputation (whether fairly or unfairly earned) of feeling superior. Counteract this reputation by approaching the communication situation as an equal communicating with an equal.

Confidence One of the most important skills in intercultural communication is tolerating ambiguity—remaining confident and comfortable in a situation that is unlike any you have been in before. Of course, avoid the obvious extreme—arrogance.

Immediacy Immediacy is used to unite people and to surmount the differences that exist between individuals. In intercultural communication this quality takes on special importance because of the obvious and great differences existing between you and the culturally different. Communicate a sense of togetherness to counteract the obvious intercultural differences.

Interaction Management Be especially sensitive to the differences in turn-taking. Many Americans, especially those from large urban centers, have the habit of interrupting the other person or of completing the other person's sentences. Some cultures consider this especially rude.

Further, recognize that different cultures will define satisfying communications in different ways. For example, Michael Hecht and Sidney Ribeau report that Hispanics perceive a satisfying communication as centering on the acceptance of self, while white and black groups stress the future of the relationship. Further, they note that black speakers require "deeper, more intimate topical involvement" than do whites and that intimacy, for blacks, must involve trust. All this is to say that we need to know something of the culture before we can judge what, to the other, constitutes "satisfying communication."

Expressiveness When differences among people are great, some feel uneasy and unsure of themselves. Counteract this by communicating genuine involvement in the interaction. Let the other person know that you are enjoying the interaction; smile and in general allow your facial muscles to express your interest and concern.

Other-Orientation   Recognize that each person has a share in the communication interaction. Do not monopolize the conversation by talking only of yourself, choosing the topics to talk about, and relating only your experiences. Instead, orient the conversation to the other by asking questions, practicing the skills of effective and active listening, and demonstrating interest in the things that interest the other.

SUMMARY

1. *Language relativity* refers to the theory that language influences our perceptions and behaviors, and that persons speaking widely differing languages will see the world and behave differently as a result of the differences in their languages.

2. Among the barriers to intercultural communication are these: ignoring differences between yourself and the culturally different, ignoring differences among the culturally different (stereotyping), ignoring meaning differences in verbal and nonverbal messages, violating the cultural rules and customs that regulate the content and flow of communication, evaluating differences negatively, and culture shock.

3. *Culture shock* may be defined as the psychological reaction to being placed in a culture very different from one's own or from what one is used to—a feeling of alienation and conspicuousness over being different.

4. Achieving effective intercultural communication involves first, the avoidance of the common barriers: recognize differences between self and other; recognize differences among group members; remember that meaning is in the person, not in the words or gestures; be aware of the cultural rules operating in any intercultural context; avoid negative evaluation; and guard against culture shock.

5. Effective intercultural communication may be further enhanced by employing those characteristics that characterize effective interpersonal interaction—namely, openness, empathy, supportiveness, positiveness, equality, confidence, immediacy, interaction management, expressiveness, and other-orientation.

SOURCES

For language relativity, see the writings of Benjamin Lee Whorf, in John B. Carroll, ed., *Language, Thought and Reality: Selected Writings of Benjamin Lee Whorf* (New York: Wiley, 1956). For a summary of the theory and research in language relativity, see my *Psychology of Speech and Language: An Introduction to Psycholinguistics* (Washington, D.C.: University Press of America, 1981). The grouping experiment referred to in Figures 28.1 and 28.2 was conducted by John Carroll. See John B. Carroll and Joseph B. Casagrande, "The Function of Language Classifications in Behavior," in Eleanor E. Maccoby, Theodore M. Newcomb, and Eugene L. Hartley, eds., *Readings in Social Psychology,* 3d ed. (New York: Holt, Rinehart and Winston, 1958), pp. 18–31. Casagrande's experiment on grammar and behavior may be found in Carroll and Casagrande, noted above. On barriers to intercultural communications, see the works cited in the previous unit, and the articles by LaRay M. Barna, "Stumbling Blocks in Intercultural Communication" and Brent D. Ruben, "Human Communication and Cross-Cultural Effectiveness" in Larry A. Samovar and Richard E. Porter, eds., *Intercultural Communication: A Reader,* 4th ed. (Belmont, Calif.: Wadsworth, 1985), pp. 330–338 and 338–346, respectively. These articles were helpful in conceptualizing the barriers identified in this unit. I drew on them for numerous insights. On culture shock, see the original article by K. Oberg, "Cultural Shock: Adjustment to New Cultural Environments," *Practical Anthropology* 7 (1960): 177–182, and the excellent review of research and theory in Adrian Furnham and Stephen Bochner, *Culture Shock: Psychological Reactions to Unfamiliar Environments* (New York: Methuen, 1986). On cultural differences in communication satisfaction, see Michael Hecht and Sidney Ribeau, "Ethnic Communication: A Comparative Analysis of Satisfying Communication," *International Journal of Intercultural Relations* 8 (1984), 135–151.

SKILL DEVELOPMENT SUMMARY

1. Beware of **ethnocentrism** in others as well as in yourself. Avoid evaluating your own cultural values, beliefs, and ways of behaving as being more positive than others simply because they are your own.

2. Recognize that in a state of **mindlessness,** you will often operate on the basis of assumptions that would not stand the normal tests of logic.

3. Remember that one's **culture influences** the form and substance of the messages sent and the messages received. Recognize these influences in your own communications and in those of others.

4. The **subcultural groups** one belongs to will also influence the form and substance of one's communications. Be mindful of these influences as you communicate with members from other subcultures.

5. Keep in mind the implications of **language and cultural relativity.** Remember that people who speak widely differing languages will tend to see the world somewhat differently. Look for these differences. Remember that translations only approximate similarity in meaning. Don't overlook the differences that may exist in the minds of the speaker-listener. Remember that all communication systems reflect the culture of which they are a part. The larger the cultural differences, the larger the communication differences, and hence the more difficult will be meaningful communication and the greater will be the need to study intercultural communication.

6. Recognize the differences between yourself and the culturally different. Avoid **assuming similarities.**

7. Recognize the differences among group members. Avoid **stereotyping** and overgeneralizing.

8. Remember that **meaning is in the person** and not in the words or in the gestures. Whenever in doubt, check with the person for the intended meaning.

9. Sensitize yourself to the **cultural rules** operating in any intercultural communication situation; do not assume that the rules from your culture will operate here also.

10. Avoid **negative evaluation** of cultural differences.

11. Guard against **culture shock** by learning as much as you can about the new culture you will enter.

12. Be open to **cultural differences**—to different values, beliefs, and attitudes as well as ways of behaving.

13. **Empathize.** Be willing to see the world from the cultural perspective of the other person, and communicate this willingness to the other person.

14. Be **descriptive rather than evaluative,** spontaneous rather than strategic, and provisional rather than certain.

15. Communicate **positive regard** for others, especially those from different cultures.

16. Practice **equality.** Approach the intercultural situation as an equal communicating with an equal.

17. Learn to tolerate ambiguity and communicate **confidence** and a sense of comfort and ease in culturally different situations.

18. Communicate **immediacy**—a sense of togetherness—to counteract the obvious intercultural differences.

19. Practice effective **interaction management** skills. Be especially sensitive to cultural differences in turn-taking.

20. Communicate **expressiveness.** Counteract feelings of discomfort by communicating genuine involvement in the interaction: Smile, lean forward, and express interest and attention.

21. Practice **other-orientation.** Orient the conversation to the other person by asking questions, practicing the skills of effective and active listening, and demonstrating interest in what interests the other.

PART EIGHT
MASS
COMMUNICATION

29. PRELIMINARIES TO MASS COMMUNICATION: COMPONENTS, FORMS, AND FUNCTIONS

30. THEORIES OF MASS COMMUNICATION

In this final part of the text, we consider mass communication. In the "Preliminaries" unit we cover the nature of mass communication, its major forms, and the functions that mass communications serve—from the obvious "to entertain" to the not so obvious "to narcotize" and "to ethicize."

In the final unit, we discuss the major theories of mass communication and attempt to explain how these various theories account for the influence that mass communications have on individuals and on society. Also considered are the roles of opinion leaders and gatekeepers in transmitting the messages of the mass media throughout society.

Unlike many of the previous topics throughout this book, the area of mass communication is approached from the point of view of the consumer rather than the originator or sender. The emphasis here is on understanding the role of the media in contemporary society, how we are influenced by the media (and how we in turn may influence the media), and how we might improve our skills as intelligent users of the media.

UNIT 29
PRELIMINARIES TO MASS COMMUNICATION:
Components, Forms, and Functions

LEARNING GOALS

After completing this unit, you should be able to

1. identify the five components of mass communication and explain how these operate in any given mass communication situation
2. identify the three types of audience discussed in this unit
3. identify and explain the major forms of mass communication and the major functions that each serves
4. identify and explain at least six functions of mass communication
5. provide at least one example of how the media perform each of the functions identified in this unit
6. explain the distinction between functional and dysfunctional effects of the media
7. define the narcotizing and the ethicizing functions of the media

The mass media are all around us. To live even one day without mass communication would be impossible for most people. We have come to the point of "needing" our morning newspaper, our stereo on the way to school or work, our television, our movies, and our records. Without these, life would be drastically different and, for most of us, extremely difficult.

In this unit, we introduce the topic of mass communication and attempt to define this form of communication. We do this first by offering a definition of its essential characteristics. Second, we examine selected mass communication forms. Third, we explore the varied functions the mass media serve.

A DEFINITION OF MASS COMMUNICATION

Mass communication is best defined by noting its essential characteristics. We may consider these most efficiently by focusing on the five variables involved in any communication act and then particularizing them for the mass media.

Source

The mass communicator is a complex organization that goes to great expense to construct and transmit messages. Donna Cross, in *Mediaspeak*, notes that a 30-second commercial costs $250,000 to produce. At this rate, a 2-hour movie would cost approximately $60,000,000. *Indiana Jones and the Temple of Doom* cost a "mere" $27,000,000.

Although mass communications cost a great deal to produce, they cost the receiver or consumer very little, at least directly. Books are perhaps the most expensive media products because the price of a book must meet the entire cost of production. It costs us nothing to watch a television program or to listen to a radio show because we pay for the shows indirectly by purchasing the advertisers' products. The advertiser assumes the direct cost through the purchase of "air time" for commercials. What this seemingly free ride comes down to, as Donna Cross phrases it, is "double shafting: first manufacturers convince you to purchase products you might not ordinarily want or need, then they charge you for the cost of their advertising efforts."

Audience

Mass communications are addressed to the masses—an extremely large audience. Because of the vastness of the audience and because it is essential for the media to adapt to its audience—to give the audience what it wants—at least generally, the messages of mass communication systems must be directed at some typical or average type of viewer. In this way, the media attempt to secure the largest number of possible receivers as their audience. However, this works only for certain widely used products and hence certain programs. More and more, the media and the advertisers carefully research and divide the mass audience into smaller, more clearly defined targets, After all, the audiences for Hanes Panty Hose, Flintstone Vitamins, and Budweiser Beer are quite different. This process of segmenting a large audience (for example, the television audience) into more narrowly defined small groups (for example, children from 6 to 10, housewives from 25 to 40, or teenage boys) is referred to as *demassification.*

Through demassification the advertisers can direct their appeals to the specific group they wish to reach. Even though *Family Circle* magazine has a circulation close to 7 million, an ad for a motorcycle would probably be less effective there than in, for example, *Cycle World* (circulation 332,304) or *Road and Track* (circulation 730,814), which have fewer but more interested readers.

Media theorist John Merrill has identified three basic subgroups of mass communication audiences, a classification that provides us with additional insight.

The Illiterates

The *illiterates* constitute the largest group, perhaps some 60 percent of the mass communication audience. Some of these are functionally illiterate, while others are merely attitudinally illiterate—that is, even though they are able to read, they choose not to. These people rely on the picture media (television, films) rather than the print media (newspapers, books). They are passive rather than active members of society. They are oriented to fulfilling their own needs rather than to concentrating on ideas. Economically, they constitute the poor classes.

The Pragmatists

The *pragmatists* constitute about 30 percent of the total mass audience. Unlike the illiterates, the pragmatists are active; they are doers rather than watchers. They expose themselves to numerous different media; they watch television and go to the movies, but they also read newspapers, magazines, and books. They are ambitious and status-conscious; they seek information so they can advance in business or in the eyes of their peers. These people are more concerned with material attainments than with ideas, and so they are the major audience the advertiser seeks.

The Intellectuals

The *intellectuals* constitute the remaining 10 percent of the entire audience. The term *intellectual* should not be taken to mean "intelligent," although many in this group would normally be labeled intelligent. These people are concerned with issues, ideas, esthetics, and philosophy rather than with material things. As with the illiterates, the advertisers have little to work with here. Intellectuals do not care much for mass communications because they cater to the lower levels of society. This group seeks mental rather than physical or material stimulation.

Messages

The entire mass communication experience is a public one; everyone has access to the messages of the mass media. Unlike a talk at a bar or a classroom lecture, mass communications may be received by anyone. The communication is also rapid; the messages are sent to an audience as soon as they are received by the communicators. This characteristic—speed—has a number of qualifications, however: A novel may take years to write and a television series years to put together, yet once they are completed, there is little time lost in the transmission of the message. This rapid nature of mass communication refers most specifically to the broadcasting of news items and events. We can see fires, robberies, political rallies, and speeches while they are in progress. This, to use Marshall McLuhan's term, has turned us into a "global village," where world events are common knowledge.

Process

In considering process, we need to look at two dimensions: (1) the process by which the messages travel, which is essentially a one-way process; and (2) the process of selection, which is essentially a two-way process.

Mass communication is essentially one-way, going from source or sources to receivers, whereas in interpersonal communication, communication goes from source to receiver and then from receiver back to source and continues to alternate between the parties involved. In mass communication the messages flow from the media to the receivers but not back again, except in the form of letters to the editor, audience ratings, box office receipts, and the like. It is true, as Nicholas Johnson says, that we can talk back to our television sets, but we can do so only indirectly and with considerable delay, at least with network television. This special kind of message (feedback) is discussed in Unit 1.

There is a two-way *selection* process involved. The first part of this selection process refers to the media selecting the portion of the total population that it will attempt to make its audience. For example, the media might attempt to gain unmarried women in their twenties and thirties as their principal audience, and so will direct their messages to this particular group of people. The second part of this selection process refers to the selection, from all the media available, of that particular subsection of media to which a given individual will attend. Some will read *Photoplay*, while others will read *Ms., Time, Playboy,* and so on.

Context

Mass communications operate in a social context; the media both influence and are influenced by that social context. There is, in other words, a transactional relationship between the media and the society in which each influences the other. Thus, for example, the media influence the economic conditions of the society, but they are influenced by the economic conditions as well. Similarly, the media influence the political environment and at the same time are influenced by the same political environment.

FORMS OF MASS COMMUNICATION

Another approach to the definition of mass communication is to define its most significant forms. Of the numerous forms of mass communication, seven are singled out for consideration (see Figure 29.1).

Television

Without a doubt, television is the most pervasive and the most popular of all the mass media in this country and throughout a large part of the world. The televisionless world is shrinking rapidly and will soon be gone completely.

It is reported that the average television set is on approximately seven hours per day. This is a total of over 2500 hours per year, or about 106 complete days per year. Each week this comes to 47 hours, which is considerably more than the amount of time people work or sleep. It is, in short, a significant and vital part of the American way of life. Although we might argue over whether

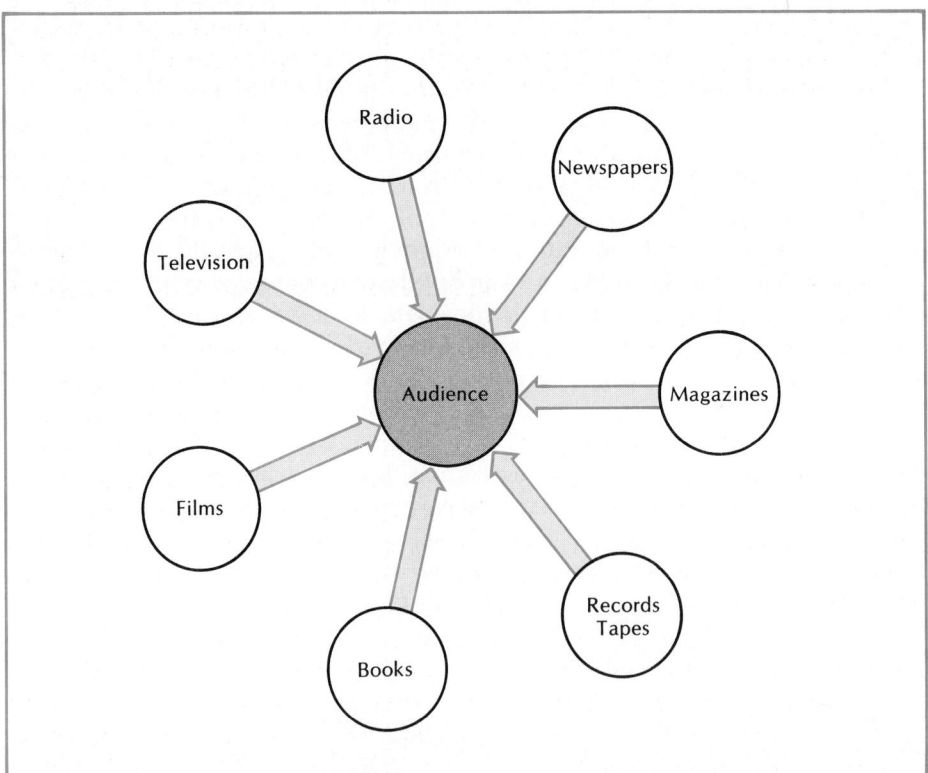

FIGURE 29.1 The mass media. Perhaps the most widely quoted of all media theorists, Marshall McLuhan saw the audience at the center of numerous attacks by the different media, as depicted here. McLuhan referred to this phenomenon as a *media implosion*: The media are directed toward the audience and bombard the audience with all sorts of sensory stimulation.

Television seems by far the most influential of all communication media. In what ways does television influence you? For example, does television influence your self-image or self-concept? Does television influence your interpersonal interactions? How does it influence your small group behavior?

this is for better or for worse, we would have to agree that American life without television would be drastically different.

Over the past 10 or 15 years television has changed drastically, and during the next 10 or 15 years it will change a great deal more. Cable TV, originally designed to provide improved reception in poor-reception areas, now operates to provide more specialized programming and is found in over 30 million homes. X-rated movies, counterculture stations and programs, and programs directed at small groups would have been impossible without cable television. Satellite television is now an important part of television and will in the next several years increase in influence. Intelsat or Early Bird goes back only to 1965, but today the entire world is connected through satellite television.

Perhaps the development of most interest to most people is the video cassette recorder (VCR), which provides the viewer with control over the television rather than the television having control over the viewer. Because VCRs can tape shows at preset times even when the viewer is not at home, the viewer now can watch shows at any time and can watch them repeatedly. With enough VCRs, reruns of popular movies would be virtually ignored, since most viewers would have already recorded *Superman*, *Star Wars*, or *Gone With the Wind*. The fact that the viewer may edit out commercials has created considerable difficulty for the advertising industry. Some television sets now come equipped with video recorders built into the set, much as cassette players are built with stereo systems and memories are built into calculators and typewriters.

Radio

Before the advent of television, radio was the dominant mass communication system. Just as families now gather to watch the hit television shows, families used to gather to listen to the hit radio shows—"Jack Benny," "Charlie McCarthy," "The Shadow," and "The Lone Ranger"—shows we remember from trivia quizzes and from stories told by those in their forties, fifties, and sixties.

Television has usurped the dominant role of radio, and radio has had to redirect its focus. Instead of appealing to the large audience that television has permanently won over, radio has concentrated on the smaller audiences and attempts to cater to these more specialized interests—for example, opera and symphonic music lovers; news enthusiasts; country and western, disco, or rock and roll fans; and so on. At the same time, radio remains dominant in those situations in which sufficient visual attention cannot be given to the media, and it serves as a kind of background noise while one is resting on the beach, working in the office, or driving to school.

Radio apparently plays an important role for youngsters who have few close interpersonal relationships. In a study of sixth-grade boys and girls, media researcher Joseph Dominick found that those having few close interpersonal relationships listened to radio a great deal more than their peers with more interpersonal relationships. Further, those with few interpersonal relationships listened more for informational reasons and less for entertainment. Interestingly enough, there were no differences between those with few and those with many interpersonal relationships in their use of other media; television viewing, magazine reading, and movie attendance were the same for both groups.

Newspapers

Although newspapers are clearly a form of mass communication, they are less "mass" than, say, radio or television. Newspapers are read by the more educated and by older people. Generally, people between the ages of 21 and 35 rely little on newspapers.

Newspapers serve two general functions. First, they are sources of information about what is happening throughout the world and locally. Older and more educated readers use newspapers for this function. Part of this news is presented to persuade us to a particular point of view—a function that is clearly not limited to the editorial page. Some news deals with important political, economic, and social issues; some deals with "unimportant" gossip about TV and Hollywood stars, advice to the lovelorn, and human interest stories about lost dogs, stray cats, and kindly old people; and some tries to persuade us to buy everything from stocks and bonds to underwear, cologne, and meat and potatoes. The second major function is to entertain, and it is for this function that the young and the less educated generally use newspapers—whether that entertainment is in the arts, in sports, or in comics.

Many newspapers are today faced with declining readership. When this happens, advertisers put their money elsewhere. This loss of revenue forces the newspaper to cut back on various features or coverage, which further reduces readership, which further cuts down advertising revenues. The end result of this spiral is the closing of the paper—an event that is not uncommon today. Among the reasons people have given for their declining readership is that television news serves their needs in an easier and more efficient way; newspapers contain too much politics and too much crime; and newspapers are not personalized enough to serve their individual needs.

This declining readership should not lead you to assume that newspapers are not influential: They are. It has been estimated that something over 60 million copies of daily newspapers are sold each day. That represents a lot of news, a lot of advertisements, and, in general, a lot of influence.

Magazines

Much that applies to newspapers also applies to magazines. Magazines are both general and specialized. The general magazines include *Reader's Digest*, *TV Guide*, and *Family Circle*. The specialized magazines include all those that appeal to specific and relatively small audiences. For example, *Science* appeals to that relatively small group of persons concerned with sophisticated scientific developments. *Scientific American* appeals to a similar audience but one that is somewhat less specialized. *Gentlemen's Quarterly* appeals to fashion-conscious men, much as *Vogue* appeals to fashion-conscious women. *Sports Illustrated*, *Modern Bride*, *Stereo Review*, *Road and Track*, *Field and Stream*, and similar magazines, as their titles imply, likewise appeal to fairly specialized interests and audiences.

Magazines are now very big business and, in fact, most of the larger magazines are owned and controlled by major corporations. Time, Inc., for example, owns *Time*, *Life*, *Fortune*, *Sports Illustrated*, *People*, and *Money*. The Hearst Corporation owns *Good Housekeeping*, *Cosmopolitan*, *Harper's Bazaar*, *Popular Mechanics*, and *House Beautiful*. The Johnson Publishing Corporation owns *Ebony*, *Jet*, and *Tan*, and Condé Nast owns *Glamour*, *Vogue*, *House and Garden*, and *Mademoiselle*. Thus, although there are numerous different magazines, they are actually controlled by relatively few corporations, and the points of view— on significant political, social, and economic issues—are likewise relatively few.

Films

Films represent a paradox. On the one hand, television cuts severely into the profits of the movie industry, leading to the closing of numerous theaters throughout the country and to a drop in the percentage of entertainment income spent on the movies. On the other hand, films are today better than ever. Some of the most creative writing, the most expert photography, and the most ingenious music are being directed into contemporary film.

Today, films are youth-oriented and constitute one of the most convenient places for the social activities of today's teenagers. They are relatively inexpensive and easily accessible to the young. At the same time they afford the young a judicious mixture of the company of peers and yet an opportunity to maintain sufficient privacy.

Although we often think of film as synonymous with entertainment, many films serve numerous other functions, and in fact even the entertainment film does more than "just entertain." Films like *The Deer Hunter* and *Platoon* showed us how horrible war really is, *Norma Rae* showed us how unskilled workers are often exploited, and the *Rocky* movies tried to demonstrate that the American dream can be a reality. But there are other films that function primarily to influence and persuade.

The film of information is being used with considerable success in schools and business organizations. Concepts such as nonverbal communication, conference and public speaking techniques, and anatomical and physiological aspects of speech and hearing—to name just a few of those in the area of communication—are so much easier to teach with the help of films. That these films also make for greater enjoyment seems almost universally agreed.

Books

Of all the mass media, books are perhaps the most elitist. They are read by the intelligentsia of the mass communication audience, and this is true even when we add the popular pornographic or romance pocket books to this list. Generally, people who read books earn higher incomes, have attained a higher level of education, and live in the city rather than in rural areas.

Books are both entertainment and education; they offer a historical record of the past, guidance for the present, and direction for the future. Approximately 30,000 trade books (nontexts) are issued each year; approximately 5 percent (only 1,500) will sell over 5,000 copies. The vast majority will fail to secure an audience and to make money.

Records-Tapes-Cassettes-Compact Discs

Records, tapes, cassettes, and, most recently, compact discs are becoming increasingly important in entertainment and education. College students spend more on these recordings than on books. The periodic lags in such spending seem always to be countered by some new technology—stereo, tapes and cassettes, and now laser discs—that encourages even greater spending, now counted in the billions of dollars. Their recent combination with videos, popularized beyond industry expectations by Michael Jackson's "Thriller," have added a new dimension to audio-recordings. Even when only listening, many can now visualize the video.

Like film, records are designed primarily to entertain, but at the same time they influence attitudes and values. This function is seen most clearly during times of political and social turmoil. The Vietnam War, for example spawned numerous records directed at influencing attitudes and behaviors. Joan Baez and Buffy Sainte-Marie, for example, had considerable impact during this time, particularly with college students.

Today, the persuasive agents and their messages are somewhat different. Large groups have banded together to popularize and raise money for a variety of humanitarian causes. The Live Aid concert in 1985, for example, which raised some $70 million for Africa's poor, was perhaps the most widely publicized and the most successful. With Live Aid and various similar concerts, huge organizations had to be formed to coordinate the efforts of hundreds of recording stars and to collect and distribute the monies raised.

Live Aid and, for example, Willie Nelson's concerts to raise money for the farmers, gave a new dimension to the role of concerts and of musicians generally. Whereas the Woodstock concert of 1969 represented drugs, antiwar and antigovernment sentiment, and freedom from society's rules and regulations, these concerts of the 1980s seem more to represent participating actively in changing the world, helping the less fortunate, and, in general, using music and the musician's fame and talent as social forces.

THE FUNCTIONS OF MASS COMMUNICATION

The popularity and pervasive influence of the mass media can be maintained only by their serving a variety of significant functions. Nine of the most important functions are discussed here.

To Entertain

The media design their programs to entertain. In reality, of course, they attempt to entertain in order to secure the attention of the largest possible group so that they may sell this attention to advertisers. This seems to be the major reason that mass communications exist. In societies where the state supports the media or where advertising is banned from various media (as in Sweden) the process is different. In the United States and in most democracies, however, if the media did not entertain, they would no longer have viewers or readers and would quickly be out of business.

To Reinforce

It is difficult for anyone to convert someone from one attitudinal extreme to another, and the media, with all the resources and power at their disposal, are no exception. For the most part the media rarely achieve conversion, but they do function to reinforce or make stronger our beliefs, attitudes, values, and opinions. Democrats will expose themselves to democratic persuasion and will emerge reinforced from the experience. Similarly, religious people will expose themselves to messages in line with their beliefs and will emerge reinforced or stronger in their convictions.

The problem the media face in achieving something beyond reinforcement, of course, is that we are the ones who choose the messages to which we will attend, and we generally do not choose to expose ourselves to messages that may contradict our existing belief structure.

This reinforcement view applies to situations in which people are relatively polarized in their beliefs, values, and opinions. The media will achieve some conversions with those who are in the middle on any individual dimension. Thus, those who are torn between the Republicans and the Democrats may well find themselves converted to one side or the other on the basis of media messages.

Even those communications we think are changing attitudes often only reinforce existing ones. For example, it had long been assumed that "All in the Family" was changing attitudes toward prejudice and stereotyping. The entire program was assumed by many to be a satire on prejudice. Archie, in particular, was assumed to be close to an idiot, constantly being put down by his daughter and son-in-law. But the studies on this show and similar shows indicate that this is not the case. For example, Neil Vidmar and Milton Rokeach, in their study "Archie Bunker's Bigotry," found that the show reinforced rather than reduced racial and ethnic prejudice. "The data," note Vidmar and Rokeach, "seem to support those who have argued that the program is not uniformly seen as satire and those who have argued that it exploits or appeals to bigotry."

To Change or Persuade

Most often, as noted in the next unit, the media and our interpersonal interactions work together to effect persuasion—to change our attitudes, beliefs, or behaviors. We hear something on TV, discuss it with friends, read about it in the newspaper, and discuss it with family members or in class. On the basis of these media presentations as well as the interpersonal encounters, we may change our attitudes, beliefs, or behaviors.

Some changes seem to be caused by the media alone. Often these concern "insignificant" or "trivial" issues. For example, the changes in our toilet-paper buying behavior may well be greatly or even totally influenced by the media. Most people, it seems, have little interpersonal discussion about toilet paper. Except to toilet paper manufacturers, our choice of toilet paper is unimportant. Political preferences, religious attitudes, and social commitments—especially those about which we feel strongly—are not so easily changed.

Once an attitude is formed or a behavior pattern is established, the media function to *canalize* it—to channel it in specific directions. For example, once the pattern of paying $40 for a pair of jeans is established (concurrently by the media exposure to attractive models, appeals to status, and the like *and* our interpersonal interactions), the media can relatively easily channel that behavior, that value, to Guess, Calvin Klein, Sasson, or in fact to any jean with a high price tag, preferably a tag that can be easily seen.

To Educate

When we think of education we generally think of a formal school situation, with a teacher in front of the classroom and the students taking notes, hoping to get down on paper what will eventually appear on an examination. But most of our information has been learned not from the schoolroom, but from the media. We have learned music, politics, film, art, sociology, psychology, economics, and a host of other subjects from the media and not from high school or college classrooms. We learn about other places and other times from seeing a good movie as well as from reading a history textbook.

One type of education (or is it persuasion?) is to teach the viewers the values, opinions, and rules that society judges to be proper and just. That is, part of the educational function of the media is directed at socializing the audience. They do this in dramas, sitcoms, stories, discussions, articles, comics, and advertisements and commercials. In all these situations, the values of the society are expressed in an almost unspoken manner. We are taught how to dress for different occasions, what it means to be a "good" citizen, what a proper meal should consist of, how to hold a discussion or conversation, how to respond to people of different national and racial groups, how to behave in strange places, and so on.

One of the nice things about learning from the media is that it is less "painful" than learning in schools (at least in too many cases). One of the not-so-nice things about education from the media is that it is often at variance with reality. Evidence supplied by media researcher George Gerbner and reported by Donna Cross shows that heavy television viewers form an image of reality that is consistent with the image presented by television but inconsistent with the fact. For example, heavy viewers see the chances of being a victim of a crime to be 1 in 10 (in reality it is 1 in 50), think that 20 percent of the world's population lives in the United States (in reality it is 5 percent), and believe that the percentage of workers in managerial or professional jobs is 25 percent (in reality it is 5 percent). Frederick Williams, commenting on these same studies, observes:

> People who are heavy viewers of television often have stereotyped attitudes about sex roles, physicians, doctors, gangsters, or the usual inhabitants of television shows. . . . In their world, housewives may be more concerned with keeping the "bathroom bowl" clean than anything else. Husbands are bumblers who exist in situation comedies. Police officials have minute-by-minute exciting days. People "die" without all the agonies of death, and gangsters are all evil-looking.

To Confer Status

If you were to list the 100 most important people in the world, they would undoubtedly be people who have been given a great deal of mass media exposure. Without such exposure the people would not in fact be important— at least not in the popular mind. Paul Lazarsfeld and Robert Merton, in their influential "Mass Communication, Popular Taste, and Organized Social Action," put it this way: "If you really matter, you will be at the focus of mass attention and, if you are at the focus of mass attention, then surely you must really matter." Conversely, of course, if you do not get mass attention, then you do not matter, and if you do not matter, then you do not get mass attention.

Agenda-Setting

The media can also confer status (or perhaps in this case, "focus attention" is a better phrase) on issues and problems. This function is often referred to as *agenda-setting*. The media in effect tell us what is and what is not important.

Notice the things we think are important. They are in fact the very things on which the media concentrate. The obvious question is whether they are important and the media therefore concentrate on them, or whether the media concentrate on them and they therefore become important. What does seem clear is that the media surely do lead us to focus attention on their choices of subjects. Although there is clearly no one-to-one relationship between media attention and popular perception of importance (other factors—for example, interpersonal ones—are also operating), the media do set our agendas to some probably significant degree.

Recognize too that the media are controlled by persons of enormous wealth and power (whether network owners and executives, advertisers, or directors of multimillion-dollar corporations) who want to retain and increase such wealth and power. What gets attention from the media and influences the bias the media present is dictated largely by this small but extremely influential group that controls the media. The media exist to make profit for this group.

To Activate

From the advertiser's point of view, the most important function is to activate—to move consumers to action. Put simply, the media function to get the viewer or reader to buy the bread, to use Gillette, to choose Brut and not Old Spice, and in general to make all the "trivial" decisions advertisers and manufacturers consider "crucial."

The advertisers' objective is to get us to buy their product and not someone else's, as well as to buy their product instead of nothing. Room deodorizers, for example, should be a substitute for cleanliness though it is never put in these terms. If we did not buy what advertisers want us to buy, they would no longer pay for the time or space to advertise, and we would no longer have the variety of media we now have.

To Narcotize

One of the most interesting and most overlooked functions of the media is the narcotizing function. This refers to the media's function of providing the receiver with information that is confused, by the receiver, with doing something about something. The individual is drugged into inactivity as if under the influence of a narcotic. As Lazarsfeld and Merton explain it:

> The individual reads accounts of issues and problems and may even discuss alternative lines of action. But this rather intellectualized, rather remote connection with organized social action is not activated. The interested and informed citizen can congratulate himself on his lofty state of interest and information and neglect to see that he has abstained from decision and action. In short, he takes his secondary contact with the world of political reality—his reading and listening and thinking—as a vicarious performance. He comes to mistake *knowing* about problems of the day with *doing* something about them.

Lazarsfeld and Merton term this *dysfunctional* rather than functional "on the assumption that it is not in the interest of modern complex society to have large masses of the population politically apathetic and inert.'' And with seven hours of television viewing each day, there is little wonder that knowledge of problems and issues is confused with or is a substitute for action.

To Create Ties of Union

One of the functions of mass communication few people ever think of is its ability to make us feel like a member of a group. Consider the lone television viewer, sitting in his or her apartment watching television while eating a TV dinner. The television programs make this lone soul feel a part of some larger group. Whether the individual is watching members of his or her own racial group, or those who think or worship as he or she does, the viewer is made to feel a part of this larger and, by virtue of the media coverage, important group of people. These ties of union, however, are artificial; the viewers are not joined with others; they only think some connection is established between them and the actors on the small screen.

Parasocial Relationships

Many viewers develop ''parasocial'' relationships with media personalities and even with dramatic characters, and will see these people or characters as friends and advisers. As a result of this perceived relationship, viewers may wave to an actor whom they see on the street as if they are friends, write to a television doctor or lawyer for medical or legal advice, and send warning letters to their ''friends'' who are about to be murdered on the latest soap opera. As can be expected, these parasocial relationships are more important to those who spend a great deal of time with the media and who have few interpersonal relationships.

Privatization

The media, however, also function to establish the opposite of union and relationships—namely, *privatization*—the tendency for an individual to retreat from social groups into a world of his or her own. Some theorists have proposed that the tremendous quantities of information almost forced upon us by the media may overwhelm us and make us feel inadequate. Wars, inflation, crime rate, robberies, deterioration in housing, and unemployment make some people feel so inadequate and helpless in dealing with or changing such issues that they retreat into their own private worlds to concentrate on matters they can control. In many cases, this takes the form of concentrating on the trivial issues and problems that are really insignificant in the total scheme of things—the problems of getting the apartment painted, which pair of designer jeans to buy, and what restaurant to go to.

To Ethicize

By making public certain deviations from the norm, the media arouse people to change the situation. They provide viewers with a collective ethic or ethical system. For example, without the media coverage of Watergate, it seems unlikely that there would have been such a public outcry over the events that eventually led Richard Nixon to resign. Writing some 15 years before Watergate, Lazarsfeld and Merton note:

> In mass society this function of public exposure is institutionalized in the mass media of communication. Press, radio, and television expose fairly well-known deviations to public view, and as a rule, this exposure forces some degree of public action against what has been privately tolerated. The mass media may, for example, introduce severe strains on polite ethnic discrimination by calling public attention to these practices that are at odds with the norm of nondiscrimination. At times, the media may organize exposure activities into a "crusade."

Evaluating Media Functions

In evaluating and analyzing these functions of the media, keep in mind at least three related issues. First, each time we turn on the television, read a newspaper, or listen to a radio, we do so for a *unique* reason. Each and every mass communication event serves a unique function, which is at least a little bit different from every previous function. Second, every mass communication event serves a different function for each individual viewer-reader-listener. The same television program may serve to entertain one person, to educate another, and to narcotize still another. Third, the functions served by any mass communication event for any individual will be different from one time to the next. Where a particular record once served to entertain, it may now function to socialize or to create ties of union.

Earlier it was pointed out that the narcotizing function of the media is a dysfunctional one in the sense that it is detrimental to the social system; it hinders rather than fosters development and needed change. Actually, all nine functions may be viewed from a functional-dysfunctional perspective. For example, the media as entertainment are generally viewed as functional or positive; the media provide viewers with convenient, inexpensive entertainment much needed after a day's work. On the other hand, the steady and constant flow of entertainment may prove dysfunctional in discouraging people to engage in interpersonal communication, to study, to learn, to work, and so on. The media's conferral of status is functional if those gaining the status prove deserving and socially productive but dysfunctional if they prove undeserving and socially unproductive. Note, for example, that those who get the most media coverage are for the most part film and television actors—persons who usually have little of value to say and who have contributed relatively little to the betterment of society. And yet, the media tell us (by giving these people extensive coverage) that these are the people who really matter. Scientists, educators, and religious leaders, for example, get much less media coverage. In its present mode of operation, the conferral of status is frequently dysfunctional.

Each of the nine functions, then, should be seen as neither positive or negative, but as functional or dysfunctional to a certain degree. Even the most noble purpose may have some dysfunctional aspects, and even the most negative may have some functional aspects.

Manifest and Latent Functions

Each of the nine functions should also be viewed as *manifest* or *latent*. Robert Merton introduced these terms in his influential *Social Theory and Social Structure* in 1957. Manifest functions are those the media intend; they are purposeful functions. Latent functions, on the other hand, are unintended; these are functions the media accomplish without intention. For example, an advertisement may have as its manifest function the selling of a certain soap, but it may also influence our attitudes toward the role of women in society. By portraying only women in soap advertisements, the ad is teaching us values and attitudes concerning women, and this is its latent function. You would be hard-pressed to identify a mass media message that did not have both manifest and latent functions.

SUMMARY

1. The source of mass communications is generally a complex organization that goes to great expense to construct and transmit messages.

2. The audience of mass communication is extremely large and varied, making it difficult for advertisers to target their messages to a specific audience. As a result, this large and heterogeneous audience is segmented into more narrowly defined small groups—a process referred to as *demassification*.

3. John Merrill divides the mass communication audience into three subgroups: (1) The *illiterates*, about 60 percent of the mass communication audience, rely on picture rather than print media and are passive rather than active members of society; (2) the *pragmatists*, about 30 percent of the audience, are active doers rather than passive watchers and expose themselves to different media—print as well as television, and books as well as magazines; (3) the *intellectuals*, about 10 percent of the audience, are concerned with ideas and issues—with philosophy rather than material things.

4. Mass communication messages are public ones; everyone has access to the messages of the media.

5. The process by which mass communication messages travel is essentially one-way; the messages go from source to receiver but seldom from receiver to source. The process of selection is two-way; the media sources select the group to which they wish to appeal, and the receivers select the media to which they wish to attend.

6. The media operate within a social context and both influence and are influenced by that context.

7. Mass communication may also be defined by identifying its more significant forms: television, radio, newspapers, magazines, films, books, and records-tapes-cassettes-compact discs.

8. Mass communications serve a variety of functions: to entertain, reinforce, change or persuade, educate, confer status, activate, narcotize, create ties of union, and ethicize.

9. Media are most frequently used for their entertainment function, especially by the young.

10. Media are generally viewed as reinforcing existing attitudes and beliefs, since people generally expose themselves to communications with which they already agree.

11. When media function to change our attitudes and beliefs, this is usually accomplished in conjunction with interpersonal interactions.

12. The media function to educate by implicitly teaching viewers the values, opinions, and rules of society.

13. The media confer status on those individuals on which they focus their attention. The general belief seems to be that if a person is chosen for attention by the media, then that person must be important; conversely, if a person is ignored by the media, that person must be unimportant.

14. The media activate the audience; they move audience members to action—usually, to buy advertised products.

15. The media narcotize the audience by providing the receiver with information that is confused, by the receiver, with doing something about something. That is, the media drug the viewers into inactivity.

16. The media create ties of union by allowing viewers to see themselves as members of some larger group. Many viewers, in fact, develop parasocial relationships with media personalities and characters. The media also function to encourage *privatization,* the tendency for viewers to retreat from social groups into worlds of their own.

17. The media function to ethicize the audience members—to provide them with a collective ethic or ethical system.

SOURCES

For an overview of the mass communication process, see Wilbur Schramm and William E. Porter, *Men, Women, Messages and Media: Understanding Human Communication* (New York: Harper & Row, 1982). For the audiences of mass media, see Schramm and Porter, cited above, and John C. Merrill and Ralph L. Lowenstein, *Media, Messages, and Men: New Perspectives in Communication* (New York: Longman, 1979). The study of radio and interpersonal relationships was conducted by Joseph R. Dominick, "The Portable Friend: Peer Group Membership and Radio Usage," *Journal of Broadcasting* 18 (spring 1974): 161–170. On the definition of mass communication, see Charles Wright, *Mass Communication: A Sociological Perspective,* 3d ed. (New York: Random House, 1986). For a readable examination of television and its effects on society, see Donna Woolfolk Cross, *Mediaspeak: How Television Makes Up Your Mind* (New York: New American Library, 1983). On demassification, see Frederick Williams, *The New Communications* (Belmont, Calif.: Wadsworth, 1984).

On the functions of mass communication, see the seminal paper by Paul F. Lazarsfeld and Robert K. Merton, "Mass Communication, Popular Taste, and

Organized Social Action," in Lyman Bryson, ed., *The Communication of Ideas* (New York: Harper & Row, 1951), pp. 95–118, and the works by Schramm and Porter and by Wright, cited above. A thorough discussion appears in Samuel L. Becker, *Discovering Mass Communication* (Glenview, Ill.: Scott, Foresman, 1983).

For the study on "All in the Family" cited in the text and a review of previous studies in this area, see Neil Vidmar and Milton Rokeach, "Archie Bunker's Bigotry: A Study in Selective Perception and Exposure," *Journal of Communication* 24 (winter 1974): 36–47. A particularly thorough discussion of mass media, covering many of the issues considered here, is Warren K. Agee, Phillip H. Ault, and Edwin Emery, *Introduction to Mass Communications*, 8th ed. (New York: Harper & Row, 1986).

UNIT 30
THEORIES OF MASS COMMUNICATION

LEARNING GOALS

After completing this unit, you should be able to

1. define the one-step, the two-step, and the multistep views of mass communication and identify some of their limitations as explanations of how the media have an effect
2. define the play theory of mass communication
3. explain the diffusion of innovations theory
4. explain the uses and gratification approach to mass communication
5. identify the characteristics of the opinion leader
6. explain the difference between the cosmopolitan and the local opinion leader
7. define *monomorphism* and *polymorphism*
8. define *gatekeeping* and explain how this process operates in mass communication

In this final unit we examine some theories of mass communication and, in the process, gain some added understanding of the structure and function of the mass media and their role in contemporary society. Although there is no single, universally accepted theory of mass communication powerful enough to answer all our questions, the theories to be examined, taken together, provide us with considerable insight into the mass media—how they function, interact with viewers-listeners, and exert an influence on the individual and on society in general.

STEP THEORIES

A number of theories that attempt to account for how the mass media have an effect on viewers and listeners may be conveniently viewed as step theories.

The One-Step Theory

The one-step theory holds the influence of the media to be direct and immediate. People read newspapers, watch television, or listen to the radio and are persuaded by what they read, see, and hear. As a result, they change their thoughts and behaviors in accordance with the media's injunctions. Messages go only one step—from the media to the reader-viewer-listener.

A variant of this theory has been called the *silver bullet theory* by theorist Wilbur Schramm. This theory holds that the media work like bullets aimed at a target. If the gun is loaded correctly and aimed accurately, the bullet will penetrate the target—that is, the media will have the desired effect on their target audience. In this view the audience, like the target, is passive and offers no resistance. Just as the target cannot resist being penetrated, neither can the audience.

This bullet theory developed largely from the fear people had of wartime propaganda. It was assumed and feared that enemy governments would be able to change basic values and beliefs simply by firing the right messages. But receivers are active, not passive participants. Message receivers mold, shape, alter, and otherwise re-create the messages they receive. Further, listeners are selective in what they expose themselves to and what they remember. The most influential media have to be invited into a receiver's consciousness; it is the receiver who has to buy the newspaper, turn on the television, or go to the movie. And it is the receiver who decides to read or not to read the morning's editorial, who chooses to watch one station rather than another, and who sees one movie but avoids ten others. Similarly, what we remember is based largely on what we want to remember and on what is important to us.

The media, for all their power and resources, are still guests that may be invited in or locked out of our consciousness. All this is not to deny the sometimes-influential subliminal messages, and the messages that somehow get through despite our attempts to keep them out. Nevertheless, and for the most part, exposure to the vast majority of media messages is controlled by the individual.

But perhaps the major inadequacy with this one-step theory is its neglect of interpersonal interaction. Before we internalize an opinion or change an attitude, we seek interpersonal support and confirmation. The one-step approach neglects this crucial element and other interpersonal dynamics. This neglect of interpersonal influence led researchers to modify the one-step into a two-step theory.

The Two-Step Theory

A somewhat more sophisticated proposal was presented by Paul Lazarsfeld, Bernard Berelson, and Helen Gaudet in *The People's Choice.* In this study of the voters in the 1940 presidential election, these Columbia University researchers found that people were influenced more by other people and less by the mass media (then, primarily newspapers and radio). Those who did the influencing were termed *opinion leaders.* Mass communications, the researchers proposed, do not affect people directly. Instead of this one-step process, they proposed a two-step process, in which messages from the mass communications influence opinion leaders, and these opinion leaders then influence the general population in more interpersonal situations. Elihu Katz, in his 1957 "The Two-Step Flow of Communication: An Up-to-Date Report on an Hypothesis," concluded that "most opinion leaders are primarily affected not by the communication media but by still other people."

As Wilbur Schramm has noted, the two-step concept, although useful and revealing, is perhaps a bit too simple. For one thing, it is not always true; much of our information comes right from the media—whether television, newspapers, or magazines. As the media become more and more a part of our everyday life, they grow as our initial source for information on a variety of issues. Further, the media today, especially television, enjoy extremely high credibility. Many people accept as true what they see and hear on the tube without need of local opinion leaders.

Second, the concept of an opinion leader must be examined in relative rather than absolute terms. Some opinion leaders are stronger opinion leaders than others. Some are leaders of leaders, whereas others are leaders of followers. Some leaders therefore get their information from the media, whereas others get their information from other leaders. Recognize, too, that many of the opinion leaders we turn to today are themselves media personalities—the Sam Donaldsons and the Ted Koppels, for example. These people have become cohabitors with us; we let them into our homes every day, and we trust them implicitly. We have today, therefore, much less need of the local interpersonal opinion leader. Also, we are less likely to turn to interpersonal opinion leaders because we now have access to basically the same information they do. Why look to the local leader, for example, when we too can go directly to the network anchorperson?

The Multistep Theory

Developed largely out of the criticism of the two-step theory, the multistep theory holds that the influence process is a reciprocal one, which goes back and forth from the media to the people, then back to the media, then back to the people, and so on. There are, in short, many steps that must be examined before the effects of the media can begin to be explained.

This back-and-forth process seems especially true today, with media so much a part of our lives. It also seems logical in terms of the finding that people who expose themselves to one medium will often expose themselves to others as well. Inevitably the same issues and news items will be covered in the different media, and we must further assume that interpersonal interaction occurs in between. Throughout these exposures (to both media and interpersonal interactions), we are influenced and we influence others. For example, we may be influenced by the media in the morning. A friend at work might then strengthen our belief. The evening newspaper may cast some doubt on our beliefs or perhaps give us sufficient reasons for changing our attitude completely. The discussion with the family might lead us to reconsider our original beliefs, and so on. Throughout this process, we are also on the influencing side. We may influence our friend or our family, and may also influence the media in a variety of ways—by writing to the editor, by buying or not buying the products advertised on a particular show, by buying one newspaper rather than another, by picketing the studio, by calling the television station to voice our opinion, and so on.

This multistep theory seems much more accurate in describing what happens in opinion and attitude formation. And it is particularly valuable in illustrating that each person is influenced by both the media and interpersonal interactions, and in turn influences the media and others. This does not mean that the issue of media effects is now solved; we still know very little about media influence. We need to combine this multistep theory with the insights provided by a number of other theories to which we now turn.

PLAY THEORY

The *play theory* of mass communication was formulated by British theorist William Stephenson in *The Play Theory of Communication*. Stephenson draws a contrast between work and play. *Work* he defines as activity dealing with earning a living and with meeting the needs of one's body for food, clothing, and shelter. Work is a productive activity; it results in tangible benefits that are needed or desired by the individual. *Play,* on the other hand, is an unproductive activity; it accomplishes nothing other than the enjoyment or satisfaction it provides. It is fun.

Communication may be viewed in a similar way. In communication pleasure, nothing is accomplished; the participants are just having fun—they're playing. In communication *un*pleasure or communication pain, communications are intended to do work, to accomplish something—for example, to change opinion, raise money, or solicit support.

According to Stephenson, the mass media are pleasure-oriented; their primary function is to allow us to escape work and to enjoy ourselves. Audiences look to the mass media for entertainment or play, not for information, improvement, or education. The popularity of any mass medium is directly related to the degree to which it serves this function. If it allows us to escape work and gives us pleasure, it will prove popular; if it fails in this, it will prove unpopular and eventually fade out of existence.

The play theory does not explain the whole of media influence and media viewing. It does, however, draw our attention to the role of play in the success and survival of any mass communication program or system. Theories that fail to take into consideration the importance of play are sure to be inadequate and incomplete explanations.

DIFFUSION OF INNOVATIONS THEORY

A theory directed at a somewhat different aspect of media influence—the way in which communications, especially those of the mass media, influence people to adopt something new or different—is that known as the *diffusion of innovations theory.*

Diffusion refers to the new information, the innovation, or the new process as it passes through the society at large or through the relevant social system. The innovation may be of any type—for example, contact lenses, computers, electronic typewriters, food processors, behavioral objectives in teaching, experiential learning, or multimedia instruction. *Adoption* refers to individuals' positive reactions to the innovation and their incorporation of it into their habitual behavior patterns. In the process of adoption, William McEwen identifies three general stages:

1. *Information acquisition*—the information relevant to the innovation is secured and understood (for example, a teacher learns about a new approach to teaching mass communication).
2. *Information evaluation*—the information relevant to the innovation is evaluated as good, bad, or anywhere in between (for example, the teacher recognizes that the new method is more effective than the old one).
3. *Adoption or rejection*—the innovation is adopted or rejected by the individual (for example, the teacher begins to teach mass communication by this new method).

Obviously all people do not choose to adopt or reject the innovation at the same time. Researchers in the area of information diffusion generally distinguish five types of adopters (Figure 30.1).

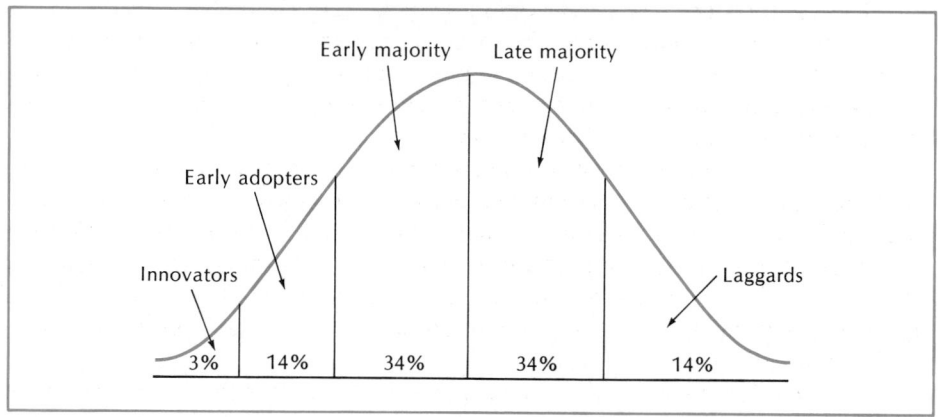

FIGURE 30.1 The five types of adopters as represented in the population.

1. *Innovators.* These are the first to adopt the innovation and constitute less than 3 percent of the total population. The innovators are not necessarily the originators of the new idea; rather, they are the ones who introduce the idea on a reasonably broad scale.
2. *Early adopters.* These people adopt the innovation next and make up about 14 percent of the total population. Sometimes called "the influentials," these people legitimize the idea and make it acceptable to people in general.
3. *Early majority.* These adopt the innovation next and constitute about 34 percent. This group follows the influentials and further legitimizes the innovation.
4. *Late majority.* This group also constitutes about 34 percent of the total population and is next-to-last in adopting the innovation. People in this group may follow either the influentials or the early majority.
5. *Laggards.* This group is the last to adopt the innovation and constitutes about 14 percent of the total population. People in this group may take the lead from people in any of the previous three groups.

These five groups constitute almost 100 percent of the population. The remaining portion are referred to as "diehards," and these are people who never adopt the innovation. These are the cooks who never use the blender or the food processor, the teachers who refuse to use audiovisual materials in their teaching, the doctors who refuse to use newly discovered medication, and so on. There are some instances in which there are no diehards. For example, teachers may wish to continue using a particular textbook, but when it goes out of print, they are forced to change and join the group of laggards.

Early as opposed to late adopters—the innovators as compared with the laggards—generally are younger, are of a higher socioeconomic status, have more specialized occupations, are more empathic, are less dogmatic, are more oriented toward change, make more use of available information, and closer to the actual agents of change, have a more cosmopolitan orientation, and are generally opinion leaders.

USES AND GRATIFICATION THEORY

In any given situation, we may reasonably ask why an audience chooses to select a particular medium. Wilbur Schramm, in his *Men, Messages, and Media,* proposes a formula:

$$\frac{\text{promise of reward}}{\text{effort required}} = \text{probability of selection}$$

Under the promise of reward, Schramm includes both immediate and delayed rewards. The rewards would focus basically on satisfying the needs of the audience—that is, we attend to a particular mass communication because it satisfies some need. The specific nature of these needs is covered from a somewhat different perspective in our discussion of the functions of mass communication.

The effort required for attending to mass communications may be looked at in terms of the availability of the media and the ease with which we may use them. We must also consider such factors as the expense involved and the time investment. For example, there is less effort required—less expense, less time lost, extreme ease—in watching television than in going to a movie, and there is less effort in going to a movie than there is in going to a play. When we divide the *effort required* into the *promise of reward,* we obtain the *probability of selection* of a particular mass communication medium.

This approach to media has come to be referred to as the *uses and gratifications approach.* It assumes that people's interaction with the media can best be understood (1) by the uses they put the media to, and (2) by the gratifications they derive. This represents a distinct move away from the concentration on what the media do *to* people. Typical gratifications are escape from everyday worries, relief from loneliness, emotional support, the acquisition of information helpful in dealing with the outside world, social contact, and numerous other benefits covered more formally in the discussion of the functions of mass communication. The main assumption of this approach is that audience members actively and consciously link themselves to certain media for certain purposes—that is, to obtain certain gratifications. The media are seen in this approach as competing with other sources (largely interpersonal) to serve the needs of the audience.

OPINION LEADERS AND GATEKEEPERS

Any consideration of media influence needs to give special attention to both opinion leaders and gatekeepers—two types of person who influence the flow of communication from media to individual and from individual to media.

Opinion Leaders

The opinion leader is differentiated from the people who are influenced in a number of ways. Opinion leaders have more formal education, greater wealth,

Video cassettes have become an essential part of our media. How has the advent of the video cassette influenced your media behavior? Has it influenced your interpersonal and small group interactions? In what ways?

higher social status, and more exposure to mass communications than those they influence. They also participate in social activities to a greater extent and are more innovative, cosmopolitan, competent, and accessible than those they influence.

Possessing these characteristics does not ensure that someone will become an opinion leader, and yet when opinion leaders are studied, they are found to possess these characteristics. If you look at the people to whom you turn for opinion leadership, you will probably find that they possess a good number of the characteristics noted. We would hardly turn for opinion leadership to someone who was less competent, had less formal education, and was less innovative (to name just a few characteristics) than ourselves.

These characteristics are all relative. The opinion leader does not possess these characteristics in an absolute sense, but possesses them to a greater extent than the individual who is influenced. Thus, for example, a graduate student in economics might be looked to by some people for opinion leadership concerning inflation and taxes. The graduate student possesses more formal education and more competence than those seeking such information. But that same graduate student would hardly be looked to for this opinion leadership by the graduate faculty in economics of Harvard or Yale.

Cosmopolitan and Local Opinion Leaders
Much as opinion leaders differ from the people they influence, they also differ from one another. Some opinion leaders are cosmopolitan; others are local. The cosmopolitan leader is concerned with national and international issues. Today, the cosmopolitan leader would be concerned with such issues

as the Iranian arms deals, proposed drug tests for new teachers, and the sale of arms to South Africa. The local opinion leader, on the other hand, is concerned with issues that are more immediate, more localized. The issues with which a local opinion leader would be concerned today would depend on where that leader was. If in New York City, this leader might be concerned with the rise in serious crimes in the city, the possible Long Island Rail Road strike, and the plans for the renovation of the Times Square area.

Monomorphism and Polymorphism

The cosmopolitan leader is generally restricted to one field of expertise, whereas the local leader is generally more broadly based. A cosmopolitan leader might, for example, be restricted to economic issues, to Central American affairs, or to Soviet-American relations. A local opinion leader is looked to for guidance and information on a broad variety of issues. Robert Merton introduced the terms *monomorphism* and *polymorphism* to highlight this distinction. The terms are, in a way, self-explanatory. *Monomorphism* refers to the tendency to serve as a leader for one topic (for example, national politics, contemporary fiction, or carpentry); monomorphism generally characterizes cosmopolitan leaders. *Polymorphism,* on the other hand, refers to the tendency for a leader to serve as a leader for a number of different topics; polymorphism generally characterizes local opinion leaders.

Gatekeepers

In the passage of a message from the source of mass media to the actual individual viewer or listener, there intervenes what is referred to as a *gatekeeper.* The term *gatekeeping,* originally used by Kurt Lewin in his *Human Relations* (1947), refers to (1) the process by which a message passes through various gates, as well as to (2) the people or groups that allow the message to pass (gatekeepers). Gatekeepers may be individuals or a group through which a message passes in going from sender to receiver. A gatekeeper's main function is to filter the messages an individual receives. Teachers are perfect examples of gatekeepers.

Teachers read the various books in an area of study, read journal articles, listen to convention papers, talk among themselves about developments in the field, and conduct their own research in the field. From all this information they pass some of it on to the students and at the same time prevent other information from getting through. In the passage of the information from researchers to students, the teacher filters what he or she knows about an area of study. Editors of magazines and publishing houses are gatekeepers; they allow certain information to get through and not other information.

As computers continue to change the ways in which we communicate, the role of the gatekeeper and even the definition of gatekeeping will change drastically. Information is stored in data banks and catalogued in various different ways in order to make its access quick and easy for most purposes. But the ways in which such information is catalogued and the descriptors that must be used for accessing such information will influence how the information is accessed and who will be most and least likely to access it. These functions will be served by the new gatekeepers. These gatekeepers will determine what data banks the information gets sent to, how the information is to be catalogued, and in what ways it must be accessed. These decisions, in turn, will influence who gets the information, the ease with which the information can be accessed, the expense involved in accessing the information, and a host of related questions.

Everyone functions to some extent as a gatekeeper. For example, of all the messages that come to you during the day, you select certain of these to be passed on to, say, your parents, friends, teachers, and so on. In passing them on, you may modify them in any number of ways for any number of reasons. Other messages may not be passed on at all; these may be messages that are too insignificant to repeat, or those that are too personal and become your secrets.

The gatekeeper, then, limits the messages we receive. The teacher, for example, limits the information the students receive. Without the teacher, however, the students would learn a great deal less. The teacher expands the informational awareness of the students through his or her distillation of the material, organization of the information, and analysis of the findings and results of study. That is, without gatekeepers we would not get half the information we now receive.

We might diagram the gatekeeping process as in Figure 30.2. Note that the messages (M_1, M_2, M_3) received by the gatekeeper come from different sources (S_1, S_2, S_3), so one of the functions the gatekeeper serves is to select the messages to be communicated and reject the ones that will not be allowed to pass. The gatekeeper then selectively transmits numerous messages (M_A, M_B, M_C) to different receivers (R_1, R_2, R_3). Teachers, for example, do not pass on the same messages to different classes: Advanced courses get very different messages

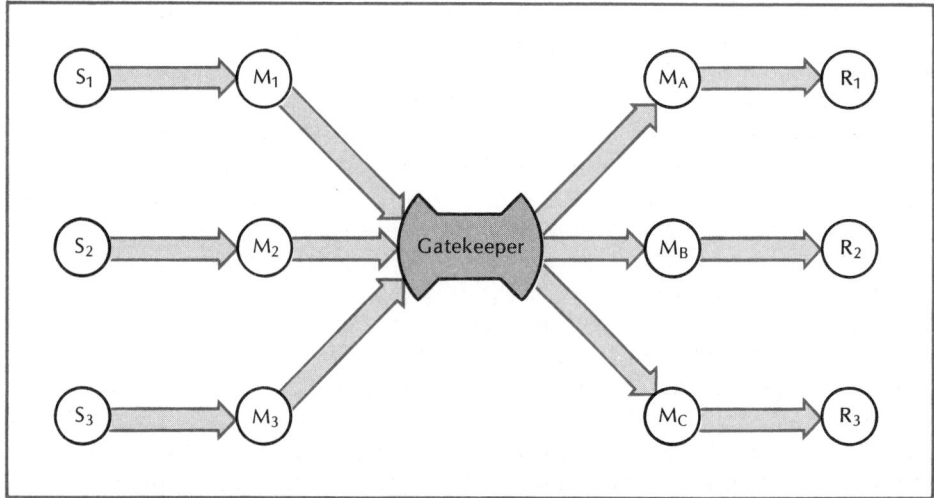

FIGURE 30.2 The gatekeeping process.

from elementary courses. Perhaps the most important aspect to note about this process is that messages received by the gatekeeper (M_1, M_2, M_3) are not the same as the messages the gatekeeper sends (M_A, M_B, M_C); the extent to which they differ is the measure of the gatekeeper's changes.

SUMMARY

1. The one-step theory of mass communication holds that the audience is influenced directly and immediately by the media. One variant of this theory is the silver bullet theory, which holds that the media's messages work much as do bullets aimed at a target.

2. The two-step theory holds that the media influence opinion leaders, who in turn influence the general population.

3. The multistep theory holds that the influence process is a reciprocal one that goes back and forth from the media to the people, then back to the media, then back to the people, and so on.

4. The play theory of mass communication holds that the media gain their audience by entertaining; the media are pleasure-oriented and their primary function is to allow us to escape work and enjoy ourselves.

5. The diffusion of innovations theory is concerned with the role of the media in influencing people to adopt something new or different. Three stages are identified: information acquisition, information evaluation, and adoption or rejection of the innovation. Five types of adopters are identified: innovators (3 percent of the audience), early adopters (14 percent), early majority (34 percent), late majority (34 percent), and laggards (14 percent). The remaining portion, the diehards, never adopt the innovation.

6. The uses and gratifications theory explains people's interaction with the media in terms of the uses to which they put the media and the gratifications they derive from the media. The media are attended to when they are easy to use or require little effort and provide great gratifications or rewards.

7. Monomorphic leaders serve as leaders for one topic, polymorphic leaders serve as leaders for a number of different topics and issues.

8. Gatekeepers are those persons or institutions that receive messages and then pass them on to others or prevent such messages from reaching others. Often the messages are changed (most often in the direction of simplification) by the gatekeepers before they are passed on.

SOURCES

For the discussion of gatekeeping, I relied on the work of Ray Eldon Hiebert, Donald F. Ungurait, and Thomas W. Bohn, *Mass Media: An Introduction to Modern*

Communication (New York: David McKay, 1974). For the two-step hypothesis, see Paul F. Lazarsfeld, Bernard Berelson, and Helen Gaudet, *The People's Choice* (New York: Duell, Sloan and Pearce, 1944), and Elihu Katz, "The Two-Step Flow of Communication: An Up-to-Date Report on an Hypothesis," *Public Opinion Quarterly* 21 (spring 1957): 61–78. For the diffusion of information discussion, see E. M. Rogers, *Diffusion of Innovations*, 3d ed. (Riverside, N.J.: Free Press, 1983).

For the play theory of mass communication, see William Stephenson, *The Play Theory of Communication* (Chicago: University of Chicago Press, 1967). Wilbur Schramm and William Porter, in their *Men, Women, Messages, and Media: Understanding Human Communication* (New York: Harper & Row, 1982), cover a wide variety of theories and offer insightful evaluations, as do Melvin L. DeFleur and Sandra Ball-Rokeach, *Theories of Mass Communication*, 4th ed. (New York: Longman, 1982). Some of the new technologies and their implications for the media are presented by Harvey C. Jassem and Roger Jon Desmond, "Theory Construction and Research in Mass Communication: The Implications of New Technologies," paper delivered at the Eastern Communication Association Convention, Philadelphia, Pennsylvania (March 1984), and by Warren K. Agee, Phillip H. Ault, and Edwin Emery, *Introduction to Mass Communications*, 8th ed. (New York: Harper & Row, 1986).

SKILL DEVELOPMENT SUMMARY

1. Use a **variety of media** to secure relevant information. Your chances of getting more accurate information will be increased by your use of several media sources.

2. Recognize that the media operate in a **social context** that is influenced by and influences the media. The interrelationships are so tightly interwoven that it would be impossible to separate one from the other.

3. Exert your **influence over the media** through buying or not buying the advertised product, writing letters to the media, and exercising interpersonal influence.

4. Remember that the media usually serve **several functions** at the same time. Even when the most obvious function is to entertain (say with "Dynasty," "Falcon Crest," or "Dallas"), remember that you are also being bombarded with messages that will influence your values, attitudes, and beliefs about a wide variety of economic, social, and political issues.

5. Be especially alert to the ways in which the media (especially television) may influence our views of **minority groups and women.** Remember that for the most part, media depictions are designed to sell products and not to present what is right, just, or honorable.

6. Do not confuse **media education** with objective education. Remember that the media almost invariably have a point of view that influences the information they present and the way they present it.

7. Do not confuse **media popularity** with social significance. Those who receive great media attention are not necessarily those who are most deserving of this attention, nor are those who do not get media exposure necessarily undeserving, unworthy, or insignificant.

8. Do not allow the media to **narcotize** you—to drug you into inactivity.

9. Always keep clearly in mind the distinction between real interpersonal relationships and **parasocial relationships**—imagined relationships with media personalities.

10. Analyze and evaluate the media's **ethicizing function** before internalizing the values and beliefs that the media attempt to instill.

11. Remember that we have a tendency (called the **sleeper effect**) to dissociate the source from the message, and eventually to forget the source (often a low-credibility source) and remember the message. Therefore, always distinguish clearly between information that is supported by evidence and research, and information presented as entertainment, propaganda, or advertisements.

12. Remember the **selective exposure principle** (discussed in Unit 26)—our tendency to approach information that is consistent with our beliefs and

values, and to avoid information that is inconsistent with our beliefs and values. In forming intelligent and well-reasoned opinions, we need to expose ourselves to the many sides of an issue and not only to the side that confirms our preconceptions.

13. Use the media (ideally, several media) and **interpersonal interactions** to develop and refine your ideas about local, national, or international events.

14. Cultivate your **opinion leadership** skills by securing relevant and up-to-date information and by communicating effectively—by using the skills of effective communication stressed throughout this text and course.

15. Recognize the role of the **gatekeeper** in all aspects of information transfer. Remember that what you receive (from television, radio, and even the best newspapers) is material that has been distilled, revised, edited, and condensed by numerous gatekeepers all along the process from source to receiver.

A HANDBOOK OF EXPERIENTIAL VEHICLES IN HUMAN COMMUNICATION

In this handbook are grouped a series of 25 Experimental Vehicles—exercises designed to enable you to work actively with the concepts and processes discussed in this book. Each Experiential Vehicle is prefaced with the part and/or unit title(s) to which it seems most appropriate.

1. MODELS OF COMMUNICATION

PRELIMINARIES TO HUMAN COMMUNICATION ■ EIGHT POSTULATES OF
COMMUNICATION ■ PRELIMINARIES TO INTERPERSONAL, GROUP, PUBLIC,
INTERCULTURAL, AND MASS COMMUNICATION

This experiential vehicle consists of two parts: In the first we explore the
components of the communication process, and in the second we attempt to
construct a wide variety of models for various different communication situations.

I. UNDERSTANDING THE COMMUNICATION PROCESS

Examine the following diagram of the communication process and respond to
the questions with reference to this diagram.

THE COMMUNICATION PROCESS DIAGRAMED

Context of the Communication Act

Channel

Originator of message (source) — Message — Receiver of message (destination)

Feedback from oneself   Feedback from receivers

Noise

1. Who or what might be designated as a *source* of communication? Identify
   as many different types of communication sources as you can.
2. Who or what might be designated by the term *destination?* Identify as many
   different types of communication destinations as you can.
3. What forms might noise take? That is, what types of noise might enter or
   interfere with a communication system? From what sources might noise
   originate?
4. How can noise be reduced? Might a communication system ever be noise-
   free? Explain.
5. What kinds of information can be fed back from the destination to the
   source?

6. Of what value to the source is information fed back from the destination?
7. What kinds of information might the source receive from his or her own communications?
8. Of what value is information that the source receives from his or her own communications?
9. What forms can a message take? That is, what signals can be used to communicate information?
10. Over what channels might a message be communicated? That is, what senses can be used by the source and by the receiver in sending and receiving information? What advantages and limitations do each of the senses have in terms of communication?
11. What are the dimensions or significant aspects of the context of the communication act? That is, in analyzing the context of communication, what factors would have to be investigated?
12. How might *interpersonal communication, small group communication, public communication, intercultural communication,* and *mass communication* be defined and distinguished from one another on the basis of the elements noted in the diagram?

II. MODEL BUILDING

In groups of five or six, construct a diagrammatic model of the essential elements and processes involved in one of the following communication situations. This model's primary function should be to describe what elements are involved and what processes operate in the specific situation chosen. (It may be useful to define the situation chosen in more detail before constructing the model.)

1. Sitting silently on a bus
2. Thinking
3. Asking for a date on the phone
4. Conversing with a very close friend
5. Talking with three or four acquaintances
6. Delivering a lecture to a class
7. Watching television
8. Participating in a formal group discussion
9. Writing a speech for a political candidate
10. Talking with a member of a different culture
11. Performing in a movie
12. Acting a role in a play
13. Arguing with your instructor
14. Selling insurance door-to-door
15. Persuading an angry crowd to disband

Each group should share their models with the rest of the class. Discussion might center on the following:

1. How adequately do the models explain the processes they are supposed to represent? Do they incorporate all the essential elements and processes? Are the relationships among the elements and processes clear?
2. What insight into the actual processes of communication do these models provide? What new ideas or information may be found in these models?
3. What elements and processes included here might also be included in the general models of communication discussed in Unit 1?
4. What functions do these models serve? Explain.

2. ANALYZING AN INTERACTION

EIGHT POSTULATES OF COMMUNICATION

The eight postulates of human communication discussed in Unit 2 should prove useful in analyzing any communication interaction. To help you understand these postulates better and to provide some practice in applying them to an actual interaction, the following interaction is presented. Carefully read this interaction and analyze each of the eight postulates of communication identified below.

AN INTERPERSONAL TRANSACTION

Participants

- Margaret: mother, housewife, junior high school history teacher; 41 years old
- Fred: father, gas station attendant; 46 years old
- Diane: daughter, receptionist in an art gallery; 22 years old
- Stephen: son, college freshman; 18 years old

Margaret is in the kitchen finishing preparing dinner—lamb chops, Fred's favorite, though she does not care much for them. Diane is going through some records. Stephen is reading one of his textbooks. Fred comes in from work and throws his jacket over the couch; it falls to the floor.

FRED [*bored but angry, looking at Stephen*]: What the hell did you do with the car last night? It stunk like hell. And you left all your damn school papers all over the back seat.

STEPHEN [*as if expecting the angry remarks*]: What did I do now?

FRED: You stunk up the car with your damn pot or whatever you kids smoke, and you left the car looking like hell. Can't you hear?

STEPHEN [*says nothing; goes back to looking at his book but without really reading*].

MARGARET: Dinner's almost ready. Come on. Wash up and sit down.

[*At dinner*]

DIANE: Mom, I'm going to go to the shore for the weekend with some friends from work.

MARGARET: Okay. When will you be leaving?

DIANE: Friday afternoon, right after work.

FRED: Like hell you're going. No more going to the shore with *that* group.

MARGARET: Fred, they're nice people. Why shouldn't she go?

FRED: Because I said so, okay? Finished. Closed.

DIANE [*mumbling*]: I'm 22 years old and he gives me problems. You make me feel like a kid, like some stupid little kid.

FRED: Get married and then you can tell your husband what to do.

DIANE: I wish I could.

STEPHEN: But nobody'll ask her.

MARGARET: Why should she get married? She's got a good life—good job, nice friends, good home. Listen, I was talking with Elizabeth and Cara this morning and they both feel they've just wasted their lives. They raised a family and what have they got? They got *nothing*. [*To Diane*]: And don't think sex is so great either; it isn't, believe me.

FRED: Well, they're idiots.

MARGARET [*snidely*]: They're idiots? Yeah, I guess they are.

DIANE: Joanne's getting married.

MARGARET: Who's Joanne?

STEPHEN: That creature who lives with that guy Michael.

FRED: Watch your mouth, wise-ass. Don't be disrespectful to your mother or I'll teach you how to act right.

MARGARET: Well, how do you like the dinner?

[*Prolonged silence.*]

DIANE: Do you think I should be in the wedding party if Joanne asks me? I think she will; we always said we'd be in each other's wedding.

MARGARET: Sure, why not. It'll be nice.

FRED: I'm not going to no wedding, no matter who's in it.

STEPHEN: Me neither.

DIANE: I hope you'll both feel that way when I get married.

STEPHEN: By then I'll be too old to remember I got a sister.

MARGARET: How's school?

STEPHEN: I hate it. It's so big. Nobody knows anyone. You sit in these big lecture halls and listen to some creep talk. I really feel lonely and isolated, like nobody knows I'm alive.

FRED: Listen to that college talk bullshit. Get yourself a woman and you won't feel lonely, instead of hanging out with those pothead faggots.

DIANE [*looking to Margaret, giving a sigh as if to say, "Here we go again"*].

MARGARET [*to Diane, in whisper*]: I know.

DIANE: Mom? Do you think I'm getting fat?

STEPHEN: Yes.

FRED: Just don't get fat in the stomach or you'll get thrown out of here.

MARGARET: No, I don't notice it.

DIANE: Well, I just thought I might be.

STEPHEN [*pushing his plate away*]: I'm finished; I'm going out.

FRED: Sit down and finish your damn supper. You think I work all day for you to throw the food away? You wanna go smoke your dope?

STEPHEN: No. I just want to get away from you—forever.

MARGARET: You mean we both work all day; it's just that I earn a lot more than you do.

FRED: *No,* I mean I work and you baby-sit.

MARGARET: Teaching junior high school history isn't baby-sitting.

FRED: What the hell is it then? You don't teach them anything.

MARGARET [*to Diane*]: You see? You're better off single. I should've stayed single. Instead . . . Oh, well. I was young and stupid. It was my own fault for getting involved with a loser. Just don't you make the same mistake.

FRED [*to Stephen*]: Go ahead. Leave the table. Leave the house. Who cares what you do?

1. Communication is transactional.
   a. How is the process nature of communication illustrated in this interaction? For example, why is it impossible to identify specific beginnings and specific endings for any of the varied interactions? Are there instances in which individual characters attempt to deny the process nature of interpersonal interaction?
   b. Can you illustrate how the messages of the different characters are interdependent?
   c. In what ways do the characters act and react as wholes?
2. Communication is inevitable.
   a. Do the characters communicate significant messages, even though they may attempt not to communicate?
   b. In what ways do the characters communicate simply by their physical presence or by the role they occupy in the family?
   c. What attempts do the characters make not to communicate? Why are these attempts not successful?
3. Communication is irreversible.
   a. Are any messages communicated that you think the characters would have (at a later date) wished they had not communicated? Why do you think so?

     b. Do any of the characters attempt to reverse the communication process—that is, to "uncommunicate"?

4. **Communication is a package of signals.**
     a. What instances can you locate of communication being a package of signals?
     b. Are there any examples of mixed or contradictory messages?
     c. What effects do you suppose these messages will have on subsequent interactions?

5. **Communication involves both content and relationship dimensions.**
     a. How do each of the characters deal with the self-definitions of the other characters? For example, how does Fred deal with the self-definition of Margaret? How does Margaret deal with the self-definition of Fred?
     b. Are any problems caused by the failure to recognize the distinction between the content and the relationship levels of communication?
     c. Select one topic of conversation and identify both the content and the relationship messages communicated.

6. **Communication is a process of adjustment.**
     a. Can any of the failures to communicate be traced to the lack of adjustment?
     b. Throughout the interaction, how do the characters adjust to one another?
     c. What suggestions would you offer this family for increasing their abilities to adjust to one another?

7. **Communication sequences are punctuated for processing.**
     a. Select any two characters and indicate how they differ in their punctuation of any specific sequence of events. Do the characters realize that they are each arbitrarily punctuating the sequence of events differently?
     b. What problems might a failure to recognize the arbitrary nature of punctuation create?

8. **Communication involves symmetrical and complementary transactions.**
     a. What type of relationship do you suppose exists between Fred and Margaret? Between Fred and Diane? Between Fred and Stephen? Between Diane and Stephen? Between Margaret and Stephen?
     b. Can any instances of rigid complementarity be found? What problems might rigid complementarity cause this particular family?

    As an alternative to analyzing this interaction, the entire class may watch a situation comedy show, television drama, or film and explore the eight communication postulates in these presentations. The questions used in this exercise should prove useful in formulating parallel questions for the television program or film. Another way of approaching this topic is to have all students watch the same television programs for an entire evening and have groups of students focus on the operation of different postulates. Thus, one group would focus on examples and illustrations of the impossibility of not communicating, one group on the content and relationship dimensions of messages, and so on. Each group can then report their findings and insights to the entire class.

3. I'D PREFER TO BE

THE SELF IN COMMUNICATION ▪ LISTENING ▪ PERCEPTION ▪ INTERPERSONAL COMMUNICATION ▪ INTERCULTURAL COMMUNICATION ▪ GROUP AND ORGANIZATIONAL COMMUNICATION

This exercise should enable members of the class to get to know one another better and at the same time get to know themselves better. The questions asked here should encourage each individual to increase awareness of some facet(s) of his or her thoughts or behaviors.

RULES OF THE GAME

The "I'd Prefer To Be" game is played in a group of four to six people, using the following category listing. General procedure is as follows:

1. Each member individually rank-orders each of the 15 groups, using 1 for the most-preferred and 3 for the least-preferred choice.
2. The group then considers each of the 15 categories in turn, with each member giving his or her rank order.
3. Members may refuse to reveal their rankings for any category by saying, "I pass." The group is not permitted to question the reasons for any member's passing.
4. When a member has revealed his or her rankings for a category, the group members may ask questions relevant to that category. These questions may be asked after any individual member's account or may be reserved until all members have given their rankings for a particular category.
5. In addition to these general procedures, the group may establish any additional rules it wishes—appointing a leader, establishing time limits, and so forth.

"I'D PREFER TO BE"

1. _____ intelligent
   _____ wealthy
   _____ physically attractive

2. _____ movie star
   _____ senator
   _____ successful businessperson

3. _____ blind
   _____ deaf
   _____ mute

4. _____ on a date
   _____ reading a book
   _____ watching television

5. _____ loved
   _____ feared
   _____ respected

6. _____ alone
   _____ with a group of people
   _____ with one person

7. _____ brave
   _____ reliable
   _____ insightful

8. _____ communicating by phone
   _____ communicating by letter
   _____ communicating face-to-face

9. _____ traitor to a friend
   _____ traitor to my country
   _____ traitor to myself

10. _____ bisexual
    _____ heterosexual
    _____ homosexual

11. _____ the loved
    _____ the lover
    _____ the good friend

12. _____ introvert
    _____ extrovert
    _____ ambivert

13. _____ a tree
    _____ a rock
    _____ a flower

14. _____ a leader
    _____ a follower
    _____ a loner

15. (Ten years from now)
    _____ married
    _____ single
    _____ living with someone but unmarried

AREAS FOR DISCUSSION

Here are some of the areas for discussion that might prove of value:

1. What are the reasons for the individual choices? Note that the reasons for the least-preferred choice may often be as important or even more important than the reasons for the most-preferred choice.
2. What do the choices reveal about the individual? Can persons be differentiated on the basis of their choices to these and similar alternatives?
3. What is the homogeneity/heterogeneity of the group as a whole? Do the members evidence relatively similar choices or wide differences? What does this mean in terms of the members' ability to communicate with one another?
4. Do the members accept/reject the choices of other members? Are some members disturbed by the choices other members make? If so, why? Are some apathetic? Why? Did hearing the choices of one or more members make you want to get to know them better?
5. Did any of the choices make you aware of preferences you were not aware of before?
6. Are members reluctant to share their preferences with the group? Why?

4. SELF-DISCLOSURE QUESTIONNAIRE

THE SELF IN COMMUNICATION ■ PRELIMINARIES TO INTERPERSONAL COMMUNICATION AND RELATIONSHIPS

Complete the accompanying questionnaire by indicating in the appropriate spaces your willingness-unwillingness to self-disclose these matters to members of a group of students chosen at random from this class.

In a group of five or six persons, discuss the questionnaires, self-disclosing or not, as you prefer. Consider at least the following:

1. Are there any discrepancies between what you indicated you would self-disclose and what you were actually willing to self-disclose?
2. In what areas were people most unwilling to self-disclose? Why? Discuss these reasons in terms of conditioning.
3. After the group got going and a number of people self-disclosed, did you feel more willing to self-disclose? Explain your feelings.
4. Were negative qualities (or perceived negative qualities) more likely to remain undisclosed? Why?
5. How would the results of your questionnaire differ if this information were to be disclosed to your parents, a stranger you would never see again, a counselor, or a best friend? Would the results differ depending on the sex of the individual to whom the disclosures were to be made? Explain the reasons.

5. A SELF-DISCLOSURE EXPERIENCE

THE SELF IN COMMUNICATION ▪ PRELIMINARIES TO INTERPERSONAL COMMUNICATION AND RELATIONSHIPS

On an index card write a statement of information that is currently in the hidden self. Do not put your names on these cards; the statements are to be dealt with anonymously. These cards will be collected and read aloud to the entire group.*

DISCUSSION OF STATEMENTS AND MODEL

1. Classify the statements into categories—for example, sexual problems, attitudes toward family, self-doubts, and so forth.
2. Why do you suppose this type of information is kept to the hidden self? What advantages might hiding this information have? What disadvantages?
3. How would you react to people who disclosed such statements to you? For example, what difference, if any, would it make in your relationship?
4. What type of person is likely to have a large hidden self and a small open self? A large open self and a small hidden self?
5. In relation to the other group members, would your open self be larger? Smaller? The same size? Would your hidden self be larger? Smaller? The same size?

---

* The general idea for this exercise comes from Gerard Egan, *Encounter* (Belmont, Calif.: Brooks/Cole, 1970).

	Would definitely self-disclose	Would probably self-disclose	Don't know	Would probably not self-disclose	Would definitely not self-disclose
1. My religious beliefs					
2. My attitudes toward other religions					
3. My attitudes toward different races					
4. My political beliefs					
5. My economic status					
6. My views on abortion					
7. My views on pornography					
8. My views on premarital relations					
9. My major pastime					
10. My parents' attitudes toward other religions					
11. My parents' attitudes toward different races					
12. My parents' political beliefs					
13. My parents' economic status					
14. My relationship with my parents					
15. My sexual fantasies					
16. My past sexual experiences					
17. My perceived sexual attractiveness					
18. My desired physical attractiveness					
19. My most negative physical attribute					
20. My physical condition or health					
21. My ideal mate					
22. My drinking behavior					
23. My drug behavior					
24. My gambling behavior					
25. My personal goals					
26. My most embarrassing moment					
27. My unfulfilled desires					
28. My major weaknesses					
29. My major worry					
30. My major strengths					
31. My present happiness-unhappiness					
32. My major mistakes					
33. My general attractiveness					
34. My general self-concept					
35. My general adequacy					

6. ETHICAL ISSUES IN HUMAN COMMUNICATION

PRELIMINARIES TO HUMAN COMMUNICATION ■ PRINCIPLES OF LANGUAGE AND VERBAL INTERACTION ■ THE PERSUASIVE SPEECH ■ PRELIMINARIES TO MASS COMMUNICATION

This exercise is designed to raise only a few of the many questions that could be raised concerning the ethics of communication, and to encourage you to think in concrete terms about some of the relevant issues. The purpose is not to persuade you to adopt a particular point of view, but to encourage you to formulate your own point of view.

The exercises consist of a series of cases, each raising somewhat different ethical questions. These exercises will probably work best if you respond to each of the cases individually and then discuss your decisions and the implications in groups of five or six. In these small groups, simply discuss those cases you found most interesting. The most interesting cases for small group discussion will probably be those that were the most difficult for you to respond to—that is, those that involved the most internal conflict. A general discussion in which the various groups share their decisions and insights may conclude the session.

For each case, respond to three questions:

1. What should you do?
2. What would you do?
3. What general principle of ethics influences this decision?

PAT AND CHRIS

You have been friends with Pat ever since elementary school. Last year Pat became engaged to Chris and for the last few months, everything has been going well. Last night, however, you saw Chris in a romantic encounter with some stranger. There is no doubt that the person was Chris, that the encounter was romantic, and that the "other person" was not Pat. You do not want to interfere with the relationship between Pat and Chris, but yet you wonder if you have an obligation to Pat.

MANAGING A RADIO STATION

You are the manager of a college radio station and are in charge of all aspects of production. All decisions are made by you—the type of music to be played, the news to be reported, and the commercials to be presented. The American Nazi Party asks to buy radio time to announce the formation of a local chapter of the ANP in your community and to ask for contributions to its cause. You personally disagree with the aims and policies of the American Nazi Party, but you wonder whether it would be unfair (and unethical) to deny them the right of free speech.

BORROWING A TERM PAPER

In your communication theory course an extensive term paper is required. If you were to earn a high enough grade on this paper (at least an A−), you would receive an A in the course. You want this A because it will help a great deal in getting you into graduate school and perhaps even in getting you a fellowship of some kind. Your problem is that you are too pressed for time to do justice to this paper. Your friend, who took a similar course at another university, has completed such a paper and earned an A. Your instructor is sure to evaluate it the same way. Your friend offers you the paper; all you have to do is have it retyped.

SCHOLARSHIP COMPETITION

You are competing with another student for a full scholarship to law school. Both of you need the scholarship and both of you seem to deserve it equally— your grades, service to the school and community, law board scores, and so on are about the same. Unfortunately, there is only one scholarship to be awarded. The committee charged with selecting the winner is a conservative group and would vote against candidates of whose personal lives they disapproved. You have recently learned that your competitor is an exconvict. You could easily leak this information to the committee, in which case you would surely get the scholarship. No one (not even the members of the committee) would know that you were the source of this information.

FREE LUNCH

You have been asked by a local organization concerned with the elderly to raise money for a free lunch program for the elderly in your community. You consider inviting the local townspeople to a community board meeting and then having a few particularly moving elderly persons deliver impassioned speeches on how desperately they need this free lunch program. The elderly would stress how many of them would have to go without lunch if this program were not instituted. You are certain that the townspeople would donate if appealed to in this way and that other means of persuasion would have no chance of working. You want to institute this free lunch program and the elderly need it, and yet you wonder if you are justified in using emotional rather than logical appeals.

7. CAUSAL ATTRIBUTION

PERCEPTION

For each of the following examples, indicate whether you think the behavior of the individual was due to *internal causes*—for example, personality characteristics and traits or various personal motives—or *external causes*—for example, the particular situation, the demands of others who might be in positions of authority, or the behaviors of others. The behavior in question appears underlined.

1. <u>Pat has just quit his job.</u> No one else that we know has quit that job. Pat has quit a number of jobs in the last five years and has in fact quit this same job once before.

2. <u>Mary has just failed her chemistry test.</u> A number of other students (in fact, some 40 percent of the class) have failed the test. Mary has never failed a chemistry test before and, in fact, has never failed any other test in her life.

3. <u>Liz tasted the wine, rejected it, and complained to the waiter.</u> No one else in the place seemed to complain about the wine. Liz has complained about the wine before and has frequently complained that her food was seasoned incorrectly, that the coffee was not hot enough, and so on.

4. <u>Russel took the children to the zoo.</u> Russel works for the board of education in a small town, and taking the children on trips is one of his major functions. All people previously in the job have taken the children to the zoo. Russel has never taken any other children to the zoo.

5. <u>John ran from the dog.</u> A number of other people also ran from this dog. I was surprised to see John do this because he has never run from other animals before and never from this particular dog.

6. <u>Donna received all A's on her film projects.</u> In fact, everyone in the class got A's. This was the first A that Donna has ever received in film and in fact the first A she has ever received in any course.

After you have responded to all six examples, identify the information contained in the brief behavioral descriptions that enabled you to make judgments concerning (1) consensus, (2) consistency, and (3) distinctiveness. What combination of these three principles would lead you to conclude that the behavior was internally motivated? What combination would lead you to conclude that the behavior was externally motivated?

8. SEQUENTIAL COMMUNICATION*

LISTENING

This exercise is designed to illustrate some of the processes involved in what might be called "sequential communication"—communication that is passed on from one individual to another.

This exercise consists of both a visual and a verbal part; they are performed in essentially the same manner. Taking the visual communication experience first, six subjects are selected to participate. Five of these leave the room while

* This exercise was inspired by William V. Haney, "Serial Communication of Information in Organizations," in *Communication: Concepts and Processes*, 3d ed., Joseph A. DeVito, ed. (Englewood Cliffs, N.J.: Prentice-Hall, 1981).

the first subject is shown the visual communication. He or she is told to try to remember as much as possible, as he or she will be asked to reproduce it in as much detail as possible. After studying the diagram, the first subject reproduces it on the blackboard. The second subject then enters the room and studies the reproduced diagram. The first diagram is then erased, and the second subject draws his or her version. The process is continued until all subjects have drawn the diagram. The last reproduction and the original drawing are then compared on the basis of the processes listed below.

The verbal portion is performed in basically the same way. Here the first subject is read the statement once, twice, or even three times; the subject should feel comfortable that he or she has grasped it fully. The second subject then enters the room and listens carefully to the first subject's restatement of the communication. The second subject then attempts to repeat it to the third subject, and so on until all subjects have restated the communication. Again, the last restatement and the original are compared on the basis of the processes listed below.

Members of the class not serving as subjects should be provided with copies of both the visual and the verbal communications and should record the changes made in the various reproductions and restatements.

Special attention should be given to the following basic processes in sequential communication.

1. *Omissions.* What kinds of information are omitted? At what point in the chain of communication are such omissions introduced? Do the omissions follow any pattern?
2. *Additions.* What kinds of information are added? When? Can patterns be discerned here, or are the additions totally random?
3. *Distortions.* What kinds of information are distorted? When? Are there any patterns? Can the types of distortions be classified in any way? Are the distortions in the direction of increased simplicity? Increased complexity? Can the sources of or reasons for the distortions be identified?

NONVERBAL COMMUNICATION

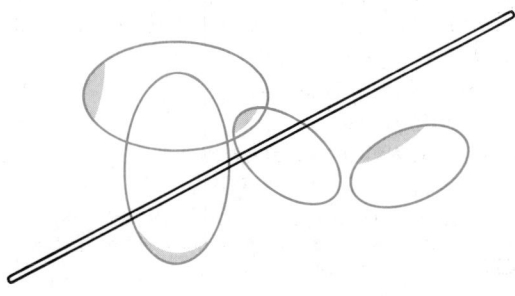

VERBAL COMMUNICATION

A verbal communication that works well comes from William Haney's "Serial Communication of Information in Organizations":

Every year at State University, the eagles in front of the Psi Gamma fraternity house were mysteriously sprayed during the night. Whenever this happened, it cost the Psi Gams from $75 to $100 to have the eagles cleaned. The Psi Gams complained to officials and were promised by the president that if ever any students were caught painting the eagles, they would be expelled from school.

9. PRACTICING ACTIVE LISTENING

LISTENING

A few situations are identified briefly. For each one, indicate appropriate and effective active listening responses, including paraphrase, expressions of understanding of feelings, and questions.

1. After breaking an engagement, a friend tells you of his loneliness and depression: *"I feel so alone, so depressed. I just can't think of what I'll do."*

2. A friend just won $20,000 on a quiz show but is depressed because she lost the championship and the chance to compete for the grand prize of $100,000: *"I knew the answer, but I just couldn't think fast enough. That money could have solved all my problems."*

3. One of your grandparents has just lost the lottery by one number and tells you of all the things that the money could have bought: *"I wanted to buy your father that new car he needs so badly and put something away for each of the grandchildren. I was so close."*

4. Your professor has just been notified that his contract for next year has not been renewed: *"I guess I thought I'd always be teaching here, and now—in just two months—I'll be on the unemployment line. I can't believe they would not renew my contract."*

5. Your friend has just received a rejection from the graduate school of her choice: *"I guess I'll just have to go to Podunk with the rest of the idiots."*

6. Your brother has just found out that his girlfriend is seeing his best friend: *"I hear they're serious about each other. And nobody has said a word to me. Everybody must know about them. I'm the only fool. I can't believe it. But I still love her. I must be crazy."*

7. In the last game, a member of the college baseball team struck out with bases loaded in the bottom of the ninth inning with a tie score. In extra innings the game was lost: *"I'm going to quit the team. I've had it. No more sports for me. I'm just wasting my time. I must have been stupid to think I could play professionally."*

8. Your classmate has to give a speech in one of her classes and is extremely nervous: *"I just can't give that speech. I'm going to drop the course. I could never get up in front of a whole class. They'd laugh at me."*

9. Your friend has just gotten engaged and is overjoyed: *"I can't believe it. I'm engaged. I'm so happy I could scream."*

10. Your mother has just broken a favorite vase that has been in the family for three generations, and she is depressed: *"How could I have done such a thing— such a stupid clumsy thing?"*

10. FACTS AND INFERENCES

BARRIERS IN LANGUAGE AND VERBAL INTERACTION

Carefully read the following report and the observations based on it.* Indicate whether you think the observations are true, false, or doubtful on the basis of information presented in the report. Circle *T* if the observation is definitely true, *F* if the observation is definitely false, and *?* if the observation may be either true or false. Judge each observation in order. Do not reread the observations after you have indicated your judgment and do not change any of your answers.

A well-liked college teacher had just completed making up the final examinations and had turned off the lights in the office. Just then a tall, dark broad figure appeared and demanded the examination. The professor opened the drawer. Everything in the drawer was picked up and the individual ran down the corridor. The dean was notified immediately.

1. The thief was tall, dark, and broad.	T	F	?
2. The professor turned off the lights.	T	F	?
3. A tall figure demanded the examination.	T	F	?
4. The examination was picked up by someone.	T	F	?
5. The examination was picked up by the professor.	T	F	?
6. A tall, dark figure appeared after the professor turned off the lights in the office.	T	F	?
7. The man who opened the drawer was the professor.	T	F	?
8. The professor ran down the corridor.	T	F	?
9. The drawer was never actually opened.	T	F	?
10. In this report three persons are referred to.	T	F	?

* This experiential vehicle is taken from Joseph A. DeVito, *General Semantics: Guide and Workbook,* rev. ed. (Deland, Fla.: Everett/Edwards, 1974), p. 55, and is modeled on those developed by William V. Haney.

11. HAPTICS: BODY ACCESSIBILITY

SPACE, TERRITORIALITY, AND TOUCH COMMUNICATION

Assume that the figures below represent your body.

1. The first figure is your body as touched by your mother.
2. The second figure is your body as touched by your father.
3. The third figure is your body as touched by your closest friend of the same sex.
4. The fourth figure is your body as touched by your closest friend of the opposite sex.

Indicate the frequency with which each part of your body is or has been touched by the four persons named. Use the following scale:

Very little = ▨
Somewhat = ▩
Pretty often = ▨
Very often = ■

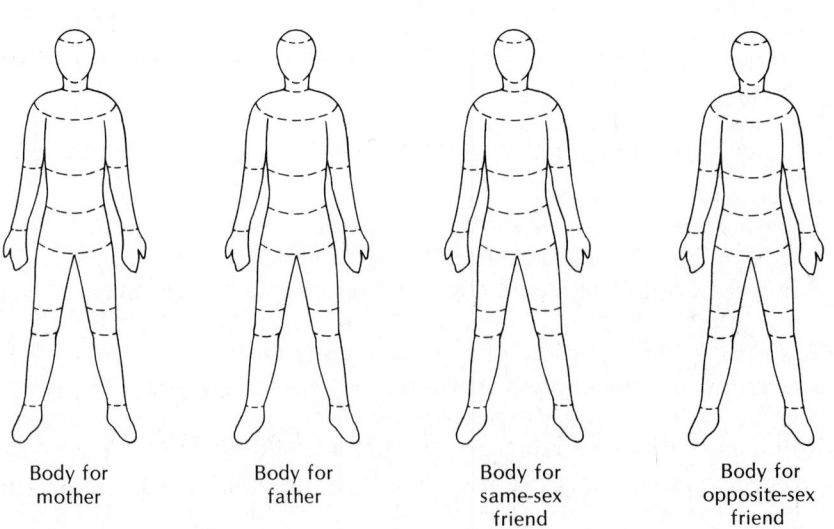

| Body for mother | Body for father | Body for same-sex friend | Body for opposite-sex friend |

After you have completed these figures, examine those presented in Unit 12. How do your figures compare with those obtained from the other studies? How might you account for the differences?

12. GENDER DIFFERENCES IN NONVERBAL COMMUNICATION

PART THREE. NONVERBAL COMMUNICATION

The following statements summarize some of the research findings on sex differences in nonverbal communication. For each statement, insert *men* or *women* in each blank space. After completing all 15 statements, consider the questions for discussion.

1. _____ seem to be slightly more accurate at judging emotions from observing facial expression than _____.

2. _____ seem better able to communicate emotions by facial expressions than _____.

3. _____ smile more than _____.

4. _____ are generally approached more closely than _____.

5. _____ reveal their emotions facially more readily than _____.

6. _____ extend their bodies more and take up greater areas of space than _____.

7. _____ maintain more eye contact than _____ in mixed-sex dyads.

8. Both men and women, when speaking, look at _____ more than at _____.

9. In mixed-sex dyads, _____ interrupt _____ more often.

10. Some research indicates that _____ speak with greater volume than _____.

11. If a man and a woman are walking toward each other, the _____ will be more apt to move out of the _____'s way.

12. Unattractive _____ seem to be less accepted than are unattractive _____.

13. _____ both touch and are touched more than _____.

14. _____ engage in greater mutual eye contact with a same-sex partner than _____.

15. Same-sex pairs of _____ sit more closely together than do same-sex pairs of _____ .

QUESTIONS FOR DISCUSSION

1. On what basis did you think that the nonverbal behavior was more accurately ascribed to one sex than the other?
2. What do you think might account for the differences in nonverbal behavior?
3. Are there types of women or men in which these differences are especially pronounced? Almost absent? Totally absent? On what basis do you make these predictions?
4. How would you go about testing one of these statements for accuracy?
5. Do the answers given by research findings seem to be consistent with your own observations? Note each that is not. How might you account for this discrepancy?

13. WHO?

PERCEPTION ▪ PART TWO. LANGUAGE AND VERBAL INTERACTION ▪ PART THREE. NONVERBAL COMMUNICATION

The purpose of this exercise is to explore some of the verbal and nonverbal cues that people give off and that others receive and use in formulating inferences about the knowledge, abilities, and personality of these others. The exercise should serve as a useful summary of the concepts and principles of verbal and nonverbal communication and of interpersonal perception.

The entire class should form a circle so that each member may see each other member without straining. If members do not know all the names of their classmates, some system of name tags should be used for this exercise.

Each student should examine the following list of phrases and should write the name of one student to whom he or she feels each statement applies in the column marked "Who." Be certain to respond to all statements. Although one name may be used more than once, the experience will prove more effective if a wide variety of names are chosen. Unless the class is very small, no name should be used more than 2 times.

Next to each student's name, record a *certainty rating* in the column labeled "CR," indicating how sure you are of your choices. Use a five-point scale with 5 indicating great certainty and 1 indicating great uncertainty.

After the names and certainty ratings have been written for *each* statement by *each* student, the following procedure may prove useful. The instructor or group leader selects a statement (there is no need to tackle the statements in the order they are given here), and asks someone specifically, or the class generally, what names were put down. Before the person whose name was put down is asked if the phrase is correctly or incorrectly attributed to him or her, some or all of the following questions should be considered.

1. Why did you select the name you did? What was there about this person that led you to think that this phrase applied to him or her? What *specific* verbal or nonverbal cues led you to your conclusion?
2. What additional verbal and/or nonverbal cues would you need to raise your degree of certainty?
3. Is your response at all a function of a stereotype you might have of this individual's ethnic, religious, racial, or sexual identification? For example, how many women's names were put down for the questions or phrases about the saws or pistons? How many men's names were put down for the statements pertaining to cooking or using a sewing machine?
4. Did anyone give off contradictory cues such that some of them would indicate that they were appropriate for a specific phrase and others would indicate that they were not appropriate? Explain the nature of these contradictory cues.
5. How pleased or disappointed are the people whose names have been proposed? Why? Were there any surprises? Why were some of these guesses unexpected?
6. How do you communicate your "self" to others? How do you communicate what you know, think, feel, and do to your peers?

WHO	CR	
_____	___	1. Goes to the professional theatre a few times a year
_____	___	2. Has taken a vacation outside the country in the last 12 months
_____	___	3. Likes to cook
_____	___	4. Watches soap operas on a fairly regular basis
_____	___	5. Knows the function of a car's pistons
_____	___	6. Attends sporting events with a fair degree of regularity
_____	___	7. Has seen a pornographic (XXX-rated) movie within the last 3 months
_____	___	8. Has been to an opera
_____	___	9. Knows how to use a sewing machine
_____	___	10. Is a member of an organized sports team
_____	___	11. Watches television for an average of 3 or more hours per day
_____	___	12. Has cried over a movie in the last few months
_____	___	13. Fluently speaks a foreign language
_____	___	14. Has many close friends
_____	___	15. Knows how potatoes should be planted
_____	___	16. Knows the difference among a hacksaw, a jigsaw, and a coping saw
_____	___	17. Knows the ingredients of a bloody Mary
_____	___	18. Knows how to make a hollandaise sauce

WHO	CR	
_____	___	19. Can name all 12 signs of the zodiac
_____	___	20. Has a car in his or her immediate family costing over $20,000
_____	___	21. Would come to the aid of a friend even at great personal sacrifice
_____	___	22. Has read a book on the best-seller list in the last year
_____	___	23. Is frequently infatuated (or in love)
_____	___	24. Would like, perhaps secretly, to be a movie star
_____	___	25. Writes poetry
_____	___	26. Could name the last 12 U.S. presidents
_____	___	27. Knows where Liechtenstein is
_____	___	28. Knows the legal status of Puerto Rico
_____	___	29. Keeps a diary or a journal
_____	___	30. Knows what *prime rate* means
_____	___	31. Was a member of the Boy Scouts or Girl Scouts
_____	___	32. Is very religious
_____	___	33. Would describe himself or herself as a political activist
_____	___	34. Wants to go to graduate, law, or medical school
_____	___	35. Would vote in favor of gay rights legislation
_____	___	36. Is planning to get married within the next 12 months
_____	___	37. Is going to make a significant contribution to society
_____	___	38. Is going to be a millionaire
_____	___	39. Is a real romantic
_____	___	40. Would emerge as a leader in a small group situation

14. THE GREETING CARD

PART FOUR. INTERPERSONAL COMMUNICATION AND RELATIONSHIPS

The objectives of this exercise are

1. to familiarize you with some of the popular conceptions and sentiments concerning interpersonal relationships
2. to introduce a wide variety of concepts important in the study of interpersonal relationships
3. to provide an opportunity for group members to get to know one another

METHODS AND PROCEDURES

1. Bring to class one greeting card expressing a sentiment that is significant for any one of the following reasons. This list is not exhaustive and the items are not mutually exclusive.

   - it expresses a popular sentiment that is correct or true
   - it expresses a popular sentiment that is incorrect or false

- it expresses a sentiment that incorporates a concept or theory that can assist us in understanding interpersonal relationships
- it illustrates a popular problem in interpersonal relationships
- it illustrates a useful strategy for relationship development, maintenance, repair, or dissolution
- it illustrates a significant concept or theory in interpersonal relationships
- it suggests a useful question (or hypothesis for scientific study) that should be asked in the study of interpersonal relationships
- it supports or contradicts some currently accepted theory in interpersonal relationships
(Remember: sentiments in greeting cards are communicated through a number of different channels. Therefore, consider the sentiments communicated through the verbal message but also consider the messages communicated through the illustrations, colors, physical form of the card, type of print, etc.)

2. Be prepared to explain the greeting card sentiment as it relates to the study of interpersonal relationships in a brief discussion (three to five minutes).
3. Identify one principle of interpersonal communication that is suggested by this card.

15. MALE AND FEMALE

PRELIMINARIES TO INTERPERSONAL COMMUNICATION AND RELATIONSHIPS

This exercise is designed to increase awareness of some matters that may prevent meaningful interpersonal communication between the sexes. It is also designed to encourage meaningful dialogue among class members.

The women and the men are separated; one group goes into another classroom and one group stays in the original room. The task of each group is to write on the board all the things they dislike having the other sex think, believe, do, and/or say about them. The women write on the board all the unpleasant things men think, believe, say, or do in reference to women—things that prevent meaningful interpersonal communication from taking place. The men do likewise, but in reference to women.

After this is completed, the groups change rooms. The men go into the room in which the women have written their dislikes, and the women go into the room in which the men have written their dislikes. The men discuss what the women have written and the women discuss what the men have written. After satisfactory discussion has taken place, the groups should get together in the original room. Discussion might center on the following:

1. Were there any surprises?
2. Were there any disagreements? That is, did the men (or women) write anything that the women (or men) argued they do not believe, think, do, or say, or that they did not believe was negative?

3. How do you suppose the ideas about the other sex started?
4. Is there any reliable evidence in support of the beliefs of the men about the women or the women about the men?
5. What is the basis for the things that are disliked? Put differently, why was each statement written on the blackboard?
6. What kind of education or training program (if any) do you feel is needed to eliminate these problems?
7. Specifically, how do these beliefs, thoughts, actions, and statements prevent meaningful interpersonal communication?
8. How do you feel now that these matters have been discussed?

16. UP AND DOWN WITH JACK AND JILL

—————

PART FOUR. INTERPERSONAL COMMUNICATION AND RELATIONSHIPS

—————

The following dialogue was written to illustrate some of the more common violations of the principles of effective interpersonal interaction and conflict management that we discussed in Units 14, 15, and especially 16. Carefully read the dialogue and (1) identify the principles that Jack and Jill violate and (2) indicate what they might have said that could have been more effective. This exercise may be completed individually, in small groups, or with the entire class.

Jack and Jill are evening students at Hunter College. They met in the first class they took, some 6 years ago. They dated since that time, and about two years ago married. This is their last semester; they will graduate this month. Both are busy looking for jobs in their respective fields. Jack majored in physical education and plans to get a job as an athletic coach for a local junior high school. Jill majored in communications and is planning to get a job in publishing. She hopes to be an editor someday.

This dialogue takes place in their living room at around 5 P.M.

JACK: Did you see this letter? I can't believe it! I was hoping to get a job in a junior high? Look at this, Hammerhead University, in Indiana, has invited me to apply for a job coaching their first class hockey team.

JILL: They probably sent that letter to hundreds of people. Be serious. How could they want you? You just barely made it through your BA.

JACK: Thanks. I appreciate that. You're always so complimentary. Just what a wife should be.

JILL: Well, you did just barely get through. After all, a 2.1 index isn't exactly Dean's List.

JACK: But, I know how to coach. And that's what they're interested in.

JILL: Billy thinks you'd be too easy with the players.

JACK: Don't be an idiot. Stick to what you know about. At any rate, Hammerhead wants me! I'm going to love Indiana. Did you know I was born in Illinois, just twenty miles from the Indiana border?

JILL: I'm not going to Indiana. I'm going to stay right here in New York. That's where publishing is, and that's where I intend to be.

JACK: Don't be stupid. I'm sure going to try to get that job and I'm off to Indiana.

JILL: If you wanted to split up, you didn't have to get a job in another state. You could have had a divorce anytime you wanted it. You're no bargain. I can easily do a lot better.

JACK: Yeah, like Bob the wimp and Harry the moose? Real winners, they were. If you could have done better, you would have; you've always been an opportunist. Just like your father.

JILL: My father at least looks out for my benefit. More than I can say for you. All you're concerned with is what is good for Jack. How can we benefit Jack? What can we do for Jack?

JACK: Speaking of what's good for Jack, what's for dinner?

JILL: *Swanson's*: meatloaf, fried chicken, or turkey breast. Oh, I'm having the fried chicken. You can have the meatloaf or the turkey.

JACK: Frozen dinners and a filthy house. That's really great. Thanks for such a great choice of dinners in such a great setting. I'll take the fried chicken on the dirty table.

JILL: Why don't you clean the house? You don't put any effort in your classes. Physical education! Do you have any classes?

JACK: When you don't know what you're talking about, keep your mouth shut so you can hear: I'll take the fried chicken on the dirty table.

JILL: I'm eating the fried chicken. And anyway, I thought you didn't like fried chicken. Meatloaf or turkey breast?

JACK: *Fried chicken, damn it. Fried chicken!*

JILL: Allright, allright. Take the chicken. I'll have the meatloaf.

JACK: Call me when it's ready. I'm going to sit in the tub.

JILL: No, you call me when it's ready. I'll go sit in the tub.

JACK [*gives Jill a dirty look, walks into the bathroom, and slams the door*].

JILL: I worked just as hard as you did. You never give me a break. You always want the best treatment for yourself but never want to give it to anyone else.

JACK [*yelling over the sound of the water filling the tub*]: Is it ready?

JILL: I should have listened to my friends when they said you were a loser. You *are* a loser.

JACK: *Is it ready?*

JILL: *You are a loser. Did you know that? You're a loser.*
[*Prolonged silence.*]

JACK [*exits the bathroom, drying his hair*].

JILL: You don't have to worry about your hair. Another week or so and it'll be all gone anyway.

JACK [*speaking to no one in particular*]: Why did I marry this nightmare? What did I do wrong to deserve this?

JILL: Why did you marry me? Why did I marry you? I should have listened to Sara and John. They told me you were never going to amount to anything. Just like your father—an alcoholic freeloader.

JACK: Alcohol is the only thing that keeps me from going crazy living with you.

JILL: Blame me. Go ahead. You blame me for everything else, you might as well blame me for your being a drunk.

JACK: Where the hell is the chicken?

JILL: On the table.

JACK: Are you ever going to cook anything besides frozen dinners?

JILL: Are you ever going to do anything besides complain?

JACK: Yes, I am. In fact, I'm going out tonight to play cards with the guys.

JILL: No, you're not. You're staying home and fixing the wallpaper. You promised to fix that paper two months ago.

JACK: I couldn't care less about the damn paper. I always hated that paper anyway, so let it fall down.

JILL: I love that paper. All my friends love it too.

JACK: But, I hate it. I always hated it.

JILL: You hate everything. You're always so negative about everything, I can't stand it.

JACK: Well, I'm not fixing the paper. I'm playing cards.

JILL: You're always going out. I never get a chance to go out.

JACK: So, go out. Who cares? Or isn't there anyone who would go with you?

JILL: You know there is. And he's always waiting for me. So don't threaten me.

JACK: Who cares? Go ahead. Go out with your toad. Who cares? Who cares?

JILL: I will go out with Ted. At least he cares about me.

JACK: Go ahead. Anyway, I'm going to Hammerhead.
[*Walks out of the house.*]

17. THE IDEAL RELATIONAL COUPLE

The objectives of this exercise are:

1. to identify some of the characteristics that make an individual a "good" relational partner

2. to identify some of the characteristics that might define a "good" relational couple
3. to identify some of the strategies ideal couples use in developing, maintaining, repairing, and perhaps dissolving relationships
4. to sensitize us to the role of the media in promoting relational stereotypes, in suggesting relational strategies, and in informing us (correctly or incorrectly) about assorted dimensions of relationships

METHODS AND PROCEDURES

Select one relational couple from literature, television, film, comic books, or any other similar source.

1. Define the individuals and the relationship. Tell us something about who the individuals are (that is, demographics such as age, sex, nationality, race, status, educational level) and what the nature of their relationship is (for example, the type of relationship, whether friendship, love, family; the length of time they have been in this relationship; the network of significant others that affect this relationship).
2. Describe (in a brief informal talk with the class) the individuals and the relationship in terms of some or all of the following issues:

- the personal qualities or behavior patterns that the individuals exemplify and that contribute to their being "good" relational partners
- the personal qualities or behavior patterns that the couple exemplifies and that make them candidates for the "ideal relational couple"
- the qualities of effective interpersonal interaction that this couple illustrates (for example, openness, empathy, supportiveness, positiveness, equality, confidence, immediacy, interaction management, expressiveness, and other-orientation) and the specific ways in which they illustrate these qualities

18. WIN AS MUCH AS YOU CAN*

IMPROVING INTERPERSONAL COMMUNICATION AND CONFLICT MANAGEMENT ▪ PART FIVE. GROUP COMMUNICATION

This exercise is designed to explore some of the concepts of communication and conflict considered in this text. "Clusters" of eight persons are formed. Each cluster consists of four teams of two members each. Visualizing the area as a clock, the four teams are placed at 12, 3, 6, and 9 o'clock. The teams should

---

* This exercise owes its formulation to an exercise by William Gellerman in J. William Pfeiffer and John E. Jones, eds., *A Handbook of Structured Experiences for Human Relations Training,* vol. 2 (La Jolla, Calif.: University Associates, 1974).

be far enough apart so they can communicate without the other teams' hearing them.

The game consist of 10 rounds. In each round each team selects X or Y. The selection is made on the basis of each team's prediction of what the other teams will select and the itemized "payoffs" as presented in the following Payoff Table. For each round each team must select either X or Y. Both team members must agree on which letter to select.

The sequence of events should follow the Score Sheet (presented following the Payoff Table). For each round the teams are allowed a certain amount of time (listed in the column headed "Time") in which to make their selection of X or Y. After they reach their decision, the X or Y is recorded in the column headed "Choice."

PAYOFF TABLE

4 X's	lose 1 point each
3 X's 1 Y	win 1 point each lose 3 points each
2 X's 2 Y's	win 2 points each lose 2 points each
1 X 3 Y's	win 3 points each lose 1 point each
4 Y's	win 1 point each

SCORE SHEET

Round	Time (in minutes)	Conference	Choice	Points won	Points lost	Balance
1	2	partner				
2	1	partner				
3	1	partner				
4	1	partner				
5	3 1	cluster partner		× 3 =	× 3 =	
6	1	partner				
7	1	partner				
8	3 1	cluster partner		× 5 =	× 5 =	
9	1	partner				
10	3 1	cluster partner		× 10 =	× 10 =	Total =

Only after each team has recorded its choices are the choices revealed. When the choices are revealed, refer to the Payoff Table to determine how many points were won or lost. For example, if two teams selected X and two teams selected Y, then according to the Payoff Table the teams selecting X would each win 2 points and the teams selecting Y would each lose 2 points. Another example: If one team selected Y and three teams selected X, the team that selected Y would lose 3 points and the teams that selected X would win one point each.

The amount won or lost for each round should be noted in the appropriate column, and a balance should be noted in the column headed "Balance."

Note that for rounds 5, 8, and 10 the game is played a bit differently. Before conferring with one's partner, all teams in the cluster confer for three minutes. Here the teams may talk about anything they wish, but they may not mark their choices at this time. They can mark their choices only after private consultations with their partners, which take place immediately after the cluster conferences. Note also that these three rounds are bonus rounds; the amount won or lost in that round is multiplied by 3 in round 5, by 5 in round 8, and by 10 in round 10.

Consider the following questions only *after* you have played the game.

1. How would you describe the behavior of the members of the cluster? How would you describe your own behavior?
2. Is this behavior typical? That is, did you behave here as you would in a real-life situation?
3. How do you feel about the way you played the game? Are you pleased? Disappointed? Sorry? Guilty? Explain the basis for your feelings.
4. If you were playing for points on an examination or even for points toward your final grade in the course, would you have played differently? Explain. What if you were playing for money—say, $1 per point?
5. Were you surprised at the way in which other members of your cluster played? Explain.

19. GROUP COMMUNICATION PATTERNS

PRELIMINARIES TO GROUP COMMUNICATION ▪ ORGANIZATIONAL COMMUNICATION ▪ MEMBERS AND LEADERS IN GROUP COMMUNICATION

In this exercise we attempt to explore the efficiency and satisfaction of communication. Five groups of equal numbers are formed according to the following patterns:

Circle   Wheel   Y

Chain   All channel

Arrows connecting two individuals indicate that communication may take place between them. Individuals not connected by arrows may communicate only indirectly through the individual(s) with whom they are connected. The problem is the same for all groups. Each group is to reach *unanimous* agreement on how many squares are contained in the following diagram:

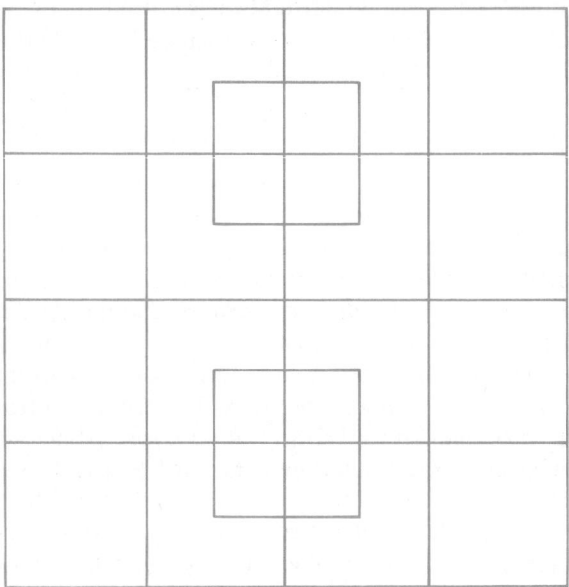

All messages are to be written on individual pieces of paper. Members may pass to other members only those messages they themselves have written. Thus, if members receive a message they wish to pass on to another member, they must rewrite the message.

EFFICIENCY AND SATISFACTION INDEXES

The efficiency of the groups should be indexed in at least two ways. First, the time necessary for completion should be carefully noted. Second, the messages sent should be saved and counted. Efficiency will thus be indexed by the time it took to arrive at the correct answer and by the number of messages needed for communicating.

The satisfaction of the group members should be indexed by responses on the following scales:

Rate your *participation in the task* on the following scales:

interesting ____ : ____ : ____ : ____ : ____ : ____ : ____ boring
enjoyable ____ : ____ : ____ : ____ : ____ : ____ : ____ unenjoyable
dynamic ____ : ____ : ____ : ____ : ____ : ____ : ____ static
useful ____ : ____ : ____ : ____ : ____ : ____ : ____ useless
good ____ : ____ : ____ : ____ : ____ : ____ : ____ bad

Compute your mean score for these scales as follows: (1) number the scales from 7 to 1 from left to right, (2) total the scores from all five scales (this number should range from 5 to 35), and (3) divide by 5 to get your mean score.

EFFICIENCY AND SATISFACTION SCORES

Channel Patterns	Efficiency		Satisfaction
	Time	Number of Messages	Group Mean Scores
Circle	_____	_____	_____
Wheel	_____	_____	_____
Y	_____	_____	_____
Chain	_____	_____	_____
All-channel	_____	_____	_____

Each group should then compute the group mean score by totaling the individual mean scores and dividing the sum by the number of participants.

FOR DISCUSSION

1. Which patterns are most effective in ensuring rapid and accurate communication? Which patterns are least effective? Would this be true with all problems? With what types of problems would it be different? Why?
2. Which patterns result in the greatest degree of member satisfaction? Which patterns result in least satisfaction? How is this related to the leader's role in the group?
3. Are there realistic counterparts to these five communication structures? Do we find these communication structures and patterns in the "real world"? Where? What are some of the consequences of these various patterns?
4. How does structure influence function? Examine your own group situation and consider how the structure of the group (the positioning of the members, for example) influenced the functions the members played. Does this have a realistic counterpart? In what ways do you function differently as a result of the structure in which you find yourself?
5. What implications would you be willing to draw from this experience for improved communication in the classroom?

20. INTERVIEWS: EXPERIENCING AND ANALYZING

INTERVIEWING ▪ ORGANIZATIONAL COMMUNICATION

Triads should be formed, preferably among persons who do not know each other well or who have had relatively little interaction. One person should be designated the interviewer, another the interviewee, and the third the interview analyst. One of the following situations should be chosen by the interview analyst:

1. An interview for the position of camp counselor for retarded children
2. An interview for a part in a new Broadway musical
3. A therapy interview to focus on communication problems in relating to superiors
4. An interview between teacher and student in which the teacher is attempting to discover why the course taught last semester was such a dismal failure

After the situation is chosen, the interviewer should interview the interviewee for approximately ten minutes. During this time, the analyst should observe the interview but not interfere in any way, verbally or nonverbally. After the interview is over, the analyst should offer a thorough and detailed analysis, considering each of the following questions:

1. What happened during the interview (essentially a description of the interaction)?
2. What was well handled?
3. What went wrong? What aspects of the interview were not handled as effectively as they might have been?
4. What could have been done to make the interview more effective?

The analysts for each triad may then be called upon to report their major findings to the class as a whole. A compendium of "common faults" or "suggestions for improving interviews" may then be developed by the instructor or group leader in response to these analyses.

.21. DEALING WITH UNLAWFUL QUESTIONS

INTERVIEWING ■ ORGANIZATIONAL COMMUNICATION

The following questions are in many cases regarded as unlawful, and an interviewee is not required to answer any of them as a condition of employment. The difficulty for the interviewee, of course, is to avoid answering the questions without antagonizing the interviewer and thus losing the job. This exercise is designed to raise some of the questions that may be unlawful and therefore unnecessary for you to answer, and to provide you with at least some practice in developing responses that are effective in protecting your privacy and at the same time maintaining a positive relationship with the interviewer.

Indicate how you would deal with each of the following questions. Write your responses and then compare them with those of other students, either in groups or with the class as a whole. Another alternative is to form dyads and role-play the interviewer-interviewee situation. To make this more realistic, the person playing the interviewer should press for an answer to the question, while the interviewee should continue to avoid answering the question, yet respond positively and cordially. As you will discover, this is not always easy; tempers are frequently lost in this type of interaction.

1. I see that you've been married for two years. Any plans for having children?
2. I notice a gap in your employment record from 1978 to 1982. Did you by any chance serve time in prison?
3. "Jones?" Is that a family name or did you change it?
4. I see you've written two articles on lesbian feminism. Do you personally identify with this philosophy? Would you define yourself as a lesbian feminist?
5. You've been working in the field—I see from your resumé—for 23 years. That must put you pretty close to retirement age, no?
6. Are you married?
7. I notice that you were exempt from physical education class in college. Do you have any physical disabilities?
8. You seem to be in your middle to late thirties and yet I don't notice any reference to marital status. Have you ever been married?
9. It's most helpful that you have fluency in Korean and Spanish. Which was your native language?
10. When I called the other day to arrange this interview, a man answered the phone. Do you live with a man?

22. ANALYZING THE PUBLIC SPEECH

PART SIX. PUBLIC COMMUNICATION

After hearing a specific speech (in class or on television) or after reading one in a newspaper or periodical, respond to each of the following questions, individually or in small groups. In doing so, you should accomplish at least two major goals. First, your analysis will fix in your mind more concretely the various steps in preparing a public speech. Second, this exercise should provide you with some experience in analyzing a public speech and should sharpen your evaluative and critical skills.

The questions presented here follow the eight steps identified in Unit 21.

I. The topic and purpose
   a. Is the topic a worthwhile one?
   b. Is the topic relevant and interesting to the audience?

c. Is the topic sufficiently narrow in scope?

d. Is the purpose appropriate to the audience?

II. The audience

    a. Have the audience, occasion, and context been analyzed?

    b. Has the speaker adapted to this specific audience, occasion, and context?

    c. How has this analysis and adaptation been manifested in the speech? Cite specific passages.

III. Research

    a. Has the speech topic been thoroughly researched?

    b. How is this research manifested in the speech? Cite specific passages.

IV. Thesis and major propositions

    a. What is the thesis of the speech?

    b. What are the major propositions of the speech?

    c. Has the speaker clearly identified the thesis and the major propositions?

V. Supporting the major propositions

    a. What types of supporting materials are used in the speech?

    b. Are these supporting materials effective? Appropriate to the speech topic? The audience? The purpose of the speech?

VI. Organization

    a. What organizational pattern is used?

    b. Is this pattern appropriate to the topic and purpose?

    c. Does the organizational pattern contribute to ease of comprehension?

    d. Does the pattern advance the persuasive purpose?

VII. Wording the speech

    a. Was the style clear? Was it economical? Did it use specific terms and numbers? Guide phrases? Short, familiar, and high-frequency terms? Did it incorporate repetition, restatement, and internal summaries?

    b. Was the style vivid? Did it make use of active verbs, strong verbs, figures of speech, and imagery?

    c. Was the style appropriate? Did the speaker speak on a proper level of formality-informality? Were unfamiliar terms, slang, and vulgar expressions avoided? Were offensive expressions avoided?

    d. Was the style personal? Did the speaker use personal pronouns, questions addressed to the audience, and immediacy expressions?

    e. Was the style forceful? Did the speaker avoid weakeners, bromides, and clichés? Was intensity varied appropriately?

    f. Were the sentences short, direct, active, and positive? Were the sentences varied in type and length? Were parallel, antithetical, and periodic sentences used to give the speech variety and force?

VIII. Introduction and conclusion

    a. Does the introduction gain attention? Through what means?

    b. Does the introduction orient the audience as to what is to follow?

    c. Does the conclusion summarize the speech?

    d. Does the conclusion provide a crisp, defined closure?

23. THE TEACHER AND THE STUDENT

EIGHT POSTULATES OF COMMUNICATION PERCEPTION ▪ LISTENING
BARRIERS IN LANGUAGE AND VERBAL INTERACTION ▪ PRINCIPLES OF
LANGUAGE AND VERBAL INTERACTION ▪ IMPROVING INTERPERSONAL
COMMUNICATION AND CONFLICT MANAGEMENT ▪ INTERCULTURAL
COMMUNICATION: BARRIERS AND GATEWAYS

This brief dialogue was composed to illustrate a wide variety of communication problems and may be used effectively with a number of different units (as noted above). Select one unit in the text which you feel is especially relevant to this dialogue and use the principles and theories of that unit to analyze the dialogue. Regardless of the unit you select, be sure to indicate in specific terms (1) what is going wrong and (2) what could have or should have been done to make for greater communication effectiveness.

This dialogue takes places between John Dawson, a junior at Cicero College majoring in communication, and Rita Williams, a professor in the communication department. The setting is Professor Williams's office.

DAWSON: Professor Williams? Do you have a few minutes? I'd like to ask you something.

WILLIAMS: Well, what's your problem?

DAWSON: I, I, I guess I was, I mean, I wasn't sure if I understood the term paper assignment. None of the students understood it, actually.

WILLIAMS: Well, it was clear, I know.

DAWSON [*prolonged silence, shifting of posture, and general awkwardness*].

WILLIAMS: Well, what part couldn't you understand? I have a department meeting in a little while.

DAWSON: Well, I wasn't sure about what you wanted in the paper.

WILLIAMS: Did you read the assignment sheet? It spells out what's required.

DAWSON: No, I didn't get a chance to read it but I figured, I mean I thought that from what you said in class that . . .

WILLIAMS: Here's the assignment: Select an area of organizational communication that was discussed in class, research it, and write a review and synthesis of the literature.

DAWSON: You mean like find articles in the newspapers?

WILLIAMS: No, articles in scholarly journals. Dawson, you're a junior in college. You should know what to do at this point. Don't you think? You really should pay more attention in class.

DAWSON: I guess so.

WILLIAMS: O.K.? Anything else?

DAWSON: How many articles should we read?

WILLIAMS: You mean how many should you read to get an A? You people are so concerned with grades, I can't stand it. Aren't you at all interested in learning something without worrying about the grade?

DAWSON: No, that's not, well I mean that's not why I came here.

WILLIAMS: Oh, I see. Right.

DAWSON: No, I mean like how many should we read for the paper? You didn't say in class.

WILLIAMS: Well, read until you've learned enough. That's all I can tell you.

DAWSON: O.K., I'll try.

WILLIAMS: You know there are a lot of absences in class. What's wrong with the students here? Don't they want to learn anything?

DAWSON: They say they can't understand you.

WILLIAMS: I explained those concepts three times. How many times should I do it?

DAWSON: I don't know. I just heard some people saying they find it difficult to understand you.

WILLIAMS: If they can't understand simple concepts and theories, then maybe they shouldn't be in college.

DAWSON: I guess so.

WILLIAMS: Do you find it difficult to understand me?

DAWSON: Sometimes, I guess.

WILLIAMS: Well, not everything in life is easy. Try harder. Is there anything else?

DAWSON: They say that it's boring just sitting in class doing nothing.

WILLIAMS: Oh, another complaint. Well, if they're bored, that's their problem, not mine. Not everything in life is exciting. Sometimes we have to sit through boring lectures.

DAWSON: I didn't mean that all the lectures were boring. I mean just sometimes.

WILLIAMS: I have to be getting to my meeting.

DAWSON: Thanks for the help.

WILLIAMS: Right.

24. MOTIVATIONAL ANALYSIS AND THE ADVERTISEMENT

THE PERSUASIVE SPEECH ■ PRELIMINARIES TO MASS COMMUNICATION

This exercise is designed to provide you with an opportunity to gain greater insight into the nature and function of motivational appeals. Here the focus is on analyzing the motivational appeals in advertisements.

Each student should select (and bring to class) an advertisement from a recent magazine or newspaper that relies heavily on motivational appeals, and explain to the class—in an informal talk of about five minutes—the operation of psychological appeals in the advertisement. More specifically, analyze the advertisement in terms of the principles of motivation and the specific appeals. The following questions are presented as guidelines for your analysis, though you need not (and should not) restrict yourself to them.

1. To what specific audience is the advertisement addressed? On what do you base your assumption? Can you point to specific messages (verbal and/or nonverbal) in the advertisement that led you to make the assumption you did?
2. What is (are) the specific purpose(s) of the advertisement? (Observe carefully: Few advertisements have just one purpose.) How is this purpose stated? Verbally? Nonverbally? Directly? Indirectly?
3. What motivational appeals are used and how are they used? Fear? Power/control/influence? Affiliation? Achievement? Financial gain? Status? Any others?

25. TELEVISION AND VALUES

PRELIMINARIES TO MASS COMMUNICATION ■ THEORIES OF MASS COMMUNICATION

Listed below are eight values found to be significant among college students in a Daniel Yankelovich survey and reported in Barry Tarshis, The "Average American" Book (New York: Atheneum/SMI, 1979). The percentage figures represent the proportion of the respondents who identified the value as "very important."

1. Self-fulfillment, 87 percent   _____
2. Education, 76 percent   _____
3. Family, 68 percent   _____
4. Hard work, 43 percent   _____
5. Having children, 31 percent   _____

6. Religion, 28 percent _____

7. Money, 20 percent _____

8. Patriotism, 19 percent _____

Examine the list of values and next to each value identify one, two, or three television characters who best seem to exemplify that value. After you have identified at least one character for each value, the entire class should pool their results and discuss them, considering some or all of the following questions. It may facilitate discussion if the values are written on the chalkboard and some of the more frequently named characters are listed next to the value. Do not read any further until you have identified the several characters requested above.

1. Are there any sex differences? That is, do male and female characters exemplify the same or different values? What are the implications of these similarities or differences for television serving an educational function? Reinforcing function? Persuasive function?

2. Are there differences based on age, race, religion, nationality? Again, what are the implications of these similarities or differences?

3. What type of character would you like to see achieve some prominence on television? For example, at the least, identify the sex, race, nationality, religion, occupation, affectional preference, age, intelligence level, marital status, and general physical condition of the character you would like to see on television. What values would you like to see this character embody? What media functions would you particularly like to influence?

4. What type of character would you like to see less of on television? Identify specific characters. Why?

5. Are the characters in the movies similar to those on TV? Explain the reasons for the differences (if any).

6. Television characters seem not to have achieved the kind of prominence that many characters in novels and dramas have. For example, Scarlett O'Hara, Huck Finn, Willie Loman, George and Martha, and so many others have achieved a level of prominence television characters rarely, if ever, achieve. What factors might account for these differences in universal and lasting fame? One possible exception that comes quickly to mind is Archie Bunker. Are there other "exceptions"?

GLOSSARY

Listed here are definitions of the technical terms of human communication—the words that are peculiar or unique to this discipline. These definitions should make new or difficult terms a bit easier to understand. For the most part the words included here are used in this text. Also included, however, are other terms that may be used during a course in communication. For additional and more extended definitions, see my *Communication Handbook: A Dictionary* (New York: Harper & Row, 1986).

Abstraction A general concept derived from a class of objects; a part representation of some whole.

Abstraction process The process by which a general concept is derived from specifics; the process by which some (never all) characteristics of an object, person, or event are perceived by the senses or included in some term, phrase, or sentence.

Accent The stress or emphasis placed on a syllable when pronounced.

Accommodation A state of cold-war conflict; a condition in which the parties, although still in conflict, agree not to battle; a state in which the conflicting individuals have adjusted to each other's position and in which interpersonal communication may take place, though real cooperation is absent.

Action language Movements of the body—for example, the way one walks, runs, sits.

Active listening A process of putting together into some meaningful whole the listener's understanding of the speaker's total message—the verbal and the nonverbal, the content and the feelings.

Adaptors Nonverbal behaviors that, when emitted in private or in public without being seen, serve some kind of need and occur in their entirety—for example, scratching one's head until the itch is eliminated.

Adjustment principle The principle of verbal interaction claiming that communication can take place only to the extent that the parties communicating share the same system of signals.

Affect displays Movements of the facial area and body that convey emotional meaning—for example, anger, fear, and surprise.

Agenda-setting The effect of the media in focusing attention on certain issues and problems. This media attention or inattention influences people to see various issues as important or unimportant; generally, the more media attention given an issue, the more will people think it is important.

Allness The assumption that all can be known or is known about a given person, issue, object, or event.

Ambiguity The condition in which a word or phrase may be interpreted as having more than one meaning.

Antithetical sentences Sentences in which contrasting ideas are juxtaposed in parallel fashion.

Appraisal interview A type of interview in which the interviewee's performance is assessed by management or by more experienced colleagues.

Arbitrariness The feature of human language that refers to the fact that there is no real or inherent relationship between the form of a word and its meaning. If we do not know anything of a particular language, we could not examine the form of a word and thereby discover its meaning.

Argot A kind of *sublanguage;* the sublanguage of a particular class, generally an underworld or criminal class, which is difficult and sometimes impossible for outsiders to understand.

Articulation The physiological movements of the speech organs as they modify and interrupt the air stream emitted from the lungs.

Artifactual communication Communication that takes place through the wearing and arrangement of various artifacts—for example, clothing, jewelry, buttons, or the furniture in your house and its arrangement.

Assimilation The process of message distortion in which messages are reworked to conform to our own attitudes, prejudices, needs, and values.

Attention The process of responding to a stimulus or stimuli.

Attitude A predisposition to respond for or against an object.

Attraction The state or process by which one individual is drawn to another, by having a highly positive evaluation of that other person.

Attractiveness principle A principle of persuasion stating that a speaker will be more persuasive if he or she is perceived as attractive and well liked.

Attribution A process through which we attempt to understand the behaviors of others (as well as our own), particularly the reasons or motivations for these behaviors.

Audience participation principle A principle of persuasion stating that persuasion is achieved more effectively when the audience participates actively.

Authoritarian leader A group leader who determines the group policies or makes decisions without consulting or securing agreement from group members.

Avoidance An unproductive conflict strategy in which we take mental or physical flight from the actual conflict.

Behavioral synchrony The similarity in the behavior, usually nonverbal, of two people. Generally, behavioral synchrony is an index of mutual liking.

Belief Confidence in the existence or truth of something; conviction.

Beltlining An unproductive conflict strategy in which we hit the other person with insults below his or her level of tolerance—that is, below the belt.

Biological time The dimension of time that refers to the physiological cycles of the body and how these influence our communication behavior. See *biorhythms*.

Biorhythms Regular cycles that our bodies supposedly go through. Generally, three cycles are identified: the physical cycle controls strength, energy, and coordination; the emotional cycle controls mood; and the intellectual cycle controls cognitive and intellectual abilities and activities.

Blame An unproductive conflict strategy in which we attribute the cause of the conflict to the other person or devote our energies to discovering who is the cause and avoid tackling the issues causing the conflict.

Blindering A misevaluation in which a label prevents us from seeing as much of the object as we might see; a process of concentrating on the verbal level while neglecting the nonverbal levels; a form of *intensional orientation*.

Blind self The part of the self that contains information about the self that is known to others but unknown to oneself.

Body English Popularly, *tactile communication*.

Body language A form of nonverbal communication in which messages are communicated by gesture, posture, spatial relations, and so forth; a popular phrase to denote all aspects of nonverbal communication.

Body territories The area encompassed by one's body and its movements and gestures.

Boundary markers *Markers* separating territories—for example, the armrests in a theater that separate one person's space from another's.

Brainstorming A technique for generating ideas among people.

Breadth The number of topics about which individuals in a relationship communicate.

Bromides Sentences that are trite and worn out by constant usage.

Bypassing A pattern of misevaluation in which people fail to communicate their intended meaning. Bypassing may take either of two forms: (1) when two people use different words but give them the same meaning, resulting in apparent disagreement that hides the underlying agreement; and (2) when two people use the same words but each gives them different meaning, resulting in apparent agreement that hides the underlying disagreement.

Cant A kind of *sublanguage;* the conversational language of any nonprofessional (usually noncriminal) group, which is generally understood only by members of the subculture.

Censorship Legal restrictions imposed on one's right to produce, distribute, or receive various communications.

Central markers Items placed in a territory that are intended to reserve it for us—for example, a jacket left on a library chair.

Certainty An attitude of closed-mindedness that creates a defensiveness among communication participants; opposite to *provisionalism.*

Channel The vehicle or medium through which signals are sent.

Channel capacity The maximum amount of information a communication system can handle at any given time.

Cherishing behaviors Small behaviors that we enjoy receiving from a relational partner—for example, a kiss, a smile, or being given flowers.

Chronemics The study of communicative nature of time—how we treat time and how we use it to communicate. Three general areas of chronemics are usually distinguished: *biological time, cultural time,* and *psychological time.*

Clichés Overused phrases that have lost their novelty and part of their meaning, and that call attention to themselves because of their overuse.

Closed-mindedness An unwillingness to receive certain communication messages.

Code A set of symbols used to translate a message from one form to another.

Cognitive complexity The state of having numerous different concepts for describing people.

Cohesiveness The property of togetherness. Applied to group communication situations, it refers to the mutual attractiveness among members; a measure of the extent to which individual members of a group work together as a group.

COIK Acronym for "clear only if known," referring to messages that are unintelligible for anyone who does not already know what the messages refer to.

Colloquy A small group format in which a subject is explored through the interaction of two panels (one asking and one answering questions) or through the panel members responding to questions from audience members.

Communication (1) The process or act of communicating; (2) the actual message or messages sent and received; and (3) the study of the processes involved in the sending and receiving of messages. [The term *communicology* (q.v.) is suggested for the third definition.]

Communication gap The inability to communicate on a meaningful level because of some difference between the parties—for example, age, sex, political orientation, or religion.

Communication network The pathways of messages; the organizational structure through which messages are sent and received.

Communicology The study of communication and particularly that subsection concerned with human communication.

Competence *Language competence* is a speaker's ability to use the language; a knowledge of the elements and rules of the language. *Communication competence* refers to the rules of the more social or interpersonal dimensions of communication and is often used to refer to those qualities that make for effectiveness in interpersonal communication. See *performance.*

Competition An interpersonal process in which persons strive to attain something and at the same time to prevent others from attaining it.

Complementary relationship A relationship in which the behavior of one person serves as the stimulus for the complementary behavior of the other; in complementary relationships, behavior differences are maximized.

Conditioning An approach to the control of behavior in which the learning or unlearning of behaviors is dependent on their consequences.

Confidence The absence of social anxiety; the communication of comfortableness in social situations. One of the qualities of effective interpersonal communication.

Confirmation A communication pattern in which we acknowledge the presence of the other person and also indicate our acceptance of this person, this person's definition of self, and our relationship as defined or viewed by this other person. Opposite to *disconfirmation*.

Conflict A disagreement between or among individuals.

Connotation The feeling or emotional aspect of meaning, generally viewed as consisting of the evaluative (for example, good-bad), potency (strong-weak), and activity (fast-slow) dimensions; the associations of a term. See *denotation*.

Consensus A principle of attribution through which we attempt to establish whether other people react or behave in the same way as the person on whom we are now focusing; if the person is acting in accordance with the general consensus, then we seek reasons for the behavior outside the individual; if the person is not acting in accordance with the general consensus, then we seek reasons that are internal to the individual.

Consistency (1) A perceptual process that influences us to maintain balance among our perceptions; a process that influences us to see what we expect to see and to be uncomfortable when our perceptions contradict our expectations; (2) a principle of attribution through which we attempt to establish whether this person behaves the same way in similar situations; if there is consistency, we are likely to attribute the behavior to the person, to some internal motivation; if there is no consistency, we are likely to attribute the behavior to some external factor.

Contamination The process by which one renders a territory impure through encroachment. See *territorial encroachment*.

Content and relationship dimensions A principle of communication holding that messages refer both to content (the world external to both speaker and listener) and to relationship dimensions (the relationship existing between the individuals interacting).

Context of communication The physical, social-psychological, and temporal environment in which communication takes place.

Conversational turns The changing (or maintaining) of the speaker or listener role during a conversation. These turns are generally signaled nonverbally. Four major types of conversational turns may be identified: turn-maintaining, by which we indicate our desire to continue in the role of speaker; turn-yielding, by which we indicate our desire to change roles from speaker to listener; turn-requesting, by which we indicate our desire to speak; and turn-denying, by which we indicate our desire not to assume the role of speaker.

Cooperation An interpersonal process by which individuals work together for a common end; the pooling of efforts to produce a mutually desired outcome.

Cosmopolitan leader An opinion leader who is concerned with national and international (as opposed to local) issues. See *local leader*.

Counseling interview A type of interview in which the interviewer tries to learn about the interviewee in an attempt to provide some form of guidance, advice, or insight.

Credibility The degree to which a receiver perceives the speaker to be believable. See *ethos*.

Credibility gap A tendency between or among people to disbelieve each other and to doubt the honesty and integrity of each other; the difference between the image a person tries to convey (highly positive) and the image a receiver perceives (usually less positive), which is often taken as a measure of the extent to which the public image is disbelieved.

Cultural time The communication function of time as regulated and as perceived by a particular culture. Generally, three types of cultural time are identified: *technical time* refers to precise scientific time; *formal time* refers to the divisions of time that a culture makes (for example, dividing a semester into 14 weeks); and *informal time* refers to the rather loose use of such time terms as *immediately*, *soon*, and *right away*.

Culture The relatively specialized life-style of a group of people—consisting of their values, beliefs, artifacts, ways of behaving, and ways of communicating—that is passed on from one generation to the next.

Culture shock The psychological reaction one experiences at being placed in a culture very different from one's own or from what one is used to.

Date An extensional device used to emphasize the notion of constant change and symbolized by a subscript: for example, John Smith$_{1972}$ is not John Smith$_{1988}$.

Decoder What takes a message in one form (for example, sound waves) and translates it into another code (for example, nerve impulses) from which meaning can be formulated. In human communication, the decoder is the auditory mechanism; in electronic communication, the decoder is, for example, the telephone earpiece. See *encoder.*

Decoding The process of extracting a message from a code—for example, translating speech sounds into nerve impulses. See *encoding.*

Delayed reactions Reactions that are consciously delayed while the situation is analyzed; a symbolic reaction.

Demassification The process of segmenting the general audience mass communication into smaller, more clearly defined groups. This is primarily done so that media and advertising may be more precisely targeted to a more homogeneous audience.

Democratic leader A group leader who stimulates self-direction and self-actualization of the group members.

Denotation Referential meaning; the objective or descriptive meaning of a word. See *connotation.*

Depth The degree to which the inner personality—the inner core of an individual—is penetrated in interpersonal interaction.

Determinism, principle of The principle of verbal interaction holding that all verbalizations are to some extent purposeful—that there is a reason for every verbalization.

Dialect A specific variant of a language used by persons from a specific area or social class; dialects may differ from the "standard" language in phonology, semantics, or syntax, but they are intelligible to other speakers of the language.

Diffused time orientation An orientation to time that is approximate rather than exact. Opposite to *displaced time orientation.*

Diffusion of innovation theory A theory of media that concentrates on how the media influence people to adopt something new or different.

Digital communication Communication signals that are discrete rather than continuous; opposite to *analogic communication.*

Directive function of communication Communication intended to persuade; communication that serves to direct the receiver's thoughts or behaviors.

Disconfirmation A communication pattern in which we ignore the presence of the other person as well as this person's communications. Opposite to *confirmation.*

Displaced speech Speech used to refer to what is not present or in the immediate perceptual field.

Displaced time orientation An orientation to time that is exact and precise. Opposite to *diffused time orientation.*

Distinctiveness A principle of attribution in which we ask whether this person reacts in similar ways in different situations; if the person does, there is low distinctiveness and we are likely to conclude there is an internal cause or motivation for the behavior; if there is high distinctiveness, we are likely to seek the cause in some external factors.

Dogmatism Closed-mindedness in dealing with communications.

Double-bind message A particular kind of contradictory message possessing the following characteristics: (1) The persons interacting share a relatively intense relationship; (2) two messages are communicated at the same time, demanding different and incompatible responses; (3) at least one person in the double bind cannot escape from the contradictory messages; (4) there is a threat of punishment for noncompliance.

Downward communication Communication in which the messages originate at the higher levels of an organization or hierarchy and are sent to lower levels—for example, management to line worker.

Dyadic communication Two-person communication.

Dyadic consciousness An awareness of an interpersonal relationship or pairing of two individuals, distinguished from situations in which two individuals are together but do not perceive themselves as being a unit or twosome.

Dyadic effect The tendency for the behavior of one person in a dyad to influence a similar behavior in the other person. Used most often to refer to the reciprocal nature of self-disclosure.

Dynamic judgments Perceptual judgments that refer to those characteristics of another person that change relatively rapidly. See *static judgments.*

Dysfunctional effects of mass communication Effects of the media that are not in the interest of society.

Ear markers Identifying marks that indicate that the territory or object belongs to you—for example, initials on an attaché case.

Ectomorphy The skinny dimension of body build.

Ego states More or less stable patterns of feelings that correspond to patterns of behaviors; in *transactional analysis* three such ego states are defined: *parent ego state, adult ego state,* and *child ego state.*

Elementalism The process of dividing verbally what cannot be divided nonverbally—for example, speaking of body and mind as separate and distinct entities.

Emblems Nonverbal behaviors that directly translate words or phrases—for example, the signs for okay and peace.

Empathy A quality of effective interpersonal communication that refers to the ability to feel another's feelings as that other person does and the ability to communicate that similarity of feeling.

Employment interview A type of interview in which the interviewee is questioned to ascertain his or her suitability for a particular job.

Encoder Something that takes a message in one form (for example, nerve impulses) and translates it into another form (for example, sound waves). In human communication the encoder is the speaking mechanism; in electronic communication the encoder is, for example, the telephone mouthpiece. See *decoder.*

Encoding The process of putting a message into a code—for example, translating nerve impulses into speech sounds. See *decoding.*

Enculturation The process by which culture is transmitted from one generation to another.

Endomorphy The fatty dimension of body build.

E-Prime A form of the language that omits the verb *to be* except when used as an auxiliary or in statements of existence. Designed to eliminate the tendency toward *projection,* or assuming that characteristics that one attributes to a person (for example, "Pat is brave") are actually in that person instead of in the observer's perception of that person.

Equality A quality of effective interpersonal communication in which the equality of personalities is recognized, and both individuals are seen as worthwhile, valuable contributors to the total interaction.

Equity theory A theory claiming that we experience relational satisfaction when there is an equal distribution of rewards and costs between the two persons in the relationship.

Etc. An extensional device used to emphasize the notion of infinite complexity; since one can never know all about anything, any statement about the world or event must end with an explicit or implicit *etc.*

Ethicizing function of communication The media's function of providing viewers with a collective ethic or ethical system.

Ethics The branch of philosophy that deals with the rightness or wrongness of actions; the study of moral values.

Ethnocentrism The tendency to see others and their behaviors through our own cultural filters, often as distortions of our own behaviors; the tendency to evaluate the values and beliefs of one's own culture more positively than those of another culture.

Ethos The aspect of persuasiveness that depends on the audience's perception of the character of the speaker; to Aristotle *ethos* or ethical proof depended upon the speaker's perceived good will, knowledge, and moral character. *Ethos* is more commonly referred to as *speaker credibility.*

Euphemism A polite word or phrase used to substitute for some taboo or otherwise offensive term.

Evaluation A process whereby a value is placed on some person, object, or event.

Exit interview A type of interview designed to establish why an employee (the interviewee) is leaving the organization.

Experiential limitation The limit of an individual's ability to communicate, as set by the nature and extent of his or her experiences.

Expressiveness A quality of effective interpersonal communication referring to the skill of communicating genuine involvement in the interpersonal interaction.

Extemporaneous speech A speech that is thoroughly prepared and organized in detail and in which certain aspects of style are predetermined.

Extensional devices Those linguistic devices proposed by Alfred Korzybski for keeping language as a more accurate means for talking about the world. The extensional devices include the *etc., date,* and *index*—the working devices; and the *hyphen* and *quotes*—the safety devices.

Extensional orientation A point of view in which the primary consideration is given to the world of experience and only secondary consideration is given to the labels. See *intensional orientation.*

Extrinsic credibility The credibility or believability the communicator is seen to possess before the actual communication begins; the communicator's initial credibility. See *intrinsic credibility.*

Fact-inference confusion A misevaluation in which one makes an inference, regards it as a fact, and acts upon it as if it were a fact.

Factual statement A statement made by the observer after observation, and limited to the observed. See *inferential statement.*

Fear appeal The appeal to fear to persuade an individual or group of individuals to believe or to act in a certain way.

Feedback Information that is fed back to the source. Feedback may come from the source's own messages (as when we hear what we are saying) or from the receiver(s) in the form of applause, yawning, puzzled looks, questions, letters to the editor of a newspaper, increased or decreased subscriptions to a magazine, and so forth. See *negative feedback, positive feedback.*

Field of experience The sum total of an individual's experiences, which influences his or her ability to communicate. In some views of communication, two people can communicate only to the extent that their fields of experience overlap.

Force An unproductive conflict strategy in which one attempts to win an argument by physical force or threats of force.

Forum A small group format in which members of the group answer questions from the audience; often follows a *symposium.*

Free information Information about a person that one can see or that is dropped into the conversation, and that can serve as a topic of conversation.

Frozen evaluation See *static evaluation.*

Gain-loss theory The theory holding that increases in rewards have greater impact than unvariant rewards.

Game A simulation of some situation with rules governing the behaviors of the participants and with some payoff for winning; in *transactional analysis, game* refers to a series of ulterior transactions that lead to a payoff; in TA, *game* also refers to a basically dishonest kind of transaction in which participants hide their true feelings.

Gatekeeping The process of filtering messages from source to receiver. In this process some messages are allowed to pass through, and others are changed or not allowed to pass at all.

General semantics The study of the relationships among language, thought, and behavior.

Ghostwriting The procedure by which one writes or prepares messages for someone else, and the identity of the real author is kept hidden.

Gobbledygook Double-talk or language that is needlessly complex.

Grammar The set of rules of syntax, semantics, and phonology. *Prescriptive grammar* deals with how educated speakers ought to speak; *descriptive grammar* deals with the knowledge (competence) speakers have of their language.

Grapevine The informal lines through which messages in an organization may travel; these informal lines resemble the physical grapevine, with its unpredictable pattern of branches.

Group A collection of individuals related to each other with some common purpose and with some structure among them.

Groupthink A tendency observed in some groups in which agreement among members becomes more important than the exploration of the issues at hand.

Gunnysacking An unproductive conflict strategy in which we store up grievances against the other person and unload these during a conflict encounter.

Haptics Touch or tactile communication.

Hidden self The part of the self that contains information about the self known to oneself, but unknown to and hidden from others.

High-order abstraction A very general or abstract term or statement; an inference made on the basis of another inference. See *level of abstraction.*

Home territories Territories for which individuals have a sense of intimacy and over which they exercise control—for example, a child's club house.

Honorific Expressing high regard or respect. In some languages certain pronouns of address are honorific and are used to address those of high status. In English such expressions as "Dr.," "Professor," and the Honorable" are honorific.

Humanistic model of interpersonal effectiveness An approach to interpersonal communication effectiveness based on the qualities that should characterize meaningful interpersonal interaction. Five such qualities are identified: *openness, empathy, supportiveness, positiveness,* and *equality.*

Human relations approach to organizations An approach to organizations holding that increases in worker satisfaction lead to increases in productivity; the function of management is to keep workers happy and satisfied so that workers, in turn, will be productive.

Hyphen An *extensional device* used to illustrate that what may be separated verbally may not be separable on the event or nonverbal level; although one may talk about body and mind as if they were separable, in reality they are better referred to as body-mind.

Iconic signals Signals that bear real or nonarbitrary relationships to their referents; opposite to *arbitrariness.*

Identification In general semantics, a misevaluation whereby two or more items are considered identical; according to Kenneth Burke, a process of becoming similar to another individual; a process of aligning one's interests to those of another. Burke sees identification as a necessary process for persuasion.

Idiolect An individual's personalized variation of the language.

Illustrators Nonverbal behaviors that accompany and literally illustrate the verbal messages—for example, upward movements that accompany the verbalization "It's up there."

Immanent reference, principle of The principle of verbal interaction holding that all verbalizations make some reference to the present, to the specific context, to the speaker, and to the receivers.

Immediacy A quality of effective interpersonal communication referring to the creation of a feeling of togetherness and oneness with another person.

Implicit personality theory A theory of personality that each individual maintains, complete with rules or systems, and through which others are perceived.

Impromptu speech A speech given without any direct prior preparation.

Index An *extensional device* used to emphasize the notion of nonidentity (no two things are the same) and symbolized by a subscript—for example, politician$_1$ is not politician$_2$.

Indiscrimination A misevaluation caused by categorizing people or events or objects into a particular class and responding to specific members only as members of the class; a failure to recognize that each individual is an individual and is unique; a failure to apply the *index*.

Inevitability A principle of communication referring to the fact that communication cannot be avoided; all behavior in an interactional setting is communication.

Inferential statement A statement that can be made by anyone, is not limited to the observed, and can be made at any time. See *factual statement*.

Information That which reduces uncertainty.

Informative interview A type of interview in which the interviewer asks the interviewee, usually a person of some reputation and accomplishment, questions designed to elicit his or her views, predictions, perspectives, and the like on specific topics.

Information overload That condition in which the amount of information is too great to be dealt with effectively; the condition in which the number or complexity of messages is so great that the individual or organization is not able to deal with them.

Initial credibility See *extrinsic credibility*.

Inoculation principle A principle of persuasion stating that persuasion will be more difficult to achieve when beliefs and attitudes that have already been challenged previously are attacked, because the individual has built up defenses against such attacks in a manner similar to inoculation.

Insulation A reaction to *territorial encroachment* in which we erect some sort of barrier between ourselves and the invaders.

Intensional orientation A point of view in which primary consideration is given to the way in which things are labeled and only secondary consideration (if any) to the world of experience. See *extensional orientation*.

Interaction diagrams Diagrams used to record the number of messages sent from one person to another.

Interaction management A quality of effective interpersonal communication referring to the ability to control the interpersonal interaction to the satisfaction of both participants.

Interaction process analysis A content analysis method that classifies messages into four general categories: social emotional positive, social emotional negative, attempted answers, and questions.

Interactional territories Territories in which people gather socially—for example, at a party.

Interchangeability The feature of language that makes possible the reversal of roles between senders and receivers of messages. Because of interchangeability, all adult members of a speech community may serve as both senders and receivers; people may produce any linguistic message they can understand.

Intercultural communication Communication that takes place between persons of different cultures or who have different cultural beliefs, values, or ways of behaving.

Interethnic communication Communication between members of different ethnic groups.

International communication Communication between nations.

Interpersonal communication Communication between two persons or among a small group of persons and distinguished from public or mass communication; communication of a personal nature and distinguished from impersonal communication; communication between or among intimates or those involved in a close relationship; often, intrapersonal, dyadic, and small group communication in general.

Interpersonal conflict A conflict or disagreement between two persons; a conflict within an individual caused by his or her relationships with other people.

Interracial communication Communication between members of different races.

Interview A particular form of interpersonal communication in which two persons interact largely by question-and-answer format for the purpose of achieving specific goals.

Intimate distance The shortest proxemic distance, ranging from touching to 6 to 18 inches.

Intrapersonal communication Communication with oneself.

Intrinsic credibility The credibility or believability a listener perceives a communicator to possess based on what takes place during the actual communication encounter. See *extrinsic credibility.*

Irreversibility A principle of communication referring to the fact that communication cannot be reversed; once something has been communicated, it cannot be uncommunicated.

Invasion The unwarranted entrance into another's territory that changes the meaning of the territory. See *territorial encroachment.*

Jargon A kind of *sublanguage;* the language of any special group, often a professional class, which is unintelligible to individuals not belonging to the group; the "shop talk" of the group.

Kinesics The study of the communicative dimension of face and body movements.

Laissez-faire leader A group leader who allows the group to develop and progress or make mistakes on its own.

Language The rules of *syntax, semantics,* and *phonology;* a potentially self-reflexive structured system of symbols that catalogs the objects, events, and relations in the world. A *language* is an infinite set of grammatical sentences generated by the grammar of any language—for example, English, Italian, Banut, or Chinese.

Language relativity hypothesis The theory that the language we speak influences our perceptions and our behaviors of the world, and that therefore persons speaking widely differing languages will perceive and behave differently as a result of the language differences. Also referred to as the *Sapir-Whorf hypothesis* and the *Whorfian hypothesis.*

Lateral communication Communication among equals—for example, manager to manager, worker to worker.

Leadership That quality by which one individual directs or influences the thoughts and/or the behaviors of others. See *laissez-faire leader, democratic leader,* and *authoritarian leader.*

Learnability The feature of language that refers to the fact that any normal human being is capable of learning any language as a first language. Learnability is dependent on and follows from language being traditionally or culturally transmitted.

Leveling A process of message distortion in which a message is repeated, but the number of details is reduced, some details are omitted entirely, and some details lose their complexity.

Level of abstraction The relative distance of a term or statement from the actual perception; a low-order abstraction would be a description of the perception, whereas a high-order abstraction would consist of inferences about inferences about descriptions of a perception.

Linguistic collusion A reaction to *territorial encroachment* in which we speak in a language unknown to the intruders and thus separate ourselves from them.

Linguistic determinism A theory holding that language determines what we do, say, and think and in fact limits what we are able to do, say, and think.

Linguistics The study of language; the study of the system of rules by which meanings are paired with sounds.

Listening An active process of receiving aural stimuli.

Local leader An opinion leader who is concerned with local rather than national or international issues. See *cosmopolitan leader.*

Loving An interpersonal process in which one feels closeness, caring, warmth, and excitement for another person.

Low-order abstraction A description of what is perceived. See *level of abstraction*.

Macroscopic approach to communication The focus on broad and general aspects of communication.

Magnitude of change principle A principle of persuasion stating that the greater and more important the change desired by the speaker, the more difficult its achievement will be.

Manipulation An unproductive conflict strategy in which open conflict is avoided; instead, attempts are made to divert the conflict by being especially charming and getting the other person into a noncombative frame of mind.

Manuscript speech A speech designed to be read from a script verbatim.

Markers Devices through which we signal to others that a particular territory belongs to us.

Mass communication Communication addressed to an extremely large audience, mediated by audio and/or visual transmitters, and processed by gatekeepers before transmission.

Matching hypothesis The assumption that persons date and mate people who are approximately the same as they are in terms of physical attractiveness.

Mere exposure hypothesis The theory holding that repeated or prolonged exposure to a stimulus may result in attitude change toward the stimulus object, generally in the direction of increased positiveness.

Mesomorphy The muscular dimension of body build.

Message Any signal or combination of signals that serve as *stimuli* for a receiver.

Metacommunication Communication about communication.

Metalanguage Language used to talk about language.

Micromomentary expressions Extremely brief movements that are not consciously perceived and that are thought to reveal a person's real emotional state.

Microscopic approach to communication The focus on minute and specific aspects of communication.

Mindfulness and mindlessness States of relative awareness. In a mindful state we are aware of the logic and rationality of our behaviors and the logical connections existing among elements. In a mindless state we are unaware of this logic and rationality.

Minimization An unproductive conflict strategy in which we make light of the other person's disagreements or of the conflict as a whole.

Model A physical representation of an object or process.

Monochronism A time orientation of persons or cultures in which one thing is scheduled per unit of time and everything occurs in sequences. Opposite to *polychronism*.

Monomorphism The tendency to serve as a leader for one topic; generally characterizes cosmopolitan leaders. See *polymorphism*.

Motivated sequence An organizational pattern for arranging the information in a discourse to motivate an audience to respond positively to one's purpose.

Multiordinality In general semantics, a condition whereby a term may exist on different levels of abstraction.

Multivalued orientation A point of view emphasizing that there are many sides (rather than only one or two) to any issue.

Narcotizing function of communication The media's function of providing receivers with information, the knowledge of which is, in turn, confused by receivers with doing something about something.

Negative feedback Feedback that serves a corrective function by informing the source that his or her message is not being received in the way intended. Negative feedback serves to redirect the source's behavior. Looks of boredom, shouts of disagreement, and letters critical of newspaper policy would be examples of negative feedback.

Neutrality A response pattern lacking in personal involvement; encourages *defensiveness;* opposite to *empathy.*

Noise Anything that distorts or interferes with the message in the communication system. Noise is present in communication to the extent that the message sent differs from the message received. *Physical noise* interferes with the physical transmission of the signal or message—for example, the static in radio transmission. *Psychological noise* refers to distortions created by such psychological processes as prejudice and biases. *Semantic noise* refers to distortions created by a failure to understand each other's words.

Nonallness An attitude or point of view in which it is recognized that one can never know all about anything and that what we know or say or hear is only a part of what there is to know, say, or hear.

Nonelementalism See *elementalism.*

Nonnegotiation An unproductive conflict strategy in which the individual refuses to discuss the conflict or the disagreement, or to listen to the other person.

Object language Language used to communicate about objects, events, and relations in the world; the structure of the object language is described in a *metalanguage;* the display of physical objects—for example, flower arranging and the colors of the clothes we wear.

Obstinate audience A view of the audience, particularly the public and mass communication audience, as critical, selective, and active.

Olfactory communication Communication by smell.

Openness A quality of effective interpersonal communication that refers to (1) the willingness to engage in appropriate self-disclosure, (2) the willingness to react honestly to incoming stimuli, and (3) the willingness to own one's own feelings and thoughts. Also see *productivity.*

Open self The part of the self that contains information about the self that is known to oneself and to others.

Opinion A tentative conclusion concerning some object, person, or event.

Opinion leader Persons looked to for opinion leadership; those who mold public opinion.

Oral style The style of spoken discourse that, when compared with *written style,* consists of shorter, simpler, and more familiar words; more qualification, self-reference terms, allness terms, verbs and adverbs; and more concrete terms and terms indicative of consciousness of projection—for example, *as I see it.*

Organization A group of individuals organized for the achievement of specific goals.

Other-orientation A quality of effective interpersonal interaction referring to one's ability to adapt to the other person's needs and desires during the interpersonal encounter.

Panel or round table A small group format in which participants are arranged in a circular pattern and speak without any set pattern.

Paralanguage The vocal (but nonverbal) aspect of speech. Paralanguage consists of voice qualities (for example, pitch range, resonance, tempo), vocal characterizers (for example, laughing or crying, yelling or whispering), vocal qualifiers (for example, intensity, pitch height), and vocal segregates (for example, *uh-uh* meaning "no," or *sh* meaning "silence").

Parallel sentences Sentences that are phrased in similar or matching grammatical structure.

Perception The process of becoming aware of objects and events from the senses.

Perceptual accentuation A process that leads us to see what we expect to see and what we want to see; for example, we see people we like as better looking and smarter than people we do not like.

Performance The actual utterances a speaker speaks and a hearer hears. See *competence.*

Periodic sentences Sentences in which the key word that completes the meaning and the grammatical structure of the sentence is presented last.

Personal distance The second-shortest proxemic distance, range from 1½ to 4 feet.

Personal rejection An unproductive conflict strategy in which the individual withholds love and affection, and seeks to win the argument by getting the other person to break down under this withdrawal.

Persuasion The process of influencing attitudes and behavior.

Persuasive interview A type of interview in which the interviewer attempts to change the interviewee's attitudes or behavior.

Phatic communion Communication that is primarily social; communication designed to open the channels of communication rather than to communicate something about the external world; "Hello," and "How are you?" in everyday interaction are common examples.

Phonology The area of linguistics concerned with sound.

Pitch The highness or lowness of the vocal tone.

Play theory of mass communication A theory of media that emphasizes the role of play; the mass media are seen as pleasure-oriented; their primary function is to allow us to escape work and to enjoy ourselves; the media are popular to the extent that they serve this function.

Polarization A form of fallacious reasoning by which only the two extremes are considered; also referred as to "black-and-white"and "either-or" thinking.

Polychronism A time orientation of persons or cultures in which several things may be scheduled at one time; events overlap and blend into one another. Opposite to *monochronism*.

Polymorphism The tendency to serve as a leader for a number of different topics; generally characterizes local opinion leaders. See *monomorphism*.

Positive feedback Feedback that supports or reinforces behavior along the lines it is already proceeding in—for example, applause during a speech.

Positiveness A quality of effective interpersonal communication referring to the communication of positiveness toward the self, the other, and the communication situation generally, and willingness to stroke the other person as appropriate.

Prevarication The feature of human language that makes lying possible. This feature depends on and is a function of displacement, openness or productivity, and semanticity.

Primacy effect The condition by which what comes first exerts greater influence than what follows. See *recency effect*.

Primary affect displays The communication of the six primary emotions: happiness, surprise, fear, anger, sadness, and disgust/contempt. See *affect displays*.

Problem orientation A focus on a problem and its possible solutions rather than on controlling the group processes; encourages *supportiveness*; opposite to *control*.

Process Ongoing activity; nonstatic; communication is referred to as a process to emphasize that it is always changing and always in motion.

Productivity The feature of language that makes possible the creation and understanding of novel utterances. With human language we can talk about matters that have never been talked about before, and we can understand utterances we have never heard before. Also referred to as *openness*.

Projection A psychological process whereby we attribute characteristics or feelings of our own to others; often used to refer to the process whereby we attribute our own faults to others.

Pronunciation The production of syllables or words according to some accepted standard, as presented, for example, in a dictionary.

Provisionalism An attitude of open-mindedness that leads to the creation of *supportiveness*; opposite to *certainty*.

Proxemics The study of the communicative function of space; the study of how people unconsciously structure their space—the distance between people in their interactions, the organization of space in homes and offices, and even the design of cities.

Public communication Communication in which the source is one person and the receiver is an audience of many persons.

Public distance The longest proxemic distance, ranging from 12 to over 25 feet.

Public speaking Communication that occurs when a speaker delivers a relatively prepared, continuous address in a specific setting to a large audience that provides little immediate feedback.

Public territories Territories in which we have freedom of access simply by virtue of our citizenship—for example, public streets.

Punctuation of communication The breaking up of continuous communication sequences into short sequences with identifiable beginnings and endings, or stimuli and responses.

Punishment Noxious or aversive stimulation.

Pupillometrics The study of communication through changes in the size of the pupils of the eyes.

Pragmatic model of interpersonal effectiveness An approach to interpersonal communication effectiveness that stresses the behaviors that speakers should focus on to gain their desired goal. Generally, five characteristics are identified: *confidence, immediacy, interaction management, expressiveness, other-orientation*.

Psychological time The importance that we place on past time, in which particular regard is shown for the past and its values and methods; present time, in which we live in the present for the enjoyment of the present; and future time, in which we devote our energies to planning for the future.

Purr words Highly positive words that express the feelings of the speaker rather than refer to any objective reality; opposite to *snarl words*.

Pygmalion effect The condition in which one makes a prediction and then proceeds to fulfill it; a type of self-fulfilling prophecy but one that refers to others and to our evaluation of others rather than to ourselves.

Quotes An *extensional device* used to emphasize that a word or phrase is being used in a special sense and should therefore be given special attention.

Rapid fading The evanescent or impermanent quality of speech signals.

Rate The speed with which we speak, generally measured in words per minute.

Rational emotive therapy (RET) A therapeutic procedure that may be applied to speaker apprehension. The general method is to substitute rational sentences or ideas for the irrational ones that the subject has internalized.

Receiver Any person or thing that takes in messages. Receivers may be individuals listening or reading a message, a group of persons hearing a speech, a scattered television audience, or a machine that stores information.

Recency effect The condition in which what comes last (that is, most recently) exerts greater influence than what comes first. See *primacy effect*.

Redefinition An unproductive conflict strategy in which the conflict is given another definition so that the source of the conflict disappears.

Redundancy The quality of a message that makes it totally predictable and therefore lacking in information. A message of zero redundancy would be completely unpredictable; a message of 100 percent redundancy would be completely predictable. All human languages contain some degree of built-in redundancy, generally estimated to be about 50 percent.

Reflexiveness The feature of language referring to the fact that human language can be used to refer to itself; that is, we can talk about our talk and create a *metalanguage*—a language for talking about language. See *self-reflexiveness*.

Regulators Nonverbal behaviors that regulate, monitor, or control the communications of another person.

Reinforcement The strengthening of a particular response.

Reinforcement/packaging, principle of The principle of verbal interaction holding that in most interactions, messages are transmitted simultaneously through a number of different channels that normally reinforce each other; messages come in packages.

Rejection A response to an individual that rejects or denies the validity of an individual's self-view.

Relational communication Communication between or among intimates or those in close relationships; term used by some theorists as synonymous with interpersonal communication.

Rigid complementarity The inability to change the type of relationship between oneself and another even though the individuals, the context, and a host of other variables have changed.

Role The part an individual plays in a group; an individual's function or expected behavior.

Scientific approach to organizations An approach to organizations holding that scientific methods should be applied to the organization to increase productivity; through the use of scientifically controlled studies, management can identify the ways and means for increasing productivity and ultimately profit.

Selective exposure principle A principle of persuasion stating that listeners will actively seek out information that supports their opinions and actively avoid information that contradicts their existing opinions, beliefs, attitudes, and values.

Self-acceptance Being satisfied with ourselves, and our virtues, vices, abilities, and limitations.

Self-attribution A process through which we seek to account for and understand the reasons and motivations for our own behaviors.

Self-concept An individual's self-evaluation; an individual's self-appraisal.

Self-disclosure The process of revealing something significant about ourselves to another individual or to a group—something that would not normally be known by them.

Self-fulfilling prophecy The situation in which we make a prediction or prophecy and fulfill it ourselves—for example, expecting a class to be boring and then fulfilling this expectation by perceiving it as boring.

Self-monitoring The manipulation of the image that we present to others in our interpersonal interactions. High self-monitors carefully adjust their behaviors on the basis of feedback from others so that they can project the desired image. Low self-monitors do not consciously manipulate their images.

Self-reflexiveness The property of being able to refer back to itself; for example, language is self-reflexive because it can be used to refer to itself. See *reflexiveness*.

Self-serving bias A bias that operates in the self-attribution process and leads us to take credit for the positive consequences and to deny responsibility for the negative consequences of our behaviors.

Semanticity The feature of human language referring to the fact that some words have denotations in the objective world. All human languages possess semanticity, but not all words have denotations (for example, *of, the,* and *is* do not have objective referents in the real world).

Semantics The area of language study concerned with meaning.

Sequential communication Communication in which messages are passed A to B, B to C, C to D, and so on; linear communication.

Sexist language Language derogatory to one sex, generally women.

Sharpening A process of message distortion in which the details of messages, when repeated, are crystallized and heightened.

Shyness The condition of discomfort and uneasiness in interpersonal situations.

Sign Something that stands for something else and that bears a natural, nonarbitrary relationship to it—for example, dark clouds as a sign of rain. See *symbol*.

Signal and noise, relativity of The principle of verbal interaction holding that what is signal (meaningful) and what is noise (interference) is relative to the communication analyst, the participants, and the context.

Sign language Gesture language that is highly codified—for example, a hitchhiker's gesture.

Silence The absence of vocal communication; often misunderstood to refer to the absence of any and all communication.

Silencers Unproductive conflict strategies that literally silence the other person—for example, crying, or feigning emotional or physical disturbance.

Slang The language used by special groups, which is not considered proper by the general society; the language made up of the *argot, cant,* and *jargon* of various subcultures, known by the general public.

Small group communication Communication among a collection of individuals, small enough in number that all members may interact with relative ease as both senders and receivers, the members being related to each other by some common purpose and with some degree of organization or structure among them.

Snarl words Highly negative words that express the feelings of the speaker rather than refer to any objective reality; opposite to *purr words.*

Social comparison processes The processes by which we compare ourselves (for example, our abilities, opinions, and values) with others and then assess and evaluate ourselves.

Social distance The third proxemic distance, ranging from 4 to 12 feet; the distance at which business is usually conducted.

Social exchange theory A theory claiming that we develop and maintain relationships in which the rewards or profits are greater than the costs.

Somatotype Body type measured in terms of the degree to which one is fat, muscular, or skinny.

Source Any person or thing that creates messages. A source may be an individual speaking, writing, or gesturing or a computer solving a problem.

Speaker apprehension A fear of engaging in communication transactions; a decrease in the frequency, strength, and likelihood of engaging in communication transactions.

Speech Messages utilizing a vocal-auditory channel.

Speech community A group of persons using the same language.

Spontaneity The communication pattern in which one verbalizes what one is thinking without attempting to develop strategies for control; encourages *supportiveness;* opposite to *strategy.*

Stability The principle of perception referring to the fact that our perceptions of things and people are relatively consistent with our previous conceptions.

Static evaluation An orientation that fails to recognize that the world is characterized by constant change; an attitude that sees people and events as fixed rather than as constantly changing.

Static judgments Perceptual judgments referring to those characteristics of another person that are relatively unchanging—for example, race, occupation, age, and nationality. See *dynamic judgments.*

Status The relative level one occupies in a hierarchy; status always involves a comparison, and thus one's status is only relative to the status of another. In our culture, occupation, financial position, age, and educational level are significant determinants of status.

Step theories of mass communication A group of theories holding that the media have their effects on viewers and listeners in steps. The one-step theory holds that the media influence people directly; the two-step theory holds that the media influence opinion leaders, who in turn influence the majority of others; the multistep theory holds that the media's influence is a reciprocal one, a process that goes back and forth, from the media to the people, then back to the media, then back to the people, and so on.

Stereotype In communication, a fixed impression of a group of people through which we then perceive specific individuals; stereotypes are most often negative (Martians are stupid, uneducated, and dirty), but may also be positive (Venusians are scientific, industrious, and helpful).

Stimulus Any external or internal change that impinges on or arouses an organism.

Stimulus-response models of communication Models of communication assuming that the process of communication is a linear one, beginning with a stimulus that then leads to a response.

Strategy The use of some plan for control of other members of a communication inter-action that guides one's own communications; encourages *defensiveness;* opposite to *spontaneity.*

Subjectivity The principle of perception referring to the fact that one's perceptions are not objective, but are influenced by one's wants and needs and one's expectations and predictions of the perceiver.

Sublanguage A variation from the general language used by a particular subculture; *argot, cant,* and *jargon* are particular kinds of sublanguages.

Superiority A point of view or attitude assuming that others are not equal to oneself; encourages *defensiveness;* opposite to *equality.*

Supportiveness A quality of effective interpersonal communication in which one is descriptive rather than evaluative, spontaneous rather than strategic, and provisional rather than certain.

Symbol Something that stands for something else but that bears no natural relationship to it—for example, purple is a symbol of mourning. Words are symbols in that they bear no natural relationship to the meaning they symbolize. See *sign.*

Symmetrical relationship A relation between two or more persons in which one person's behavior serves as a stimulus for the same type of behavior in the other person(s). Examples of such relationships include situations in which anger in one person en-courages or serves as a stimulus for anger in another person, or in which a critical comment by one person leads the other to respond in like manner.

Symposium A small group format in which each member of the group delivers a relatively prepared talk on some aspect of the topic. Often combined with a *forum.*

Syntax The area of language study concerned with the rules for combining words into sentences.

Systematic desensitization A procedure used in reducing irrational fears—for example, speaker apprehension. The general method is to learn to relax while visualizing selected behaviors. These behaviors are arranged in a hierarchy; the subject begins visualization with the least nonthreatening behavior and eventually works up to the specific behavior that is to be mastered.

Systems approach to organizations An approach to organizations that stresses the interaction of all parts of the organization; each part influences each other part. The organization should be seen as an open system in which the physical and physiological factors and the social and psychological factors interact, each influencing the other.

Taboo Forbidden; culturally censored. Taboo language is what is frowned upon by "polite society." Themes and specific words may be considered taboo—for example, death, sex, certain forms of illness, and various words denoting sexual activities and excretory functions.

Tactile communication Communication by touch; communication received by the skin.

Territorial encroachment The trespassing on, use of, or appropriation of one's territory by another. The major types of territorial encroachment are *violation, invasion,* and *contamination.*

Territoriality A possessive or ownership reaction to an area of space or to particular objects.

Theory A general statement or principle applicable to a number of related phenomena.

Thesis The main assertion of a message—for example, the theme of a public speech.

Total feedback The quality of speech that refers to one's ability to receive all the communications one sends.

Touch avoidance The tendency we have to avoid touching and being touched by others.

Traditional transmission The feature of language referring to the fact that human lan-guages (at least in their outer surface form) are learned. Unlike various forms of animal language, which are innate, human languages are transmitted traditionally or culturally. This feature of language does not deny the possibility that certain aspects of language may be innate. Also referred to as *cultural transmission*.

Transactional The relationship among elements in which each influences and is influenced by each other element; communication is a transactional process, since no element is independent of any other element.

Trust Faith in the behavior of another person; confidence in another person that leads us to feel that whatever we risk will not be lost.

Turf defense The most extreme reaction to *territorial encroachment* through which one defends one's territory and expels the intruders.

Two-step flow of communication A hypothesis stating that the influence of the media occurs in two steps: (1) The media influence opinion leaders, and (2) the opinion leaders influence the general population through interpersonal communication.

Two-valued orientation A point of view in which events are seen or questions are evaluated in terms of two values—for example, right or wrong, good or bad. Often referred to as the fallacy of black-and-white and *polarization*.

Undelayed reaction A reaction that is immediate; a signal response; a reaction made without any conscious deliberation.

Universal of communication A feature of communication common to all communication acts.

Universal of language A feature of language common to all known languages.

Unknown self That part of the self that contains information about the self that is unknown to oneself and to others, but that is inferred to exist on the basis of various projective tests, slips of the tongue, dream analyses, and the like.

Upward communication Communication in which the messages originate from the lower levels of an organization or hierarchy and are sent to upper levels—for example, line worker to management.

Uses and gratifications A theory of mass media that seeks to explain the influence of the media in terms of the uses to which people put the media and the gratifications they derive from those uses.

Value Relative worth of an object; a quality that makes something desirable or undesirable; ideals or customs about which we have emotional responses, whether positive or negative.

Violation Unwarranted use of another's territory. See *territorial encroachment*.

Volume The relative loudness of the voice

Withdrawal A reaction to *territorial encroachment* in which we leave the territory.

Written style See *oral style*.

INDEX

A

Abstractions, 85
Accent errors, 370
Acronyms, 355
Action, 334
Activation, in mass communication, 466
Active listening, 69–72
  function of, 70
  techniques of, 71
Adaptors, 148
Adjustment, communication as process of, 22
Adopters of innovation, 477
Adoption of innovation, 476
Affect displays, 147, 149
Agenda-setting, 465
Alliteration, 353
Allness, 97–99
Allport, Gordon, 285
Altman, Irwin, 193
Andersen, Peter, 164
Antithesis, 354
Antithetical sentences, 360
Appraisal interview, 292–293
Apprehension, 322–324
  dealing with, 323–324
Appropriateness of language, 355–356
Arbitrariness in language, 82, 83
Archer, Richard, 36
Argot, 123
Aronson, Elliot, 197
Articulation, 368–369
  problems in, 369
Artifactual communication, 138–139

Assertiveness training group, 252
Assimilation, 285
Attention, 333
Attractiveness, 195
Attribution, 55–58
Audience, mass communication, 455
Audience analysis in public communication, 313–316
Audiovisual aids, 388–392
Auditory imagery, 354
Authoritarian leader, 269
Avoidance, 233
Avoidance of touch, 164

B

Bach, George, 236
Back, Kurt, 195
Balance, 111
Barriers in language, 91–102
Behavioral synchrony, 137
Believability and nonverbal communication, 140–141
Berelson, Bernard, 474
Berg, John, 36
Biological time, 175
Biorhythms, 175
Birdwhistell, Ray, 140, 141
Blame, 235
Blind self, 30
Blumstein, Philip, 211ff
Bodily action in public communication, 371–373
Body communication, 145–154
  movements, 146–148
Bok, Sissela, 114

Books, 462
Boundary markers, 162
Brainstorming, 251
Breadth of relationships, 192
Breathiness, 368
Bromides, 357–358
Brougher, Toni, 223
Burgoon, Judee, 140
Bypassing, 96–97

C

Camden, Carl, 108
Cant, 123
Cassettes, 462
Cause-effect pattern, 333
Central markers, 162
Channels, 7
Cherishing behaviors, 231
Choice and ethics, 10–12
Civil inattention, 152
Clarity of language, 351–353
Clichés, 357–358
Climax, 354
Closure, 49
Cody, Michael, 141
Colloquy, 255
Communication
    definition of, 4
    flow in organizations, 282–288
    networks, 279–282
    in organizations, 275–276
    privacy, 121–122
    purposes, 12
    as transaction, 18–20
    universals of, 4–12
Compact discs, 462
Competence, 6
Complementarity, 198
Complementary transactions, 24
Complimenting, 107
Componential definition of inter-
    personal communication, 187
Conclusions, 337–339
    after the, 339–340
    closure in, 338–339
    faults with, 339

in public communication, 321
    summary in, 338
Conferral of status in mass com-
    munication, 465
Confidence, 226, 447
Confidentiality, 114
Confirmation, 115
Conflict, 232–237
    and allness, 99
    management, 232–237
Connotation, 86–88
Consciousness-raising group, 252–
    254
    procedures in, 253–254
Consensus in attribution, 56
Consistency, 52
    in attribution, 56
Contamination, 161
Content and relationship dimen-
    sions of communication, 21
Context of communication, 4
    in mass communication, 457
Contradictory messages, 20
Conversational turns, 173
Cosmopolitan opinion leader, 479
Cosmopolite, 276
Counseling interview, 293–294
Criticism, 107
Cross-cultural communication, 433
Cultural approach to organiza-
    tions, 278–279
Cultural time, 176–177
Cultural transmission, 82–83
Culture, 430
Culture shock, 441–444

D

Date, 100
Davis, K. E., 55
Davis, Keith, 286–287
Davis, Murray, 206
Deception, 215
Decoding-encoding, 6
Definition, 386–388
Delivery in public communication,
    362–377

methods of, 363–365
outline for, 345–346
Democratic leader, 268
Denasality, 367–368
Denotation, 86–88
Depenetration, 193
Depth of relationships, 192
Descriptiveness, 223
Developmental definition of inter-
    personal communication, 188–
    189
Diffusion of innovations, 476
Disconfirmation, 114
Displacement in language, 81
Distinctiveness in attribution, 56
Downward communication, 283–
    284
    problems with, 284
Downward talk, 105
Dysfunctional roles, 261
Dysfunctions of mass communica-
    tion, 468

E

Ear markers, 162
Educational group, 254–255
Education in mass communication,
    464
Effect-cause pattern, 333
Effects of communication, 10
Ekman, Paul, 141, 146, 148, 149
Ellsworth, Phoebe, 148
Emblems, 146
Empathy, 222, 446
Employment interview, 293
Encoding-decoding, 6
Encounter group, 252
Entertainment in mass communi-
    cation, 463
Equality, 107, 225, 447
Equity, 212, 220, 231
Etc., 99
Ethicizing in mass communication,
    467
Ethics, 10–12
    and gossip, 114

Ethnocentrism, 429
Euphemism, 124–126
Examples, 384–385
Exit interview, 293
Expressiveness, 228, 447
Extemporaneous delivery, 364–365
    guidelines in, 365
Extensional orientation, 93
Eye avoidance, 152
Eye contact, 371
Eye movements, 150–153
    functions of, 151–152

F

Facial Affect Scoring Technique,
    149–150
Facial expression, 371
Facial movements, 148
Fact-inference confusion, 94–96
Fairness, 112
FAST, 149–150
Feedback, 8–9, 254
    immediate and delayed, 8
    positive and negative, 8
    sources of, 8
Festinger, Leon, 195
Field of experience, 10
Figures of speech, 353–354
Films, 461
Filtering out messages, 67
Force, 233
Forcefulness in language, 357
Formal and informal communica-
    tions, 276
Forum, 255
Foster, Myrna, 141
Free information, 204
Friesen, Wallace V., 146, 148

G

Gain-loss theory, 197
Gatekeepers, 275, 480–482
Gaudet, Helen, 474
Gestures, 371–372
Gibb, Cecil, 269

Gifts as nonverbal messages, 137–138
Gobbledygook, 106
Goffman, Erving, 152
Gonzalez, Alexander, 177
Gossip, 112–114
Grapevine, 286–287
Group-building roles, 260–261
Group-task roles, 259–260
Groupthink, 263
Gudykunst, William, 433
Gunnysacking, 235

H

Hall, Edward T., 156ff
Haney, William, 96–97
Hayakawa, S. I., 86
Hecht, Michael, 447
Henley, Nancy, 163
Hess, Ekhard, 152–153
Hidden self, 32
Hoarseness, 368
Honesty, 107, 111
Humanism, 220
Humanistic approach to interpersonal effectiveness, 220–226
Human relations approach to organizations, 277
Hyperbole, 354

I

Idea generation group, 251–252
Illiterates, 456
Illustrations, 384–385
Illustrators, 147
Imagery, 354
I-messages, 221
Immediacy, 227, 357, 447
Implicit personality theory, 52
Impromptu method of delivery, 363
Inclusion, 104
Index, 101
Indiscrimination, 100–101

Individual role, 261
Informal and formal communications, 276
Information interview, 292
Information overload, 287–288
Informative speaking, 378–393
    amplifying materials in, 384–392
    of definition, 380–381
    of demonstration, 380–382
    of description, 379, 381
    principles of, 382–383
    purposes, 379–382
    types of, 379–380
Ingham, Harry, 29
In-group talk, 104
Insulation, 161
Intellectuals, 456
Intensional orientation, 93
Intensity in language, 358
Interaction management, 227, 447
Intercultural communication, 3, 422–451
    barriers, 442–445
    difficulty in studying, 428–431
    forms of, 432
    gateways, 445–448
    importance of, 426–428
    model of, 431
    nature of, 430–432
Interethnic communication, 432
Internal motivation in attribution, 57
Internal summaries, 330–332
International communication, 432
Interpersonal attraction, 194–199
Interpersonal communication, 3, 184–242
    definitions of, 187–189
    effectiveness in, 219–238
Interpersonal relationships, 184–242
Interpersonal skills in interviews, 300–301
Interracial communication, 432
Interviewing, 290–305

definition of, 291
kinds of, 292–294
preparation for, 295
sequence in, 294–302
Intimacy claims, 209
Intimate distance, 156
Introductions in public communi-
    cation, 335–337
attention in, 335–336
before the, 339–340
faults with, 337
orientation in, 335–337
in public speaking, 322
Invasion, 161
Irony, 354
Irreversibility of communication,
    19

J

Jargon, 123, 355
Johari window, 29–32
Johnson, Wendell, 83–84
Jones, E. E., 55
Jones, Stanley, 162
Jourard, Sidney, 39, 164ff

K

Katz, Elihu, 474
Kelly, H. H., 55
Kim, Young, 433
Knapp, Mark, 151
Korzybski, Alfred, 99

L

Laissez-faire leader, 268
Langer, Ellen, 430
Language, 78–130
as meaning system, 83
in the public speech, 349–361
relativity, 436–442
as social institution, 119
as symbol system, 81

Lateral communication, 284–285
problems with, 284–285
Lazarsfeld, Paul, 474
Leader's functions, 266
Leadership in small group commu-
    nication, 266–271
evaluation form, 266–270
styles of, 268–269
Learning group, 254–255
Leathers, Dale, 149
Lederer, William, 231
Leibowitz, Ken, 164
Leveling, 285
Lewin, Kurt, 480
Liaison, 275
Linguistic collusion, 162
Listening, 61–73
active, 69–72
active-passive, 65
effectively, 64
empathic and objective, 65
nature of, 62
nonjudgmental and judgmental,
    66
significance of, 62
surface-deep, 67
types of, 63
Local opinion leader, 479
Luft, Joseph, 29, 30
Lying, 82, 108–111

M

McEwen, William, 476
McGill, Michael, 36
MacLachlan, John, 174–175
McLuhan, Marshall, 458
Maintenance roles, 261–262
Manipulation, 236
Manuscript method of delivery,
    363–364
Markers, 162
Marshall, Evan, 151
Marston, Peter, 141
Mass communication, 3, 452–485
definition of, 455

Mass communication (*Continued*)
  functions of, 463–469
  theories of, 472–482
Matching hypothesis, 198
Meaning, 83
  levels of, 69
Media implosion, 458
Mehrabian, Albert, 140
Member participation in groups,
    261–263
Member roles, 259–261
Members in small group communi-
    cation, 259–263
Memorized method of delivery,
    364
Mencken, H. L., 124, 126
Mere exposure, 196
Messages, 7
  in mass communication, 457
Metacommunication, 142
Metaphor, 354
Metonymy, 354
Micromomentary expressions, 150
Mindfulness, 430
Mindlessness, 430
Miller, Gerald, 188–189
Minimization, 234
Monomorphism, 479
Morale in organizations, 281–282
Morris, Desmond, 141, 163
Motivated sequence pattern, 333–
    335
Motley, Michael, 108
Movement, 373
Multistep theory of mass commu-
    nication, 475

N

Naisbitt, John, 7
Narcotizing in mass communica-
    tion, 466
Nasality, 367–368
Need, 333–334
Network productivity and morale,
    281–282

Networks, communication, 279–
    282
Network structures, 280–281
Newspapers, 461
Nias, David, 199
Nirenberg, Jesse S., 63
Noise, 9
Nonnegotiation, 233
Nonverbal communication, 132–
    182
  body communication, 145–154
  eye movements, 150–153
  facial movements, 148–150
  functions of, 135–136
  paralanguage, 171–175
  preliminaries to, 134–144
  space communication, 156–160
  temporal communication, 175–
    179
  territoriality, 160–162
  touch communication, 162–167
  universals of, 136–143
Notes, using in public speaking,
    373

O

Oberg, Kalervo, 445
Offensive language, 355–356
Openness, 221
Open self, 29
Opinion leaders, 276, 474, 478–479
  cosmopolitan and local, 479
  monomorphism and polymor-
    phism, 479
Oral sytle, 350–351
Organization, definition of, 274
Organizational communication,
    273–289
  approaches to, 276–279
  networks, 279–282
Organization in public communica-
    tion, 319–321
Organizations
  approaches to, 276–279
  characteristics of excellent, 279

Other-orientation, 230, 448
Other talk, 111
Outline for speech, 340–346
   delivery, 345–346
   identifying data, 340–341
   mechanics of, 342–345
Overload of information, 287–288

P

Package of signals, communication
   as, 20
Panel, 255
Paralanguage, 170–175
   and conversational turns, 173
   and effectiveness, 174–175
   and people perception, 171–173
Parallel sentences, 360
Parallel style, 330
Parasocial relationships, 467
Pauses, 370–371
Pearson, Judy, 37
Pease, Allan, 141
Penetration, 193
Perception, 47–60
   processes influencing, 50–55
   process of, 48–49
Perceptual accentuation, 51
Periodic sentences, 360
Personal distance, 157
Personal growth group, 252–254
Personalness in language, 356–357
Personification, 354
Persuasion as purpose of commu-
   nication, 14
Persuasion in mass communica-
   tion, 464
Persuasive interview, 292
Peters, Thomas, 279
Phatic communion, 88–89
Physical noise, 9
Pitch in public communication,
   366–367
Play as purpose of communication,
   14

Play theory of mass communica-
   tion, 475
Polarization, 92–93
Polymorphism, 479
Positiveness, 224
Postman, Leo, 285
Power, 151
Power games, 105–106
Pragmatic approach to interper-
   sonal effectiveness, 226–230
Pragmatic implications, 95
Pragmatism, 220
Pragmatists, 456
Prejudgment, 66
Prestige suggestion, 94
Primacy-recency, 50
Privatization, 467
Problem-solution pattern, 319–320
Problem-solving group, 248–251
   steps in problem solving, 248–
   251
Process of mass communication,
   457
Productivity
   in language, 81
   in organizations, 281–282
Progressive differentiation, 26
Pronunciation, 368–370
Propositions in public communica-
   tion, 316–319
Provisionalism, 224
Proxemics, 156, 372–373
Proximity, 48–49, 195
Psychological noise, 9
Psychological time, 177–179
Public communication, 3, 308–420
Public distance, 158
Public speech, preparation of, 311–
   322
Punctuation, 23
Pupil dilation, 152
Purpose in public communication,
   311–312
   narrowing, 312
Purposes of communication, 12–14
Purr words, 86

Q

Qualifiers, 204
Quality in public communication, 367–368
Questions in interviews, 302–304

R

Racism, 112
Radio, 460
Rapid fading in language, 82
Rate in public communication, 366
Recency-primacy, 50
Receivers-sources, 5
Records, 462
Redefinition, 233
Regulators, 147
Rehearsal in public communication, 373–376
  goals of, 374
  procedures, 374–376
Reik, Theodore, 199
Reinforcement, 196
  in mass communication, 463
Rejection, personal, 236
Relational definition of interpersonal communication, 187
Relationship and content dimensions of communication, 21
Relationship deterioration, 206–216
  causes of, 207
  communication in, 214–216
  nature of, 206–207
Relationship development, 202–206
  initiating, 203
  reasons for, 202
Request behaviors, 216
Research sources, 318–319
Research topic, 316
Résumé, 298–300
Rhetorical question, 354
Ribeau, Sidney, 447
Rigid complementarity, 24
Rosenfeld, Lawrence, 37–38
Rothwell, J. Daniel, 106
Round table, 255

Rules and nonverbal communication, 141
Rumor, 285

S

Safire, William, 126
Satisfaction, 334
Schachter, Stanley, 195
Schismogenesis, 26
Schramm, Wilbur, 473, 474, 478
Schwartz, Pepper, 211ff
Scientific approach to organizations, 276–277
Self-attribution, 57
Self-awareness, 29–35
  growing, in, 33–35
Self-disclosure, 35–44, 215
  avoidance, 37
  dangers of, 40
  factors influencing, 36
  guidelines for, 41
  nature of, 35
  rewards of, 38
Self-fulfilling prophecy, 51
Self in communication, 28–46
Self-monitoring, 227–229
Self-talk, 111
Semantic noise, 9
Sentences in public communication, 359
Serial communication, 285–286
  problems with, 285–286
Sexism, 112
Sharpening, 285
Silencers, 235
Silver bullet theory of mass communication, 473
Similarity, 198
Simile, 354
Slang, 123, 355
Small group communication, 3, 246–272
  definition, 247
  formats for, 255–256
  leaders in, 264–270
  members in, 259–264

Snarl words, 86
Snyder, Mark, 227–229
Social comparison processes, 13
Social distance, 158
Social exchange theory, 220
    approach to effectiveness, 230–
        232
Social penetration, 193
Sources-receivers, 5
Source in mass communication,
    455
Space communication, 155–162
    influences on, 158–160
Spatial distances, 156
Spatial pattern, 332
Spontaneity, 223
Stages in relationships, 189–192
Static evaluation, 99–100
Stephenson, William, 475
Step theories in mass communica-
    tion, 473
Stereotype, 53, 101
Stroking, 224–225
Style in the public speech, 349–361
Subcultural communication, 120–
    121
Subcultural identification, 121
Subculture, 119, 431
Subject in public communication,
    311–312
Sublanguages, 118–127
    functions of, 120
    kinds of, 123
Support in public communication,
    317–319
Supportiveness, 215, 223
Symmetrical transactions, 24
Symposium, 255
Symposium-forum, 255–256
Synchrony, 137
Systems approach to organiza-
    tions, 277

T

Taboo, 124–126
    effects, 125
    origins, 124
    variations, 124
Tactile imagery, 354
Tapes, 462
Taylor, Dalmas, 193
Television, 458
Temporal communication, 175–179
    and appropriateness, 178
    and status, 178
Temporal pattern, 320
Territoriality, 160–162
    encroachment, 161
    reactions to encroachment, 161
Testimony, 385–386
Thesis formulation, 316–317
Thought patterns, 319–321, 332–
    335
Ties of union in mass communica-
    tion, 467
Topical pattern, 320–321
Topics for public communication,
    314–315
Touch avoidance, 164
Touch communication, 162–167
    meanings of, 162
Transactional process, communica-
    tion as, 18–20
Transitions, 330–331
Truax, C., 222
Turf defense, 161
Turn cues, 173
Two-step theory of mass commu-
    nication, 474

U

Universals of communication
    model, 5
Unknown self, 31
Unlawful interview questions, 302–
    304
Upward communication, 282–283
    problems with, 283
Upward talk, 106
Uses and gratification theory in
    mass communication, 478

V

Violation, 161
Visual dominance behavior, 151
Visual imagery, 354
Visualization, 334
Vividness in language, 353–354
Voice in public communication,
    365–371
Volume in public communication,
    365–366

W

Waterman, Robert, 279
Weakeners, 357

Who Am I test, 33
Wilson, Ann, 108
Wilson, Glenn, 199
Withdrawal, 162
Word choice, 351–359
Wording the speech, 321
Wyden, Peter

Y

Yarbrough, Elaine, 162

Z

Zimbardo, Philip, 177